Constitutionali
Transnational Govern

Edited by

Ernst-Ulrich Petersmann
Armin Steinbach

BRILL | NIJHOFF

LEIDEN | BOSTON

Co-funded by the HEC S&O Institute and the European Union. Views and opinions expressed are however those of the author(s) only and do not necessarily reflect those of the European Union or the European Education and Culture Executive Agency (EACEA). Neither the European Union nor EACEA can be held responsible for them.

The Library of Congress Cataloging-in-Publication Data is available online at https://catalog.loc.gov
LC record available at https://lccn.loc.gov/2024002938

Typeface for the Latin, Greek, and Cyrillic scripts: "Brill". See and download: brill.com/brill-typeface.

ISSN 2405-9331
ISBN 978-90-04-69371-5 (hardback)
ISBN 978-90-04-69372-2 (e-book)
DOI 10.1163/9789004693722

This book is printed on acid-free paper and produced in a sustainable manner.

Contents

Constitutionalism and Transnational Governance Failures

World Trade Institute Advanced Studies

VOLUME 16

The titles published in this series are listed at *brill.com/wtia*

Foreword

In the face of contemporary challenges – global warming, ecological degradation, warfare, gross violations of human rights, increasing inequality, poverty and migration – conventional wisdom mostly tends to blame the weaknesses of international law. The legal mind still operates under the distinction of domestic and international law; the legal quality of the later is often questioned in light of the usual absence of effective international policing powers and law enforcement. There is no shortage of international law providing guidance and aspirations, ranging from general principles of law, human rights, SDGs and principles of non-discrimination and transparency. But, so it is said, the well-known weaknesses of international law and institutions explain the frequent absence of effective transnational public goods.

The present volume challenges such conventional wisdom. In fact, many of these transnational problems are rather caused by the tradition of introverted national constitutions and political systems than by international law. National constitutions are shaped to, and operate in, the pursuit of domestic interests in foreign affairs. Thus, they often are unable to contribute and produce global public goods addressing common concerns of humankind. Instead, sovereignty in defence of national interests, of western democracy, or of authoritarian rule, prevails with a purely national and territorial focus. They often do not allow international law to apply. Free-riding and beggar-your-neighbour policies result, to the detriment of others and global welfare.

Editors and authors of this volume identify and analyse dysfunctional governance as a result of introverted constitutional law and the lack of appropriate interaction with international law, civil society and the private sector. The volume offers a broad framework of transnational constitutionalism beyond the nation state, bringing all components together while recognising and struggling with the fact of largely diverse values and political systems. True, the project was inspired, and is informed, by the unique experience of European integration. Yet, it does not purport to simply extrapolate the latter to global governance. While conceptually European, and based on ordo-liberal philosophy represented by the editors, authors from all continents with different backgrounds contribute to produce evidence of a fascinating variety and plurality of different regulatory traditions and approaches. These case studies are at the heart of the volume. Importantly, they are not limited to intergovernmental relations, but include all actors and contribute to the advent of transnational law. They take stock in different fields, not limited to trade and investment, the core areas of international economic law. They show strength and weaknesses in different systems, and offer important groundwork for subsequent work in further developing the theory of multi-level governance and transnational constitutionalism.

Many of the conclusions drawn, and proposals made, insist on enhanced communication and interaction between different actors and different regulatory fields. They show that domestic and foreign affairs no longer can be separated. They show that domestic constitutions need to respect and enforce international law. They need to develop tools, unilaterally contributing to global public goods, thus overcoming traditional perspectives of national and territorial self-interest. Carrot and sticks are indispensable tools of transnational constitutionalism. The contributions show that transnational markets are not a given, but are constituted in law. Foremost, they imply the necessity of a strong and undivided rule of law, no longer adhering to the Austinian divide of domestic and international law. And such a rule of law must be anchored within domestic constitutional law, irrespective of the great spectrum of different political systems. Only countries making this commitment form part of effective transnational constitutionalism.

The contributions are mainly written with great powers in mind. But they are of equal, and perhaps greater, importance to small and middle-sized countries, dependent upon a rule-based international order and devoid of power politics. Switzerland, perhaps, is a case in point, upon which transnational constitutionalism and vertical checks and balances in the daily life of law can build. The country has a long and proud tradition friendly to international law, a monist doctrine, granting citizens the right to invoke international law. Recognising the respect of international law in the Federal Constitution as a means to protect minorities in direct democracy, constitutional review of Swiss federal legislations is essentially based upon the European Convention for the Protection of Human rights, and not the Federal Constitution itself which limits, from a federalist perspective, constitutional review to the laws of Cantons. The Convention thus is an integral part of the domestic constitutional system. Populist initiatives to reverse this achievement were voted down by the Swiss with strong majorities. Swiss people rely upon transnational constitutionalism. There is no fundamental divide in the rule of law. The model can also inspire the rule of law in international economic relations where courts of law, including in the EU, have been more reluctant, taking recourse to political questions doctrine and to powers of parliaments. Existing weaknesses can be addressed taking recourse to transnational constitutionalism. The volume will assist the implied transition of domestic constitutional law within an overarching framework. It offers a most valuable contribution to the doctrine of multi-level governance.

This work is the legacy of Ernst-Ulrich Petersmann, in association with Armin Steinbach who takes up the torch for the next generation in building and developing transnational constitutionalism in the face of contemporary challenges. It shows how far Ulli travelled, from insisting on economic rights of citizens to full protection of human rights and transnational constitutional theory in the pursuit of happiness of humans in the 21st Century. The many contributions in this book pay tribute in their way to a far sighted mind, and so does this preface in gratitude. The volume also shows how much work lies ahead, inspiring a new generation of scholars.

Berne, August 2023
Thomas Cottier

Figures and Tables

Figures

Tables

Notes on Contributors

Julien Chaisse
is a professor at the School of Law, City University of Hong Kong (CityU), specialising in international economic law, cyberlaw, and international dispute resolution. With expertise in trade, investment, and tax matters, he has garnered recognition for his contributions to the field, including receiving the prestigious *Smit-Lowenfeld* Prize from the International Arbitration Club of New York in 2020. Dr. Chaisse's extensive experience extends beyond academia, as he serves on corporate and advisory boards for international organisations. As the President and Chair of the Asia Pacific FDI Network, he leads collaborative research on foreign direct investment. Additionally, Dr. Chaisse is a distinguished senior arbitrator listed on the panels of major arbitration institutions.

Erin Daly
is a Professor of Law and Director of the Dignity Rights Clinic, Widener University Delaware Law School and former Director of Global Network for Human Rights and the Environment (GNHRE) 2017–2021. Major publications include: Dignity Rights: Courts, Constitutions, and the Worth of the Human Person (2d ed. U. Penn 2020); with James R. May: Dignity Law: Global Recognition, Cases, and Perspectives (W.S. Hein 2020) (Casebook); Global Environmental Constitutionalism (Cambridge University Press 2015); Human Rights and the Environment: Indivisibility, Dignity, Legality, Geography, Encyclopedia of Environmental Law (Edward Elgar Press 2019), (ed.); Implementing Environmental Constitutionalism: Current Global Challenges (Cambridge University Press 2018) (ed.); and Reconciliation in Divided Societies: Finding Common Ground (U. Penn., Human Rights Series 2006; paperback 2010), with Jeremy Sarkin.

John W.H. Denton AO
is Secretary-General of the International Chamber of Commerce, Paris. John was formerly Partner and CEO of Corrs Chambers Westgarth. He is a member of the Board of the global infrastructure investor – IFM Global Investors and a member of the Board of the UN Global Compact. He was a member of the Australian Government advisory panel overseeing the development of the 'Australia in the Asian Century' White Paper. John has a Bachelor of Arts (Honours) and a Bachelor of Law from the University of Melbourne and is a Harvard Business School Alumnus.

Christina Eckes
is professor of European law at the University of Amsterdam and director of the Amsterdam Centre for European Law and Governance (ACELG). She has published widely on the internal constitutional consequences of the European Union's external actions, a comprehensive account of which was published as a monograph entitled EU Powers under External Pressure – How the EU's External Actions Alter its Internal Structures (Oxford University Press, 2019). Her current research interests are the separation of powers in 21st century Europe, the legal exceptionalism of climate litigation, climate constitutionalisation, the normative relevance of climate science, and climate governance in the growing dissensus on liberal democracy.

Elaine Fahey
is Professor of Law at the Institute for the Study of European Law (ISEL), the City Law School, City, University of London and Deputy Head of Department (academic programmes) and co-convener of the Institute for the Study of European Law (ISEL), City Law School. She has been awarded a Jean Monnet Chair in Law and Transatlantic Relations 2019-2022. In 2022/2023 she is Senior Land Steiermark Fellow of Law and Innovation at the University of Graz, Austria and a visiting Professor at Washington College of Law (WCL), American University, Washington DC. Her monograph, *the EU as a Global Digital Actor* was published by Hart in 2023 and she has recently edited the *Routledge Research Handbook on Transatlantic Relations*, published in 2023.

James Flett
was until recently Deputy to the Director of the Trade Policy and WTO Team of the European Commission Legal Service. He has represented the European Commission before the European Court of Justice and the European Union before the WTO in more than 300 proceedings. Mr. Flett graduated from the London School of Economics and Political Science, and has a Master's degree in European law from the College of Europe, Bruges. He is a qualified solicitor. Before joining the Commission Legal Service, he spent several years working for two international law firms in London and Brussels. He has published widely on international trade law and teaches WTO Law at Leuven University, WTO dispute settlement law at the Academy of International Economic Law and Policy and WTO subsidies law at the World Trade Institute.

Henry Gao
is Professor of Law at Singapore Management University and Senior Fellow at CIGI. With law degrees from three continents, he started his career as the first

Chinese lawyer at the WTO Secretariat. He has been an advisor on trade issues for many national governments as well as the WTO, UN, World Bank, ADB, APEC, ASEAN and the World Economic Forum. Widely published on China and WTO and digital trade issues, he sits on the Advisory Board of the WTO Chairs Program, as well as the editorial boards of the Journal of International Economic Law and Journal of Financial Regulation.

Merit E. Janow
is an internationally recognized expert in international economic law and policy. She was Dean of the Faculty of SIPA from 2013–2021, and remains on the faculty. Janow has had three periods of government service: from 2003–2008, she served as the North American member of the WTO Appellate Body; from 1997–2000, Janow served as the Executive Director of the first international antitrust advisory committee to the Attorney General. From 1989 to 1993, Janow served as Deputy Assistant USTR for Japan and China. Janow has extensive corporate and nonprofit board experience. She speaks Japanese and has a JD from Columbia Law School and a BA in Asian Studies from the University of Michigan.

Pascal Lamy
is the former President of the Paris Peace Forum, and the current President of the European branch of the Brunswick Group. He coordinates the Jacques Delors Institutes (Paris, Berlin, Brussels). He is an affiliated professor at the China Europe International Business School CEIBS (Shanghai) and at HEC (Paris). From 2005 to 2013, Lamy served two consecutive terms as Director-General of the World Trade Organization. He was previously Trade Commissioner, Director General of Crédit Lyonnais, Chief of Staff of the President of the European Commission, Jacques Delors and his G7 Sherpa, Deputy Chief of Staff of the French Prime Minister and to the French Minister of the Economy and Finance.

Maria Laura Marceddu
specializes in international investment law. She is Visiting Max Weber Fellow (EUI). She obtained her PhD at King's College London where she has been appointed a fellow at the Center of European Law. She is also fellow at the Edinburgh Center for International and Global Law (ECIGL). Since 2018 she has been treasurer of the Society of International Economic Law, where she also chairs the SIEL Online Conversations.

Ernst-Ulrich Petersmann
worked as legal counsel in Germany's Ministry of Economic Affairs, GATT and the WTO, and taught international and European law at the Universities of St. Gallen, Fribourg, Geneva and the European University Institute at Florence, where he served as head of the Law Department. He taught at the Hague and Xiamen Academies of International Law, the EUI Academy of European Law, and at numerous Universities in Germany, Switzerland, Italy, Spain, the USA, Latin-America, South-Africa, China, India and Singapore. His publications include more than 35 books and 380 contributions to books and academic journals.

Armin Steinbach
holds the Jean Monnet Chair of EU Law and Economics and the HEC Foundation Chair of Law at the École des hautes études commerciales (HEC) in Paris. He is also research affiliate at the Max Planck Institute for Research on Collective Goods (Bonn, Germany) and non-resident fellow at the Brussels-based economic think tank Bruegel. As government official for more than ten years, Armin headed the fiscal policy division in the German Ministry of Finance, the economic policy division in the Ministry of Economic and Energy Affairs, and served as ministerial secondment in the German parliament. He worked at the World Trade Organization (WTO) and as attorney-at-law with the law firm Cleary Gottlieb Steen & Hamilton.

Maria Antonia Tigre
is a Senior Fellow, Global Climate Change Litigation, Sabin Center for Climate Change Law at Columbia Law School and Deputy Director of Global Network for Human Rights and the Environment (GNHRE). Major publications include: Regional Cooperation in Amazonia: A Comparative Environmental Law Analysis (Brill|Nijhoff, 2017); Gaps in International Environmental Law: Toward a Global Pact for the Environment (ELI Press, 2020); Exploring the Bedrock of Earth Jurisprudence, 22 Rutgers Journal of Law & Religion 223–313 (2022); Climate Change and Indigenous Groups: The Rise of Indigenous Voices in Climate Litigation, 9(3) E-Publica 214 (2022).

Natalia Urzola
is a S.J.D student, Elisabeth Haub School of Law, Pace University. LL.M, University of California at Berkeley (2020). Chief Operating Officer at the Global Network for Human Rights and the Environment (GNHRE). Recent publications include: Climate litigation in Latin America: is the region quietly leading a revolution? (with Maria A. Tigre and Alexandra Goodman, Journal

of Human Rights and the Environment); The human right to a healthy environment and the rights of racialized groups: applying critical race theory as a framework for (re)constructing environmental rights through foundational transformation (in D. Lupin *A Research Agenda for Human Rights and the Environment*, Edward Elgar Publishing); Gender-based Environmental Violence in Colombia: Problematising Dominant Notions of Gender-based Violence during Peacebuilding (with Maria P. González, Australian Feminist Law Journal).

Peter Van den Bossche
is Director of Studies of the World Trade Institute and Professor of International Economic Law, University of Bern, Switzerland; President of the Society of International Economic Law (SIEL); and former Member and Chair of the Appellate Body of the World Trade Organization, Geneva, Switzerland (2009–2019).

Weihuan Zhou
is Associate Professor and Co-Director of the China International Business and Economic Law (CIBEL) Centre at the Faculty of Law and Justice, University of New South Wales Sydney. He publishes widely in the field of international economic law, particularly on the nexus between international trade law and China. His work has been cited in reports of the European Parliament, the Parliament of Australia, Australia's Productivity Commission, US Congressional Research Services and World Economic Forum. Dr Zhou is co-Secretary of the Society of International Economic Law (SIEL) and sits on the editorial boards of the World Trade Review and the Journal of International Trade Law and Policy.

CHAPTER 1

Introduction and Conclusions

Ernst-Ulrich Petersmann and Armin Steinbach

This Introduction summarizes the contents and explains the methodology of the book and of its main policy conclusions on how constitutional democracies should respond to the increasing governance failures inside and beyond states. All UN member states have employed constitutional law for providing national public goods (PGs) such as protection of the environment; they also participate in multilateral treaties of a higher legal rank and multilevel governance institutions for protecting transnational PGs such as UN rules and institutions for the protection of the environment and human rights. However, international treaty commitments are often not effectively implemented inside UN member states, for instance if UN member states prioritize national communitarian values over internationally binding agreements (e.g. in Anglo-Saxon democracies with parliamentary supremacy); or if they continue being governed by authoritarian governments insisting on the UN Charter principle of 'sovereign equality of states' even if multilateral treaties and human and democratic rights are not effectively protected by governments. The 2030 UN Sustainable Development Agenda (SDA) emphasizes the need for international cooperation in protecting 17 universally agreed sustainable development goals (SDGs) based on respect for human rights, democratic governance and rule-of-law. Yet, these 'constitutional principles' and SDGs are not effectively protected inside and among many UN member states, especially if their domestic legal systems fail to subject foreign policy powers to effective constitutional restraints.[1]

The increasing 'executive power politics' and transnational 'governance failures' are influenced by numerous political, legal, economic and social causes. For instance, legal civilization in terms of protecting rights and judicial remedies of citizens (*cives*) in democratic and republican city states around the Mediterranean Sea 2500 years ago, and during Europe's medieval constitutionalism, had no parallel traditions outside Europe. Following the 'democratic enlightenment revolutions' in the Americas and Europe since the 18th century,

1 Like those in the 2009 Lisbon Treaty on European Union (TEU), whose Articles 3 and 21 require the EU to respect human rights, rule-of-law, democratic governance and other constitutional EU governance principles and judicial remedies also in the EU's external relations.

 | DOI:10.1163/9789004693722_002

domestic constitutionalism and constitutionalization of foreign policies continued to develop in diverse ways. Today's reality of 'constitutional pluralism' also includes 'fake constitutions' enabling authoritarian rulers (e.g. in China and Russia) to abuse domestic and foreign policy powers without effective democratic, legal and judicial accountability. Among democracies, process-oriented governance prioritizing legislative supremacy over individual rights differs from rights-based, multilevel democratic and economic constitutionalism. While the EU Charter of Fundamental Rights (EUCFR) and the Lisbon Treaty on European Union recognize human rights and diverse democracies as co-constitutive of Europe's multilevel constitutional democracies,[2] citizens and governments outside Europe often argue 'against constitutionalism beyond states', for instance on the ground that 'it institutes a system of rule that is unlikely to carry popular support'.[3] As illustrated by increasing 'executive power politics', this may even culminate in the violation of treaties ratified by parliaments for the benefit of citizens. The conflicting value premises and conceptions of international law among authoritarian, neoliberal and ordo-liberal state systems, as discussed throughout the Paris conference and in the book contributions, draw attention to the unresolved 'constitutional problems' of today's 'multipolar world' where diverse social conceptions of justice (e.g in the sense of socially accepted justifications of international law and governance of PGs) pose challenges to the UN and WTO governance of the SDGs.

Part I of this book explains why – notwithstanding this reality of 'constitutional pluralism' based on diverse cultural and constitutional traditions among the 193 UN member states – constitutionalism, constitutional politics, and constitutional economics offer the most coherent, analytical methods for explaining, and responding to, transnational 'governance failures' in protecting the SDGs, also in the 'interface relations' between democratic and authoritarian UN member states. Parts II and III of this book offer case-studies explaining the importance of 'environmental constitutionalism' and of multilevel democratic constitutionalism for strengthening multilevel governance of the SDGs through democratic participation, private-public partnerships and stronger 'stakeholder responsibilities'. These case-studies must be seen in the

2 Cf E.U. Petersmann, *Multilevel Constitutionalism for Multilevel Governance of Public Goods* (Oxford: Hart 2017).

3 Cf Martin Loughlin, *Against Constitutionalism* (Harvard UP 2022), at 202, who rejects European 'ordo-constitutionalism' and 'cosmopolitan constitutionalism' as being inconsistent with his nationalist conception of representative democracy – without offering any solutions for limiting transnational governance failures and responding to citizen demand for protecting transnational PGs more democratically and more effectively.

broader context of 'structural transformations' of societies, international relations and international law since World War II. As social, economic, political and legal systems are interdependent, mere liberalization of some economic sub-structures (e.g. in China and Russia) was unlikely, anyhow, to protect equal freedoms in the political, legal and social systems of authoritarian states.[4]

1 Structural Transformations of the International Legal System

In contrast to the 'international law of coexistence' (1648–1945) and failures of the League of Nations to protect human rights and transnational rule-of-law, the UN Charter and the 15 UN Specialized Agencies established a new kind of 'international law of cooperation' (W.Friedmann) for multilevel governance of transnational PGs. The decisive US leadership in defeating imperialism (e.g., through World Wars I and II, the dissolution of the Soviet Union at the end of the cold war) and in elaborating and globalizing UN and GATT/WTO law promoted decolonization and 'constitutionalization' of the post-1945 transnational relations based on increasing respect for individual and democratic self-determination in a rules-based, neoliberal economic order. The accession of authoritarian states like China (2001) and Russia (2012) to the World Trade Organization (WTO) enabled also authoritarian rulers to reform their dysfunctional economies. However, their continuing authoritarian suppression of human and democratic rights provoked new geopolitical rivalries – like Russian wars of aggression, the trade war started by US President Trump against China, and the US disruption of the WTO legal and dispute settlement system – demonstrating the politically unrealistic nature of the UN and WTO objectives of a rules-based and market-driven, liberal world order.[5]

Since the 1950s, European states used the GATT provisions for free trade areas and customs unions for transforming international law in Europe into multilevel legal, democratic and judicial protection of human and constitutional rights of EU citizens in a common market among more than 30 European democracies practicing new kinds of multilevel, democratic constitutionalism protecting peace and unprecedented social welfare. In the 1990s, following the end of the cold war, the EU commitments to promoting

4 On this 'interdependence of orders' emphasized by ordoliberalism see E.U. Petersmann, Neoliberalism, Ordoliberalism and the Future of Economic Governance, in *JIEL* 26 (2023) 836–842.

5 See E.U. Petersmann, The Future of International Economic Law in the Asian Century, in *JIEL* 26 (2023) 595–613.

transnational rule-of-law led to adoption of compulsory third-party adjudication also in WTO law, international investment law, the UN Convention on the Law of the Sea (UNCLOS), and in the 1998 Rome Statute of the International Criminal Court. Yet, as discussed in Part I, the geopolitical rivalries of the 21st century increasingly prompt China, Russia and the USA to oppose judicial protection of transnational rule-of-law; and, as discussed in Parts II and III, while the increasing number of UN environmental conferences and environmental agreements since the 1972 Stockholm Conference and the 1992 Rio Conference have led to universal acceptance of the environment and of climate change mitigation as global PGs, enforcing multilateral trade and environmental agreements through multilevel legal and judicial protection of economic, environmental and human rights – as successfully practiced in Europe – remains deeply contested by hegemonic and many other states outside Europe.

As described in Chapters 2, 4 and 5 of this book, the progressive 'constitutionalization' of EU environmental law and policies enabled a leading role of the EU also in the negotiations and domestic legal implementation of the UN Framework Convention on Climate Change (UNFCCC 1992) and the related Kyoto (1997) and Paris Agreements (2015), as illustrated by the EU's emission trading system and complementary Carbon Border Adjustment Mechanism (CBAM) inducing third countries to tax and restrict carbon emissions. Yet, just as the EU insistence on inserting 'human rights clauses' and providing for compulsory adjudication of disputes in international agreements remains contested by third countries, so are many WTO members challenging the legal consistency with UN and WTO law of EU environmental measures (like the CBAM and EU import restrictions on palm oil produced in illegally deforested tropical lands). If international law is defined by treaties, customary rules and general principles of law (as in Article 38 of the Statute of the International Court of Justice), the changing structures of international law may not be obvious. This book focuses on the dynamic interactions between international rules and related *legal practices* (like abuses of the WTO Appellate Body system, plurilateral countermeasures like multi-party interim arbitration in the WTO, increasing challenges to investor-state arbitration), and on plurilateral and regional agreements such as the Regional Comprehensive Economic Partnership (RCEP) in Asia, the Comprehensive and Progressive Agreement for Trans-Pacific Partnership (CPTPP), transatlantic cooperation among the EU and the USA, and the EU's CBAM in response to insufficient greenhouse gas emission reductions in third countries; arguably, these legal practices (e.g. favoring plurilateral reforms in response to failures of the UN and WTO legal systems) reveal structural changes in the international legal system.

2 Research Questions and Methodology of This Book

The editors of this book share the view underlying Europe's multilevel constitutionalism that ordoliberal and constitutional methodologies could inspire a humane rebuilding also beyond European integration of the world trading, investment and environmental systems if it should ever be possible to reform the suppression of human rights in authoritarian UN member states and neoliberal nationalism (as illustrated by the 'Brexit' and by money-driven US protectionism) disrupting multilateral economic order.[6] Yet, the realities of 'constitutional pluralism' suggest that the diverse constitutional traditions of European, American, African and Asian countries will continue promoting regulatory competition, geopolitical rivalries and transnational governance failures like the 'executive power politics' disrupting the UN and WTO 'world order treaties'. How should reasonable citizens and democratically accountable governments respond to such governance failures like suppression of human and democratic rights, abuses of veto powers, and insufficient cooperation in responding to health pandemics, climate change, food crises, Russian wars of aggression and threats of using nuclear weapons? Europe's legal commitment to 'competitive social market economies' (Article 3 TEU) is based on Europe's social experiences that citizens must be empowered by human and constitutional rights and social security to develop their human capacities and adjust to, and support, the changes imposed in open societies with economic and democratic competition. The current human disasters – like illegal wars of aggression, global health pandemics, climate change, ocean pollution, overfishing and other biodiversity losses, non-compliance with UN and WTO law and dispute settlement systems – reflect transnational governance failures and 'constitutional failures' to protect human and democratic rights and the SDGs. Both left-wing and right-wing 'populist politicians' polarize societies by blaming science-based elites (e.g. demonstrating man-made climate change) and pluralist societies (e.g. defending human rights, democratic accountability and protection of minorities); they call for returning to authoritarian governance so that 'strongmen politics' can impose 'social peace' and 'social justice'. Yet, social inequalities, political exclusion, corruption and suppression of human and democratic rights remain much more characteristic of authoritarian states than of constitutional democracies. This book explores how to

---

6 See Petersmann (n 4), reviewing *The Oxford Handbook of Ordoliberalism* edited by T. Biebricher/ W. Bonefeld/P. Nedergaard (Oxford University Press, 2022); *idem*, Transforming Trade, Investment and Environmental Law for Sustainable Development?, *Austrian Review of International and European Law* 26 (2023), 1–38.

rethink constitutionalism and governance of global PG by using the analytical lenses of 'constitutional politics' (e.g. emphasizing the need for transforming 'constitutional contracts' into democratic legislation and administrative and judicial protection of rule-of-law at national and international levels of governance of PGs) and of 'constitutional economics' (e.g. exploring the limitation of market failures, governance failures and constitutional failures by multilevel constitutionalism).

The book aims to explain transnational governance failures as well as how to remedy them, building on 'constitutional pluralism' in rules-based approaches to mitigating climate change and to other regulatory challenges in UN and WTO governance of PGs. The term 'constitutionalism' is used in a broad sense for constituting, limiting, regulating and justifying multilevel rules and governance institutions of a higher legal rank for providing PGs.[7] It covers evolutionary constitutionalism (e.g. as emphasized in the chapter by J. Flett), transformative national constitutionalism (e.g. as elaborated by E. Daly/M. Tigre/N. Urzola for the Americas), and constructive, multilevel constitutionalism at national and international levels of governance (e.g. as emphasized by

7 This 'open definition' differs from the state-centered definition proposed by Loughlin (n 3, pages 6–7), according to whom a modern Constitution '(1) establishes a comprehensive scheme of government, founded (2) on the principle of representative government and (3) on the need to divide, channel, and constrain governmental powers for the purpose of safeguarding individual liberty. That constitution is also envisaged (4) as creating a permanent governing framework that (5) is conceived as establishing a system of fundamental law supervised by a judiciary charged with elaborating the requirements of public reason, so that (6) the constitution is able to assume its true status as the authoritative expression of the regime's collective political identity'. From the point of view of European constitutionalism, such traditional definitions neglect the transformation of most *national* into *transnational PGs* resulting from globalization, the 'republican task' of constitutions to respond to demand by citizens for protecting such transnational PGs, and the democratic task of constitutionalism to protect democratic input-legitimacy and output-legitimacy of multilevel governance of global PGs, which no single state can protect without international law and multilevel governance institutions. Mere constitutional nationalism without regard to transnational governance failures has become parochial and democratically irresponsible. The public disinformation of the nationalist 'Brexit politics' is also increasingly recognized in Britain; cf Martin Sandbu, *No, there isn't a 'democratic deficit' in the EU,* Financial Times 14 August 2023. See also Philip Stevens, *The EU is doing more – lots more,* Financial Times of 18 August 2023 (explaining why – contrary to the predictions during the Brexit referendum in 2016 that a leave vote would see the EU collapse under the weight of its intrusions into national affairs – the new EU migration, health, environmental and common defense policies responding to the migration, COVID-19, climate change and security crises continue being supported by EU citizens and their democratic institutions). Even if recent opinion polls in the UK now show clear and consistent expressions of regret that the country left the EU, 'rejoining the EU remains a very distant dream' (Robert Shrimsley, *Financial Times* 31 August 2023).

European lawyers and in the negotiations on reforming investor-state arbitration); Anglo-Saxon claims 'against constitutionalism' (e.g. based on nationalist conceptions of representative democracy and insufficient popular support for constitutionalism beyond states) offer no coherent responses for protecting transnational PGs; in Europe, they have been refuted by the effectiveness of European constitutional law and by the 'constitutional patriotism' of EU citizens supporting multilevel democratic and republican constitutionalism for limiting national governance failures, as discussed in various chapters of this book.

The legal, political, economic and social processes of constitutionalism – like democratic 'constitutional politics' transforming agreed 'constitutional contracts' (e.g. on national Constitutions) into democratic legislation and administrative and judicial protection of rule-of-law – are complicated by globalization, its transformation of *national* into *transnational* PGs (like protection of the environment, rule of law, public health), and by the reality of 'constitutional pluralism'. Depending on their historical evolution and democratic preferences, UN member states often prioritize conflicting values (like state sovereignty, popular sovereignty, inalienable rights of citizens) ushering in regulatory competition and geopolitical rivalries. The linking of economic, environmental and social rules with human rights and rule-of-law principles in the UN SDA could not prevent transnational governance failures undermining the universally agreed SDGs like food security (SDG2), healthy lives (SDG3), climate change mitigation (SDG13) and protection of other environmental commons (SDGs 14 and 15), access to justice and rule-of-law (SDG16). Exploring 'constitutional pluralism' reveals fundamental divergences on how to protect PGs, as illustrated by the diverse EU and US climate change legislation and litigation analyzed in Part II of this book. The protection of civil, political, economic and social human rights in the national constitutional systems of the member states of the EU and of the broader European Economic Area (EEA) – reinforced by EU law, EEA law, the European Convention of Human Rights (ECHR) and UN human rights law – has no equivalent in Africa, the Americas and Asia. Europe's multilevel 'constitutional politics' (e.g. in national and European parliaments), like the 'constitutional economics' underlying Europe's unique economic and environmental constitutionalism, are characterized by multilevel legal, democratic and judicial restraints on abuses of public and private power, 'institutional checks and balances', science-based regulatory agencies, and legal protection of individual preferences (e.g. by judicial protection of human and fundamental rights and non-discriminatory competition as a discovery procedure and as restraint on abuses of power). The editors share the EU's ordo-liberal commitment to 'normative and methodological individualism', which is justified by

UN and European human rights law (HRL). The 1948 Universal Declaration of Human Rights acknowledges the perennial human search for morality, reasonableness and universal protection of human rights (cf Article 1 UDHR); the social and political nature of human beings as reflected in human rights to individual and democratic self-development (cf the Preamble and Articles 19–21 UDHR); the limitation of 'human dignity' by human passions provoking perennial abuses of public and private power (as recalled in the Preamble of the UDHR), resulting in the need for institutionalizing public reason and democratic constitutionalism based on rule-of-law and communitarian, democratic and judicial institutions protecting PGs (cf Articles 27–29 UDHR), including also undistorted market competition as a decentralized information, coordination and sanctioning mechanism inducing citizens to supply and demand scarce goods and services.[8] Yet, the realities of 'constitutional pluralism' based on diverse conceptions and traditions of constitutionalism are reflected in the chapters of this book written by authors from diverse continents. The ubiquity of transnational governance failures illustrates how UN HRL is not effectively implemented through 'constitutional politics' and 'constitutional economics' in many UN member states. Constitutional economics (as discussed in *Chapter 3*) aims at protecting 'consumer sovereignty' in Europe's common market and 'citizen sovereignty' in Europe's constitutional democracies; its normative individualism (acknowledging voluntary, informed consent of citizens as primary source of democratic and economic values) goes far beyond the basic principles of the Bretton Woods agreements, GATT, the WTO, international investment and environmental law, which – even though historically designed by and for market economies – include only insufficient legal disciplines for non-discriminatory conditions of competition and rule-of-law, notably in state-capitalist countries. 'Constitutional economics' as economic discipline originated in the USA.

8 For a human rights approach to international economic regulation challenging the neoliberal focus on the utility-maximizing rationality of the *homo economicus* (as emphasized by utilitarian neoliberalism as advocated by UK Prime Minister Thatcher and US President Reagan during the 1980s) by acknowledging the social and political vulnerability of the *homo laborans* and *homo politicus* see: E.U. Petersmann, *International Economic Law in the 21st Century. Constitutional Pluralism and Multilevel Governance of Interdependent Public Goods* (Hart 2012). The editors of this book emphasize that the needed legal protection of general interests in non-discriminatory conditions of market competition (e.g. by protecting 'consumer sovereignty' in economic markets and 'citizen sovereignty' in democratic markets) must be complemented by legal safeguards of special interests (e.g. for protecting decent working conditions) and by democratic and judicial 'balancing procedures' (e.g. for promoting social justice, reconciling investor rights and shareholder interests in profit-maximization with larger 'stakeholder interests' in sustainable development).

Yet, its multilevel policy implementation remained essentially limited to economic agreements among democracies in Europe and in third countries (like Canada), which concluded free trade agreements (FTAs) with human rights guarantees with the EU. Neither constitutional economics nor the liberal, economic principles underlying the IMF, GATT and WTO agreements (like monetary convertibility, protection of private rights, rules-based open markets aimed at non-discriminatory conditions of competition) are effectively protected in authoritarian states like China and Russia, which acceded to the Bretton Woods and WTO agreements without effectively implementing their underlying 'embedded liberalism'.

UN and WTO law have not prevented public and private abuses of power nurturing geopolitical rivalries undermining HRL and WTO rules for non-discriminatory conditions of trade. In contrast to Europe, the responses by African, American and Asian governments to the global governance challenges remain guided by diverse constitutional and political governance traditions, as discussed in the various chapters of this book. Cultural, social, and legal diversity fosters economic and legal incoherencies between neoliberal, ordoliberal, totalitarian and 'third world' approaches to multilevel governance of PGs (like the SDGs). Russian wars of aggression and trade wars between China and the USA have made 'constitutional reforms' of UN and WTO law unlikely. The 'unipolar moment' after the dissolution of the Soviet Union (1991) has given rise to a new multipolar world with increasing regulatory competition and transnational governance failures disrupting the diverse UN/WTO governance regimes for PGs.[9] This book explores reasonable responses to the global governance crises.

3 Part I: Constitutional Pluralism, Constitutional Politics and Constitutional Economics

Chapter 2 on *Constitutional pluralism, regulatory competition and transnational governance failures* proceeds from the fact that all UN member states use constitutionalism for protecting national PGs. The current human disasters – like illegal wars of aggression, violent suppression of human and democratic

9 For a discussion of the different kinds of (trans)national PGs (like non-rival and non-excludable 'pure PGs', excludable 'club goods', and exhaustible 'common pool resources'), which require diverse policy responses, see E.U. Petersmann (n 2), at 190 ff. On the lack of rights-and citizen-based 'legal civilization' in many non-European countries with non-democratic, communitarian cultures see Petersmann (n 5).

rights, global health pandemics, climate change, ocean pollution, overfishing and other biodiversity losses, and non-compliance with UN and WTO law and dispute settlement systems – reflect transnational governance failures and 'constitutional failures' to protect human and democratic rights and the SDGs. Since the 1950s, Europe's multilevel constitutionalism succeeded in progressively limiting transnational governance failures; yet, it is not followed outside Europe. Geopolitical power politics and constitutional nationalism prompted China, Russia and the USA to resist constitutional reforms of UN/WTO governance and 'environmental constitutionalism'. Constitutionally unbound 'totalitarian states' (like China and Russia) and Anglo-Saxon neo-liberal interest group politics (notably in the USA) disrupt the rules-based world trading system. The more globalization is perceived as creating vulnerabilities justifying national security restrictions (e.g. against spread of viruses, weaponization of interdependence), the more important become plurilateral second-best responses like free trade and investment agreements prescribing respect for human rights and judicial remedies, 'de-risking' global supply chains, and 'climate protection clubs' conditioning market access on greenhouse gas reductions. The sociological insight underlying the ordoliberal objective of a 'social market economy' – that citizens must be empowered by human and constitutional rights and social security to adjust to, and support, the changes imposed in open societies with economic and democratic competition – remains true also for the needed transformation of international economic law (IEL) to better protect the universally agreed SDGs. The neoliberal paradigm of a utility-maximizing *homo economicus* must be supplemented by the human rights paradigm of individual and democratic self-determination by reasonable citizens who remain socially and politically vulnerable unless they are protected by civil, political, economic, social and cultural rights to develop their diverse human capacities. Yet, authoritarian rulers reject this primacy of reasonable citizen interests and the legal-institutional framework for market economies and constitutional democracies reconciling the individual pursuit of self-interests with the common citizen interests in PGs and social justice.

Chapter 3 on *Constitutional economics and transnational governance failures* explains 'constitutional economics' as a methodology for analyzing legal strategies aimed at 'constitutionalizing' foreign policy powers and the law of international organizations. Constitutional economics distinguishes between 'market failures' (like distortions of competition, environmental pollution, social injustices), 'governance failures' (like insufficient protection of PG like the SDGs, suppression of human and democratic rights), and 'constitutional failures' (like non-existence of rules of higher rank limiting market and governance failures, inadequate rule of law, lack of democratic governance institutions). These three types of transnational governance failures disrupt equal human and constitutional rights and different policy fields characterized by collective action dilemmas (like climate change mitigation, international rule-of-law, division of labor through international trade and investments). With its 'normative individualism' prioritizing mutual agreeability of constitutional arrangements for all members of society aimed at protecting 'consumer sovereignty' and 'citizen sovereignty', constitutional economics has been the conceptual underpinning of European multilevel governance; it could promote also UN/WTO governance protecting legislative, administrative and adjudicative rule of law and equal rights inside and beyond states through international rules of a higher legal rank. Disentangling policy failures into *market*, *governance* and *constitutional* failures offers analytical insights and normative guidance for responding to the causes of policy failures. The distinctions clarify responsibilities and allow targeting policy responses; they reveal deficiency of rules and inform their re-design; and highlight systemic rivalries between rules-based, state-controlled, and business-determined governance regimes. Many countries outside Europe reject Europe's 'normative individualism' for protecting non-discriminatory market competition through multilevel democratic protection of human and constitutional rights and independent regulatory and judicial institutions.

Chapters 1–3 form Part I which discusses and defines 'transnational governance failures' by the failure of markets, governments and international organizations to protect transnational PGs (like compliance with UN and WTO law as ratified by national parliaments) and to effectively contribute to the universally agreed 17 SDGs. The emergence of a multi-polar world with authoritarian governments disregarding UN and WTO law entails regulatory competition and systemic rivalries undermining the UN SDA and human rights. Transnational governance failures violating international law confirm that path-dependent governance methods – like constitutional nationalism, intergovernmental power politics, and conceptions of international organizations as 'international functionalism' among states (rather than as multilevel governance for the benefit of citizens) – may not suffice for realizing the universally agreed SDGs. Part I explains the methods suggested by the book editors (i.e. normative and methodological individualism) for exploring alternative policy responses remedying collective action problems (such as climate mitigation) and maintaining international rule-of-law (e.g. through reforms of trade, investment and environmental rules and dispute settlement procedures, plurilateral agreements on carbon taxes and carbon-border adjustment measures). The following three research questions had been proposed by the book editors for the elaboration of all book chapters in view of their universal importance for realizing the SDGs:

(1) To what extent will the realities of the 'multipolar world' undermine the supply of transnational PGs such as the rule-of-law objectives of the UN SDA (SDG16) and environmental preservation (cf SDGs13–15)? Can the lack of effective UN and WTO legal disciplines on 'market failures' (like restraints of competition, external effects, information asymmetries), 'governance failures' (e.g. to respect rule-of-law and protect PGs) and 'constitutional failures' (e.g. in terms of protecting human rights against authoritarian power politics) be compensated by more decentralized private-public partnerships (e.g. for decarbonizing and digitalizing economies, inventing and distributing vaccines for everybody) and plurilateral agreements? Contributions in this book offer multiple avenues towards the supply of transnational PGs. Private-public partnerships are at the core of the contributions by Lamy and Denton, whose recommendations aim at moving from a state-centered Westphalian order towards one that emphasizes the different contributions of societal actors (societal groups, business, individuals, states) towards the achievement of the SDG. The shift towards plurilateral approaches looms behind the EU's endeavour to introduce a CBAM (discussed by Flett) as core element of a 'climate club' that would offer incentives for more ambitious SDG efforts.

(2) Can republican constitutionalism be extended to multilevel governance of transnational PGs (like compulsory judicial remedies in WTO law) and remain democratically and legally accountable to citizens and their representative institutions? The policy responses discussed in Part III explore how new and decentralized forms of cooperation may contribute to effective PG supply (Lamy, Denton), or how regional and plurilateral cooperation may offer 'second-best policies' for preserving rules-based cooperation overcoming collective action dilemmas (Chaisse, Fahey) and disagreements on trade and investment adjudication (van den Bossche, Marceddu).

(3) Are there lessons from Europe's multilevel constitutionalism for reforming multilevel governance of global PGs like the SDGs? This book does *not* claim that the European experiences with transforming governance failures (e.g. in monetary, competition, environmental and human rights policies) into multilateral constitutional reforms should serve as a role model for governance reforms in different global and regional contexts. The 'interdependence of orders' (like social, cultural, economic, political and legal systems) and the unique context of European

integration may exclude such 'policy transfers' to diverse institutional, legal, and cultural traditions. For example, Europe's focus on individual rights limiting 'market failures' (e.g. by competition, environmental and social rights and judicial remedies), 'governance failures' (e.g. by rule-of-law requirements, institutional 'checks and balances') and 'constitutional failures' (e.g. protecting human and constitutional rights of EU citizens) has no equivalent in constitutionalism in Africa, the Americas or Asia. Yet, as discussed in Part II of this book, the EU's climate change litigation and 'environmental constitutionalism' are influencing environmental governance and 'climate litigation' also in some countries outside Europe (like Brazil and Colombia) (Daly/Tiger/Urzola). The more geopolitical rivalries prompt hegemonic governments to disrupt UN and WTO governance and related third-party adjudication, the more important become regional and functionally limited, plurilateral alliances of countries and private-public partnerships (e.g. for decarbonizing and digitalizing economies, providing vaccines to all countries) supporting global PGs like transnational rule-of-law (van den Bossche, Marceddu).

4 Part II: Constitutional Pluralism, Rule-of-Law and Climate Change Mitigation: How to Limit Transnational Governance Failures in Climate Change Mitigation?

The contributions in Part II explore origins and remedies of transnational governance failures by using the example of the perennial failures of mitigating climate change effectively in the context of the 1992 UN Framework Convention on Climate Change (UNFCCC). The 2015 Paris Agreement on climate change mitigation recognizes the sovereignty of its more than 190 contracting states to decide on their 'nationally determined contributions' (NDCs) – subject to periodic, international surveillance procedures – for realizing the universally agreed goal of decarbonizing economies to limit global temperature rises to 1.5°C, and to keep them 'well below' 2.0°C above pre-industrial times. The authors from Europe, the US and Asia explain why European, US and Asian views on 'environmental constitutionalism' differ fundamentally among these three regions of the world. This entails what Part I described as regulatory competition among competing conceptions of regulation. Comparative studies of EU, US, Latin American, Chinese, Japanese and UN environmental policies demonstrate how diverse constitutional contexts contribute to diverse environmental and climate change regulations and policies. Constitutionalism, decarbonizing economies, regulatory competition and perceived national security risks interact dynamically; they explain some of the environmental governance failures (like insufficient phasing-out of fossil fuels, lack of support in the US Congress for carbon taxes, 'carbon leakage' caused by diverse regulatory standards and regulatory competition for attracting 'green investments'). 'Environmental constitutionalism' – inspired also by constitutional economics insights – increasingly influences European environmental practices (like EU primary and secondary law, environmental litigation) and also some Latin American countries prone to transformative constitutionalism; yet, it remains contested outside the EU (e.g. in US federal courts exercising 'judicial deference' vis-à-vis democratic legislatures), and seems to play no role in authoritarian countries like China and Russia.

The 'implementation deficits' undermining the SDGs can be reduced by bottom-up approaches promoting parliamentary, participatory and deliberative, democratic constitutionalism where possible, particularly in the EU with its tradition of fundamental rights recognition, economic and environmental constitutionalism and climate litigation (as discussed in the chapter by Eckes). The EU's constitutional requirements to protect the EU's internal constitutional principles also in the EU's external policies prompted the EU legislation on introducing WTO-consistent Carbon Border Adjustment Measures (CBAMs) as discussed in the chapter by Flett. Rights-based trade and climate litigation exists also in Latin American countries like Brazil and Colombia; it remains resisted in more process-oriented governance systems like the US and its constitutional nationalism (as discussed in the chapter by Daly/Tigre/Urzola). In Anglo-Saxon federal states (like Australia and the USA), regional or state-level bottom-up constitutionalism could be more promising rather than top-down federal obligations (Daly). Similarly, in China, regional autonomy offers potential leverage (e.g. for 'green cities') to promote bottom-up environmentalism; but it has also enabled resistance against top-down reforms (e.g. for phasing-out of coal-based energy plants at the request of China's central government), as discussed by Gao and Zhou.

The EU's *'environmental constitutionalisation'* has evolved from a sectoral policy to one of the core, transversal and guiding components of the EU legal order. The constitutional dimension of environmental protection is reflected in environmental objectives, principles and rules in EU primary and secondary law, which have promoted 'environmental democracy' and an environmental dimension also in the EUCFR. The EU's environmental constitutionalism responds to global environmental challenges emphasizing the 'intrinsic value' of environmental protection within the EU legal order and the *'constitutional consensus'* among EU Member States that environmental protection warrants high levels of legal and judicial protection. Environmental transition is particularly visible in EU secondary law following the approval, in 2020, of the EU Green Deal for decarbonizing and greening the EU's economy. The multiple policy tools and mandatory standards aim at a socially 'just transition' with active industrial policies to secure continuing economic growth. Their promotion of 'climate change litigation' and of external 'carbon border adjustment measures' confirm the transformative nature of the EU's environmental constitutionalism.

Chapter 4 on *Governance failures in court: How litigation constitutionalizes norms on climate change mitigation* illustrates the citizen-driven dimension of the EU's environmental constitutionalism and of the central role of individual preference orientation that constitutional economics posits. The contribution emphasizes the role of individuals in claiming effective supply of environmental PGs and strengthening multilevel 'climate constitutionalism' in Europe through strategic climate litigation relying on international or regional environmental commitments that originate outside the domestic legal order, with a higher legal rank than the domestic executive and legislative actions and inactions that they challenge. Often, later cases replicate successful legal arguments and strategies from earlier cases and vest them with additional authority. Some climate litigation relies on international and European human rights norms – like the right to life (Article 2 ECHR) and the right to respect for private and family life (Article 8 ECHR) – and norms relating to states' responsibility for adaptation and mitigation, such as the 2015 Paris Agreement and the 2021 Glasgow Climate Pact. Ratifying and participating in the UNFCCC has repeatedly been viewed as justification for demanding greater mitigation efforts than originally planned by national institutions. While the European Court of Human Rights had earlier interpreted human rights to cover situations where people's lives were affected by environmental pollution, the court pioneered by interpreting Articles 2 and 8 ECHR to entail an obligation to mitigate climate change.

Chapter 5 on *EU Proposals for WTO-consistent Carbon Border Adjustment Mechanisms* emphasizes the evolutionary nature of the process by which States construct appropriate multilateral governance in response to their search for proper governance of PGs. The EU's quest for WTO-consistent, multilateral solutions respects the realities of constitutional pluralism. This is also why each WTO Member only has one vote (there is no weighting); why, even though voting is provided for, in practice no Member ever calls for a vote and decisions are taken by consensus; and there is no independent executive. Mandatory and binding adjudication is a step down the evolutionary path but is temporarily partially obstructed by the United States. In these circumstances, geopolitical rivalry and power play are inevitable elements of international governance and can be used by states in pursuit of the protection of the transnational PG, as illustrated by the EU proposal for a Carbon Border Adjustment Mechanism. This 'CBAM' is quite particular because credit is given for any carbon price already paid in the third country; this is central both to establishing its exclusively environmental credentials and to understanding the very specific regulatory nudge created for third countries providing, in the current circumstances, the best available model for propelling the evolutionary protection of sustainable global governance of PGs.

In contrast to Europe's 'environmental constitutionalism', the United States' climate and environmental regulations can be characterized as a process-based – rather than rights-based – regulatory approach. This absence of US environmental constitutionalism is also influenced by regulatory competition favoring the use of second-best policy instruments in the 2022 US Inflation Reduction Action Act aimed at reducing CO_2 emissions (as a transnational PG). The US Supreme Court has not recognized constitutional rights to protection of the environment, for example in terms of negative rights against harmful externalities (built on a commitment to end uninternalized externalities). The U.S. Congress – rather than introducing non-discriminatory carbon taxes – has chosen second-best, discriminatory 'subsidies strategies' for climate change in the 2022 US Inflation Reduction Act, which sets strong incentives for industry investments into green technologies. The co-existence of diverse NDCs under the 2015 Paris Agreement – such as emission trading systems, carbon taxes and related carbon border tariffs, green subsidies, environmental standards and other NDCs – intensifies regulatory competition and potential trade disputes over discriminatory CBAMs, for instance if such CBAMs focus only on explicit domestic carbon prices without taking into account other NDCs like the phasing-out of fossil fuel subsidies.

Chapter 6 on *'Environmental constitutionalism' for improving UN environmental law and governance: Latin American and US perspectives* discusses the different forms which environmental constitutionalism has taken in the Americas in response to climate change mitigation. This contribution describes recent developments in the United States, Colombia, and Brazil, highlighting the divergent constitutional and legal approaches to climate protection. Notwithstanding the rhetoric of rights in the popular imagination, rights-based approaches have never driven policy in the United States, either in the context of environmental and climate policy or otherwise. Nor has popular will often impelled government action. Nor for that matter has the U.S. tended to be swayed by international winds. Instead, the U.S. tends to rely on a combination of market-based approaches and administrative enforcement of broad legislative principles to advance national well-being, in the belief that markets, rather than political or judicial elites, are more likely to be responsive to both existing conditions and popular will. Where pursuit of national welfare meets with geoeconomic competition, business-driven approaches marry with state intervention engaging in discriminatory and protective means in order to protect domestic business. In this regard, the Inflation Reduction Act of 2022, which contains the most innovative and ambitious climate mitigation goals in the country's history, exemplifies this approach. This contrasts with the more constitutional economic approaches elsewhere in the Americas: rights-based approaches have held sway as constitutional courts have been especially responsive to individual and collective claims for environmental protection and climate change mitigation in the context of robust environmental constitutionalism. In particular, the courts of Colombia and Brazil have been global pioneers in the recognition of environmental and even climate rights to galvanize political action. Colombia's Constitutional and Supreme Courts have for many years protected environmental rights as part of an integrated web of human rights including rights to food, water, shelter, health, education and dignity for indigenous and non-indigenous communities. Brazil's judiciary has been equally committed to environmental protection; in the summer of 2022, the Brazilian Federal Supreme Tribunal held that the obligation to comply with the Paris Agreement creates enforceable human rights that individuals can vindicate in court and that the government is obligated to respect; failure to establish a climate fund, for instance, is not only a violation of the accord but an actionable violation of a constitutional and human right that controls the government. While the US may provide a model of political and economic approaches to climate mitigation, courts in Latin America, as exemplified by Brazil and Colombia, are providing a model of progressive rights-based action. This chapter analyzes these national examples from a comparative perspective, assessing their effectiveness to climate mitigation and their connection to the editors' analytical framework. The transformative constitutionalism of some Latin American countries can be likened with the constitutional economics approach and the assertive role of European courts in enforcing individual rights.

Chapter 7 on *Constitutional Failures or Market Failures: China, Climate Change and Energy Transition* analyzes Chinese climate change mitigation policies embedded into state planning and state-authoritarian approaches to the protection of the environment. China's greenhouse gas emissions exceed those of all OECD market economies. In September 2016, China formally ratified the Paris Agreement. Four years later, President Xi announced China's plan to further scale up its intended NDCs, which aim to have CO_2 emissions peak before 2030 and achieve carbon neutrality before 2060. Due to China's unique political system, many people expect China to be a leader in climate change mitigation given the personal commitment of the top leader to climate issues. Can state-authoritarian systems ignoring individual rights be a role model in effectively supplying environmental PGs? This paper illustrates the complex political economic tensions between the different stakeholders behind China's climate policy, especially between the central and local governments, through a case study on the reduction of the reliance on coal power, as announced by China in April 2021. As the result, in 2021, China's new coal power plants saw a reduction of 57% compared to 2020. However, the good progress in energy transition was interrupted by the power outage sprawling over 20 provinces in China in September 2021, which resulted in a U-turn in the policy. As the consequence, China reversed its course of action, with more coal power plants approved in the last month of 2021 than all 11 months before combined. This chapter explores the reasons behind China's policy shift; the major domestic factors driving China's policy; the major players involved in the decision-making; whether this kind of policy-making engenders transnational policy failures; how conflicts between national and subnational interests and approaches have been resolved; and how the bargaining between different domestic players impacts China's approaches in FTAs and other trade and investment negotiations.

At the HEC conference at Paris in September 2022, an additional presentation on *Japanese and Asian leadership for climate change mitigation?* described how Japan's climate law and policy have always been driven by international developments of climate policy, especially international climate treaties. The Climate Action Plan of Government is a key tool to implement climate policy under the 1998 Law Concerning the Promotion of Measures to Cope with Global Warming (1998 Law); yet, it looks as a mere compilation of measures taken or planned by relevant ministries rather than as a comprehensive strategy. The minimal intervention of law in climate actions is another feature; it barely obliges private entities to undertake climate actions. Japan's climate law and policy raise problems of effectiveness and equity. Since acknowledgment of the net zero by 2050 goal in October 2020 and its aligned pledge (in its 2030 NDC) to reduce carbon emissions by 46 to 50 per cent below 2013 levels, significant changes have emerged. Climate change consideration permeates also other areas of laws and policies such as circular economy regulation and aviation law, aligned with the net zero by 2050 goal. The long-term goal drives climate law and policy toward a more integrated system and its 'constitutionalization'. Private sectors' behaviour has been changing through integration and mainstreaming of climate consideration into its business and management, promoted by financial institutions requesting sustainability reporting and undertaking ESG investing. Integration and convergence of sustainability reporting standards by private sector at the global level are in progress through elaboration of rules for sustainability reporting by the International Sustainability Standard Board. The private standard-making impacts and interacts with rule making by public authorities. However, voluntary actions by companies and social sanction from capital market may cause problems of effectiveness, of equity and of legitimacy. Transforming existing rules consistent with net zero goal to enhance actions by private sectors is more essential than ever, for instance through legalization of sustainability reporting, modernization of the Energy Charter Treaty and of trade rules. For Japan and Asian countries where spontaneous drivers for stringent climate actions are relatively weak, international norm-making is more critical than in other parts of the globe. Japanese and Asian leadership will be determined by whether and what appropriate public policy at all levels, especially at the international one, should be introduced for decarbonization.

5 Part III: Policy Proposals for Limiting Transnational Governance Failures

SDG 16 recalls obligations to 'promote the rule of law at the national and international levels and ensure equal access to justice for all', including in international trade and investments whose systemic importance for sustainable development and for decarbonization of economies the SDA acknowledges. With transnational governance failures challenging the rule of law in international trade, investment, and environmental policies, Part III discusses reforms of UN and WTO governance (Chapters 8 and 9), of transatlantic leadership for reforming international trade, investment and environmental regulation (Chapters 10 and 11), of the WTO dispute settlement system (Chapter 12) and investor-state arbitration (Chapter 13). The realities of 'constitutional pluralism', regulatory competition, power rivalries and unilateralism undermine UN and WTO law and related 'economic constitutionalization' (like compulsory third-party adjudication in WTO law, in investment agreements and in the UN Law of the Sea Convention), thereby weakening legal accountability for transnational governance failures and provoking additional power rivalries. The concluding Chapter 14 explains how Asian countries seek to maintain the advantages of rules-based trade and investment integration by concluding an increasing number of regional trade and investment agreements influenced by Asia's communitarian rather than individualist, constitutional traditions.

In *Chapter 8* on *Reforming UN and WTO governance: Multilateralism and polylateralism*, former WTO Director-General Pascal Lamy emphasizes the multiple types of transnational policy failure resulting from interpreting UN and WTO governance as based on inter-national treaties, member-driven institutions and state sovereignty. Human rights and UN law failed to prevent President Putin's illegal war of aggression, Russia's interpretation of UN law as a framework for intergovernmental power politics, and Russia's public disinformation and authoritarian suppression of democratic rights. Similarly, business-driven neoliberalism prevented prioritization of citizen interests and regulation of market failures like global pollution and climate change. Power-oriented 'Westphalian conceptions of law' facilitate abuses of power unless citizens, democratic and judicial institutions, NGOs, multinational corporations, major cities and science-based institutions are effectively empowered to participate in purpose-driven, multi-stakeholder coalitions protecting transnational PGs. Such 'polylateralism' has been tested at the Paris Peace Forum, a five years old promising innovation in global governance, as evidenced by several successes in various domains such as the environment, supply of vaccines, financial support of independent media, SDG benchmarks for transnational corporations, Internet protection of children, and protection of Antarctica. Citizens should not expect too much from intergovernmental multilateralism and invest more in polylateralism.

In *Chapter 9* on *Business views on transnational 'governance failures' and 'corporate responsibilities'*, the Secretary-General of the International Chamber of Commerce, John W.H. Denton AO, explains why the member-driven character of international organizations undermines the contribution of non-members to effective problem-solving. The current institutional governance architecture is inadequate in light of the rapidly changing context of technological progress, digitization and environmental challenges driven by nongovernmental actors. Recent crises such as COVID-19 have demonstrated the value of cooperation between states and non-state actors in responding to governance crises more effectively (like state-sponsored cyber-attacks, production and distribution of vaccines in response to global health pandemics, private financial and food assistance, development of green technologies). The International Chamber of Commerce and its global network of national chambers of commerce (coordinating some 50 million enterprises) can strengthen the contribution of non-state actors (like pharmaceutical industries, environmental technology industries, global internet companies) in multilevel governance of PGs. Intergovernmental institutions (like the WTO, the WHO, the FAO) must cooperate more closely with private stakeholders to effectively respond to global health pandemics, the need for decarbonizing economies, limiting ocean pollution and over-fishing. Negotiations on reforming the UN and WTO governance architectures should provide for stronger business advisory groups capable of practically harnessing the expertise, resources and ideas of non-state actors.

In *Chapter 10* on *U.S. Trade and Multilateralism*, former WTO Appellate Body member Merit Janow describes the evolution of US trade policies from being a key architect of the postwar GATT/WTO trading system to the current US blockage of the WTO Appellate Body system and frequent disregard for WTO law by the US Congress and executive trade policies. While acknowledging the importance of a functioning WTO and multilateralism, the Biden Administration is intensely focused on domestic issues in the US economy. Recent US legislation and executive measures aim at incentivizing domestic investment and production, bringing supply chains back to the US ('homeshoring') or nearby, expanding trade and supply chain resilience with 'friendly' nations, promoting production of semiconductors and clean technologies, and reducing technology dependency and interaction with China.

Chapter 11 on *Democratic Leadership through Transatlantic Cooperation for Trade and Environmental reforms?* explores transatlantic relations as a case study for responding to transnational policy failures, as a major platform of experimentation, and as a political and legal willingness to lead. Since the 1990s, the Transatlantic Partnership mostly provides evidence of 'law-light' 'institution light' commitments to bilateral law-making at best, and at worst to many failed global governance experiments. Civil society has historically been excluded. The establishment of the Trade and Technology Council (TTC) illustrates how trade and technology are now viewed by the EU and US as the lynchpins of solutions to global challenges. The paper considers the place of soft law and institutions in transatlantic cooperation, the place of multilateralism and international law within this framing. It focuses on two case studies: the 2022 US CHIPS and Science Act relating to subsidies and microchips; and the promotion of clean technologies for climate change mitigation through the 2022 US Inflation Reduction Act. The TTC offers potential for inclusion of civil society and responsiveness to policy needs; but its intergovernmental coordination opens the door also to regulatory capture and power politics.

In *Chapter 12*, former WTO Appellate Body member Peter van den Bossche examines: *Can the WTO Dispute Settlement System be Revived? Options for Addressing a Major Governance Failure of the World Trade Organization'.* He discusses the nature of the crisis, its impact on the rule of law in world trade, and the 'concerns' of the United States regarding the functioning of the Appellate Body, which triggered this crisis – underscoring how weak constitutional restraints on power politics and on business-driven regulatory capture lead to transnational governance failure. The analysis then examines how the paralysis of the Appellate Body since December 2019 has affected the WTO dispute settlement system as a whole and has resulted in a significant weakening of the rule of law in world trade. The paralysis of the Appellate Body has left many disputes in legal limbo, has caused a drastic drop in the number of disputes brought to the WTO for resolution, and has triggered recourse to unilateral action in response to alleged breaches of WTO law. This chapter explores what kind of reform would be needed to 'revive' the Appellate Body and restore binding WTO dispute settlement. It questions whether the adoption of a more deferential standard of appellate review, more flexibility regarding the time frame for appellate review, enlarging the Appellate Body and strengthening its independence, and/or establishing a Dispute Settlement Review Committee to oversee the Appellate Body, are elements of the reform needed. It emphasizes that any reform of the Appellate Body would need to be accompanied by a reform of the panel process and of the remedies for breach of WTO law. There is also a need to address the WTO's institutional imbalance by strengthening its negotiation/rule-making function. Finally, the chapter discusses the lessons for the governance of international adjudication that can, and should, be drawn from the crisis of the Appellate Body, and offers some views on the prospects for overcoming the crisis. Considering current international and national political realities and constitutional pluralism, the article considers it unlikely that it will be possible to overcome the crisis any time soon. This sad state of affairs may, however, give room for experimentation with other methods of trade dispute settlement, such as mediation, conciliation, arbitration or regional dispute resolution.

Chapter 13 on *EU and UN Proposals for reforming investor-state arbitration* explores the dissatisfaction with investment arbitration, which has grown considerably both in academia and the political debate. More than ever, the investment regime is nowadays under scrutiny and contested, mostly because the system has evolved into a complex regime in which foreign investments have to be accommodated with other needs that go beyond the purely economic sphere – for example, health, environmental, social and labor issues. The current efforts to reform investor-state dispute settlement, undertaken by the European Union, the United Nations Commission on International Trade Law (UNCITRAL), and the United Nation Conference on Trade and Development (UNCTAD) respond to these non-economic needs. The article, first, considers justice as *openness*. In democratic adjudicative processes, powers like those of arbitrators reviewing matters of public interest and issuing compensation from public funds need to be exercised publicly to ensure accountability and fairness. Second, it investigates justice in the decision-making process. Unlike other adjudicative systems, investment arbitration lacks institutional safeguards of judicial independence and procedural fairness. To this end, institutionalization and judicialization are advanced, especially by the European Commission, as remedies to enduring systemic malaise. Third, justice is conceived as a remedy to failures and social injustice. The investment arbitration system is rather asymmetric given that access is permitted to the claimant investor and the respondent government, but other parties, whose rights or interests may be affected by the decision-making, have no standing in the process.

Chapter 14 on *The future of regional economic cooperation and rivalries in Asia: Open regionalism or closed clubs?* explores Asia Pacific as home to two of the largest FTAs in the world: the Comprehensive and Progressive Trans-Pacific Partnership (CPTPP) and the Regional Comprehensive Economic Partnership (RCEP). In addition to these normative developments, the Indo-Pacific Economic Framework (IPEF) was launched in 2022, which has the potential to foster even greater economic and regulatory integration. This chapter explores the reasons for the proliferation of trade pacts in Asia Pacific, and discusses the future of regional economic cooperation in the region by drawing from a few key trends: the rise of China; the pivot to Asia by the US; the rivalry between the US and China; the competition and convergence of regional blocs; non-traditional agreements such as the Digital Economy Partnership Agreement (DEPA), the Singapore-New Zealand Declaration on Trade in Essential Goods, and IPEF; and the role of small open economies. The chapter reflects on whether the future will lead to open regionalism or closed clubs, as well as on transnational governance failures.

6 Policy Conclusions

Realizing the SDGs, and 'global survival governance' responding to transnational PGs (such as climate change mitigation and 'rule of law'), require maintaining and, to the extent possible, further developing UN and WTO law and governance and judicial remedies protecting transnational rule-of-law in multilevel governance of PGs. Yet, the increasing violations of UN and WTO law – a result of systemic rivalry and the reality of constitutional pluralism – by UN member states reflect transnational governance failures undermining the input-and output-legitimacy of UN and WTO governance and the effective protection of the SDGs. Among the many analytical findings and policy recommendations in the following 13 book chapters, the following conclusions of the editors are singled out:

(1) Human rights and democratic constitutionalism require UN member states to protect 'normative individualism' (e.g. respect for, and legal protection of informed, individual and democratic consent as most legitimate sources of values) in their legal design of multilevel governance of PGs like the SDGs, as confirmed by the EU Treaty requirements to protect human rights and rule-of law also in EU external relations (Part I).

(2) In order to circumvent state-centered opposition and respond to governance crises more effectively (like state-sponsored cyber-attacks, production and distribution of vaccines in response to global health pandemics, private financial and food assistance for less-developed countries, development of green technologies), the contribution of non-state actors (like pharmaceutical industries, environmental technology industries, global internet companies, the International Chamber of Commerce and its global network of national chambers of commerce coordinating some 50 million enterprises) needs to be strengthened and institutionalized (Denton); such 'polycentric governance approaches' leveraging more flexible stakeholder cooperation integrating and incentivizing civil society actors (Lamy) are increasingly important in multilevel governance of PGs (like cyber security, decarbonization of economies and investment law reforms).

(3) Intergovernmental institutions (like the WTO, the WHO, the FAO) must cooperate more closely among each other and with private stakeholders (like pharmaceutical industries protected by intellectual property rights, shipping companies capable of transporting wheat exports from Ukraine) in order to effectively respond to global health pandemics and to the need for decarbonizing economies (Denton). Conceptualization of international organizations as 'international functionalism' among states ('member-driven governance') disregards the need for cooperating with non-governmental actors and civil societies in the implementation of international rules (Lamy). A human rights approach insists on democratic input-and output-legitimacy of multilevel governance of PGs for the benefit of citizens (Petersmann).

(4) Path-dependent standard tools of formal and hard law approaches to rule-making may need to be relativized in favor of informal 'law-light policy dialogues' attenuating formal conceptions of 'sovereign veto powers' by pragmatic expert cooperation (Lamy, Fahey). Constitutional commitments to sustainable development (such as laid down in EU, UN and WTO law) need to be politically, judicially and scientifically clarified (e.g. by monitoring climate change governance by

expert-driven surveillance based on scientific indicators); they can be rendered more effective by legal and judicial remedies (see the chapters by Eckes, van den Bossche, Flett). Even in the absence of formal changes of treaties, customary rules and general principles of international law, the dynamic interactions between rules and legal practices reveal structural changes in the international legal system (Chapter 1).

(5) The realities of 'constitutional pluralism' render impossible a one-size-fits-all constitutionalism that could remedy the diverse kinds of transnational governance failures identified in this book. Neither the 'constitutional politics' required for transforming UN and WTO governance principles into effective legislation and administrative and judicial protection of rule-of-law, nor the 'constitutional economics' underlying UN and WTO law and European integration law are effectively implemented in many jurisdictions. The *normative* goal of constitutional economics – like individual and democratic consent to rules of a higher legal rank protecting 'consumer sovereignty' and 'citizen sovereignty' through equal fundamental rights, democratic and social inclusion – remain contested inside and outside Europe, notably in authoritarian countries (Petersmann and Steinbach).

(6) 'Sovereign equality' of states and related 'constitutional pluralism' (e.g. maintaining power-based political and legal traditions) foster 'regulatory competition' and hegemonic rivalries among states prioritizing diverse values (like human rights, representative democracy, authoritarian traditions); such competition is often abused, for instance by extra-territorial power politics of stronger actors (e.g. if governments like the US Trump administration welcome the adoption by the WTO Dispute Settlement Body of 'constructive WTO dispute settlement rulings' supporting their own legal complaints vis-à-vis other WTO members, but reject similar WTO dispute settlement findings against themselves as defendant on the ground that the rulings create 'new obligations' not consented to by their government).[10] Institutional economics explains the need for legal institutions limiting 'moral hazards' inside multilevel governance and federal states, with rules on governing bailouts of banks and states (as controversially discussed in the Eurozone) as prominent examples.

---

10 On the illegal blocking and contradictory criticism by the United States of the WTO dispute settlement system see E.U. Petersmann, *Transforming World Trade and Investment Law for Sustainable Development* (OUP 2022), Chapter 3; *idem*, 'How Should WTO Members React to their WTO Governance Crises?' (2019) 18 *World Trade Review* 503.

(7) The interdependencies among social, economic, political and legal orders require designing rules and institutions with due regard to the political economy environment (e.g. political election campaign financing by business) in order to limit 'rent-seeking interest group politics' and 'regulatory capture' by protectionist interest groups. Decentralized supply of PGs (like invention, testing and production of pharmaceutical products and 'green technologies') requires private-public partnerships and 'corporate responsibilities' extending inter-state cooperation to private business and civil societies ('polylateralism' as proposed by Lamy).

(8) The normative recognition of citizen-oriented, reasonable 'constitutional choices' respecting human dignity (human and democratic rights), protection of human capabilities, constitutional rights of citizens (like equal access to education, health protection, satisfaction of basic needs), social justice (e.g. promoting 'social market economies' reducing unjust income distribution) and the principal-agent relationships between citizens and governance agents with limited, delegated powers remains limited to democratic jurisdictions, especially those with ordo-liberal traditions recognizing the need for limiting market failures, governance failures and constitutional failures; process-based neo-liberal traditions (e.g. in the USA) and authoritarianism (e.g. in China and Russia) favor different approaches to multilevel governance of transnational PGs.

(9) Successful pursuit of the UN SDGs requires plurilateral reforms (like 'climate clubs') and rules-based third-party adjudication of trade and investment disputes as envisaged in SDG16 (Flett). Rules-based trade and investments remain crucial for realizing the SDGs (like ending poverty and hunger, decarbonizing economies). Yet, geopolitical rivalries and China's successful economic and social transformation, which is expected to make China the world's largest economy and increasingly limit US military and economic hegemony and political leadership, risk to further disrupt international trade and investment law, energy supply, climate change mitigation (e.g. by carbon taxes, CBAMs, limitation of fossil fuel subsidies, GHG emission trading systems), WTO adjudication, investor-state arbitration, and the UN and European collective security systems. The regulatory problems of 'free-riding' and geopolitical rivalries can be reduced by transforming global PGs into 'club goods' conditioning membership on GHG reductions and rule-of-law commitments.

(10) In view of diverging perceptions of vulnerabilities justifying national security restrictions (e.g. against foreign technologies, spread of viruses, weaponization of interdependence), plurilateral second-best responses become more important, like trade, investment and environmental agreements conditioning market access on respect for human rights and greenhouse gas reductions. With heterogenous policy preferences and systemic rivalries requiring policy space, transnational governance must strike a balance between constitutional flexibility towards national approaches reflecting divergent value choices, and a constitutional architecture reinforcing national contributions to PGs such as climate change mitigation and respect for multilateral trade rules. Hence, flexibility building on the subsidiarity principle, as enshrined in several multilateral architectures offering national policy leeway (e.g. GATT Articles XX, XXI), and the 'embedded liberalism compromise' underlying WTO law may justify more flexible, legal interpretations (e.g. of WTO trade remedy rules for protecting domestic industries against foreign market distortions, use of WTO exception clauses and WTO 'waivers' for decentralized production of vaccines and for making CBAMs WTO-consistent so as to limit GHG emissions and 'carbon leakage'). If geopolitical power politics should prevent reforms of WTO negotiations and of the WTO dispute settlement system, decentralized reforms of world trade rules through (inter) regional and bilateral agreements among 'willing' and like-minded governments are inevitable. The non-discrimination and reciprocity principles underlying trade and investment law require maintaining third-party adjudication and transnational rule-of-law de-politicizing disputes.

(11) With flexibility on the one side, multilevel governance promoting the SDGs requires, on the other hand, a transnational constitutional architecture overcoming the collective action problems, such as climate change mitigation suffering from insufficient commitments under the 2015 Paris Agreement. In Europe and some Latin-American countries, judicial empowerment of individuals invoking their human and environmental rights (like rights to life) has helped to achieve higher levels of climate protection efforts, as illustrated by climate litigation invoking human rights (e.g. to live in an environment without pollution endangering human health) for clarifying legal duties of states to reduce GHG emissions.[11] Reconciling legal interpretation of human

11 Climate change litigation is discussed in the book chapters by Daly, Tigre, Urzola and Eckes.

rights law with the economic PG character of the environment can improve remedies to solve market failures and constitutional failures (Eckes, Daly/Tigre/Urzola).

(12) Constitutional approaches to multilevel governance of PGs must avoid 'one-size-fits-all claims' of constitutionalism, for instance taking one regional approach (like the individual rights experiences of the EU) as role model to be followed around the globe. Yet, they should learn from the normative tenets of HRL and constitutional economics prioritizing 'citizen sovereignty' and 'consumer sovereignty' as paradigms for how societal choices and market choices should be made and can be legally protected by equal rights. Criticism of totalitarian and neo-liberal variants of constitutionalism and 'constitutional failures' must be taken more seriously, even if 'constitutional pluralism' and the obvious lack of a global *'constituent power'* will remain permanent facts. UN HRL can be construed as requiring that also international law must remain democratically and legally accountable to democratic self-government in national democracies. History suggests that constitutionally unrestrained governance powers risk being abused more than constitutionally limited powers subject to 'institutional checks and balances' protecting equal rights of citizens. Constitutionalization should neither be understood as striving for an empire of uniformity (e.g. disregarding the legitimately diverse political cultures of nation states and of their people) nor as contrary to representative democracy and its popular support by citizens (Petersmann).

(13) The controversial relationship between constitutionalism and fragmentation in international law raises the question of what procedures and mechanisms of constitutionalization are suitable for coordinating specialized international organizations and for reconciling diverging rationales of special branches of international law. The political reality of constitutional pluralism and the legitimate diversity of constitutional theories and traditions (e.g. regarding 'optimal levels' of legal and judicial protection of individual rights) requires also re-thinking how Europe's unique multilevel constitutionalism constraining domestic and foreign EU policies should be reconciled in relations with hegemonic and authoritarian governments disregarding human rights. For instance, it remains an open question whether UN climate change law and its international surveillance mechanisms can promote a functionally limited 'common good constitutionalism' protecting humanity against the existential risks of climate change. The obvious governance failures in authoritarian states (as illustrated by their suppression of

human rights and threats of wars, weaponization of energy and food supplies) require 'de-risking interdependencies'.

(14) Multilevel constitutional politics and constitutional economics remain under-researched. Their focus on market failures, governance failures and constitutional failures in multilevel governance of PGs offers innovative, analytic insights and policy proposals – also for authoritarian countries, which joined the open WTO trading system without political willingness to legally limit their state-capitalism and authoritarian government powers. Europe's ordo-liberal focus in EU and WTO law on legal limitations of market failures, governance failures and constitutional failures (e.g. in EU common market and constitutional law, multilevel WTO adjudication protecting non-discriminatory conditions of competition and rule-of-law as approved by national parliaments) rejects neoliberal conceptions of 'laissez faire competition' and of discriminatory trade protectionism (e.g. based on 'regulatory capture' of US trade remedy regulations by rent-seeking US industries). Some WTO agreements (e.g. on antidumping and trade-related intellectual property rights) reflect business-driven industry pressures without adequate regard for promoting non-discriminatory conditions of competition; other WTO agreements (e.g. on agricultural and textiles trade, the WTO Dispute Settlement Understanding) limit discriminatory trade distortions in order to protect rules-based, non-discriminatory competition. Equating constitutionalization of international economic governance (e.g. through compulsory WTO appellate jurisprudence) with neoliberal de-regulation favoring business interests to the detriment of general consumer welfare – as suggested by Loughlin[12] and by Slobodian[13] – disregards the categorical differences between utilitarian Anglo-Saxon neo-liberalism and rights-based, European

12 Cf Loughlin (n 3), at 184, 186, who wrongly likens ordo-liberal constitutionalism to a neo-liberal stance for 'laissez-faire' regimes and minimum regulatory and legal restraints on economic activities. It is rather Loughlin's rejection of transnational constitutional restraints which promotes neoliberal power politics.

13 Q. Slobodian, *Globalists. The End of Empire and the Birth of Neoliberalism* (Harvard UP 2018) at 23–25. Slobodian describes the WTO as 'the paradigmatic product of Geneva School neoliberalism', and the 'creation of the WTO (as) a crowning victory of the neoliberal project of finding an extra-economic enforcer for the world economy in the twentieth century'. On Slobodian's misunderstandings of the categorical differences among rights-based, ordoliberal constitutionalism and utilitarian, neoliberal nationalism see E.U. Petersmann, Book review of Q. Slobodian, Globalists: The End of Empire and the Birth of Neo-liberalism (Harvard University Press 2017), in: JIEL 21 (2018), 915–921.

ordo-liberalism: The German, European and Virginia Schools of ordo-liberalism perceive markets as legal constructs of reasonable citizens (rather than as gifts of nature), who cannot maximize their general consumer welfare without legal limitations of market failures, governance failures and 'constitutional failures'.[14] GATT/WTO jurisprudence (e.g. on interpreting GATT/WTO rules as protecting non-discriminatory conditions of competition) emphasized the systemic, ordoliberal functions of the GATT/WTO legal and dispute settlement systems as 'guardians' of non-discriminatory conditions of competition. China's compliance with most WTO dispute settlement findings would have enabled using WTO jurisprudence for progressively clarifying the vague WTO disciplines on state-trading enterprises and the 'WTO plus' obligations accepted by China in its WTO accession protocol. Yet, the US trade war against China and the US disruption of the WTO Appellate Body system risk promoting authoritarian alliances rejecting the 'embedded liberalism' underlying UN/WTO law and the relevance of 'constitutional economics' for the changing structures of worldwide and regional IEL and its insufficient regulation of state-trading enterprises and state-capitalism.

14 Cf Petersmann (n 10), Chapters 3 and 4.

CHAPTER 2

Constitutional Pluralism, Regulatory Competition and Transnational Governance Failures

Ernst-Ulrich Petersmann

1 How to Respond to UN and WTO Governance Failures?

This contribution uses the term 'constitutionalism' in a broad sense for constituting, limiting, regulating and justifying multilevel rules and governance institutions of a higher legal rank for providing public goods (PGs). It explains why globalization, its transformation of *national* into *transnational* PGs, and the demand by citizens for more effective protection of transnational PGs (such as climate change mitigation) require extending 'constitutional safeguards' to multilevel governance of PGs; and why human and democratic rights protecting informed, individual and democratic consent of free and equal citizens must remain the 'co-constitutive legitimation' of transnational constitutionalism.[1] All UN member states adopted national Constitutions (written or unwritten) constituting, regulating and justifying national governance of PGs. The 'constitutional politics' necessary for transforming agreed constitutional principles into democratic constitutionalism was described by the American philosopher Rawls as a 'four-stage sequence' as reflected in the history of the US Constitution: reasonable citizens, after having agreed (1) on their constitutional 'principles of justice' (e.g. in the 1776 US Declaration of Independence

1 cf Ernst-Ulrich Petersmann, *Multilevel Constitutionalism for Multilevel Governance of Public Goods* (Hart 2017). Martin Loughlin, *Against Constitutionalism* (Harvard UP 2022), rejects Europe's 'ordo-constitutionalism' and 'cosmopolitan constitutionalism' as being inconsistent with his nationalist conception of British democracy (as represented by 'the Crown, the Lords and the Commons' claiming 'parliamentary sovereignty') – without offering any solutions for limiting transnational governance failures and responding to citizen demand for protecting transnational PGs more democratically and more effectively. His preference for nationalism and its greater solidarity and 'common sympathy' neglects the social welfare, rule-of-law and solidarity created by Europe's 'social market economy' and monetary union limiting individual and nationalist egoisms. Anglo-Saxon neoliberalism and constitutionally unrestrained foreign policy discretion favor populist and feudal abuses of representative democracies, where 'ordinary politics' is typically driven by narrow self-interests and money-driven interest group politics; cf Bruce Ackerman, *We the People: Foundations* (Harvard UP 1991).

 | DOI:10.1163/9789004693722_003

and Virginia Bill of Rights), (2) elaborate national Constitutions (e.g. the US Federal Constitution of 1787) providing for basic rights and legislative, executive and judicial institutions; (3) democratic legislation must progressively implement and protect the constitutional principles of justice for the benefit of citizens; and (4) the agreed constitutional and legislative rules need to be applied and enforced by administrations and courts of justice in particular cases so as to protect equal rights and rule of law.[2] National constitutional practices differ enormously among countries, as illustrated by the greater reliance on evolutionary constitutionalism in common law jurisdictions (like the United Kingdom) compared with constitutional constructivism (e.g. in India and Switzerland with their frequent constitutional amendments). All countries joined multilateral treaties of a higher legal rank for protecting transnational PGs like human rights and rule-of-law. But transnational 'constitutional politics' constituting, limiting and regulating multilevel legislative, executive and judicial governance institutions beyond states remain contested and underdeveloped outside Europe. Similarly, the 'constitutional economics' underlying UN and WTO law is not effectively implemented inside many states. This contribution explains why constitutional nationalism and disregard for 'constitutional economics' undermine democratic protection of the sustainable development goals (SDGs) like food security (SDG2) undermined by Russian wars of aggression, climate change mitigation (SDG15) undermined by China's and India's use of coal-powered energy, and transnational rule-of-law (SDG16) undermined by hegemonic disregard for judicial protection of transnational rule-of-law.

The more globalization transforms *national* into *transnational PGs* (like human rights, rule of law, most SDGs) which – in a globally interdependent world composed of 200 sovereign states – no state can unilaterally protect without international law and multilevel governance institutions, the more '*national constitutionalism 1.0*' has become an incomplete system for governing transnational 'aggregate PGs'. In European integration among constitutional democracies since the 1950s, the demands by EU citizens for regional and global PGs transformed *national* into *multilevel constitutionalism* extending the national 'four-stage sequence' to (5) international law, (6) multilevel governance institutions, (7) communitarian domestic law effects of EU law (like legal primacy, direct effects and direct applicability by citizens of precise, unconditional EU rules) and (8) domestic implementation of EU law

2 cf John Rawls, *A Theory of Justice* (rev edn Harvard UP 1999) 171–173.

inside member states protecting PGs across national borders (cf Section 2).[3] Following the fall of the 'Berlin wall' (1989) and the dissolution of the Soviet Union (1991), democratic constitutionalism also contributed to worldwide recognition of multilevel judicial protection of rule of law in UN law (e.g. in the UN Convention on the Law of the Sea (UNCLOS)), trade law (e.g. in WTO law), in investor-state arbitration, and in international criminal law. Yet, transforming *national* into *multilevel constitutionalism* remains resisted by authoritarian and nationalist rulers avoiding democratic and judicial restraints on foreign policy powers. For example,

- the UN Security Council system is rendered ineffective by authoritarian abuses of veto-powers and illegal aggression and threats of military force;
- the UN human rights system fails to prevent violations of human and democratic rights in many UN member states;
- the 1992 UN Framework Convention on Climate Change (UNFCCC) failed to prevent climate change;
- UN environmental law and institutions also failed to prevent ocean pollution, over-fishing and biodiversity losses;
- the World Health Organization (WHO) failed to prevent and effectively respond to global health pandemics;
- the Food and Agriculture Organization (FAO) failed to protect food security for currently more than 200 million people;
- the Bretton-Woods Agreements failed to prevent the 2008 financial crises and remain one-sidedly dominated by the industrialized G7 countries; and
- China, Russia and the USA increasingly reject international adjudication if judicial rulings limit their foreign policy decisions to violate UN or WTO law; the increasing number of abuses of military power (e.g. in Central Africa) reinforce this trend towards power politics.

1.1 *How to Define and Explain 'Transnational Governance Failures'?*

Constitutionalism proceeds from the insight that constitutional contracts among free and reasonable citizens can limit abuses of public and private power and promote voluntary, mutually beneficial cooperation by institutionalizing public reason. The diverse forms of *democratic constitutionalism* (e.g. since the ancient Athenian democracy), *republican constitutionalism*

3 cf Giuliano Amato and others (eds), *The History of the European Union: Constructing Utopia* (Hart 2019).

(e.g. since the ancient Italian city republics), and of *common law constitutionalism* (e.g. in Anglo-Saxon democracies) aim at limiting 'governance failures' through commitments to agreed 'principles of justice' (like human rights, democratic self-governance, separation of powers) and institutions of a higher legal rank (like democratic and judicial protection of rule-of-law). Principles of democratic constitutionalism agreed upon since ancient Athens (like citizenship, democratic governance, courts of justice, 'mixed government'), of republican constitutionalism since ancient Rome (like separation of power, rule-of-law, *jus gentium*), and of common law constitutionalism (like judicial and parliamentary protection of equal freedoms and rights of property owners) have been progressively developed and incorporated into modern, written Constitutions as necessary for protecting PGs. The 2030 UN Sustainable Development Agenda (SDA) links economic, environmental and social rules with human rights, democratic governance and rule-of-law also for multilevel governance of transnational PGs like the universally agreed 17 SDGs. Yet, as discussed in Section 3, the 'constitutional principles' underlying UN human rights law (HRL) and the SDA are neither effectively implemented ('constitutionalized') in the legislative, administrative and judicial practices inside and among many states (e.g. authoritarian states like China, Iran, Myanmar, North Korea, Russia, Syria etc) nor in UN law. The current economic, environmental, food and migration crises, global health pandemics, Russia's unprovoked military aggression and war crimes in Ukraine confirm the constitutional insight (e.g. of Kantian legal theory) that national Constitutions and 'inter-national law' cannot protect citizens against external human disasters unless abuses of policy discretion are legally limited also in external relations for the benefit of all citizens. Democratic constitutionalism – in the sense of citizen-driven constitutional politics, constitutional economics and constitutional law as restraints on market failures and governance failures and as safeguards for protecting informed, individual consent of citizens and their individual and democratic self-development of human capacities as foundational values justifying market economies and democratic governance of PGs – is under increasing attack also inside business-driven, neoliberal democracies with high social inequalities as inside the USA.

Transnational governance failures can be narrowly defined in terms of violations of international law and arbitrary disregard for the universally agreed SDGs; but they may also be defined more broadly by the lack of justifiable 'principles of justice', as illustrated in the chapter by Marceddu on the reforms of international investor-state arbitration. Understanding the causes of governance failures and remedial options requires distinguishing market failures (like distortions of competition, external effects, social injustices, information asymmetries), government failures (e.g. to protect PGs, human and democratic rights, and limit market failures) and constitutional failures (e.g. to protect transnational PGs like the SDGs). Public choice theories explain why public and private actors may benefit from exploiting such 'failures' (like corruption, externalization of pollution costs, related 'rent-seeking' at the expense of social costs). Transnational governance failures violating international law confirm that path-dependent governance methods – like constitutional nationalism, intergovernmental power politics, and conceptions of international organizations as mere 'international functionalism' (rather than as multilevel governance of PGs) – may not suffice for realizing the universally agreed SDGs. In contrast to 'realism' prioritizing power-oriented, individual and national self-interests (like maximization of relative power, income and self-help), democratic constitutionalism prioritizes protection of equal individual and democratic freedoms and related PGs – in both the economy and the polity – through rules and institutions of a higher legal rank. This 'normative individualism' perceives voluntary, informed individual and democratic consent to 'just rules' and 'institutionalization of public reason' as most important sources of values and as necessary constitutional restraints against abuses of public and private power. Hence, state sovereignty derives value from protecting individual and democratic self-determination (e.g. as protected by UN HRL) rather than from authoritarian power politics. From such a citizen perspective prioritizing equal human and constitutional rights, the UN and WTO governance crises can be explained in terms of 'constitutional failures' (e.g. to protect human rights, rule-of-law and the SDGs), related 'governance failures' (including both public and private abuses of power) and 'market failures' (like restraints of non-discriminatory competition, environmental pollution, social injustices). Even though human and democratic preferences and constitutional agreements differ among countries, UN and WTO law and the SDGs offer multilaterally agreed benchmarks for defining 'transnational governance failures'.

1.2 *Diverse Constitutional Responses to Transnational Governance Failures*

UN member states tend to define – and respond to – transnational governance failures in diverse ways depending on which UN legal values their governments prioritize:

- *Process-based, representative democracies* (e.g. in Anglo-Saxon countries with parliamentary supremacy) prioritize constitutional nationalism, majoritarian institutions, their democratic accountability, civil and political liberties over economic, social and cultural rights of citizens, and discretionary foreign policy powers;[4] arguably, their prioritization of business-driven market processes ('markets know best') and of money-driven, democratic majority decision-making (e.g. in US federal elections financed by business interests) is distorted by high social and financial inequalities and only selective enforcement of competition and environmental laws (e.g. inside the USA).

– *Rights-based, multilevel democratic constitutionalism* is practiced notably in the 27 EU member states interpreting their Treaties on European Union (TEU), on the Functioning of the EU (TFEU) and the EU Charter of Fundamental Rights (EUCFR) as functionally limited 'treaty constitutions' restraining market failures (e.g. by competition, environmental and social rules protecting individual and common market freedoms, social rights and judicial remedies), constitutional failures (e.g. by constituting democratic, judicial and regulatory EU institutions protecting human and constitutional rights of EU citizens, transnational PGs and 'national identities'), and governance failures (e.g. by rule-of-law enforcemenet, institutional 'checks and balances');[5] arguably, the EU's normative and methodological individualism (explaining social phenomena like competition in terms of the interplay of individual actions and rights) justifies the EU's more comprehensive, multilevel legal, democratic and judicial protection of equal civil, political, economic, social and cultural rights of EU citizens (e.g. as codified in the EUCFR and clarified and enforced through

4 Loughlin (n 1) claims that the people and their elected representatives, rather than citizens and courts of justice invoking and defending human and constitutional rights, should define the nation's political identity and make its most important policy decisions (pp. 124–35). His focus on nation states neglects multilevel protection of human and constitutional rights and transnational constitutional, parliamentary, participatory and deliberative democracy as prescribed in EU law (e.g. Arts 9–12 TEU), including protection of transnational PGs as a task of 'living democratic constitutionalism'. The focus in US courts on 'negative freedoms' from coercion by government – and on judicial deference to 'political questions' to be decided by the US Congress (like the regulatory powers of the US Environmental Protection Agency) – impedes judicial recognition of 'positive constitutional rights' (e.g. to health and environmental protection) if they have not been explicitly recognized in legislation.

5 As discussed in Sections 2 and 5, European courts perceive their judicial mandates as 'constitutional guardians' more broadly in view of the multilevel guarantees of human and constitutional rights and related PGs in Europe's multilevel, democratic constitutionalism. On the need for more 'progressive constitutionalism' also in the USA challenging 'originalist interpretations' of the US Constitution see: Joseph Fishkin and William E Forbath, The Anti-Oligarchy Constitution: Reconstructing the Economic Foundations of American Democracy (Harvard UP 2022); Adrian Vermeule, Common Good Constitutionalism (Polity Press 2021).

multilevel judicial remedies), including Europe's greater trust in science-based, independent regulatory institutions.[6]

– *Authoritarian states* (like China and Russia) often adopt 'fake constitutions' that neither effectively constrain power monopolies (e.g. of China's communist party, the oligarchic rulers in the Kremlin) nor protect independent, democratic and judicial remedies and human rights. Dictatorships often challenge UN law as being based on 'Western values' in order to justify disregard of human and democratic rights and rule-of-law inside and beyond their national borders.

This reality of constitutional pluralism (also in less-developed countries with particular development priorities) suggests that diverse preferences, regulatory competition, geopolitical rivalries and authoritarian opposition against 'constitutional UN and WTO reforms' will remain permanent facts. Russia's wars of aggression, war crimes and 'weaponization' of energy and food supplies illustrate how – the more the UN and WTO systems are undermined by

6 The democratically defined mandates of such science-based regulatory agencies, and their limitation of market and governance failures subject to judicial remedies of citizens and democratic oversight, justify such 'ordo-liberal agencies'; they refute neo-liberal criticism (e.g. by Friedrich August Hayek, *Knowledge, Evolution and Society*, Adam Smith Institute 1983) of their 'inevitable ignorance' and 'pretense of knowledge'; cf. Ernst-Ulrich Petersmann, Competition-oriented Reforms of the WTO World Trade System – Proposals and Policy Options, in: Roger Zäch (ed.), *Towards WTO Competition Rules* (Kluwer 1999), 43–71. On the categorical differences between utilitarian neoliberalism (as illustrated by the prioritization of legal protection of intellectual property rights and rejection of WTO competition disciplines) and rights-based ordoliberalism see Ernst-Ulrich Petersmann, Neoliberalism, Ordoliberalism and the Future of Economic Governance, in *JIEL* 26 (2023) 836–842. The neglect of these value differences prompts frequent 'neo-liberal mis-interpretations' of European economic regulation (e.g. by Emma Luce Scali, *Sovereign Debt and Socio-Economic Rights Beyond Crisis*, Cambridge UP 2022, who attributes the 'austerity-conditionality' of the EU's financial assistance in response to Greece's sovereign debt crises to 'Hayekian neo-liberalism' (grounded in F.A. Hayek's explanation of market competition as information-, coordination-and sanctioning-mechanism) rather than to the 'democratic constitutionalism' emphasized in the relevant jurisprudence by the German Constitutional Court). Similarly, Loughlin (n 1) conflates EU ordoliberalism with neoliberalism (e.g. on p. 186, 195) by overlooking that the multilevel legal and judicial protection of social, labor and human rights co-constituting Europe's 'social market economy' aims at protecting the autonomy, dignity and capabilities of all EU citizens by limiting the neoliberal prioritization of property rights and of market distortions benefitting the powerful. Cosmopolitan constitutionalism is not inconsistent with Loughlin's claim that 'constitutional democracy remains our best hope of maintaining the conditions of civilized existence' (p.24); yet, his dismissal of democratic constitutionalism as baseless 'faith' (p.149) amounts to a neoliberal recipe for human disaster and continued human failure to protect global PGs demanded by, and of existential importance for citizens.

abuses of powers – UN and WTO law and governance, and the 'regulatory competition' among authoritarian and democratic countries, risk failing to protect the universally agreed SDGs. The successful, albeit modest results of the WTO Ministerial Conference in June 2022 confirm the need for continuing global cooperation in protecting the SDGs. Yet, the realities of power politics in UN and WTO governance call for second-best, *plurilateral* reforms among 'willing countries' (e.g. through democratic defense alliances like NATO, 'climate protection clubs' conditioning market access on protection of the SDGs).

1.3 *Citizen Struggles for Justice and Democratic Governance beyond Borders*

Do the realities of intergovernmental power politics – and the difficulties of multilevel democratic governance of PGs – justify the frequent disregard of transnational constitutionalism, for instance by arguing 'against constitutionalism' beyond constitutional democracies and by pragmatic focus on 'what works', whether successful arrangements in one field can be replicated in others, and on the interests, incentives, power, costs and benefits of the actors involved?[7] As Europe's multilevel constitutional guarantees of civil, political, economic and social rights have protected mutually beneficial cooperation in protecting transnational PGs (like rule-of-law, the common market) more effectively than constitutional nationalism: Why is it that national welfare economics (e.g. examining costs and benefits of alternative policy instruments within the given constitutional context of states) and power-oriented,

---

7 cf Loughlin (n 1), who argues 'against constitutionalism' without offering any strategy for protecting transnational PGs like the SDGs, notwithstanding his acknowledgment (e.g. on p 202) that constitutional democracy has proven to be the most effective method for protecting peace, security and welfare. Loughlin's argument against constitutionalism 'rests on the claim that it institutes a system of rule that is unlikely to carry popular support' (p. 202); yet, EU citizenship rights, EU constitutional rights and remedies, EU parliamentary, deliberative and participatory 'demoi-cracy' have promoted transnational 'constitutional patriotism' (Günther Habermas) justifying and supporting EU law and acknowledging past 'constitutional failures' in national governance systems. The case-studies of this book confirm that legal empowerment of citizens beyond states and private-public partnerships can render transnational governance (e.g. for producing and distributing food and vaccines, holding governments accountable through climate litigation) more legitimate and more effective. See also the report by George Papaconstantinou and Jean Pisani-Ferry (eds), *New World, New Rules? Final report on the Transformation of Global Governance Project 2018–2021* (EUI 2022), which admits that 'a new world requires new rules' (p. 40), and that 'top-down constitutionalisation through treaties and law' (p. 120) is no realistic template for global governance reforms in a multipolar world (cf. p. 19). Yet it hardly discusses Europe's historical experience that multilevel, bottom-up democratic constitutionalism remains crucial for protecting transnational PGs at regional and plurilateral levels of governance.

intergovernmental pursuit of national self-interests remain the prevailing paradigms for analyzing international politics outside Europe? This chapter proceeds from the constitutional insight that constitutionalism offers the most convincing response to 'bounded rationality', human passions, rational egoism and psychopathic autocrats (e.g. using and threatening military force at home and abroad) as perennial challenges to peaceful cooperation among citizens. It criticizes path-dependent nationalism for neglecting how 'constitutional economics' (e.g. underlying EU common market law) and transnational 'constitutional politics' (like EU human rights and environmental constitutionalism) have promoted economic and social welfare, for instance by empowering EU citizens and promoting transnational constitutional, parliamentary, participatory and deliberative democracy at national and European levels of governance (as prescribed in Articles 9–12 TEU). Also European 'moonshot management' (e.g. for responding to the COVID-19 health crises, the climate crisis, and to the European security crisis caused by Russia's war against Ukraine) has become more legitimate and more effective by embedding it into mutually beneficial constitutional restraints, efficient rule-of-law principles, democratic civil society support and successful 'PGs litigation' reinforcing democratic accountability of governments. Due to the interdependence of social, economic, political and legal orders, Europe's post-1945 struggles for a coherent 'constitutional house' protecting social peace and justice remain grounded in respect for human dignity (e.g. in the sense of respecting individual and democratic diversity by protecting equal freedoms) and diverse human capacities (e.g. through protecting 'positive human rights' to education, food, decent work, non-discrimination, democratic participation) promoting mutually beneficial cooperation and reasonable, individual and democratic self-development. Informed, individual consent to constitutional rules protecting 'consumer sovereignty' in economic markets, 'citizen sovereignty' in political markets, and rule-of law – rather than mere national politics, utilitarian cost-benefit analyses, and neoliberal interest group politics cloaked as 'representative democracy' – justify multilevel legal protection of equal rights of citizens and of inclusive social, economic, democratic and legal policy responses to transnational regulatory challenges.

The policy question underlying constitutionalism – how to constitute, limit, regulate and justify governance institutions and rules of a higher legal rank protecting informed, individual consent to collective supply of PGs? – remains of existential importance for reasonable citizens in all states. National Constitutions differ among countries according to their histories and preferences. Their diverse value priorities and 'implementation deficits' entail geopolitical rivalries, regulatory competition, and authoritarian opposition against multilateral restraints on power politics (like President Putin withdrawing

Russia from European institutions, China suppressing human and democratic rights, President Trump withdrawing the USA from some UN and regional treaties). The multilateral treaties establishing the 15 UN Specialized Agencies governing special PGs differ among each other in response to their diverse collective action problems. Yet, their effectiveness depends on private-public partnerships as discussed in this book; their multilevel governance regimes remain embedded into the UN Charter and limited by general principles of UN law, just as the various EU institutions remain embedded into general EU constitutional law principles (e.g. as codified in the European Convention on Human Rights (ECHR) and the EUCFR); also national legislatures, executives, judiciaries and independent regulatory bodies remain constrained by agreed constitutional rules in their joint governance of PGs. The diverse constitutional structures, principles, human and democratic rights and duties protect private-public partnerships, legal and democratic accountability for limiting transnational governance failures, and guidelines for *normative governance reforms* (e.g. for protecting universal access to vaccines, decarbonizing economies, educating and institutionalizing public reason, constraining disinformation by populist demagogues, judicial remedies protecting equal rights and rule-of-law, countermeasures against Russia's war crimes and *jus cogens* violations).

Arguably, constitutionalism offers citizens also the most reasonable strategy for preventing that 'de-globalisation' between democracies and authoritarian regimes provokes, once again, devastating conflicts similar to those caused by the 'first de-globalisation' (1914–1945) provoking World Wars I and II, the great economic depression, the rise in dictatorships responsible for the killing of millions of people, and other abuses of public and private power.[8] Authoritarian abuses of power and disinformation also increase the 'paradox of globalization', i.e., the rational ignorance of most people (including populist rulers) towards global regulatory challenges (like the UN and WTO legal systems protecting transnational freedoms and rule-of-law). European integration law has demonstrated that – by empowering citizens through human and constitutional rights, rule-of-law and democratic governance beyond

8 On this 'paradox of freedom' – i.e., that insufficient legal and institutional protection of equal freedoms favors abuses of public and private power disrupting order and social peace, as already discussed in Plato's book on *The Laws* – see: Ernst-Ulrich Petersmann, *International Economic Law in the 21st Century* (Oxford: Hart 2012) 61–66; Tara Zahra, *Against the World: Anti-Globalism and Mass Politics between the World Wars* (New York: Norton 2023). Modern democratic constitutionalism has reversed Europe's long history of feudalism and absolutism by reconciling liberty, equality, solidarity and democratic inclusion.

states and legally limiting market failures, governance failures and nationalist 'constitutional failures' – transnational 'social market economies' (Article 3 TEU) and democratic governance of PGs can be promoted more effectively than by constitutional nationalism and populism disregarding transnational governance failures. Authoritarian 'survival governance' cannot be trusted; hence, transnational governance must remain limited by constitutional rights, remedies, 'checks and balances', and by 'de-risking' cooperation with constitutionally unrestrained autocrats 'weaponizing' economic dependencies (e.g. on Russian energy and food exports).

1.4 *Insights from 'Constitutional Economics' and 'Constitutional Politics'*

'*Constitutional economics*' (explaining the welfare effects of constitutional agreements among citizens protecting equal freedoms and limiting 'market failures' and 'governance failures') and '*constitutional politics*' (transforming agreed constitutional 'principles of justice' into multilevel legislative, administrative and judicial protection of rule-of-law and PGs) remain neglected in state-capitalist and business-driven, neo-liberal governance regimes and in academic research on multilevel governance of global PGs.[9] 'Constitutional failures' and 'constitutional implementation deficits' aggravate market failures, governance failures and the current, worldwide human disasters undermining the SDGs. Constitutional economics suggests examining – and limiting – the man-made causes of the current environmental, health, food, security and rule-of-law crises, including 'market failures' (like harmful externalities), 'constitutional failures' (like insufficient constitution of democratic governance institutions protecting human rights) and related 'governance failures' (like disregard for rule-of-law) beyond national legal systems.[10] For

9 See note 7 above. For example, the acclaimed book by Mariana Mazzucato, *Mission Economy: A Moonshot Guide to Changing Capitalism* (Penguin 2020), recommends managerial 'mission-oriented approaches' for realizing the SDGs without acknowledging that most SDGs are 'aggregate PGs' (like ending poverty and hunger for all) requiring international cooperation among UN member states for overcoming collective action problems, which are fundamentally different from 'single best efforts PGs' (like inventing vaccines and sending astronauts to the moon, which may be realized by a single state). On the different kinds of PGs and their diverse 'collective action problems' see Ernst-Ulrich Petersmann, *Transforming World Trade and Investment Law for Sustainable Development* (OUP 2022) chapts 4 and 5.

10 On 'constitutional economics' and 'economic constitutionalism' see Chapter 3 in this book and Petersmann (n 9); Stefan Voigt, *Constitutional Economics: A Primer* (CUP 2020). Constitutional economics' justifications of protecting the common, reasonable interests of all citizens (like 'consumer sovereignty' in economic markets, 'citizen sovereignty' in democratic markets) complement moral, constitutional and democratic justifications of protecting individual, national and cosmopolitan citizen interests (e.g. in protection of

example, without taking into account 'pollution externalities', economists cannot even know to what extent the global division of labor increases consumer and citizen welfare. Rather than focusing only on result-oriented cost-benefit analyses within the limits of existing laws, constitutional economics explores enhancing economic welfare through mutually agreed, inclusive rules limiting market failures (like 'harmful externalities') and governance failures (like arbitrary domination). Europe's multilevel constitutionalism has, however, no equivalent in Africa, the Americas or Asia, where national constitutionalism often fails to effectively constrain abuses of power and to transform 'collective action problems' into constitutional reforms – not only in totalitarian states (like China and Russia), but also in other BRICS countries (like Brazil, India, South Africa) and Anglo-Saxon democracies (like 'Brexit Britain' and the USA under President Trump, cf Sections 3–5). Similar to EU law, also UN law and the SDA link economic, environmental and social rules with human rights, democratic governance and rule-of-law for protecting the SDGs. Yet, UN HRL and UN/WTO remedies do not effectively constrain ('constitutionalize') power politics (Sections 3–4). The 'regulatory competition' among neoliberal, state-capitalist and ordoliberal conceptions of governance is aggravated by the lack of effective UN and WTO legal disciplines on 'market failures' (like restraints of competition, adverse externalities, information asymmetries, social injustices), 'governance failures' (e.g. to respect rule-of-law and protect PGs), and 'constitutional failures' (e.g. in terms of protecting human rights against authoritarian power politics). The needed global cooperation in UN and WTO institutions is further eroded by regional power politics (e.g. in Eurasia) and related countermeasures (e.g. by democratic alliances sanctioning suppression of human rights in China and Russia by trade and investment restrictions). This contribution concludes that the UN SDA risks becoming a *utopia* unless democracies extend their diverse forms of constitutionalism to plurilateral protection of transnational 'aggregate PGs' (like public health and climate change mitigation) by empowering private and public, national and transnational actors to hold multilevel governance of PGs more accountable.

human rights, worker rights, property rights, refugee rights) and input- as well as output-legitimacy of rules and (self)governance.

2 Europe's Multilevel Constitutionalism Has No Equivalent outside Europe

Since the 1950s, the successful transformation of *national* into *multilevel European constitutionalism* protecting human rights and democratic peace among most European countries has confirmed the historical experience that democratic constitutionalism remains the most important 'political invention' for limiting transnational governance failures like abuses of public and private power caused by 'bounded rationality' of human beings. Citizens often remain dominated by their passions and selfish utility-maximization (as illustrated by millennia of wars, slavery and gender discrimination) rather than by their reasonableness and morality. European constitutional law emerged in response to unprecedented governance failures like WWII; it demonstrated that – also beyond states – constitutional self-limitations can limit abuses of public and private power by 'tying one's hand to the mast' (following the ancient wisdom of Ulysses) of agreed principles of justice (like human rights, democratic self-determination, rule-of-law) and inclusive institutions of a higher legal rank. WWII prompted all 193 UN member states to strengthen such 'legal self-commitments' at national and international levels of law and governance. 'Constitutional politics'[11] adjusting national Constitutions to global regulatory challenges remains, however, neglected by most citizens and governments outside Europe notwithstanding their universal experience that intergovernmental power politics (like colonialism and imperial wars) undermined democratic peace and welfare all over the world. Just as WWI led to communist dictatorships (e.g. following the Bolshevik revolution in 1917) and civil wars (e.g. in the dissolution of the Chinese and European empires), the Russian wars of aggression, current geopolitical rivalries and trade wars require 'de-risking' international relations through new forms of plurilateral, economic and political cooperation preventing autocratic 'strongmen' from realizing their threats of nuclear war, war crimes and environmental disasters, including new forms of transnational constitutional restraints on 'bounded human rationality'.

11 The term 'constitutional politics' is used here for describing dynamic democratic and judicial processes of implementing agreed 'constitutional principles of justice' in multilevel governance of PGs and for challenging the 'non-implementation deficits' causing constitutional-, governance- and market-failures.

2.1 *Constitutional Self-limitations of 'Market Failures' and 'Governance Failures' in Europe*

Europe's multilevel constitutionalism extended national constitutionalism to functionally limited 'treaty constitutions' constituting, limiting, regulating and justifying European governance of transnational PGs (like the human rights protected in the ECHR, the common market freedoms and rule-of-law principles of Europe's common market and monetary constitutionalism). The Lisbon Treaty's micro-economic 'common market constitution' for a 'competitive social market economy' limits national and EU powers through constitutional, competition, environmental, social rules and institutions of a higher legal rank restricting 'market failures' (like abuses of market power, cartel agreements, environmental pollution, information asymmetries, social injustices) and related 'governance failures' (like public-private collusion exploiting consumers and taxpayers for the benefit of 'rent-seeking' industries). Inside the EU and in the external relations with European Free Trade Association (EFTA) countries, multilevel constitutionalism induced all EU and EFTA countries to cooperate in their multilevel implementation of European and national competition, environmental, 'social market economy' rules, data protection and digital services regulations. The institutionalization of multilevel competition, environmental, monetary and other EU regulatory agencies, and of related democratic and judicial remedies, limited governance failures through multilevel network governance of independent competition, monetary and other regulatory agencies, democratic institutions and courts of justice.

The 'regulatory competition' among EU member states, EFTA states and third European states remained 'constitutionally restrained', for instance due to the ECHR and related constitutional law principles protected by multilevel cooperation among European courts (like the European Court of Human Rights, the EFTA Court, the European Court of Justice) and national courts.[12] The common membership of European countries in the General Agreement on Tariffs and Trade (GATT 1947), the 1979 Tokyo Round Agreements, and the 1994 Agreement establishing the WTO offered additional legal disciplines, political institutions and judicial remedies for resolving disputes if diverse European regulatory systems and economic and trade policies created conflicts over perceived governance failures. The – relatively few – GATT and WTO disputes initiated by third European countries (like Norway and Turkey) challenging EU regulations confirmed how European integration law promoted 'democratic

12 For recent examples see Giovanni de Gregorio, *Digital Constitutionalism in Europe. Reframing Rights and Powers in the Algorithmic Society* (CUP 2022).

peace'. Whenever financial, public debt, monetary, migration, public health and other (e.g. energy) crises inside the EU revealed 'constitutional failures' to secure rule-of-law and protect PGs, EU institutions responded by seeking to reform EU law, for example by monetary and fiscal integration in response to the financial crises since 2008, a 'health union' in response to the COVID-19 health pandemic of 2020, legal protection of privacy rights in digital services, and common migration, energy, foreign and defense policies in response to Russia's military aggression against Ukraine since 2014.

2.2 *Multilevel 'Constitutional Politics' Protecting Transnational European PGs*

European law responds to the fact that globalization transforms *national* into *transnational* PGs, thereby rendering national Constitutions incomplete. Globalization requires complementary, multilevel constitutionalism constituting, limiting and justifying multilevel governance of transnational PGs. European law illustrates how path-dependent 'constitutionalism 1.0' based on (1) national constitutional contracts (like the 1789 French Declaration of the Rights of Man and the Citizen), (2) national Constitutions, (3) democratic legislation and (4) administrative and judicial protection of rule-of-law for the benefit of citizens can be extended to international law and institutions for legally constituting *transnational* PGs, which no single state can protect without rules-based international cooperation. Maintaining the input-and output-legitimacy of functionally limited 'treaty constitutions 2.0' among states (like the 2009 Lisbon TEU) constituting and regulating such multilevel governance requires also 'cosmopolitan constitutionalism 3.0' (as codified in the EUCFR) based on multilevel, institutional protection of human and constitutional rights, transnational rule-of-law and multilevel implementing regulations respecting 'constitutional pluralism'. In Europe, the demands by EU citizens for regional and global PGs transformed *national 4-stage constitutionalism* into *multilevel constitutionalism* by 'constitutionalizing' (5) international law among EU and EFTA states, (6) multilevel governance institutions, (7) communitarian domestic law effects of EU rules and (8) domestic implementation of EU law inside member states protecting PGs across national borders. The emergence of 'illiberal' EU member states (e.g. in Hungary and Poland) illustrated why the 'normative pull' of human rights depends on their 'normative push' through 'constitutional politics', i.e., their effective legal implementation through constitutional law, democratic legislation, administration and adjudication, international treaties, multilevel governance institutions, 'secondary law' of international institutions (like the jurisprudence of European economic and human rights courts) and its domestic, legal implementation.

Such multilevel 'constitutional politics' remained democratically acceptable due to its 'bottom-up construction' based on principles of subsidiarity, proportionality, protection of 'national identities', multilevel democracy and 'EU citizen rights' without a supranational 'European state'. The limitation of EU membership to constitutional democracies – and the democratic, regulatory and judicial EU institutions – promoted citizen-driven enforcement of EU law through multilevel, judicial protection of constitutional guarantees of civil, political, economic and social rights and common market freedoms (like free movements of goods, services, persons, capital and related payments, freedom of profession) across national borders, which the more than 450 million EU citizens never enjoyed before the creation of the European community. The EU law commitments (e.g. in Arts 3, 21 TEU) to protecting human rights and rule-of-law also in the EU's external relations contributed to worldwide recognition of multilevel judicial protection of rule-of-law beyond the EU, for instance in trade and investment agreements (e.g. by prompting the EU to insist on compulsory trade adjudication in WTO law and on investment adjudication also in the EU's external investment treaties), in international criminal law (e.g. by constituting transnational criminal courts), and in other multilateral treaties with compulsory adjudication like the UNCLOS. Europe's historical experiences with centuries of wars, the institutionalized cooperation of 46 neighboring democracies in the Council of Europe, their common experiences of 'constitutional failures' (like feudalism, dictatorships, the holocaust) ushering in World Wars I and II and the 'cold war', and the positive 'constitutional transformation experiences' of EU citizens were major driving forces for Europe's multilevel constitutionalism.

2.3 *Opposition against Multilevel Democratic Constitutionalism outside Europe*

In Asia and North-America, constitutional nationalism continues to prevail in the shadow of regional hegemons. Among African and Latin-American democracies, regional human rights conventions and common markets promoted much weaker 'constitutional reforms' compared with European integration, often due to populist politicians prioritizing nationalist over cosmopolitan responses to global governance crises, challenging science-based regulatory agencies and independent courts of justice, and promoting non-pluralist conceptions of society (e.g. by suppressing human rights and independent media). Asian countries did not conclude effective regional human rights conventions due to their communitarian governance traditions. The social, economic, political, and legal context of multilevel, European integration – like transnational 'social market economies' (Article 3 TEU) helping citizens to adjust to the economic and social changes in open societies – have no equivalent outside Europe, where many less-developed countries prioritize nation-building and the domestic rather than transnational challenges of the SDGs. EU common market, competition and human rights law prioritizes normative individualism (using individual welfare and informed, individual consent as relevant normative standards) and methodological individualism promoting economic 'consumer sovereignty', democratic 'citizen sovereignty' and voluntary, mutually beneficial agreements among citizens (like democratic elections), with informed, individual consent as ultimate source of values. Europe's millennia of republican and individualist legal traditions (e.g. in city states around the Mediterranean sea) have no equivalent in Africa, the Americas or Asia with their often more communitarian or neo-liberal, business-driven cultures. Authoritarian rulers tend to prioritize collectivist state-values like re-conquering historical Russian territories in sovereign neighboring states, restoring China's ancient rule over most of the South China sea in violation of UNCLOS rules, and suppressing human and democratic rights inside and beyond authoritarian states. Recognition of human dignity and human rights in European law reflect legal recognition of EU citizens as being vulnerable and depending on social assistance for developing their human capacities, as illustrated by the EU's huge financial project (*Next Generation EU*) and new '*Social Climate Fund*' supporting the *European Green Deal* for climate change mitigation (as discussed below), and by multilevel EU assistance for responding to other global challenges (like health pandemics, migration, foreign debt and rule-of-law crises, Russian disruption of energy and military security). Societies and citizenship outside Europe remain national with lesser, transnational adjustment assistance and multilevel, legal restraints on the *homo economicus* and on oligarchic distortions of societies.[13]

3 Has UN Constitutionalism Become a *Utopia* in a Multipolar World?

The constitution, limitation, regulation and justification of legislative, executive and judicial UN institutions and procedures in the UN Charter and the 1948 Universal Declaration of Human Rights (UDHR) initiated revolutionary transformations and decolonization of the international legal system.

13 cf Loic Azoulay, 'The Law of European Society' (2022) 59 Common Market Law Review 203. Loughlin's nationalist conception of constitutional democracies (see notes 1, 4, 6–7) disregards the enormous social welfare and solidarity promoted by EU law among EU member countries and 'EU citizens'.

National constitutionalism and UN HRL induced some UN institutions to recommend 'constitutional governance models' (including protection of human rights, democracy, separation of powers, checks and balances, judicial remedies, rule-of-law) also for multilevel governance of the SDGs.[14] Yet, the proposed constitutional reforms remained limited to a few policy areas like compulsory adjudication in WTO law, investment law and in the UNCLOS; political UN and WTO institutions only rarely invoked 'constitutional arguments'. Without compulsory judicial remedies, UN HRL cannot be effectively enforced. The UN Security Council system continues being blocked by abuses of veto-powers. Only in exceptional situations did the UN Security Council (SC) assert 'legislative powers', for example to establish international criminal courts; the SC responses to international health pandemics remained political, for instance by adopting UN SC Resolutions 2532 and 2565 (2020) acknowledging that 'the unprecedented extent of the COVID-19 pandemic is likely to endanger the maintenance of international peace and security'[15] and calling 'upon all parties to armed conflicts to engage immediately in a durable humanitarian pause' to provide humanitarian assistance to the world's most vulnerable in conflict zones.[16] Similar UN Security Council responses to environmental crises remain unlikely, notwithstanding the universal recognition of the need for decarbonizing economies and for protecting the potentially millions of climate refugees against the risks of climate change and rises in sea levels inundating countries and cities.

3.1 *Disagreements on Human Rights*

The disagreements – also among the five veto-powers in the UN SC – on the scope of UN HRL reflect the incomplete ratification and implementation of UN human rights conventions:

- China has ratified the International Covenant on Economic, Social and Cultural Rights (ICESCR) but not the UN Covenant on Civil and Political Rights (ICCPR) in order to shield its communist party's political monopoly;

---

14 cf Giuliana Ziccardi Capaldo, 'Global Constitutionalism and Global Governance: Towards a UN-Driven Global Constitutional Governance Model' in Mahmoud Cherif Bassiouni (ed), *Globalization and its Impact on the Future of Human Rights and International Criminal Justice* (OUP 2015) 629.

15 SC Res 2532 (1 July 2020) para 11; SC Res 2565 (26 February 2021) para 17.

16 SC Resolution 2532 (1 July 2020) para 2.

- the USA has ratified the ICCPR but not the ICESCR in view of US political preferences for business-driven, neo-liberalism and prioritization of civil and political over economic, social and cultural rights;
- most European countries have ratified both the ICCPR and the ICESCR; in contrast to the rejection by China and the USA of individual UN complaint mechanisms and of regional human rights conventions and human rights courts, they protect civil, political, economic, social and cultural rights also through individual UN complaint procedures and regional HRL (like the ECHR and the EUCFR) with individual access to national and European courts;
- Russia does not effectively implement human rights conventions; its oligarchic rulers suppress human rights (e.g. of political dissidents, freedom of information) and democratic self-determination at home and abroad.

The universal recognition of civil, political, economic and social rights in the UDHR illustrates how human struggles for freedom and peace, and for truth and justice (e.g. in the sense of 'reasonable justification'), are inseparably linked. Democratic self-constitution based on agreed 'principles of justice' (like equal freedoms as 'first principle of justice' as explained by I.Kant and J.Rawls) enables societies to strengthen social peace and mutually beneficial cooperation. Public disinformation and suppression of human rights characterize authoritarian governance in unfree societies like China and Russia. Constitutional economics perceives informed individual consent to reasonable, mutually beneficial rules – rather than only cost-benefit analyses – as primary source of consumer welfare and citizen welfare (e.g. in the sense of 'development as freedom' to realize one's human capacities).[17] The 'embedded liberalism' and rule-of-law systems underlying the UN and WTO sustainable development obligations are, however, increasingly disregarded by authoritarian rulers, as illustrated by

- China's refusal to comply with the 2016 UNCLOS arbitral award on China's illegal extension of sovereign rights in the South China Sea, and China's disregard for human rights inside China;
- the illegal US blocking of the WTO Appellate Body (AB) system since 2017, which reflected President Trump's efforts at politicizing and weakening judicial control also inside the USA; and

17 For developing international economic law from such citizen-oriented theories of justice see Petersmann (n 8).

– Russia's refusal to comply with the 2022 judicial orders by the International Court of Justice and the European Court of Human Rights to suspend its illegal suppression of human rights in Ukraine and inside Russia.

Disregard for human and democratic rights is the main reason for unprovoked and unjustified wars of aggression and related war crimes (as currently in Ukraine) and for 'constitutional implementation deficits' in UN and WTO legal practices ushering in governance failures to prevent unnecessary poverty (SDG1) and protect food security (SDG2), public health (SDG3) and public education for all (SDG4), gender equality (SDG5), access to water and sanitation for all (SDG6), the environment (SDGs 13–15) and many other SDGs like 'access to justice' (SDG16).[18] The annual UN reports on progress towards the SDGs document how 'decades of development progress have been halted or reversed' as a result of Russia's military aggression against Ukraine (e.g. forcing more than 15 million people inside Ukraine to flee from their homes), global health pandemics, related food and economic crises and violent conflicts.[19] The realities of power politics blocking constitutional reforms of UN and WTO governance do not exclude cooperation among 'willing countries', for instance at the WTO Ministerial Conference in June 2022 and in regional free trade agreements (FTAs). Yet, power politics impedes the 'constitutional functions' of UN/WTO law for limiting collective action problems and protecting PGs demanded by citizens by transforming constitutional nationalism into multilevel protection of transnational PGs.

3.2 *Executive Power Politics Undermines Democratic Constitutionalism*

Constitutional rules and international law – including also peremptory rules of law (like democratic self-determination, prohibition of the use of force and of denial of basic human rights) and prohibitions to recognize as lawful situations that were created by serious breaches of *jus cogens* (like Russia's aggression, annexation and 'Russification' of Ukrainian territories aimed at annihilating the people of Ukraine) – are recognized as 'higher law' vis-à-vis

18 The importance of democratically inclusive 'good governance' and of 'inclusive institutions' for promoting sustainable development in its economic, social, environmental and legal dimensions is empirically proven; see: Stefan Dercon, *Gambling on Development: Why Some Countries Win and Others Lose* (Hurst 2022); Daron Acemoglu and James Robinson, *Why Nations Fail: The Origins of Power, Prosperity and Poverty* (Profile RBP 2011).

19 UN Economic and Social Council, Report of the Secretary-General (advance un-edited version) E/2022/XXX.

post-constitutional legal practices. As the collective action problems inside and among states often differ, also the 15 UN Specialized Agencies provide for diverse 'treaty constitutions' for multilevel governance of specific PGs, as illustrated by the 'constitutions' (*sic*) establishing

- the International Labor Organization (e.g. providing for labor rights and tri-partite ILO membership of governments, employer and employee representatives),
- the World Health Organization (WHO, e.g. protecting health rights through international health regulations and conventions),
- the Food and Agriculture Organization (FAO, e.g. protecting food security and related human rights of access to food) and the
- UN Educational, Scientific and Cultural Organization (UNESCO, e.g. protecting rights of access to education).

Likewise, the collective action problems of regulating private goods, PGs, 'club goods' with limited membership, exhaustible common pool resources and 'global commons' (like outer space, the High Seas, Antarctica, the atmosphere, cyberspace, biodiversity, cultural heritage) differ among each other. Democratic support for their multilevel regulation is impeded by the fact that most citizens tend to prioritize their 'local lives' (e.g. as members of families, villages, and professional organizations); they often remain 'rationally ignorant' toward global governance in distant organizations dominated by academic and political elites. The (inter)governmental power politics dominating UN institutions (like abuses of veto-powers in the UN SC, China's lack of full cooperation in WHO attempts at clarifying the origins of the COVID-19 pandemic in Wuhan) undermines UN protection of human rights and related PGs. Some of the agreed governance principles (like benefit-and burden-sharing, protection of the environment) for the 'global commons' are disregarded (e.g. by pollution of the atmosphere and the High Seas). The diverse regulatory regimes (like UNCLOS as the legal 'constitution of the oceans', the UNFCCC as legal 'constitution of the atmosphere') remain distorted by market and governance failures (as illustrated by ocean pollution, over-fishing and climate change). Without enforcement of the *jus cogens* limits of 'higher' international and constitutional rules protecting 'planetary boundaries', the prevailing power politics continues undermining the legitimacy and effectiveness of UN and WTO law.[20]

---

20 cf Petersmann (n 1) and the work of the International Law Commission on codification of the international law rules on *jus cogens*.

3.3 *Constitutional Economics Remains Neglected in UN and WTO Legal Practices*

State-capitalist countries and business-driven, neoliberal economies rely more on management approaches to economic and environmental regulation than ordoliberal economies (e.g. inside the EU) restrained by multilevel constitutionalism. Mazzucato's acclaimed book on 'Mission Economy: A Moonshot Guide to Changing Capitalism' (2020) argued for managerial 'mission approaches' to organizing economies and realizing the SDGs, for instance following the example of the inclusive 'Green Deal' advocated by the EU Commission. Such approaches are appropriate for 'single best effort PGs' that can be supplied by a single state (like inventing medicines, exploring the moon) as well as for the pursuit of 'aggregate PGs' within regional communities like the EU. Yet, globalization has transformed most PGs into global 'aggregate PGs' (like human rights, rule-of-law, most SDGs) dependent on global 'aggregation' of local, national and transnational PGs, which no state can secure without cooperation with other states. Overcoming global collective action problems (e.g. in controlling 'rogue governments' circumventing nuclear non-proliferation as a PG, preventing 'wrong GATT panel reports' by mandating the GATT/WTO Secretariats to 'assist' GATT/WTO panel proceedings) requires legal restraints limiting managerial discretion and 'technological solutions' proposed for multilevel regulatory challenges (like geo-engineering aimed at mitigating climate change, artificial intelligence regulating social media). Europe's 'constitutional constructivism' illustrates how 'evolutionary constitutionalism' (e.g. as clarified in European and national jurisprudence on general constitutional principles) and Europe's functionally limited – and periodically adjusted – 'treaty constitutions' interact dynamically. Without multilevel cooperation (as among national and European governments, parliaments, courts, central banks, competition and other regulatory authorities, civil societies), constitutional reforms of UN and WTO law risk being blocked (e.g. by veto powers in UN institutions and WTO consensus practices). Similarly, the impunity of war crimes (as in Russia's war of aggression in Ukraine), distortions of economic competition (e.g. by state subsidies, state-trading practices, environmental pollution), 'pollution externalities' and neoliberal 'rent-seeking' in WTO member states call for stronger legal restraints.

Both inside the EU and in the wider European Economic Area (EEA) with EFTA countries, human, constitutional and economic rights were enforced by citizens protected by multilevel democratic, judicial and regulatory institutions and treaty systems like the EUCFR, the ECHR, the EU's common market constitution, its partial extension to EFTA countries, the EU's incomplete monetary constitution and functionally limited 'foreign policy constitution' (e.g. as codified in Arts 3, 21 TEU). The institutional 'checks and balances' constraining 'executive emergency governance' inside the EU during economic, financial, public health and environmental crises confirmed how human rights became more effective if citizens could invoke and enforce (e.g. in national and European courts) precise, unconditional, international rules and judicial remedies for challenging power politics. Rather than relying only on result-oriented, macro-economic 'Kaldor-Hicks efficiency gains' and 'welfare economics' within the existing framework of national constitutionalism, Europe's multilevel economic constitutionalism is based on 'constitutional economics' deriving values from voluntary, informed consent of EU citizens to common market, monetary, competition and environmental rules and EU policies promoting mutually beneficial, human and constitutional rights and non-discriminatory conditions of competition for a 'competitive social market economy' (Art. 3 TEU) enhancing general consumer welfare and 'citizen sovereignty'. In contrast to British, Chinese, US and Russian executives claiming 'sovereign powers' to violate international treaties ratified by parliaments (e.g. for realizing 'Brexit', starting US trade wars against China and NATO allies, concluding hundreds of 'executive trade deals' without asking for approval by the US Congress), EU executive powers are constitutionally more constrained, for example by respect for human rights and rule-of-law (Arts 3, 21 TEU) and for the common market freedoms, customs union rules and judicial remedies in the EU's common market constitution. *Constitutional economics* confirms the welfare-enhancing effects of changes in constitutional rules (like EU common market freedoms, constitutional and social rights of access to food, public health and environmental protection);[21] it explains, *inter alia,*

- why economic and social welfare functions must be defined through democratic constitutionalism (e.g. respecting demand of citizens for equal freedoms, human rights and other PGs) with due respect also for multilateral treaties protecting transnational PGs;
- why mutually complementary economic and democratic constitutionalism tend to avoid human disasters (like famines, abuses of

21 cf n 10. Institutional and constitutional economics share with neoclassical economics certain fundamental assumptions (such as methodological and normative individualism, pursuit of efficiency gains). Yet, they extend economic analyses to aspects that are typically ignored in neoclassical economics, such as the interdependencies between democratic constitutionalism (e.g. protecting civil and political freedoms, voter preferences, limitation of all government powers, democratic accountability) and transnational, economic constitutionalism (e.g. protecting economic and social rights, consumer preferences, non-discriminatory competition, legal accountability and consumer welfare by limiting business-driven neo-liberal politics and social inequalities).

military power) that have been tolerated in dictatorships (e.g. under Stalin, Mao and colonialism); and
- why legal institutions limiting 'moral hazards' (e.g. by 'balanced budget rules', the fiscal and debt disciplines prescribed in the TFEU) and prohibiting gender and racial discrimination are likely to increase economic welfare inside states.

Economic analyses of international, legal and political systems can enhance their respective contribution to economic welfare. For instance, GATT/WTO law and their legal ranking of alternative trade policy instruments according to their economic welfare effects enabled all 164 WTO members to reduce poverty and enhance national welfare for the benefit of their citizens. Out of the 10 most productive countries in 2021/22 (measured by GDP by hour worked), seven were EU members, and two were EEA/EFTA members following most EU common market rules. Constitutional economics insists on citizen-consent to reasonable 'constitutional choices' respecting human dignity (human and democratic rights), protecting human capabilities, constitutional rights of citizens (like equal access to education, health protection, satisfaction of basic needs), social justice (e.g. promoting 'social market economies' reducing unjust income distribution) and the principal-agent relationships between citizens and governance agents with limited, delegated powers – not only on moral, democratic and legal, but also on economic grounds. Yet, rules and institutions must be designed with due regard to diverse political economy environments. For instance, invention, clinical testing and production of vaccines by pharmaceutical industries supported by intellectual property rights, subsidies and government procurement may offer efficient health policy strategies for industrialized market economies (provided 'rent-seeking interest group politics' and 'regulatory capture' are limited); less-developed and state-capitalist countries, however, may justify different health policies. The 'rational ignorance' of most citizens towards complex foreign policy challenges (like abuses of discriminatory tariffs for taxing and redistributing domestic income) justifies constitutional restraints on foreign policy discretion (e.g. as prescribed in the EU's 'foreign policy constitution' set out in Arts 3, 21 TEU). The emergence of the 'anthropocene' caused by human transgressions of laws of nature provoking climate change, biodiversity losses, and disruption of other ecosystems (like water and land uses) reinforced insistence by EU citizens on 'environmental constitutionalism', as illustrated by the regulation of environmental rights, duties, principles and policy goals in the EUCFR (e.g. Article 37), in the Lisbon Treaty (e.g. Arts 11, 191–193 TFEU) as well as in national Constitutions and HRL empowering citizens to complement the constitutional, parliamentary, participatory and deliberative dimensions of European democracy (cf Articles 9–12 TEU) by engaging in 'strategic climate litigation' (as discussed below).

Business-driven economic regulation in the USA and GATT/WTO practices often prioritize macro-economic 'Kaldor-Hicks efficiency gains' rather than related social costs (e.g. of tobacco consumption and pollution costs).[22] The EU rules governing Europe's 'competitive social market economy' limit market failures and discriminatory protectionism systematically. Britain's 'Brexit' and the US withdrawal from the draft Transatlantic Trade and Investment Partnership (TTIP) illustrated the conflicts between utilitarian, neoliberal nationalism and multilevel, constitutional ordoliberalism. In many UN member states (like China, Iran, North Korea, Myanmar and Russia), the lack of rule-of-law, of independent, judicial protection of human rights, and of non-discriminatory conditions of competition reflect suppression of democratic constitutionalism and constitutional economics. Also some UN governance institutions, like the monetary and financial Bretton Woods institutions dominated by US policies (e.g. defending the US dollar as global reserve currency and preventing a more equitable redistribution of quotas), remain driven by neoliberal power politics.

3.4 *UN Climate Law Prioritizes State Sovereignty over Environmental Constitutionalism*

Intergovernmental climate politics since the 1992 UNFCCC failed to prevent climate change and the increasing heat waves, droughts, floods and related threats to SDGs (like access to food and water). This transgression of 'earth system boundaries' for sustainable development is bound to create increasing social injustices (e.g. due to the richest 1% of the world population causing twice as much carbon dioxide emissions as the poorest 50%, China causing more carbon emissions than all 38 OECD countries) and political conflicts (e.g. over hosting the 140 million climate refugees predicted by the UN for 2050).

The 2015 Paris Agreement prioritizes national sovereignty by focusing on 'nationally determined contributions', which differ enormously among UN

22 cf Petersmann (n 9) 189–191. In contrast to neoliberal conceptions of self-regulatory markets and competition as gift of nature subject to 'governmental fixes', Europe's ordoliberalism perceives markets and non-discriminatory conditions of competition as legal constructs requiring systemic legal restraints of market failures, constitutional failures and related governance failures. On the differences between national schools of law and economics (like the Freiburg and Cologne schools in Germany, the Chicago and Virginia schools in the USA) and transnational schools of law and economics (like the Brussels and Geneva schools in Europe, the 'Washington consensus' promoted by the Bretton Woods institutions) see Petersmann (n 9) ch 2.

member states (e.g. regarding phasing-out of fossil-fuel subsidies and of coal-based energy). The regular 'conferences of the parties' (COP) to the UNFCCC, and their science-based and political review mechanisms, exert pressures for progressive legal clarifications of greenhouse gas (GHG) reduction obligations. Multilevel democratic, parliamentary, executive and judicial climate mitigation governance in the context of Europe's 'environmental constitutionalism' is more legally developed compared with UN climate mitigation policies and their authoritarian neglect in many UN member states.

In Europe, Articles 2 and 8 ECHR prompted ever more courts to protect human rights to life and family life against harmful environmental pollution and climate change. Some European states adjusted their national Constitutions by recognizing environmental rights or constitutional duties to protect the environment (as in Article 20a German Basic Law). According to Article 37 EUCFR, a 'high level of environmental protection and the improvement of the quality of the environment must be integrated into the policies of the Union and ensured in accordance with the principle of sustainable development'. Combatting climate change, promoting sustainable development in cooperation with third states, and principles of 'environmental constitutionalism' (like the principles of precaution, prevention and rectifying pollution at source, the 'polluter pays' principle) are included into the EU Treaty provisions on EU environmental policies (e.g. Arts 11, 191–193 TFEU). It was in response to democratic and parliamentary pressures that the EU's comprehensive climate legislation – notably the European climate law approved in June 2021 and the 13 legislative EU Commission proposals published on 14 July 2021 aimed at making Europe the first carbon-neutral continent by 2050 – offered leadership for implementing the Paris Agreement on climate change mitigation, for instance by making the goals of 'at least' 55% GHG reductions by 2030 and a climate-neutral European economy by 2050 legally binding for EU and member state policies. The multiple policy tools and mandatory standards aim at a socially 'just transition' with active industrial policies to secure continuing economic growth. The EU emissions trading system (ETS) will be complemented by carbon border adjustment measures (CBAM) aimed at preventing 'carbon leakage' and distortions of competition in countries with more ambitious climate change policies. Climate litigation increasingly acknowledges invocation by private and public complainants of GHG reduction obligations of governments as recognized in EU law and UN law.[23] The EU climate mitigation objectives, principles and legal obligations are more precise, more uniform,

23 cf the chapter by Eckes to this book.

more democratically controlled and judicially enforceable than the respective objectives, principles and legal obligations under UN law.

Rights to the protection of the environment are increasingly recognized in the laws of now more than 150 states, regional treaties, and by the UN General Assembly Resolution of 28 July 2022 recognizing human rights to a clean, healthy and sustainable development.[24] Environmental rights have been invoked by litigants all over the world in hundreds of judicial proceedings on protection of environmental interests. In national and European environmental litigation, courts holding governments legally accountable for climate mitigation measures increasingly refer to human rights, constitutional principles, and to international GHG reduction commitments in order to hold governments and also companies legally accountable for climate change mitigation. For example, the ruling of the Dutch Supreme Court on 20 December 2019 in *State of the Netherlands v Urgenda* confirmed that Articles 2 (right to life) and 8 ECHR (right to private and family life) entail legal duties of the Dutch government to reduce GHG emissions by at least 25% (compared to 1990 levels) by the end of 2020. The judgment clarified that human rights and related constitutional and environmental law guarantees (like the 1998 Aarhus Convention on access to justice in environmental matters) may be invoked by citizens to enforce positive obligations to take appropriate measures mitigating climate change.[25] The ruling of the District Court of The Hague on 26 May 2021 in *Milieudefensie v Royal Dutch Shell* was the first judgment in which a multinational corporation was held responsible for its contribution to climate change based on national and international law.[26] The case was brought as a public interest class action by a Dutch NGO; it does not focus on compensation for past damages but on corporate obligations to reduce emissions and invest

24 See Res. A/76/L.75, confirming the previous Resolution 48/13 adopted by the Human Rights Council of 8 October 2021 recognizing that having a clean, healthy and sustainable environment is a human right.

25 *State of the Netherlands v Stichting Urgenda* [2019] ECLI:NL:HR:2019:2007 (Supreme Court). For comparative overviews of climate litigation see: César Rodriguez-Garavito (ed), *Litigating the Climate Emergency: How Human Rights, Courts, and Legal Mobilization can Bolster Climate Action* (CUP 2021); Francesco Sindico and Makane M Mbengue, *Comparative Climate Change Litigation* (Springer Publishing 2021). For systemic collections of climate cases see: Margaretha Wewerinke-Singh and Sarah Mead, 'Fighting Dangerous Climate Change: A Best Practice Guide for Judges and Courts' (World Commission of Environmental Law, 19 January 2022) <https://www.iucn.org/news/world-commission-environmental-law/202201/a-climate-law-primer-forthcoming-book-offers-guidance-judges> accessed 28 August 2023. See also the chapter by C. Eckes in this book.

26 *Milieudefensie et al. v. Shell* [2021] ECLI:NL: RBDHA:2021:5339 (The Hague District Court).

more in cleaner fuels to protect the common interest of current and future generations in preventing dangerous climate change. Similar litigation against energy companies focusing on corporate responsibilities for climate change is pending in many countries. Even though the judgment is based on corporate duties of care under Dutch tort law, the Court's references to international law and to the shared responsibilities of corporate actors may influence the reasoning in future judgments by other courts. The Court found that the total CO_2 emissions of the Shell group exceeded the emissions of many states, including the Netherlands. The group's global CO_2 emissions contributed to global warming and climate change in the Netherlands; they entailed significant risks for residents of that country. The court agreed with the complainants that Shell had an obligation to reduce CO_2 emissions of the Shell group's entire energy portfolio, holding that:

- Shell is obliged to reduce the CO_2 emissions of the Shell group's activities by net 45 per cent by the end of 2030 relative to 2019 through the Shell group's corporate policy;
- the policy, policy intentions, and ambitions of the Shell group imply an imminent violation of this obligation;
- the Court, therefore, allowed the claimed order for compliance with this legal obligation.

The judgment considered human rights and the Paris Agreement in its interpretation of the unwritten standard of care. The Court also referred to the UN Guiding Principles on Business and Human Rights (UNGP), which it found to constitute an authoritative, internationally endorsed soft law instrument setting out the responsibilities of states and businesses in relation to human rights; the UNGP 'are suitable as a guideline in the interpretation of the unwritten standard of care'. According to the Court, the responsibility to respect human rights encompasses the company's entire value chain' including the end-users of the products produced and traded by the Shell group. The Court concluded that the human rights standards, the UNGP, and the Paris agreement all support the conclusion that Shell should be ordered to reduce the CO_2 emissions of the Shell group's activities by net 45 per cent at the end of 2030 relative to 2019 through the group's corporate policy. In the USA, by contrast, similar constitutional and human rights tend to be denied by US courts, for instance on grounds of judicial deference towards 'political questions' left open in the US Constitution and not (yet) decided by the US Congress, which remains reluctant to enact legislation recognizing new human, constitutional or environmental rights and prescribing climate change mitigation based on the 'polluter pays principle' (aimed at enhancing 'total welfare' protecting all citizens against environmental harms) rather than on macro-economic 'Kaldor-Hicks-efficiencies' (justifying also polluting industries). The US Inflation Reduction Act (IRA) adopted in August 2022 uses discriminatory tax credits, domestic content requirements and trade discrimination for promoting de-carbonization of the US economy, thereby further undermining WTO law and increasing trade conflicts. While the IRA's financial incentives for 'green investments' are important, their economic discrimination will undermine non-discriminatory conditions of trade and competition. The EU's response to the US's announcement that it would plough $369bn-worth of tax credits and subsidies into its clean tech industries – a key part of President Biden's IRA – marks a return to mutually competing industrial policies at a time when the WTO dispute settlement system has been undermined by the USA.

4 Disruption of WTO Law by Executive Power Politics

Authoritarian states (like China and Russia) do not protect effective constitutional and judicial remedies of their citizens against executive suppression of human and democratic rights (like freedoms of information and of political opposition). Nor do their power monopolies and state-capitalism protect non-discriminatory conditions of competition. GATT/WTO law provides for insufficient legal disciplines on state-trading companies, subsidies and other distortions of trade and competition. Hence, market economies increasingly introduce countermeasures in their trade relations with China and Russia aimed at limiting competitive distortions and perceived violations of the 'embedded liberalism'[27] underlying WTO law. China's 'unlimited partnership' with Russia of February 2022, and its network of bilateral 'Belt and Road Agreements' with over 80 countries, lay the foundations for an alternative trade regime dominated by bilateral power-politics without multilateral rules, independent judicial remedies and guarantees of human and democratic rights of citizens.

Abuses of executive powers by populist demagogues (e.g. disregarding international obligations like the EU-UK Brexit Agreement and the Paris Agreement on Climate Change) are an increasing challenge also inside democratic countries. US President Trump (2017–2021) interpreted his executive powers under Article II of the US Constitution very broadly as allowing him to do whatever

27 Arguably, the 'embedded liberalism' underlying WTO law has evolved beyond its limited meaning under GATT 1947, for instance by including new UN and WTO legal obligations like human rights and the recognition of four Chinese customs territories as subjects of international law.

he wanted in the foreign policy area (e.g. withdrawing the US from multilateral treaties like the WHO Constitution and the 2015 Paris Agreement). The 'tribal support' from Republican party majorities in the US Congress for President Trump undermined parliamentary control of executive politics (like President Trump's 'big lies' denying the 2020 federal election outcome, his 'putsch attempt' on 6 January 2021), including congressional control of US trade policies which are now based on hundreds of 'executive deals' without oversight by the US Congress. Following the refusal by the US Congress to ratify the GATT 1947 and the 1948 Havana Charter for an International Trade Organization, the US Congress did adopt implementing legislation for the 1979 Tokyo Round Agreements and the 1994 Uruguay Round Agreements establishing the WTO. As this implementing legislation does not recognize a power of the US President to unilaterally withdraw the USA from the WTO and change the pertinent US trade laws without involving the US Congress, US constitutional lawyers disagree on whether President Trump's executive orders blocking the functioning of the WTO AB and ordering discriminatory import restrictions in clear violation of WTO law are justifiable under US constitutional law.[28] Since the 1980s, US President Reagan's neoliberal policies promoted business-driven economic regulation, money-driven democratic elections, 'rent-seeking' limitations of trade and competition (e.g. by protecting domestic producers through ever more discriminatory 'trade remedies', subsidies, regulatory standards, tax reductions, intellectual property rights, only selective enforcement of US antitrust laws) and increasing social inequalities. Unilateral US trade sanctions (e.g. against foreign violations of US intellectual property rights) and US interest group politics in the 'GATT Rounds' of multilateral trade negotiations reinforced selective US import protection (e.g. for domestic agricultural, cotton, textiles and steel producers) and export opportunities for dominant US suppliers (notably for services trade and US 'tech empires' protected by intellectual property rights and systemic tax avoidance).

4.1 *'Regulatory Capture' of US Trade Policies Distorts Competition*

Under the US Trump administration, the 'regulatory capture' of US trade policies (e.g. for import protection for steel and aluminum industries), the US withdrawal from various multilateral treaties by executive orders of President Trump, and the illegal US disruption of the WTO AB revealed some of the systemic conflicts between utilitarian, business-driven US neo-liberalism

28 Cf Ernst-Ulrich Petersmann, 'The 2018 Trade Wars as a Threat to the World Trading System and to Constitutional Democracies' (2018) 10(2) Trade, Law and Development 179.

and Europe's ordoliberal, multilevel economic constitutionalism. US Trade Representative (USTR) Lighthizer, his deputy ambassador Shea, and US secretary of commerce Ross had all been long-standing business lobbyists who, like President Trump himself, identified US business interests (e.g. in rejecting WTO judicial findings limiting US trade policy discretion) with the national US interest. President Trump's decisions to withdraw the USA from UN agreements (e.g. on the WHO, the 2015 Paris Agreement) and from regional trade agreements (like the 2016 Trans-Pacific Partnership, the draft TTIP agreement) were taken unilaterally without requesting approval by the US Congress. The 2020 USTR Report criticizing the AB jurisprudence[29] perceived WTO law as an instrument of US power politics; it ignored the (quasi)judicial mandates of WTO dispute settlement bodies and their (quasi)judicial methodologies by insisting on controversial US interpretations of WTO rules, yet without identifying violations by the AB of the customary law rules of treaty interpretation. The USTR Report – notwithstanding its valid criticism of some WTO rules and dispute settlement practices (e.g. that the AB no longer consulted with the parties when deciding to disregard the Article 17.5 deadline) – suffered from legal biases and false claims characteristic for the US Trump presidency and for Trump's 'big lies' (e.g. about having won the 2020 US federal elections):

- US denial of (quasi)judicial functions of WTO third-party adjudication, even though numerous WTO publications and WTO dispute settlement reports over more than 20 years acknowledged the (quasi)judicial mandates of WTO dispute settlement bodies (*i.e.*, WTO panel and AB reports as adopted by the DSB);
- US disregard for judicial AB arguments in the performance of the Dispute Settlement Understanding (DSU)'s mandate 'to clarify the existing provisions of those agreements in accordance with customary rules of interpretation of public international law' (Article 3 DSU), for instance whenever the AB found compliance with the time limit of 90 days (Article 17.5 DSU) – which was imposed by US negotiators in 1993 notwithstanding the widespread criticism that no other court seems to be limited by such an unreasonably short time

29 See USTR, 'Report on the Appellate Body of the WTO' (2007–2021 Press Releases, 11 February 2020) <https://ustr.gov/about-us/policy-offices/press-office/press-releases/2020/february/ustr-issues-report-wto-appellate-body> accessed 28 August 2023. For a detailed refutation of the false USTR legal claims see: Jens Lehne, *Crisis at the WTO: Is the Blocking of Appointments to the WTO Appellate Body by the United States Legally Justified?* (Berlin: Grossmann 2019); Petersmann (n 9) ch 3.

limit – impossible to reconcile with the other AB tasks (e.g. due to illegal US blocking of the filling of AB vacancies);

- contradictory USTR claims that AB legal findings against the US violated the DSU prohibition to 'add or diminish the rights and obligations in the covered agreements' (Article 3.2 DSU) – even if the AB had justified these legal findings on the basis of the customary rules of treaty interpretation and its (quasi)judicial mandate-, notwithstanding the USTR's regular support of AB reports accepting 'creative WTO interpretations' advocated by the USTR as a legal complainant;
- US description of US 'zeroing practices' as a 'common-sense method of calculating the extent of dumping' even if their biases had been consistently condemned by the AB and DSB as violations of the WTO obligations of 'fair price comparisons' (which are hardly mentioned in the USTR report);
- one-sided focus on WTO texts as interpreted by US negotiators without regard to the customary law and DSU requirements to clarify the meaning of the – often indeterminate – WTO provisions with due regard also to WTO legal texts revealing the 'context, object and purpose' of WTO provisions and the explicitly recognized 'systemic character' of what the WTO Agreement calls 'this multilateral trading system' (Preamble) and its 'dispute settlement system' (Article 3 DSU);
- denigration of AB members as 'three unelected and unaccountable persons' whose 'overreaching violates the basic principles of the United States Government',[30] notwithstanding the election of AB members through consensus decisions of 164 DSB member governments (including the USA), their (quasi)judicial mandate, and the approval of WTO agreements (including the DSU) by the US government and US Congress;
- insulting claims that the AB Secretariat had weakened the WTO dispute settlement system by not respecting WTO rights and obligations.[31]

The financial and political influence of protectionist US interest groups on the US Congress prevented the US Trump and Biden administrations to accept compromise solutions for reforming the DSU. Most WTO members continue to reject US propositions for exempting trade remedies and unilateral invocations of WTO 'security exceptions' (e.g. for justifying the US trade war against

30 See the Introduction to the USTR Report (n 29) 8, 13.

31 USTR Report (n 29) 120.

China) from WTO third-party adjudication. The disruption of the WTO dispute settlement system by a dysfunctional AB led to non-adoption of ever more WTO panel reports due to their 'appeal into the void' of a no longer functioning AB system. The 'Economic and Trade Agreement' signed by the Chinese and US governments on 15 January 2020 provided for discriminatory Chinese commitments to buy US products, discriminatory US import tariffs and US trade restrictions (e.g. targeting Chinese technology companies) without third-party adjudication. This bilateral 'opt-out' – by the two largest trading nations – from their WTO legal and dispute settlement obligations was subsequently continued and deepened (e.g. by additional US export restrictions on technology products as of 2022) by the US Biden administration in order to contain China's rise as a new military and technology threat openly challenging human and democratic rights and other UN legal obligations (e.g. on maritime boundaries and freedom of the seas as defined in UNCLOS).

4.2 *Geopolitical Disruption of the Rules-Based Trading System Endangers the SDGs*

The SDA explicitly acknowledges (e.g. in paras 17.10–12) that realizing most SDGs – like ending poverty for everybody, securing access to food, water and medicines, and de-carbonizing economies – requires a 'rules-based, open, non-discriminatory and equitable multilateral trading system under the WTO'. Without a multilateral WTO dispute settlement system, successful realization of climate change mitigation, of future WTO negotiations, and of inducing market-oriented reforms in China's totalitarian state-capitalism are unlikely to succeed. President Trump's arbitrary destruction of the WTO AB – and the lack of majority support in the US Congress for restoring the WTO AB system, for concluding new FTAs, and for introducing carbon taxes as the most efficient policy instrument for carbon reductions aimed at climate change mitigation – illustrate some of the continuing differences between business-driven US neoliberalism (e.g. US preferences for power-oriented trade protectionism unrestrained by impartial adjudication), compared with EU ordoliberalism (like leadership for introducing Multi-Party Interim WTO arbitration in 2020, for adopting the European climate law in June 2021, and for implementing the currently 14 legislative EU Commission proposals aimed at making Europe the first carbon-neutral continent by 2050, thereby exercising EU leadership inside and beyond Europe for implementing the Paris Agreement on climate change mitigation).[32]

32 cf Petersmann (n 9) ch 9; European Commission, 'Communication from the Commission to the European Parliament, the Council, the European Economic and Social Committee

The recent support by the IMF and World Bank of activist fiscal, economic, health, and environmental policies in response to the global health pandemic, climate change, security and food crises illustrates how distinctions between 'neoliberalism', 'state-capitalism', and 'ordoliberalism' refer to policy trends that continue to evolve and elude precise definitions. Also in the USA, government spending, budget deficits, central bank interventions, welfare payments and corporate bailouts have increased over the past decades. The neoliberal focus on business efficiency in terms of consumer prices is now challenged by focusing also on the welfare of workers, farmers, house owners, and citizens adversely affected by media concentration, rising health and housing costs, and environmental harm. The focus on more systematic legal limitations of 'market failures', 'governance failures' and 'constitutional failures' through multilevel constitutionalism continues, however, to distinguish European ordoliberalism from Anglo-Saxon and authoritarian, constitutional nationalism. The money-driven US elections and business-driven US economic legislation (e.g. on import protection, domestic sales of guns and tobacco, discriminatory environmental regulation and tax benefits) undermine US leadership for protecting the SDGs. For example, the US Inflation Reduction Act – as the most important climate change mitigation legislation in US history – could be adopted in August 2022 only in exchange for numerous protectionist discriminations (like tax credits, local content requirements) favoring US industries in violation of WTO law; the Act also failed to respond to the 2022 US Supreme Court ruling limiting the regulatory powers of the US Environmental Protection Agency. Without congressional and judicial recognition of human and constitutional rights to climate change mitigation inside the USA, democratic support and judicial remedies for climate change mitigation rest much weaker inside the USA (as the world's *per capita* biggest emitter of GHG) than in Europe.

5 Conclusions: UN and WTO Governance Failures Require Plurilateral Responses

This contribution explained the successful evolution of European integration law since the 1950s as resulting from dialectic transformations of *national* into *multilevel, European constitutionalism* limiting transnational governance failures through multilevel protection of European PGs (like the ECHR, the

and the Committee of the Regions: Trade Policy Review – An Open, Sustainable and Assertive Trade Policy' COM/2021/66 final, 18 February 2021.

EUCFR, the EU common market, monetary and environmental constitutionalism). Europe's 'social market economy' promoted the social adjustments, 'human capabilities' and structural changes needed for citizen support of economic and democratic competition in open market societies. The EU's 'foreign policy constitution' (e.g. Arts 3, 21 TEU) extended constitutionalism to foreign policymaking, for instance by requiring the EU to respect and pursue domestic constitutional principles (like human rights, democracy, rule-of-law, sustainable development, compliance with UN law) also in the EU's common foreign and security policies. This 'multilevel constitutionalism' based on multilevel human and constitutional rights and democratic, judicial and regulatory remedies and institutions enabled the EU to exercise leadership for constitutional reforms of UN and WTO law and governance (e.g. by pushing for compulsory third-party adjudication in the UNCLOS, trade and investment law). Constitutionalism made EU foreign policies more transparent, reasonable and predictable. Yet, different constitutional traditions and increasing geopolitical rivalries entail that authoritarian rulers resist constitutional reforms of UN and WTO law aimed at better protecting human rights and the SDGs. Russia's wars against Ukraine, Russian threats of nuclear aggression, the US destruction of the WTO AB adjudication system, and China's suppression of human rights illustrate transnational governance failures undermining global PGs. Constitutional UN reforms (e.g. of the ineffective UN Security Council system) and WTO reforms (like compliance with Article 17 DSU) appear ever more unlikely. For instance, Pascal Lamy remained the only WTO Director-General who emphasized synergies between HRL and WTO law, and invited the Inter-Parliamentary Union to convene regular parliamentary meetings inside the WTO in order to promote democratic support and accountability of trade policies; Lamy's call for 'cosmopolitics' aimed at enhancing the legitimacy and coherence of the world trading system, of its global governance, and of its support by civil societies and 'cosmopolitan constituencies'.[33] Outside Europe, as discussed in Sections 2–4, nationalism, the difficulties of amending national Constitutions, process-rather than rights-based constitutional traditions, power politics and neo-liberal 'business capture' of economic legislation (e.g. by the US Congress) impede 'multilevel democracy' and rights-based 'multilevel constitutionalism' as policy strategies for protecting the SDGs.

33 cf Pascal Lamy, *The Geneva Consensus. Making Trade Work for All* (CUP 2013); Steve Charnovitz, 'The WTO and Cosmopolitics', in Ernst-Ulrich Petersmann (ed), *Reforming the World Trading System. Legitimacy, Efficiency and Democratic Governance* (OUP 2005) 437.

5.1 *Bounded Rationality: Geopolitical Rivalries as Permanent Facts*

The authoritarian 'strong man politics' in China, Russia and in the US Republican Party suggest that nationalism and hegemonic power politics will continue undermining UN and WTO law and politics by supporting market failures, governance failures and related constitutional failures. The 'Beijing consensus' imposed by the power monopoly of China's communist party[34] is not effectively constrained by China's national Constitution (e.g. as citizens cannot invoke and enforce human and constitutional rights through judicial remedies in independent Chinese courts). Similarly, Russia's President Putin and his kleptocratic oligarchs dominate Russia's police state without effective 'constitutional checks and balances'; their executive governance suspended human and democratic rights inside Russia (e.g. of the political opposition and public media) and outside Russia (e.g. ordering illegal invasions into neighboring countries, annexation and 'Russification' of occupied territories like Crimea and the Donbass in Ukraine). Totalitarian power politics – like China's secretive 'polit-bureau politics', 'surveillance capitalism', disproportionate health-lockdowns, Orwellian 'social credit systems', suppression of human and minority rights and threats of military force (e.g. in the South China sea and vis-à-vis Taiwan) – force democracies to respond by forming collective defense alliances and protecting their citizens against foreign 'weaponization' of economic interdependence. State-capitalism undermines citizen-driven market-competition, for instance by means of non-transparent business privileges, subsidies, state-owned enterprises and manipulation of non-convertible currencies. Russia's political domination of the Eurasian Economic Community, like China's political domination of bilateral 'Belt & Road agreements' on financial, trade and infrastructure networks, related Eurasian agreements on regional Asian institutions and 'China-Russia strategic cooperation' are based on power-oriented cooperation among authoritarian governments without multilateral rules and institutions protecting human and democratic rights. This focus on rulers and power-monopolies – rather than on protection of citizens through independent media and remedies – is also characteristic of many governments in former Soviet republics in Eurasia and less-developed countries (like Iran, Myanmar, North Korea, Syria) and their opportunistic conduct (e.g. in buying oil and gas from Russia undermining countermeasures against illegal aggression by Russia, abstention from UN General Assembly

34 At the Communist Party congress in November 2022, President Xi Jinping followed the example of Mao of unifying his personal control over the Party, the state and the military apparatus and of evading constitutional time limits for his concentration of personal power and his exclusion of political critics in the standing polit-bureau.

resolutions condemning Russia for its illegal invasion of Ukraine and related violations of *erga omnes* UN legal obligations like respect for democratic self-determination). The regulatory competition among neo-liberal, state-capitalist, ordoliberal constitutional and authoritarian paradigms of economic regulation undermines the UN and WTO 'world order treaties'. EU efforts at reforming the WTO appellate review system and investor-state arbitration, and strengthening environmental policies by embedding them into the WTO legal and dispute settlement system, are resisted by hegemonic power politics.[35] Human rights, democratic governance, rule-of-law and 'corporate responsibilities' remain insufficiently protected also in the legal practices of the more than 10,000 transnational corporations participating in the 'UN Global Compact' on business and human rights. The 'politicization' of the WTO trading system is likely to continue, for instance if WTO members fail to extend the 'COVID-19 waiver' and the WTO agreement on unreported fishing subsidies of June 2022 and to agree on a 'climate waiver' for CBAMs. The more authoritarian governments disregard global rules limiting 'market failures', 'governance failures' and 'constitutional failures', the stronger becomes the risk of economic disintegration, for instance between 'authoritarian alliances' (e.g. among China, Russia and other Eurasian countries), FTAs among democracies, and the non-aligned 'global south' prioritizing national development. The 'polarization politics' by populist 'strong men' promoting anti-pluralist policies contributed to the rising number of authoritarian governments (e.g. also in 'illiberal' EU member states like Hungary and Poland) and to the declining number of democracies, thereby rendering democratic leadership for protecting the SDGs more difficult. A re-election of Donald Trump as US President in 2024 could mean the end of democratic US leadership for multilateral protection of the SDGs.

5.2 *Transatlantic Leadership beyond NATO Remains Fragile*

Anglo-Saxon neoliberalism prioritizes constitutional nationalism (as illustrated by the 'Brexit') and 'process-based constitutionalism' (as illustrated by the unwritten British Constitution, the lack of references in written Anglo-Saxon Constitutions to the SDGs) rather than rights-based, multilevel constitutionalism requiring all branches of government to protect PGs (like UN HRL, regional common markets, global environmental protection).[36] Europe's multilevel constitutionalism perceives democratic constitutions as expressing dynamically evolving 'living constitutions' responding to changing regulatory challenges and needs of citizens; HRL is interpreted as requiring both

35 cf Petersmann (n 9) chs 3, 7–8.

36 cf notes 4 and 5 above and related text.

democratic legislators and the judiciary as 'constitutional guardians' to interpret and develop laws and policies responding to citizen demand for protecting PGs.[37] Conflicting regulatory and foreign policy conceptions were the main reason for the long-standing failures of the Transatlantic Partnership cooperation since 1990.[38] The 'Brexiters' pursue a 'Singapore at Thames' as a deregulated competitor for the EU with more restrained judicial powers; like former US President Trump, they assert national sovereignty to disregard international agreements (like the EU-UK Brexit Agreement of 2020) and European adjudication. Business-driven economic regulation and related 'regulatory capture' are today more restrained inside the EU (e.g. due to its public financing of political election campaigns) than in the USA, where business-financed presidential and congressional elections often lead to appointment of business leaders (like US President Trump, his Secretary of Commerce W.Ross), business lobbyists (like USTR R.Lighthizer, his deputy USTR D.Shea) and congressmen financed by business interests (like coal, steel, cotton, tobacco, gun and pharmaceutical lobbies). The Biden administration temporarily settled some of the EU-US trade disputes (e.g. over subsidies for aircraft makers Airbus and Boeing, European digital taxes on US tech groups, the US Section 232 tariffs on EU aluminum and steel). The Transatlantic Trade and Technology Council did, however, not prevent the illegal trade discrimination in the 2022 Inflation Reduction Act (e.g. in favor of producing electric vehicles and their batteries in the USA); it may also prove incapable of preventing re-introduction of discriminatory US steel tariffs if the EU should not accept the US proposals for imposing 'carbon tariffs' on 'dirty steel products' produced in China. NATO cooperation remains strong in implementing countermeasures against Russia's illegal wars of aggression. Yet, it is uncertain whether China's longstanding support for dictatorships (like Iran, Myanmar, North Korea, Russia)

37 Fishkin and Forbath (n 5) similarly argue for 'affirmative constitutional obligations' (21–23) of both legislative and judicial institutions to prevent oligarchic domination of the US economy resulting in socially unjust inequalities and failures to protect PGs, as they were recognized during most periods of US constitutionalism (like the early Republic, the post-civil war reconstruction and the New Deal legislation, when 'constitutional economic order hinged on a governmental duty to assure decent work and livelihoods, collective bargaining, social insurance, and other social goods to all Americans', 254–55). Yet, progressive arguments using 'living constitutionalism' for advocating political reforms as being constitutionally required remain challenged by US conservatives using 'originalist constitutional interpretation' for opposing such reforms. Given the Supreme Court's conservative view of the US Constitution and the difficulties of amending the US Constitution, US advocates of the SDGs often avoid constitutional interpretations and human rights arguments in support of the SDGs.

38 See the chapter by Fahey.

and Chinese military aggression against Taiwan will promote common transatlantic countermeasures similar to those introduced against Russia's military aggression. The lack of US trade policy leadership (e.g. through concluding transatlantic and transpacific FTAs updating trade rules among democracies) will inevitably increase the relative power of 'authoritarian alliances' like the Shanghai Cooperation Organization as the world's largest regional economic and security organization in terms of territory and population. Europe remains a regional rather than global power in view of its military, economic and technological dependencies on the USA.

5.3 *Plurilateral Protection of SDGs Depends on Democratic Bottom-up Constitutionalism*

As democracies cannot trust totalitarian power politics, they increasingly resort to pluri-or unilateral policy responses and collective countermeasures. The EU's multilevel constitutionalism, UN HRL and the recognition of affirmative constitutional duties to protect PGs (like protection of the environment) remain driven by multilevel constitutional, participatory and deliberative democracy as protected in Articles 9–12 TEU. The defense of democracy in Ukraine against Russia's illegal aggression illustrates how rule-of-law and the survival of democracies may require 'democratic wars of independence' based on active citizenship[39] and defense alliances among 'militant democracies'. As the current health, environmental, economic, food, migration and security crises were provoked by governance failures, democracies and the EU have good reasons to base their foreign policies on defending democratic constitutionalism, as prescribed in Arts 3 and 21 Lisbon Treaty. For instance, the EU has introduced new regulations for

- screening foreign investments inside the EU;
- limiting access of non-EU companies to government procurement inside the EU unless reciprocal access of EU companies is secured;
- avoiding 'carbon leakage' through unilateral EU carbon border adjustment measures;
- EU 'anti-coercion measures' providing for unilateral EU countermeasures against economic sanctions by third countries (like China);
- EU 'sustainability sanctions' in response to foreign violations of labor rights, human rights and of sustainable development commitments;

39 cf Jon Alexander and Ariane Conrad, *Citizens: Why the Key to Fixing Everything is All of Us* (Canbury Press 2022).

- EU emergency powers for responding to supply chain problems (as they emerged during the COVID-19 and energy crises); and
- stronger EU anti-subsidy and emergency export control regimes.[40]

Similarly, the failures of the WTO 'single undertaking'-and consensus-practices prompt ever more WTO members to conclude plurilateral 'club agreements' like

- FTAs and similar preferential trade agreements (e.g. under Article XXIV GATT);
- 'critical mass agreements' like the 1996 WTO Information Technology Agreement, which was initially negotiated among 29 WTO members and progressively extended on a most-favored nation basis covering now 97% of world trade in information technology products among 83 countries; and
- other plurilateral agreements like the WTO Government Procurement and Aircraft Agreements.

Constitutionalism suggests embedding CBAMS into broader 'GHG reduction clubs' making market access conditional on, *inter alia*, agreed 'green product standards', agreed procedures for calculating 'embedded carbon' in products and equivalence of diverse GHG reduction policies, reductions of fossil fuel subsidies, agreed rules for renewable fuel subsidies, and the elimination of tariffs on environmental goods and services, with due respect for the WTO principles of special and differential treatment of less-developed countries and the environmental law principle of common but differentiated responsibilities.[41] Just

40 cf Alan Hervé, 'European unilateralism as a tool for regulating international trade: a necessary evil in a collapsing multilateral system' *Fondation Robert Schuman* (28 March 2022) <https://www.robert-schuman.eu/en/european-issues/0626-european-unilateralism-as-a-tool-for-regulating-international-trade-a-necessary-evil-in-a>accessed28August 2023.

41 On the problems of linking diverse CBAM systems see the various contributions to the symposium on 'Taxing, Regulating, and Trading Carbon' (2022) 116 AJIL Unbound 191. Arguably (as explained in the chapter by J. Flett), the EU's CBAM is justifiable under GATT Article XX, a (EU protection of the human right to climate change mitigation), XX, b (health protection), XX, d (a non-discriminatory EU emission trading system) and XX, g (non-discriminatory conservation of exhaustible natural resources) as well as under the heading of Article XX GATT (EU leadership for reducing GHG emissions through a non-discriminatory emission trading system multilaterally agreed among EU and EFTA states); it does not violate the Paris Agreement (e.g. on 'common but differentiated responsibilities'), which the EU continues to support and which does not limit sovereign rights under Article XX GATT. Following a G7 initiative for promoting 'carbon clubs' in June 2022, trade ministers representing more than 50 WTO members launched an initiative for promoting trade-related climate mitigation rules in January 2023.

as the multilaterally agreed trade restrictions in the UN Convention on Trade in Endangered Species and in the Montreal Protocol and Basel Convention on Transboundary Movement of Hazardous Wastes were never challenged in WTO dispute settlement proceedings, multilaterally agreed GHG reduction clubs, 'environmental goods agreements', newly agreed subsidy rules and fossil fuel disciplines should set incentives for plurilateral cooperation with 'critical mass membership' promoting non-discriminatory treatment without free-riding. Consensus on a 'package deal' and 'grand bargain' might require a broader 'WTO sustainability agenda' on how to promote the broader policy objectives of a 'circular economy' (e.g. reducing waste and plastic pollution by re-cycling), sustainable agriculture (e.g. addressing bio-diversity, water and food security issues), greening of transport services, the 'blue economy' (like over-fishing, ocean pollution) and a 'just transition' assisting less-developed countries through financial and technical assistance.

The diversity of governmental and private company pledges of GHG reductions also calls for promoting civil society incentives for active participation in decentralized monitoring of market failures (like pollution harms) and governance failures (like non-implementation of GHG pledges). Enhancing synergies between human and legal rights to protection of the environment can strengthen democratic and judicial remedies and citizen participation. Arguably, an effective 'circular economy' (e.g. avoiding harmful externalities) requires 'circular constitutional democracies' empowering citizens to challenge pollution externalities through equal rights, democratic and judicial remedies. As prices of internationally traded goods often do not reflect their environmental and social costs, the UN and WTO sustainable development goals must factor in the pollution costs, human and labor rights, and the 'planetary boundaries' to promote social welfare, just as neo-liberal 'shareholder conceptions' of company goals must be replaced by more inclusive 'stakeholder conceptions' and 'social corporate responsibilities'. This requires not only stronger reporting requirements of companies on their environmental, social and governance (ESG) performance. The 'constitutional politics'-and 'constitutional economics'-methodologies argue more broadly that constitutional democracies can remain effective only if the human and constitutional rights of citizens are protected by democratic legislation, administration and adjudication protecting rule-of-law and empowering citizens. Even if Europe's multilevel constitutionalism has no equivalent outside Europe, the transformation of *national* into *transnational 'aggregate PGs'* (like the SDGs) requires extending national constitutionalism to transnational governance of PGs. History suggests that such constitutional reforms require perennial struggles of citizens for collective protection of human rights limiting abuses of power.

In a globalized 'world on fire', reasonable citizens must recognize themselves as human beings with cosmopolitan responsibilities rather than only as national citizens of this or that state. Without such a cosmopolitan 'Sisyphus morality' and stronger leadership from constitutional democracies, realizing the SDGs remains a *utopia*.

Even if preference heterogeneity requires second-best strategies for protecting the SDGs, the EU countries should continue challenging protectionist discriminations as those in the 2022 US Inflation Reduction Act and those applied by authoritarian WTO members. Continued EU leadership for reforming WTO third-party adjudication and investor-state arbitration remains necessary for protecting the SDGs, human rights and non-discriminatory conditions of competition – at least in the external relations of the EU. If plurilateral cooperation among like-minded countries – rather than global economic integration also among geopolitical rivals – should become the new security policy paradigm, UN and WTO governance will become even less capable of protecting the SDGs. The entry into force, on 1 January 2022, of the Regional Comprehensive Economic Partnership (RCEP) between China and 14 Asia-Pacific countries, and its regulatory competition with the Comprehensive and Progressive Agreement for Trans-Pacific Partnership (CPTPP),[42] illustrates how Asian countries – similar to African countries participating in the Pan-African FTA, American countries participating in regional FTAs in Southern, Central and North America, and European countries participating in the EU, EFTA, EEA and external FTAs with third countries – remain determined to protect the advantages of rules-based, liberal trading systems, notwithstanding increasing challenges of the WTO system. The lack of provisions on labor rights and environmental protection in the RCEP agreement, as in most bilateral 'Belt & Road' agreements concluded by China, illustrates China's lack of leadership for the human rights and environmental dimensions of the SDGs. By involving domestic democratic institutions, non-governmental actors (like business and 'green cities'), science-based regulatory agencies and epistemic communities, democratic support and 'checks and balances' can be enhanced.[43] The UN's

---

42 The CPTPP is an FTA between Australia, Brunei Darussalam, Canada, Chile, Japan, Malaysia, Mexico, Peru, New Zealand, Singapore and Vietnam, which entered into force in 2018 after US President Trump withdrew the USA in spite of the earlier signing of the agreement by the Obama administration.

43 See Chapters 4 and 5; on the problematic relationships between democratic and 'stakeholder governance': Harris Gleckman, *Multistakeholder Governance and Democracy. A Global Challenge* (Routledge 2018); Liliana B Andonova, Moira V Faul and Dario Piselli (eds), *Partnerships for Sustainability in Contemporary Global Governance* (Routledge 2022).

'constitutional governance model' and Europe's multilevel constitutionalism are reminders that – without empowering citizens through human and democratic rights, parliamentary and judicial protection of transnational rule-of-law, and transnational democratic cultures – transnational rule-of-law, social justice and other PGs are unlikely to be effectively protected for the benefit of all citizens. As explained by the 'paradox of freedom', they risk being eroded by abuses of public and private power.[44]

Bibliography

Acemoglu D and Robinson J, *Why Nations Fail: The Origins of Power, Prosperity and Poverty* (Profile RBP 2011).

Alexander J and Conrad A, *Citizens: Why the Key to Fixing Everything is All of Us* (Canbury Press 2022).

Amato G, Moavero-Milanesi E, Pasquino G and Reichlin L (eds), *The History of the European Union: Constructing Utopia* (Hart 2019).

Andonova LB, Faul MV and Piselli D (eds), *Partnerships for Sustainability in Contemporary Global Governance* (Routledge 2022).

Bassiouni MC (ed), *Globalization and its Impact on the Future of Human Rights and International Criminal Justice* (OUP 2015).

Charnovitz S, 'The WTO and Cosmopolitics' in Petersmann EU (ed), *Reforming the World Trading System. Legitimacy, Efficiency and Democratic Governance* (OUP 2005) 437.

Dercon S, *Gambling on Development: Why Some Countries Win and Others Lose* (Hurst 2022).

44 Loughlin's criticism (e.g. on pp 150, 162, 186ff, 194–202) of the 'rights revolution', 'judicial revolution', and of 'invisible constitutions' protecting a new 'constitutional legality' undermining his conception of representative democracy neglects that – in multilevel governance of global PGs among diverse 'demoi-cracies' in the 21st century – globalization renders judicial clarification and enforcement of transnational constitutional restraints on power-oriented inter-governmentalism indispensable for rules-based protection of PGs – provided diverse traditions of 'democratic constitutionalism' based on human rights and democratic governance of free and equal world citizens are respected. This need for rules-based reconciliation of private and democratic autonomy based on agreed constitutional principles (like subsidiarity, proportionality, rule-of-law) requires also strengthening human rights and multilevel, democratic constitutionalism in international economic law. Human rights and judicial remedies empowering citizens set incentives for 'participatory' and 'deliberative democracy' limiting the 'rational ignorance' of many citizens towards global PGs and challenging the insufficient parliamentary control of distant, worldwide governance organizations.

Fishkin J and Forbath WE, *The Anti-Oligarchy Constitution: Reconstructing the Economic Foundations of American Democracy* (Harvard UP 2022).

Gleckman H, *Multistakeholder Governance and Democracy. A Global Challenge* (Routledge 2018).

Gregorio de G, *Digital Constitutionalism in Europe. Reframing Rights and Powers in the Algorithmic Society* (CUP 2022).

Hayek FA, *Knowledge, Evolution and Society* (Adam Smith Institute 1983).

Lamy P, *The Geneva Consensus. Making Trade Work for All* (CUP 2013).

Lehne J, *Crisis at the WTO: Is the Blocking of Appointments to the WTO Appellate Body by the United States Legally Justified?* (Berlin: Grossmann 2019).

Loughlin M, *Against Constitutionalism* (Harvard University Press 2022).

Papaconstantinou G and Pisani-Ferry J (eds), *New World, New Rules? Final report on the Transformation of Global Governance Project 2018–2021* (European University Institute 2022).

Petersmann EU, *International Economic Law in the 21st Century* (Hart 2012).

Petersmann EU, *Multilevel Constitutionalism for Multilevel Governance of Public Goods* (Hart 2017).

Petersmann EU, *Transforming World Trade and Investment Law for Sustainable Development* (OUP 2022).

Rawls J, *A Theory of Justice* (rev edn Harvard University Press 1999).

Rodriguez-Garavito C (ed), *Litigating the Climate Emergency: How Human Rights, Courts, and Legal Mobilization can Bolster Climate Action* (CUP 2021).

Sindico F and Mbengue M, *Comparative Climate Change Litigation* (Springer Publishing 2021).

Vermeule A, *Common Good Constitutionalism* (Polity Press 2021).

Voigt S, *Constitutional Economics: A Primer* (CUP 2020).

Zahra T, *Against the World: Anti-Globalism and Mass Politics between the World Wars* (Norton 2023).

CHAPTER 3

Constitutional Economics and Transnational Governance Failures

Armin Steinbach

1 Introduction

Failure is a negatively connotated label.[1] Blaming mistakes and failures is standard practice of rhetoric rivalry between political opponents[2] and even extends to the diplomacy-based world of international relations.[3] In international law, failure is possibly most salient as analytical and normative reference in relation to the 'failed state'. Rooted in the traditional thinking of the Westphalian system, the failed state carries the narrative of a state's incapacity to live up to the classical international law ideal, notably to ensure a minimum authority over territory and citizens and refers to the collapse and dissolution of States.[4] Failing states share characteristics of inadequate structural competency, including, inter alia, the inability to advance human welfare and security.[5]

1 Michael Howlett, 'The Lessons of Failure: Learning and Blame Avoidance in Public Policy-Making' (2012) 33 International Political Science Review 539.

2 Andreas Kruck, Kai Oppermann and Alexander Spencer, 'Introduction: Mistakes and Failures in International Relations' in Andreas Kruck, Kai Oppermann, Alexander Spencer (eds), *Political Mistakes and Policy Failures in International Relations* (Palgrave Macmillan 2018) 5, 18 ("The close link between labelling a policy a failure, blaming its originators and reaping political benefits from succeeding in the blame game crucially contributes to making the designation of a policy as a failure so political, powerful and contested.").

3 Mark Bovens and Paul 't Hart, 'Revisiting the Study of Policy Failures' (2016) 23 Journal of European Public Policy 653; Annika Brändström and Sanneke Kuipers, 'From 'Normal Incidents' to Political Crises: Understanding the Selective Politicization of Policy Failures' (2003) 38 Government and Opposition 279; Krebs, 'How Dominant Narratives Rise and Fall: Military Conflict, Politics, and the Cold War Consensus' (2015) 69 International Organization 809.

4 Rosa Ehrenreich Brooks, 'Failed States, or the State as Failure?' (2005) 72 The University of Chicago Law Review 1159.

5 Mario Silva, *State Legitimacy and Failure in International Law* (Brill Njhoff 2014).

 | DOI:10.1163/9789004693722_004

At the same time, failures are the source of enlightenment,[6] learning[7] and political impetus.[8] They offer the genuine rationale for states to enter into international cooperation and produce international law ushering into a regional and international agreements which may be understood as response to failed domestic-only policies. Historically, any shift in governance occurring vertically (between sovereign states and transnational or supranational entities) or horizontally (shifting competence between or within domestic or transnational entities, e.g. altering competences between EU institutions) is preceded by applying benchmarks of, *inter alia*, inadequacy, ineffectiveness, unfairness – and hence implicitly posit a failure judgment on a given governance structure.[9] The EU, as most sophisticated construct of supranationality, evolved through various stages of institutional, political, and economic failures that gave rise to a unique architecture of rights, obligations, and competences.

Failure also became a popular analytical category amidst the loss of control of nation states to regulate an interconnected world by domestic means. Constitutionalism and transnational governance are inevitably connected to failure, as nations have not only lost their grip on setting rules effectively but also struggle to manage the disruptive process of globalization and social, cultural, and legal interconnectedness. Local and national actions and decisions

6 "Trial-and-error" is at the heart of "Critical Rationalism" as developed by *Karl Popper*. The permanent learning process through failing is inherent to the trial and error process; this process is open to criticism and corrections and denies any deterministic approach by recognizing error and failure as sources for progress. Karl R Popper, *Auf der Suche nach einer besseren Welt: Vorträge und Aufsätze aus dreißig Jahren* (8th edn, Piper 1995) 79.

7 On the learning effect from policy failures also Michael Howlett, 'The Lessons of Failure: Learning and Blame Avoidance in Public Policy-Making' (2012) 33 International Political Science Review 539; Pat Gray, 'Disastrous Explanations – Or Explanations of Disaster? A Reply to Patrick Dunleavy' (1996) 11 Public Policy and Administration 74.

8 Political speeches often refer to failures as reference point for political change and to differentiate past and future political action. For example, Macron's famous speech on the future of the European continent in 2017 at Sorbonne University referred to failure four times; similarly, Macron referred to failure in his Speech at the closing ceremony of the Conference on the Future of Europe in 2022; former German foreign minister Joschka Fischer in his famous speech on "From Confederacy to Federation – Thoughts on the finality of European integration" at Humboldt University referred to policy failures two times. For failure as element of political narrative see Arjen Boin, Paul 't Hart, and Allan McConnell, 'Crisis Exploitation: Political and Policy Impacts of Framing Contests' (2009) 16 Journal of European Public Policy 81.

9 Michael Howlett, 'The Lessons of Failure: Learning and Blame Avoidance in Public Policy-Making' (2012) 33(5) International Political Science Review 539, 541–542; Allan McConnell, 'Policy Success, Policy Failure and Grey Areas In-Between' (2010) 30(3) Journal of Public Policy 345, 349–351.

produce increasingly extraterritorial effects, for instance by way of trade and environmental changes, which cannot be solved only at the domestic level. Complex cross-border interdependencies and side-effects ensue from free trade in goods, services, and financial capital.[10] Revolutionary advances in knowledge and technology have changed the preconditions of nation states as the legitimate and effective entities of decision-making and problem-solving. Modern societies interconnecting knowledge, technology, governmental and non-governmental interaction across borders do not longer coincide with territorially-bound regulation and the traditional sources of legitimacy.[11]

The world's increasing interconnectedness and transboundary mutation imply national public goods to turn into transnational public goods, and domestic and international policy proponents of a political order endorsing the protection of public goods may hence easily take recourse to policy failures as analytical and normative argument. The provision and protection of public goods is traditionally plagued by failures, but the interconnected world has rendered effective provision of public goods even more prone to failure, as the community affected by external effects has expanded in size and heterogeneity.

The core contribution put forward in this chapter is to invoke constitutional economics to better understand the failures plaguing the governance of transnational public goods and offering avenues to overcome it. The thrust of this approach is to abandon the dominant lens of welfare economics with its neoclassical 'maximization paradigm' and rational choice focus that underlies realist theories in international relations.[12] Rather, the constitutional economic premise rests on 'constitutional contract/exchange paradigms', notably mutual individual and collective gains enabled by constitutional cooperation improving the 'laws and institutions' of the economic-political order protecting informed, individual and democratic preferences. Constitutional economics re-directs the focus of economic analysis away from individual utility maximization towards designing markets and political arenas such that 'consumer sovereignty' on markets and 'citizen sovereignty' in political domains form the analytical and normative benchmark. In political practice, however, constitutional economics has been fertile only in European constitutionalism, where 'constitutionalizing' the ubiquity of abuses of public and private power in the economy were progressively embedded into multilevel theories

10 Inger-Johanne Sand, 'Polycontextuality as an Alternative to Constitutionalism' in Christian Joerges, Inger-Johanne Sand and Gunther Teubner (eds), *Transnational Governance and Constitutionalism* (Hart Publishing 2004) 48.

11 ibid 58.

12 Carmen E Pavel, *Law Beyond the State* (Oxford University Press 2021) 58–85.

of democratic constitutionalism and social justice. Constitutional economics does not offer normative appeal to regimes characterized by authoritarian and neoliberal governments. The respective problem-solving capacities of authoritarian power politics and business-dominated politics are difficult to align with constitutional economics in light of diverse value priorities (e.g. individual vs collectivist values) and diverse types of competition (e.g. conflictual struggle-type rivalries vs rules-based competition limiting monopoly powers and other restraints of competition). Systemic rivalry undermines constitutional economics arguments for multilevel protection of human and constitutional rights and effective third-party adjudication enabling individuals to pursue both their diverse private self-interests and their common public interests in mutually coherent ways.[13]

While limited in normative appeal to political systems undermining economic and social inclusion of individuals or those over-emphasizing utilitarian individualism as policy orientation, constitutional economics offers analytical rigor in underscoring 'market failures', 'governance failures' and 'constitutional failures' as sources of transnational governance failures. Constitutional economics offers a framework to explain why 'intergovernmental supply of public goods' requires 'institutional checks and balances' limiting abuses of public and private powers and judicial protection of rule-of-law to promote individual and democratic autonomy by assisting citizens and governments in maximizing long-term benefits and minimizing costs in the pursuit of individual and collective preferences.[14]

Against this background, this chapter proceeds as follows: Section 2 unfolds the analytical framework of constitutional economics and spells out its notion of mutual agreeability of constitutional arrangements for all members of society. 'Consumer sovereignty' and 'citizen sovereignty' guide the quest for inclusive social and economic arrangements that meet basic needs of all citizens and consumers requiring mutually agreed protection through constitutional rights. However, the normativity of constitutional economics has been limited to the EU constitutionalism, yet meets deaf ears under process-oriented, authoritarian, or business-biased concepts of political and economic governance. Building on the constitutional economic insight, Section 3 disentangles market, governance and constitutional failures in the supply of transnational

13 Ernst-Ulrich Petersmann, 'Neoliberalism, Ordoliberalism and the Future of Economic Governance' (2023) Journal of International Economic Law (book review).

14 Ernst-Ulrich Petersmann and Armin Steinbach, 'Neo-liberalism, State-capitalism and Ordo-liberalism: "Institutional Economics" and "Constitutional Choices" in Multilevel Trade Regulation' (2021) 22 Journal of World Investment and Trade 1.

public goods. These failure types have historically stood in variable relationship to each other and drew policy-makers efforts to remedy to a different degree. Constitutional economics further requires, as discussed in Section 4, correction of market failures to the protection of public goods, notably by widening the narrow focus on cost-benefit analysis and instead locating the ultimate sources of choices and preferences in individuals and in their informed exchange contracts. With policy failures increasingly shifting from domestic government to transnational governance levels, 'citizen sovereignty' emphasizes the case for implementation of legislative, administrative and adjudicative protection of rule of law and equal rights in transnational governance (Section 5).

2 The (Limited) Value of Constitutional Economics for the Study of Transnational Governance Failures

Neoclassical economics offers valuable analytical tools in addressing international law and economic regulation. Rational choice analysis of law has been applied productively to international law and cooperation.[15] For instance, scholarship has put emphasis on the issue of compliance with or disregard for international law rules and the extent to which this may be influenced by economic considerations and choices.[16] It offered the descriptive and prescriptive yardstick for realist theories to cast doubt on the relevance of international law, and instead consider states as rational egoists in a self-help world.[17] The underlying neoclassical Walrasian tradition in economics posits the "maximization paradigm" of individual utility in a world populated by perfectly rational homines oeconomici.[18] While behavioral economics offers some relaxations to the rationality paradigm,[19] constitutional economics questions the efficiency-focused and utility-only perspective more fundamentally. This

15 See, e.g., Jeffrey Dunoff and Joel P Trachtman, 'Economic Analysis of International Law' (1999) 24 Yale Journal of International Law 1; Jagdeep S Bhandari and Alan O Sykes, *Economic Dimensions In International Law: Comparative and Empirical Perspectives* (Cambridge University Press 1998).

16 Cf. Joel P Trachtman, *The Economic Structure of International Law* (Harvard UP 2008).

17 John J. Mearsheimer, 'The False Promise of International Institutions' (1994) 19 International Security 5; Eric Posner, *The Perils of Global Legalism* (Reprint, University of Chicago Press 2009).

18 Tracing back to Lionel Robbins, *An Essay on the Nature and Significance of Economic Science* (2nd edn, Macmillan 1935) 16.

19 Anne van Aaken, 'Behavioral International Law and Economics' (2014) 55 Harvard Journal of International Law 427.

disciplinary strand draws from the work of James M. Buchanan,[20] the work on limited knowledge of state planners by F.A. Hayek, and emphasizes the choice of rules and institutions by offering a process-oriented rather than an outcome-focused view on the optimal design of institutions. If economics is about the arrangements within which individuals and collective actors make 'efficient choices' in response to scarcity, it is important to distinguish choices within existing constraints (as studied by ordinary economics) from choices among alternative legal and institutional constraints (as studied by constitutional and 'institutional economics').[21] The focus on comparative rule design rests on the basic premise that the order of rules affects the resulting order of actions.[22] Interested in the institutional structure of an economy rather than its outcome, Buchanan conceptualizes the rules governing markets as determining private market choices and the rules leading to political decision-making as matters of collective-political choice – on both markets and politics the normative benchmark is that sovereign individuals enter into voluntary agreement among sovereign individuals.[23]

Constitutional economics does not draw from maximizing utility (as motivating realists theories). It instead emphasizes individual freedom of choice as a constitutional value (e.g. grounded in respect for human dignity and human rights) and the procedural concept of ensuring mutual benefits from voluntary cooperation and gains from trade.[24] To some extent this approach aligns with welfare economics pertaining to the market dimension, with voluntary market-exchanges as safeguard for efficient and mutually beneficial market transactions; but constitutional economics extends the "mutual gains from trade" notion to voluntary co-operation more generally understood, including arrangements for collective action, private and public.[25] Mutual benefits accrue in situations where transactions or arrangements generate benefits to

20 Geoffrey Brennan and James M Buchanan, *The Reason of Rules – Constitutional Political Economy* (Cambridge University Press 1985); James M. Buchanan, 'The Domain of Constitutional Economics' (1990) 1 Constitutional Political Economy 1.

21 On institutional economics Ludwig Van den Hauwe, 'Public Choice, Constitutional Political Economy and Law and Economics' in Boudewijn Bouckaert and Gerrit De Geest (eds), *Encyclopedia of Law and Economics* (Vol. 1, Edward Elgar 2000) 603.

22 Friedrich A. Hayek, 'Rechtsordnung und Handelsordnung' in Friedrich A. Hayek, *Freiburger Studien* (J. C. B. Mohr (Paul Siebeck) 1969) 161.

23 Viktor Vanberg, 'Market and state: The perspective of constitutional political economy' (2005) 1 Journal of Institutional Economics 23, 42.

24 James M Buchanan, *The Economics and Ethics of Constitutional Order* (The University of Michigan Press 1991) 31.

25 James M Buchanan, *What Should Economists Do?* (Liberty Press 1979) 27–31.

all parties involved.[26] The 'mutual benefit'-requirement plays out particularly for public goods, which typically suffer from (positive and negative) externalities and collective actions dilemmas. Mutual benefits do not allow environmental harm to be passed on to the society, nor does it permit decision-making practices inflicting harm on others not agreeing to it, nor to impose arbitrary sway on other sovereigns or individuals. Mutual benefits must be safeguarded through inclusive participation in political decision-making, fundamental rights and social and economic inclusiveness.

Despite a wide range of economic perspectives on legal rules, constitutional economics' focus on legal rules offers a suitable, albeit under-researched framework and interdisciplinary approach to studying international law.[27] To the extent that neoclassical economics assumes the existence and market-clearing function of 'perfect competition' and the absence of transactions costs (allowing what is typically referred to as the Coase theorem), constitutional economics instills what lawyers may find more realistic when dealing with interpreting and analyzing legal rules – that in the real world without 'perfect market competition' and without equal access to human capabilities, economic resources and opportunities, a move toward 'free markets' may not enhance efficiency;[28] that the political economy environment with its heterogeneity of stakeholders and interests matters for the design of legal rules; that given the persistence of transactions costs, legal institutions offer plausible solutions to deal with transactions costs in cost-effective manners; and that emphasis should be given to constitutional choices regarding protection of human capabilities, constitutional rights of citizens (like equal access to education, health protection, satisfaction of basic needs) and the principal-agent relationships between citizens and governance agents with limited, delegated powers.[29] The added-value of constitutional economics emphasizing the gains-from-trade paradigm lies in

26 As such, this concept turns against strong realist theories that normative guidelines for state conduct should be to enter only in those transactions that secure relative gains (rather than absolute gains), see John J Mearsheimer, 'The False Promise of International Institutions' (1994) 19(3) International Security 5, 12–13.

27 For an overview on general collective action issues pertaining to political systems and democratic institutions Stefan Voigt, *Constitutional Economics: A Primer* (Cambridge University Press 2020).

28 On the history of feudal, capitalist, communist and neo-liberal 'inequality regimes' distorting market competition, the distribution of incomes and wealth see: Thomas Piketty, *Capital and Ideology* (Belknap Press 2019).

29 Ernst-Ulrich Petersmann and Armin Steinbach, 'Neo-liberalism, State-capitalism and Ordo-liberalism: "Institutional Economics" and "Constitutional Choices" in Multilevel Trade Regulation' (2021) 22 Journal of World Investment and Trade 1.

its procedural logic offered by the institutional framework within which individuals choose, whether individually and separately in markets, or collectively in politics and in organizational arrangements more generally.[30]

Constitutional economics lends itself to *descriptive* and *normative* analysis: In its descriptive dimension, it remains committed to methodological individualism in the sense that it seeks to explain social phenomena and individual choices in terms of the actions of individual human beings.[31] Descriptive analysis may uncover institutional differences shaped by fundamentally divergent paradigms. For example, 'constitutional reforms' (e.g. in communist economies) may be of more existential importance for citizens than the utility maximization paradigm of 'efficient choices within existing constraints' (like use of 'black markets'). In its normative dimension, constitutional economics seeks to design markets and political choices such that individuals enter into voluntary agreements, which implies that individuals must themselves be respected as the ultimate judges on what qualifies as desirable in their social and market transactions. The focus lies on improving the legal-institutional frameworks of markets and of politics in a way that enables mutually beneficial transactions to be realized. With legitimacy thus rooted in the notion of voluntary agreement, constitutional economists address the constitutional question of how people can live together in liberty, peace and prosperity by using the 'exchange paradigm' for exploring efficient 'choices of constraints': How should constitutional rights, obligations and institutions be designed in order to protect democratic preferences and ensure individual freedoms responding to democratic preferences and citizen demand for public goods?

Constitutional economics can be re-phrased as exploring and proposing the 'rules of the game', be it on markets or in the political arena, under which individuals are allowed to pursue their own interests.[32] Markets and political arenas follow different constitutions, with different rules of the game and different actors. With respect for equal individual freedoms of consumers as the normative nucleus for designing markets and political arenas with the aim of mutual benefit, constitutional economics suggests a normative design of these constitutions, as initially coined by William H. Hutt[33] and elaborated by Viktor

30 Viktor Vanberg, 'Market and state: The perspective of constitutional political economy' (2005) 1(1) Journal of Institutional Economics 23, 35.

31 ibid, 24.

32 Geoffrey Brennan and Alan Hamlin, 'Constitutional Economics' in P Newman (ed), *The New Palgrave Dictionary of Economics and the Law* (Vol I, London: Macmillan 1998) 401.

33 William H Hutt, *Plan for Reconstruction: A Project for Victory in War and Peace* (London: Kegan Paul 1943) 215.

Vanberg:[34] an economic constitution that enhances *consumer sovereignty*, and a political constitution that enhances *citizen sovereignty*.

Standard economics assesses efficiency of constitutional arrangements in terms of the market outcome or political outcome, which remain untestable personal utility preferences and perceptions. In turn, the process-oriented perspective emphasized by constitutional economics explores the processes that unfold under alternative legal-institutional frameworks, notably the extent to which they enable agents to realize mutual gains from voluntary cooperation. Ultimately, there can be no other test of "mutual advantage" than the agreement of the parties involved. Performance of markets are thus assessed against the benchmark of whether consumers are able to enter into voluntary commercial relations, free of power dominance.[35] Market failures occur where producers undermine consumers as ultimate judges by escaping the constraints of competition, either through abusing dominant market positions or by insufficiently taking account of harmful effects on society or consumers.

In turn, 'citizen sovereignty' looks at the collective arrangements in the political arenas, allowing formation of political will through "cooperative ventures for mutual advantage".[36] In analogy to consumer sovereignty, citizen sovereignty places the individual at the heart of a democratic polity, in whose common interests the polity should be operated. Accordingly, the political process should be institutionally framed in a manner that makes citizens' common interests its principal controlling force.[37] Citizen sovereignty requires that political institutions, domestic politicians and bureaucracies as well as international organizations are made most responsive to citizens' common interests. Institutions, decision-making process, fundamental rights protection and adjudication must be implemented and respected in a way so as to maximize the prospects that the political process works to the mutual advantage of all citizens. Applying citizen sovereignty as normative and comparative benchmark means that potential alternative rules and institutions of democratic politics are analyzed with regard to their capacity to enable citizens to realize mutual gains – and to what extent these arrangements can protect consumers from being dominated by potent market actors and citizens from being dominated by political agents.[38]

---

34 Viktor J Vanberg, 'Market and state: The perspective of constitutional political economy' (2005) 1(1) Journal of Institutional Economics 23, 37.

35 Viktor J Vanberg, *Wettbewerb und Regelordnung* (Mohr Siebeck Verlag 2008).

36 John Rawls, *A Theory of Justice* (Harvard University Press 1971) 84.

37 Viktor J Vanberg, 'Market and state: The perspective of constitutional political economy' (2005) 1(1) Journal of Institutional Economics 23, 42.

38 ibid.

Normative constitutional economics concerned about citizen sovereignty pertains to issue of societal self-government: How should societies proceed in order to bring about constitutional rules that ensure agreeability to all members of society? Which issues should be dealt with in the constitution – and which should be left to post-constitutional choice?[39] Constitutional economics hence searches for optimal rules of higher rank building on consensus and free political will of citizens safeguarded through equal fundamental rights, democratic and social inclusions.

Europe's multilevel democratic, economic, and human rights constitutionalism offers probably the most developed governance system aligning with consumer and citizens sovereignty as normative benchmarks through protecting equal freedoms, non-discriminatory conditions of competition, and democratically agreed principles of 'constitutional justice' for democratic governance of public goods. For example, the EU Charter of Fundamental Rights (EUCFR) guarantees civil, political, economic, social and 'European citizenship rights' that protect not only 'negative freedoms' (e.g. constraining abuses of public and private power). Rights empowering individuals to exercise 'positive freedoms' (e.g. human rights to education, health protection, freedom of association, decent life and work conditions) through governmental protection of individual self-development (e.g. 'human dignity') can be seen as constitutional core values balancing economic liberties with social rights based on the idea of economic and social inclusion.

Yet 'constitutional pluralism' at national levels of governance is a reality. Rights-based constitutional democracies and functionally limited international constitutional democracies adopting a strong focus on individual rights (such as the EU) stand in stark contrast to process-based constitutional democracies (for example, US, Australia). Process-based national constitutionalism prioritizes democratic elections, majoritarian institutions like the US Congress, democratic accountability and international 'unilateralism' if needed to limit the influence of unelected international institutions and of 'anti-democratic world constitutionalism' on democratic self-government by the American people. The 2022 US Supreme Court judgments construing constitutional rights and delegated executive powers (e.g. of the US Environmental Protection Agency) narrowly as long as related 'political questions' (like limiting greenhouse gas emissions caused by fossil fuels) are not decided by the US

39 Cf. Viktor J. Vanberg, *The Constitution of Markets. Essays in Political Economy* (Routledge, 2001); Robert B McKenzie (ed), *Constitutional Economics. Containing the Economic Powers of Government* (Lexington Books, 1984); James M Buchanan, *The Economics and the Ethics of Constitutional Order* (University of Michigan Press 1991).

Congress reveals a bias of majoritarianism to the detriment of constitutional individual rights and balance of powers.

Likewise, authoritarian state-capitalism prioritizing power monopolies (e.g. of China's communist party state, Russia's oligarchic government structures) does not prevent executive power monopolies from undermining human and democratic rights. In turn, Anglo-Saxon economic and societal governance has long prioritized liberties, trade liberalization, deregulation, privatization and 'financialization' of economies, business-driven regulation and market competition as decentralized information-, coordination-and sanctioning mechanism.[40] These systems engender dangers of 'regulatory capture' (e.g. by rent-seeking business actors or political party monopolies), thus contravening the concepts of consumer and citizen sovereignty.

This reveals a mixed record of constitutional economics serving as normative rulebook. Normative guidance on market design and political will formation was adopted only in the European constitutionalization process, one that inspired also the 'Brussels and Geneva Schools of ordoliberalism' with its impetus to shape the multilateral economic governance as to safeguard multilevel legal, institutional and judicial guarantees of non-discriminatory market competition limiting abuses of public and private powers beyond European integration.[41] Other states reject legal constitutionalism at national levels (e.g. China's 'communist party state' and military power are not subject to legal constitutionalism), yet support and participate in international 'constitutional systems' (like the UN Security Council, the compulsory WTO dispute settlement system).

---

40 The recent support by the IMF and World Bank of activist fiscal, economic, health and environmental policies in response to the global health pandemics and climate change illustrates that distinctions between 'neo-liberalism', 'state-capitalism', and 'ordoliberalism' refer to policy trends that elude precise legal definitions. Even in the USA, government spending, budget deficits, central bank interventions, welfare payments and corporate bailouts have increased over the past decades. The neo-liberal focus (as promoted notably by British Prime Minister Thatcher and US President Reagan) on business efficiency in terms of consumer prices is now challenged also in the USA by focusing on the welfare of workers, farmers, house owners, and citizens adversely affected by media concentration, rising health, energy and housing costs, and environmental harm.

41 For a comparative discussion of the various strands underpinning the 'Washington consensus', the 'Brussels consensus' and the 'Geneva consensus' see Heinz Hauser *et alii*, 'The Contribution of Jan Tumlir to the Development of a Constitutional Theory of International Trade Rules (in German with English summary)' (1988) 39 *Ordo – Jahrbuch für die Ordnung von Wirtschaft und Gesellschaft* 219; Ernst-Ulrich Petersmann, *Transforming World Trade and Investment Law for Sustainable Development* (Oxford University Press 2022) chs 2.4, 2.5, and 4.4.

3 Constitutional Economics Revealing Market, Governance and Constitutional Failure Types

Constitutional economics uncovers market failure, governance failures, and constitutional failures in the supply of transnational public goods. More generally, failure in effectively supplying and safeguarding transnational public goods can be assessed through two lenses: actor-based and rules-oriented perspectives. 'Actor-based' inquiry into failure quests for origin and responsibility of the failure.[42] By looking at conduct of private and public authorities, governments, international organisations, intergovernmental or supranational entities, an actor-focused analysis of failure explores – descriptively – how and why actors fail or succeed in supplying public goods (e.g. through private market-based transactions or government decision failing to take decisions in account of negative spillovers for others) and – normatively – how actors should align their decision such that they remedy collective actions problems or to avoid harming others. Typically, there is congruence between the formal institutional distribution of authority and the distribution of responsibility, not only in the national political arena but also in international contexts. However, in complex multi-level governance systems the responsibility attributions are much less obvious than in domestic context due to their institutional complexity, leading to diffuse public responsibility attributions.[43] This actor focus also encompasses actions channeled through markets mechanisms. With markets serving as cybernetic information-, coordination-and sanctioning mechanisms, they produce and determine private and public actions. This connects to, but differs from, 'rules orientation' which examines existing rules and institutions and how they should be adjusted. A rule-oriented perspective inquires about the role of legal principles of higher rank, with constitutional rules offering the framework within which actors are expected to bring their individual rationality in line with societal imperatives. Related, an institution-based view lends itself to the tenets of institutional economics that depart from narrow assumption of neoclassical paradigms and acknowledges the communitarian

42 Andreas Kruck, Kai Oppermann and Alexander Spencer, 'Introduction: Mistakes and Failures in International Relations' in Andreas Kruck, Kai Oppermann, Alexander Spencer (eds), *Political Mistakes and Policy Failures in International Relations* (Palgrave Macmillan 2018) 8.

43 Sarah B Hobolt and James Tilley, Blaming Europe? Responsibility Without Accountability in the European Union (Oxford University Press 2014).

dimensions of individuals, their civil, political, economic, social and cultural rights and voluntary cooperation.[44]

Approaching policy failure by distinction between actors, rules and institutions informs the academic and policy debate in two regards. First, it allows a multidisciplinary approach to transnational governance: political science and sociological approaches typically focus on empirical (rather than normative) analysis of the types of actors involved,[45] the rationales guiding their conduct,[46] or the processes through which the content of transnational rules is determined.[47] International relations and foreign policy analysis identify broad ranges of possible causes of mistakes and failures in international relations, relating to: individual decision-makers, the decision-making process, domestic politics and the structure of the international system.[48] Economists apply normative efficiency and welfare standards and explore whether desirable outcomes can be achieved through market transactions or public policy intervention and why the private and public actors pursue self-serving interests yielding socially suboptimal results.[49] Lawyers emphasize less the empirical incentive structure of individual actors but rather inquire into the normative design of the legal framework guiding actions of private and public parties, in particular pertaining to whether the legal principles of higher rank should guide transnational conduct and how they should be designed and enforced. Put differently, economics informs roots and remedies to market and government failure, international relations and political science identify

---

44 Claude Menard and Mary M Shirley (eds), *Introduction to a Research Agenda for New Institutional Economics* (Elgar Publishing 2018); Erik Furubotn and Rudolf Richter, *Institutions and Economic Theory: The Contribution of the New Institutional Economics* (2nd edn, University of Michigan Press 2005).

45 Charles Roger and Peter Dauvergne, 'The Rise of Transnational Governance as a Field of Study' (2016) 18(3) International Studies Review 415.

46 E.g. Graham T Allison, *Essence of Decision: Explaining the Cuban Missile Crisis* (Little, Brown and Company 1971); Lawrence Busch, *Standards: Recipes for Reality* (MIT Press 2011); Matthew Potoski and Aseem Prakash, *Voluntary Programs: A Club Theory Perspective* (MIT Press 2009).

47 Tim Büthe and Walter Mattli, *The New Global Rulers: The Privatization of Regulation in the World Economy* (Princeton University Press 2011); Matthew Potoski and Aseem Prakash, *Voluntary Programs: A Club Theory Perspective* (MIT Press 2009).

48 Andreas Kruck, Kai Oppermann and Alexander Spencer, 'Introduction: Mistakes and Failures in International Relations' in Andreas Kruck, Kai Oppermann, Alexander Spencer (eds), *Political Mistakes and Policy Failures in International Relations* (Palgrave Macmillan 2018) 8.

49 Glenn Furton and Adam Martin, 'Beyond market failure and government failure' (2019) 178 Public Choice 197; William R Keech and Michael C Munger, 'The anatomy of government failure' (2015) 164 Public Choice 1.

political and governance failures, and international law informs the debate on constitutional failure and constitutionalization.

Second, from policy perspective, differentiating between actors and rules permits to trace and formulate forward looking remedies to overcome failure: policy inferences can be made from findings, for instance, that market actors neglect societal concerns such as public goods (e.g., private investment decision irrespective of the CO_2 intensity and environmental impact of an investment) leading markets to inefficient results; that governmental actors or international bureaucrats pursue their own non-welfare oriented interests (e.g. by power politics detrimental to the society such as Brexit disintegration from European common market) or value domestic interests over the legitimate interests of the global community in avoiding negative impact (e.g. by free-riding of governments on climate mitigation undertaken by other countries). Remedying failure thus invites focusing on the respective source of failure, such as markets to be redesigned or regulated in order to modify the conduct of private actors; change domestic rules and regulations in order to confine public authorities to welfare orientation; or modify the domestic or transnational design of constitutional rules in order to safeguard legal principles of higher rank (e.g. strengthening third-party adjudication).

The constitutional economics perspective unfolded above, with further distinctions between actors and rules allows to classify and distinguish between three types of transnational governance failures.[50] With public goods transforming from domestic public goods to transnational public goods, market failures, constitutional failures, and governance failures occur in policy fields characterized by collective action dilemmas, notably turning previously domestically perceived and tackled crisis into transnational governance crisis – like irreversible climate change, biodiversity losses, global health pandemics, food crises, unprovoked and unjustified wars of aggression and related war crimes (as currently in Ukraine), refugee and migration crises.

3.1 *Market Failures*

'*Market failures*' capture dysfunctions of market and price mechanisms in delivering decentralized information, coordination and sanctioning mechanisms

50 Howlett offers a classification of failures based on magnitude and salience see Michael Howlett, 'The Lessons of Failure: Learning and Blame Avoidance in Public Policy-Making' (2012) 33(5) International Political Science Review 539; McConnell in contrast differentiates between process, programme and political failure, Allan McConnell, 'A Public Policy Approach to Understanding the Nature and Causes of Foreign Policy Failure' (2016) 23(5) Journal European Public Policy 667, 672–675.

to maximize consumer welfare and contribute to the supply of public goods. Specifically, market failures occur in different guises: restrictions of competition, induced by anti-competitive conduct, engender harmful effects for consumers or competitors, or both; external effects occur where market actors do not internalize the social costs of their market activity (e.g. environmental externalities); asymmetric information entails uninformed decision-making and inefficient market results; market failures can lead to or compound inequitable access to services. Market failure undermines consumer sovereignty as required by constitutional economics. Consumer sovereignty builds on the proposition that non-discriminatory market competition and internalized externalities generate welfare maximizing outcome. History shows however that consumer sovereignty can only be insufficiently achieved through 'negative integration' minimizing state intervention, but that embeddedness of market liberties into legal architecture (e.g. legal protection of equal freedoms, property rights, constitutional-, competition-, environmental-and social rules limiting abuses of public and private power) require 'positive integration' in order for markets to minimize societal harm. Standard economics explains the vulnerability of markets to settle in bad equilibria such as abuses of market power, cartel agreements, negative external effects like environmental pollution, unseized positive externalities like public health protection, all of them leading to diminished efficiency and reduce overall welfare. The ambivalence of market results and the inevitable nature of market failures is illustrated by WTO memberships of China and Russia. Productive efficiency gains of market orientation boosted macroeconomic output and lifted many domestic citizens out of poverty through international trade, sidelined, however, by significant societal costs due to exploding inequality caused by non-transparent corruption and social and legal inequalities inside oligarchic governance systems. From an actor perspective, market failure points at the limits of markets as sole welfare generating actors implying that it remains incumbent on domestic government, intergovernmental cooperation or international agreement to set rules guiding the conduct of market actors (actor perspective) by designing or modifying constitutional arrangements on transnational level (rules perspective).

3.2 *Governance Failures*

Market failures give rise to '*governance failures*' referring to failures of public and private governance actors to limit 'market failures', undermining both consumer sovereignty and citizen sovereignty in constitutional economic parlance. In the above example of WTO memberships boosting growth with significant side-effects, domestic governance institutions fail to protect consumer sovereignty and to contain these market failures, nor do UN and WTO law offer the adequate constitutional framework for competition, environmental, social rules, legislative procedures and judicial remedies. Market failures are thus exacerbated by governance failure (and are not prevented by constitutional design suggesting constitutional failure), with citizen sovereignty impaired as governments fail to act to protect consumers and citizens from distortive and power-dominated market structures. As long as states were the central (and sole) actor in national and international legal systems, it was predominantly 'government failure' that failed to limit market failures and implement their constitutional mandates, e.g. through appropriate law-making, administration, adjudication and other protection of private and public goods demanded by citizens like human rights and rule-of-law. The standard conceptualization of government failure in international relations scholarship was provided by Putnam's two-level games, in which the key yardstick for success or failure becomes whether or not decision-makers are able to adopt policies on the international level that pass the domestic policy arena. Failure occurs when decision-makers are unable to implement domestically what they have agreed to internationally, either because they have misjudged their domestic constraints or because these constraints have changed.[51]

Yet, the more national governments are constrained by the realities of today's multi-polar world and by global interdependencies between civil, political, economic, social, environmental, cultural and technological interactions, the more necessary appears the analytical focus on 'governance failures' (widening the focus to include private and public market actors, governments, international organizations and governance institutions to) or even 'multilevel governance failures' to capture the interplay between domestic with supranational entities, international organisations or intergovernmental actions. Impediments to citizens sovereignty may occur no matter on which level of governance, with national governments as well as regional and global institutions bearing the responsibility to maintain what is required from constitutional economics perspective: to design markets and political choices such that individuals enter into voluntary agreements, which implies that individuals are enabled to realize mutually beneficial transactions. Governance failure also empirically demonstrates that path-dependent governance

51 Robert D Putnam, 'Diplomacy and Domestic Politics: The Logic of Two-Level Games' (1988) 43 International Organization 427; Andreas Kruck, Kai Oppermann and Alexander Spencer, 'Introduction: Mistakes and Failures in International Relations' in Andreas Kruck, Kai Oppermann, Alexander Spencer (eds), *Political Mistakes and Policy Failures in International Relations* (Palgrave Macmillan 2018) 11.

methods – like intergovernmental power politics or welfare nationalism – are insufficient for realizing the universally agreed UN sustainable development goals. Governance failure thus spots the increased range of actors involved in failure – from domestic governments to transnational plethora of actors and institutions (actor focus) –, and allows to identify the relevance of post-constitutional rules which are, if ill-defined, not existent, or not enforced, at the roots of governance failure (rules perspective).

3.3 *Constitutional Failures*

'*Constitutional failures*' reveal that legal principles of higher rank are not in place to the effect that transnational public goods are sufficiently protected. Constitutional failures connect to protecting citizen sovereignty. It relies on constitutional commitments organized through collective action that serves to define and enforce the "rules of the game" to which the members of a group are subject. They offer a framework to allow mutually agreeable decisions in their social and market transactions. National and international constitutional rules and institutions of a higher legal rank may be lacking, ill-defined, misinterpreted, unenforceable or simply ignored, thus rendering constitutional rules ineffective to regulate and limit market failures and governance failures. Constitutional failures may appear in different guises, most generally occurring as inadequate measures to protect human and constitutional rights of citizens through representative democratic institutions, judicial remedies, fundamental rights requiring minimum social regulation to contain negative effects of market failures, and other 'institutional checks and balances' like independent central banks and science-based health and environmental agencies. Constitutionally secured fundamental rights may be safeguarded through independence of state agencies and bureaucracies in order to prevent dangers of 'regulatory capture' (e.g. by rent-seeking business actors, political party monopolies). Arguably, UN and WTO law reflect the insight that improving multilevel governance of the SDGs requires more effective, multilevel regulation of constitutional and governance failures (e.g. to protect human rights, rule-of-law, decarbonize national economies).

History documents the variable interaction between market failure, government failure, and constitutional failures, driven by a changing awareness and perception of these failures. The emergence and functioning of local markets (e.g. responding to supply and demand for local goods and services) depended, *inter alia*, on legal guarantees of contract law (*pacta sunt servanda*), private property rights, monetary means of payment or barter, tort and criminal law (e.g. limiting fraud). Markets required to be embedded in legal and constitutional systems in order for markets to unleash their welfare increasing effect by protecting consumer sovereignty. Likewise, in response to governance failures such as abuses of monetary and police powers entailing legal insecurity and market distortions, for the protection of citizen sovereignty democratic and republican city states (e.g. since the ancient Greek and Italian city republics) introduced republican laws limiting monetary, tax and fiscal powers of governments, and regulating monetary, trade, investment and health policies, related contractual and property rights, and transnational trade and investment agreements (e.g. among city republics around the Mediterranean Sea, the 'Hanse cities' around the Baltic seas).[52] The 1944 Bretton Woods Agreements and decolonization initiated progressive worldwide, legal and institutional reforms of economic regulation aimed at limiting government failures, notably common abuses of power (e.g. in authoritarian and imperial trade regimes) and protecting transnational public goods.[53] The evolutionary pattern of transnational governance shows how new forms of (transnational) governance reacted to market failures, while constitutional arrangements were implemented to respond to market and government failure.

Take the evolution of transnational trade governance as one example: Historic development of international economic law shows the evolution from narrow market failure orientation towards addressing government failures up until the point in which constitutional failures (on national and international level) are at stake. The lense provided by institutional economics enables the analysis to differentiate the variable influence of different economic schools on international cooperation and on legal institutions, which they have fostered or undermined. The Bretton Woods agreement and the 1947 General Agreement on Tariffs and Trade (GATT) had been negotiated and progressively implemented under the leadership of the United States; they were strongly influenced by Anglo-Saxon, economic liberalism aimed at liberalizing trade barriers and promoting monetary stability and convertibility of currencies.[54] However, while driven by liberal market paradigms underpinned by a narrow role for the state to frame markets, they were a first step of institutionalization and rules-generation with the aim to restrain political and economic

52 For 'institutional economics analyses' of the ancient economies of Rome and Greece see: Taco T Terpstra, 'Neo-Institutionalism in Ancient Economic History' in Claude Menard and Mary M Shirley (eds), *Introduction to a Research Agenda for New Institutional Economics* (Elgar Publishing 2018) ch 26.

53 Ernst-Ulrich Petersmann and Armin Steinbach, 'Neo-liberalism, State-capitalism and Ordo-liberalism: "Institutional Economics" and "Constitutional Choices" in Multilevel Trade Regulation' (2021) 22 Journal of World Investment and Trade 1.

54 ibid.

power. Government failures and constitutional failures played a minor role, the focus was on a narrow correction effort to contain market failure. From an institutional economics perspective, the Bretton Woods environment established an institutional setting that, while maintaining the hegemonic predominance of the US economy (e.g. due to the use of the dollar as global reserve currency and its convertibility into gold). With little constitutionalization and deference to domestic policies provoking government failures (e.g. rent seeking, trade wars), legal uncertainty in international relations remained and predictability were fostered only through a successively built web of international treaties.

While market framing disciplines such as non-discrimination principles contributed to offer *substantive* rules to contain government failure, it became clear that constitutional rules beyond substantive obligations were required in order to safeguard compliance with rules. The development of *procedural* rules such as the GATT's dispute settlement system fostered legal security, progressively evolving through decisions of the GATT Contracting Parties and additional trade agreements resulting from eight 'GATT Rounds' of multilateral trade negotiations. With the inception of the WTO institutions and multilevel WTO dispute settlement system implemented through the multilateral Uruguay Round negotiations (1986–1994) and ushering in the 1994 Agreement establishing the WTO and its Dispute Settlement Understanding (DSU), a major shift towards constitutionalization of state-like principles such as checks and balances and binding adjudication ensued. The WTO Agreement recognizes the separation of legislative, executive and judicial powers of WTO institutions (cf. Article III WTO), it places the WTO within the multilevel governance structures with its Member States (cf. Article IV), and coordinates WTO activities with those of other worldwide and regional organizations (cf. Articles V WTO, XXIV GATT) – taken together, the multilevel architecture emancipated trade governance from the logic of retaining market and government failure by establishing constitutional mechanisms that contained domestic constitutional failures (e.g. insufficient rule of law and fundamental rights to pursue trade-oriented economic activities). This turns the WTO towards a more ordoliberal foundation of international cooperation (e.g. strengthening fundamental rights through binding state-to-state adjudication and third-party adjudication of trade disputes, rule of law, multilateral treaties).[55]

This development is illustrative also of a changing view about the cause of failure. The neoliberal turn throughout the '80s trusted in market power and

55 ibid.

the self-healing forces of market failures denying the role of the state to frame market forces and ensure through positive (rather than negative) integration a minimum social and economic equality. The focus was on government failure with bureaucracies and governments acting in self-interest rather than for common good seen as the source of failure, hence retrenching government influences on markets. 'Small governments' was the cure to the insights offered by public choice, rather than thinking about constitutional remedies such as well-defined checks and balances pushing back on business influence on governments decision and independence safeguards of governments preventing regulatory capture. Lifting binding adjudication to transnational level offering adjudication by independent panelists supported by a neutral WTO Secretariat, hence cutting off the outreach of business interests, was a turn to recognize domestic governance failures. No longer trusting in self-healing market forces but seeing that constitutional and governance failures is "causally prior" to the operation of markets and therefore markets can fail because of insufficient constitutional arrangements.

With three failure types shedding light on responsible actors and on (in)adequate rules architecture, transnational governance can be analyzed both from descriptive perspective (why do failures occur and through whose action?) and normative perspective (how can failure be remedied and by whom?).

4 'Consumer Sovereignty' Requires Correction of Market Outcomes to Promote Transnational Public Goods

While constitutional economics is concerned with mutual gains from voluntary co-operation and voluntary joint commitment, it is not blind to self-interested agents searching for unilateral gains by taking advantage of others. Exploitative strategies are common, and the constitutional economist does not ignore the omnipresence of opportunities for gaining at the expense of others.[56] Public goods are particularly vulnerable to exploitative strategies. By extending the definition of public goods from the economic to the legal sphere, public goods can be defined as goods that benefit and can be consumed by all citizens and whose supply is plagued by problems of collective action and free riding – like the rule of law, international security or climate stability.[57] For transnational

56 Viktor J Vanberg, 'Market and State: The Perspective of Constitutional Political Economy' (2005) 1(1) Journal of Institutional Economics 23, 28.

57 Inge Kaul, et al (eds.), *Providing Global Public Goods: Managing Globalization* (Oxford University Press 2003).

public goods to be supplied and safeguarded, extensive participation must be achieved. Yet, even though the rationale of the multilateral framework as response to the collective action problem is reasonable in theory and formally addressed by the universal recognition of legal arrangements (such as the universal treaty-based recognition of human rights), collective action problems such as 'free-riding' can diminish the effectiveness of global regimes (e.g. by domestically minimizing the scope of environmental human rights, thus shifting the burden of climate mitigation to other countries that recognize stronger environmental rights).[58] Similarly, international legal cooperation governing national defense, adherence to the rule of law or the absence of armed threat typically allow all citizens to enjoy the associated benefits, yet at the same time gives rise to collective action problems. International agreements may suffer from fairness and efficiency deficits as they are biased by power politics; or countries threaten security or peace due to short-sighted selfish reasons inflicting negative externalities on other states.

Welfare economics struggled in translating its notion of efficiency into operational terms for real world policies. Narrow Pareto efficiency requiring for a state of society to be preferred only if the new state does not make anyone in society worse off, is an unrealistic efficiency benchmark, as any policy decision produces distributional effects leaving at least some groups of society worse off (e.g. taxation, infrastructure, pricing CO_2 consumption). Less strict concepts of Pareto efficiency allow some groups to be better off, and others to be worse off and require negotiation (or re-distribution) to the end that the gains compensate the losses.[59] With unanimity of citizens being the condition to accept a new state of society, this wide Pareto concept may guide many policy decisions. However, unanimity involves high transaction costs and thus hinders an assertive state action and policy implementation. The least challenging criterion of Kaldor-Hicks, in turn, renounces the need for actual negotiations and compensation between winners and losers and lets it suffice that benefits exceed costs and hypothetical compensation suffices. The policy relevance of the classical welfare economics concepts is thus severely limited.

Constitutional economics extends the narrow focus on cost-benefit analysis inherent in welfare concepts and their focus on utility-maximization and assumptions of 'perfect market competition' without transaction costs. It

58 Ernst-Ulrich Petersmann (ed), *Multilevel Governance of Interdependent Public Goods: Theories, Rules and Institutions for the Central Policy Challenge in the 21st Century* (RSCAS 2012/13).

59 William R Keech and Michael C Munger, 'The anatomy of government failure' (2015) 164 Public Choice 1, 5.

focuses on constitutional designs that maximize the likelihood of being voluntarily agreeable to all members of society. This promotes economic growth satisfying the basic needs of all citizens, enhancement of 'human capacities' (A.K. Sen) and their mutually agreed protection through constitutional rights, which offer better benchmarks for human well-being. Specifically, market-specific 'consumer sovereignty' constitutionalizes market arenas by going beyond assessing efficiency only by way of cost-benefit studies; free consumer choice limits particularistic interests undermining the common good and constrains government powers to discriminate (e.g. in response to rent-seeking pressures). 'Consumer sovereignty' locates the ultimate sources of choices and preferences in individuals and in their informed exchange contracts. Yet, the 'consumer sovereignty' ideal of consumers making reasonably informed market choices is often confronted with the reality that economic actors and political regulators have only limited knowledge of the complex interactions among private and public, national, transnational and international legal, economic, political and social rules and institutions.[60] Their decisions may be influenced also by 'rational ignorance' and intuitive or irrational motives, as illustrated by the diversity of 'social contract' theories and assumptions.[61] Market failure is therefore often intertwined with governance failures, as governments, who define the framework within which markets unfold, are incapable of designing market rules such that public goods are not harmed. How then does constitutional economics inform the address of governance failures?

5 Domestic Government Failure and Transnational Governance Failure Undermine 'Citizen Sovereignty'

While 'consumer sovereignty' requires market failures to be addressed, it is 'citizen sovereignty' that searches for inclusive, reasonable agreements among citizens protecting democratic preferences. Both 'consumer sovereignty' and 'citizen sovereignty' endorse a set of normative values putting choices of

60 Cf. Geoffrey Brennan and James M Buchanan, *The Reason of Rules. Constitutional Political Economy* (Cambridge University Press 1985).

61 On behavioral economics exploring intuitive or irrational economic behavior see, e.g.: Anne van Aaken and Jürgen Kurtz, 'Beyond Rational Choice: International Trade Law and the Behavioral Political Economy of Protectionism' (2020) 22 Journal of International Economic Law 601. On the historical evolution and institutional diversity of social contract theories see e.g.: David Boucher and Paul Kelly (eds), *The Social Contract from Hobbes to Rawls* (Routledge 1994).

individuals at the core of legitimacy of market and governance design – the normative individualism hence builds on the respect for human dignity and the recognition of individual rights pertaining to the making of individual consumer choices as well as political preferences. With citizens as sovereigns in whose interest the polity should be operated, politicians and bureaucrats should be responsive to citizens' common interests. Like consumer sovereignty, citizen sovereignty is a procedural criterion, not one of specific outcomes. That is, the constitutional economic concept of 'citizen sovereignty' leaves space for constitutional plurality – modes of participation and free will-based decision making may vary as long as it remains responsive to the free will of citizens and as long as citizens' common interests remain its principal controlling force.[62]

Public choice scholars argued that government failures are often far more disastrous than market failures.[63] Governments sometimes fail to provide the fundamental requirements of law and order or even actively foment humanitarian crises; they fail to implement property rights and legal institutions, all of them as preconditions for markets to thrive.[64] Public choice literature casts doubts on the notion of benevolent governments performing taxation, regulation and administration with a general welfare objective, but rather emphasizes government agents' decision-making biases and explores why they fail to achieve efficient outcomes. This feeds into multiple government failures related to the supply of public goods – political actors trust in markets even though they should regulate, hence perpetuating market failures; they fail to resist to regulatory capture and rent seeking by business interest; corrupt leaders deprive society of welfare for selfish reasons; insufficient domestic checks-and-balances, weak judiciary etc. undermine societal interests taken into account; or welfare losses result from insufficient account of transnational public goods by nationalist welfare perspective or discount of future generations' welfare (e.g. climate).

Government failure often translates into transnational governance failure, as illustrated by the US withdrawal from the 2015 Paris Agreement and by the US assault on the WTO legal and dispute settlement system. Populist governments

62 Viktor Vanberg, 'Market and State: The Perspective of Constitutional Political Economy' (2005) 1(1) Journal of Institutional Economics 23, 42.

63 James M Buchanan, *Cost and Choice: An Inquiry in Economic Theory* (University of Chicago Press 1979); Gordon Tullock, 'Problems of Majority Voting' (1959) 67(6) Journal of Political Economy 571; Gordon Tullock, *Bureaucracy* (CK Rowley ed, Liberty Fund 2005).

64 Ronald H Coase, 'The Problem of Social Cost' (1960) 3(1) The Journal of Law and Economics 1; Elinor Ostrom, *Governing the Commons: The Evolution of Institutional Forms of Collective Action* (Cambridge University Press 1990).

ushered into trade wars by the US Trump administration and the 'Brexit' confirming that global cooperation is no longer a one-way development towards more rules-orientation. The return of hegemonic, mercantilist power politics and neo-liberal interest group politics undermine an order of international cooperation that builds on mutual respect and necessarily conflicts with public goods, as short-run nationalist interests are placed before a common interest of the international community. Consequently, there is a revival of political and economic forces which the trade order was intended to restrain by rules-based market competition and adjudication. This development is embedded more broadly into the rising influence of authoritarian state-capitalism threatening to undermine the rules-based trading system through state-induced, anti-competitive practices in guises as different as hidden subsidy practices, forced technology transfers, indirect discrimination, other market distortions and trade sanctions for political reasons. Subsidy schemes in state-capitalist countries like China not only distort competition on world markets (creating government-induced market failures), they also conflict with WTO subsidy rules and more broadly with a rules-based trading system building on a level-playing field and non-discrimination.

With governance shifting increasingly from domestic to international, transnational and supranational levels, failures appear in different guises: they can occur as decisions and actions plagued by biases due to rent-seeking (favoring some countries, groups, or businesses' interests), for example by letting market power proliferate in favor of big digital companies, insufficient financial regulation giving rise to too big to fail dilemmas, or letting companies undermine individual rights to privacy; governments can fall afoul of international law obligations due to power-mongering or domestic policy reasons; or international organisations take or prepare decisions that lack sufficient commitment to the collective action problem of public goods, for example if their decisions are biased to favor the interest of (big) Member States[65] (or the largest financial contributors to the organization) like the UN Security Council adopting policies in the interest of dominant veto powers, for example by Russia's abuse of veto power to block assertive climate action by the UN Security Council,[66] to

65 See the case study of the WHO's handling of the 2009 H1N1 influenza pandemic and the 2014 West African Ebola outbreak giving rise to failure due to the WHO secretariat's aversion to offending member states, Adam Kamradt-Scott, 'What Went Wrong? The World Health Organization from Swine Flu to Ebola' in Political Mistakes and Policy Failures in International Relations [2017] Springer Nature 193–215.

66 See the UN Security Council rejection to adopt resolution integrating climate-Related security risk into conflict-prevention strategies at its 8926th meeting on December 13, 2021, SC/14732; Shirley V Scott, 'Implications of climate change for the UN Security

the detriment of other members of the international community undermining the idea of equal rights. International organizations may insufficiently remedy rule-of-law violations (as they are required by international law) if their internal decision-making does not prevent power-politics, with the EU only half-heartedly tackling assault on rule-of-law in some EU member states like Hungary and Poland as one example. Also, judicial decisions by international tribunal and courts can be skewed due to political biases or by judges not being able to act entirely independent from their domestic governments' interests or from the parties selecting judges or arbitrators. The EU initiatives respond to such development by aiming to replace investor-state arbitration inside the EU – as well as in the external relations of the EU – by new kinds of multilevel adjudication responding to the increasing civil society challenges of 'investor biases' and insufficient guarantees of public interests in international investment arbitration.[67]

In some cases, the mandate of international organisations is more generally not well-designed to constrain governments from taking recourse to welfare-nationalistic policies. In international trade, the WTO law has never followed consistently the embedded liberalism underlying GATT 1947, as it contained elements of power imbalances reflecting neo-liberal Anglo-Saxon interest-group politics (e.g. resulting in the WTO Anti-dumping and Trade-related Intellectual Property Rights (TRIPS) Agreements).[68] Arguably, drawing from the GATT's embedded liberalism to the challenges of decolonization, the embedded liberalism underlying the WTO trading system needs to be adjusted not only to the 'new nationalism' inspiring hegemonic mercantilism, the United Kingdom's 'Brexit' from the European Union (EU), and protectionism in BRICS countries (Brazil, Russia, India, China, South Africa). In order to enable WTO members to realize their 'sustainable development' objectives, WTO rules and institutions must also adjust to the 2015 Paris Agreement aimed at mitigating climate change.

Public choice scholars have offered a number of solutions to government failures. Among them, competition between jurisdictions has been viewed as

---

Council: mapping the range of potential policy responses' (2015) 91(6) International Affairs 1317–1333.

67 Cf. Maria L Marceddu and Pietro Ortolani, 'What is Wrong with Investment Arbitration?' (2020) 31 The European Journal of International Law 405.

68 Hanns Ullrich *et alii* (eds), *TRIPS Plus 20. From Trade Rules to Market Principles*, (Springer 2016).

a suitable tool to reduce failure.[69] The 'sovereign equality' of states and related legal freedoms foster 'regulatory competition' among states, with competition placing a natural limit on government predation. If citizens, capital and labor can move freely from jurisdiction to jurisdiction, policy makers are incentivized to select more favorable bundles of policies.[70] The notion of institutional competition normatively inspires the idea of political competition for, within and between government(s) in order to produce benefits for citizens similar to those generated by economic market competition, for instance by promoting regulatory competition. On that account, legal-institutional pluralism promotes institutional competition between jurisdictions, thereby furthering knowledge, enhancing efficiency, restraining power and promoting experimentation with innovative legal-institutional arrangements.[71] Institutional competition can promote variability and quality, for instance if socially and economically viable institutions are imitated while unsuccessful policies are refused by competing jurisdictions. But competition may not be working in many instances because barriers between markets remain high and regulatory competition is often abused, which plays out in particular in the context of transnational governance. Power biases trump fair jurisdictional competition. Transnational governance is also prone to failure where unequal distribution of human and economic resources risks aggravating social inequalities to a point that citizens lose trust (e.g. in social justice, political elites), or circumvent the law (e.g. through tax avoidance, black markets, illegal transactions).[72]

Insight from constitutional economics offers to overcome the pitfalls of jurisdictional competition by strengthening the role of judiciary and multi-level governance. Barry Weingast has argued that, rather than emphasizing competition, the devolution of power can function as a credible commitment to policy reform. Drawing from English constitutional history, Weingast shows that the shifting of power from monarchs to Parliament raised the transaction

69 Friedrich A Hayek, *The Economic Conditions of Interstate Federalism' in Individualism and Economic Order* (University of Chicago Press 1948); Charles M Tiebout, 'A Pure Theory of Local Expenditures' (1956) 64 The Journal of Political Economy 416.

70 Glenn Furton and Adam Martin, 'Beyond Market Failure and Government Failure' (2019) 178 Public Choice 197, 202.

71 Lüder Gerken, 'Institutional Competition: An Orientative Framework' in Lüder Gerken (ed), *Competition among Institutions* (Palgrave Macmillan 1995); Wallace E. Oates, 'An Essay on Fiscal Federalism' (1999) 37 Journal of Economic Literature 1120, 1132.

72 Cf. Anne Case and Angus Deaton, *Deaths of Despair and the Future of Capitalism* (Princeton University Press 2019).

costs of potential rent seekers and hence reduced government failure.[73] He infers that competitive judiciary is key to remedy government failure.[74] By extension, in the same way in which national constitutions have transformed their constitutional rules towards balancing democratic legislation, administration and adjudication protecting rule of law and equal rights of citizens, the 'world order treaties' – like the UN Charter and the WTO Agreement – can deliver governance of transnational public goods only though additional legislative, administrative and judicial implementing acts (like political or judicial interpretations clarifying indeterminate treaty provisions).

Normative constitutional economics therefore emphasizes the need for 'social embedding' of international economic regulation, for instance through protecting also social rights and 'social peace', and for 'institutionalizing public reason', safeguarded by independent regulatory authorities, impartial third-party adjudication protecting rule-of-law and equal rights of citizens. Constitutional economics hence offers a rationale why 'intergovernmental supply of public goods' requires 'institutional checks and balances' limiting abuses of public and private powers: Just as executive powers inside national jurisdictions have often been abused until democratic and republican constitutionalism progressively succeeded – in many countries – in protecting constitutional rights of citizens and collective supply of national public goods, so have the multilevel constitutional 'checks and balances' and judicial protection of constitutional and human rights inside the EU – or the multilevel judicial protection of transnational rule of law among the 164 WTO members – enhanced multilevel governance of transnational public goods by containing abuses of detrimental geopolitical power by means of trade policy.[75]

6 Conclusion

Governance failures of transnational governance abound in an interconnected world, as local and national actions and decisions produce increasingly

73 Barry R Weingast, 'The Economic Role of Political Institutions: Market-Preserving Federalism and Economic Development' (1995) 11(1) Journal of Law Economics and Organization 1.

74 Glenn Furton and Adam Martin, 'Beyond Market Failure and Government Failure' (2019) 178(1) Public Choice 197, 203.

75 Ernst-Ulrich Petersmann and Armin Steinbach, 'Neo-liberalism, State-capitalism and Ordo-liberalism: "Institutional Economics" and "Constitutional Choices" in Multilevel Trade Regulation' (2021) 22 Journal of World Investment and Trade 1, 8–9.

extraterritorial effects. While market failure reveals insufficient transaction-based market solutions in promoting and protecting public goods, and governance failures reveal public or private actions undermining public goods, constitutional failures focus on the adequacy of constitutional rules, notably legal norms of higher rank, in governing transnational public goods.

Constitutional economics engages in the search for legal restraints on abuses of public and private power, for 'institutional checks and balances' and for legal protection of individual preferences (e.g. by means of legal protection of human and fundamental rights). It focuses on ensuring equal freedoms of consumers ('consumer sovereignty') and of citizens ('citizen sovereignty') that require constitutional arrangements to ensure mutual agreeability of market rules, political decision-making and exercise of domestic and transnational political power.[76] Yet, the 'social contract ideal' of citizens making reasonably informed 'constitutional choices' is often confronted with the reality that economic actors and political regulators have only limited knowledge of the complex interactions among private and public, national, transnational and international legal, economic, political and social rules and institutions.[77]

In political practice, constitutional economics is a European project. The normative persuasiveness of constitutional economics has been limited to inspire European integration ushering into multilevel democratic, economic, and human rights constitutionalism, thereby offering the most developed treaty practices aiming at securing consumer sovereignty and citizen sovereignty; this has led the EU to strengthen multilateral rules-based fora such as the WTO and to ratify most UN human rights conventions. Yet, the European tradition of rules-based constraints making governments responsive to citizens' interests is not shared widely. Its normative appeal vanishes in process-based constitutionalism placing democratic elections over rights-based adjudication of political issues. More generally, authoritarian regimes and those driven by business-interests undermine core principles developed under constitutional economics. Geopolitical rivalries and geoeconomic interests are likely to deepen these rifts further as illustrated by the promulgation of divisive policy slogans such as 'friend-shoring' or 'systemic rivalries', with even the EU being at risk to abandon its DNA as normative power to enter instead power-based international 'cooperation'.[78]

---

76 Viktor J Vanberg, 'Market and state: The perspective of constitutional political economy' (2005) 1(1) Journal of Institutional Economics 23.

77 Cf. Geoffrey Brennan and James M. Buchanan, *The Reason of Rules. Constitutional Political Economy* (Cambridge University Press 1985).

78 Armin Steinbach, 'The EU's turn to 'strategic autonomy': leeway for policy action and points of conflict' (forthcoming).

Bibliography

Allison GT, *Essence of Decision: Explaining the Cuban Missile Crisis* (Little, Brown and Company 1971).

Bhandari JS and Sykes AO, *Economic Dimensions In International Law: Comparative and Empirical Perspectives* (Cambridge University Press 1998).

Boin A, 't Hart P and McConnell A, 'Crisis Exploitation: Political and Policy Impacts of Framing Contests' (2009) 16 Journal of European Public Policy 81.

Boucher D and Kelly P (eds), *The Social Contract from Hobbes to Rawls* (Routledge 1994).

Bovens M and 't Hart P, 'Revisiting the Study of Policy Failures' (2016) 23 Journal of European Public Policy 653.

Brändström A and Kuipers S, 'From 'Normal Incidents' to Political Crises: Understanding the Selective Politicization of Policy Failures' (2003) 38 Government and Opposition 279.

Brennan G and Buchanan JM, *The Reason of Rules – Constitutional Political Economy* (Cambridge University Press 1985).

Brennan G and Hamlin A, 'Constitutional Economics' in P Newman (ed), *The New Palgrave Dictionary of Economics and the Law* (Vol I, London: Macmillan 1998) 401.

Brooks RE, 'Failed States, or the State as Failure?' (2005) 72 The University of Chicago Law Review 1159.

Buchanan JM, 'The Domain of Constitutional Economics' (1990) 1 Constitutional Political Economy 1.

Buchanan JM, *Cost and Choice: An Inquiry in Economic Theory* (University of Chicago Press 1979).

Buchanan JM, *The Economics and Ethics of Constitutional Order* (The University of Michigan Press 1991).

Buchanan JM, *What Should Economists Do?* (Liberty Press 1979).

Busch L, *Standards: Recipes for Reality* (MIT Press 2011).

Büthe T and Mattli W, *The New Global Rulers: The Privatization of Regulation in the World Economy* (Princeton University Press 2011).

Case A and Deaton A, *Deaths of Despair and the Future of Capitalism* (Princeton University Press 2019).

Coase RH, 'The Problem of Social Cost' (1960) 3(1) The Journal of Law and Economics 1.

Dunoff J and Trachtman JP, 'Economic Analysis of International Law' (1999) 24 Yale Journal of International Law 1.

Furton G and Martin A, 'Beyond Market Failure and Government Failure' (2019) 178 Public Choice 197.

Furubotn E and Richter R, *Institutions and Economic Theory: The Contribution of the New Institutional Economics* (2nd edn, University of Michigan Press 2005).

Gerken L (ed), *Competition among Institutions* (Palgrave Macmillan 1995).

Gray P, 'Disastrous Explanations – Or Explanations of Disaster? A Reply to Patrick Dunleavy' (1996) 11 Public Policy and Administration 74.

Hauser H, Moser O, Planta R, and Schmid R, 'The Contribution of Jan Tumlir to the Development of a Constitutional Theory of International Trade Rules (in German with English summary)' (1988) 39 Ordo – Jahrbuch für die Ordnung von Wirtschaft und Gesellschaft 219.

Hayek FA, 'Rechtsordnung und Handelsordnung' in Friedrich A. Hayek, *Freiburger Studien* (J. C. B. Mohr (Paul Siebeck) 1969).

Hayek FA, *The Economic Conditions of Interstate Federalism' in Individualism and Economic Orde*r (University of Chicago Press 1948).

Hobolt SB and Tilley J, *Blaming Europe? Responsibility Without Accountability in the European Union* (Oxford University Press 2014).

Howlett M, 'The Lessons of Failure: Learning and Blame Avoidance in Public Policy-Making' (2012) 33 International Political Science Review 539.

Hutt WH, *Plan for Reconstruction: A Project for Victory in War and Peace* (London: Kegan Paul 1943).

Kaul I (ed), *Providing Global Public Goods: Managing Globalization* (Oxford University Press 2003).

Keech WR and Munger MC, 'The anatomy of government failure' (2015) 164 Public Choice 1.

Krebs, 'How Dominant Narratives Rise and Fall: Military Conflict, Politics, and the Cold War Consensus' (2015) 69 International Organization 809.

Kruck A, Oppermann K and Spencer A, 'Introduction: Mistakes and Failures in International Relations' in Andreas Kruck, Kai Oppermann, Alexander Spencer (eds), *Political Mistakes and Policy Failures in International Relations* (Palgrave Macmillan 2018).

Marceddu ML and Ortolani P, 'What is Wrong with Investment Arbitration?' (2020) 31 The European Journal of International Law 405.

McConnell A, 'Policy Success, Policy Failure and Grey Areas In-Between' (2010) 30(3) Journal of Public Policy 345.

McKenzie RB (ed), *Constitutional Economics. Containing the Economic Powers of Government* (Lexington Books, 1984).

Mearsheimer JJ, 'The False Promise of International Institutions' (1994) 19 International Security 5.

Menard C and Shirley MM (eds), *Introduction to a Research Agenda for New Institutional Economics* (Elgar Publishing 2018).

Oates WE, 'An Essay on Fiscal Federalism' (1999) 37 Journal of Economic Literature 1120, 1132.

Ostrom E, *Governing the Commons: The Evolution of Institutional Forms of Collective Action* (Cambridge University Press 1990).

Pavel CE, *Law Beyond the State* (Oxford University Press 2021).

Petersmann EU (ed), *Multilevel Governance of Interdependent Public Goods: Theories, Rules and Institutions for the Central Policy Challenge in the 21st Century* (RSCAS 2012/13).

Petersmann EU and Steinbach A, 'Neo-liberalism, State-capitalism and Ordo-liberalism: "Institutional Economics" and "Constitutional Choices" in Multilevel Trade Regulation' (2021) 22 Journal of World Investment and Trade 1.

Petersmann EU, 'Neoliberalism, Ordoliberalism and the Future of Economic Governance' (2023) Journal of International Economic Law (book review).

Petersmann EU, *Transforming World Trade and Investment Law for Sustainable Development* (Oxford University Press 2022).

Piketty T, *Capital and Ideology* (Belknap Press 2019).

Posner E, *The Perils of Global Legalism* (Reprint, University of Chicago Press 2009).

Potoski M and Prakash A, *Voluntary Programs: A Club Theory Perspective* (MIT Press 2009).

Putnam RD, 'Diplomacy and Domestic Politics: The Logic of Two-Level Games' (1988) 43 International Organization 427.

Rawls J, *A Theory of Justice* (Harvard University Press 1971).

Robbins L, *An Essay on the Nature and Significance of Economic Science* (2nd edn, Macmillan 1935).

Roger C and Dauvergne PD, 'The Rise of Transnational Governance as a Field of Study' (2016) 18(3) International Studies Review 415.

Sand IJ, 'Polycontextuality as an Alternative to Constitutionalism' in Joerges C, Sand IJ and Teubner G (eds), *Transnational Governance and Constitutionalism* (Hart Publishing 2004).

Scott SV, 'Implications of climate change for the UN Security Council: mapping the range of potential policy responses' (2015) 91(6) International Affairs 1317.

Silva M, *State Legitimacy and Failure in International Law* (Brill Njhoff 2014).

Steinbach A, 'The EU's turn to 'strategic autonomy': leeway for policy action and points of conflict', European Journal of International Law (forthcoming).

Terpstra TT, 'Neo-Institutionalism in Ancient Economic History' in Menard C and Shirley MM (eds), *Introduction to a Research Agenda for New Institutional Economics* (Elgar Publishing 2018).

Tiebout CM, 'A Pure Theory of Local Expenditures' (1956) 64 The Journal of Political Economy 416.

Trachtman JP, *The Economic Structure of International Law* (Harvard UP 2008).

Tullock G, 'Problems of Majority Voting' (1959) 67(6) Journal of Political Economy 571.

Tullock G, *Bureaucracy* (CK Rowley ed, Liberty Fund 2005).

Ullrich H, Hilty RM, Lamping M and Drexl J (eds), *TRIPS Plus 20. From Trade Rules to Market Principles* (Springer 2016).

Van Aaken A and Kurtz J, 'Beyond Rational Choice: International Trade Law and the Behavioral Political Economy of Protectionism' (2020) 22 Journal of International Economic Law 601.

Van Aaken A, 'Behavioral International Law and Economics' (2014) 55 Harvard Journal of International Law 427.

Van den Hauwe L, 'Public Choice, Constitutional Political Economy and Law and Economics' in Bouckaert B and De Geest G (eds), *Encyclopedia of Law and Economics* (Vol. 1, Edward Elgar 2000).

Vanberg VJ, 'Market and state: The perspective of constitutional political economy' (2005) 1 Journal of Institutional Economics 23.

Vanberg VJ, *The Constitution of Markets. Essays in Political Economy* (Routledge, 2001).

Vanberg VJ, *Wettbewerb und Regelordnung* (Mohr Siebeck Verlag 2008).

Voigt S, *Constitutional Economics: A Primer* (Cambridge University Press 2020).

Weingast BR, 'The Economic Role of Political Institutions: Market-Preserving Federalism and Economic Development' (1995) 11(1) Journal of Law Economics and Organization 1.

CHAPTER 4

Constitutionalising Climate Mitigation Norms in Europe

Christina Eckes

1 Introduction

Climate Litigation is emerging in many jurisdictions in Europe, in the national context but also before the European Court of Human Rights (ECtHR). A category of these cases, that is particularly salient for constitutionalisation of mitigation norms, targets states for failing to reduce emissions in line with their international commitments within the context of the UN Framework Convention on Climate Change (UNFCCC). The first successful case against a state worldwide was the Dutch *Urgenda* case,[1] followed by the Irish climate case,[2] and *Neubauer* in Germany.[3] Other partially successful cases of this kind are the *Grande-Synthe* and *Notre Affaire à Tous* in France,[4] *Klimaatzaak* in Belgium,[5] and *Net Zero Strategy* case in UK.[6] The (ultimately) unsuccessful cases of *Plan B* in UK,[7] *Natur og Ungdom* in Norway,[8] the ongoing case of *Klimatická žaloba ČR* in Czech Republic,[9] the Finnish climate case,[10] and *Klimaseniorinnen* in

1 *State of the Netherlands (Ministry of Economic Affairs and Climate Policy) v Stichting Urgenda* [2019] ECLI:NL:HR:2019:2007 (Supreme Court of the Netherlands, Civil Division).

2 *Friends of the Irish Environment CLG v The Government of Ireland, Ireland and the Attorney General* [2020] Appeal no. 205/19 (Supreme Court) (*Irish case*).

3 *Neubauer and Others v Germany* [2021] 1 BvR 2656/18, 1 BvR 96/20, 1 BvR 78/20, 1 BvR 288/20, 1 BvR 96/20, 1 BvR 78/20 (German Federal Constitutional Court).

4 *Commune de Grande-Synthe v France* [2021] No. 427301 (Conseil d'Etat); *Notre Affaire à Tous and Others v France* [2021] Nos. 1904967, 1904968, 1904972, 1904976/4–1 (Paris Administrative Court).

5 *VZW Klimaatzaak v Kingdom of Belgium & Others* [2021] 2015/4585/A (Brussels Court of First Instance).

6 *R v Secretary of State for Business Energy and Industrial Strategy* [2022] EWHC 1841 (*'Net Zero Strategy Case'*).

7 *Plan B Earth et al v Secretary of State for Transport* [2020] EWCA Civ 214.

8 *Nature and Youth Norway and others v Norway* [2020] HR-2020-24720P (Supreme Court).

9 *Klimatická žaloba ČR v Czech Republic* [2023] 9 As 116/2022 – 166 (Czech Supreme Court).

10 *Greenpeace Nordic and the Finnish Association for Nature Conservation v Finland* [2023] ECLI:FI:KHO:2023:62 (Supreme Administrative Court of Finland) (*'Finnish climate case'*). See for an analysis in English: K Kulovesi et al, 'Finland's first climate judgment: Putting

DOI:10.1163/9789004693722_005

Switzerland,[11] while not imposing emission reduction obligations, contributed to the ongoing climate constitutionalisation. Some of these unsuccessful cases have been escalated (*Klimaseniorinnen*[12] and *Carême/Grande-Synthe*[13]) and new cases (*Duarte Augustino*[14]) have been brought to the ECtHR.

This chapter examines the emerging phenomenon of '*climate* constitutionalisation'[15] in the multi-layered legal landscape of Europe. It focusses on cases against states attempting to address governance failure to mitigate climate change by relying on international or regional norms. Mushrooming climate cases against states directly and indirectly vest these norms that originate outside the domestic legal order with a higher legal rank than the domestic executive and legislative actions and choices to remain inactive that they challenge. This constitutionalises these norms relating to mitigation commitments and makes them into (enforceable) legal obligations. Often, later cases replicate successful legal arguments and strategies of earlier cases and hereby confers additional authority on their reasoning and outcome.[16]

Climate constitutionalism is a new and multifaceted phenomenon. We can see it emerging as the result of judges acknowledging the relevance of a stable climate for the enjoyment of fundamental rights, interpreting constitutional provisions in relation to the climate emergency, or vesting (international) political commitments with legal force by connecting them directly or via ordinary law with constitutional norms or human rights.

This chapter takes a 'court-centric approach', different from other approaches that have focused on the constitutionalisation of the climate in

---

the government on notice' (CCEEL, 12 June 2023) <https://sites.uef.fi/cceel/finlands-first-climate-judgment-putting-the-government-on-notice> accessed 15 June 2023.

11 *KlimaSeniorinnen Schweiz et al v Federal Department of the Environment, Transport, Energy and Communications* [2020] 1C_37/2019 (Switzerland Supreme Court).

12 *KlimaSeniorinnen Schweiz et al v Switzerland*, no. 53600/20 (application communicated to the Swiss Government in March 2021 – Relinquishment in favour of the Grand Chamber in April 2022).

13 *Carême v France*, no. 7189/21 (Relinquishment in favour of the Grand Chamber in May 2022).

14 *Duarte Agostinho and Others v Portugal and 32 Other States*, no. 39371/20 (application communicated to the defending governments in November 2020 – Relinquishment in favour of the Grand Chamber in June 2022).

15 N Singh Ghaleigh, J Setzer and A Welikala, 'The Complexities of Comparative Climate Constitutionalism' (2022) 34 Journal of Environmental Law 517; J Jaria-Manzano and S Borrás (eds), *Research Handbook on Global Climate Constitutionalism* (Edward Elgar 2019).

16 M Wewerinke-Singh and S Mead (eds), *Judicial Handbook on Climate Litigation, lawyers and legal scholars* (project of IUCN's World Commission on Environmental Law (WCEL) Climate Change Law Specialist Group (CCLSG), 2023).

codified norms.[17] It only engages with *European cases* and only with climate cases *against states that aims for general emission reduction*. This chapter contributes a perspective different from earlier work in at least two ways: First, it focusses on multi-layered legal interaction in climate litigation that is characteristic for *Europe*. Its approach is hence limited geographically and includes cases pending before ECtHR. Second, it pays specific attention to how judicial decisions attach legal value to political commitments within the context of the UNFCCC, predominantly by reading them in light of open-textured binding legal norms. This leads us to examine in particular the implications of constitutionalisation for the powers of the three branches of government, i.e. the implications for separation of powers.

In terms of legal basis, human rights norms are at the centre of climate constitutionalisation. The Dutch Supreme Court in *Urgenda,* for example, relied on the right to life (Article 2 ECHR) and the right to respect for private and family life (Article 8 ECHR) in order to oblige the state to reduce the overall emissions from its territory.[18] Neither of these provisions directly refers to the climate or even the environment. While the ECtHR had earlier interpreted these rights to cover situations where people's (private) lives were affected by environmental pollution, the courts in *Urgenda* pioneered by interpreting Articles 2 and 8 ECHR to entail an obligation to mitigate climate change.

These legally binding norms are interpreted in light of strong and repeated political commitments and interpretations. Political leaders and governments have for their states repeatedly stated what they consider necessary to mitigate climate change. They have repeatedly strengthened and tightened their commitments considering the climate emergency that is currently unfolding. The judicial reasoning process uses these political commitments as means of interpretation to concretise what open-textured legally binding norms mean in practice and for the individual case. The concomitant of this process is that these political commitments, when they are (repeatedly) relied on by judges, are vested with legal legitimacy. This chapter traces the process of constitutionalisation, identifies the implications of its multi-layered dimension in

---

17 For other 'court-centric approaches' see: C Rodríguez-Garavito, 'Human Rights: The Global South's Route to Climate Litigation' (2020) 114 American Journal of International Law 40; JR May and E Daly, 'Global climate constitutionalism and justice in the courts' in J Jaria-Manzano and S Borrás (eds), *Research Handbook on Global Climate Constitutionalism* (Edward Elgar 2019). For an approach also concentrating on codified law: N Singh Ghaleigh, J Setzer and A Welikala, 'The Complexities of Comparative Climate Constitutionalism' (n 15).

18 So have the cases now pending before the ECtHR (see n 12–14).

Europe, and examines its implications through a lens of separation of powers. The chapter argues that climate constitutionalisation strengthens the judiciary but rather than undermining democratic will-formation, it contributes to an institutional setting where will-formation of the polity is enabled to deal with longer-term challenges and maintain credibility in an era of fast-moving over-information.

Section 2 offers conceptual clarifications, background considerations, and links constitutionalisation to separation of powers considerations. Section 3 analyses the entire population of all general mitigation cases against states in Europe that have been decided until 31 December 2022. This population comprises seven (partially) successful and five unsuccessful cases, some of which have not been decided in final instance.[19] It demonstrates the constitutionalisation of the climate emergency as a human rights issue (3.1), of political climate commitments (3.2), and of the normative effects of climate science (3.3). Section 4 turns to the ECtHR as an additional layer of climate constitutionalisation that, because of the great relevance and status of the Strasbourg Court, will be one factor that either strengthens or slows down the stringency of judicial review, once the decisions in the first climate cases are delivered. It introduces the pending cases and sketches how the applications and the eventual decisions may contribute to constitutionalizing climate related understanding of human rights norms. Section 5 explains the role of climate litigation in demanding justification for inaction. Section 6 concludes.

2 Climate Constitutionalisation, Separation of Powers, and Democratic Will-Formation

2.1 *Climate Constitutionalisation*

'*Climate* constitutionalism'[20] refers to an outcome of a process of establishing and consolidating legal (constitutional) principles governing the climate emergency. Developing a vocabulary, i.e., a stock of shared concepts that are

19 Successful: *Urgenda* [2019] (n 1); *Friends of the Irish Environment/Irish case* [2020] (n 2); *Neubauer* [2021] (n 3); *Notre Affaire à Tous* [2021] (n 4); *Grande-Synthe* [2021] (n 4); *VZW Klimaatzaak* [2021] (n 5); *Net Zero Strategy* Case [2022] (n 6). Unsuccessful: *Nature and Youth* [2020] (n 8) *KlimaSeniorinnen* [2020] (n 11); *Plan B Earth* [2020] (n 7); *Klimatická žaloba ČR* [2023] (n 9); Finnish Climate Case (n 10).

20 N Singh Ghaleigh, J Setzer and A Welikala, 'The Complexities of Comparative Climate Constitutionalism' (n 15). J Jaria-Manzano and S Borrás (eds), *Research Handbook on Global Climate Constitutionalism* (n 15).

or become comprehensible beyond the individual case. It builds on an equally ongoing process of 'environmental constitutionalisation'[21] and has direct implications for the division of powers between the three branches of government, the legislature, executive and judiciary.

One of the 'more powerful conventions of the legal argument', that Duncan Kennedy points out in a very different context, is helpful to understand the relevance of constitutionalisation: namely, that 'arguments proceed, both within a given case and over a series of cases, from the more general choices to the more particular, arguing and then re-arguing, rather than debating the merits of a point on the continuum versus all the other points on the continuum'.[22] Few legal scholars dispute that legal reasoning is a process of choosing between alternatives and that the stakes differ depending on whether one goes down one path or the other with the argumentation in any given case. At the same time and this is also implied in Kennedy's quote, the process of norm interpreting and creating is prone to unfold in a path-dependent way. Climate constitutionalism is no exception. Interpretations and norm constructions of the past shape the arguments of the parties and the reasoning of the courts in future cases.

On the one hand, climate litigation contribute to a norm interpretation that concretises legal rights and obligations in relation to the climate emergency. On the other hand, climate litigation makes visible what the legal obstacles are that stand in the way of meeting the demands of those who are climate victims. Usually, the legal process focusses on a limited, legally determined realm of arguments and actors. It is not able to include or even disclose the vast array of situational considerations, affected interests, and involved persons. Often, unsuccessful cases contribute to better understanding the legal opportunity structures and allow for more strategic choices for future climate litigation.[23]

In addition, what has been legally established frames the argumentation of plaintiffs and judges. Interpretations by higher instance courts and references

---

21 Cf., inter alia, JR May and E Daly, *Environmental Constitutionalism* (Cambridge University Press 2015); L Kotzé, *Global Environmental Constitutionalism in the Anthropocene* (Hart 2016) – also touched upon in G Ganguly, J Setzer and V Heyvaert, 'If at First You Don't Succeed: Suing Corporations for Climate Change' (2018) 38 Oxford Journal of Legal Studies 841.

22 D Kennedy, 'A Semiotics of Legal Argument' (1991) 42 Syracuse Law Review 75, 101.

23 See for learning from failure: A Steinbach, 'Constitutional economics and transnational governance failures' in this volume; for literature on strategic choices and legal opportunity structures: L Vanhalla, 'Legal opportunity structures and the legal mobilization by the environmental movement in the UK' (2012) 46 Law & Society Review 523. See also: R Verheyen, *Wir alle haben ein Recht auf Zukunft* (DTV Verlag 2023), 13.

to constitutional norms have a particularly authoritative value. They create norms of higher rank, which are taken as a point of reference rather than a point of discussion in the exchanges before lower instance courts – a point of reference from which one can distinguish one's own case and argument but that cannot be changed through argumentation. Overall, climate litigation has opened new understandings and opportunities to use the law and in particular constitutional law to force those in charge and those with exceptionally high emissions to take climate action.

Judges must decide. On the one hand, courts may only act when cases are brought to them. On the other hand, when a case is brought to them, judges must deliver justice.[24] They may of course deny or decline jurisdiction but also the decision not to exercise jurisdiction contributes to the understanding of the law, i.e., what conflicts and situations it governs and what it does not govern or what boundaries separation of powers considerations imposes on the judiciary. In other words, climate litigation necessarily develops the law – whether it considers the climate emergency as a matter of constitutional nature or not.

2.2 *Separation of Powers*

Constitutionalism is intrinsically linked to the concept of separation of powers. It is based on the understanding that the exercise of public power must be controlled in light of pre-determined norms of higher rank than those flowing form that very exercise of public power.[25] The climate emergency is widely seen as (one of) the greatest challenge to human rights and democracy in the 21st century.[26] It is a challenge to the functioning of our democratic state institutions. Central issues in the many different attempts to grapple, internationally, regionally, nationally, and locally, with this exceptional and existential challenge, relate to the power division, responsibility, and duty to act. In this

---

24 *E.g.*, Art. 13 Wet AB neergelegde verbod van rechtsweigering (prohibition to deny justice). This is also how 'duty' is read in the famous citation: 'It is emphatically the province and duty of the judicial department to say what the law is' form *Marbury v Madison* [1803] 5 U.S. (1 Cranch) 137 (1803) (US Supreme Court).

25 MJC Vile, *Constitutionalism and the Separation of Powers* (Oxford University Press 1967), 1.

26 *E.g.*, World Health Organisation, 'Health and climate change' (*WHO News Room*, 5 December 2018) <https://www.who.int/news-room/facts-in-pictures/detail/health-and-climate-change> accessed 15 June 2023; *e.g.*, E Darian-Smith, *Global Burning: Rising Anti-Democracy and the Climate Crisis* (Stanford University Press 2022). This is also widely the perception: see UNESCO, 'UNESCO 'World in 2023' Survey Report highlights youth concerns over climate change and biodiversity loss' (*UNESCO*, 31 March 2021) <https://en.unesco.org/news/unesco-world-2030-survey-report-highlights-youth-concerns-over-climate-change-and-biodiversity> accessed 15 June 2023.

context, the question arises of who is competent or even mandated to frame and decide these issues. This question concerns the horizontal (between the three branches of government) and vertical (which layer of law and governance) separation of powers.

Climate cases brought against states pursue the objective of compelling states to accelerate their efforts to implement emissions reduction targets, exposing that national goals are insufficiently ambitious, or holding states responsible for their contribution to the climate emergency.[27] Because of the objective of 'forcing the hand of the executive and the legislature' climate cases against states are generally considered to be particularly controversial from a separation of powers perspective as they regularly ask the judge to impose foreword looking policy goals concretised into specific reduction percentages, which often need to be deduced relying on internationally agreed (not legally binding) political commitments, legally binding but open-textured human rights norms, and complex climate science expressing probabilities of consequences.[28] One could argue that, in mitigation cases against states, the judiciary is faced with a request by the litigants to engage in pro-active expert law-making – to force the policymakers to act and justify their actions in light of 'best available science'.

Separation of powers is the well-known and time-tested foundation of modern democracies committed to the rule of law. Not only in practice but also as an ideal, separation of powers refers to a designation and delimitation (rather than strict separation) of powers that enables constructive interaction as well as mutual constraints between the three branches. I here purport a *relational* understanding that emphasises the need for constructive interaction, while acknowledging the need for mutual control.[29] I distinguish between separation of powers as a *concept* that serves as a regulatory ideal that has an

27 Insufficiently ambitious: *Friends of the Irish Environment/Irish case* [2020] (n 2); *Family Farmers and Greenpeace Germany v Germany* [2018] 00271/17/R/SP (Administrative Court Berlin).

28 B Mayer, 'Climate Change Mitigation as an Obligation Under Human Rights Treaties?' (2021) 115 American Journal of International Law 409; L Besselink, 'The National and EU Targets for Reduction of Greenhouse Gas Emissions Infringe the ECHR: The Judicial Review of General Policy Objectives: Hoge Raad (Netherlands Supreme Court) 20 December 2019, Urgenda v The State of the Netherlands' (2022) 18 European Constitutional Law Review 155.

29 A relational understanding can be contrasted with the functionalist approach of *e.g.*, MJC Vile, *Constitutionalism and the Separation of Powers* (n 25); J Waldron, 'Separation of Powers in Thought and Practice' (2013) 54 Boston College Law Review 441, referring to John Locke.

identifiable purpose but cannot (logically) be realised entirely and the different *conceptions* of separation of powers, *i.e.*, realisations of that purpose in different jurisdictions.

The purpose of the *concept* of separation of powers is primarily to prevent the concentration of power in a single source as opposed to pursuing any identifiable substantive outcome.[30] Its focus is on the procedural and institutional 'how' of law-making. The non-concentration of power aims to serve the double objectives of collective will-formation and control of those in power.[31] Public will-formation is ensured by establishing through the means of separated powers a process of expressing, mediating, and mitigating – and, indeed, protecting and perpetuating – the at times contradictory claims of individual and collective autonomy; put differently, between liberalism and a republican-Rousseauist idea.[32] Separated powers create the institutional conditions for discursive justificatory exchanges, in which no one branch can in the long run dominate the others. The judiciary traditionally represents individual autonomy (*ex post*) in these exchanges and is mandated to require public justification for human rights interferences by the other branches.

As a natural part of democratic processes, the understanding of the different *conceptions* of separation of powers are subject to change, including changes that affect the precise division of powers between the branches. They are legally prescribed but dynamically develop through practice. One driving question in the analysis of the suitability of any specific understanding of separation of powers, including the interpretations given to the different (usually national) conceptions of separation of powers in climate litigation, should therefore be whether that understanding establishes a process of reason-giving and hereby establishes institutional interactions that contribute to creating the conditions that activate will-formation.

Considering the common constitutional duty of courts to protect fundamental rights[33] it may seem odd that some argue that the judiciary has little to no role in addressing the climate emergency as the most pressing concern for human rights of this century. This impression is reinforced by the fact that the

30 C Möllers, *The Three Branches: A Comparative Model of Separation of Powers* (Oxford University Press 2013), 77–79.

31 Ibid.

32 Ibid, 108; see also: J Habermas, *Between Facts and Norms: Contribution to a Discourse Theory of Law and Democracy* (MIT Press 1996).

33 E.g., in Germany, Article 94(1)4a GG, setting out the German Constitutional Court's duty and mandate to review the exercise of public power for its compatibility with fundamental rights; in Ireland the 'solemn duty' of courts to review executive action: *Efe v. Minister for Justice, Equality and Law Reform* [2011] 2 IR 798, [813].

legislature and the executive widely fail to adequately address this concern. What is and should be the role of the judiciary?

In climate cases against states, a distinction can be made between cases that challenge the actions or more often *inactions* of, on the one hand, the executive and, on the other, the legislature.[34] The trailblazer of climate cases against states for general emission reduction, the *Urgenda* case, is an example that could be said to concern both the executive and the legislature.[35] The Dutch state was required to adopt mitigation measures that required government to take actions, likely including making legislative proposals to parliament. Yet, parliament could not be obliged to adopt these proposals but always retained the right to reject them.

In all climate cases against states, the judiciary is asked to specify legal limits to acceptable actions or inactions of the other branches. A growing consensus is emerging that even though addressing climate change requires reconciling numerous interests pulling in different directions, which is a task for the legislature and the executive, courts must play a role in response to challenges pointing out the blatant inadequacy of climate action in light of science.[36] This is a form of exerting political influence. Court decisions can influence the political debate.[37] They provide legal, symbolic, and argumentative reasons for or against action that are used by political actors who prefer policies in line with these reasons.[38] These reasons usually have a longevity beyond a short election cycle.

However, this is not to be misunderstood that litigation is the perfect fix. Courts equally struggle to give climate justice beyond borders any legal relevance.[39] Their constitutional mandate is given and limited by a specific

34 Examples of the former are: *Friends of the Irish Environment* [2020] (n 2); *Net Zero Strategy* Case [2022] (n 6); *Notre Affaire à Tous* [2021] (n 4). Examples of the latter are: *Neubauer* [2021] (n 3); Plan B Earth [2020] (n 7).

35 *Urgenda* [2019] (n 1); *State of the Netherlands v Stichting Urgenda* [2018] ECLI:NL:GHDHA:2018:2591 (Court of Appeal); *Stichting Urgenda v State of the Netherlands* [2015] ECLI:NL:RBDHA:2015:7196 (District Court).

36 C Eckes, J Nedevska and J Setzer, 'Climate litigation and separation of powers' in M Wewerinke-Singh and S Mead (eds), *Judicial Handbook on Climate Litigation, lawyers and legal scholars* (project of IUCN's World Commission on Environmental Law (WCEL) Climate Change Law Specialist Group (CCLSG), 2023).

37 Dutch Minister for climate and energy Rob Jetten at: Al Jazeera English, 'The Case for the Climate: Forcing systems change in court | earthrise' (26 April 2023) <https://www.youtube.com/watch?v=MJXpOooZwpc> accessed 15 June 2023.

38 Ibid.

39 May and Daly, 'Global Climate Constitutionalism and Justice in the Courts' (n 17).

jurisdiction. Judicial process is slow. Judges need to look towards the past, even if they establish prospective obligations.

2.3 *Climate Change and Democratic Will-Formation*

The climate emergency is an exceptional test of the capacities of our democracies.[40] So far, our democracies are failing to 'prevent dangerous anthropogenic interference with the climate system'.[41] The consequences are already felt today and will be much greater in the future.[42] The climate emergency is 'crying out for action from leaders around the world.'[43]

Increasingly, scholars and courts are identifying the tensions between the 'democracy's short-sightedness that makes politics stumble in our increasingly connected world'[44] and the need to mitigate climate change, which may first seem to come with steep costs. Some argue that they have higher costs than benefits for those states that are the greatest polluters.[45] However, first, already today, one needs to also take into account adaptation, loss and damage, as well as diffuse social-economic costs that are often, because of the long causation chains, difficult to directly link to climate change. Second, ultimately, the lack of mitigating actions today will increase all these costs in the future. Hence, the calculation of costs and benefits strongly depends on the time frame and geographical focus (place), as well as how wholistic diffuse and indirect costs of climate change are considered. Political organisation is still largely concentrated in the nation-state and hence reasons from that perspective. Politicians work in incentive structures that relate to the short-term interests of present-day voters. The rights and interests of future generations are structurally insufficiently represented in the political institutions.

---

40 D Fiorino, *Can Democracy Handle Climate Change?* (Polity Press 2018); F Fischer, 'Ecological Crisis and Climate Change: From States of Emergency to 'Fortress World'?' in F Fischer (ed), *Climate Crisis and the Democratic Prospect: Participatory Governance in Sustainable Communities* (Oxford University Press 2017); S Dover, 'Sustainability: Demands on Policy' (1997) 16 Journal of Public Policy 303; D Shearman and JW Smith, *The Climate Challenge and the Failure of Democracy* (Praeger 2007).

41 Art. 2 UNFCCC.

42 IPCC, *Global Warming of 1.5°C* (IPCC 2019) <https://www.ipcc.ch/sr15/download/> accessed 15 June 2023.

43 Olivier Knox, 'The Daily 202: The Alarming Climate Report Is Also a Huge Politics Story' (*Washington Post* 10 August 2021) <https://www.washingtonpost.com/politics/2021/08/10/daily-202-alarming-climate-report-is-also-huge-politics-story/> accessed 15 June 2023.

44 J Zielonka, *The Lost Future and How to Reclaim It* (Yale University Press 2023).

45 B Mayer, 'The Contribution of Urgenda to the Mitigation of Climate Change' (2022) 20 Journal of Environmental Law 1.

The German Constitutional Court framed this tension between climate change and institutional conditions of democracies pointedly:

> [T]he democratic political process is organised along more short-term lines based on election cycles, placing it at a structural risk of being less responsive to tackling the ecological issues that need to be pursued over the long term. […] [F]uture generations – those who will be most affected – naturally have no voice of their own in shaping the current political agenda.[46]

3 A Repeat Game under Increasing Pressure: Climate Litigation in Europe

Obligations under international treaties regularly require implementation within domestic legal orders. In this case, domestic courts are 'the first port of call and the last line of defense for the interpretation and application of international law'.[47] In climate cases, we see how courts weave together international, regional, and national obligations and give meaning to them considering scientific facts and political acknowledgement of these facts. This leads them to draw conclusions on what is legally necessary for the state to meet its duty of care and protection of its citizens. It also highlights the widespread and continuous governance failures when it comes to mitigating climate change.

Increasingly, climate litigation relies on human rights, globally and in Europe.[48] In the United States, where numerically most climate case are brought international norms and political commitments have a very different value in court. This is a confirmation of the need for and relevance of a study of climate constitutionalisation in the European context, where commitment to

---

46 *Neubauer* [2021] (n 3), p. 61.

47 A Tzanakopoulos, 'Domestic Courts in International Law: The International Judicial Function of National Courts' (2011) 34 Loy. L.A. Int'l & Comp. L. Rev 33.

48 See for the human rights trend: G Ganguly, 'Judicial transnationalization' in V Heyvaert and LA Duvic-Paoli (eds), *Research Handbook on Transnational Environmental Law* (Edward Elgar 2020), Section 3.2; C Rodríguez-Garavito, *International Human Rights and Climate Governance: The 'Rights Turn' in Climate Litigation* (Unpublished manuscript), and for the exception of the US: J Peel and H Osofsky, 'Climate Change Litigation' (2020) 16 Annual Review of Law and Social Science 21. See specifically for Economic, Social, and Cultural Rights: S Gloppen and C Vallejo, 'The climate crisis: litigation and economic, social and cultural rights' in J Dugard et al (eds), *Research Handbook on Economic, Social and Cultural Rights as Human Rights* (Edward Elgar 2020).

and compliance with international law, including human rights treaties, such as the ECHR, create a very different legal landscape for climate litigation.

3.1 *Reliance on Human Rights Norms*

A rights-based approach as opposed to other legal grounds gives equal emphasis to the individual autonomy of all humans, including underrepresented and disadvantaged groups.[49] Considering that the climate emergency exacerbates inequalities both between countries and within countries, and that its impacts are affecting persons of different race, gender, and class, very differently,[50] human rights are a way of empowering each individual person.

At the same time, a rights-based approach bears the interrelated dangers of either having to demonstrate the *individualised* rights-impact of climate change to meet standing requirements and establish a violation and empowering courts to carry out a balancing of general interests that is – in light of separation of powers considerations – traditionally reserved for the legislature. Protecting individualised interests is the core function of the judiciary; however, litigating for the public good stands inherently in tension with demonstrating an individualised rights infringement. While climate cases aim to protect individual rights of those affected by climate change, regularly these rights are invoked by public interest organisations or large number of citizens that are affected in a way comparable to many other citizens of that state or even all those states that are in a similar geographical and economic position. Arguably, the climate emergency 'threatens the world's entire population'.[51] However, when courts protect the rights of the collective and no specific individual is distinguishable by the gravity of the rights violation that they are facing, courts are asked to consider and balance general interests. This blurs the

49 Amnesty International, 'After UN Climate Action Summit, Urgent Action Needed by All States to Avoid Human Rights Violations on Massive Scale' (Public statement, Index number IOR 40/1239/2019, Amnesty International 2019) <https://www.amnesty.org/en/documents/ior40/1239/2019/en/> accessed 2 April 2023; UNEP, 'Climate Change and Human Rights' (Report, UNEP 2015) <https://www.unep.org/resources/report/climate-change-and-human-rights> accessed 2 April 2023.

50 N Taconet, A Méjean and C Guivarch, 'Influence of climate change impacts and mitigation costs on inequality between countries' (2020) 160 Climatic Change 15; Serhan Cevik and João Tovar Jalles, *For Whom the Bell Tolls: Climate Change and Income Inequality* (IMF 2022); L Chancel et al, *Climate Inequality Report 2023* (World Inequality Lab Study 2023/1) <https://wid.world/wp-content/uploads/2023/01/CBV2023-ClimateInequalityReport-3.pdf> accessed 15 June 2023.

51 Conclusion of Procurator General in *State of the Netherlands (Ministry of Economic Affairs and Climate Policy) v Stichting Urgenda* [2019], ECLI:NL:PHR:2019:887.

distinction between individual autonomy and the collective and puts pressure on the function of the judiciary, as outlined above.

The *Urgenda* case[52] was initiated based on the unwritten duty of care under Dutch tort law (District Court, 2015). In second and third instance, the Court of Appeal (2018) and the Dutch Supreme Court (2019), however, ruled based on Articles 2 and 8 ECHR. In *Urgenda*, human rights moved to the centre stage of the case as it moved up to the higher instances. In the highest instance, the judges established a duty of care based on human rights norms, considering international commitments of the Dutch State and climate science. In many respects, the move to human rights as the legal grounding of this duty of care has strengthened the replicability of the reasoning and added an important element to climate constitutionalism across Europe.

Human rights were also central to the German case of *Neubauer*, decided by the German Constitutional Court in 2021. However, *Neubauer* differs from *Urgenda* in the role of human rights at least in two important respects: First, the judges in the *Neubauer* case in Germany found a human rights violation but did not conclude that a duty of care was infringed. Second, they could rely on the national incorporation of international climate commitments in the national climate protection act.[53] In other words, they did not have to rely on international (political) commitments but could rely on the temperature goal of 'well below 2°C above preindustrial levels and pursuing efforts to limit the temperature increase to 1.5°C above pre-industrial levels' confirmed by the German legislature in the legally binding national climate protection act.[54]

In the French case of *Notre Affaire à Tous*, the plaintiffs asked the court, in an action for failure to act, to hold the French State in breach of obligations under the 2015 Paris Agreement.[55] They aimed among other things to establish a statutory duty to act in compliance with the state's own goals for reducing emissions. This duty was based on the French Charter for the Environment, the ECHR, and the general principle of law establishing a right to a preserved climate system. The plaintiffs requested the court to order France first to take proper measures to reduce greenhouse gas emissions in the atmosphere – in due proportion considering global emissions, and taking into account the particular responsibility accepted by developed countries – at a level compatible with the objective to contain the rise of the average temperature of the planet below the threshold of 1.5 °C compared to pre-industrial levels; and second to

52 *Urgenda* [2019] (n 1).

53 *Neubauer* [2021] (n 3).

54 Paragraph 1 on the objective of the law.

55 *Notre Affaire à Tous* [2021] (n 4).

take, at least, all necessary measures to achieve France's targets for reducing greenhouse gas emissions.[56] In final instance, the courts obliged the French State to adopt immediate and concrete climate measures and, importantly, to repair the damage caused by its inaction by the end of 2022.

Equally in France, in *Carême/Grande-Synthe I*, the Conseil d'Etat disallowed the claim of the *mayor* of the municipality of Grande-Synthe to challenge the national government's climate policies. It *allowed the claim of the municipality* together with several other affected municipalities, because of their 'direct and certain' exposure to climate change impacts.[57] However, the legal position of these municipalities was not grounded in human rights. The claim of the mayor of Grande-Synthe, Mr. Carême, was rejected and is now pending before the ECtHR.[58]

The plaintiffs in the Belgian *Klimaatzaak*, decided by the Court of First Instance in Brussels in 2021, took the *Urgenda* case in first instance as their blueprint.[59] Their claim is based both on alleged civil liability of a public authority (Art 1382 of the Belgian Civil Code) and an alleged violation of human rights, namely Articles 2 and 8 ECHR and Articles 6 and 24 International Convention on the Rights of the Child. In addition, the court considered access to justice for alleged violations of national environmental law within the meaning of Article 9(3) Aarhus Convention in the context of its assessment of the admissibility of the case. The Court of First Instance in *Klimaatzaak*, which is currently under appeal, found both civil liability and a violation of the plaintiffs' rights under the ECHR.[60] It explicitly agreed with the Supreme Court in *Urgenda* that the global dimension of the climate emergency could not absolve the Belgian state from its responsibility (rejection of the drop in the ocean argument).[61] Based on explicit separation of powers considerations, the court denied the plaintiffs' request for an injunction ordering the defendants to take the necessary mitigation measures.[62]

By contrast, the Irish Supreme Court invalidated the Government's National Mitigation Plan on narrow legal grounds of *ultra vires* action rather than human rights grounds.[63] In other words, the Irish Climate Case, while

56 C Cournil, A Le Dylio and P Mougeolle, 'L'Affaire du Siecle: French Climate Litigation between Continuity and Legal Innovations' (2020) 14 CCLR 40.

57 *Grande-Synthe* [2021] (n 4), [3].

58 *Carême v France* (n 13).

59 *VZW Klimaatzaak* [2021] (n 5).

60 Not under the International Convention on the Rights of the Child.

61 *ZW Klimaatzaak* [2021] (n 5), Section 1.2.

62 Ibid, Section 2.3.2.

63 *Friends of the Irish Environment* [2020] (n 2).

successful in imposing climate obligations on the state, did not bolster the potential of human rights as a basis for future climate litigation.[64] This is similar to the courts' position in Plan B. Here, the plaintiffs challenging the legality of building a third runway at Heathrow in *Plan B* arguing their case also based on the ECHR; yet, the courts restricted themselves to the narrow question of the respective powers of the political branches, i.e. whether the executive exercised its powers in line with the legal framework established by the national legislature.[65]

In *Natur og Ungdom v Norway*, environmental groups asked the Oslo District Court, the Court of Appeal and the Supreme Court to declare that Norway's Ministry of Petroleum and Energy violated the Norwegian constitution by issuing oil and gas licenses for deep-sea extraction in the Barents Sea.[66] Their claim was rejected in all three instances, with the Supreme Court upholding the licences in December 2020 and declaring that Articles 2 and 8 ECHR were not violated. The case is hence an 'unsuccessful' example of climate litigation. This comes with low expectations of what it could contribute to climate constitutionalisation. Nonetheless, it contributed, albeit in a limited fashion, to establishing and consolidating legal principles governing the climate emergency, while taking a quite conservative position on other aspects.[67] In terms of consolidation, the Supreme Court confirmed for example that the right to a healthy and natural environment in the Norwegian constitution (Art 112) is 'not merely a declaration of principle, but a provision with a certain legal content.'[68] Under certain circumstances, this provision can directly be invoked in court. The case is now pending before the ECtHR.[69]

Similarly, in the *Klimaseniorinnen* case a group of senior women challenged in 2016 the alleged omissions of the Swiss federal government to adopt a regulatory framework to develop adequate climate protection policy. Their claim was based on Articles 2 and 8, as well as Articles 6 and 13 ECHR. It was rejected by Swiss courts in three instances and is now pending before the ECtHR.[70] The

64 V Adelmant, P Alston and M Blainey, 'Human Rights and Climate Change Litigation: One Step Forward, Two Steps Backwards in the Irish Supreme Court' (2021) 13 Journal of Human Rights Practice 1, 6.

65 *Plan B Earth* [2020] (n 7), [2]; this is in some ways like the narrow approach of the court in the Irish Case.

66 *Nature and Youth* [2020] (n 8).

67 See below Section 5 on the aspects of *Nature and Youth* that confirmed weakened the law's ability to offer answers and opportunities in the face of the global climate emergency.

68 *Nature and Youth* [2020] (n 8), [144].

69 *Greenpeace Nordic and Others v Norway*, no 34068/21. The case has been communicated to Norway with the request for observations. It will hence move to the deliberation stage.

70 *KlimaSeniorinnen* [2020] (n 11).

court considered that the substance of this case is a matter for the political arena and not a violation of human rights. The ECtHR is now asked to,consider the crucial questions of whether the climate emergency (already) violates Convention rights, who is a victim of the climate emergency,[71] causal link between the emissions of a particular state and the harm suffered by the applicants, and what is the 'fair share', which is at the core of any legal challenge to the adequacy of a state's mitigation efforts.

In another 'unsuccessful case', the Finnish climate case (2023), Greenpeace and Finnish Association for Nature Conservation claimed that the governance failure to adopt additional climate measures as they were required to achieve the binding climate targets under the Finnish Climate Act of 2022 constituted a judiciable administrative act.[72] The applicants relied, besides the Aarhus Convention, on Articles 6 and 13 ECHR and, even though the court rejected the appeal, it acknowledged the relevance of these human rights norms for the climate emergency, including when no administrative decision was taken.[73] In other words, the Finnish climate case, while being unsuccessful, contributed by climate constitutionalisation by emphasising the *role of courts* in ensuring that political decision-makers act in accordance with the law and do not obstruct the enjoyment of human rights. This is a climate litigation friendly reading of separation of powers. The Court further established that climate inaction requires an effective remedy. Both in the German *Neubauer* and in the Finnish climate cases, the courts specifically considered (and in the *Neubauer* case protected) the right of future generations.

In six European countries, courts, including highest courts, have established that the climate emergency violates or at least has the potential to violate human rights.[74] In two case, this was rejected.[75] Whenever courts accept to rule on the climate emergency as a potential rights violation they establish and enforce a principled longstanding framework that sets the outer limits in which policymakers may act. This necessarily inserts a longer-term perspective into the political debate, which becomes particularly apparent when right of future generations are protected by the courts.

71 Article 34 ECHR.

72 *Finnish climate case* (n 10). See for the Finnish Climate Act 2022: <https://www.finlex.fi/fi/laki/alkup/2022/20220423>.

73 *Finnish climate case* (n 10), para 58.

74 Actual human rights violation: *Urgenda, Klimaatzaak, Neubauer, Notre Affaire à Tous*; only potentially a human rights violation: *Finnish climate case* (n 10) and Irish case (n 2).

75 *Nature and Youth v Norway* [2020] (n 8) and *KlimaSeniorinnen* [2020] (n 11).

All cases differ as to their specific jurisdictional circumstances, including procedural rules. Yet, all of them are contracting parties to the ECHR and the ECtHR's rulings in the pending climate cases are a crucial moment of opportunity in consolidating or challenging the human rights dimension of the ongoing climate constitutionalisation.

3.2 *Reference to Ratification and Participation in the UNFCCC*

The above outlined relational understanding of separation of powers places emphasis on the constructive interaction between the branches that contributes to justified decision-making and channels disagreement into the decision-making process. In this interaction, courts have a function as both part of the state and independent bodies to offer fora to those whose rights are sufficiently affected for them to be procedurally able to challenge the process or outcome of the decision-making. One core point in the constructive interaction is to ensure that public actors are accountable for their words and actions, not necessarily legally but in any event politically. Climate cases offer a context for pointing out deep running inconsistencies in governments' actions if they repeatedly, and usually internationally pledge climate actions but do not take adequate steps towards such actions. Many cases have brought to light the deep contradictions of governments' (international) political commitments and domestic (legal) actions by reference to the positions that they take under the United Nations Framework Convention on Climate Change (UNFCCC).

The UNFCCC aims to 'stabilize the greenhouse gas concentrations in the atmosphere at a level that would prevent dangerous anthropogenic interference with the climate system'.[76] Enhancing the implementation the UNFCCC, the 2015 Paris Agreement sets a long-term temperature goal, aiming at '[h]olding the increase in the global average temperature to well below 2 °C above pre-industrial levels and pursuing efforts to limit the temperature increase to 1.5 °C above pre-industrial levels'.[77] Nationally Determined Contributions (NDCs) form the basis for countries to achieve this objective of the Paris Agreement. The Intergovernmental Panel on Climate Change (IPCC) has published an NDCs Synthesis Report, detailing targets, and policies and measures for mitigation (and adaptation) aimed to achieve the objectives of the Paris Agreement.[78]

76 Article 2 UNFCCC.

77 Article 2 a) of the 2015 Paris Agreement.

78 UNFCCC, 'Nationally determined contributions under the Paris Agreement', FCCC/PA/CMA/2022/4 (Synthesis Report, UNFCC 2022) <https://unfccc.int/ndc-synthesis-report-2022> accessed 2 April 2023.

The Dutch Supreme Court in *Urgenda* set out the legal framework of the UNFCCC, explains the role of the Conferences of the Parties (COPs) in developing the parties' obligations under the UNFCCC.[79] Importantly, the court explains that while the COPs are the highest political organ they do not necessarily produce binding norms with their decisions. However, the court's reasoning demonstrates that this does not mean that these non-binding commitments and norms cannot deploy legal effects via other norms. The court lists all past COPs and their main relevant stipulations. It also sketches the findings of the two most recent assessment reports of the IPCC that precede the ruling (AR4 in 2007 and AR5 in 2013–14). Equally comprehensive in this respect is the advisory opinion of the Procurator General in *Urgenda*. It traces, as part of the 'recitation of the established facts', the international commitments of all parties to the UNFCCC at the different COPs, but also communications on the Netherlands' negotiation objectives in international climate conferences from the relevant minister to parliament and the national consultation process, leading to the adoption of the national Climate Act, with a reduction target for 2030.[80] The Procurator General explains in detail how he moved from the different political commitments to a legal obligation to reduce GHG emissions.[81] Interesting in this context is also that he makes remarks on the constraints of Dutch procedural law '[f]or the benefit of non-Dutch readers'.[82] He sets out that '[t]he literature […] shows that, when possible, the courts must base specific interpretations of standards of care on objective assumptions' and gives the following examples 'non-binding guidelines and codes of conduct (both of which are 'soft law')' and 'treaty provisions and principles of international law which do not have direct effect'.[83] He concludes that 'in implementing open standards, the national court will take international law into account as much as possible (irrespective of whether or not it has direct effect). This is the concept of reflex effect.'[84] These considerations also indirectly speak to the issue of separation of powers. While the judiciary cannot take political commitments and vest them with legal effect – this would empower it beyond its mandate to interpret the law and establish what is legal and illegal – it must

79 *Urgenda* [2019] (n 1), [5–12].

80 Conclusion of Procurator General in Urgenda [2019] (n 51), section 1.2 et seq, in particular section 1.2(xxvii) and 1.7.

81 Ibid, Sections 2.1.

82 Ibid, sections 1.35.

83 Ibid, Section 2.19.

84 Ibid, Section 2.30.

rely on relevant facts including science and political commitments to establish what open textured legal provisions mean.

In the Irish climate case, Ireland's *international commitments* played no role as the case turned on the interpretation of the executive's obligations under the national Climate Action and Low Carbon Development Act of 2015.[85] A similar situation presents itself in the German Constitutional Court's ruling in *Neubauer*. While the case referred four times to the Dutch *Urgenda* case, *e.g.*, when concluding that states cannot avoid responsibility by pointing at the emissions of other states, the construction of the legal obligation was different. The court did not (have to) rely on Germany's international commitments because the national climate protection act had incorporated the temperature goal.[86]

In *Notre Affaire à Tous*,[87] the plaintiffs referred among other things to the UNFCCC and the Paris Agreement, Rio Declaration, Stockholm Declaration and EU law. The Administrative Court of Paris ordered France to take immediate and concrete actions to comply with its emission reduction commitments and repair the damages caused by its climate inaction by 31 December 2022. More specifically, the court calculated that France, even if it lowered its emissions, emitted 62 million extra tons of emissions from 2015–2018. Interestingly, the court required France to subtract the extra emissions in the past, *i.e.*, those exceeding the targets stipulated in national legislation, by further reducing emissions between 2021 and 2022. It also confirmed that all future excess emissions will need to be compensated.

In *Grand-Synthe I*, the Conseil d'Etat argued that the international commitments of the French State may amount to legally enforceable norms, granting the executive another opportunity to justify its actions and lack thereof in light of these international commitments.[88]

In the Belgian *Klimaatzaak*, the Court of First Instance in Brussels, while being relatively concise on the science and impacts of the climate emergency, meticulously traced the international and national political agreements and commitments of the Belgian federal state and the regions.[89] As part of this overview, it emphasized Belgium's failure to meet the agreed reduction targets, including with repeated references to the EU Commission's assessment of that failure. In their appeal of the first instance ruling, the plaintiffs highlighted

85 *Friends of the Irish Environment/Irish case* [2020] (n 2).
86 *Neubauer* [2021] (n 3).
87 *Notre Affaire à Tous* [2021] (n 4).
88 *Grande-Synthe I*.
89 *VZW Klimaatzaak* [2021] (n 5); The hearing of the appeal is in September/October 2023.

that '[n]one of the respondents has disputed that, as Belgium is a party to the UNFCCC and therefore to the COP, it has adopted by consensus the various decisions that this body has taken over the years, from meeting to meeting, from the 2007 COP to the 2015 COP, and that, in so doing, the country and therefore all the respondents were necessarily fully informed of these decisions.'[90] Belgium therefore adhered by consensus to the COP decisions, setting the threshold for dangerous warming at 2°C first, then towards 1.5°C.[91] 'from COP-13 in Bali in 2007 to COP-21 in Paris in 2015, it has been agreed and re-agreed each year that, to avoid dangerous warming understood as 2°C, Annex I countries should reduce their GHG emissions by at least 25–40% by 2020'.[92] The plaintiffs on appeal extensively refer to repeated political commitments within the framework, *e.g.*, Belgium's participation in the Report of the Ad Hoc Working Group on Further Commitments for Annex I Parties, which took the '25 and 40 per cent below 1990 levels by 2020' from 'Box 13.7 of the Working Group III report' as a starting point and indicated that even greater reduction obligation could be possible.[93] They aim to demonstrate the repeated *political commitment* to the COP decisions from COP-13 in Bali in 2007 to COP-21 in Paris in 2015, it has been agreed and re-agreed each year that, to avoid dangerous warming understood as 2°C, Annex I countries should reduce their GHG emissions by at least 25–40% by 2020.[94] They emphasized that '[n]ot only were the respondents aware of the mitigation measures to be taken, but they expressly acknowledged the scientific need for them'[95] and that this is confirmed by a range of national political statements by the regional parliaments and the an executive body (Flemish Council for the Environment and Nature).[96]

In Czech Republic, the Prague Municipal Court ordered in first instance on 15 June 2022 in the case *Klimatická žaloba ČR v. Czech Republic* the state to urgently take climate mitigation measures. It held that the state's failure to take these measures was unlawful, that the plaintiffs' rights were violated and that the state should abstain from further continuing the rights violation. In lack of a national climate act, the legal basis of the obligation was the Paris Agreement and the EU Climate Law setting out the 55% emission reduction

90 Appeal of 17 November 2021 for VZW *Klimaatzaak* (unofficial translation), <http://climatecasechart.com/wp-content/uploads/sites/16/non-us-case-documents/2021/20211117_2660_appeal.pdf> accessed 2 April 2023, [38].

91 Ibid, [48].

92 Ibid, [48].

93 Ibid, [45].

94 Ibid, [47]-[48].

95 Ibid, [53].

96 Ibid, [54].

target of the Union (by 2030 as compared to 1990). While pointing out that the goals of the Paris Agreement are not legally binding, it is obvious from these legal instruments that the Czech Republic must contribute to their attainment. The court also rejected the drop in the ocean argument that the state's small contribution to overall emissions did not make a material difference.[97] In the meantime, the first instance judgment has, on appeal, been annulled by the Supreme Administrative Court.[98] The Court discusses separation of powers on several occasions, stressing the need to for judicial restraint, concluding that it is not the right body to assess compliance of concrete policies with the long-term temperature goal, and finally referring the case back to first instance court on the narrow issue of compliance with sectoral legislation.

In *Plan B* in March 2022, the UK Court of Appeal rejected the case arguing that '[t]he fundamental difficulty which the Claimants face is that there is no authority from the [ECtHR] on which they can rely, citing the Paris Agreement as being relevant to the interpretation of the ECHR, Articles 2 and 8'.[99] The claimants build their argument on 'the Paris Agreement temperature limit of 1.5°C as evidence of the international consensus on what must be done to avoid intolerable risks to life and to family life'.[100] The judge specifically mentioned that the reference to the *Urgenda* case, where the Dutch Supreme Court had interpreted the ECHR in the light of the Paris Agreement, was not alone sufficiently convincing as the constitutional context could be very different.[101] In the 2022 Net Zero Strategy case, the legal hook was the Government's duty under the 2008 Climate Act.[102] It is hence a case focused on the limits of executive action under ordinary national law.

The Court of Appeal in *Plan B* argued that the established unlawfulness of the preparation and designation of the relevant policy was based on the narrow ground that the minister had not considered the Paris Agreement. This specific point was reversed by the Supreme Court holding that the Paris Agreement did not constitute 'government policy' within the meaning of the Planning Act.[103]

---

97 *Klimatická žaloba ČR v Czech Republic* [2022] No. 14A 101/2021 (Prague Municipal Court).

98 Supreme Administrative Court, *Klimatická žaloba ČR* [2023] (n 9).

99 *Plan B and Others v Prime Minister and Others* [2022] CA-2021-003448 (Court of Appeal) <https://planb.earth/wp-content/uploads/2022/03/CA-Order-and-Judgment.pdf> accessed 2 April 2023.

100 Ibid, [4].

101 Ibid, [5].

102 *Net Zero Strategy Case* [2022] (n 6), [14].

103 *R (on the application of Friends of the Earth and Others) v Heathrow Airport* [2020] UKSC 52, [101]-[112].

By contrast, it emphasized the executive's discretion in deciding whether to consider the Paris Agreement as part of its assessment.

The unsuccessful Norwegian case of *Natur og Ungdom*, as discussed above, turned on the compliance with the Norwegian Constitution of the national executive's decision to grant petroleum licences.[104] The 'key issue raised [was] the decision's compliance with Article 112 of the Constitution on the right to a healthy environment'.[105] Within this setting reliance on Norway's international commitments to mitigate emissions can be envisaged in order to give meaning to the obligations flowing from the constitutional right to a healthy environment. However, while the appellants argued that Norway must cut its emissions by at least 60% in 2030 and that until 'a detailed legal framework and climate accounts are in place, the authorities cannot commence [fossil fuel exploitation] in new areas', the court concluded '[i]t is unlikely that the courts, when assessing an individual decision, may lay down such specific requirements based on Article 112 of the Constitution'.[106] The Court emphasised that the evaluation must start with the challenged decision instead. When the decision is taken an assessment of the climate effects must be carried out and that 'includes an assessment of the international climate commitments and targets.'[107] Hence, Norway's international commitments were not considered to inform the content of its constitutional obligations but only formed part of the considerations that must be taken into account in the procedure of applying for a license, namely in the plan presented by the licensee (that then requires approval by the executive). The Norwegian case, while weakly acknowledging their procedural relevance for the assessment of climate effects, does not contribute to the constitutionalisation of international mitigation commitments. As a result, it reduces the role of the judiciary to the guardian of procedure, disallowing the judicial stipulation of a particular minimum of climate action.

The different courts dealt quite differently with the legal and political commitments under the UNFCCC. While some drew direct conclusions from the obligations under the Paris Agreements for the mitigation obligation of the defendant state, others rejected such conclusions outright.[108] Several courts used the repeated political commitments confirming the long-term

104 *Nature and Youth* [2020] (n 8).

105 Ibid, [3].

106 Ibid, [161]-[162].

107 Ibid, [267].

108 Establishing legal obligations: *e.g.*, first instance court in *Klimatická žaloba* (n 96); *Klimaatzaak* (n 5); *Notre Affaire à Tous* (n 4); *Grande-Synthe I* (n 4); rejection: *Plan B* (n 98).

temperature goal and acknowledging the need to avoid 'dangerous climate change', as well as its predicted impacts, as factual basis to interpret the legal obligations under open textured norms, such as human rights.[109]

3.3 *The Normative Effects of IPCC Science*

Judges rely in climate cases heavily on climate science, setting out probabilistic models at a very high level of theoretical agreement. They usually refer to the leading, politically endorsed international expert body: the IPCC. In other words, the IPCC reports are the prevailing source for climate science in court. Their purpose, as stated on the IPCC's website is to 'fulfil two functions: for IPCC member governments they represent the accepted document of record arising from an intergovernmental process; for the research community, they are highly cited scientific documents that synthesize a vast body of evolving knowledge and bring prestige to those involved in writing them.'[110]

The IPCC is the United Nations body for assessing the science related to climate change. Its three working groups (WP) produce reports on the physical science basis (WP I); impacts, adaptation and vulnerability (WP II); and mitigation of climate change (WP III). It is a 'boundary institution'[111] that works on the border of and hence both with scientific and political/policy-making epistemologies, producing translation/transfer work that allows engagement of both communities with the work of the other. It does not only bring together climate science but its findings in form of the Summaries for Policy-Makers (SPM) are also politically agreed and endorsed. Over time, the IPCC has adapted its working procedures considering criticisms, *e.g.*, given more space to dissenting opinions.

The inclusive and unbiased nature of information in IPCC reports exceeds the inclusiveness and impartiality of scientific evidence advanced in most judicial proceedings.[112] As Roda Verheyen, the leading lawyer in the *Neubauer* case, formulated already in 2005 that 'no court of law could possibly deviate from IPCC findings since any expertise put before the court would never be as inclusive as that inherent in the IPCC.'[113] Because of this exceptional inclusiveness

---

109 See above all: *Urgenda* [2019] (n 1); different *Nature and Youth* [2020] (n 8).

110 IPCC, *Progress Reports* (IPCC 2021) <https://apps.ipcc.ch/eventmanager/documents/65/040320210332-INF.%208%20-%20Progress%20Report%20IG%20Publications.pdf> accessed 2 April 2023.

111 See G Ganguly, *Towards a transnational law of climate change: transnational litigation at the boundaries of science and law* (LSE PhD Thesis, 2019).

112 See for more details: www.ipcc.ch.

113 R Verheyen, *Climate Change Damage and International Law: Prevention Duties and State Liability* (Brill 2005), 20.

of and the political support for IPCC reports, they should not only be considered a reflection of the 'best available science' but also as enjoying particular *normative* authority.[114] In terms of substance, some plaintiffs in climate cases have rightly pointed out that the IPCC reports are fairly cautious. This flows from the fact that they do not only have the explicit aim to serve policymaking, but that the SPMs is agreed line by line by the climate negotiators of the governments of the contracting parties.

IPCC reports provide judges around the globe with reliable information about the 'best available science'[115] at a given point in time. Extensive reliance on a range of IPCC assessment reports by the judges in *Urgenda* (NL, 2019), *Klimaatzaak* (BE, 2020), *Notre Affaire à Tous* (FR), and *Neubauer* (DE, 2020).

The Dutch Supreme Court in *Urgenda* set out the science in considerable detail. It strongly relied on AR4 of 2007.[116] This is the case because AR4 addresses the reduction target for 2020, while the newer available AR5 focusses on the reduction target for 2030. The court build its decision of what constitutes and absolute minimum of reduction to reach the 'likely' outcome that global warming stays below 2C.[117]

In *Neubauer*, the German Constitutional Court relied on the *national* advisory council's assessment, which is based on IPCC reports.[118] As did the Norwegian Supreme Court in *Natur og Ungdom*, pointing out that the report of the Norwegian Climate Risk Commission on climate risk and the Norwegian economy of 2018 'is primarily a compilation of knowledge provided by the [IPCC] – including [AR5] and [IPCC SR on 1.5C]'.[119]

However, reference to the IPCC does not in all cases result in the same engagement with facts. In the *Klimaatzaak*, for example, the Court of First Instance, in its ruling of 17 June 2021, referred extensively to the IPCC, its establishment, its reports, but less to the scientific information contained in these reports that establishes in detail and with certainty the relations between emissions

114 See C Eckes, 'Strategic Climate Litigation: Legal Consequences of Scientific "Truth"?' (forthcoming).

115 Articles 4(1), 7(5) and 14(1) Paris Agreement 2015.

116 B Mayer, 'The Contribution of Urgenda to the Mitigation of Climate Change' (n 45).

117 Likely means greater than 60%. AR5 concluded that if the concentration GHG emissions is stabilised at around 450 ppm in the year 2100, the chance that the global temperature increase would remain under 2°C is 'likely'; however, 87% of the scenarios included in AR5 are based on assumptions regarding the possible removal of CO_2 from the atmosphere (see Conclusion of Procurator General in Urgenda [2019] (n 51), section 1.2 xiii).

118 German Advisory Council on the Environment (Sachverständigenrat für Umweltfragen – SRU), see *Neubauer* [2021] (n 3), [28], [36], [216]-[247].

119 *Nature and Youth* [2020] (n 8), [50].

and global warming, deducts emission budgets, and expresses probabilities of impacts. This becomes particularly apparent in a comparison between the ruling in first instance and the plaintiff's appeal filed on 17 November 2021. The latter dwells extensively on the science and aims to demonstrate the detailed knowledge of the climate emergency and the political agreement of Belgium to the scientific establishment of the factual situation in the IPCC's procedures and the decisions of the COPs under the UNFCCC. The appellants in *Klimaatzaak* strongly pushed that the court should *confirm the role and relevance of the IPCC*.[120] They emphasized that the IPCC is 'an emanation of the States', which 'recognise the legitimacy' of the 'scientific content' of the IPCC reports, referring specifically to the *SPMs*.[121] They also highlighted that the final report and the SPMs are endorsed by governments.[122] This endorsement of climate science by state actors is another constitutionalisation dynamic that I do not explore further here but that takes place in and of itself and is strengthened when explicated in the authoritative setting of climate litigation.

In the Finnish climate case, the Court concluded from best available science based on the reports of the IPCC that 'climate change is a question of humanity's fate, which threatens the living conditions of current and future generations on Earth, unless quick and effective measures are taken in terms of maintaining and increasing emission limits and carbon sinks'.[123] The case concerned the inaction of the Finnish government in particular in light of the collapse of the Finnish forest carbon sink and is the first to explicate the relevance of degradation of European forests for assessing a state's duty to take climate action.

Judges' reliance on climate science injects the established scientific basis, which is in principle acknowledged and agreed by all parties, into the public debate. Any debate on decision-making and problem-solving depends on the ability to reach basic agreement on what the problem is and what factors are relevant to that problem. In the case of climate change mitigation, the crux is the scientific consensus that anthropogenic emissions are the cause of the rapid climate change, projected impacts of different temperature levels, the natural science that emissions, once emitted, stay in the atmosphere

120 Appeal for *Klimaatzaak* (n 88), [11]: The IPCC calls itself "the leading international body for assessing climate change". This status is confirmed in that the 195 Member countries take (or at least should take) the IPCC reports as a starting point for their climate policy and that the IPCC reports have a special place in the 1992 UNFCCC.

121 Ibid, [12].

122 Ibid, [14].

123 English translation taken from: K Kulovesi et al, 'Finland's first climate judgment' (n 10).

for hundreds (thousands) of years, and the historical and current emissions of states and citizens (per capita) in Europe. Courts have time and again judicially established these scientific facts, related their reasoning to them, and hence brought the agreed problem and factual basis back into the public debate. The judicial process allows the parties to bring forward their evidence, which is then either formally established or rejected as fact. In the relational understanding of separation of powers, weighing and establishing facts is one way, in which the judiciary contributes to the reasoned exchange that leads to public will-formation.

4 Multi-layered Constitutionalism: Cases in Strasbourg

Nine climate cases aiming for general mitigation by States are currently pending before the ECtHR.[124] Three have been relinquished to the Grand Chamber, *Duarte Agostinho*,[125] *Klimaseniorinnen*,[126] and *Carême/Grande-Synthe*.[127] The relinquishment may, on the one hand, be considered to confirm that a section to which a case is assigned considers that this case raises serious questions of legal interpretation that require a consistent approach of a more authoritative body. On the other hand, the decisions of the Grand Chamber in these cases will enjoy greater judicial authority and hence more strongly contribute to a constitutionalisation of climate norms in Europe. The greater authority derives from the composition of the Grand Chamber, consisting of 17, rather than 7 judges, including the Court's President and Vice-Presidents, the Section Presidents and the national judge, plus other judges selected by drawing of lots.

In addition, several climate related cases before ordinary chambers are likely to contribute to establishing the position of the Strasbourg court on how

124 Three are pending before the Grand Chamber and six have been adjourned pending the Grand Chamber decisions, see here https://hudoc.echr.coe.int/app/conversion/pdf/?library=ECHR&id=003-7566368-10398533&filename=Status%20of%20climate%20applications%20before%20the%20European%20Court.pdf. The hearings in Klimaseniorinnen and Carême took place on 29 March 2023. Much of KlimaSeniorinnen focusses on the issue of what is a 'fair share' of the carbon budget for each and every case.

125 *Duarte Agostinho v Portugal and 32 other states* (n 14); Application communicated to the defending governments in November 2020 – Relinquishment in favour of the Grand Chamber in June 2022. The hearing is scheduled for 28 September 2023.

126 *KlimaSeniorinnen v Switzerland* (n 12); Application communicated to the Swiss Government in March 2021 – Relinquishment in favour of the Grand Chamber in April 2022.

127 *Carême v France* (n 13); Relinquishment in favour of the Grand Chamber in May 2022.

the rights under the ECHR relate to states' failure to adequately address the climate emergency. One is the Norwegian Youth case discussed above.[128]

Together these cases give the Strasbourg court the opportunity to contribute to the climate-related interpretations of the Convention. They will emerge as a body of case law with exceptional, either direct constitutional or at least strong interpretative weight in all jurisdictions across Europe.[129] They concern the questions of who is a victim of climate change but also very prominently the question of what is the 'fair share' of each state, i.e. how should the global carbon budget be broken down to national carbon budgets.

The relevance and status of the ECHR and decisions of the ECtHR differ tremendously between the 47 signatories. The direct legal effects of the ECtHR's decisions in the pending climate cases consequently also differs. This does not take away their great symbolic and persuasive authority in future litigation.

Germany, in which one of the successful climate cases was decided, is an example of a very dualist legal order. The German Federal Constitutional Court (GFCC) explicitly ruled that the ECHR, as any other binding international law in Germany, has the same status as ordinary laws (*Gesetzesrang*) and takes effect within the framework of the German Constitution.[130] The ECHR hence ranks below the German Constitution, with the consequence that ordinary courts must observe and apply the Convention, while before the GFCC the ECHR (only) serves as an 'interpretation aid' in determining the contents and scope of fundamental rights and fundamental principles protected under the German Constitution.[131] This also explains why the ECHR was not given any attention in the *Neubauer* case.

The Netherlands, as the other extreme, follows a (moderate) monist tradition.[132] Individuals can rely upon provisions of international treaties even if they are incompatible with the national constitution.[133] Decisions of the

---

128 *Greenpeace Nordic and Others v Norway* (n 69).

129 See for the direct legal weight of the ECHR in a selection of national jurisdictions: C Eckes, 'EU accession to the ECHR: between autonomy and adaption' (2013) 76 *Modern Law Review* 254.

130 GFCC, Decision of 14 October 2004, 2 BvR 1481/04 – (Görgülü; ECHR decision). See more recently: GFCC, Decision of 4 May 2011, 2 BvR 2365/09; 2 BvR 740/10; 2 BvR 2333/08; 2 BvR 1152/10; 2 BvR 571/10 – (Preventive Detention).

131 Eckes, 'EU accession to the ECHR' (n 129).

132 It is considered moderate because international customary law has internal effect but does not take precedence over a conflicting rule of Dutch law (*Nyugat* [1959], HR 6 March 1959, NJ 1962, 2).

133 Except for provisions of international agreements that are not binding on everyone ('een ieder verbindend'), see article 94 of the Dutch Constitution.

ECtHR can be directly invoked before national courts and the ECtHR de facto functions as the highest human rights court of the land since the Dutch Hoge Raad does not have the power of constitutional review. This strong position of the ECHR in the Netherlands is illustrated by *Urgenda*.

In the UK, the European Convention is not itself part of national law and the decisions of the ECtHR are not directly legally binding under UK law. The 1998 Human Rights Act gives domestic legal effect to the ECHR, but it does not oblige Parliament to legislate compatibly or courts to disregard laws that are incompatible with the Convention. Yet, in *Plan B*, the UK Court of Appeal explicitly looked for authoritative case law of the ECtHR supporting the case of the claimants.

Climate litigation seeks to protect the public good of a liveable planet by triggering broad political and socio-economic changes in an area of controversy and tensions about how we should pursue general mitigation objectives and what this means for who carries the costs. In this context, the credibility and social legitimacy of judicial decisions is pertinent to their ability to contribute to this change. To the extent, that court decisions form part of a broader multi-actor trend towards greater reliance on international climate norms and objectives or IPCC reports, they can also benefit for the legitimacy of the individual decision from climate constitutionalisation dynamics in Europe. Cross-references and reliance on each other's reasoning does not only strengthen constitutionalisation in the sense of giving additional authority to the international norms and political commitments/policy goals but also reinforce the authority of the judicial decisions.

The decisions before the ECtHR play an important role in this respect. Generally, the ECtHR is a well-respected interpreter of the constitutional charter of Europe. Its rulings will have interpretative value of the obligations of all the 47 contracting parties before national courts. The extra-layer of human rights review in Strasbourg, which is generally respected and followed by state institutions in Europe, has direct constitutionalising effects. It shifts the interpretation of what is a human rights violation to an external judicial body, which determines then how the binding obligations under the ECHR should be understood. The ECtHR's reading of the ECHR then guides domestic courts when they rule on future climate cases. It is also a resource for political reasoning, which originates outside the political debate and is for this reason an entrenched point of reference that cannot itself be changed within the domestic legal debate. This shifts powers to the judicial branch, both the externalised judiciary in Strasbourg but also to national courts by giving them additional arguments of internationally binding obligations when confronted with climate cases against the state. At the same time, the applicants in *Klimaseniorinnen* specifically relied before the ECtHR on the interpretation of the ECHR (Articles 2 and 8) by the Dutch Supreme Court in *Urgenda*. Hence, the reinforcement of authority also goes in the other direction.

Pending and future climate cases before the ECtHR will clarify whether a particular class of persons (*e.g.*, women above 75 years of age) that are statistically more affected by the impacts of climate change (*e.g.*, heatwaves)[134] enjoy victim status within the meaning of Article 34 ECHR. They will clarify whether the applicants have to demonstrate that their rights under the Convention are affected more or differently as compared to other citizens in their position (*e.g.*, because of a particular health condition). The ECtHR, as well as national courts, are also likely to (have to) take positions on what is a 'fair share' of the global carbon budget for each and every country. This may very well be the most far reaching and politically loaded issue underlying climate cases aiming for general emission reduction. It relates to difficult redistributive, i.e. political questions, which the ECtHR is unlikely to address head on. These include: What can an individual state claim in terms of carbon budget? How should this be established? What is the relevance of past emissions in this respect? What is the relevance of per capita calculations?

5 Democratic Decision-Making and the Right to Justification

Climate cases when based on human rights are acts that demand public justification for the alleged violation of these rights by taking inadequate climate action.[135] In a relational understanding of separation of powers, as outlined above, it falls to the judiciary to ensure that the exercise of public powers respects the individual autonomy of all persons by offering them reasons for restricting their human rights and if need be to assert a particular demand for public justification in practice.[136]

The *Urgenda* case highlights this discursive justificatory dimension of the function of the independent judiciary in a state of law.[137] The Supreme Court held that the Dutch State could not lawfully reduce emissions by less than

134 Climate Inequality Report 2023 (n 50).

135 See for a theory of human rights that places the right to justification at the origin of all human rights: R Forst, *Das Recht auf Rechtfertigung – Elemente einer konstruktivistischen Theorie der Gerechtigkeit* (Suhrkamp 2014).

136 See section 2.2 above.

137 C Eckes, 'The Urgenda Case is Separation of Powers at Work' in N de Boer, A Nieuwenhuis and JH Reestman (eds), *Liber Amicorum Besselink* (Universiteit van Amsterdam 2021).

25% in 2020 compared to emission levels in 1990 without offering a justification considering the arguments advanced by the plaintiffs based on an extensive presentation of climate science. Throughout the proceedings in three instances, the courts invited the Dutch state time and again invited to justify its failure to develop a climate policy aimed at reducing emissions by 25%. Yet, the Dutch State did not offer such justification.

In the words of the Supreme Court, 'under certain circumstances, the State must properly substantiate that the policy it pursues meets the requirements to be imposed, *i.e.*, that it pursues a policy through which it remains above the lower limit of its fair share.'[138] However, '[t]he State has not provided any insight into which measures it intends to take in the coming years, let alone why these measures, in spite of the above, would be both practically feasible and sufficient to contribute to the prevention of dangerous climate change to a sufficient extent in line with the Netherlands' share. The State has confined itself to asserting that there "are certainly possibilities" in this context'.[139] On the contrary, '[t]he State acknowledge[d] the fact' that 'any postponement of the reduction of emissions therefore means that emissions in the future will have to be reduce on an increasingly large scale in order to make up for the postponement in terms of both of time and size.' Postponement makes the necessary measures hence 'increasingly far-reaching and costly', as well as 'riskier'.[140]

Similarly, in the Irish climate case, the Supreme Court held that the public needed to be able to hold their government to account.[141] Citizens need to understand whether the government is doing its job (well enough). This is a broad and fundamental democratic argument that carries weight much beyond the narrow legal grounds on which the Irish courts ruled. Surely, the government failed to comply with the specificity requirements of the national climate law, requiring it to draw up a plan to reduce emissions. The justification requirement is substantively linked to the apparent inconsistency that the plan, while stating that Ireland was committed to achieving by 2050 an aggregate reduction in carbon emissions of at least 80 per cent in some sectors and zero net emissions in others (both compared to 1990 levels),[142] first allowed Ireland's emissions first to increase further.[143] The Irish Supreme Court held

138 *Urgenda* [2019] (n 1), para 6.5.

139 Ibid, para 7.4.6.

140 Ibid, paras. 7.4.5 and 7.4.3.

141 *Friends of the Irish Environment* [2020] (n 2), para 46(47).

142 Ibid, para 5(25).

143 Ibid, *inter alia* para 4(3).

that the proposed trajectory was deficient and that the national law required the government to specify how they were going to achieve their reduction target. The courts were not convinced by the government's response that not all the steps to achieve the envisaged reduction could be known already. The Government's plan spoke of 'endeavouring to improve our understanding' and 'further investigation will also be necessary'.[144] Most importantly, the plan alluded to carbon capture and storage (CCS) technologies by stating 'we cannot be sure what future technologies will deliver'.[145] It was in particular the postponement of (political responsibility for) emission reduction (by being insufficiently specific and by allowing in the short-term a further increase in emissions) that the courts did not accept and on which they required further explanation.

In *Grande-Synthe I*, the Conseil d'État (highest French Administrative Court) ruled that the Government had failed to pursue effective climate action. The Court gave the Government nine months (until March 2022) to take the measures necessary for reducing emissions produced on French territory to a level that complies with France's climate targets under the 2015 Paris Agreement.[146] This additional opportunity to take action is also an opportunity to offer justification. It follows the same reasoning as the Irish climate case. The Government's climate action appeared contrary to the requirements of climate science considering France's commitment to pursue the goal of keeping global warming below 1,5° C. The State must explain why this is not the case.

In the UK, *Net Zero Strategy* case, the judges confirmed the focus of the earlier Irish climate case on the lack of concretization, explanation, and quantification of how the government's plans would achieve the emissions targets set out by the legislature. For this reason, the judge found the Government's plan had failed to meet its obligations under Climate Change Act (CCA) 2008. Justice Holgate's judgment ordered the Department for Business, Energy, and Industrial Strategy to prepare and present, by April 2023, a report explaining how the government's policies in the net zero strategy would contribute towards emissions reductions.

Where courts give value to the need for public justification for human rights violations flowing from climate inaction they make an important contribution to democratic will-formation. A robust democratic space requires a forum where contradictory and insincere pledges of politicians to citizens and other

144 Ibid, para 6(43).

145 Ibid.

146 *Grande-Synthe* [2021] (n 4).

states can be exposed and evaluated. If the political branches that are mandated to balance and reconcile the different interests fail to do so and hide behind general assurances while the scientific consensus exposes that climate change structurally endangers the human rights of their citizens courts have a role in allowing citizens to demand justification.

6 Conclusions

A growing body of climate cases that is interconnected by references and takes notice of each other emerges. It contributes to exposing and, partially, sanctioning the insincerity with which European governments publicly and solemnly confirm the urgency and necessity of drastic climate actions, while in practice shying away from making the difficult concrete decisions on the ground. They are unwilling or unable to take the necessary decisions on how the numerous, both overlapping and contradicting interests should be reconciled in a sincere effort of taking the drastic climate actions necessary to avoid what they themselves see as 'dangerous climate change'.

Some (partially) unsuccessful cases also contribute to climate constitutionalisation, *e.g.*, by establishing that human rights were violated, that the national constitution gives individuals a right to a healthy environment, or that climate inaction requires an effective remedy. Climate constitutionalisation is like throwing stones into a river to be eventually able to cross to the other side.[147] In other words, climate litigation is not mushrooming in many unrelated cases but builds a connected web of arguments and references. It produces a version of constitutionalisation that relates to the climate-relevance of human rights, mitigation commitments, and climate science. Climate litigation constitutes a shift towards expert law-making in the sense that it, even if partially relating to (symbolic) damages, asks courts to establish legal obligations that have value in the political debate and aim to trigger deep socioeconomic changes for the future. As the catastrophic consequences of the climate emergency are already present and are going to increase, the pressure for more stringent climate laws is growing. For politicians, climate litigation in Europe may feel like being stuck in a repeat game with increasing stakes and decreasing chances. In Germany, another constitutional complaint was filed on 24 January 2022 (*Steinmetz*).[148]

147 See for this image: R Verheyen, *Wir allen habben ein Recht auf Zukunft* (n 23), 107.

148 For more information on the German case see: DUH, 'Climate lawsuit filed: Environmental Action Germany sues German government for ineffective climate protection measures in agriculture and forestry' (*Deutsche Umwelthilfe*, 24 November 2022)

It puts into practice what was predicted in advance, namely that the new climate protection act opens new litigation opportunities.[149]

The additional layer of the ECHR and its interpretation by the ECtHR are substantively highly relevant for the interpretation of human rights in many national jurisdictions. They also have a much wider reach because the 47 signatories to the ECHR have good reasons to take notice of the case law of the ECtHR on an issue that is a truly global action problem, for example when the Court gives meaning to political commitments that all of them have made in slightly different form and shape as they are all parties to the UNFCCC.

This chapter has traced the constitutionalising of mitigation norms emerging from human rights, international political commitments, and climate science. Many successful and some unsuccessful cases in Europe have created a web of legal interpretations, often with mutual references, on which future litigation can stand to push in different ways for climate action.

Litigation as a driver of climate constitutionalisation also has consequences for the powers of the three branches of government and their interaction. This chapter identified these consequences and demonstrated that climate cases strengthen the judiciary's position in the institutional interaction and how this contributes to a constructive exchange and offers an alternative forum, in which the agreed factual basis is publicly established and in which political decision-makers are pressed to offer justification. The judiciary is not only asked to press the other branches for justification of their inaction but also contributes to the development of legal norms in form of principles and interpretations that speak to the climate emergency and that enjoy – at least potentially – a higher rank than ordinary legislative or executive action. This becomes apparent in the authoritative interpretations of the Strasbourg Court of rights under the ECHR.

These judicially interpreted norms constitute the framework in relation to which public and private actors develop their understanding of what is lawful. This concerns both mitigation but also implementation of the politically established and endorsed targets. If law has – at least also – a justificatory function

---

<https://www.duh.de/presse/pressemitteilungen/pressemitteilung/climate-lawsuit-filed-environmental-action-germany-sues-german-government-for-ineffective-climate-p/> accessed 15 June 2023.

149 A Buser, 'Of Carbon Budgets, Factual Uncertainties, and Intergenerational Equity–The German Constitutional Court's Climate Decision' (2021) 22 *German Law Journal* 1409 explains 'how the German legislator, by going beyond what was required by the Court "trapped itself" on an ambitious reduction path, opening opportunities for future constitutional complaints'.

and acts as a moral yardstick, that sets out normative evaluations in a way that can find support by a majority and that benefits from at least some *prima facie* assumption of correctness, these norms also have an influence on the broader understanding of what is legitimate. As more and more states set net zero targets for the future, courts will be less engaged in reviewing the legality of insufficient targets and more engaged in reviewing insufficient implementation of these targets.

Bibliography

Cases

BvR 1152/10; 2 BvR 571/10 – (Preventive Detention).

Carême v France, no. 7189/21 (ECtHR).

Commune de Grande-Synthe v France [2021] no. 427301 (Conseil d'Etat).

Duarte Agostinho and Others v Portugal and 32 Other States, no. 39371/20 (ECtHR).

Efe v. Minister for Justice, Equality and Law Reform [2011] 2 IR 798.

Family Farmers and Greenpeace Germany v Germany [2018] 00271/17/R/SP (Administrative Court Berlin).

Friends of the Irish Environment CLG v The Government of Ireland, Ireland and the Attorney General [2020] Appeal no. 205/19 (Supreme Court).

GFCC, Decision of 14 October 2004, 2 BvR 1481/04 – (Görgülü; ECHR decision).

GFCC, Decision of 4 May 2011, 2 BvR 2365/09; 2 BvR 740/10; 2 BvR 2333/08; 2.

Greenpeace Nordic and Others v Norway, no. 34068/21 (ECtHR).

Greenpeace Nordic and the Finnish Association for Nature Conservation v Finland [2023] ECLI:FI:KHO:2023:62 (Supreme Administrative Court of Finland).

KlimaSeniorinnen Schweiz et al v Federal Department of the Environment, Transport, Energy and Communications [2020] 1C_37/2019 (Switzerland Supreme Court).

KlimaSeniorinnen Schweiz et al v Switzerland, no. 53600/20 (ECtHR).

Klimatická žaloba ČR v Czech Republic [2022] No. 14A 101/2021 (Prague Municipal Court).

Klimatická žaloba ČR v Czech Republic [2023] 9 As 116/2022 – 166 (Czech Supreme Court).

Marbury v Madison [1803] 5 U.S. (1 Cranch) 137 (1803) (US Supreme Court).

Nature and Youth Norway and others v Norway [2020] HR-2020-24720P (Supreme Court).

Neubauer and Others v Germany [2021] 1 BvR 2656/18, 1 BvR 96/20, 1 BvR 78/20, 1 BvR 288/20, 1 BvR 96/20, 1 BvR 78/20 (German Federal Constitutional Court).

Notre Affaire à Tous and Others v France [2021] Nos. 1904967, 1904968, 1904972, 1904976/4-1 (Paris Administrative Court).

Nyugat [1959], HR 6 March 1959, NJ 1962, 2.
Plan B and Others v Prime Minister and Others [2022] CA-2021-003448 (Court of Appeal).
Plan B Earth et al v Secretary of State for Transport [2020] EWCA Civ 214.
R (on the application of Friends of the Earth and Others) v Heathrow Airport [2020] UKSC 52.
R v Secretary of State for Business Energy and Industrial Strategy [2022] EWHC 1841.
Soubeste and 4 other applications v Austria and 11 other States, no. 31925/22 (ECtHR).
State of the Netherlands (Ministry of Economic Affairs and Climate Policy) v Stichting Urgenda [2019] ECLI:NL:HR:2019:2007 (Supreme Court of the Netherlands, Civil Division).
State of the Netherlands v Stichting Urgenda [2018] ECLI:NL:GHDHA:2018:2591 (Court of Appeal).
Stichting Urgenda v State of the Netherlands [2015] ECLI:NL:RBDHA:2015:7196 (District Court).
VZW *Klimaatzaak* (unofficial translation), Appeal of 17 November 2021, <http://climatecasechart.com/wp-content/uploads/sites/16/non-us-case-documents/2021/20211117_2660_appeal.pdf> accessed 2 April 2023.
VZW *Klimaatzaak v Kingdom of Belgium & Others* [2021] 2015/4585/A (Brussels Court of First Instance).

Literature

Adelmant V, P Alston and M Blainey, 'Human Rights and Climate Change Litigation: One Step Forward, Two Steps Backwards in the Irish Supreme Court' (2021) 13 Journal of Human Rights Practice 1.
Al Jazeera English, 'The Case for the Climate: Forcing systems change in court | earthrise' (26 April 2023) <https://www.youtube.com/watch?v=MJXpOooZwpc> accessed 15 June 2023.
Amnesty International, 'After UN Climate Action Summit, Urgent Action Needed by All States to Avoid Human Rights Violations on Massive Scale' (Public statement, Index number IOR 40/1239/2019, Amnesty International 2019) <https://www.amnesty.org/en/documents/ior40/1239/2019/en/> accessed 2 April 2023.
Besselink L, 'The National and EU Targets for Reduction of Greenhouse Gas Emissions Infringe the ECHR: The Judicial Review of General Policy Objectives: Hoge Raad (Netherlands Supreme Court) 20 December 2019, Urgenda v The State of the Netherlands' (2022) 18 European Constitutional Law Review 155.
Buser A, 'Of Carbon Budgets, Factual Uncertainties, and Intergenerational Equity– The German Constitutional Court's Climate Decision' (2021) 22 *German Law Journal* 1409.
Cevik S and J Tovar Jalles, *For Whom the Bell Tolls: Climate Change and Income Inequality* (IMF 2022).

Chancel L et al, *Climate Inequality Report 2023* (World Inequality Lab Study 2023/1) <https://wid.world/wp-content/uploads/2023/01/CBV2023-ClimateInequalityReport-3.pdf> accessed 15 June 2023.

Cournil C, A Le Dylio and Mougeolle, 'L'Affaire du Siecle: French Climate Litigation between Continuity and Legal Innovations' (2020) 14 CCLR 40.

Darian-Smith E, *Global Burning: Rising Anti-Democracy and the Climate Crisis* (Stanford University Press 2022).

Dover S, 'Sustainability: Demands on Policy' (1997) 16 Journal of Public Policy 303.

DUH, 'Climate lawsuit filed: Environmental Action Germany sues German government for ineffective climate protection measures in agriculture and forestry' (*Deutsche Umwelthilfe*, 24 November 2022) <https://www.duh.de/presse/pressemitteilungen/pressemitteilung/climate-lawsuit-filed-environmental-action-germany-sues-german-government-for-ineffective-climate-p/> accessed 15 June 2023.

Eckes C, 'EU accession to the ECHR: between autonomy and adaption' (2013) 76 *Modern Law Review* 254.

Eckes C, 'Strategic Climate Litigation: Legal Consequences of Scientific "Truth"?' (forthcoming).

Eckes C, 'The Urgenda Case is Separation of Powers at Work' in N de Boer, A Nieuwenhuis and JH Reestman (eds), *Liber Amicorum Besselink* (Universiteit van Amsterdam 2021).

Eckes C, J Nedevska and J Setzer, 'Climate litigation and separation of powers' in M Wewerinke-Singh and S Mead (eds), *Judicial Handbook on Climate Litigation, lawyers and legal scholars* (project of IUCN's World Commission on Environmental Law (WCEL) Climate Change Law Specialist Group (CCLSG)), 2023.

Fiorino D, *Can Democracy Handle Climate Change?* (Polity Press 2018).

Fischer F, 'Ecological Crisis and Climate Change: From States of Emergency to 'Fortress World'?' in F Fischer (ed), *Climate Crisis and the Democratic Prospect: Participatory Governance in Sustainable Communities* (Oxford University Press 2017).

Forst R, *Das Recht auf Rechtfertigung – Elemente einer konstruktivistischen Theorie der Gerechtigkeit* (Suhrkamp 2014).

Ganguly G, 'Judicial transnationalization' in V Heyvaert and LA Duvic-Paoli (eds), *Research Handbook on Transnational Environmental Law* (Edward Elgar 2020).

Ganguly G, J Setzer and V Heyvaert, 'If at First You Don't Succeed: Suing Corporations for Climate Change' (2018) 38 Oxford Journal of Legal Studies 841.

Ganguly G, *Towards a transnational law of climate change: transnational litigation at the boundaries of science and law* (LSE PhD Thesis, 2019).

Ghaleigh NS, J Setzer and A Welikala, 'The Complexities of Comparative Climate Constitutionalism' (2022) 34 Journal of Environmental Law 517.

Gloppen S and C Vallejo, 'The climate crisis: litigation and economic, social and cultural rights' in J Dugard et al (eds), *Research Handbook on Economic, Social and Cultural Rights as Human Rights* (Edward Elgar 2020).

Habermas J, *Between Facts and Norms: Contribution to a Discourse Theory of Law and Democracy* (MIT Press 1996).

IPCC, *Global Warming of 1.5°C* (IPCC 2019) <https://www.ipcc.ch/sr15/download/> accessed 15 June 2023.

IPCC, *Progress Reports* (IPCC 2021) <https://apps.ipcc.ch/eventmanager/documents/65/040320210332-INF.%208%20-%20Progress%20Report%20IG%20Publications.pdf> accessed 2 April 2023.

Jaria-Manzano J and S Borrás (eds), *Research Handbook on Global Climate Constitutionalism* (Edward Elgar 2019).

Kennedy D, 'A Semiotics of Legal Argument' (1991) 42 Syracuse Law Review 75.

Knox O, 'The Daily 202: The Alarming Climate Report Is Also a Huge Politics Story' (*Washington Post* 10 August 2021) <https://www.washingtonpost.com/politics/2021/08/10/daily-202-alarming-climate-report-is-also-huge-politics-story/> accessed 15 June 2023.

Kotzé L, *Global Environmental Constitutionalism in the Anthropocene* (Hart 2016).

Kulovesi K et al, 'Finland's first climate judgment: Putting the government on notice' (*CCEEL*, 12 June 2023) <https://sites.uef.fi/cceel/finlands-first-climate-judgment-putting-the-government-on-notice> accessed 15 June 2023.

May JR and E Daly, 'Global climate constitutionalism and justice in the courts' in J Jaria-Manzano and S Borrás (eds), *Research Handbook on Global Climate Constitutionalism* (Edward Elgar 2019).

May JR and E Daly, *Environmental Constitutionalism* (Cambridge University Press 2015).

Mayer B, 'Climate Change Mitigation as an Obligation Under Human Rights Treaties?' (2021) 115 American Journal of International Law 409.

Mayer B, 'The Contribution of Urgenda to the Mitigation of Climate Change' (2022) 20 Journal of Environmental Law 1.

Möllers C, *The Three Branches: A Comparative Model of Separation of Powers* (Oxford University Press 2013).

Peel J and H Osofsky, 'Climate Change Litigation' (2020) 16 Annual Review of Law and Social Science 21.

Rodríguez-Garavito C, 'Human Rights: The Global South's Route to Climate Litigation' (2020) 114 American Journal of International Law 40.

Rodríguez-Garavito C, *International Human Rights and Climate Governance: The 'Rights Turn' in Climate Litigation* (Unpublished manuscript).

Shearman D and JW Smith, *The Climate Challenge and the Failure of Democracy* (Praeger 2007).

Taconet N, A Méjean and C Guivarch, 'Influence of climate change impacts and mitigation costs on inequality between countries' (2020) 160 Climatic Change 15.

Tzanakopoulos A, 'Domestic Courts in International Law: The International Judicial Function of National Courts' (2011) 34 Loy. L.A. Int'l & Comp. L. Rev 33.

UNEP, 'Climate Change and Human Rights' (Report, UNEP 2015) <https://www.unep.org/resources/report/climate-change-and-human-rights> accessed 2 April 2023.

UNESCO, 'UNESCO 'World in 2023' Survey Report highlights youth concerns over climate change and biodiversity loss' (*UNESCO*, 31 March 2021) <https://en.unesco.org/news/unesco-world-2030-survey-report-highlights-youth-concerns-over-climate-change-and-biodiversity> accessed 15 June 2023.

UNFCCC, 'Nationally determined contributions under the Paris Agreement', FCCC/PA/CMA/2022/4 (Synthesis Report, UNFCC 2022) <https://unfccc.int/ndc-synthesis-report-2022> accessed 2 April 2023.

Vanhalla L, 'Legal opportunity structures and the legal mobilization by the environmental movement in the UK' (2012) 46 Law & Society Review 523.

Verheyen R, *Climate Change Damage and International Law: Prevention Duties and State Liability* (Brill 2005).

Verheyen R, *Wir alle haben ein Recht auf Zukunft* (DTV Verlag 2023).

Vile MJC, *Constitutionalism and the Separation of Powers* (Oxford University Press 1967).

Waldron J, 'Separation of Powers in Thought and Practice' (2013) 54 Boston College Law Review 441.

Wewerinke-Singh M and S Mead (eds), *Judicial Handbook on Climate Litigation, lawyers and legal scholars* (project of IUCN's World Commission on Environmental Law (WCEL) Climate Change Law Specialist Group (CCLSG), 2023).

World Health Organisation, 'Health and climate change' (*WHO News Room*, 5 December 2018) <https://www.who.int/news-room/facts-in-pictures/detail/health-and-climate-change> accessed 15 June 2023.

Zielonka J, *The Lost Future and How to Reclaim It* (Yale University Press 2023).

CHAPTER 5

The EU Carbon Border Adjustment Mechanism: a Transnational Governance Instrument Whose Time Has Come

James Flett

1 Introduction

This chapter assimilates the conceptual themes of the book. However, drawing on the author's experiences of the gradual construction of the European Union, it posits that the process by which States construct multilateral governance structures, from the bottom up, in response to the need for proper governance of common goods, is necessarily evolutionary. There would not appear to be any other method reasonably available. This evolutionary process is driven economically, politically and legally, often during or after a "crisis". Usually, the solution, in one form or another, is "more EU", that is, more transnational governance. So, when we consider global governance issues, the interesting questions are, where are we on the evolutionary track and what is the next logical step? The WTO looks the way it does today, constitutionally, institutionally and in terms of legal policy, simply because it represents a relatively early stage in the global evolutionary process. This is inevitable and could not be otherwise. As so many diverse States attempt to reach agreement on such diverse matters, especially through the lens of trade, the early stages were always going to be marginal and replete with attenuated constructive ambiguities. This is also why each WTO Member only has one vote (there is no weighting); why, even though voting is provided for, in practice no Member ever calls for a vote and all decisions are taken by consensus; and there is no independent executive. Mandatory and binding adjudication is a step down the evolutionary path but is temporarily partially obstructed by the United States. In these circumstances, and as well-illustrated by the history of the European Union, the only logical way forward, down the evolutionary path, is for larger States to leverage their markets to create regulatory incentives for others to follow. This is the best democratic proxy available for the time being.

By way of a practical example of a step towards better transnational governance of a common good, this chapter focuses on legislation recently adopted

 | DOI:10.1163/9789004693722_006

by the European Union: the Carbon Border Adjustment Mechanism (CBAM),[1] which is the principal measure in the European Green Deal,[2] the defining policy of the current European Commission. The EU aims to reduce carbon emissions by 55 % by 2030 and become climate neutral by 2050. The CBAM requires that, for all products subject to the relevant legislation,[3] whether domestic or imported, a carbon price is paid commensurate with the carbon emissions generated during production. If, for an imported product, a carbon price has already been paid in the non-EU country, no adjustment is required upon import to the EU. If not, an adjustment must be made, equivalent to the carbon price that would have been paid if the product had been produced in the EU. The purpose of the measure is to address climate change by giving effect to the 'polluter pays' principle, that is, by internalising the otherwise exogenous environmental costs of carbon emissions. Specifically, the CBAM is designed to prevent so-called carbon leakage: the risk that, as the EU increases the level of its environmental ambition, industry simply shifts offshore, continuing to serve the EU market from non-EU countries with less regulated markets, without diminishing carbon emissions.

The chapter will situate CBAM, as a legitimate, if partial, response to transnational governance failure, in the context of the EU's international obligations and rights, particularly as regards World Trade Organization (WTO) law and explain why it is consistent with those obligations and rights. It will explain why the CBAM is an idea, and a measure, whose time has come. In this respect, whilst it may be characterised as a "second-best" response, if one rather takes as a premise the absence of transnational constitutionalism,[4] at least for the time being, measures such as CBAM can also been seen as the "lesser evil", and therefore the most rational way forward at this point.

To put the matter in context, the chapter will briefly describe certain aspects of the historical development of international trade law, which is rather similar to EU law (the law of international economic integration), albeit with some important differences. It will consider how the context has changed from one in which states and firms were primarily or even only concerned with boosting exports and keeping imports out ('Where can I sell my stuff?') to one in

1 Regulation (EU) 2023/956 of the European Parliament and of the Council of 10 May 2023 establishing a carbon border adjustment mechanism [2002] OJ L130/52.

2 European Commission, Commission communication – 'Fit for 55': Delivering the EU's 2030 climate target on the way to climate neutrality, COM(2021) 550 final.

3 Essentially: iron and steel, cement, fertilisers, aluminium, electricity and hydrogen.

4 See: Chapter 2, Ernst-Ulrich Petersmann, 'Constitutional Pluralism, Regulatory Competition and Transnational Governance Failures', at page [1].

which states and firms are now just as concerned about where they get their inputs from ('Where do I make my stuff?'). A changing context that has, in some respects, brought transnational governance failures more clearly into the foreground.

The chapter will also explain how, in this new globalised world, states are collectively presented with new problems that demand (preferably collective) action, of which climate change is the prime example. It will identify a specific activity that, historically, the WTO legal establishment has assumed is not normal regulatory activity. This is the regulation of so-called non-product-related processes and production methods (PPMs) – that is, those that do not manifest themselves in the characteristics of the product – in a third country. It is because of this historical assumption that such measures, if non-discriminatory, are not obviously regulated by the General Agreement on Tariffs and Trade (GATT), which one can see as a specific example of governance failure in the principal instruments of international trade law. This has thrown up a whole series of intellectual problems that have been resolved in various ways. This is also the reason why such measures are largely excluded from the relevant subsidiary WTO agreements (the TBT Agreement and the SPS Agreement).[5] The chapter will explain that, although relatively novel, measures such as CBAM are consistent with WTO law, if their design and architecture ensures that they treat imports and domestic products in an even-handed manner and that any differences flow exclusively from the pursuit of the relevant legitimate regulatory objectives (particularly, in this case, the protection of the environment). In other words, CBAM is a novel but legitimate and effective response to transnational governance failures, and the only type of response realistically available at this point.[6]

5 The WTO Agreement on Technical Barriers to Trade, which applies to technical regulations, standards and conformity assessment procedures, and the WTO Agreement on the Application of Sanitary and Phytosanitary Measures, which applies specifically to measures adopted to protect human, animal or plant life or health on the territory of the regulating member.

6 See: Chapter 3, Armin Steinbach, 'Constitutional Economics and Transnational Governance Failures', at page [26]. CBAM differs from the so-called carbon club concept because it is specifically about carbon pricing, which is a market-related mechanism, and therefore has a different focus compared to other regulatory measures. CBAM is: quantitative, being based on a market mechanism, as opposed to qualitative, which would demand complex, time-consuming and controversial procedures for quantification and comparison; dynamic, since the price can vary daily, as opposed to static, meaning that the re-assessment of changing qualitative measures can only be done over an extended period of time; and calibrated, meaning that a prior partial payment of the carbon price will be taken into account, as opposed to binary, meaning one is either in the club, or not.

As part of the explanation, this chapter will shift to a higher level of abstraction and explain that much of the law is about not how it is to be interpreted in isolation from particular fact patterns but, rather, how it is to be applied to particular and changing fact patterns. This is particularly true of WTO law, because it is replete with so-called constructive ambiguity. This is an inevitable feature of WTO law, given that it is created based on what many different states are capable of agreeing to, despite their very different interests and stakeholders. This often results in rules that are stated in somewhat general and abstract terms. What this means is that, even though important parts of WTO law (notably the GATT) are essentially unchanged since they were first agreed in 1947, the fact patterns to which the law is to be applied have certainly changed, and it is here that we find the flexibility to accommodate measures such as CBAM. As others have observed, a judge, in adjudicating, must not be influenced by the weather of the day, but must surely be sensitive to the climate of the era (a particularly apt observation in this context).[7] Novel ways of interpreting and applying existing law thus constitute a key policy tool for addressing transnational governance failures.

2 Climate Change and Transnational Governance Failures

It is not the purpose of this chapter to rehearse the evidence regarding climate change and its consequences. Suffice it to say that the European Green Deal and the CBAM are grounded in the propositions that climate change and its consequences are real and serious and that they must be addressed through reductions in carbon emissions. If a complainant in international trade litigation were to assert or suggest otherwise, that would surely only make the task of the defendant easier.

International negotiations with the objective of reducing carbon emissions have been continuing for some years, notably within the four corners of the Paris Agreement.[8] Consensus among participating countries is required, which has proved difficult to reach, and understandably so. Least developed and developing countries take the reasonable view that developed countries should bear a greater burden in addressing climate change since they carry a greater responsibility, having already industrialised and polluted, and are

---

7 Professor Paul Freund, Harvard University, often referenced by Ruth Bader Ginsburg, Justice of the US Supreme Court.

8 See, generally, United Nations Climate Change, 'The Paris Agreement' <https://unfccc.int/process-and-meetings/the-paris-agreement/the-paris-agreement> (accessed 29 June 2023).

better able to shoulder the burden. China, in particular, continues to characterise itself as a developing country (there is no formal definition in WTO law of what constitutes a developing country) and still tends to put the development objective ahead of the environmental objective. However, a precise formula for calibrating responsibility and allocating the burden of compliance between least developed and developing countries on the one hand and developed countries on the other hand has proved elusive, as has a formula for allocating responsibility among least developed and developing countries. The inevitable result has been a fudge, in the form of the so-called principle of combined but differentiated responsibility. National commitments to reduce carbon emissions are not binding and cannot be enforced. The level of ambition is simply not high enough, and the available mechanisms incapable of delivering the necessary outcome. It is a paradigm example of the kind of transnational governance failure identified elsewhere in this book.

Against this background, the European Green Deal and the CBAM are grounded in the proposition that, faced with such a transnational governance failure, the only way forward at this point is to adopt more of a bottom-up approach. That is not to say that the approach is simply 'unilateral'. One may reasonably point out that when a country continues to pollute a common good, which all the citizens of the world have a right to enjoy, including EU citizens, it is in fact that country that is acting 'unilaterally'. In any event, the EU approach is not simply unilateral, because, while taking necessary action, the EU continues to engage with other countries, and in particular with its main trading partners, in an effort to explain the reasons for the measures it has adopted and to encourage them to follow suit. Furthermore, the EU does not have the pretension to direct non-EU countries as to how they must produce for their own market, or for markets in other non-EU countries. We may hope that our measures contribute to further movement in that direction, but we do not seek direct regulation of those matters. Rather, we condition access to our market on a requirement that a carbon price has been paid for the product, either in the non-EU country where it was produced or at the EU border. At this point, there is simply no other choice. It has been said in the past that globalisation is not a policy choice but a fact; one may equally state today that taking action with respect to climate change is not a policy choice but an overwhelming governmental and moral imperative, which demands that new ways are found to overcome pressing transnational governance failures. In this sense, in adopting CBAM, the European Union is, in some measure, a "regulatory exporter", in that it is conditioning access to its market on a carbon price having been paid, and, in addition, hoping to "nudge" third countries to follow the same path. This means that, although it may be the case that Europe's multilevel constitutionalism has no equivalent outside Europe,[9] CBAM, and other measures like it, are, in effect, "exporting" or at least projecting relevant European values into the international arena.

3 A Governance Failure in WTO Law: Non-product Related Production Methods, *de facto* Discrimination, and the Environmental Exception

At this point, it is perhaps helpful to step back and consider the law of economic integration, and particularly WTO law, which is something of an analogue of EU law, albeit with more participants (164 compared with 27 states) and somewhat less complete. We are speaking of the law of economic integration between states, through treaty law. That is, the entire structure is conceptualised through the lens of states as the basic building blocks, both as the authors of the agreements and as the subjects of the law. There is nothing particularly objective about this; it is just historically the case. Thus, the very concept of trade, in terms of volume and/or value, as something that occurs between states, as a protected interest, flows from the state-centred lens on which the entire structure is based. We should constantly bear in mind that trade is just a subset of economic activity more generally (including transactions within states). It is precisely such conceptual assumptions, even as written into the relevant treaties, that come under increasing stress as the processes of integration and globalisation progress. Citizens are simply becoming progressively more central to the thinking.[10]

We also need to bear in mind that we are speaking of the World Trade Organization, not the World Organization for the Protection of the Environment. Trade is an interest protected by the WTO by definition; the environment is not (in the absence of any specific environmental agreement to that effect). States may act for environmental reasons and their measures may be tested by the WTO to ensure that they are not excessively trade restrictive. But the WTO will never tell a state that it must do more to protect the environment.

Finally, we must also be aware of the concepts of absolute and comparative advantage; the latter explains why least developed and developing countries have an interest in participating in the system. A particular developed country

9 See: Chapter 2, Ernst-Ulrich Petersmann, 'Constitutional Pluralism, Regulatory Competition and Transnational Governance Failures', Section 2, at page [8].

10 See, for example, Ernst-Ulrich Petersmann, *Constitutional Functions and Constitutional Problems of International Economic Law* (1st edition, Routledge 2020).

may have an absolute advantage over a particular developing country with respect to two different products (making the first two times more efficiently and the second three times more efficiently). The developing country does not have an absolute advantage with respect to either product; however, it has a comparative advantage with respect to the product that it makes only two times less efficiently. The developed country has an absolute advantage with respect to both products but a comparative advantage only with respect to the product it makes three times more efficiently. It is rational for the developing country to specialise in the first product, for the developed country to specialise in the second product, and for the two countries to trade. It is this economic theory of comparative advantage that explains why developing countries have an interest in participating in the international trade system even if they do not have an absolute advantage with respect to any product. We will return to this point below.

Against that background, the structure of the main relevant treaty, GATT 1994 (which originally dates from 1947), is conceptually straightforward. The main rule is that each member must treat goods from other members in a non-discriminatory way (that is, no discrimination between goods on grounds of origin). The rule covering non-discrimination between other members is known as the most favoured nation (MFN) rule; that covering non-discriminatory treatment of domestic and imported goods is known as the national treatment rule.[11] Naturally, what happens at the border is regulated. In principle, the only tariffs that can be applied are those in the agreed schedule of concessions (unless, exceptionally, anti-dumping or countervailing duties are justified).[12] Quantitative restrictions on imports are also generally prohibited (unless the conditions for a safeguard measure are present).[13] Internal measures, both fiscal and regulatory, are also regulated: they must be non-discriminatory.[14] Internal taxes and regulations enforced at the border are analysed under Article III, as opposed to Article XI.[15] If a subsidy is used as a policy instrument (as opposed to a fiscal measure or regulation), it is acceptable for it to be granted only to firms on the territory of the subsidising member (the member does not have to make the subsidy available globally), provided that it is not

11 GATT 1994, Articles I and III.

12 GATT 1994, Articles II and VI; Agreement on Implementation of Article VI of GATT 1994 (Anti-Dumping Agreement); Agreement on Subsidies and Countervailing Measures (SCM Agreement).

13 GATT 1994, Articles XI and XIX; Agreement on Safeguards.

14 GATT, Articles III:1, III:2 and III:4.

15 Note Ad Article III.

contingent upon export or the use of domestic over imported goods and does not adversely affect the interests of trading partners.[16]

Importantly, for indirect fiscal measures such as value added tax (VAT) the law provides for the operation of the so-called destination principle. According to this principle, the rate of tax to be paid is that applicable in the country in which the product is sold. Thus, when an imported product enters a country, it is subject to the tax applicable in that country; when a domestically produced product is exported, it is not subject to that tax, or a rebate applies. Such rebates are specifically carved out of subsidies law – that is, they are deemed not to be subsidies.[17] Critically, as discussed below, no such mechanism exists for regulatory measures.

The treaty states that nothing in the GATT is to be construed as preventing a member from adopting a measure necessary to protect an enumerated list of protected legitimate policy objectives, including the protection of public morals, or human, animal or plant life or health, or the conservation of exhaustible natural resources. There is also a provision covering security-related exceptions.[18]

Traditionally, the treaty has been interpreted and applied by taking a bifurcated approach to the obligations (such as the MFN rule) on the one hand and the rights or exceptions (such as the so-called environmental exception) on the other hand. Following this approach, one speaks of a 'violation' of an obligation and then considers whether that violation is 'justified' by one of the rights. However, this is not how the treaty is actually written. Rather, it is written in a more integrated or unitary manner, providing that nothing in the GATT is to be construed as preventing the adoption of a measure that pursues one of the enumerated legitimate policy objectives. There is a difference between a violation that is justified and a measure that, as a whole, is consistent with the balance of obligations and rights under the treaty.[19] This is a point to which we shall also return.

With this summary of the design and architecture of the GATT in mind, we may see how it functions with regard to the regulation of product characteristics. Traditionally, countries may regulate the characteristics of products sold

---

16 GATT, Article III:8(b); SCM Agreement, Articles 3.1(a) and (b) and Part III.

17 Note to Article XVI of GATT 1994; SCM Agreement, footnote 1 and Annex I, particularly items (e) and (h) and footnote 58.

18 GATT 1994, Articles XX and XXI, particularly Articles XX(g), XX(b) and XX(a).

19 See, for example, Joseph Weiler, 'Law, culture and values in the WTO: gazing into the crystal ball' in Daniel Bethlehem, Donald McRae, Rodney Neufeld and Isabelle Van Damme (eds), *Oxford Handbook of International Trade Law* (Oxford University Press 2009).

in their market on the grounds that these may have implications for, notably, human, animal or plant life or health, or the environment. Similarly, countries may also regulate production processes, including those carried out in other countries, to the extent that they are expressed in the characteristics of the product. However, traditionally, countries do not normally or extensively regulate production processes in other countries that are not expressed in the characteristics of a product sold into the market of the regulating member. One can see this as a specific governance failure in the texts regulating international trade law, as least from an historical perspective.

It is important to note that, in accepting non-discriminatory but autonomous national regulation, the system accommodates limitations on the protected trade interest. That is, while it welcomes and encourages internationally agreed rules, at the same time it accepts in principle a situation in which each of the 164 WTO members may have a different regulation concerning the product characteristics of a particular item (such as a plug), with respect both to domestic production and imports. Obviously, this is not ideal for achieving economies of scale or for specialisation or, thus, for exploiting comparative advantages, but it is inherent in the design and architecture of the system. It is a compromise.

Finally, we must consider the problem of the regulatory measure that is non-discriminatory on its face. Without more, this would not appear to be caught. It would not appear to violate the rules against discrimination on grounds of origin, or the rules regarding the schedule of concessions, or the rules regarding quantitative restrictions. Thus, without more, the measure would never be subject to the necessity test under Article XX of the GATT (that is, it would never be scrutinised in order to ensure that it was the least trade restrictive measure available and that there was no alternative, less trade-restrictive possibility that would make an equivalent contribution to the legitimate policy objective).

The main solution to this problem[20] has been the development of the concept of so-called *de facto* discrimination. This concept is based on the provisions concerning internal taxation, which seem to create a second category, leaving aside measures that expressly discriminate on grounds of origin.[21] This

20 An earlier theory posited that non-product-related PPM regulations are controlled by Article XI of GATT 1994, which prohibits quantitative restrictions on imports. See, for example, GATT Panel Report, *US-Tuna (Mexico)*, paras. 5.11–5.14 (unadopted by the Dispute Settlement Body); GATT Panel Report, *US-Tuna (EEC)*, paras. 5.8–5.10 (unadopted by the Dispute Settlement Body). This theory has now been largely discredited.

21 GATT 1994, Article III:2, first and second sentences.

category consists of measures that are origin neutral on their face but are nevertheless applied so as to afford protection to domestic production. Apparently, the concept requires that the measure may be expected to have an asymmetrical economic impact on imports and competing domestic products. This is already a problematic proposition, because the situation under scrutiny may result in part from the measure but equally in part because of the decisions made by economic operators in the exporting country. In addition, most academic commentators support the view that, conceptually and intellectually, the notion of *de facto* discrimination necessarily requires regulatory purpose to be taken into account. That is because a genuine environmental measure that is origin neutral on its face may well impact existing economic operators differently, and indeed is likely to do so. This does not mean that it discriminates on grounds of origin. Despite this, the WTO's Appellate Body has decided that the concept of *de facto* discrimination in the GATT need not involve any consideration of regulatory purpose (this being a matter reserved eventually for the interpretation and application of Article XX of the GATT).[22] This is the case for both fiscal and regulatory measures, and for the national treatment and MFN rules. In practice, since it is essentially impossible to design an origin-neutral measure that impacts all of the other 163 WTO members equally, this means that all regulations will violate some obligation, and therefore all regulations will be subject to the necessity test under Article XX of the GATT. In effect, the necessity test introduced in Article 2 of the TBT Agreement (further discussed below) has been reverse-engineered into the GATT. The end result is to make the analysis required less like a bifurcated approach and more akin to an integrated or unitary approach.

An important part of this puzzle is the concept of 'like product', about which a great deal has been written and which is much misunderstood. The correct approach is actually quite simple. First, one has to consider what is the definition of the product – that is, which things can be grouped together and referred to as one product. There is no 'right' answer to this question, because it depends on the cross-price elasticities of demand (and to a lesser extent supply) that are deemed sufficient to establish that two things compete sufficiently closely to be grouped together as a single product. Next, in examining whether or not there is *de facto* discrimination, and in particular whether or not there is an asymmetrical adverse impact on imports, one must define the domestic product and the imported product, categorically, in identical terms.

22 Appellate Body Report, *European Communities – Measures prohibiting the importation and marketing of seal products*, paras. 5.101–5.530.

Then, one must examine the entire content of the domestic category and the entire content of the imported category for the purposes of reaching a conclusion regarding *de facto* discrimination. What one is not permitted to do is to compare one domestic subcategory with one different imported subcategory; such a comparison is just economic and legal nonsense.[23]

In considering whether or not two things compete it is legitimate to take into account not just their physical characteristics but also other considerations relevant to the operation of the forces of supply and demand, including the manner in which they have been produced. Consider, for example, two identical items, one of which has been produced in an environmentally friendly manner and the other of which has not. It is possible to argue that, if consumers care about the environment and are informed by an appropriate label, a situation might in theory be reached in which all consumers always choose the environmentally friendly item, there being no price difference at which they would switch to the other. In that case, one might argue that the two items were in different markets – that is, that they did not compete at all. Accordingly, one could argue that a regulation banning the environmentally unfriendly item (both domestically and with respect to imports) does not give rise to *de facto* discrimination. One could even try to develop this argument by focusing only on those consumers who always choose the environmentally friendly product and asserting that they constitute a different market. However, such an argument is hardly realistic. In the real world, price will continue to play a role. One also needs to be wary of situations that are created by the measure under scrutiny itself. But perhaps most importantly, one has to be alert to the fact that there is no way an international trade adjudicator is going to sign off on a relatively intrusive non-product-related PPM regulation on the grounds that it is non-discriminatory. This would represent a binary analysis and outcome. Instead, the adjudicator will always seek, and find, a way to get to the calibrated necessity test under Article XX of GATT 1994, and with good reason.

Layered on top of the GATT is the TBT Agreement, the two agreements applying concurrently. The TBT Agreement, which dates from 1995, controls technical regulations and standards, which are precisely defined. Article 2.2 of the TBT Agreement contains a necessity test that is an analogue of the necessity test in Article XX of the GATT. The problem of getting to the necessity test is thus solved, since the TBT Agreement simply applies to the relevant types of

23 James Flett, 'WTO space for national regulation: requiem for a diagonal vector test' [2013] Journal of International Economic Law, Vol. 16, No. 1, 37.

measures (arguably, it requires that the measure may have a significant effect on trade, but this is probably an extremely low threshold). While there has been some controversy about the issue, it appears that the TBT Agreement does not apply to non-product-related PPM regulations, except, possibly, to the extent that they deal with terminology, symbols, packing, marking or labelling requirements.[24] Similarly, the SPS Agreement only applies to the protection of interests on the territory of the regulating member. This drafting probably reflects a (misconceived) assumption that WTO members do not generally regulate non-product-related PPMs, an assumption that one may characterise as a transnational governance failure in international trade law. Were it not for the expansive understanding of the concept of *de facto* discrimination described above, this would have created an anomalous situation in which non-product-related PPM regulations (which are potentially highly intrusive on the policy calculus of trading partners) would have been subject to limited scrutiny. In summary, from a legal policy point of view, the expansive approach to the concept of *de facto* discrimination kills two birds with one stone: it makes the GATT necessity test generally applicable, and it ensures that non-product-related PPM regulations are subject to the same intensity of control as other types of regulation, notwithstanding their exclusion from the TBT Agreement.

4 The European Union Emissions Trading System: Governance Failure with Respect to the Transnational Dimension

With the foregoing observations in mind, the next step is to consider the EU emissions trading system (ETS),[25] which is a 'cap and trade' system. The objective of the EU ETS is environmental, and specifically to reduce carbon emissions by putting a price on them. It reflects the fact that the EU is pursuing a particular level of environmental ambition, in terms of reducing carbon emissions, higher than that of certain of its trading partners, and indeed higher than that of the Paris Agreement.

Under the ETS, firms producing the designated products in the EU are required to purchase and surrender certificates entitling them to do that. Because this relates to production in the EU, it does not apply to imports, an aspect that leaves the system incomplete and that may be characterised as a

24 Appellate Body Report, *European Communities – Measures prohibiting the importation and marketing of seal products*, paras. 5.8–5.12.

25 See, generally, European Commission, 'Climate action' <https://ec.europa.eu/clima/index_en> (accessed 29 June 2023).

transnational governance failure. The total number of available certificates is fixed in such a way as to exert downward pressure on the carbon emissions of EU industry. The certificates can be traded. This introduces certain market-based mechanisms into the process. The system creates an incentive for firms to consider alternatives to carbon emissions (and the associated purchase and surrender of certificates). They can decide instead to produce in a more efficient manner, avoiding carbon emissions and thus avoiding the obligation to purchase and surrender certificates. In this way, firms compete with each other not just in terms of price or product characteristics but also in terms of carbon emissions. In other words, the otherwise exogenous environmental costs of carbon emissions are internalised in the market mechanism, and ultimately through prices, subject to the disciplines of consumer demand. It is important to note that what is not going on here is that the government is intervening directly to require, for example, the use of greener technology. That would be a different approach. The two approaches are not mutually exclusive, and indeed, in the EU, there is a significant amount of regulation that falls into this latter category. The ETS, however, is something quite different. What it represents is not direct regulation of specific actions by firms but rather the general framing, through regulation, of the parameters of a market, including carbon costs, within which the forces of supply and demand will be allowed to play out. The sectors covered by the system are those with the highest carbon emissions, taking into account what can reasonably be achieved, at least as a first step, in administrative terms.

It is in the nature of economic integration from the bottom up that this type of regulatory measure entails what might be termed a 'first-mover disadvantage'. That is, by comparison with its trading partners, the EU has increased its level of environmental ambition, specifically with respect to domestic production. This creates the regulatory problem of carbon leakage, on both the import side and the export side. In other words, all other things being equal, EU producers will have an incentive to shift offshore, to a non-EU country that is less regulated in terms of carbon price, in order to continue serving the EU market with imports. On the export side, they have an incentive to move to the less regulated non-EU country in order to produce there and serve that market. This is a particular problem when one is speaking of a common good such as the environment, which is adversely affected by carbon emissions everywhere. Thus, without more, the very purpose of the EU ETS, which is to reduce carbon emissions, would be frustrated, because industry would just shift offshore and continue polluting, and there would be no impact on climate change.

The solution to this has been to provide for free allowances to those sectors covered by the ETS that are most at risk of delocalisation – that is, the issuance of a certain number of certificates free of charge. This is, of course, a compromise, because it diminishes the environmental effectiveness of the ETS. However, it has the advantage of not burdening imports. On the export side, the free allowances have been considered by at least one trading partner to constitute subsidies (a financial contribution in the form of revenue otherwise due foregone), conferring a benefit, that are specific, and to cause material injury to the domestic industry of that other WTO member, giving rise to countervailing duties. It must be doubtful that a subsidy re-establishing a level playing field in terms of environmental competition can reasonably be said to cause price and thus volume effects for the less regulated industry in the other country, but such countervailing duties have not, to date, been challenged at the WTO. Importantly, any such subsidy relates indistinctly to domestic production and exports, so cannot be said to be a prohibited subsidy, contingent, in law or in fact, upon export. Export subsidies and import substitution subsidies are prohibited, without it being necessary to demonstrate that they cause injury or adverse effects to the interests of another WTO member. Prohibited subsidies cannot benefit from the general exceptions under Article XX of GATT 1994, including the environmental exception, because that provision refers to 'this Agreement', meaning GATT 1994 and not the SCM Agreement. In any event, a prohibited subsidy would never pass the necessity test, because such subsidies are considered to be particularly trade distorting, and there would always be an alternative, less trade-restrictive measure equally capable of contributing to the legitimate policy objective.

The EU ETS has reached the point at which it needs to be updated and complemented with the CBAM. The tension inherent in the system between the relatively increased level of environmental protection and the granting of free allowances can be sustained only up to a point. It is clear that the Paris Agreement is not delivering a timely solution to the problem of climate change, which is itself a transnational governance failure. The level of environmental ambition must be raised further. This means that the free allowances must go. And this means in turn that the problem of carbon leakage, on both the import side and the export side, returns.

5 Transnational Governance of Production Processes Unrelated to Product Characteristics in International Trade Law

Before turning to the CBAM itself, it is opportune to explore in more detail the issue of the regulation of production processes unrelated to product characteristics in international trade law. As explained above, traditionally, this has not been a focus of regulatory efforts, which have been more concerned with the regulation of product characteristics. The introduction of measures to regulate such processes reflects an evolution in the legitimate concerns of trading countries and their regulatory authorities. That is, an attempt to respond to as yet unregulated transnational governance issues. However, they are relatively rare, and have not usually been controversial, with some exceptions.[26]

It is helpful to understand the reticence with which such measures have been considered by the trade establishment in Geneva. As explained above, even in the case of the regulation of product characteristics, multiple national regulations have the effect of fragmenting markets and diminishing the benefits of trade, although this is a compromise that is accepted by the system. The regulation of non-product-related PPMs exacerbates that effect. A national producer in one WTO member might in theory need not just 163 different versions of their product but 163 different production lines. This does more than just hinder economies of scale and the exploitation of comparative advantage; it entirely negates them, because it makes economies of scale impossible to achieve in practice. In addition, another member might legitimately complain that such regulation was relatively intrusive on its domestic policy calculus. It might affirm, for example, that it cared just as much about the environment but had a relatively impoverished population to feed, as a priority. If all 164 WTO members were to adopt non-product-related PPM regulations on all matters of concern to them, the whole international trading system would probably grind to a halt.

However, the fact remains that WTO law does not *per se* prohibit the regulation of non-product-related PPMs. It may be that, when the GATT was originally written in 1947, this was not something that the drafters were thinking about. But the notional intent of a small group of people involved in the negotiation of an agreement is an illusory basis on which to interpret and apply the law. Rather, we must look at the law itself – that is, the words that are actually in the treaty – and, by studying the design and architecture of the relevant provisions, understand their purpose. This is an objective notion of 'intent' or 'object and purpose'. It is the same way that we can look at a hammer and understand that it is for nails, and look at a screwdriver and understand that it is for screws.

26 These include, notably, the *US-Shrimp/Turtle*, *US-Tuna/Dolphin* and *EC-Seals* cases. The EU already has measures of this type in place, for example covering genetically modified organisms, the protection of animals at the time of slaughter, the use of animal testing in the development of cosmetics, the labelling of eggs, the use of leghold traps, the sale of cat and dog fur, and the killing of seals.

Furthermore, and critically, we must understand that a great deal of the law is about not how the law is to be interpreted in abstract terms, divorced from any particular fact pattern, but, rather, how the law is to be applied to a particular fact pattern. This is particularly true of the WTO Agreement, which is replete with constructive ambiguity – that is, rules written in a general and abstract manner in order to facilitate agreement. Thus, when, for example, in the *Shrimp/Turtle* dispute, WTO adjudicators accepted that turtles could be an 'exhaustible natural resource' within the meaning of Article XX(g),[27] even though this was probably not in the minds of the original drafters, they were not bending or distorting the law inappropriately. They were simply applying the law, in a balanced and reasonable way, to new fact patterns arising today, as they were bound to do.

Thus, when we examine the GATT, we do not, in truth, find any prohibition on the regulation of non-product-related PPMs. They cannot be said to somehow violate the rules against quantitative restrictions or non-discrimination *per se*, and to be incapable of justification. Article XX of GATT 1994 does not contain a territorial limitation.[28] On the contrary, certain subparagraphs, such as subparagraph (e) ('relating to the products of prison labour') appear to strongly suggest that such measures are possible. The chapeau of Article XX itself refers to 'countries where the same conditions prevail', apparently directing the reader to consider the conditions prevailing in the third country or countries, and not just the characteristics of the regulated product.

The problem, then, is to try to understand how the system finds a reasonable balance between the acceptable regulation of non-product-related PPMs and a regulation of non-product-related PPMs that would be excessive. The key to this is the necessity test, particularly when applied in the context of a common good, such as the climate – that is, when it is in the nature of the problem being addressed that it necessitates the regulation of non-product-related PPMs. And that brings us, finally, to the CBAM and WTO law.

27 Appellate Body Report, *United States – Import prohibition of certain shrimp and shrimp products*, paras. 127–134.

28 GATT Panel Report, *US-Tuna* (*EEC*), paras. 5.14–5.20; Appellate Body Report, *US-Shrimp*, para. 133 (basing its reasoning on the observation that the relevant species of turtle migrates also in US waters, without ruling on the question of whether or not there is an implied territorial limitation in Article XX(g)).

6 The EU Carbon Border Adjustment Mechanism: a Step (Albeit Imperfect) along the Evolutionary Path towards Transnational Governance

Aware of the complexity of the problem, and the controversy surrounding it, the EU has for years been engaged in discussions with its trading partners and with other countries in order to address the problem of carbon emissions and climate change. There have been extensive exchanges of information and analysis directed towards that outcome, and this continues to be the case today. However, at some point it becomes clear that, in addition to continuing discussions, some further action is necessary, even if it needs to be autonomous. That point has been reached. The climate emergency is extremely serious and accelerating. Urgent action is required. European citizens demand it. They will simply not accept that being a member of the WTO and participating in the international trading system has as a consequence that we must sit on our hands while the planet burns. Nor will European consumers accept that they must continue to use goods that have not paid a carbon price, effectively dumping the problem, or at least responsibility for it, on someone else's doorstep. In effect, EU citizens demand that new ways of thinking about, interpreting and applying international trade law be found, in order to allow their legitimate concerns to be addressed. In moving forward, the EU has very carefully selected the least trade-restrictive measure reasonably available, and the only one that creates a regulatory incentive for other countries to follow suit.

6.1 *The Overall Regulatory and Governance Response*

The first point to make is that the matter can only reasonably be considered by looking at the ETS/CBAM as a whole. That is because the CBAM has been designed to complete and complement the ETS and is dependent upon it. No doubt, complainants may be particularly interested in the CBAM, because it applies to imports, and less interested in the ETS, because it does not. But it is not, or at least should not be, the subjective trade or perceived legal interests of complainants that determines what reasonably constitutes the subject of the discussion.

In WTO case-law there is a certain amount of focus on what constitutes 'the measure at issue'. Lawyers in particular tend to become very focused on this. They like to get absolutely clear from the start what 'the measure at issue' is and then carry that analytical clarity with them all the way through the case. So the question is, is 'the measure at issue' inconsistent with the obligation, is 'the measure at issue' justified by the exception, and so forth. There is certainly some merit in this approach. It brings some analytical clarity and order to debates. But, like anything else, it is possible to have too much of a good thing. In truth, the question of what is 'the measure at issue' is generally rather more subtle than that. One might, for example, begin by identifying a particular piece of legislation set out in a document. Then one might realise that it is a particular article that is the focus of the concern, and perhaps a particular paragraph or subparagraph, or even a particular phrase. But then one might also realise that one can only understand the complaint being made by referring to other provisions in the same piece of legislation. The point at which these are part of 'the measure at issue' or just part of the context in which 'the measure at issue' exists is quite often far from clear. If the identified provision includes qualifying language, is 'the measure at issue' the general rule or the exception, or both, separately or together? The matter can become even more complicated if it is necessary to look at several documents, or to think not just about the words on the page of the legislative provision but how they have been applied in practice to a particular fact pattern. Further complexity arises if the complainant seeks to identify 'the measure at issue' not by referring directly to particular terms used in municipal law but, rather, using more abstract terms selected by the complainant.

The answer here is that, while it is reasonable to do what is necessary to comply with the procedural requirement that 'the measure at issue' be appropriately identified, one should not overstate the point. As observed above, for example, complainants will no doubt wish to focus on the CBAM, but this should not release them from properly analysing it in the context of the ETS or allow them to ignore the overall design and architecture of the ETS/CBAM. If complainants accept in principle that a measure of this type is possible (which they should), we should not need to read lengthy arguments directed against the regulation of non-product-related PPMS *per se*. To the extent that this implies that there must be a specific aspect of the ETS/CBAM with which complainants may wish to take issue, such as product coverage, we should expect it to be reasonably identified from the outset. And so forth.

There is also a certain line in WTO case-law, consistent with the above point, to the effect that it is in principle for the complainant to identify what 'the measure at issue' is. This is a reasonable point of departure. After all, the complainant should know what it is complaining about. It is not for the defendant or the panel to guess what that might be. That said, as always, there are certainly limits to this proposition. For example, it is probably fair to say that one of the consequences of some of the 'over-lawyering' that has sometimes taken place in WTO litigation is that, having analysed the case, lawyers have attempted to manipulate the process by artificially circumscribing what they assert is 'the measure at issue'. To take a somewhat simplified but obvious example, if

Article 1 imposes a tax of 20 % on domestic products and Article 2 imposes a tax of 20 % on imports, one cannot reasonably attempt to limit the definition of 'the measure at issue' to Article 2, then make a claim of discrimination. In an extreme case, I have seen a complainant define the alleged 'measure at issue' in abstract terms of its own invention that by definition violated the relevant obligation, and then simply assert the existence of such a measure, even in the absence of any direct or compelling evidence to that effect.

Linked to this discussion is the fact that the WTO Dispute Settlement Understanding has been interpreted and applied in such a way that the terms of reference of a panel are defined only by the panel request. There is no statement of defence integrated into the terms of reference (even though this is something that could have been done). Such a statement of defence would give the defendant an opportunity to indicate whether or not it considers the description of 'the measure at issue' advanced by the complainant reasonable (as opposed to under-inclusive or indeed over-inclusive).

The answer here, again, is that one should not overstate the point. While complainants may be expected to identify 'the measure at issue', they should not be permitted to artificially and unfairly control the conduct of the case, including the manner in which the panel eventually frames its analysis, without regard to a more reasonable and objective view about what is or should be the subject of the discussion.

6.2 *Incomplete Governance: Product Coverage*

Based on experiences in similar cases, one may expect that one of the issues that may come up is product coverage and alleged *de facto* discrimination. The argument goes like this: here is a product that is covered by the ETS/CBAM; here is another product that is not and that competes in some degree; I make or would like to make the product that is covered; regulatory purpose is irrelevant; so there is a violation of the non-discrimination rules. We continue the analysis under Article XX of GATT 1994, according to which the defendant has the burden of proof.

This kind of argument is profoundly unsatisfactory in many ways, legally and intellectually, for the reasons already explained above. At its heart is a concept of *de facto* discrimination that has, at this point, practically become an empty shell – that is, a very low or even non-existent hurdle on the way to Article XX of GATT 1994. As explained above, one cannot meaningfully compare two different products; one must consider the entire category on both sides of the comparison. One cannot reasonably ignore the fact that the situation complained of results, at least in part, from decisions made by the industry of the complainant, or to be made (allegedly) by it in the future. And one cannot reasonably ignore regulatory purpose. The problem is that, if one attempts to argue these points as the defendant, unsuccessfully (because the legal cards have at this point been stacked in favour of the complainant), one arrives at consideration of Article XX as a 'violator' of the rules against discrimination on grounds of origin – and this in a very binary manner (one either violates or not, there being no calibration). And as one tries to explain that one's measure is in truth even-handed, one finds oneself running up against the very same kinds of arguments that one has just lost. This is not conducive to a fair hearing of the defence.

Here is what has, in fact, occurred.

First, the product scope of the ETS was chosen by focusing on sectors with relatively high carbon emissions, but also taking into account what was administratively feasible (the SPS Agreement refers to what is reasonably available, taking into account technical and economic feasibility). No one could even sensibly suggest that, in fixing the product scope of the ETS, the EU was engaging in *de facto* discrimination against imports. The ETS does not even apply to imports. Exactly the reverse is true. In adopting the ETS, the EU was autonomously increasing the level of its environmental ambition, placing a burden on domestic production that was not placed on imports at all. That is, by its own terms, the ETS represents reverse discrimination. In other words, under the ETS, imports are treated more favourably than domestic products. To characterise this as *de facto* discrimination would be indeed surreal.

Second, the CBAM simply adopts as a starting point the same product scope as the ETS, in order to complete the regulatory structure and eliminate the reverse discrimination. The regulation, therefore, specifically identifies the product scope of the CBAM on the basis of objective criteria, including carbon emissions and the risk of carbon leakage, taking into account what can reasonably be achieved at this point in time, having regard to technical and economic feasibility.

Third, it is certainly the case that some WTO members will produce or assert that they wish to produce a product covered by the ETS/CBAM that competes in some degree with a product that is not covered or not yet covered by the ETS/CBAM. As WTO law has to date been interpreted and applied, it would be impossible to design a measure without this result.

Fourth, one cannot reasonably expect a WTO member seeking to regulate from the bottom up on an issue such as climate change to regulate everything at once. WTO members are permitted to approach a complex and extensive problem progressively when regulating. That is what the EU is doing, with the extension of the ETS/CBAM to more sectors already under discussion and consideration.

Fifth, none of this detracts from the basic observation that the ETS/CBAM is even-handed, that it pursues an exclusively environmental objective and that it does not constitute a means of arbitrary or unjustifiable discrimination between countries where the same conditions exist, or a disguised restriction on international trade. In other words, by far the better approach is to adopt an integrated or unitary perspective, rather than a bifurcated one. And any such integrated analysis must also be properly calibrated to take into account such things as the relative remoteness of asserted competitive relationships, the relative propensity of the non-EU country to produce the relevant product as opposed to some other product and the relative implausibility of the proposition that the entire ETS/CBAM edifice has been set up by the EU for protectionist as opposed to environmental reasons. In truth, one could observe that complainants should probably not be attacking the EU at all; they should be thanking it for assuming a large part of the regulatory burden of addressing climate change – an additional environmental effort upon which complainants are, in fact, free-riding.

Sixth, complainants making such arguments should take great care that they do not get what they wish for. WTO law does not dictate how adverse panel findings are to be implemented. A discrimination finding can be implemented by aligning either with the lower or the higher standard. Thus, if the best a complainant can do is complain that a particular product is covered while another is not, it would be a simple matter to implement such findings by extending the product scope of the ETS/CBAM, which would, of course, not be the result actually sought by complainants. In bringing the case, the complainant would in fact be doing the environmental lobby in the EU a big favour. Potential complainants should probably therefore think very carefully before acting as to what they are trying to achieve, and not be misled by enthusiastic lawyers, who will have their own agenda.

6.3 *The Legitimacy of the Environmental Governance Objective*

One of the points that will come up in the litigation is the question of what objectives the EU is pursuing in adopting the ETS/CBAM. The EU will explain that it is pursuing an environmental objective, seeking to address climate change by reducing carbon emissions.[29] There cannot be any doubt that this comfortably meets the requirements of Article XX(g) of GATT 1994, which

29 As indicated above, other general exceptions are or may be relevant, including those under Article XX(b) (measures to protect human, animal or plant life or health), Article XX(a) (public morals) and Article XX(d) (measures necessary to secure compliance with law or regulations not inconsistent with GATT 1994).

refers to 'the conservation of exhaustible natural resources', or that the CBAM is made effective in conjunction with restrictions on domestic production or consumption. It also falls within the scope of Article XX(a) (public morals). There is nothing to prevent the subparagraphs of Article XX overlapping. One cannot, in this case, deny the public morals aspect of the measure, and this does have consequences. Specifically, the concept of concurrent defences (to mirror the concept of concurrent obligations) has yet to be properly developed in WTO law. What this means is that one should not split the measure into a public morals element and an environmental element (something that would surely be impossible in this case in any event) and analyse each element separately under each exemption. Nor should one assess the defences in the alternative – that is, first test the entire measure against the environmental objective, then test the entire measure against the public morals objective. Rather, the defences are invoked concurrently: there is a single measure with a double objective. The specific consequence of this is that any alternative mooted by the complainant must make an equivalent contribution to both legitimate policy objectives, a point we return to below.

Complainants are likely to assert that one of the objectives of the CBAM is to raise revenues. That is not particularly the case. Like many such measures, the ETS/CBAM may reasonably be expected, at least in the short term, to have both a behaviour-changing and a revenue-raising outcome. Taxes often have both consequences and are rarely set so as to be entirely behaviour changing (that is, prohibitive) or entirely revenue raising (that is, with no impact on behaviour). But the fact remains that, in the ideal world that the EU would like to see evolve, all its trading partners would introduce carbon pricing, and no one would ever pay a CBAM charge. In any event, raising revenue is an entirely respectable exercise for all WTO members, and they all do it all of the time, so the fact that the ETS/CBAM may have that outcome, at least in the short term, certainly does not take it outside Article XX of GATT 1994.

Of course, the term 'exclusively' here is important. It means that the adjudicators will need to be satisfied that the design and architecture of the ETS/CBAM is 'pure', in the sense that it pursues legitimate policy objectives (notably, the protection of the environment and public morals), even if there is some revenue raising at least in the short term, and taking into account what is reasonably achievable from a technical and economic point of view. In other words, they will need to be satisfied that the design and architecture of the ETS/CBAM does not reveal that it has the objective of discriminating between countries where the same conditions prevail or of creating unnecessary obstacles to international trade (that is, that it is protectionist).

6.4 *Improving Governance with Respect to Imports*

We may also anticipate that complainants will repeatedly affirm that the EU is acting to address carbon leakage on the import side only because it does not want its industry to shift offshore, for industrial policy reasons. They will argue that this is an end in itself and sufficient to establish the protectionist nature of the measures. However, the measures themselves explain at great length, and this is also very clear from the context and from the design and architecture of the measures, that they address the problem of carbon leakage on the import side not as an end in itself but only as a necessary means of achieving the overarching environmental objective. This is a subtle but important distinction.

6.5 *Respect of the Environmental Governance Principle: The Measure Is Always Calibrated to Carbon Emissions*

Keeping in mind the foregoing discussions regarding the concept of *de facto* discrimination, the important point to note is that the ETS/CBAM is even-handed because it is always calibrated to carbon emissions. That is, it merely sets out to ensure that all the relevant products produced or sold in the EU have paid a carbon price at least once. If a carbon price has not been paid in the non-EU country, a CBAM payment will be due. If a carbon price has been paid in the non-EU country, no CBAM payment will be due.

It is important in this context to think carefully about what one means by the concept of discrimination on grounds of origin. What that concept actually means is that two identical products are treated differently only because of their origin. If they are treated differently for any other reason, one is not looking at discrimination on grounds of origin at all but at discrimination on grounds of whatever that other difference may be. Here, the difference is whether or not a carbon price has been paid. In other words, once it is demonstrated that the ETS/CBAM is consistent with Article XX of GATT 1994, the logical conclusion is actually that it does not involve *de facto* discrimination at all. Hence the observation that what is really going on, or at least what should really be going on, is not a bifurcated analysis but rather an integrated or unitary analysis.

No doubt complainants will seek to scrutinise any differences between the ETS and the CBAM. Such differences certainly exist for a variety of very good reasons. For example, the ETS is a cap and trade system. One could not have such a cap and trade system on the import side without introducing quantitative restrictions, which would be more trade restrictive. And in any event one could not reasonably, as a regulating authority, have the pretension to cap production in non-EU countries.

Consistent with the EU pursuit of higher environmental regulatory ambition, the carbon price is set by the European Union, not on the basis of some kind of global analysis, as some have argued. Such a calculation would essentially be impossible, since carbon pricing depends precisely on regulation, which is absent in many third countries. And in any event, it would be impossible to gather accurate data necessary for making the calculation.

6.6 *Nudging Trading Partners to Price Carbon as a Legitimate Governance Objective*

It should now be apparent from the foregoing discussion that the key feature of the measure is the regulatory incentive for non-EU countries to introduce carbon pricing of their own, at least for exports to the EU. This is the regulatory nudge that is designed to overcome the blockage at the level of the Paris Agreement and to catalyse the necessary action by other countries. In this respect, the EU is not conditioning access to its market by using a stick. It is using instead a carrot, albeit one that has been created by designing a particular, non-discriminatory, regulatory framework. That is, it is creating a situation in which the exporting member faces a choice: either it does not introduce carbon pricing and pays CBAM (to the EU), or it introduces carbon pricing, collects the relevant funds itself, redistributes them as it sees fit and pays no CBAM. All other things being equal, the hope is that this relatively simply calculus will produce the desired result. And the EU hopes that the process may spill over into carbon pricing for the domestic market of the non-EU country and its other export markets, even if this is not directly the object of the measures it has adopted.

This feature confirms that the ETS/CBAM is not a tax but a regulatory measure. There is a certain amount of pseudo-technical analysis that has gone into the question of which substantive obligations under GATT 1994 may be employed in order to assess the ETS/CBAM – that is, whether it is a border or internal measure, a tax (whether direct or indirect) or a regulation. This does not need to be the centre of gravity of the debate, and one should not get lost in the detail, since it will not, or at least should not, change the outcome. The most straightforward observation one can reasonably make is that the ETS/CBAM is, in essence, a behaviour-changing regulatory measure that pursues exclusively legitimate objectives and, at this point, is the least trade-restrictive option available to address the urgent problem of climate change.

It should also be clear that creating an incentive for non-EU countries to adopt carbon pricing, at least for exports to the EU, is a legitimate objective, even though it is in some sense extra-territorial. That flows from the nature of the climate as a common good. The EU cannot simply address itself to the European climate. We must, necessarily, address the climate as a whole.

A carbon price based on the destination principle would not make the same contribution to achieving the overarching legitimate policy objectives of the EU. It would not create the same regulatory nudge for non-EU countries, because no credit would be given for carbon pricing in the non-EU country. In other words, it would not create any incentive for non-EU countries to introduce carbon pricing of their own. Furthermore, on the export side, it would not make the same contribution to the legitimate objectives being pursued (because there would be a rebate). Finally, even though subsidising or supporting exports might seem to enhance trade, when trade deflection and diversion effects are taken into account such measures actually tend to introduce inefficiencies, and at least in this sense would be more trade restrictive. We will return to the question of subsidies, but at this point we may observe that the necessarily relatively intrusive nature of the ETS/CBAM on the import side is nicely and appropriately balanced by forbearance on the export side, given the absence of the rebates that would be associated with a tax based on the destination principle.

6.7 *Transnational Governance on an Even-Handed Basis*

As explained at the beginning of this chapter, an important part of the discussion in the context of the Paris Agreement relates to the balance to be struck between the environmental objective and the development objective, taking into account, in particular, the costs of past industrialisation and pollution. This is quintessentially a matter of international climate change politics, which is precisely why the discussion is stuck and is unlikely to progress further in a timely manner – an unobtainable "*Utopia*" for the time being.[30]

However, the question that we must ask ourselves as lawyers is whether or not, as a matter of law, the WTO requires the EU to integrate the development objective into the ETS/CBAM. The answer to that question is that clearly it does not. The key provision is the chapeau of Article XX of GATT 1994, which refers to countries where the same conditions exist. The question, of course, is what are the relevant conditions – that is, what is the metric by reference to which sameness is to be determined as present or not. Clearly, it cannot be all the characteristics of a country, since no two countries are the same, and if this were the meaning the term 'where the same conditions exist' would be

30 See: Chapter 2, Ernst-Ulrich Petersmann, 'Constitutional Pluralism, Regulatory Competition and Transnational Governance Failures', Section 3, at page [12].

redundant. The answer is that the metric can only be the metric determined by the measure that is being adopted, which here is environmental, and not developmental. There is simply no language in Article XX or in any other provision of GATT 1994 that compels or even supports a different conclusion.

That is not to say that the EU is not concerned about such matters. It is, and there is a host of flanking measures adopted by the EU that are designed to help other countries, including in particular least developed countries and developing countries, to adjust to the EU's new environmental measures and to deal with the challenges posed by climate change. But the point is that, legally, the EU is not required to integrate these concerns into the ETS/CBAM.

6.8 *Transnational Governance Issues with Respect to Exports*

We turn now to briefly address the final piece of the puzzle, which relates to the problem of carbon leakage on the export side. As explained above, in the case of a fiscal measure, the WTO agreements provide for the operation of the destination principle. This means that the rate of tax paid is that in the country where the product is sold. Consistently with this, rebates are granted on exports and the tax at destination imposed on imports. Such arrangements are carved out of WTO subsidies law.[31]

However, as we have also explained above, the ETS/CBAM is not a tax but a regulatory measure, whose purpose is in essence behaviour changing, which is why credit is given for a carbon price paid in the non-EU country. For regulatory measures, there is no equivalent to the destination principle. The SCM Agreement applies. This means that, if subsidies are given (for example, in the form of free allowances), they may not be contingent, in law or in fact, upon export. These would be prohibited subsidies that could not benefit, in law or in fact, from the exceptions in Article XX of GATT 1994.

However, what is perfectly possible is that the EU can grant subsidies that are available indistinctly as regards domestic sales and export sales, such as subsidies for green innovation. We are entitled to do this precisely in order to retain industry on our territory; we are not required to make the subsidies available to firms in all parts of the world.[32] This therefore provides a legitimate policy tool for the EU to address the problem of carbon leakage on the export side. In this respect, it is important to note that the case-law makes it clear that it is not the reason for which a subsidy is granted that determines whether or not it is a subsidy contingent in law or in fact upon export, but

31 SCM Agreement, footnote 1.

32 GATT 1994, Article III:8(b).

rather whether or not it is tied specifically to exports, which would not be the case, for example, with green technology subsidies.

7 Conclusion

As indicated at the outset, this Chapter assimilates the analyses of Petersmann and Steinbach set out elsewhere in this book. However, it is grounded in the "bounded rationalism" both refer to. In the presence of constitutional pluralism, the live question is what, at this point, can realistically be done to address transnational governance failure, specifically with respect to climate change. Answering that question is not about describing a *Utopia*. Rather, drawing from the lessons of history, including the development of the European Union, the live question is more modest: what can be done to set matters in the right *direction of travel*, gradually nudging the global regulatory process towards the essential objective. In the history of economic integration large markets have always in some measure leveraged that characteristic in order to be, in effect, "regulatory exporters". This may be an imperfect approach, but it can be effective. CBAM is the main current example of this process. Critically, it has not been adopted in contravention of the European Union's international trade law obligations and rights, something that could itself be characterised as a transnational governance failure. Rather, from its inception, as explained in this Chapter, it has been carefully designed to be consistent with the balance of those obligations and rights. As such, it represents a legitimate policy tool for responding to transnational governance failures, and probably the only effective model currently available.

Bibliography

Flett J, 'WTO space for national regulation: requiem for a diagonal vector test' [2013] Journal of International Economic Law, Vol. 16, No. 1, 37.

Petersmann E-U, *Constitutional Functions and Constitutional Problems of International Economic Law* (re-print of the 1991 1st edition, Routledge 2020).

Weiler J, 'Law, culture and values in the WTO: gazing into the crystal ball', in Daniel Bethlehem, Donald McRae, Rodney Neufeld and Isabelle Van Damme (eds), *Oxford Handbook of International Trade Law* (Oxford University Press 2009).

CHAPTER 6

Common but Differentiated Constitutionalisms

Does 'Environmental Constitutionalism' Offer Realistic Policy Options for Improving UN Environmental Law and Governance? US and Latin American Perspectives

Erin Daly, Maria Antonia Tigre and Natalia Urzola

1 Introduction

Environmental law and governance have taken many different forms in the Americas in response to climate change mitigation. This chapter describes recent developments in the United States (U.S.), Colombia, and Brazil, highlighting the divergent approaches to climate protection. Notwithstanding the rhetoric of rights in the popular imagination, rights-based approaches have never driven policy in the United States, either in the context of environmental and climate policy or otherwise. Nor has popular will often impelled government action. Nor for that matter has the U.S. tended to be swayed by international winds. Instead, the U.S. tends to rely on a combination of market-based approaches and administrative enforcement of broad legislative principles to advance well-being, in the belief that markets, rather than political or judicial elites, are more likely to be responsive to both existing conditions and popular will. The Inflation Reduction Act of 2022, which contains the most innovative and ambitious climate mitigation goals in the country's history, exemplifies this approach.

Elsewhere in the Americas, however, rights-based approaches have held sway as constitutional courts have been especially responsive to individual and collective claims for environmental protection and climate change mitigation. This has taken the form of increasingly robust environmental constitutionalism. In particular, the courts of Colombia and Brazil have been global pioneers in the recognition of environmental and even climate rights to galvanize political action. Colombia's Constitutional and Supreme Courts have for many years protected environmental rights as part of an integrated web of human rights including rights to food, water, shelter, health, education and dignity for indigenous and non-indigenous communities. Brazil's judiciary has been equally committed to environmental protection. In the summer of 2022, the Brazilian Federal Supreme Tribunal held that the obligation to comply with the Paris Agreement creates enforceable human rights that individuals can vindicate in court and that the government is obligated to respect; failure to establish a climate fund, for instance, is not only a violation of the accord but an actionable violation of a constitutional and human right that controls the government. While the U.S. may provide a model of political and economic approaches to climate mitigation, courts in Latin America, as exemplified by Brazil and Colombia, are providing a model of progressive rights-based judicial action. This chapter analyzes these national examples from a comparative perspective, assessing their promise for climate mitigation and adaptation.

2 Climate Accountability in the United States

In 1981, President Ronald Reagan announced his vision for his presidency in his first inaugural address by boldly declaring: "Government is not the solution to our problem; government is the problem."[1] This echoed another popular president, John F. Kennedy who, in his inaugural address twenty years earlier, invited his "fellow Americans" to "ask not what your country can do for you – ask what you can do for your country."[2] These phrases resonate in the American psyche and reinforce a particular relationship between people and the government, one that looks to private entrepreneurs rather than public servants to address problems that Americans face. Thus, the American government is mostly a negative one, designed to stay out of the way, more than to engage helpfully in the lives of citizens. And that view has remained largely static from the nation's 19th century founding to today, even while the rest of the world has demanded more of their governments and bent the arc of sovereignty around the needs of human and ecological dignity.

2.1 *Strong Constitutionalism across the Globe*

It is perhaps easiest to see the basic structure of American constitutionalism in relief against the backdrop of constitutionalism in the modern world. For most of the world, including Europe, the Americas (outside the United States), Asia, and much of Africa, states are set up, according to their constitutions, to provide for some version of the good life for their citizens.

1 President Ronald Reagan, Inaugural Address (January 20, 1981) available at https://www.reaganfoundation.org/media/128614/inaguration.pdf.

2 President John F. Kennedy's Inaugural Address (*National Archives*, 1961) <www.archives.gov/milestone-documents/president-john-f-kennedys-inaugural-address#:~:text=My%20fellow%20citizens%20of%20the,for%20the%20freedom%20of%20ma> accessed 8 June 2023.

According to Constitution Project, out of the 193 constitutions in force, 140 mention free education, 84 constitutions contain a right to shelter, 63 mention health care, and 44 establish a Human Rights Commission.[3] These numbers reveal the prevalence of social and economic rights in constitutions and, by implication, demonstrate the extent to which people look to the state to solve social problems, to advance social progress, and to progressively realize social justice. The turn toward the social state continues to be relevant both in Europe and in Latin America, where it began roughly simultaneously in the early 20th century – to the point where countries like Colombia, as will be seen below, commit to being an *Estado Social De Derecho* – a social state of rights. Brazil's Constitution contains a single chapter on the social order that is longer than the entire United States Constitution including its amendments, and the Colombian Constitution's 83 articles on Fundamental Rights amount to slightly less than the length of the US Constitution.

For present purposes, the extent and quality of the satisfaction of these promises is not as important as the fact that people expect governments to commit to them and may seek to hold them responsible if they fail to provide. In these countries, the state is looked not only to pass laws and execute them, not only to provide for national security, and to protect economic interests, but to do so in a way that promotes human dignity (mentioned in 161 constitutions[4]); indeed, some constitutions identify the promotion of dignity as the foundation of the constitutional order,[5] or as the very purpose of the state: for example, the Peruvian Constitution asserts that "The defense of the human person and respect for his dignity are the supreme purpose of the society and the State,"[6] and the Dominican Republic puts it this way: "The State bases itself on respect for the dignity of the person and organizes itself for the real and effective protection of the fundamental rights that are inherent to it. The

3 Constitute Project, <https://www.constituteproject.org> accessed 8 June 2023.

4 Constitute Project, <https://www.constituteproject.org/constitutions?lang=en&q=dignity&status=in_force> accessed 8 June 2023.

5 Latvia (1922) was the first to do so: "Latvia as democratic, socially responsible and national state is based on the rule of law and on respect for human dignity and freedom; it recognises and protects fundamental human rights and respects ethnic minorities." (Preamble) and "The State shall protect human honour and dignity." (Art. 95). Latvia Constitution of 1992, reinstated in 1991 with Amendments through 2016 (1992), <https://www.constituteproject.org/constitution/Latvia_2016.pdf?lang=en> accessed 8 June 2023.

6 Constitución Política del Perú (1993), Art. 1. <https://www.congreso.gob.pe/constitucionyreglamento/#:~:text=La%20Constituci%C3%B3n%20Pol%C3%ADtica%20del%20Per%C3%BA,y%20organizaci%C3%B3n%20del%20Estado%20peruano> accessed 8 June 2023.

dignity of the human being is sacred, innate, and inviolable; its respect and protection constitute an essential responsibility of the public powers."[7]

Insisting that states take responsibility for the dignity of people is also evident in Europe at the national and regional levels, where political and judicial bodies routinely use their authority to solve the problems of the day, whether they be economic, social, or political.[8] Here, the very purpose of state sovereignty is to bring about the good life, as Pascal Lamy put it during the conference, both by protecting people from threats (whether they be environmental or anthropogenic or both) and by ensuring that every person is able to live with a modicum of dignity, or a minimum existence.[9] In this view (as described by some of the participants in this conference), the government is not the barrier to international cooperation but its conduit, harnessing (differentiated) sovereign power to address (common) global and regional challenges.

Thus, for most nations on earth, given the varied situations in which people live and the pervasiveness of poverty and discrimination throughout the world, the line between the positive and negative obligations of the state are blurred. This understanding of constitutionalism can be transformative, as the very purpose of the constitutional state evolves over time, always in the direction of "social progress and better standards of life in larger freedom," as the UN Charter proclaims.[10]

2.2 *Thin Constitutionalism in the United States*

This is not so in the United States, whose constitution is famously old and terse. It does not protect against discrimination (as the so-called "Jim Crow" era proved in mandating racial segregation and injustice from cradle to grave well into the post-war era); it includes no social, economic, cultural, or

---

7 Constitución Política de la República Dominicana (2010) Title II Chapter I Section I Art. 38 Human Dignity, <https://observatoriop10.cepal.org/sites/default/files/documents/constitucion_republica_dominicana.pdf> accessed 8 June 2023.

8 As the democratically elected European Parliament explains: Members of the European parliament "fight against new and old attacks on essential liberties. ... Some of these freedoms are as old as Europe: life and liberty, thought and expression. But others have had to be redefined to keep pace with the times. Protecting personal data or prohibiting human cloning were far from the minds of the first elected MEPs, some four decades ago." European Parliament, <https://www.europarl.europa.eu/about-parliament/en/democracy-and-human-rights> accessed 8 June 2023.

9 For the German concept, see I. Leijten, 'The German Right to an Existenzminimum, Human Dignity, and the Possibility of Minimum Core Socioeconomic Rights Protection' (2015) 16(1) German Law Journal 23–48. doi:10.1017/S2071832200019416.

10 United Nations Charter (1945) Preamble, <https://www.un.org/en/about-us/un-charter> accessed 8 June 2023.

environmental rights, nor a right to affirmative action to redress past harms; it contains no privacy rights, nor even a right to vote[11] – much less the rights of indigenous peoples, or other rights extensively protected in constitutions such as Brazil's and Colombia's.

This is all by design. Perhaps the U.S. is unique in having been established by people who did not believe in a strong central government, but rather by slave owners and mercantilists who believed that the less the government did, the more they would prosper. The United States government was designed precisely to keep the peace among the states while ensuring that men could profit financially without concern for the burden it would impose on any others in present and future generations. It was established not to respect human dignity but to allow commerce (including the slave trade) to thrive, to allow states to establish their own rules of conduct (including allowing the establishment of churches, the genocide of native populations, and again the ownership, rape and abuse of other human beings). If there were problems to be solved, the drafters of the national constitution left them to the states to address. The entirety of the national legislative power in the original constitution is contained in 429 words[12] and (with the exception of a trio of powers addressing the end of slavery), it has never been expanded nor amended to permit the government to address social problems. Indeed, most federal legislation designed to tackle the most significant challenges of the day must still be justified either as regulations of interstate commerce or as exercises of federal authority to tax and to spend money, as the 2022 Inflation Reduction Act is.[13] It is well established that the federal government has no general power to act simply to improve the lives of people or to respond to social challenges.[14]

11 The equality right simply prohibits a state from denying "equal protection of the laws," (Amends. V and XIV) but it has been interpreted to prohibit only intentional discrimination (Washington v Davis, 426 U.S. 229 (1976)) and only where the government cannot justify the discrimination, and only on the basis of race and a very few other characteristics. There is no right to privacy, Dobbs v Jackson, and there is no right to vote in federal elections, but simply a prohibition of discrimination in the right to vote on the basis of race (Amend XV), sex (XIX), wealth (XXIV), or age over 18 (XXVI).

12 United States Constitution, Art. I, s. 8, <https://www.archives.gov/founding-docs/constitution-transcript> accessed 8 June 2023.

13 The Affordable Care Act was invalidated as an exercise of the interstate commerce power and upheld only as an exercise of the federal power to spend. National Federation of Independent Business v. Sebelius, 567 U.S. 519 (2012).

14 As the Supreme Court explained in striking down a law that would have prevented people from bringing guns to school zones: "We start with first principles. The Constitution creates a Federal Government of enumerated powers. See Art. I, § 8. As James Madison wrote: "The powers delegated by the proposed Constitution to the federal government are few and defined. Those which are to remain in the State governments are numerous and

Nor has the constitution been updated by text or interpretation since the 19th century. In the 235 years of its existence, it has been amended a scant 27 times: this includes 12 amendments in the first decade after its adoption, another three to end the Civil War and abolish slavery, another 2 dealing with the sale of alcohol, and only 3 in the 20th century expanding individual rights – all prohibiting discrimination in voting.[15] The last time it was amended to expand rights was 1971.[16] The last time it was amended at all was in 1992, making it one of only 28 countries whose constitutions have not been adopted or amended in the 21st century.[17]

One might think that under such circumstances, the courts charged with constitutional application and implementation would ensure that the constitution was relevant to the conditions and needs of the times by interpreting it as a "living instrument," as Colombia and the European Court of Human Rights (ECtHR) do,[18] or as a "living tree" in the Canadian sense.[19] But for most of its history, the United States Supreme Court has taken the opposite view. Rather, it has held tight to the view of the Constitution that many of its framers had: that the limits of federal authority must be strictly adhered to, to ensure maximal opportunity for capitalist enterprise. In the last 10 years alone, as the world has witnessed with increasing alarm the devastation that climate change produces, the U.S. Supreme Court has consistently withheld authority from the federal government to protect the environment, in favor of private interests.[20]

---

indefinite." The Federalist No. 45, pp. 292–293 (C. Rossiter ed. 1961). ... The Constitution ... withhold[s] from Congress a plenary police power that would authorize enactment of every type of legislation. See Art. I, § 8." United States v. Lopez, 514 U.S. 549, 552, 567 (1995).

15 None of these guarantees a right to vote; rather, they all prohibit the denial of the franchise on account of sex (Amend. XIX), poverty (Amend. XXIV), and age for people over 18 (Amend. XXVI).

16 United States Constitution (n 12), Amend. XXVI (prohibiting denial or abridgment of the right to vote of 18-, 19-, and 20-year olds on account of their age).

17 Constitute Project (n 3).

18 Tyrer v. United Kingdom, 26 Eur. Ct. H.R. (ser. A) 26 (1978) at para. 31: "The Court must also recall that the Convention is a living instrument which, as the Commission rightly stressed, must be interpreted in the light of present-day conditions. In the case now before it the Court cannot but be influenced by the developments and commonly accepted standards in the penal policy of the member States of the Council of Europe in this field. Indeed, the Attorney-General for the Isle of Man mentioned that, for many years, the provisions of Manx legislation concerning judicial corporal punishment had been under review."

19 Reference Re Same Sex Marriage, 2004 SCC 79 (CanLII), para. 22: "[O]ur Constitution is a living tree which, by way of progressive interpretation, accommodates and addresses the realities of modern life."

20 See Los Angeles County Flood Control Dist. v. NRDC, 568 U.S. 78 (2013) (limiting EPA's authority under the Clean Water Act); Utility Air Regulatory Group v. EPA, 573 U.S. 302

Most recently, in 2023, the Supreme Court again limited the EPA's authority to regulate wetlands to waters encompassing "only those relatively permanent, standing or continuously flowing bodies of water 'forming geographic[al] features' that are described in ordinary parlance as 'streams, oceans, rivers, and lakes,'" quoting nothing more than an earlier case and two dictionary entries. This holding can have a "catastrophic"[21] effect on the federal government's ability to protect wetlands throughout the country, which increases the risks associated with climate change. As the NRDC explains, "wetlands 'are among the most productive ecosystems in the world, comparable to rainforests and coral reefs.' By regulating water flow, they dramatically lessen the impact of both floods and droughts. They provide habitat for all manner of fish, birds, mammals, insects, reptiles, and amphibians. And they do all of these things while storing massive amounts of carbon in their abundant vegetation – making safeguarding wetlands a valuable natural climate solution."[22] The world loses, but the owners of waterfront property will now be able to develop it without having to seek prior authorization from the federal government, just as their 18th century property-owning forebearers could.

Thus, the Supreme Court has usually adhered to a historic view of constitutional application, thereby closing avenues to demand more of government than a few elite men from over 200 years ago would have wanted. Procedurally as well, the Supreme Court has more often closed the doors to the courthouse than opened them: it has developed extraordinarily high barriers to establish standing, for instance, and has never developed the kinds of procedures accepted in other countries to hold government accountable, such as Brazil's claim for noncompliance, or Colombia's *tutela* action, discussed below. Furthermore, among the 20th and 21st century innovations that the Supreme Court has rejected is the integration of international, and especially international human rights, law into its domestic constitutionalism. While some

---

(2014) (limiting EPA's authority under the Clean Air Act to treat greenhouse gases as a pollutant for certain purposes); Michigan v. Envtl. Prot. Agency, 576 U.S. ___ (2015) (requiring EPA to consider corporate costs in the decision whether to regulate power plants); West Virginia v. Environmental Protection Agency, 597 U.S. ___ (2022) (limiting EPA authority to regulate power plants).

21 Earthjustice, "Supreme Court Catastrophically Undermines Clean Water Protections," https://earthjustice.org/brief/2023/supreme-court-sackett-clean-water-act (noting that "More than half of the 118 million acres of wetlands in the United States are threatened by this ruling.").

22 NRDC, "What the Supreme Court's Sackett v. EPA Ruling Means for Wetlands and Other Waterways: How the twisting of words in the Clean Water Act spells disaster," quoting the EPA, at https://www.nrdc.org/stories/what-you-need-know-about-sackett-v-epa.

constitutions require this,[23] and some countries – like Colombia – see themselves as monist in terms of the integration of international law, the United States is not among them, and its Supreme Court usually declines to look abroad for guidance or incorporate international norms, including *jus cogens*, into its analysis. Indeed, its refusal to engage with environmental and climate justice is just one example of its willingness to be a global outlier.

The United States' deeply rooted commitment to a limited national government is not necessarily a rejection of popular will. Rather, it could be seen as a choice to understand popular will as reflected in market choices rather than as the product of electoral decisions. Through its spending power, the Congress can advance a social policy not by compelling behavior (with all the bureaucracy and consistency and expense of enforcement that regulation requires in order to be effective) but by providing additional choices to people about how, when, and how much to comply and by incentivizing, rather than compelling, policy choices. Using its spending power, Congress can offer financial benefits to those who choose a certain course of conduct over another – essentially offering carrots to those who change their behavior rather than using stick against those who do not. For instance, in the last few years, the Congress has used not its regulatory authority but its spending power to accomplish systemic health care reform,[24] respond to the economic crisis resulting from the COVID crisis,[25] and improve infrastructure.[26] In a certain sense, this too advances dignity by enhancing opportunities for agency and reasoned decision-making and limiting regulatory compulsion. It is too early to tell if this approach is

23 See, e.g. South Africa Constitution, Art. 39.1: "39. Interpretation of Bill of Rights: When interpreting the Bill of Rights, a court, tribunal or forum a. must promote the values that underlie an open and democratic society based on human dignity, equality and freedom; b. must consider international law; and c. may consider foreign law." The Constitution of the Republic of South Africa (1996) <https://www.gov.za/documents/constitution/constitution-republic-south-africa-1996-1> accessed 8 June 2023; Spain Constitution, Part I, Section 10: "Provisions relating to the fundamental rights and liberties recognized by the Constitution shall be construed in conformity with the Universal Declaration of Human Rights and international treaties and agreements thereon ratified by Spain." Constitución Española (1978) <https://www.boe.es/legislacion/documentos/ConstitucionCASTELLANO.pdf> accessed 8 June 2023.

24 Patient Protection and Affordable Care Act of 2010, Pub. L. No. 111–148, 124 Stat. 119 (2010).

25 H.R.1319 – 117th Congress (2021–2022): American Rescue Plan Act of 2021, H.R.1319, 117th Cong. (2021), <https://www.congress.gov/bill/117th-congress/house-bill/1319/text> accessed 8 June 2023.

26 H.R.3684 – 117th Congress (2021–2022): Infrastructure Investment and Jobs Act, H.R.3684, 117th Cong. (2021), <https://www.congress.gov/bill/117th-congress/house-bill/3684> accessed 8 June 2023.

as effective as regulation to address climate change; we do know that waiting for the national government to respond legislatively or regulatorily to climate change has produced not behavioral change but more climate change. And courts have not been eager to intervene. With this in mind, it is not hard to see why environmental constitutionalism would not fare well as a regulatory matter in the form of command-and-control legislation as is popular in Europe, nor in the federal courts of the United States. As we will see, elsewhere in the Americas – notably in Brazil and Colombia – judicially managed environmental constitutionalism is the approach of choice.

2.3 *A Market-Based Approach to Climate Change: the Inflation Reduction Act of 2022*

In 2022, the United States Congress adopted landmark legislation designed to mitigate and adapt to the impacts of climate change in a way that is aligned with American (U.S.) sensibilities about the role of the federal government in responding to major social issues and adhering to faith in the markets over faith in government regulation to solve social problems.

Many things about the legislation havc garnered attention. First, the spending commitment is enormous: most estimates put it at $369 billion,[27] but some estimate that the overall impact could be as much as $800 billion.[28] Second, it is the private sector, rather than government, that is expected to do the work of mitigation[29] (just as Presidents Kennedy and Reagan suggested it should

27 According to the Secretary of the Treasury, "The Inflation Reduction Act is the single most significant legislation to combat climate change in our nation's history, investing a total of $369 billion to help build a clean energy economy. Nearly three-quarters of that climate change investment – an estimated $270 billion – is delivered through tax incentives, putting Treasury at the forefront of this landmark legislation." 'Treasury Announces Guideline on Inflation Reduction Act's Strong Labor Protections,' (*US Department of the Treasury*, 29 November 2022) <https://home.treasury.gov/news/press-releases/jy1128> accessed 8 June 2023.

28 "In fact, Credit Suisse estimates total federal spending at double the headline figure – to over USD 800 billion – sending the total public and private spending mobilized by the IRA to nearly USD 1.7 trillion over the next ten years." 'US Inflation Reduction Act: A catalyst for climate action' (*Credit Suisse*, November 2022) <https://www.credit-suisse.com/about-us-news/en/articles/news-and-expertise/us-inflation-reduction-act-a-catalyst-for-climate-action-202211.html> accessed 8 June 2023.

29 See ibid: "The public spending will likely trigger private sector investment (i.e. the "leverage effect"). The multiplier generally ranges from 1.1x to 1.6x[2], meaning for every dollar of public spending, at least 1.1 dollar would be spent by the private sector. Subsidized lending from the Department of Energy's loan program and Greenhouse Gas Reduction Fund (i.e. green banks) will supercharge green financing."

be). Third, it is expected to be effective in reducing carbon emissions.[30] As one analysis explains: "The legislation includes $369 billion for climate and energy provisions and will contribute to reducing carbon emissions from 2005 levels by approximately 40 percent by 2030 by accelerating the decarbonization of electricity production and other carbon-intensive sectors."[31] According to another, it may even enable the United States to meet its nationally determined contributions under the 2015 Paris Agreement.[32] Moreover, the "significant commitment to a sustainable future aligns the legislation with the principles of" Environmental and Social Governance (ESG).[33] But it accomplishes this not by command-and-control regulation but by extending and enhancing "existing energy-related tax credits and incentives, including those for: Renewable electricity investment and production, Energy storage, Carbon capture, Production of clean hydrogen, Sustainable aviation and biofuels, Electric vehicles and charging infrastructure, Advanced domestic manufacturing, [and] Greenhouse gas reductions."[34]

It will not be known for some time whether the promises of the legislation will be fulfilled. But it is quite likely to be more effective in moving the American economy in a more environmentally sensitive direction than would

30 "Multiple independent analyses show the bill will reduce U.S. greenhouse gas emissions some 40% below 2005 levels by 2030, a big step toward President Biden's goal of cutting them in half by 2030." Fred Krupp, 'The biggest thing Congress has ever done to address climate change' (*Environmental Defense Fund*, August 2022), <https://www.edf.org/blog/2022/08/12/biggest-thing-congress-has-ever-done-address-climate-change> accessed 8 June 2023.

31 ERM, 'Issue Briefing: "Inflation Reduction Act of 2022: Climate and Energy Provisions"' (*ERM*, October 2022), <https://www.erm.com/globalassets/documents/insights/2022/issue-brief-ira-climate-2022-climate-energy-provisions.pdf> accessed 8 June 2023.

32 "Under a business-as-usual scenario (without the IRA), the U.S. would be expected to reduce greenhouse gas (GHG) emissions by between 24% and 35% by 2030 compared to 2005 levels. This reduction is a far cry from the 50–52% reduction target set in the latest U.S. nationally determined contribution (NDC). With the passage of the IRA, GHG reductions are expected to reach 31% to 44% by 2030. When combined with renewed ambition from executive agencies like the EPA and Department of Agriculture, as well as states and cities, the Rhodium Group's modeling suggests that the U.S. can meet its NDC commitment." Melissa Barbanell, 'A Brief Summary of the Climate and Energy Provisions of the Inflation Reduction Act of 2022,' (*World Resources Institute*, October 2022) <https://www.wri.org/update/brief-summary-climate-and-energy-provisions-inflation-reduction-act-2022> accessed 8 June 2023.

33 Michael Stavish, Gabe Rubio & Lisa Kieth, 'ESG and the Inflation Reduction Act of 2022,' (*BDO USA*, October 2022), <https://www.bdo.com/insights/tax/esg-and-the-inflation-reduction-act-of-2022> accessed 8 June 2023.

34 Ibid.

constitutional litigation in the federal or state courts. It thus has the potential to be more environmentally transformative than a judicial order would be in the United States. Environmental litigation, however, has been extremely successful in other parts of the Americas and we turn next to models of environmental constitutionalism from Brazil and then Colombia.

3 The Right to a Healthy Environment in Brazil: the Decision in PSB et al. v. Brazil (on Climate Fund)

In Brazil, the scenario is quite different. Brazil has adopted in 1988 – after the end of the military dictatorship – a carefully crafted constitutional right to a healthy environment with an individual and collective dimension, as well as related responsibilities of governments (national and sub-national). This responsibility has evolved through decades of environmental litigation, and, more recently, through a growing trend of expanding climate litigation.

3.1 *Brazil's Environmental Constitutionalism*

Among the fundamental rights enshrined in Brazil's 1988 constitution is the protection of an ecologically balanced environment, which is essential to the quality of life and belongs to present and future generations.[35] The constitutional protection effectively links environmental protection and human rights by ensuring that a healthy environment is essential for the fulfilment of the fundamental right to human dignity. The right to a healthy environment has an individual and a collective dimension. An infringement of the right can be claimed individually, similarly – and in relation to – violations of other traditional human rights through direct or indirect repercussions. However, the right also has a collective dimension, which applies due to its universal interest for present and future generations. The Brazilian Supreme Court – the country's constitutional court and highest court – has repeatedly affirmed the importance of environmental protection since the constitutional recognition of the right to an ecologically balanced environment.[36] The court considers the

---

35 Constituição da República Federativa do Brasil (1988) art. 225, <https://www.gov.br/cade/en/content-hubs/legislation/brazilian-constitution> accessed 8 June 2023.

36 See, e.g.: (1) Case Antonio de Andrade Ribeiro Junqueira, Supreme Court, Writ of Mandamus [Mandado de Segurança – MS 22164/SP], Merits. Judgment 30.10.1995. 1155–1190; (2) Case Partido Progressista – PP, Supreme Court, Declaratory Action of Constitutionality [Ação Declaratória de Constitucionalidade – ADC 42/DF], Merits. Judgment 28.02.2018; (3) Case Associação Nacional dos Procuradores do Trabalho – ANPT, Supreme Court, Direct Action of Unconstitutionality [Ação Direta de Inconstitucionalidade – ADI 4066/DF],

right to environmental integrity a 'collective right', which both enshrines the principle of solidarity and integrates the process of recognition and expansion of the content of human rights.[37]

Relatedly, the right to a healthy environment sets a positive duty of the government and other stakeholders to defend and protect the environment for present and future generations. As a fundamental right, and therefore different from ordinary duties arising from the relationship with the respective rights and those directly set by the legal text, the right to a healthy environment requires effective implementation through infra-constitutional regulation. Minister Herman Benjamin, a judge at Brazil's superior tribunal, clarifies that one of the characteristics of environmental law in Brazil is that the right and correlated duty have an 'aversion for empty discourse.' Environmental law is, therefore, 'a legal discipline of result, that is only justified by what it reaches, definitely, in the social framework of degrading interventions'.[38]

3.2 *Political Backsliding and Judicial Engagement*

This positive duty became even more pressing during the recent widespread backsliding of environmental and climate laws and policies during Jair Bolsonaro's administration. Bolsonaro, who served as Brazil's president from 2019 to 2022, was criticized for his stance on the environment and his efforts to roll back protections for the Amazon rainforest and other critical ecosystems.[39] One of Bolsonaro's main priorities was to boost economic growth and development, and he took a series of steps to relax environmental regulations and open protected areas for exploitation. This included weakening enforcement of environmental laws, emptying capacities of environmental bodies, reducing the size of protected areas, excluding civil society organizations from participation in environmental policy, reducing the resources available to environmental agencies, and weakening Brazil's environmental and climate

Merits. Judgment 24.08.2017; (4) Case Presidente da República, Supreme Court, Claim for Noncompliance with a Fundamental Precept [Arguição de Descumprimento de Preceito Fundamental – ADPF 101/DF], Merits. Judgment 24.06.2009; and (5) Case Procurador Geral da República, Supreme Court, Direct Action of Unconstitutionality [Ação Direta de Inconstitucionalidade – ADI 3540/DF], Court judgment on injunction (medida cautelar). Judgment 01.09.2005. 408–475.

37 See ibid Case Antonio de Andrade Ribeiro Junqueira.

38 Antônio Herman Benjamin, *Direito Constitucional Ambiental Brasileiro* (Saraiva, 2010).

39 Barnabé Lucas de Oliveira Neto, 'Da lama ao caos: o retrocesso da política e liderança ambiental do Brasil sob o governo Bolsonaro' (2022) 25(2) *Novos Cadernos NAEA* 59.

commitments at the international level.[40] Bolsonaro was skeptical of the Paris Agreement, claiming it jeopardized Brazil's sovereignty over the Amazon rainforest,[41] and he extensively criticized the global effort to combat climate change as a threat to Brazil's economic growth.

The environmental rollbacks by the federal government resulted in a significant increase in GHG emissions.[42] Placed within the wider context of deregulation of environmental laws, this has led certain political parties to bring a series of constitutional actions to the Brazilian Constitutional Court challenging state responsibility for the climate crisis. These cases, analyzed here, are part of a broader movement by civil society organizations that brought a series of climate litigation cases in Brazil, demanding compliance with the obligations established in national legislation and international law, and implementation of public policies to protect the environment, including concerning the climate crisis.[43] During the period 2022–2023, the Constitutional Court analyzed environmental and climate cases (the "Green Agenda"), marking a historical moment that established the court as a climate action actor.[44] The cases bring an abstract review of constitutional law before the Supreme Court in light of an apparent conflict between federal law, state law, or other normative acts and the federal constitution. These types of concentrated control cases, or abstract cases, are characterized by "abstraction, generality, and

40 ISA, 'A anatomia do desmonte das políticas socioambientais' (*Instituto Socioambiental*, January 2019), <https://site-antigo.socioambiental.org/pt-br/blog/blog-do-isa/a-anatomia-do-desmonte-das-politicas-socioambientais> accessed 8 June 2023.

41 GAIER, 'R. V. Bolsonaro diz que pode retirar Brasil do Acordo de Paris se for eleito' (*UOL*, September 2018), <https://noticias.uol.com.br/politica/eleicoes/2018/noticias/reuters/2018/09/03/bolsonaro-diz-que-pode-retirar-brasil-do-acordo-de-paris-se-for-eleito.htm> accessed 8 June 2023.

42 Joana Setzer, Guilherme JS Leal, & Caio Borges, 'Climate Change Litigation in Brazil: Will Green Courts Become Greener' in Ivano Alogna, Christine Bakker & Jean-Pierre Gauci (eds), *Climate Change Litigation: Global Perspectives* (Leiden, Boston: Brill Nijhoff, 2021) 143–172. ISBN: 978-90-04-44761-5 (e-book).

43 Julia M. Neiva & Gabriel AS Mantelli, '¿Existe un enfoque brasileño para los litigios climáticos? La crisis climática, la inestabilidad política y las posibilidades de litigio en Brasil' in C. G. Rodríguez (ed) *Litigar la emergencia climática*, (Ciudad Autónoma de Buenos Aires: Siglo XXI Editores Argentina, 2022) 393; 403; Alessandra Lehmen, 'Advancing Strategic Climate Litigation in Brazil' (2021) 22(3) German Law Journal 1471; 1472.

44 Política Por Inteiro, 'Pauta verde no STF abre caminho para retomar a política climática brasileira' (*Política por Inteiro*, March 2021) <https://www.politicaporinteiro.org/2022/03/29/pauta-verde-stf/> accessed 8 June 2023.

impersonality," and can be brought by a limited type of actors and are directly analyzed by the constitutional court.[45]

3.3 *The Incorporation of Climate Treaties into Domestic Law: the Supranational Obligation to Mitigate Climate Impacts*

The case analyzed here was brought in 2020 using a constitutional mechanism called Claim for Noncompliance with a Fundamental Precept (Arguição de Descumprimento de Preceito Fundamental – ADPF). In 2019, political parties filed ADPF 708, requiring the Brazilian government to combat climate change as part of their constitutional right to a healthy environment. In particular, plaintiffs claimed that Climate Fund payments had not been disbursed. Brazil's Climate Fund was created in 2009 as a financial instrument of its National Policy on Climate Change.[46] Its annual budget is to be allocated to projects and studies aimed at mitigating and adapting to climate change. However, in 2019 and 2020, the Bolsonaro administration failed to allocate the available resources. Therefore, the plaintiffs sought a declaration of 'unconstitutional omission' against the paralysis of the Fund's operations and governance and an injunction compelling the government to reactivate the Fund.

Grounded in the right to a healthy environment, the case specifically challenges the procedural duties of the state as it pertains to its political accountability in the context of climate change (i.e., providing reliable scientific information on climate change, transparency of policies and allocation of funds, and participation of communities in climate policies).[47] The plaintiffs argued that the government's failure to fulfill its obligations to reduce greenhouse gas emissions and protect the environment resulted in negative impacts on the health and well-being of the Brazilian people and jeopardized ecosystems and essential ecological processes. In July 2022, the Supreme Court found, in an unprecedented decision, that the Paris Agreement is a human rights treaty and that, as such, has supra-national status that binds the political

45 The heads of the executive power at the federal and state levels, legislative powers at the federal and state levels, the Attorney General of the Republic, the Brazilian Bar Association, political parties, and trade union confederation or class entities. Art. 103, Brazilian Constitution n 34.

46 Maria A. Tigre, 'Brazil's First Climate Case to Reach the Supreme Court' (*OpinioJuris*, October 2020). <http://opiniojuris.org/2020/10/13/brazils-first-climate-case-to-reach-the-supreme-court/> accessed 8 June 2023.

47 Gabrielle Albuquerque, Gabrielle Tabares Fagundez, & Roger Fabre, 'Emergência Climática e Direitos Humanos: o caso do Fundo Clima no Brasil e as obrigações de Direito Internacional' (2022) 19(1) Brazilian Journal of International Law 126.

branches of the state.[48] The Supreme Court thus confirmed that there is a 'constitutional, supra-legal and legal duty' to protect the environment and combat climate change.

When the Paris Agreement was negotiated, there was much disagreement about the extent of its commitment to human rights. In the end, human rights were relegated to a passing reference in the preamble, which notes that 'climate change is a common concern of humankind' and 'Parties should, when taking action to address climate change, respect, promote and consider their respective obligations on human rights'.[49] While the former UN special rapporteur on human rights and the environment, John Knox, has previously argued that the Paris Agreement is a human rights treaty,[50] the Brazilian court is the first to recognize it as such formally.[51]

Furthermore, the Supreme Court clarified that environmental law treaties constitute a particular type of human rights treaty, which enjoy 'supranational' status. This 'supralegality' of human rights treaties means that they are above 'ordinary' laws in the legal hierarchy.[52] Thus, according to the decision, there is no legally valid option to simply not act in the fight against climate change.[53] If a law passed by Congress conflicts with a provision of a human rights treaty, the human rights treaty (and based on this ruling, environmental and climate treaties) prevails. In practice, the law in question is overridden by the treaty. Accordingly, any Brazilian law or decree that contradicts the Paris Agreement, including the Nationally Determined Contributions, may be invalidated. Any action or omission contrary to this protection directly violates the constitution

---

48 PSB et al. v. Brazil (on Climate Fund) (ADPF 708) <http://climatecasechart.com/non-us-case/psb-et-al-v-federal-union/> accessed 8 June 2023.

49 Conference of the Parties, Adoption of the Paris Agreement, Dec. 12, 2015, U.N. Doc. FCCC/CP/2015/L.9/Rev/1 (Dec. 12, 2015), Preamble. <https://unfccc.int/resource/docs/2015/cop21/eng/l09r01.pdf> accessed 8 June 2023.

50 John Knox, 'The Paris Agreement as a Human Rights Treaty', in Dapo Akande and others (eds), *Human Rights and 21st Century Challenges: Poverty, Conflict, and the Environment* (Oxford, 2020).

51 Maria A. Tigre, 'Advancements in Climate Rights in Courts Around the World' (*Climate Law Blog*, 2022) <https://blogs.law.columbia.edu/climatechange/2022/07/01/advancements-in-climate-rights-in-courts-around-the-world/> accessed 8 June 2023.

52 Antonio M. Maués, 'Supra-Legality of International Human Rights Treaties and Constitutional Interpretation' (2013) 10(18) International journal on human rights Sur, [English edition]: 205–223. <https://sur.conectas.org/wp-content/uploads/2017/11/sur18-eng-antonio-moreira-maues.pdf> accessed 8 June 2023; Maria A. Tigre, 'South America' in Lavanya Rajamani and Jaqueline Peel (eds), *The Oxford Handbook of International Environmental Law*. (Oxford: Oxford University Press, 2021).

53 Tigre, n 50.

and human rights. Therefore, as Justice Roberto Barroso explained, any doubts that the climate issue falls within the context of Article 225 and concerns a fundamental human right are dispelled.[54]

The government had contended that the Climate Fund, deriving from Brazil's international commitments within the scope of multilateral treaties on climate change, does not bind the government to its mandatory compliance since it is not a Brazilian law. However, the majority ruled that climate protection is a constitutional value. As such, the government's constitutional environmental protection mandate is not a discretionary political decision but a mandatory obligation.[55] The constitutional duty to allocate the funds effectively means that there is an obligation to mitigate climate change considering the international commitments under the climate change framework.[56] Accordingly, the executive branch has a constitutional duty to execute and allocate the funds of the Climate Fund to mitigate climate change based on the separation of powers and the constitutional right to a healthy environment. The court further found that the judiciary, in turn, must act to avoid the regression of environmental – and climate – protection. Finally, the Court held that the government's discretion in allocating the funds is subject to judicial review.[57] The decision prohibits the 'contingency' of such amounts based on the constitutional right to a healthy environment.

Justice Barroso, writing for the majority, also emphasized the role of the Court in preventing setbacks to the protection of fundamental rights.[58] This, too, is a binding obligation and not a matter of 'free political choice'. The court determined that the executive must allocate resources to operate the Climate Fund, curing its intentional and wrongful omissions in violation of Articles 225 and 5, § 2, of the Federal Constitution.[59]

---

54 Moreira, D.A. et al., Rights-based climate litigation in Brazil: An assessment of constitutional cases before the Brazilian Supreme Court, Journal of Human Rights Practice (forthcoming, 2023).

55 De Azevedo et al., 'O Fundo Clima e as lições do Ministro Barroso' (*Migalhas*, June 2022) <https://www.migalhas.com.br/depeso/368577/o-fundo-clima-e-as-licoes-do-ministro-barroso> accessed 8 June 2023.

56 Tigre, n 50.

57 Ibid.

58 ADPF Nº 708, Supremo Tribunal Federal, 01.07.2022, 8 <http://climatecasechart.com/non-us-case/psb-et-al-v-federal-union/> accessed 8 June 2023.

59 Id., at 2.

3.4 *Implications for Brazil's Climate Constitutionalism*

De Azevedo et al. argue that the ADPF 708 case mandates the duty to efficiently allocate the Fund's resources to preserve its original function.[60] This advancement can avoid the mismanagement of funds intended for mitigation and adaptation. Furthermore, the decision contributes to unravelling the much-needed climate finance to a net zero transition in Brazil's economy.[61] The resources from the Climate Fund (estimated to be around R$ 1.1 billion) are, therefore, essential in ensuring the implementation of policies to increase Brazil's ambition.

This case and others like it have advanced the argument that the climate system should be understood as an integral part of an ecologically balanced environment.[62] Plaintiffs have increasingly argued that the effectiveness of the fundamental human right to a healthy environment depends, at least in part, on climatic conditions that enable a dignified life.[63] The diversity of constitutional human rights cited in climate disputes demonstrates the essential interdependence between the right to an ecologically balanced environment and other fundamental rights.[64] There is a close correlation between Article 225 and several other fundamental rights in Brazilian climate cases: the rights to life (Article 5), health (Articles 6 and 196), and free enterprise (Article 170) – the latter lists environmental defense as one of its guiding principles (Article 170, item VI) – as well as the rights of indigenous peoples (Article 231), children and adolescents (Article 227). The rights of indigenous populations are invoked mainly in cases seeking to combat the advance of deforestation in Brazil. The violation of native communities' rights also draws attention to the unequal impact of climate change on indigenous peoples due to their close relationship with and dependency on the natural environment. In line with the terms of Advisory Opinion 23/2017 of the IACtHR, the right

60 De Azevedo et al., n 54.

61 Caio Borges, 'STF reconhece Acordo de Paris como tratado de direitos humanos (e por que isso importa)' (*re/set,* July 2022) <https://www.capitalreset.com/stf-reconhece-acordo-de-paris-como-tratado-de-direitos-humanos-e-por-que-isso-importa/> accessed 8 June 2023.

62 Danielle de Andrade Moreira, *Litigância climática no Brasil: argumentos jurídicos para a inserção da variável climática no licenciamento ambiental*. (Coleção Interseções. Série Estudos, Rio de Janeiro: Editora PUC-Rio, 2021) ISBN: 978-65-88831-32-8 (e-book). <http://www.editora.puc-rio.br/cgi/cgilua.exe/sys/start.htm?infoid=956&sid=3> accessed 8 June 2023.

63 Moreira et al., n 53.

64 The UN Special Rapporteur on Human Rights and the Environment has already recognized the interdependence and the impact of the climate crisis in the enjoyment of human rights (UN General Assembly 2019: 18–24).

to a healthy environment constitutes a human right in and of itself and it is the basis for the enjoyment of other rights necessary for a dignified minimum existence.[65]

The decision in the ADPF 708 case has been widely recognized as the most important judgment on climate litigation in Brazil to date.[66] Environmental advocates have hailed it as a significant victory, underscoring the importance of using the courts to address the pressing issue of climate change. The case has been commended for its role in addressing the urgent problem of climate change and is considered a landmark in the field of environmental law, setting a precedent for similar cases worldwide. Its significance lies in its contribution to Brazil's efforts to combat climate change and its impact on the constitutional interpretation of the right to a healthy environment.

Specifically, the ADPF 708 case provides practical implementation of the right to a healthy environment by clarifying its scope and meaning in relation to climate change and the mismanagement of funds essential to tackling the climate crisis. It is therefore an important development in the constitutional interpretation of the right to a healthy environment. Procedurally, the case has enabled direct engagement with the constitutional court, providing a more effective way to promote access to justice and ensure that the matter is dealt with rapidly. This is in contrast to an ordinary action, which would likely take years to reach the constitutional court. Subsequent actions that rely on the Paris Agreement and seek to ensure its implementation can now draw on the constitutional interpretation of the right to the environment provided by the Court, which is more favorable to pro-climate plaintiffs.

65 Maria A. Tigre & Natalia Urzola, 'The 2017 Inter-American Court's Advisory Opinion: Changing the Paradigm for International Environmental Law in the Anthropocene' (2021) 12(1) Journal of Human Rights and the Environment 24–50. https://doi.org/10.1111/reel.12400.

66 Isabella Kaminski, 'Brazilian court world's first to recognise Paris Agreement as human rights treaty' (*Clima Home News*, 2022) <https://www.climatechangenews.com/2022/07/07/brazilian-court-worlds-first-to-recognise-paris-agreement-as-human-rights-treaty/> accessed 8 June 2023; Duda Menegassi, 'Em vitória histórica, STF reconhece proteção do clima como dever constitucional' (*Jornal O Eco*, 2022) <https://oeco.org.br/noticias/em-vitoria-historica-stf-reconhece-protecao-do-clima-como-dever-constitucional/> accessed 8 June 2023.

4 Lessons from Colombia's Constitutional Expansionism

Colombia's 1991 Constitution was groundbreaking in the country's civil law tradition.[67] Based on an *Estado Social de Derecho* model,[68] the Constitution places significant emphasis on social and economic rights as the basis of human dignity.[69] In particular, the Constitution establishes a list of 'fundamental' rights, centered on both individual and collective interests. These fundamental rights are regarded as the most basic rights of all Colombian citizens and as such have been granted the highest standard of protection.[70] The Constitution divides them into individual and collective rights according to the interest they protect and the mechanism designed to uphold them. Among these latter set of rights are environmental rights.[71] As widely discussed by prominent scholars, the special emphasis on environmental rights, with over 30 articles dedicated to environmental protection, makes Colombia's constitution a true ecological constitution.[72]

The Constitution also established the Constitutional Court (CC) as the court of final review of all constitutional law issues[73] and created an expedited judicial mechanism specifically designed and exclusively applied to the protection against the violation or threat of violation of fundamental individual rights.[74]

---

67 Luz Estella Nagle, 'Evolution of the Colombian Judiciary and the Constitutional Court' (1995) 6(1) Indiana International and Comparative Law Review 59–90; 60.

68 "[A] social state under the rule of law, organized in the form of a unitary republic, decentralized, with autonomy of its territorial units, democratic, participatory, and pluralistic, based on the respect of human dignity, the work and solidarity of the individuals who belong to it, and the prevalence of the general interest". Elizabeth Macpherson, et al., 'Where ordinary laws fall short: 'riverine rights' and constitutionalism' (2021) 30(3) Griffith Law Review 438–473, 448 DOI: 10.1080/10383441.2021.1982119

69 Chris Thornhill & Carina Rodrigues de Araújo Calabria, 'Global Constitutionalism and Democracy: The case of Colombia' (2020) 2 Jus Cogens 155–183; 161. https://doi.org/10.1007/s42439-020-00024-z. See also, Laura Betancur-Restrepo, 'The Colombian Legal Framework for Social Rights and the Challenges of a Post-conflict Society', in Katharina Boele-Woelki & Diego Fernández Arroyo (eds) 52 *Ius Comparatum – Global Studies in Comparative Law* (Springer, Cham., 2021) 47–78; 48–49. https://doi.org/10.1007/978-3-030-57324-9_2.

70 Constitution Política de Colombia (1991), art. 4 and 5, and Title II. <http://www.secretariasenado.gov.co/senado/basedoc/constitucion_politica_1991.html> accessed 8 June 2023.

71 Ibid., art. 79, 80 and 81. Also included in arts. 1, 2, 8, 49, 86, 88, 95, 333, 366.

72 Macpherson et al., n 67 at 448.

73 Nagle, n 66 at 59.

74 Colombian Constitution n 69, art. 86. See also Decree 2591 of 1991 for further rules of procedure. <http://www.secretariasenado.gov.co/senado/basedoc/decreto_2591_1991.html> accessed 8 June 2023.

The *tutela*, as it is known in Colombian constitutional law, (similar to *amparo* mechanism in other jurisdictions) has become the preferred mechanism to uphold fundamental individual rights in Colombia in part because it holds priority over other judicial proceedings, and judicial bodies are bound to very strict decision times.[75] Furthermore, every judicial entity in Colombia has competence to hear matters brought before them through *tutelas*, albeit subject to specific competences based on subject-matter jurisdiction.[76] However, the CC is Colombia's highest judicial body in constitutional matters and as such is the main entity to uphold constitutional provisions.[77] The CC receives all *tutela* decisions and submit them to a judicial review procedure where only some are selected depending on different criteria, such as the need to unify a particular fundamental rights interpretation (known as unifying rulings-*sentencias de unificación-*) or the importance of a particular case of fundamental rights violations (known as *tutela* judicial review – *sentencia de revisión de tutela*).[78] The third type of decisions the CC adopts are exclusive to this body and relate to the constitutionality of a specific provision, legislation or statute (known as constitutionality rulings-*sentencias de constitucionalidad-*).[79]

A second device to assert constitutional rights is the acción popular.[80] This device was intended to allow any person, regardless of standing or particular interest in the matter, to bring action to protect collective rights and interests, including the right to a healthy environment.[81] Notably, unlike the *tutela*, the *acción popular* does not convey the same preferential treatment. It must comply with standard rules of procedure and is not subject to judicial review by the Constitutional Court. As a result, many claims regarding the protection of the environment are often delayed in time. However, if a fundamental right of individual nature is being threatened or violated in tandem with the right to a healthy environment, the case will acquire priority due to related actions criterion (*conexidad*) and can be heard via the *tutela*.[82] Due to the increasing recognition of the link and interdependence between the right to a healthy

75 Ibid.

76 Decree 2591 of 1991 n 73, arts. 37 to 41.

77 Ibid., art. 33.

78 Colombian Constitution n 69, art. 241.

79 Ibid.

80 Ibid., art. 88. See also Law 472 of 1998 for further rules of procedure. <http://www.secretariasenado.gov.co/senado/basedoc/ley_0472_1998.html> accessed 8 June 2023.

81 Nagle, n 66 at 84.

82 See, e.g., Constitutional Court Decision T-341/16 (2016), <https://www.corteconstitucional.gov.co/relatoria/2016/t-341-16.htm> accessed 8 June 2023. See also Betancur-Restrepo, n 68 at 57.

environment and the enjoyment of other fundamental individual rights, many environmental claims in Colombia are being heard via *tutela*.

Hence, the entirety of the judicial branch in Colombia hears fundamental rights cases, resulting in diverse and progressive decisions throughout the country. Sometimes these decisions coincide in their overall interpretation of the situation, whereas other times contradictory decisions have been made, which has occasionally led to turmoil and unrest. In any case, judges across the country have started to put forth innovative theories resulting in what can be called rights expansionism. The following subsection will dive deeper on what rights expansionism looks like in Colombia regarding environmental rights.

4.1 *Rights Expansionism through Stakeholders' Recognition*

Colombia's judiciary, remarkably the CC, is transformative and progressive, despite its civil law tradition.[83] Colombian judges have shown openness towards expanding dominant visions of democratic constitutionalism and rights' creation and interpretation to extend their benefits to historically marginalized groups.[84] Rights expansionism in Colombia has taken many forms, one of which is the increasing recognition of subjects of rights outside the dominant standard. Colombia's constitution is considered a living instrument and as such its judicial interpretation allows broadening its initial scope, albeit not without restriction.[85] Furthermore, Colombia follows a monist tradition where international agreements and treaties ratified by the country acquire a constitutional status in the country's normative hierarchy, in addition to the comprehensive bill of fundamental rights.[86] In particular, international human rights law has acquired a privileged position in Colombia's legal framework, where human rights have precedence over domestic norms and human rights treaties should act as interpretative guides for the realization of all constitutional rights and duties.[87] This is predominantly relevant to environmental rights since Colombia is signatory and has ratified most of the international and regional commitments on environmental protection and climate action.

Since its inception, the CC has used progressive approaches to constitutional law. In one of its first decisions, the court asserted its competence to determine

83 Macpherson et al., n 67 at 449. See also Betancur-Restrepo n 68 at 49.

84 Ibid.

85 Thornhill et al., n 68 at 161.

86 Colombian Constitution n 69, arts. 11–15, 93. See also Rodrigo Uprimny, 'The Recent Transformation of Constitutional Law in Latin America: Trends and Challenges' (2011) 89 Texas Law Review 1587–1609; 1591.

87 Thornhill et al., n 68 at 163.

which rights are fundamental and should be protected as such.[88] Thus, many novel interpretations of fundamental rights followed. Furthermore, other courts have also exercised their progressive reasoning through *tutela* decisions, namely the Supreme Court (which is the highest-ranking court on matters of private law) as discussed in detail below. This section examines two sets of decisions adopted via *tutela* (one by the Constitutional Court and the other by the Supreme Court) that demonstrate the country's openness to rights expansionism in the context of environmental rights and climate change.

4.1.1 Rights of Nature: Rivers, the Amazon and Ecosystems

In Colombia, courts have granted legal rights to specific ecosystems, such as the Atrato River,[89] and Colombia's Amazon basin.[90] In that case, Afro-Colombian and Indigenous communities filed a *tutela* against the Colombian government and private companies for the violation of their fundamental rights to life, health, water, food security, culture and territory, along with their right to a healthy environment as a result of the pollution caused by mining activities in the River. The CC agreed, granting protection to the plaintiffs' rights and issuing orders to eradicate mining and decontaminate the river.

Significantly, the CC went beyond the customary recognition of human rights violation of plaintiffs and expanded this protection *to* the Atrato River. The CC ordered the recognition of the river as a subject of rights invoking the ecological nature of the Colombian Constitution.[91] The CC concluded that the superior interest of nature could be explained through an eco-centric perspective, where nature is considered a right-bearing entity and where plural worldviews take center stage.[92] The CC supported this decision

88 Ibid. at 165.

89 Constitutional Court of Colombia, Judgment T-622/16, 10 November 2016 (Atrato River Case unofficial translation) <https://delawarelaw.widener.edu/files/resources/riveratr atodecisionenglishdrpdellaw.pdf> accessed 8 June 2023. See also Héctor Herrera-Santoyo, 'The Rights of Nature (Rivers) and Constitutional Actions in Colombia' (*GNHRE*, July 2019) <https://gnhre.org/2019/07/08/the-rights-of-nature-rivers-and-constitutional-acti ons-in-colombia/#_ftn3> accessed 8 June 2023.

90 Paola Andrea Acosta Alvarado & Daniel Rivas-Ramírez, 'A Milestone in Environmental and Future Generations' Rights Protection: Recent Legal Developments before the Colombian Supreme Court' (2018) 30(3) Journal of Environmental Law 519–526; Paola Villavicencio Calzadilla,. 'A Paradigm Shift in Courts' Views on Nature: The Atrato River and Amazon Basin Cases in Colombia' (2019) 15 Law, Environment and Development Journal 1–11 <https://lead-journal.org/content/19049.pdf> accessed 8 June 2023.

91 Atrato River case n 88, para. 9.31 and 9.32.

92 Ibid., para 9.30.

on the *Estado Social de Derecho* and multiculturalism to grant rights to the river.[93]

Following this recognition of the rights of nature and relying almost entirely on this decision, the Supreme Court also recognized the Amazon rainforest as a subject of rights in the Future Generations case studied in the following section. This judicial reasoning has been echoed by other domestic judges who have furthered the rights of nature paradigm to accord rights to different ecosystems and features of nature throughout the country, including moors, national parks and other rivers.[94] As stated by Gómez-Betancur (2020), this approach strengthens environmental constitutionalism by extending protection beyond the human being to other living beings.[95]

4.1.2 Children, Youth and Future Generations

Usually, the judicial apparatus is set into motion by adults. Children and youth are often regarded as mere victims, whose rights need to be protected by adults who file actions on their behalf. However, in recent years children and youth have started to take matter into their own hands appearing before the courts and international negotiation bodies to demand protection of their rights.[96] They have also brought up the need to protect the rights of generations yet to come, especially as it relates to the enjoyment of a healthy environment as a precondition to the enjoyment of other human rights.[97]

One of the first decisions adopted in favor of children, youth and future generations' rights is the 2018 Colombia's Supreme Court decision known

---

93 Ibid., para 6.9 and 6.10. See also Phillip Wesche, 'Rights of Nature in Practice: A Case Study on the Impacts of the Colombian Atrato River Decision' (2021) 33(3) Journal of Environmental Law 531–555; 539, https://doi.org/10.1093/jel/eqab021.

94 Luisa Gómez-Betancur, Sandra Vilardy & David Torres, 'Ecosystem Services as a Promising Paradigm to Protect Environmental Rights of Indigenous Peoples in Latin America: the Constitutional Court Landmark Decision to Protect Arroyo Bruno in Colombia' (2022) 69 Environmental Management 768–780; 769 <https://doi.org/10.1007/s00267-021-01483-w> accessed 8 June 2023.

95 Luisa Gómez-Betancur, 'The Rights of Nature in the Colombian Amazon: Examining Challenges and Opportunities in a Transitional Justice Setting' (2020) 25(1) UCLA Journal of International Law and Foreign Affairs <https://escholarship.org/uc/item/5bk379rd> accessed 8 June 2023.

96 June Flora & Connie Roser-Renouf, 'Climate Change activism and youth', in Patrizia Faustini (ed). *The Challenges of Climate Change: Children on the front line* (Innocenti Insights UNICEF, 2014) <https://www.unicef-irc.org/publications/716-the-challenges-of-climate-change-children-on-the-front-line.html> accessed 8 June 2023.

97 OHCHR, 'Children at the forefront of climate action urge focus on child rights' (*OHCHR*, March 2017) <https://www.ohchr.org/en/stories/2017/03/children-forefront-climate-action-urge-focus-child-rights> accessed 8 June 2023.

as the Future Generations case.[98] Plaintiffs in this case are 25 children and adolescents, in tandem with Dejusticia (a Colombia-based social justice and legal NGO), who sued the Colombian government and several corporations as a result of the government's failure to comply with its international commitment derived from the Paris Agreement and other international law to ensure net-zero Amazon deforestation by 2020.[99] Plaintiffs filed a *tutela* asserting that this failure to comply amounts to a violation of their and future generations' fundamental rights to life, health, human dignity and the right to a healthy environment.[100] The Supreme Court recognized a substantial link between the government's inaction regarding its commitment to reduce deforestation, GHG emissions and the plaintiffs' fundamental rights. Furthermore, the Supreme Court invoked the principle of solidarity to conclude that every generation is entitled to environmental rights, whose protection is endowed by the responsibility of present and past generations.

The Supreme Court's rationale is supported on the recognition of the 'Other' as a rights-bearing entity that extends not only to every other person, animal or plant species on the planet, but also to future generations.[101] The Supreme Court emphasized that the rights of future generations to access natural resources should be protected from violation.[102] In doing so, the Supreme Court developed a dual reading of environmental intergenerational equity: one the one hand, it is based on the ethical duty of solidarity, and on the other on nature's intrinsic value,[103] particularly the Amazon basin deemed the 'world's lung'.[104] Hence, the Supreme Court recognized the Amazon basin as a subject of rights that is a vital ecosystem of global importance. The Supreme Court then concluded that the Colombian state's failure to curb deforestation violated human rights and international climate commitments, such as the Paris Agreement, of present and future generations.[105]

98 Joana Setzer & Lisa Benjamin, 'Climate Litigation in the Global South: Constraints and Innovations' (2020) 9(1) Transnational Environmental Law 77, 87.

99 Corte Suprema de Colombia, Andrea Lozano Barragán y otros v. Minambiente y otros, 11001-2203-000-2018-00319-01, 5 April 2018 <www.elaw.org/system/files/attachments/publicresource/Colombia%202018%20Sentencia%20Amazonas%20cambio%20climatico.pdf> accessed 8 June 2023 (Future Generations case).

100 Ibid 49.

101 Ibid 19.

102 Ibid 20.

103 Ibid 19.

104 Ibid 30.

105 Ibid 37, 39–41.

The Future Generations case was a pioneer and served as a blueprint for other youth climate lawsuits. More importantly, the case opened the door to substantially expanding constitutional provisions to future generations, following the country's progressive and transformational judicial constitutionalism.[106] Generations yet to come are now recognized as right bearers, entitled to environmental rights, thus expanding protection to previously unprotected subjects.

4.2 *Coherent Constitutionalism: the Opportunities and Pitfalls of Colombia's Environmental Constitutional Expansionism*

Colombia's rights expansionism is constantly evolving. Every year, new *tutelas* are filed, creating new opportunities for judicial transformative activism. But despite its many promises, constitutional rights expansionism also confronts some hurdles. This section will provide an overview of both benefits and challenges of constitutional expansionism as it relates to environmental rights protection from a Colombian perspective. This overview is not exhaustive but aims to outline the current state of Colombia's constitutionalism as an avenue for future research.

As Colombia deals with socio-economic development in the midst of the triple planetary crisis, environmental issues are at the core of the country's social conflicts.[107] Environmental issues are among the most salient root causes of the internal armed conflict, which has lasted more than five decades.[108] Unequitable access to land and natural resources fueled the conflict, and the climate and environmental crises exacerbate these precarious conditions.[109] Furthermore, historically marginalized communities remained excluded from decision-making spaces while suffering the hardest consequences of

106 Ibid.

107 Natalia Urzola & Maria P. González, 'When two crises collide: the effects of climate change in the Colombian environmental peacebuilding process' (*Agency for Peacebuilding*, June 2021), <https://www.peaceagency.org/colombian-environmental-peacebuilding-process/> accessed 8 June 2023.

108 This is evidenced in the commitments reached by the 2016 Peace Agreement signed between the Colombian government and the guerrilla FARC-EP. Furthermore, other conflicts are still ongoing in Colombia with other actors. See, generally, Natalia Urzola, 'Derechos de la Naturaleza: un camino hacia la construcción de paz ambiental en Colombia' in Jurisdicción Especial para la Paz, *Conflicto armado, medio ambiente y territorio: Reflexiones sobre el enfoque territorial y ambiental en la Jurisdicción Especial para la Paz* (Bogotá D.C., 2022) 49–85 <https://www.jep.gov.co/Infografas/docs/libro-comision-territorial-2022.pdf?csf=1&e=dzP9xa> accessed 8 June 2023.

109 Ibid.

the climate and peace crises.[110] The country finds itself in a constant tension between its over-reliance on extractivism and natural resource exploitation to support its economy and peace building, and environmental protection as a hub of biological and cultural diversity.[111]

Perhaps as a result, environmental constitutional expansionism appears as a way to coherently address the conflation of these complex problems. Particularly, in the aftermath of the recognition of the Atrato river as a subject of rights, and despite some implementation issues, the river's legal guardians have noticed a significant improvement in policymaking. The CC's ruling acknowledged the multiple forms of life expressed through cultural diversity and sought to integrate them to the ecosystem and territories' diversity.[112] Protection of one (biodiversity) would undoubtedly imply protection of the other (cultural diversity). Thus, environmental governance in Colombia is experiencing changes that move towards a more inclusive governance model where environmental protection is deeply intertwined with cultural protection.[113] Formerly marginalized communities are taking center stage in the collective construction of the plans to restore the Atrato river's ecosystem.[114] Likewise, the intergenerational plan envisioned by the Supreme Court to protect the Amazon basin from deforestation is expected to conflate different voices, especially from those most affected and historically neglected.

Moreover, Colombia's environmental constitutional expansionism seems to aim towards protection of the environment in and of itself, but also in relation to its importance to the enjoyment and realization of other human rights. This expansionism aims to tackle intra-and intergenerational justice, seeking to guarantee the rights of present and future generations in the context of the climate crisis and social conflict. Protecting the rights of subjects previously outside of the dominant gaze (nature, children, future generations, armed conflict actors, etc.) could prevent fueling new and old conflicts, while achieving climate-related goals. Nonetheless, further research and discussion is needed to fully understand the effects of granting rights to nature on the existing fundamental and human rights, particularly those of marginalized communities.

110 Natalia Urzola & Maria P. González, 'Gender-based Environmental Violence in Colombia: problematizing dominant notions of gender-based violence during peacebuilding' (2022) 48(2) Australian Feminist Law Journal 5, <https://doi.org/10.1080/13200968.2022.2147704> accessed 8 June 2023.

111 Gómez Betancur et al., n 93 at 770.

112 Wesche, n 92 at 539.

113 Ibid., at 540, 544.

114 Ibid., at 547.

Constitutional expansionism needs to be studied with caution. Unrestricted rights expansionism may result in a rights overreach that could eventually have the undesired effect of rendering rights ineffective or unenforceable. As mentioned, the Colombian system of fundamental rights is inherently open, which allows an expanding body of rights granted sufficient legal grounding and reasoning. Generally, fundamental rights are a powerful means to protect and promote human dignity, and rights operate on interpretation and the creation of norms.[115] As society evolves, it is not only expected but necessary that the bill of rights evolves with it to ensure human dignity remains shielded.

Some critics argue that this openness should have limits, otherwise we may risk denaturation and weakening of the concept of fundamental rights.[116] Scholars state that an unrestricted proliferation of rights could diminish human dignity by affecting the separation of powers or states' capacity to guarantee fundamental rights.[117] Openness implies an active judiciary role, which could overstep other government branches affecting the overall constitutional fiber. Scholars have warned against judicial activism that oversteps other branches of the government threatening democratic institutions.[118] Additionally, new rights impose burdens and demands on the state powers that if unmet, may hinder the protection of rights as a whole.[119] New rights could also threaten other fundamental rights by diluting their significance.[120] Nonetheless, these challenges do not imply that rights should be static or reduced (as they are in the United States). Rights are, and should be, open and dynamic. An active and progressive judicial approach is beneficial, especially if done within the framework of constitutionalism. These concerns may be overcome by approaching openness with caution and allowing it to evolve progressively and in alignment with other rights obligations. Future research could develop criteria to test emerging constitutional rights and how they interplay with existing rights in a way that is coherent.

115 Luisa Netto, 'Criteria to Scrutinize New Rights: Protecting Rights against Artificial Proliferation' (2020) 8(1) Journal of Constitutional Research 11–75; 12 doi:10.5380/rinc.v8i1.82654.
116 Ibid., at 34.
117 Ibid.
118 Laura Burgers, 'Should Judges Make Climate Change Law?' (2020) 9(1) Transnational Environmental Law: 55–75; 58. doi:10.1017/S2047102519000360.
119 Netto, n 114 at 35.
120 Ibid., at 37.

5 Conclusion

The creativity and forcefulness of the Brazilian and Colombian judiciaries, in the service of climate protection, is a model of human and environmental rights protection, though not one that the United States courts are likely to adopt any time soon. The Brazilian court imagined new legal relationships between the different levels of government necessary to commit to the environmental rule of law, holding that an environmental treaty aimed ultimately at protecting human rights globally, was binding on the national sovereign authorities; it integrated the commitments made internationally into a holistic and comprehensive vision of the nation's constitutional commitments to its own people and to the world. For their part, the Colombian courts have reimagined how different stakeholders, including human and non-human rightsholders, could all be integrated so that a multiplicity of interests and perspectives converge in the service of environmental protection for present and future generations. The United States, meanwhile, holds fast to its antiquarian view of what people can expect of their government but may, in the end, find its own way to mitigate the impacts of climate change by incentivising changes in behavior from the ground up and through the entire social economy.

Bibliography

Acosta Alvarado PA & Rivas-Ramírez D, 'A Milestone in Environmental and Future Generations' Rights Protection: Recent Legal Developments before the Colombian Supreme Court' (2018) 30(3) Journal of Environmental Law 519–526.

ADPF N° 708, Supremo Tribunal Federal, 01.07.2022, 8 <http://climatecasechart.com/non-us-case/psb-et-al-v-federal-union/> accessed 8 June 2023.

Albuquerque G, Tabares Fagundez G & Fabre R, 'Emergência Climática e Direitos Humanos: o caso do Fundo Clima no Brasil e as obrigações de Direito Internacional' (2022) 19(1) Brazilian Journal of International Law 126.

Barbanell M, 'A Brief Summary of the Climate and Energy Provisions of the Inflation Reduction Act of 2022,' (*World Resources Institute*, October 2022) <https://www.wri.org/update/brief-summary-climate-and-energy-provisions-inflation-reduction-act-2022> accessed 8 June 2023.

Benjamin AH, *Direito Constitucional Ambiental Brasileiro* (Saraiva, 2010).

Betancur-Restrepo L, 'The Colombian Legal Framework for Social Rights and the Challenges of a Post-conflict Society', in Katharina Boele-Woelki & Diego Fernández Arroyo (eds) 52 *Ius Comparatum – Global Studies in Comparative Law* (Springer, Cham., 2021) 47–78; 48–49. https://doi.org/10.1007/978-3-030-57324-9_2.

Borges C, 'STF reconhece Acordo de Paris como tratado de direitos humanos (e por que isso importa)' (*re/set*, July 2022) <https://www.capitalreset.com/stf-reconhece-acordo-de-paris-como-tratado-de-direitos-humanos-e-por-que-isso-importa/> accessed 8 June 2023.

Burgers L, 'Should Judges Make Climate Change Law?' (2020) 9(1) Transnational Environmental Law: 55–75; 58. doi:10.1017/S2047102519000360.

Case Antonio de Andrade Ribeiro Junqueira, Supreme Court, Writ of Mandamus [Mandado de Segurança – MS 22164/SP], Merits. Judgment 30.10.1995. 1155–1190.

Case Associação Nacional dos Procuradores do Trabalho – ANPT, Supreme Court, Direct Action of Unconstitutionality [Ação Direta de Inconstitucionalidade – ADI 4066/DF], Merits. Judgment 24.08.2017.

Case Partido Progressista – PP, Supreme Court, Declaratory Action of Constitutionality [Ação Declaratória de Constitucionalidade – ADC 42/DF], Merits. Judgment 28.02.2018.

Case Presidente da República, Supreme Court, Claim for Noncompliance with a Fundamental Precept [Arguição de Descumprimento de Preceito Fundamental – ADPF 101/DF], Merits. Judgment 24.06.2009.

Case Procurador Geral da República, Supreme Court, Direct Action of Unconstitutionality [Ação Direta de Inconstitucionalidade – ADI 3540/DF], Court judgment on injunction (medida cautelar). Judgment 01.09.2005. 408–475.

Conference of the Parties, Adoption of the Paris Agreement, Dec. 12, 2015, U.N. Doc. FCCC/CP/2015/L.9/Rev/1 (Dec. 12, 2015), Preamble. <https://unfccc.int/resource/docs/2015/cop21/eng/l09r01.pdf> accessed 8 June 2023.

Constitución Española (1978) <https://www.boe.es/legislacion/documentos/ConstitucionCASTELLANO.pdf> accessed 8 June 2023.

Constitución Política de la República Dominicana (2010) <https://observatoriop10.cepal.org/sites/default/files/documents/constitucion_republica_dominicana.pdf> accessed 8 June 2023.

Constitución Política del Perú (1993), <https://www.congreso.gob.pe/constitucionyreglamento/#:~:text=La%20Constituci%C3%B3n%20Pol%C3%ADtica%20del%20Per%C3%BA,y%20organizaci%C3%B3n%20del%20Estado%20peruano> accessed 8 June 2023.

Constituição da República Federativa do Brasil (1988) art. 225, <https://www.gov.br/cade/en/content-hubs/legislation/brazilian-constitution> accessed 8 June 2023.

Constitute Project, <https://www.constituteproject.org> accessed 8 June 2023.

Constitution of the Republic of South Africa (1996) <https://www.gov.za/documents/constitution/constitution-republic-south-africa-1996-1> accessed 8 June 2023;.

Constitution Política de Colombia (1991), art. 4 and 5, and Title II. <http://www.secretariasenado.gov.co/senado/basedoc/constitucion_politica_1991.html> accessed 8 June 2023.

Constitutional Court of Colombia Decision T-341/16 (2016), <https://www.corteconstitucional.gov.co/relatoria/2016/t-341-16.htm> accessed 8 June 2023.

Constitutional Court of Colombia Judgment T-622/16, 10 November 2016 (Atrato River Case unofficial translation) <https://delawarelaw.widener.edu/files/resources/riveratratodecisionenglishdrpdellaw.pdf> accessed 8 June 2023.

Corte Suprema de Colombia, Andrea Lozano Barragán y otros v. Minambiente y otros, 11001-2203-000-2018-00319-01, 5 April 2018 <www.elaw.org/system/files/attachments/publicresource/Colombia%202018%20Sentencia%20Amazonas%20cambio%20climatico.pdf> accessed 8 June 2023 (Future Generations case).

De Azevedo et al., 'O Fundo Clima e as lições do Ministro Barroso' (*Migalhas*, June 2022) <https://www.migalhas.com.br/depeso/368577/o-fundo-clima-e-as-licoes-do-ministro-barroso> accessed 8 June 2023.

de Oliveira Neto BL, 'Da lama ao caos: o retrocesso da política e liderança ambiental do Brasil sob o governo Bolsonaro' (2022) 25(2) *Novos Cadernos NAEA* 59.

Decree 2591 of 1991 for further rules of procedure. <http://www.secretariasenado.gov.co/senado/basedoc/decreto_2591_1991.html> accessed 8 June 2023.

Dobbs v. Jackson Women's Health Organization 567 U.S. (2022), slip. op. at 12.

ERM, 'Issue Briefing: "Inflation Reduction Act of 2022: Climate and Energy Provisions"' (*ERM*, October 2022), <https://www.erm.com/globalassets/documents/insights/2022/issue-brief-ira-climate-2022-climate-energy-provisions.pdf> accessed 8 June 2023.

European Parliament, <https://www.europarl.europa.eu/about-parliament/en/democracy-and-human-rights> accessed 8 June 2023.

Flora J & Roser-Renouf C, 'Climate Change activism and youth', in Faustini P (ed). *The Challenges of Climate Change: Children on the front line* (Innocenti Insights UNICEF, 2014) <https://www.unicef-irc.org/publications/716-the-challenges-of-climate-change-children-on-the-front-line.html> accessed 8 June 2023.

GAIER, 'R. V. Bolsonaro diz que pode retirar Brasil do Acordo de Paris se for eleito' (*UOL*, September 2018), <https://noticias.uol.com.br/politica/eleicoes/2018/noticias/reuters/2018/09/03/bolsonaro-diz-que-pode-retirar-brasil-do-acordo-de-paris-se-for-eleito.htm> accessed 8 June 2023.

Gómez-Betancur L, 'The Rights of Nature in the Colombian Amazon: Examining Challenges and Opportunities in a Transitional Justice Setting' (2020) 25(1) UCLA Journal of International Law and Foreign Affairs <https://escholarship.org/uc/item/5bk379rd> accessed 8 June 2023.

Gómez-Betancur L, Vilardy S & Torres D, 'Ecosystem Services as a Promising Paradigm to Protect Environmental Rights of Indigenous Peoples in Latin America: the Constitutional Court Landmark Decision to Protect Arroyo Bruno in Colombia' (2022) 69 Environmental Management 768–780; 769 <https://doi.org/10.1007/s00267-021-01483-w> accessed 8 June 2023.

H.R.1319 – 117th Congress (2021–2022): American Rescue Plan Act of 2021, H.R.1319, 117th Cong. (2021), <https://www.congress.gov/bill/117th-congress/house-bill/1319/text> accessed 8 June 2023.

H.R.3684 – 117th Congress (2021–2022): Infrastructure Investment and Jobs Act, H.R.3684, 117th Cong. (2021), <https://www.congress.gov/bill/117th-congress/house-bill/3684> accessed 8 June 2023.

Herrera-Santoyo H, 'The Rights of Nature (Rivers) and Constitutional Actions in Colombia' (*GNHRE*, July 2019) <https://gnhre.org/2019/07/08/the-rights-of-nature-rivers-and-constitutional-actions-in-colombia/#_ftn3> accessed 8 June 2023.

ISA, 'A anatomia do desmonte das políticas socioambientais' (*Instituto Socioambiental*, January 2019), <https://site-antigo.socioambiental.org/pt-br/blog/blog-do-isa/a-anatomia-do-

Jian, Betty et al. 'US Inflation Reduction Act: A catalyst for climate action' (*Credit Suisse*, November 2022) <https://www.credit-suisse.com/about-us-news/en/articles/news-and-expertise/us-inflation-reduction-act-a-catalyst-for-climate-action-202211.html> accessed 8 June 2023.

desmonte-das-politicas-socioambientais> accessed 8 June 2023.

Kaminski I, 'Brazilian court world's first to recognise Paris Agreement as human rights treaty' (*Clima Home News*, 2022) <https://www.climatechangenews.com/2022/07/07/brazilian-court-worlds-first-to-recognise-paris-agreement-as-human-rights-treaty/> accessed 8 June 2023.

Kibler T. 'The 15 Most Inspiring Presidential Speeches in American History' (*HeinOnline Blog*, February 2021), <https://home.heinonline.org/blog/2021/02/the-15-most-inspiring-presidential-speeches-in-american-history/> accessed 8 June 2023.

Knox, JH, 'The Paris Agreement as a Human Rights Treaty', in Akande D et al (eds), *Human Rights and 21st Century Challenges: Poverty, Conflict, and the Environment* (Oxford, 2020).

Krupp F. 'The biggest thing Congress has ever done to address climate change' (*Environmental Defense Fund*, August 2022), <https://www.edf.org/blog/2022/08/12/biggest-thing-congress-has-ever-done-address-climate-change> accessed 8 June 2023.

Latvia Constitution of 1992, reinstated in 1991 with Amendments through 2016 (1992), <https://www.constituteproject.org/constitution/Latvia_2016.pdf?lang=en> accessed 8 June 2023.

Law 472 of 1998 for further rules of procedure. <http://www.secretariasenado.gov.co/senado/basedoc/ley_0472_1998.html> accessed 8 June 2023.

Lehmen A, 'Advancing Strategic Climate Litigation in Brazil' (2021) 22(3) German Law Journal 1471; 1472.

Leijten I. 'The German Right to an Existenzminimum, Human Dignity, and the Possibility of Minimum Core Socioeconomic Rights Protection' (2015) 16(1) German Law Journal 23–48. doi:10.1017/S2071832200019416.

Macpherson E et al., 'Where ordinary laws fall short: 'riverine rights' and constitutionalism' (2021) 30(3) Griffith Law Review 438–473, 448 DOI: 10.1080/10383441.2021.1982119.

Maués A, 'Supra-Legality of International Human Rights Treaties and Constitutional Interpretation' (2013) 10(18) International journal on human rights Sur, [English edition]: 205–223. <https://sur.conectas.org/wp-content/uploads/2017/11/sur18-eng-antonio-moreira-maues.pdf> accessed 8 June 2023.

Menegassi D, 'Em vitória histórica, STF reconhece proteção do clima como dever constitucional' (*Jornal O Eco*, 2022) <https://oeco.org.br/noticias/em-vitoria-historica-stf-reconhece-protecao-do-clima-como-dever-constitucional/> accessed 8 June 2023.

Moreira DA et al., Rights-based climate litigation in Brazil: An assessment of constitutional cases before the Brazilian Supreme Court, Journal of Human Rights Practice (forthcoming, 2023).

Moreira DA, *Litigância climática no Brasil: argumentos jurídicos para a inserção da variável climática no licenciamento ambiental*. (Coleção Interseções. Série Estudos, Rio de Janeiro: Editora PUC-Rio, 2021) ISBN: 978-65-88831-32-8 (e-book). <http://www.editora.puc-rio.br/cgi/cgilua.exe/sys/start.htm?infoid=956&sid=3> accessed 8 June 2023.

Nagle LE, 'Evolution of the Colombian Judiciary and the Constitutional Court' (1995) 6(1) Indiana International and Comparative Law Review 59–90; 60.

National Archives, President John F. Kennedy's Inaugural Address (*National Archives*, 1961) <www.archives.gov/milestone-documents/president-john-f-kennedys-inaugural-address#:~:text=My%20fellow%20citizens%20of%20the,for%20the%20freedom%20of%20ma.> accessed 8 June 2023.

National Federation of Independent Business v. Sebelius, 567 U.S. 519 (2012).

Neiva J & Mantelli G, '¿Existe un enfoque brasileño para los litigios climáticos? La crisis climática, la inestabilidad política y las posibilidades de litigio en Brasil' in Rodríguez C (ed) *Litigar la emergencia climática*, (Ciudad Autónoma de Buenos Aires: Siglo XXI Editores Argentina, 2022) 393.

Netto L, 'Criteria to Scrutinize New Rights: Protecting Rights against Artificial Proliferation' (2020) 8(1) Journal of Constitutional Research 11–75; 12 doi:10.5380/rinc.v8i1.82654.

OHCHR, 'Children at the forefront of climate action urge focus on child rights' (*OHCHR*, March 2017) <https://www.ohchr.org/en/stories/2017/03/children-forefront-climate-action-urge-focus-child-rights> accessed 8 June 2023.

Patient Protection and Affordable Care Act of 2010, Pub. L. No. 111–148, 124 Stat. 119 (2010).

Política Por Inteiro, 'Pauta verde no STF abre caminho para retomar a política climática brasileira' (*Política por Inteiro*, March 2021) <https://www.politicaporinteiro.org/2022/03/29/pauta-verde-stf/> accessed 8 June 2023.

PSB et al. v. Brazil (on Climate Fund) (ADPF 708) <http://climatecasechart.com/non-us-case/psb-et-al-v-federal-union/> accessed 8 June 2023.

Reference Re Same Sex Marriage, 2004 SCC 79 (CanLII).

Setzer J & Benjamin L, 'Climate Litigation in the Global South: Constraints and Innovations' (2020) 9(1) Transnational Environmental Law 77, 87.

Setzer J, Benjamin L, Leal G & Borges C, 'Climate Change Litigation in Brazil: Will Green Courts Become Greener' in Alogna I, Bakker C & Gauci JP (eds), *Climate Change Litigation: Global Perspectives* (Leiden, Boston: Brill Nijhoff, 2021) 143–172. ISBN: 978-90-04-44761-5 (e-book).

Stavish M, Rubio G & Kieth L, 'ESG and the Inflation Reduction Act of 2022,' (*BDO USA*, October 2022), <https://www.bdo.com/insights/tax/esg-and-the-inflation-reduction-act-of-2022> accessed 8 June 2023.

Thornhill C & Rodrigues de Araújo Calabria C, 'Global Constitutionalism and Democracy: The case of Colombia' (2020) 2 Jus Cogens 155–183; 161. https://doi.org/10.1007/s42439-020-00024-z.

Tigre M & Urzola N, 'Advancements in Climate Rights in Courts Around the World' (*Climate Law Blog*, 2022) <https://blogs.law.columbia.edu/climatechange/2022/07/01/advancements-in-climate-rights-in-courts-around-the-world/> accessed 8 June 2023.

Tigre M & Urzola N, 'The 2017 Inter-American Court's Advisory Opinion: Changing the Paradigm for International Environmental Law in the Anthropocene' (2021) 12(1) Journal of Human Rights and the Environment 24–50. https://doi.org/10.1111/reel.12400.

Tigre M, 'Brazil's First Climate Case to Reach the Supreme Court' (*OpinioJuris*, October 2020). <http://opiniojuris.org/2020/10/13/brazils-first-climate-case-to-reach-the-supreme-court/> accessed 8 June 2023.

Tigre M, 'South America' in Lavanya Rajamani and Jaqueline Peel (eds), *The Oxford Handbook of International Environmental Law*. (Oxford: Oxford University Press, 2021).

Tyrer v. United Kingdom, 26 Eur. Ct. H.R. (ser. A) 26 (1978).

United Nations Charter (1945) Preamble, <https://www.un.org/en/about-us/un-charter> accessed 8 June 2023.

United States Constitution, <https://www.archives.gov/founding-docs/constitution-transcript> accessed 8 June 2023.

United States Department of the Treasury, 'Treasury Announces Guideline on Inflation Reduction Act's Strong Labor Protections,' (*US Department of the Treasury*, 29 November 2022) <https://home.treasury.gov/news/press-releases/jy1128> accessed 8 June 2023.

United States v. Lopez, 514 U.S. 549, 552, 567 (1995).

Uprimny R, 'The Recent Transformation of Constitutional Law in Latin America: Trends and Challenges' (2011) 89 Texas Law Review 1587–1609; 1591.

Urzola N & González M, 'Derechos de la Naturaleza: un camino hacia la construcción de paz ambiental en Colombia' in Jurisdicción Especial para la Paz, *Conflicto armado, medio ambiente y territorio: Reflexiones sobre el enfoque territorial y ambiental en la Jurisdicción Especial para la Paz* (Bogotá D.C., 2022) 49–85 <https://www.jep.gov.co/Infografas/docs/libro-comision-territorial-2022.pdf?csf=1&e=dzP9xa> accessed 8 June 2023.

Urzola N & González M, 'Gender-based Environmental Violence in Colombia: problematizing dominant notions of gender-based violence during peacebuilding' (2022) 48(2) Australian Feminist Law Journal 5, <https://doi.org/10.1080/13200968.2022.2147704> accessed 8 June 2023.

Urzola N & González M, 'When two crises collide: the effects of climate change in the Colombian environmental peacebuilding process' (*Agency for Peacebuilding*, June 2021), <https://www.peaceagency.org/colombian-environmental-peacebuilding-process/> accessed 8 June 2023.

Villavicencio Calzadilla P, 'A Paradigm Shift in Courts' Views on Nature: The Atrato River and Amazon Basin Cases in Colombia' (2019) 15 Law, Environment and Development Journal 1–11 <https://lead-journal.org/content/19049.pdf> accessed 8 June 2023.

Wesche P, 'Rights of Nature in Practice: A Case Study on the Impacts of the Colombian Atrato River Decision' (2021) 33(3) Journal of Environmental Law 531–555; 539, https://doi.org/10.1093/jel/eqab021.

CHAPTER 7

Constitutional, Governance or Market Failures: China, Climate Change and Energy Transition

Henry Gao and Weihuan Zhou***

1 Introduction

China is a major player in climate change mitigation. In September 2016, China formally ratified the Paris Agreement.[1] Four years later, President Xi Jinping announced China's plan to further scale up its Intended Nationally Determined Contributions, aiming at achieving CO_2 emissions peak before 2030 and carbon neutrality before 2060.[2] A central element of the plan is reducing China's heavy reliance on coal power. As a result, China's use of coal already saw a steady decrease between 2013 and 2018. While coal demand increased in 2019 and 2020, new coal power plants approved in 2021 declined by approximately 58% compared to 2020.[3] However, the good progress in energy transition was interrupted by the power outage sprawling over 20 provinces in China in September 2021, which resulted in a U-turn in the policy. Consequently, China reversed its course of action and approved more coal power plants in the last month of 2021 than it did in the previous eleven months combined. This trend continued in 2022, with the coal power capacity approved in the first quarter of 2022 accounting for almost half of the total capacity approved in 2021.

This paper explores the reasons behind China's policy shift, drawing from insights on the policy-making process in China's climate change mitigation

* Henry Gao is Professor of Law at Yong Pung How School of Law, Singapore Management University. Email: gaohenry@gmail.com.

** Weihuan Zhou is Associate Professor and Co-Director of the China International Business and Economic Law (CIBEL) Centre, Faculty of Law and Justice, UNSW Sydney. Email: weihuan.zhou@unsw.edu.au. All websites cited are current as of 25 June 2023.

1 Brian Spegele, 'China's Legislature Ratifies Paris Agreement on Climate Ahead of G-20 Meeting' (*The Wall Street Journal*, 2 September 2016).

2 CGTN, 'Full Text: Xi Jinping's Speech at General Debate of the 75th Session of the United Nations General Assembly' (*CGTN*, 23 September 2020).

3 Yujie Xue, 'China's approvals for new coal plants rebound amid renewed focus on energy security after last year's power crisis: Greenpeace' (*South China Morning Post*, 20 July 2022).

 | DOI:10.1163/9789004693722_008

and energy transition policy. In particular, the paper addresses the following questions: What are the major domestic factors driving China's policy and the major players involved in the decision-making? What are the conflicts between national and subnational interests and approaches, and how have these conflicts been resolved? How has the bargaining between different domestic players impacted China's approaches in trade negotiations?

The paper also compares the implementation of climate policies with the implementation of trade policies in China, discusses the potential consequences of constitutional and market failures due to "competition among purposes"[4] at both the domestic and international levels, and offers more general observations on ways to help developing countries overcome such competition and conflicts.

2 The Evolution of China's Climate Change Policy: a Brief Account

The development of climate policies in China has been shaped not only by China's overarching economic development goals and plans, but also by China's international engagements and commitments. As early as in 1972, the United Nations Conference on the Human Environment prompted China to consider environmental issues and develop its first set of environmental legislation.[5] However, it was not until the 1990s that China made major progress in advancing its environmental policy and regulatory framework. In 1990, the State Council established the National Coordination Group on Climate Change (NCGCC), which subsequently participated actively in the United Nations Conference on Environment and Development (UNCED) in 1992, also known as the Earth Summit.[6] This conference developed a blueprint for international cooperation on environmental and development issues and led to the conclusion of the United Nations Framework Convention on Climate Change (UNFCCC), the first international treaty on climate change.[7] The Convention created the Conference of the Parties (COP) to monitor the implementation of

4 Jorge E. Viñuales, *The International Law of Energy* (Cambridge University Press 2022) 28.

5 Tianbao Qin and Meng Zhang, 'Development of China's Environmental Legislation', in Eva Sternfeld (eds), *Routledge Handbook of Environmental Policy in China* (Routledge 2017) 19.

6 Ye Qi and Tong Wu, 'The Politics of Climate Change in China' (2013) 4 WIREs Climate Change 301, 303. See also United Nations, 'A new blueprint for international action on the environment' (*United Nations*, 1992).

7 United Nations, 'What is the United Nations Framework Convention on Climate Change?' (*United Nations*).

the covered commitments, promote information exchange and coordination and further international cooperation on climate actions.[8] China has actively engaged in all COPs, including the negotiations and conclusion of the Kyoto Protocol[9] at COP3 in 1997 and the Paris Agreement[10] at COP21 in 2015.

China's active engagement in climate policymaking at the international level has progressively enriched its own knowledge about climate change, leading to the gradual elevation of sustainable development and climate policies to a core, strategic national policy in China. In 1998, the NCGCC was relocated to the State Development Planning Commission, the predecessor of the National Development and Reform Commission (NDRC) and the most powerful agency in the central government.[11] The 10th Five-Year Plan (2001–2005) made a reference to climate change for the first time and emphasized the growth of renewable energy, energy conservation and environmental protection leading to the promulgation or amendments of a range of laws and regulations such as the Renewable Energy Law which took effect in 2006.[12] However, during this period the national priority was focused on economic growth, and no specific targets were set for climate actions. Due to the heavy reliance on energy-intensive industries for economic development and industrialization, China became the world's largest emitter of energy-related carbon dioxide (CO_2) in 2005.[13] The environmental degradation, especially air pollution, intensified public debate over China's environmental policy and provoked the central government to strengthen climate policy and actions in the next decade.

During the 11th Five-Year Period (2006–2010), the central government set energy efficiency targets, allocated individual targets to provinces, and required

8 See United Nations, 'United Nations Framework Convention on Climate Change' (*United Nations*, 9 May 1992) art 7.

9 United Nations, 'What is the Kyoto Protocol?' (*United Nations*) <https://unfccc.int/kyoto_protocol>.

10 United Nations, 'The Paris Agreement. What is the Paris Agreement?' (*United Nations*).

11 See above Qi and Wu, 'The Politics of Climate Change in China' (n 6) 303.

12 See David Sandalow and others, 'Guide to Chinese Climate Policy 2022' (*Oxford Institute of Energy Studies*, 2022) 32; Qin and Zhang (n 5) 21. See also The Central People's Government of the People's Republic of China, 'The Outline of the 10th Five-Year Plan for Economic and Social Development of the People's Republic of China' (中华人民共和国国民经济和社会发展第十个五年计划纲要) (*The Central People's Government of the People's Republic of China*, 15 March 2001); The Central People's Government of the People's Republic of China, 'Renewable Energy Law of the People's Republic of China' (中华人民共和国可再生能源法) (*The Central People's Government of the People's Republic of China*, 21 June 2005).

13 International Energy Agency, 'An Energy Sector Roadmap to Carbon Neutrality in China' (*IEA*, September 2021) 22.

local governments to implement.[14] In 2007, the NDRC published China's first detailed National Plan to Address Climate Change,[15] and the NCGCC was further elevated to become the National Leading Group on Climate Change. Led by the then Premier Wen Jiabao, this group included all major ministries of the central government in charge of developing national climate policies and actions, guiding China's international cooperation and negotiations, and coordinating the implementation of greenhouse gas (GHG) mitigation strategies.[16] China's effort to address environmental issues during this period, however, was compromised by the need to react to the global financial crisis in 2008–09 through the introduction of massive stimulus plans to maintain economic growth including supporting energy-intensive industries.[17] This was another notable incident which revealed the challenges faced by the Chinese government in overcoming the underlying tensions between its pursuit of climate goals and economic growth.

The 12th Five Year Plan (2011–2015) was a landmark in China's advancement of climate policy leading to a period of remarkable achievements at both domestic and international levels. The Plan set out a clear mandate to transform China's economic development model with the transition to a green economy and a sustainable development path as one of its priorities.[18] It devoted a whole chapter to climate change and set forth specific, binding targets and action plans including reducing carbon intensity and energy consumption, increasing non-fossil energy sources and government support for strategic, green industries and technologies, promoting the restructuring of the coal industry, enhancing the system for monitoring GHG emissions, planning the creation of a carbon trade market, etc.[19] More detailed plans were subsequently released in a series of implementation regulations including

---

14 See above Sandalow and others (n 12) 33–5.

15 National Development and Reform Commission, 'China's National Plan for Addressing Climate Change' (中国应对气候变化国家方案) (*National Development and Reform Commission*, June 2007).

16 See above Qi and Wu, 'The Politics of Climate Change in China' (n 6) 303. See also The State Council of the People's Republic of China, 'Introduction to the National Coordination Group for Addressing Climate Change' (*China Climate Change Info-Net*, 17 July 2006).

17 See above Sandalow and others (n 12) 34.

18 The Central People's Government of the People's Republic of China, 'The Outline of the 12th Five-Year Plan for Economic and Social Development of the People's Republic of China' (中华人民共和国国民经济和社会发展第十二个五年规划纲要) (*The Central People's Government of the People's Republic of China*, 16 March 2011).

19 For a more detailed discussion of China's climate policy and goals under the 12th Five Year Plan, see Sam Geall and others, *China's Green Revolution: Energy, Environment and the 12th Five-Year Plan* (Chinadialogue 2011).

most significantly the Work Plan for Controlling Greenhouse Gas Emission[20] published by the State Council in December 2011 and the National Plan on Climate Change issued by the NDRC in 2014.[21] The latter set out China's plans and goals relating to GHG mitigation, climate change adaptation and priorities in its green transition by 2020.

As a strong proponent for the Paris Agreement, China submitted its first "nationally determined contributions" (NDCs) to the UNFCCC in 2015, committing to specific targets for the reduction of CO_2 emissions and the increase of non-fossil fuels in primary energy consumption, amongst other commitments.[22] These targets were incorporated in China's 13th Five-Year Plan (2016–2020).[23] To achieve these targets, the central government rolled out a new set of policy documents to detail the action plans and allocate targets to provinces.[24] By the end of this period, CO_2 emissions per unit of GDP (i.e. carbon intensity) in China were approximately 48% lower than the 2005 level (or a 40–50% reduction), and the share of non-fossil fuels in primary energy consumption was approximately 16% marking "a significant increase of 8.5 percentage points compared with 2005".[25]

20 The State Council of the People's Republic of China, 'Working Plan for Greenhouse Gas Emission Control in Implementing the 12th Five-Year Plan' (国务院关于印发"十二五"控制温室气体排放工作方案的通知) (*The Central People's Government of the People's Republic of China*, 01 December 2011).

21 National Development and Reform Commission, 'The National Plan (2014–2020) for Addressing Climate Change' (国家发展改革委关于印发国家应对气候变化规划(2014–2020 年)的通知) (*National Development and Reform Commission*, 19 September 2014).

22 National Development and Reform Commission, 'Enhanced Actions on Climate Change: China's Intended Nationally Determined Contributions' (强化应对气候变化行动—中国国家自主贡献) (*National Development and Reform Commission*, 30 June 2015).

23 The Central People's Government of the People's Republic of China, 'The Outline of the 13th Five-Year Plan for Economic and Social Development of the People's Republic of China' (中华人民共和国国民经济和社会发展第十三个五年规划纲要) (*Xinhua*, 17 March 2016).

24 National Development and Reform Commission and National Energy Administration, 'The 13th Five-Year Plan for the Development of Energy' (能源发展"十三五"规划) (*National Development and Reform Commission and National Energy Administration*, 26 December 2016); The State Council of the People's Republic of China, 'The Comprehensive Working Plan for Energy Conservation and Emission Reduction for Implementing the 13th Five-Year Plan' ("十三五"节能减排综合工作方案) (*The State Council of the People's Republic of China*, 20 December 2016).

25 The State Council Information Office of the People's Republic of China, 'Full Text: Responding to Climate Change: China's Policies and Actions' (*The State Council Information Office of the People's Republic of China*, 27 October 2021).

Since 2020, President Xi Jinping reiterated, in a series of high-profile global events, China's pledges to combatting climate change through more vigorous policies and measures in order to achieve "CO_2 emissions peak before 2030 and carbon neutrality before 2060", which are known as China's "30–60" or "dual carbon" goals.[26] This commitment was incorporated in China's updated NDCs submitted to the UNFCCC prior to COP26 in October 2021.[27] More specifically, China commits to

> lower CO_2 emissions per unit of GDP by over 65% from the 2005 level, to increase the share of non-fossil fuels in primary energy consumption to around 25%, to increase the forest stock volume by 6 billion cubic meters from the 2005 level, and to bring its total installed capacity of wind and solar power to over 1.2 billion kilowatts by 2030.

These commitments and goals are also embedded in China's 14th Five-Year Plan (2021–2025)[28] and are being implemented through a range of policy documents designed to promote climate actions and compliance nationwide during the Plan period in pursuit of the "dual carbon" goals. In May 2021, the central government established a Leading Group on Carbon Peak and Carbon Neutrality to strengthen and better coordinate national climate policies and actions.[29] Through the work of this group, China adopted a "1+N" policy system under which the "1" refers to the *Working Guidance for Completely, Accurately and Comprehensively Implementing the New Development Concept and Achieving Carbon Dioxide Peak and Carbon Neutrality* (hereinafter Working Guidance 2021),[30] the overarching national plan jointly issued by the Central Committee

26 See above CGTN (n 2); Xinhua, 'Full Text: Remarks by Chinese President Xi Jinping at Leaders Summit on Climate' (*Xinhua*, 22 April 2021).

27 Ministry of Ecology and Environment of the People's Republic of China, 'China's Achievements, New Goals and New Measures for Nationally Determined Contributions' (中国落实国家自主贡献成效和新目标新举措) (*Ministry of Ecology and Environment of the People's Republic of China*, 28 October 2021).

28 The Central People's Government of the People's Republic of China, 'The Outline of the 14th Five-Year Plan for National Economic and Social Development and Long-Range Objectives for 2035 the People's Republic of China' (中华人民共和国国民经济和社会发展第是十四五个规划和2035年远景目标纲要) (*The Central People's Government of the People's Republic of China*, 13 March 2021).

29 See above Ministry of Ecology and Environment (n 27) 5–6.

30 The Central People's Government of the People's Republic of China, 'Working Guidance for Carbon Dioxide Peaking and Carbon Neutrality in Full and Faithful Implementation of the New Development Philosophy' (完整准确全面贯彻新发展理念做好碳达峰碳中和工作的意见) (*The Central People's Government of the People's Republic of China*, 22 September 2021).

of the Communist Party of China and the State Council in October 2021. The "N" refers to all subordinate policy documents including detailed action plans in different industries and sectors of the economy. For example, the issuance of the Working Guidance 2021 was accompanied by the release of the *Action Plan for Carbon Dioxide Peaking Before 2030*[31] by the State Council, which constitutes part of the "N". This design of China's climate policies, with the central government playing a leadership role, continues to reinforce China's top-down approach to climate policymaking.

3 The Coal Energy Transition: a Closer Look

The overview of the evolution of China's climate policy above shows that climate change has become "an integral part of China's development vision and strategy" and that China has committed to "more ambitious action to tackle climate change."[32] At the same time, China's climate action has faced considerable, ongoing challenges. To understand the major drivers of and challenges for China's climate action, we use as a case study coal energy transition, which is critical to the success of China's climate policy.

China's phenomenal economic development and industrialization in past decades has relied heavily on energy-intensive activities leading to massive production and consumption of fossil fuels, especially coal. As the world's largest coal user, in 2018 China's electricity and heat generation accounted for approximately 45 percent of all domestic GHG emissions, and its heavy industrial production, particularly in the steel, iron and cement sectors, accounted for approximately 85 percent of industrial CO_2 emissions.[33] Energy efficiency, renewables and reduction of coal use are therefore essential to the achievement of China's climate goals on CO_2 emissions peaking and carbon neutrality.[34] Consequently, China has progressively intensified its climate policy and actions in these areas leading to a significant growth of low-carbon fuel and technologies and reduction of coal use in power and industrial production (especially between 2013–2018).[35] Concrete actions taken in the 13th Five-Year

---

31 The State Council of the People's Republic of China, 'The Action Plan for Reaching Carbon Dioxide Peak before 2030' (2030年前碳达峰行动方案) (*The State Council of the People's Republic of China*, 24 October 2021).

32 See above International Energy Agency (n 13) 37.

33 See above Sandalow and others (n 12) 45; World Bank Group, 'Country Climate and Development Report: China' (*World Bank Group*, October 2022) 26, 45.

34 See above Sandalow and others (n 12) 14.

35 Ibid 24–6.

period involved, for instance, restricting the construction of new coal-fired power generation plants, closing existing plants which failed to comply with efficiency standards, subsidizing clean coal power generation, energy-efficiency investments, renewable energies, related technologies and R&D, etc.[36] During the current 14th Five-Year period, China remains committed to its ambitious goals in these areas. For example, by 2025, China aims to reach 20% share of non-fossil fuel in primary energy use and reduce energy intensity by 13.5% and carbon intensity by 18% from the 2020 levels.[37] It sets specific targets for the expansion of major renewable energies and the reduction of coal production and consumption in key industrial processes making coal consumption peaking a priority.[38] Apart from these internal targets, China's updated NDCs also include commitments not to build new coal-fired power projects overseas, and it has cancelled or stopped investing in 26 such projects since 2021.[39] At the same time, however, China's national policy also emphasizes the need to protect energy security and improve self-sufficiency in energy supply,[40] foreshadowing the major policy considerations that may counterbalance China's climate pledges.

There are notable driving forces behind China's entrenched commitment to climate actions. This commitment is first and foremost a strategic choice aligned with and supportive of China's own development goals and political needs. As Chinese leaders become increasingly convinced that the old "growth-at-any-cost model" cannot be sustained,[41] energy efficiency, decarbonization and sustainability enter the centrepiece of China's economic transformation. While economic growth remains a priority, Chinese leaders become increasingly aware of the political risks associated with growing social unrest due to environmental degradation and adverse effects of climate change.[42] Thus, there is a strong political will to steer China toward the new

36 Craig Hart and others, 'Mapping China's Climate & Energy Policies' (*Development Technologies International*, December 2018) 86–101.

37 See above The State Council of China (n 31).

38 Ibid.

39 See above Ministry of Ecology and Environment (n 27) 2; Isabella Suarez and Xiaojun Wang, 'Year Review: The Impact of China's Ban on Overseas Coal Power Plants on Global Climate' (*Centre for Research on Energy and Clean Air*, 22 September 2022) 3.

40 National Development and Reform Commission and National Energy Administration, 'The 14th Five-Year Plan for the Modern Energy System' ("十四五"现代能源体系规划) (*National Development and Reform Commission and National Energy Administration*, 29 January 2022).

41 Genia Kostka, 'China's Local Environmental Politics' in Eva Sternfeld (eds), *Routledge Handbook of Environmental Policy in China* (Routledge 2017) 31.

42 Ibid.

sustainable development path to balance economic growth with environmental and public health concerns and to enhance government accountability and maintain political stability.[43] At the international level, climate policies and actions play an important role in fostering China's reputation as a responsible stakeholder and trustworthy partner[44] and securing "recognition of its status as a global power and its leadership in international governance".[45] By committing to ambitious climate targets, China can use its international commitments to push domestic reforms and economic transformation.[46] With the political consensus reached within the central government, China's political system provides the foundation for its top-down approach to climate policymaking which facilitates the design of climate policies, as further discussed in Section 4.[47]

At the same time, China's climate action faces acute challenges particularly due to the need to accommodate its energy needs and the diverse interest of local governments, industries, state entities and other stakeholders in implementation. Here too, China's commitment to the reduction of coal production and consumption provides a telling example. While China took an incremental approach to reducing coal use in the past, it deviated from its coal reduction policy in September 2021, when over 20 provinces in China cut power supplies allegedly due to power outages. This in turn led to a massive approval of new coal power plants, with more approvals in the final month of 2021 than in all preceding 11 months combined.[48] The effect was also felt in 2022, with coal power capacity approved in the first quarter alone equals to half of the total approved capacity in 2021.[49]

4 Making Sense of China's Policy Shift: Gaps in Energy Transition and Governance

So what explains the policy shift in 2021? On the surface, here are a few apparent reasons, such as the rising demand, the insufficient supply from traditional

43 See above International Energy Agency (n 13) 35–6; Lisa Williams, 'China's Climate Change Policies: Actors and Drivers' (*Lowy Institute*, July 2014) 16.
44 See above Williams (n 43) 18.
45 See above Hart and others (n 36) 138.
46 See above International Energy Agency (n 13) 35.
47 See above Qi and Wu (n 6) 302.
48 Xinnan Wang, 'Provincial Approval on Coal Fired Power Revived after Power Rationing, Local State-Owned Capital Refilled Strongly' (*Greenpeace*, 20 July 2022).
49 Ibid.

coal power, and the unreliability of renewable energy.[50] However, deep down, China's policy shift must be understood in terms of the multifaceted interactions among different stakeholders at both the domestic and international levels. More specifically, the bargaining between these forces shapes not only the making of China's domestic policy and international commitments, but also the implementation (or non-implementation) of such policies.

As noted above, China's policymaking generally follows a top-down process whereby policies are made by the central leadership without much input from local governments or consultations with other stakeholders. This means that, at the front-end of policy making, China could avoid the tortuous bargaining process required in many other countries which often leads to the need to strike compromises that nobody is happy with, or even paralysis where the decision could not be made. This is reflected in China's climate policymaking, where the main decision-maker is the central government, or more specifically President Xi himself.

At the domestic level, the seriousness China has attached to climate policies is a reflection of President Xi's "New Development Concept" (新发展理念). True to the nature of Communism as an ideology, even paramount leaders have come up with new "thoughts", from Deng Xiaoping's "Socialism with Chinese Characteristics", to Jiang Zemin's "Three Represents", to Hu Jintao's "Scientific Outlook on Development", and finally to "Xi Jinping Thought on Socialism with Chinese Characteristics for a New Era", where the "New Development Concept" is an important component. This Concept emphasizes "Innovation, Coordination, Green, Openness, Sharing" as a way to shift China's economic model to one of a high-quality and low-pollution.[51] The link between the Concept and China's carbon goals is explicitly confirmed by the top policy document issued by the central government, i.e., the Working Guidance 2021.[52] By shifting the policy in a new direction, the Concept also provides a convenient way to test the loyalty of local officials based on whether they faithfully implement the Concept, which is why the Working Guidance 2021 repeatedly refers to "compacting local responsibilities"[53] and "strengthening supervision and assessment"[54] under the leadership and coordination

50 David Fishman, 'Reasons Behind China's Power Shortage in Q4 2021, Resultant Reform Measures, and the Impact on Power Markets', (Oxford Energy Forum, March 2022, Issue 131) 13–20.

51 Xinhua, 'Full and Faithful Implementation of the New Development Philosophy: Grasp the theory of 'Five Inevitable Routes' deeply and thoroughly' (*Xinhua*, 14 March 2022).

52 See above The Central People's Government (n 30).

53 Ibid.

54 Ibid.

of the central government as the way to achieve the "dual carbon" goals. In addition, the central government launched a major restructuring of agencies in 2018 to provide both the carrot and stick needed to get local governments in action. The carrot is held by the newly formed Ministry of Natural Resources (MNR), which took over the portfolio from several other agencies, including the all-important power of urban and rural planning from the NDRC and the Ministry of Housing and Urban-Rural Development.[55] The MNR "takes charge of the owner's responsibilities for all types of natural resource assets owned by the whole people", which gives it control of all natural resources as a powerful carrot.[56] On the other hand, a new Ministry of Ecology and Environment was also formed to take over the powers of anti-pollution enforcement that used to be scattered through several agencies[57] such as the former Ministry of Land and Resources, the Ministry of Water Resources, the Ministry of Agriculture, and the State Oceanic Administration, as well as the enforcement of climate change and emission reduction goals from the NDRC.[58] This provides it with a big stick as all environmental enforcement powers are now controlled by one agency.

If the *raison d'être* of "promoting high-level development" still stays true to climate goals at the domestic level, the main rationale for climate responsibility at the international level, i.e. "to foster an image of responsible power", sounds even more instrumentalist.[59] In particular, President Trump's "irresponsible"[60] decision to withdraw the US from the Paris Agreement in 2017[61] left a vacuum in climate leadership, one which China was eager to fill as a way to "enhance China's international influence and discourse power".[62] By

55 The Central People's Government of the People's Republic of China, 'The Plan for the Institutional Reform of the State Council of the People's Republic of China' (国务院机构改革方案) (*The Central People's Government of the People's Republic of China*, 17 March 2018).

56 Wang Yong, 'Explanations on the Plan for the Institutional Reform of the State Council of the People's Republic of China' (关于国务院机构改革方案的说明) (*Xinhua*, 17 March 2018).

57 Ibid.

58 Ibid.

59 Zhenhua Xie, 'Persistently Confronting Climate Change and Continuing to Involve, Contribute and Lead the Global Construction of Ecological Civilization: In the Memory of the Ratification of the Paris Agreement' (*China Environment News*, 14 December 2020).

60 Ministry of Foreign Affairs of the People's Republic of China, 'Report on the United States Prejudicing Global Environmental Governance' (*Ministry of Foreign Affairs of the People's Republic of China*, 19 October 2020).

61 Timothy Cama and Devin Henry, 'Trump: We Are Getting out of Paris Climate Deal' (*The Hill*, 1 June 2017).

62 See above The Central People's Government (n 30).

the time that the withdrawal took effect in late 2020,[63] China further realized that, given the importance that Democratic Party Presidential candidate Joe Biden attached to the Paris Agreement, climate change could provide an opening to revive bilateral cooperation between the US and China following the devastating "trade war" waged by the Trump administration, akin to the Ping-pong diplomacy which opened the door for the establishment of the bilateral diplomatic relations some 50 years ago. This point was confirmed explicitly by President Xi in his first summit with Biden in November 2021, where he emphasized that "given that China and the U.S. used to work together to make the Paris Agreement possible, climate change can definitely become a new highlight of Sino-US cooperation".[64] With such an instrumentalist approach to climate change, it is no surprise that China decided to temporarily suspend the bilateral climate change talks with the US as a counter-measure against the US when US Congress Speaker Nancy Pelosi visited Taiwan in August 2022 despite China's strong opposition.[65] As made clear by China, it "had to suspend Sino-US climate change negotiations in view of Pelosi's visit, and all consequences must be borne by the United States."[66]

While the climate change policymaking power is monopolized by the central government, when it comes to the implementation of such policies, the central government must work together with local governments and other stakeholders such as power plants and downstream user industries. This is where things get tricky, as these players often have different incentives and therefore do not always behave the same way as the central government would prefer.

As noted earlier, after the central government set forth the overarching climate goals, it allocated specific targets to different provinces for local governments to implement. Unlike their counterparts in the West,[67] the local governments in China do not have to answer to local constituencies or civil society

63 Leslie Hook and Katrina Manson, 'US Formally Withdraws from Paris Climate Agreement' (*Financial Times*, 4 November 2020).

64 Xinhua, 'President Xi Jinping's Web Conference with the US President Biden' (*Xinhua*, 16 November 2021).

65 Ministry of Foreign Affairs of the People's Republic of China, 'Sanction against Pelosi's Sneaky Visit to Taiwan' (*Ministry of Foreign Affairs of the People's Republic of China*, 5 August 2022).

66 Xinhua, 'Facts about Pelosi's Visit to Taiwan' (*Xinhua*, 25 August 2022).

67 Christopher Gore and Pamela Robinson, 'Local Government Response to Climate Change: Our Last, Best Hope?' in Henrik Selin and Stacy D VanDeveer (eds), *Changing Climates in North American Politics: Institutions, Policymaking, and Multilevel Governance* (MIT Press 2009).

groups. Instead, their main function is to implement the targets set by the central government. The promotion of local officials is decided by how well they implement such targets, which used to focus predominantly on GDP growth. In view of the growing importance of environmental issues, the central government included environmental indicators such as the achievement of climate goals in recent years to evaluate the performance of local officials. So why did the central government take such an abrupt policy shift in late 2021? We offer two explanations.

4.1 *Last-Minute Rush to Meet the Targets*

On 12 August 2021, the NDRC issued the notice on the "First half of 2021 Barometer on the completion of energy consumption dual control targets in each region", which listed in the top warning category 9 provinces for the achievement of energy intensity reduction goals, and 8 provinces for the achievement of total energy consumption control goals.[68] The NDRC also made clear that, "from the date of issuance of this notice, for regions where energy consumption intensity has risen instead of fallen, the energy-saving review of "two high" (high energy consumption, high emissions) projects will be suspended in 2021".[69] To make sure that the local governments got the message, the NDRC further issued the "Plan on the improvement of the dual control system for energy consumption intensity and total volume" on 16 September 2021,[70] which explicitly stated that the assessment results for the dual control system "will be handed over to the competent department of cadres as an important basis for the comprehensive assessment and evaluation of the leadership team and leading cadres of the Provincial Government".[71]

These documents spurred the provinces into quick action, especially those in the top warning category. This is most evident in the two provinces with the biggest industrial outputs, i.e., Guangdong and Jiangsu, which are both listed in the top warning categories for both targets.

---

68 National Development and Reform Commission, 'Report on the implementation of the dual-control of energy consumption in each province in the first half of 2021' (关于印发《2021年上半年各地区能耗双控目标完成情况晴雨表》的通知) (*National Development and Reform Commission*, 17 August 2021).

69 Ibid.

70 National Development and Reform Commission, 'Improving the plan of the dual-control of the intensity and quantity of energy consumption' (关于印发《完善能源消费强度和总量双控制度方案》的通知) (*National Development and Reform Commission*, 16 September 2021).

71 Ibid.

It might be argued, however, that there were less drastic actions available to local governments than simply cutting off the power supply. Though in a country where lower level governments are supposed to blindly follow central government orders, such drastic actions would send a strong signal up the command chain, giving the local governments some bargaining power when the central government is forced to take action in response to anger from downstream user industries including the many SOEs with deep links to the central government.

4.2 *Power Shortages and Incomplete Market Reform*

At the same time, it is also interesting to note that the above rationale might not apply to all provinces imposing restrictions on power usages. For example, none of the three provinces in the north-eastern region were in the top warning category (red). Instead, Jilin was in the green category for both targets. For Heilongjiang and Liaoning, their energy consumption and energy intensity reduction achievements were green and yellow respectively. This means that they did not really need to cut power usages to meet the mandatory targets. Rather, they seem to have real power shortage problems, as complicated by factors such as the reduction of wind, solar and hydro power and the national shortage of coal.[72]

So how could there be power shortages if the market mechanism was working? Aren't power shortages the best excuse for power plants to gear up their production and generate more power and thus more profits? The answer, it turns out, is that the market transformation is far from complete in China.

China's power prices have traditionally been set by the government. This is also reflected in China's WTO commitments, which explicitly list prices of both electricity and heating power as one of the goods and services which may be subject to price controls.[73] In 2004, in an effort to promote market reform, the government established the coal and electricity price linkage mechanism.[74] Under the new system, power prices are supposed to be adjusted upward or downward depending on the coal prices in the preceding period (normally no less than 6 months). Since mid 2016, coal prices rose rapidly and stayed

---

72 Ziwen Jiang, 'The government officially disclosed the reasons why three provinces in Northeast China were forced power rationing' (*Pengpai News*, 27 September 2021).

73 WTO, 'Protocol on the Accession of the People's Republic of China, WT/L/432' (*WTO*, 23 November 2001) Annex 4.

74 National Energy Administration, 'Guidance on establishing the mechanism of coal-electricity price linkage' (关于建立煤电价格联动机制的意见的通知) (*National Energy Administration*, 17 August 2011).

at high levels.[75] According to the formula in the coal and electricity price linkage mechanism, electricity prices were supposed to be adjusted upwards. However, in 2018,[76] in an effort to reduce the operating costs of manufacturing and business firms, the central government announced that the electricity prices would be reduced by 10%. A further 10% reduction was also announced in 2019.[77] This means that the more electricity power plants generated, the more losses they would incur. This is reflected in the financial reports of the State Grid, which incurred a loss of 17.8 billion Yuan in its power generation business in 2020, for the first time in its history.[78] This trend continued in 2021, with coal prices rising by as much as 300%,[79] and all state-owned coal power plants reportedly losing 101.7 billion Yuan in that year.[80] Thus, it is no surprise that power plants were not keen to generate more electricity. Instead, creating a gap in meeting the demand could be a way to force the central government to allow more price adjustment, and/or to seek subsidies from the government.

This strategy seemed to have worked. Right after the nation-wide power shortages, the NDRC issued the "Notice on further deepening market-oriented reform of on-grid electricity price for coal-fired power generation", which expanded the upper price fluctuations limit from 10% to 20%, while the transaction price of high energy-consuming enterprises was not even subject to the 20% upper limit.[81] In May 2022, the central government agreed to provide state-owned coal power plants with a subsidy package totalling 100 billion Yuan, along with 30 billion Yuan of additional capital injection,[82] as well as

75 National Bureau of Statistic, 'Coal production increased in rehabilitation, and the industrial layout was optimized in adjustment' (*National Bureau of Statistic*, 20 March 2018).

76 Keqiang Li, '2018 Government Work Report' (2018年政府工作报告) (*The Central People's Government of the People's Republic of China*, 05 March 2018).

77 Keqiang Li, '2019 Government Work Report' (2019年政府工作报告) (*The Central People's Government of the People's Republic of China*, 05 March 2019).

78 Jinghua Xi, 'The State Grid Corporation of China lost 17.8 billion yuan for the first time in its main business last year, and its profit hit a seven-year low' (*Jiemian*, 16 April 2021).

79 Xiaoxing Liu, 'Whether the dual-control policy of energy consumption should be responsible for power rationing?' (*China Environment News*, 08 October 2021).

80 The State Council, 'The State Council Information Office held a news conference on the economic operation of central enterprises in the first quarter of 2022' (*The Central People's Government of the People's Republic of China*, 20 April 2022).

81 National Development and Reform Commission, 'Notice on deepening the marketization reform of the on-grid price generated by coal-fired power' (关于进一步深化燃煤发电上网电价市场化改革的通知) (*National Development and Reform Commission*, 11 October 2021).

82 Zhi Li, 'Standing Committee of the State Council: Another 50 billion yuan of renewable energy subsidies will be allocated to central power generation enterprises' (*Xinhua*, 11 May 2022).

approval for them to issue 200 billion Yuan of special bonds for energy supply guarantee.[83]

5 Comparison with China's Trade Policy Making

As we can see from the above discussions on China's climate policy implementation, contrary to what might be assumed, it has not been easy to implement the policy despite China being a unitary state with a top-down power structure. This is because China is far from a monolithic entity with only one voice and one course of action. Instead, while the central government may make a policy, it might not be able to force the other actors, such as local governments and state-owned firms, to implement such policy.

This provides an interesting contrast with the implementation of China's trade policy, where the problems are mainly at the level of central government rather than local government. This is reflected in China's WTO disputes, where most of the cases brought against China are about trade remedy measures (especially subsidies measures) and various import and export restrictions that are introduced and implemented by the central government.

On the other hand, the same problems may be observed even in the trade area when the interests of the local and central governments are not aligned with each other. The best example is the protection of intellectual property (IP) rights, where the central government has for a long time been unable to enforce the IP laws due to local protectionism that results from the lack of incentives from the local government to crack down local IP-infringing firms that provide jobs and economic growth.[84] The problem was only solved after the local firms themselves became innovators, and started to pressure local governments to aggressively enforce China's own IP laws, which is also aligned with the goals of the central government to upgrade China's position in the value chain.[85]

Such misalignment of the interests of different levels of government also explains China's negotiation positions in trade agreements. So far, most of China's commitments in free trade agreements (FTAs) have been on traditional border measures such as tariffs. This is because these issues are mainly

83 The Central People's Government of the People's Republic of China, '2023 New Year Message to Enterprises' (*Zhengfu*, 22 January 2023).

84 Bryan Mercurio, 'The Protection and Enforcement of Intellectual Property in China since Accession to the WTO: Progress and Retreat' (2012) 1 China Perspectives 23, 23.

85 Ibid.

controlled by the central government and thus are easier to implement. Behind the border regulatory issues are rarely included, especially difficult ones such as environment and labor, where enforcement needs to be relegated to local governments. In FTAs which do include these issues, the environment or labor provisions are often couched in non-binding, best endeavor language. Even when China started to include stronger CPTPP-like language such as "[a] Party shall not fail to effectively enforce its environmental measures including laws and regulations, through a sustained or recurring course of action or inaction, in a manner affecting trade or investment between the Parties"[86] in its latest FTAs such as the ones with Korea and Singapore, these clauses are still excluded from the application of the dispute settlement mechanisms under the respective FTAs,[87] probably due to the concern that implementation would be a major headache for the central government.

The conundrum China faces in implementing its climate change policies also highlights the importance of implementing more market reforms, which is often fraught with difficulties. Paradoxically, compliance with China's trade commitments may sometimes further complicates the matter, as the "competition among purposes" between "different bodies of international law"[88] might lead to absurd results. Take, for example, China's export restrictions on rare earth, the subject matter of a high-profile WTO dispute in 2012.[89] Theoretically speaking, direct environmental protection measures would be more efficient than export restrictions in addressing environment problems. Yet, the lack of effective enforcement by the local governments left China with only one real option: export restrictions implemented by the central government, even though that is not the optimal policy action in theory. After the case was launched in March 2012, it was almost certain that China would lose the case

86 Ministry of Commerce of the People's Republic of China, 'Free Trade Agreement between the Government of the People's Republic of China and the Government of the Republic of Korea' (*China FTA Network*, June 2015) art 16.5; Ministry of Commerce of the People's Republic of China, 'Free Trade Agreement between the Government of the People's Republic of China and the Government of the Republic of Singapore' (*China FTA Network*, 23 October 2008) ch 17, art 4.

87 See above China-Korea FTA (n 86) art 16.9; China-Singapore FTA (n 86) ch17, art 7.

88 See above Viñuales (n 4).

89 WTO, 'Appellate Body Report, China – Measures Related to the Exportation of Rare Earths, Tungsten, and Molybdenum, WT/DS431/AB/R' (*WTO*, 7 August 2014).

based on the unfavorable precedent of the *China – Raw Materials* case.[90] As it was almost impossible to get the local government to step up the enforcement, a leading expert at the Ministry of Commerce's International Trade and Economic Cooperation Research Institute proposed to have more state control in the sector through further consolidation of rare earth firms by SOEs.[91] This is confirmed by subsequent developments, where all of the seven leading rare earth firms turned out to be SOEs.[92]

More specifically, on the relationship between climate change and trade, China has been consistently opposing the use of trade measures for climate purposes. For example, China criticises the EU's Carbon Border Adjustment Mechanism (CBAM) as being inconsistent with WTO rules and the principles and requirements of the UNFCCC and the Paris Agreement.[93] Similarly, China refused to join the EU-led Coalition of Trade Ministers on Climate when it was announced at the World Economic Forum in 2023.[94] Instead, the Chinese Minister of Commerce voiced indirect disapproval of the initiative by stressing that "climate change shall be addressed through trade and investment liberalization and facilitation, rather than through trade restrictions and subsidy competition."[95] Again, China's position partly reflects its concern that, due to the challenges it faces in effectively implementing climate policies domestically, making binding climate-oriented trade policies at the international level could severely undermine China's policy space.

90 WTO, 'Appellate Body Report, China – Measures Related to the Exportation of Various Raw Materials, WT/DS394/AB/R' (*WTO*, 30 January 2012).

91 Xinyu Mei, 'The Dispute of Rare Earth: Short-Term Response and Radical Measures' (*Securities Times*, 16 March 2012).

92 Shujuan Bi, 'Mergers and Acquisitions of China's Rare Earth Industry Accelerated' (*China United Business News*, 13 July 2012).

93 China News, 'China's response to the 'Carbon Tariff': A contravention of both WTO rules and the principles and requirements stipulated by the Paris Agreement' (*China News*, 26 July 2021).

94 European Commission, 'Trade and Climate: EU and partner countries launch the 'Coalition of Trade Ministers on Climate'' (*European Commission Press Corner*, 19 January 2023).

95 Ministry of Commerce of the People's Republic of China, 'Wang Shouwen, the negotiator and deputy minister of the Ministry of Commerce, led a delegation to attend the small ministerial meeting hosted by the WTO in Davos' (*Ministry of Commerce of the People's Republic of China*, 20 January 2023).

6 Constitutional Failures, Environmental Authoritarianism and Transnational Governance Failures

It has been argued that democracies might face limits in tackling climate change due to their tendencies to focus on short-term gains for their constituencies[96] and their susceptibility to influences from business interests which oppose environmental policies.[97] Instead, to deal with the mounting environmental challenges, authoritarianism "may become not only justifiable, but essential for the survival of humanity".[98] On the other hand, both theories have been challenged. "The limits of democracy in tackling climate change" has been partially debunked by Marina Povitkina's study which shows that democracies do tend to emit less, and that the limits to the benefits of democracy for climate change mitigation are mainly due to "the presence of corrupt institutions, which obstruct coercive capacity, extractive capacity of the state, actors' compliance, and pro-climate policy-making".[99] Similarly, Bruce Gilley notes that, while authoritarian environmentalism might be "more effective in producing policy outputs",[100] such outputs might suffer from lack of coherence, which in turn would lead to more implementation problems compared to democratic governments.[101]

As a typical authoritarian regime, China's Constitution is often perceived as lacking the substance required to achieve constitutionalism, due to the lack of judicial oversight over political power, democracy in its political system, amongst other deficiencies.[102] Yet, it has also been argued that despite these deficiencies, authoritarian constitutions, like China's, do serve some standard constitutional functions, such as setting up political mechanisms and practices, facilitating coordination among major institutions, and establishing

96 Stephen Haggard, 'Inflation and stabilization' in Gerald M. Meler (ed), *Politics and policy making in developing countries: perspectives on the new political economy* (ICS Press 1991) 233–49.

97 Philip Keefer, 'Clientelism, credibility, and the policy choices of young democracies' (2007) 51 American Journal of Political Science 804, 804–21.

98 Mark Beeson, 'The coming of environmental authoritarianism, Environmental Politics' (2010) 19 Environmental Politics 276, 289.

99 Marina Povitkina, 'The limits of democracy in tackling climate change, Environmental Politics' (2018) 27 Environmental Politics 411, 425.

100 Bruce Gilley, 'Authoritarian environmentalism and China's response to climate change' (2012) 21 Environmental Politics 287, 287.

101 Ibid 297–98.

102 Stéphanie Balme and Michael W. Dowdle, 'Introduction: Exploring for Constitutionalism in 21st Century China' in Stéphanie Balme and Michael W. Dowdle (eds), *Building Constitutionalism in China* (Palgrave Macmillan 2009) 1–20.

overarching principles, norms and policies to shape and promote the development of law, regulatory practices and social behavior.[103] While China's Communist Party maintains absolute leadership in decision-making, it does not, and has no intention to, exercise absolute control over all matters but instead leaves ample room for "power advancement for other state apparatuses and citizens' rights" which is considered necessary for economic reforms and modernization.[104] When it comes to climate actions and energy transition, the commitment of the central government is embedded in China's Constitution which incorporates environmental protection and sustainable development as general principles.[105] Although this provides the constitutional basis for China's climate actions, the deficiencies in China's constitutionalism present a cause of the challenges faced by Chinese leaders in ensuring the implementation of national policies at the local level. One major deficiency here concerns the highly centralized, non-democratic policymaking process in which local governments and stakeholders are not involved.[106] This leads to *constitutional* failures because China's climate policies and actions come out of top-down rather than bottom-up decisions which often fail to consider local differences and needs, hence engendering difficulties and tensions in implementation at the local level.[107] Such implementation problems can also be viewed as *governance* failures for at least two interrelated reasons. One concerns the incentive and promotion mechanisms imposed by the central government on local officials such as the climate targets discussed in Section 4. Since these mechanisms and targets usually do not pay "due consideration of the costs and challenges in the implementation process", they end up inducing local authorities to form strategic alliances against implementation.[108] Such alliances, based on wide and strong local networks involving supervising authorities and officials

103 Tom Ginsburg and Alberto Simpser, 'Introduction: Constitutions in Authoritarian Regimes' in Tom Ginsburg and Alberto Simpser (eds), *Constitutions in Authoritarian Regimes* (Cambridge University Press 2013) 1–18; Ma Ji and Dini Sejko, 'The Protection of Foreign Investment in China Constitutional Law: An Evolving Constant' in Ngoc S. Bui, Stuart Hargreaves and Ryan Mitchell (eds), *Routledge Handbook of Constitutional Law in Greater China* (Routledge 2023) 286–99.

104 Xin He, 'The Party's Leadership as a Living Constitution in China' in Tom Ginsburg and Alberto Simpser (eds), *Constitutions in Authoritarian Regimes* (Cambridge University Press 2013) 259.

105 The Central People's Government of the People's Republic of China, 'Constitutional Law of the People's Republic of China' (*Xinhua*, 22 March 2018) Preamble and art 26.

106 See above He (n 104) 245–64.

107 Xueguang Zhou, 'The Institutional Logic of Collusion among Local Governments in China' (2010) 36 Modern China 47, 57.

108 Ibid 64–6.

in other agencies and organizations, make enforcement mechanisms futile,[109] constituting the second cause of governance failures. In addition, the implementation problems are also a consequence of incomplete market-oriented reforms in China's energy sector due to misaligned objectives, as discussed in Section 4. While the reforms are essential for China's energy transition, it remains to be seen how the central government will address the competing interests between climate ambitions, energy transition and economic growth and the extent to which it will reduce intervention and let the market play a major role in allocating resources and setting energy prices which properly internalize environmental costs.[110]

At the international level, it has been observed that the rigid "hierarchical structure of China's policymaking processes"[111] "leaves virtually no scope for positions to be significantly adjusted on the spot during international negotiations",[112] which in turn could result in "transnational governance failures".[113] However, our discussion above shows that such "transnational governance failures" could be easily overcome when the top leader decides to make an international commitment. Nonetheless, as we can see from the abrupt policy shift in China in 2021, the much-admired efficiency of "environmental authoritarianism" in making international commitments shall not be confused with the actual implementation of such commitments. When it comes to implementation, the lack of consultation and deliberation from the relevant stakeholders often translate into the lack of understanding of the true significance of such commitments, while the lack of market and political mechanisms to allow "consumers and citizens to freely and fully engage in market-based and political transactions"[114] also make it hard for the policies to be carried out as envisaged, leading instead to fits and starts, even crises.

More broadly, China's experience with climate change and energy transition also highlights the need to not just focus on international cooperation when

---

109 Ibid 67–73.

110 For a recent recap of China's energy market reforms, see International Monetary Fund, 'People's Republic of China: Selected Issues' (*IMF Country Reports*, 10 February 2023) 51–63.

111 Mark Beeson, 'Coming to Terms with the Authoritarian Alternative: The Implications and Motivations of China's Environmental Policies' (2018) 5 Asia & the Pacific Policy Studies 34, 42.

112 Björn Conrad, 'China in Copenhagen: Reconciling the "Beijing Climate Revolution" and the "Copenhagen Climate Obstinacy"' (2012) 210 The China Quarterly 435, 443.

113 Ernst-Ulrich Petersmann, Constitutional Pluralism, Regulatory Competition and Transnational Governance Failures.

114 Armin Steinbach, Constitutional economics and transnational governance failures.

it comes to multilevel governance of public goods,[115] but also the sub-national implementations of such commitments after the conclusion of international agreements. For countries with a constitutional democracy where the sub-national governments enjoy substantive autonomy, this might be achieved through the preference of transnational governance over local or national governance once "it is established that the subsidiarity principle determines the affected and interested community to be global".[116] But for countries with no constitutional democracy, another mechanism might be needed to avoid implementation problems. In the context of international trade regulation, this was achieved through the incorporation of a special clause in China's WTO Accession Protocol.[117]

> 2. *Administration of the Trade Regime*
>
> (A) *Uniform Administration*
>
> 1. *The provisions of the WTO Agreement and this Protocol shall apply to the entire customs territory of China, including border trade regions and minority autonomous areas, Special Economic Zones, open coastal cities, economic and technical development zones and other areas where special regimes for tariffs, taxes and regulations are established (collectively referred to as "special economic areas").*
> 2. *China shall apply and administer in a uniform, impartial and reasonable manner all its laws, regulations and other measures of the central government as well as local regulations, rules and other measures issued or applied at the sub-national level (collectively referred to as "laws, regulations and other measures") pertaining to or affecting trade in goods, services, trade-related aspects of intellectual property rights ("TRIPS") or the control of foreign exchange.*
> 3. *China's local regulations, rules and other measures of local governments at the sub-national level shall conform to the obligations undertaken in the WTO Agreement and this Protocol.*

115 For the discussion of this concept, see Ernst-Ulrich Petersmann and Armin Steinbach, 'Neo-Liberalism, State-Capitalism and Ordo-Liberalism: "Institutional Economics" and "Constitutional Choices" in Multilevel Trade Regulation' (2021) 22 The Journal of World Investment & Trade 1.

116 See above Steinbach (n 114).

117 See above WTO n 73.

4. *China shall establish a mechanism under which individuals and enterprises can bring to the attention of the national authorities cases of non-uniform application of the trade regime.*

In 2014, China further stepped up the efforts to ensure local compliance with WTO rules with the State Council's " Notice on Further Strengthening Trade Policy Compliance Work",[118] which is followed by the Ministry of Commerce (MOFCOM)'s "Implementation Measures for Trade Policy Compliance (Interim)".[119] The two documents give the MOFCOM wide-ranging power to review the "regulations, normative documents and other policy measures formulated by various departments of the State Council, local people's governments at various levels and their departments concerning or affecting trade in goods, trade in services and trade-related intellectual property rights"[120] to ensure their compliance with WTO rules including China's accession commitments.[121] The problem, however, is that it is still just desk review of documents and does not cover "specific administrative measures for specific administrative subjects",[122] which means that implementation is not covered. Thus, more would be needed to deal with the gap in implementation of international commitments.

7 Concluding Thoughts

China's abrupt shift from its policy commitment to the reduction of coal use for its climate goals in 2021 provides a vivid reminder that, while climate issues are global, politics is always local. Politics is not a problem for effective implementation of climate policies in Western countries, where such policies were initially adopted in response to bottom-up demands from various local civil society groups concerned with the negative effects of climate change. However, for countries like China with a top-down decision-making process, the real challenge lies not in the formulation of climate policies but

118 The State Council of China, '国务院办公厅关于进一步加强贸易政策合规工作的通知' (*Ministry of Commerce of the People's Republic of China*, 09 June 2014).

119 The Ministry of Commerce of China, '商务部公告2014年第86号 公布《贸易政策合规工作实施办法（试行）》' (*Ministry of Commerce of the People's Republic of China*, 15 December 2014).

120 Ibid art 2.

121 See above The State Council of China (n 118) art 2.

122 Ibid art 1.

the implementation. Getting climate policies implemented at the local level can be difficult due to the misalignment of the incentives between the central and local governments, which is as much a constitutional failure as a government failure; and the lack of well-functioning market mechanisms that would respond well to market signals.

However, the policy shift should not be seen as China retreating from its climate goals. Rather, it was a temporary deviation and short-term response to one of the worst power shortages in China, which is further complicated by the impacts of the COVID-19 pandemic on the Chinese economy and the Russia-Ukraine war on global energy prices and supply. Nevertheless, the challenges China faces in balancing climate actions and energy security may well continue to drive China's incremental approach to controlling coal use and will remain a key concern in China's pursuit of climate goals.[123]

In addition, this paper provides some broader insights on understanding the difficulties facing many developing countries. Their reluctance to take climate actions might not necessarily arise from a lack of willingness to undertake commitments at the international level. Rather, it is closely related to gaps in energy transition and governance at the domestic level, including effective tools to translate international commitments into implementation by local governments, and efficient markets to align the interests of different stakeholders in service of the common goal. Thus, a more productive approach to international cooperation on climate issues should involve a more sympathetic understanding of the constraints facing developing countries, and the supply of the necessary tool-box of best practices to help them address such governance deficits. This may also provide a way to help developing countries overcome short-term problems in the implementation of climate policies, which would in turn lead to a brighter future for all mankind.

Bibliography

Balme S and Dowdle WM, 'Introduction: Exploring for Constitutionalism in 21st Century China' in Stéphanie Balme and Michael W. Dowdle (eds), *Building Constitutionalism in China* (Palgrave Macmillan 2009).

123 Wendong Wei and others, 'Toward carbon neutrality: Uncovering constraints on critical minerals in the Chinese power system' (2022) 2 Fundamental Research 367.

Beeson M, 'Coming to Terms with the Authoritarian Alternative: The Implications and Motivations of China's Environmental Policies' (2018) 5 Asia & the Pacific Policy Studies 34.

Beeson M, 'The coming of environmental authoritarianism, Environmental Politics' (2010) 19 Environmental Politics 276.

Bi S, 'Mergers and Acquisitions of China's Rare Earth Industry Accelerated' (*China United Business News*, 13 July 2012), <http://finance.sina.com.cn/roll/20120713/201512563878.shtml>.

Cama T and Henry D, 'Trump: We Are Getting out of Paris Climate Deal' (*The Hill*, 1 June 2017) <https://thehill.com/policy/energy-environment/335955-trump-pulls-us-out-of-paris-climate-deal/>.

CGTN, 'Full Text: Xi Jinping's Speech at General Debate of the 75th Session of the United Nations General Assembly' (*CGTN*, 23 September 2020) <https://news.cgtn.com/news/2020-09-23/Full-text-Xi-Jinping-s-speech-at-General-Debate-of-UNGA-U07X2dn8Ag/index.html>.

China News, 'China's response to the 'Carbon Tariff': A contravention of both WTO rules and the principles and requirements stipulated by the Paris Agreement' (*China News*, 26 July 2021) <https://www.chinanews.com.cn/cj/2021/07-26/9528890.shtml>.

Conrad B, 'China in Copenhagen: Reconciling the "Beijing Climate Revolution" and the "Copenhagen Climate Obstinacy"' (2012) 210 The China Quarterly 435.

European Commission, 'Trade and Climate: EU and partner countries launch the 'Coalition of Trade Ministers on Climate'' (*European Commission Press Corner*, 19 January 2023) <https://ec.europa.eu/commission/presscorner/detail/en/IP_23_248>.

Fishman D, 'Reasons Behind China's Power Shortage in Q4 2021, Resultant Reform Measures, and the Impact on Power Markets', (Oxford Energy Forum, March 2022, Issue 131) 13–20 <https://a9w7k6q9.stackpathcdn.com/wpcms/wp-content/uploads/2022/03/OEF-131.pdf>.

Geall S and others, *China's Green Revolution: Energy, Environment and the 12th Five-Year Plan* (Chinadialogue 2011) <https://www.greengrowthknowledge.org/sites/default/files/downloads/resource/China%E2%80%99s_Green_Revolution_Energy_Environment_and_the_12th_Five-Year_Plan_Chinadialogue.pdf>.

Gilley B, 'Authoritarian environmentalism and China's response to climate change' (2012) 21 Environmental Politics 287.

Ginsburg T and Simpser A, 'Introduction: Constitutions in Authoritarian Regimes' in Tom Ginsburg and Alberto Simpser (eds), *Constitutions in Authoritarian Regimes* (Cambridge University Press 2013).

Gore C and Robinson P, 'Local Government Response to Climate Change: Our Last, Best Hope?' in Henrik Selin and Stacy D VanDeveer (eds), *Changing Climates in*

North American Politics: Institutions, Policymaking, and Multilevel Governance (MIT Press 2009).

Haggard S, 'Inflation and stabilization' in Gerald M. Meler (ed), *Politics and policy making in developing countries: perspectives on the new political economy* (ICS Press 1991).

Hart C and others, 'Mapping China's Climate & Energy Policies' (*Development Technologies International*, December 2018) <https://assets.publishing.service.gov.uk/government/uploads/system/uploads/attachment_data/file/786518/China_Climate_Map_Public_Secured_2019-3-1.pdf>.

He X, 'The Party's Leadership as a Living Constitution in China' in Tom Ginsburg and Alberto Simpser (eds), *Constitutions in Authoritarian Regimes* (Cambridge University Press 2013).

Hook L and Manson K, 'US Formally Withdraws from Paris Climate Agreement' (*Financial Times*, 4 November 2020) <https://www.ft.com/content/54f600e0-183f-41fd-8d4b-69ab4403e331>.

International Energy Agency, 'An Energy Sector Roadmap to Carbon Neutrality in China' (*IEA*, September 2021) <https://www.iea.org/reports/an-energy-sector-roadmap-to-carbon-neutrality-in-china>.

International Monetary Fund, 'People's Republic of China: Selected Issues' (*IMF Country Reports*, 10 February 2023) <https://www.elibrary.imf.org/view/journals/002/2023/081/002.2023.issue-081-en.xml>.

Ji M and Sejko D, 'The Protection of Foreign Investment in China Constitutional Law: An Evolving Constant' in Ngoc S. Bui, Stuart Hargreaves and Ryan Mitchell (eds), *Routledge Handbook of Constitutional Law in Greater China* (Routledge 2023).

Jiang Z, 'The government officially disclosed the reasons why three provinces in Northeast China were forced power rationing' (*Pengpai News*, 27 September 2021) <https://m.thepaper.cn/newsDetail_forward_14689139>.

Keefer P, 'Clientelism, credibility, and the policy choices of young democracies' (2007) 51 American Journal of Political Science 804.

Kostka G, 'China's Local Environmental Politics' in Eva Sternfeld (eds), *Routledge Handbook of Environmental Policy in China* (Routledge 2017) 31.

Li K, '2018 Government Work Report' (2018年政府工作报告) (The Central People's Government of the People's Republic of China, 05 March 2018年政府工作报告) (2018The Central People's Government of the People's Republic of China) <http://www.gov.cn/guowuyuan/2018zfgzbg.htm>.

Li K, '2019 Government Work Report' (2019年政府工作报告) (The Central People's Government of the People's Republic of China, 05 March 2019年政府工作报告) (2019The Central People's Government of the People's Republic of China) <http://www.gov.cn/guowuyuan/2019zfgzbg.htm>.

Li Z, 'Standing Committee of the State Council: Another 50 billion yuan of renewable energy subsidies will be allocated to central power generation enterprises' (*Xinhua*, 11 May 2022) <https://www.yicai.com/news/101409372.html>.

Liu X, 'Whether the dual-control policy of energy consumption should be responsible for power rationing?' (*China Environment News*, 08 October 2021) <http://epaper.cenews.com.cn/html/2021-10/08/content_70284.htm>.

Mei X, 'The Dispute of Rare Earth: Short-Term Response and Radical Measures' (*Securities Times*, 16 March 2012) <https://business.sohu.com/20120316/n337913670.shtml>.

Mercurio B, 'The Protection and Enforcement of Intellectual Property in China since Accession to the WTO: Progress and Retreat' (2012) 1 China Perspectives 23.

Ministry of Commerce of the People's Republic of China, 'Free Trade Agreement between the Government of the People's Republic of China and the Government of the Republic of Korea' (*China FTA Network*, June 2015) <http://fta.mofcom.gov.cn/topic/enkorea.shtml>.

Ministry of Commerce of the People's Republic of China, 'Free Trade Agreement between the Government of the People's Republic of China and the Government of the Republic of Singapore' (*China FTA Network*, 23 October 2008) <http://fta.mofcom.gov.cn/topic/enkorea.shtml>.

Ministry of Commerce of the People's Republic of China, 'Wang Shouwen, the negotiator and deputy minister of the Ministry of Commerce, led a delegation to attend the small ministerial meeting hosted by the WTO in Davos' (*Ministry of Commerce of the People's Republic of China*, 20 January 2023) <http://www.mofcom.gov.cn/article/xwfb/xwbldhd/202301/20230103380415.shtml>.

Ministry of Commerce of the People's Republic of China, '商务部公告2014年第86号 公布《贸易政策合规工作实施办法（试行）》' (*Ministry of Commerce of the People's Republic of China*, 15 December 2014) <http://sms.mofcom.gov.cn/article/zt_myzchggz/lanmuone/201412/20141200833104.shtml>.

Ministry of Ecology and Environment of the People's Republic of China, 'China's Achievements, New Goals and New Measures for Nationally Determined Contributions' (中国落实国家自主贡献成效和新目标新举措) (*Ministry of Ecology and Environment of the People's Republic of China*, 28 October 2021) <https://unfccc.int/sites/default/files/ NDC/2022-06/%E4%B8%AD%E5%9B%BD%E8%90%BD%E5%AE%9E%E5%9B%BD%E5%AE %B6%E8%87%AA%E4%B8%BB%E8%B4 %A1%E7%8C%AE%E6%88%90%E6%95%88 %E5%92%8C%E6%96%B0%E7%9B%AE%E6%A0%87%E6%96%B0%E4%B8%BE%E6%8E%AA.pdf>.

Ministry of Foreign Affairs of the People's Republic of China, 'Report on the United States Prejudicing Global Environmental Governance' (*Ministry of Foreign Affairs of the People's Republic of China*, 19 October 2020) <https://www.fmprc.gov.cn/web/wjb_673085/zzjg_673183/tyfls_674667/xwlb_674669/202010/t20201019_7671146.shtml>.

Ministry of Foreign Affairs of the People's Republic of China, 'Sanction against Pelosi's Sneaky Visit to Taiwan' (*Ministry of Foreign Affairs of the People's Republic of China*,

5 August 2022) <https://www.fmprc.gov.cn/fyrbt_673021/202208/t20220805_10735604.shtml>.

National Bureau of Statistic, 'Coal production increased in rehabilitation, and the industrial layout was optimized in adjustment' (*National Bureau of Statistic*, 20 March 2018) <https://app.www.gov.cn/govdata/gov/201803/20/421737/article.html>.

National Development and Reform Commission, 'China's National Plan for Addressing Climate Change' (中国应对气候变化国家方案) (*National Development and Reform Commission*, June 2007) <https://www.ccchina.org.cn/WebSite/CCChina/UpFile/File189.pdf>.

National Development and Reform Commission, 'Enhanced Actions on Climate Change: China's Intended Nationally Determined Contributions' (强化应对气候变化行动—中国国家自主贡献) (*National Development and Reform Commission*, 30 June 2015), <https://policy.asiapacificenergy.org/sites/default/files/China%27s%20INDC%20-%20on%2030%20June%202015.pdf>.

National Development and Reform Commission, 'Improving the plan of the dual-control of the intensity and quantity of energy consumption' (关于印发《完善能源消费强度和总量双控制度方案》的通知) (*National Development and Reform Commission*, 16 September 2021), <https://www.ndrc.gov.cn/xwdt/tzgg/202109/t20210916_1296857.html?code=&state=123>.

National Development and Reform Commission, 'Notice on deepening the marketization reform of the on-grid price generated by coal-fired power' (关于进一步深化燃煤发电上网电价市场化改革的通知) (*National Development and Reform Commission*, 11 October 2021) <https://www.ndrc.gov.cn/xxgk/zcfb/tz/202110/t20211012_1299461.html>.

National Development and Reform Commission, 'Report on the implementation of the dual-control of energy consumption in each province in the first half of 2021' (关于印发《2021年上半年各地区能耗双控目标完成情况晴雨表》的通知) (*National Development and Reform Commission*, 17 August 2021) <https://www.ndrc.gov.cn/xwdt/tzgg/202108/t20210817_1293836.html>.

National Development and Reform Commission, 'The 13th Five-Year Plan for the Development of Energy' (能源发展"十三五"规划) (*National Development and Reform Commission and National Energy Administration*, 26 December 2016), <http://www.nea.gov.cn/135989417_14846217874961n.pdf>.

National Development and Reform Commission, 'The 14th Five-Year Plan for the Modern Energy System' ("十四五"现代能源体系规划) (*National Development and Reform Commission and National Energy Administration*, 29 January 2022) <http://www.nea.gov.cn/1310524241_16479412513081n.pdf>.

National Development and Reform Commission, 'The National Plan (2014–2020) for Addressing Climate Change' (国家发展改革委关于印发国家应对气候变化规划(2014–2020年)的通知) (*National Development and Reform Commission*, 19

September 2014), <https://www.ndrc.gov.cn/xxgk/zcfb/tz/201411/t20141104_963642.html>.

National Energy Administration, 'Guidance on establishing the mechanism of coal-electricity price linkage' (关于建立煤电价格联动机制的意见的通知) (*National Energy Administration*, 17 August 2011), <http://www.nea.gov.cn/2011-08/17/c_131054427.htm>.

Petersmann EU and Steinbach A, 'Neo-Liberalism, State-Capitalism and Ordo-Liberalism: "Institutional Economics" and "Constitutional Choices" in Multilevel Trade Regulation' (2021) 22 The Journal of World Investment & Trade 1.

Povitkina M, 'The limits of democracy in tackling climate change, Environmental Politics' (2018) 27 Environmental Politics 411, 425.

Qi Y and Wu T, 'The Politics of Climate Change in China' (2013) 4 WIREs Climate Change 301, 303. See also United Nations, 'A new blueprint for international action on the environment' (*United Nations*, 1992) <https://www.un.org/en/conferences/environment/rio1992>.

Qin T and Zhang M, 'Development of China's Environmental Legislation', in Eva Sternfeld (eds), *Routledge Handbook of Environmental Policy in China* (Routledge 2017) 19.

Sandalow D and others, 'Guide to Chinese Climate Policy 2022' (*Oxford Institute of Energy Studies*, 2022) <https://chineseclimatepolicy.oxfordenergy.org/> 32.

Spegele B, 'China's Legislature Ratifies Paris Agreement on Climate Ahead of G-20 Meeting' (*The Wall Street Journal*, 2 September 2016) <https://www.wsj.com/articles/chinas-legislature-ratifies-paris-agreement-on-climate-ahead-of-g-20-meeting-1472872781>.

Suarez I and Wang X, 'Year Review: The Impact of China's Ban on Overseas Coal Power Plants on Global Climate' (*Centre for Research on Energy and Clean Air*, 22 September 2022) <https://energyandcleanair.org/wp/wp-content/uploads/2022/09/ChinaBan-Report_ChV_FINAL27Sept22.pdf> 3.

The Central People's Government of the People's Republic of China, 'The Outline of the 12th Five-Year Plan for Economic and Social Development of the People's Republic of China' (中华人民共和国国民经济和社会发展第十二个五年规划纲要) (*The Central People's Government of the People's Republic of China*, 16 March 2011) <http://www.gov.cn/2011lh/content_1825838.htm>.

The Central People's Government of the People's Republic of China, 'The Outline of the 13th Five-Year Plan for Economic and Social Development of the People's Republic of China' (中华人民共和国国民经济和社会发展第十三个五年规划纲要) (*Xinhua*, 17 March 2016) <http://www.gov.cn/xinwen/2016-03/17/content_5054992.htm>.

The Central People's Government of the People's Republic of China, 'The Outline of the 14th Five-Year Plan for National Economic and Social Development and Long-Range Objectives for 2035 the People's Republic of China' (中华人民共和国国民

经济和社会发展第是十四五个规划和2035年远景目标纲要) (*The Central People's Government of the People's Republic of China*, 13 March 2021) <http://www.gov.cn/xinwen/2021-03/13/content_5592681.htm>.

The Central People's Government of the People's Republic of China, 'Working Guidance for Carbon Dioxide Peaking and Carbon Neutrality in Full and Faithful Implementation of the New Development Philosophy' (完整准确全面贯彻新发展理念做好碳达峰碳中和工作的意见) (*The Central People's Government of the People's Republic of China*, 22 September 2021) <http://www.gov.cn/zhengce/2021-10/24/content_5644613.htm>.

The Central People's Government of the People's Republic of China, 'The Plan for the Institutional Reform of the State Council of the People's Republic of China' (国务院机构改革方案) (*The Central People's Government of the People's Republic of China*, 17 March 2018) <http://www.gov.cn/guowuyuan/2018-03/17/content_5275116.htm>.

The Central People's Government of the People's Republic of China, '2023 New Year Message to Enterprises' (*Zhengfu*, 22 January 2023) <http://www.gov.cn/xinwen/2023-01/22/content_5738440.htm>.

The Central People's Government of the People's Republic of China, 'Constitutional Law of the People's Republic of China' (*Xinhua*, 22 March 2018) <https://www.gov.cn/guoqing/2018-03/22/content_5276318.htm>.

The Central People's Government of the People's Republic of China, 'The Outline of the 10th Five-Year Plan for Economic and Social Development of the People's Republic of China' (中华人民共和国国民经济和社会发展第十个五年计划纲要) (*The Central People's Government of the People's Republic of China*, 15 March 2001) <http://www.gov.cn/gongbao/content/2001/content_60699.htm>.

The Central People's Government of the People's Republic of China, 'Renewable Energy Law of the People's Republic of China' (中华人民共和国可再生能源法) (*The Central People's Government of the People's Republic of China*, 21 June 2005) <http://www.gov.cn/ziliao/flfg/2005-06/21/content_8275.htm>.

The State Council Information Office of the People's Republic of China, 'Full Text: Responding to Climate Change: China's Policies and Actions' (*The State Council Information Office of the People's Republic of China*, 27 October 2021) <http://www.scio.gov.cn/zfbps/32832/Document/1715506/1715506.htm>.

The State Council of the People's Republic of China, 'Introduction to the National Coordination Group for Addressing Climate Change' (*China Climate Change Info-Net*, 17 July 2006) <https://www.ccchina.org.cn/list.aspx?clmId=67>.

The State Council of the People's Republic of China, 'The Action Plan for Reaching Carbon Dioxide Peak before 2030' (2030年前碳达峰行动方案) (*The State Council of the People's Republic of China*, 24 October 2021) <http://www.gov.cn/zhengce/content/2021-10/26/content_5644984.htm>.

The State Council of the People's Republic of China, 'The Comprehensive Working Plan for Energy Conservation and Emission Reduction for Implementing the 13th Five-Year Plan' ("十三五"节能减排综合工作方案) (*The State Council of the People's Republic of China*, 20 December 2016) <http://www.gov.cn/zhengce/content/2017-01/05/content_5156789.htm>.

The State Council of the People's Republic of China, 'The State Council Information Office held a news conference on the economic operation of central enterprises in the first quarter of 2022' (*The Central People's Government of the People's Republic of China*, 20 April 2022) <http://www.gov.cn/xinwen/2022-04/20/content_5686227.htm>.

The State Council of the People's Republic of China, 'Working Plan for Greenhouse Gas Emission Control in Implementing the 12th Five-Year Plan' (国务院关于印发"十二五"控制温室气体排放工作方案的通知) (*The Central People's Government of the People's Republic of China*, 01 December 2011) <http://www.gov.cn/zwgk/2012-01/13/content_2043645.htm>.

The State Council of the People's Republic of China, '国务院办公厅关于进一步加强贸易政策合规工作的通知' (*Ministry of Commerce of the People's Republic of China*, 09 June 2014) <http://sms.mofcom.gov.cn/article/zt_myzchggz/lanmuone/201408/20140800686109.shtml>.

United Nations, 'The Paris Agreement. What is the Paris Agreement?' (*United Nations*) <https://unfccc.int/process-and-meetings/the-paris-agreement/the-paris-agreement>.

United Nations, 'United Nations Framework Convention on Climate Change' (*United Nations*, 9 May 1992) <https://unfccc.int/resource/docs/convkp/conveng.pdf>.

United Nations, 'What is the Kyoto Protocol?' (*United Nations*) <https://unfccc.int/kyoto_protocol>.

United Nations, 'What is the United Nations Framework Convention on Climate Change?' (*United Nations*) <https://unfccc.int/process-and-meetings/what-is-the-united-nations-framework-convention-on-climate-change>.

Viñuales JE, *The International Law of Energy* (Cambridge University Press 2022) 28.

Wang X, 'Provincial Approval on Coal Fired Power Revived after Power Rationing, Local State-Owned Capital Refilled Strongly' (*Greenpeace*, 20 July 2022) <https://www.greenpeace.org.cn/2022/07/20/2021-2022q1-coal-brieifng/>.

Wang Y, 'Explanations on the Plan for the Institutional Reform of the State Council of the People's Republic of China' (关于国务院机构改革方案的说明) (*Xinhua*, 17 March 2018) <http://www.gov.cn/guowuyuan/2018-03/14/content_5273856.htm>.

Wei W and others, 'Toward carbon neutrality: Uncovering constraints on critical minerals in the Chinese power system' (2022) 2 Fundamental Research 367.

Williams L, 'China's Climate Change Policies: Actors and Drivers' (*Lowy Institute*, July 2014) <https://www.files.ethz.ch/isn/182715/chinas-climate-change-policies.pdf>.

World Bank Group, 'Country Climate and Development Report: China' (*World Bank Group*, October 2022) <https://openknowledge.worldbank.org/bitstream/handle/10986/38136/FullReport.pdf>.

WTO, 'Appellate Body Report, China – Measures Related to the Exportation of Rare Earths, Tungsten, and Molybdenum, WT/DS431/AB/R' (*WTO*, 7 August 2014) <https://docs.wto.org/dol2fe/Pages/SS/directdoc.aspx?filename=q:/WT/DS/431ABR.pdf&Open=True>.

WTO, 'Appellate Body Report, China – Measures Related to the Exportation of Various Raw Materials, WT/DS394/AB/R' (*WTO*, 30 January 2012) <https://docs.wto.org/dol2fe/Pages/SS/directdoc.aspx?filename=Q:/WT/DS/398ABR.pdf&Open=True>.

WTO, 'Protocol on the Accession of the People's Republic of China, WT/L/432' (*WTO*, 23 November 2001) <https://docs.wto.org/dol2fe/Pages/SS/directdoc.aspx?filename=q:/WT/L/432.pdf&Open=True>.

Xi J, 'The State Grid Corporation of China lost 17.8 billion yuan for the first time in its main business last year, and its profit hit a seven-year low' (*Jiemian*, 16 April 2021) <https://www.jiemian.com/article/5961951.html>.

Xie Z, 'Persistently Confronting Climate Change and Continuing to Involve, Contribute and Lead the Global Construction of Ecological Civilization: In the Memory of the Ratification of the Paris Agreement' (*China Environment News*, 14 December 2020) <http://epaper.cenews.com.cn/html/2020-12/14/content_100353.htm>.

Xinhua, 'Facts about Pelosi's Visit to Taiwan' (*Xinhua*, 25 August 2022) <http://www.xinhuanet.com/2022-08/25/c_1128944443.htm>.

Xinhua, 'Full and Faithful Implementation of the New Development Philosophy: Grasp the theory of 'Five Inevitable Routes' deeply and thoroughly' (*Xinhua*, 14 March 2022) <http://www.gov.cn/xinwen/2022-03/14/content_5678878.htm>.

Xinhua, 'Full Text: Remarks by Chinese President Xi Jinping at Leaders Summit on Climate' (*Xinhua*, 22 April 2021) <http://www.xinhuanet.com/english/2021-04/22/c_139899289.htm>.

Xinhua, 'President Xi Jinping's Web Conference with the US President Biden' (*Xinhua*, 16 November 2021) <http://www.gov.cn/xinwen/2021-11/16/content_5651232.htm>.

Xue Y, 'China's approvals for new coal plants rebound amid renewed focus on energy security after last year's power crisis: Greenpeace' (*South China Morning Post*, 20 July 2022) <https://www.scmp.com/business/article/3185844/chinas-approvals-new-coal-plants-rebound-amid-renewed-focus-energy>.

Zhou X, 'The Institutional Logic of Collusion among Local Governments in China' (2010) 36 Modern China 47.

CHAPTER 8

Reforming International Governance: Multilateralism or Polylateralism?

Pascal Lamy

1 The Problem: Leadership, Coherence and Legitimacy in the International System

The current global challenges spanning from the risks associated with climate change, the existential danger for the planet, the Russian invasion of Ukraine and the blatant Russian violation of international law as well as, at the time of writing, the fight between Hamas and Israël are all failures in international cooperation. The current governance of international relations is not delivering any more because itis plagued by two fundamental flaws: one is structural and the second is circumstantial.

The structural flaw is associated with our international system as based on the principle of sovereignty. This is the DNA of international law and core of the Westphalian legal order. It was invented in 1648 for a variety of reasons, but the sovereignty principle stands today in the way of any global governance system. There is a fundamental barrier to international cooperation – sovereignty handicaps structurally the three main deliveries of a governance system: *leadership, coherence and legitimacy*. *Leadership* is needed to show the way to set the agenda, and to leverage delivery. These elements are missing in a sovereignty-based Westphalian system. Nobody will recognize that a sovereign is more sovereign than others, which would contradict the very premise of the concept. Nor is collective leadership in the hands of leaders of international organizations. From the perspective of my own experience as the DG of the WTO, I can tell that being the DG of the WTO does not mean that the DG of WTO exercises real leadership. The theory of the WTO is that this is a "member driven organization". *Coherence* remains difficult whenever states disagree on certain issues or have different policy preferences. In many ways, sovereignty is the privilege of incoherence. That's the reality. I remember Angela Merkel just out of the Heiligendamm G7 summit in 2007, which was her first big international experience. She thought "*this system doesn't work. I'll try to fix this with the leaders of international organizations*". And so we had a meeting later with Angela Merkel and Robert Zoellick at the World Bank, and Dominique

Strauss-Kahn at the IMF at the time and the leaders of the ILO and the OECD. And Merkel said, "*Okay guys, let's be serious. You have to organize a coherence between your organizations. You're working in different clusters, it doesn't work*". And then we spent an afternoon with her discussing and we had the opportunity to express our points. Merkel, who was absorbing this said at the end of the meeting, "*okay, I've understood. The problem of coherence is not with you, it's with me. So I've understood I have to install coherence within the German system*".

Then comes *legitimacy*. Legitimacy, in a proper governed system, is about bringing your constituencies along. And this has a lot to do with proximity. Politics are, before all, local. And by definition, international governance is not local. Legitimacy is a reverse function of distance. What is even more unfortunate is that in this inter-national system, the most legitimate organizations are inefficient and the most efficient organizations are not legitimate. The United Nations General Assembly, for instance, is a very legitimate institution. If you look at polls, people like the United Nations, but the United Nation General Assembly does not really deliver. Another example: the Animal Health Organization, which nobody knows, which has never attracted attention, is a really efficient international organization. The health of animals is much better globally organized than the health of people. Why is it so? Because it is a veterinary club. They cook their soup in their corner. But when a cow gets foot-mouth disease in a province of Argentina, then the next morning the whole world knows it, and there is no more meat trade with this place in Argentina. So that's one of the characteristics of the system.

Another, more circumstantial reason is that most inter-national organizations date from a long time ago, roughly since the end of the Second World War. They were totally Western conceived, with a western architecture. The problem being that obviously the world has changed and that in many countries of this planet, the legitimacy of the system is disputable. The notion that it's a Western creation and that new or emerging powers were not involved in their establishment has consequences. They don't fully feel part of it. Just look at the UN vote on Ukraine. Many of us discovered with shock that more than half of the population of this planet did not side with us in sanctioning Russia. And this is a formidable reverberation of why we are in this problem. If you look at the U.N. Security Council, the five veto holding powers are the victors of a war that took place 80 years ago. Does it make sense, to be frank? If you look at the IMF voting rights, the US has 17%, China has 6%, and Brazil 2%. It makes no sense. More importantly now, if you look at the way China is now trying to decouple International organizations from the Universal Declaration of Human Rights by systematically trying to get rid of any reference to this declaration, you realize that it is not just a functional problem, it's an ideological problem.

Final point about the roots of the problem. In the next decades ahead of us, the world will be dominated by the rivalry between the US and China. We have to live with that, hopefully not in a confrontational way, although the odds that it remains peaceful are probably much lower than they were ten or twenty years ago. This rivalry will inevitably have negative consequences on the way multilateralism works.

The reasons identified above – *leadership, coherence and legitimacy – are at the core* of why the traditional organizations, the one we have, do not work. But this does not mean that nothing can be done within this system.

There are a series of possible marginal improvements. Let me mention a few possible avenues, some of which have been used, including recently. Softer arrangements first: the G20. No specific legitimacy, but some capacity to provide leadership and – in a limited number of remits – coherence. The creation of the Sustainable Development Goals (SDGs), which provide a target for 2030, that we can see as a sort of agenda for the world. Another example is the 2015 Paris Agreement, which, if you compare it to the Kyoto Protocol, is a very different animal. The Kyoto Protocol was a traditional institution treaty-based with binding commitments by the signatories. The problem is that it was addressing 20% of the carbon emissions of this planet, and that couldn't work, whereas the Paris system is much softer. It is based on national contributions for carbon emission targets and, as a consequence of that, it transposes a global legitimacy beyond domestic legitimacy. Governments make commitments. And they are held accountable not by some sort of global agora but by their local domestic constituencies. I would be more careful about the "regionalisation" avenue which is often mentioned in this category. The only example of successful regional integration is the European Union, and the European Union is a very specific case. It is a non-identified political object, totally strange to the normal system of international law. In reality, if you look at the regional governance in the world today, it does not really work. Latin America had quite a lot of regional and continental governance that did not work. Africa has a lot of them, and it does not really work either. ASEAN works for a variety of reasons which are specific and which I cannot further explore here.

Then, there are probably marginal improvements. If, for instance, we would reform the way leaders of international organizations are selected. At the moment, the selection of an international organization leader is unprofessionally done with a few exceptions, and I am proud the WTO is one of those. In general, it is not merit-based, i.e. after a serious vetting of recruitment and profiles. It is very often the result of a transactional diplomatic system. I will vote for you if you vote for me. I vote for you tomorrow if you vote for me 5 years from now. And of course, there are machines in Foreign Ministries that keep stock of all these commitments, even if many of them are forgotten after a few years. This is not professional given the responsibilities that these people are entrusted with. This is not serious and it should be replaced by up to date processes.

2 The Solution: Polylateralism

Improvements can be made but only marginally. Overall, we should not expect too much from the international classical Westphalian system. This is why we have to look elsewhere. In my view, as mentioned already, the root of the problem is sovereignty. One of the avenues is to go around sovereignty by engaging in international cooperation other than sovereign states, namely NGOs, multinational companies, major philanthropic or academic organizations, cities, regions, just to name a few. Many of these stakeholders yield more influence than many of the members of the UN, and are deploying bigger capacities to cooperate and find solutions to many of the unresolved issues of our times. This is what I have called polylateralism. This theory led to the creation of the Paris Peace Forum in 2018 when Emmanuel Macron, the French President, Justin Vaisse, the founder of the Forum, and myself decided to test a new avenue to international cooperation. It is an innovative approach to the problems we are facing. And this new way consists in building, nurturing, monitoring and helping purpose-led multi-stakeholder coalitions that work on solutions.

Of course, it may not be perfect. It may solve only a part of the problem. But let's get things done. This is the spirit of the Paris Peace Forum. The diplomatic system is too diplomatic so to speak. It often looks like an exercise in elegant procrastination, whereas the Paris Peace Forum is about getting things done. And, of course, it's a very different mood. Of course, we don't dispense with diplomats. They are part of the system. But we also work a lot with other actors than diplomats. And I think this is the reason why we have a good number of achievements in a relatively short time. Let me just name a few for the sake of brevity:

- Surrounding the Antarctica continent with marine protected areas. This is something that a coalition between NGOs and some states like the US and the EU are now working on to overcome specific objections by Russia and China, who still have a vested interest in fishing around the Antarctic. To cut it short it would be terrible for global warming to not protect this area.

- We have nurtured the creation of a global fund to help develop independent media called IFPIM. This is a venture by philanthropists and by large media on this planet, including The New York Times, to foster or preserve the freedom of press in the world, which has unfortunately been shrinking in recent times.
- In 2020, in the span of a few weeks, we collected $200 million for vaccine doses. That's obviously not enough to bridge the gap of the vaccine apartheid, which is one of the reasons why we have a bigger North-South gap now, but it was a welcome addition at a crucial time.
- We created a coalition of major digital companies, NGOs and some governments, to protect children on the Internet. There is no treaty for that. There is no institution that cares for that. But it's a major problem and we have to find a solution built on multi-stakeholders' individual commitments.
- We have incubated a common taxonomy for a large number of multinationals to help them benchmark their trajectory to the SDGs. This is something that was created by academics working with CEOs, multinationals and the Paris Peace Forum.

So, as one can see with these few examples, the method is overall less institutional, but more operational. And if you want to look at what I have in mind behind this experience in terms of institutions, my model for the decades to come would rather be the board of the Global Fund against HIV AIDS, which has been a very efficient organization. But if you look at the composition of the board of the Global Fund, it is like the Paris Peace Forum. You have philanthropies, you have experts, you have states, you have NGOs. You have a lot of money that comes from various sources. It is composed very differently from the UN Security Council, and it works better than the UN Security Council.

In conclusion, the classical inter-national system does not look promising for the reasons I gave. I believe that we are living through a major shift in international relations: from a time where geoeconomics had disciplined geopolitics to a world where the balance moved the other way around. I think we are in a world for the decades to come where geopolitics are back on the front page. Geoeconomics are about rules. Global market capitalism needs rules. Addressing the environmental challenge needs rules. Geopolitics are about force. And this fundamental tension between rules and force, an old story in human history, is again ahead of us.

Among many others this is the reason why we have to innovate in international cooperation to reduce tensions and avoid new conflicts and new wars.

CHAPTER 9

Transnational Governance Failures – a Business Perspective and Roadmap for Future Action

John W.H. Denton AO

1 Introduction

The theme of transnational governance – and, more specifically its effectiveness in the real world – is one that is central to the century-long history of the International Chamber of Commerce ("ICC").

ICC was founded out of the ashes of the first world war with a vision that business could be a force for good in the world; and, perhaps more fundamentally, that cross-border commerce should be a vital driver of peace, prosperity and opportunity for all. This early vision of globalization – though admittedly simplistic – remains, I believe, a useful starting point for any discussion on transnational governance failures.

This may seem an unfashionable approach in today's geopolitical context. After all, many respected commentators have been quick to point to the limitations of the German doctrine of *Wandel durch Handel*, or "change through trade", in the context of Russia's unprovoked invasion of Ukraine. The conclusion being, to cite a recent piece by the *Financial Times* columnist John Plender, that trade "produced the wrong sort of change".

This line of argument has, to be sure, a certain instinctive attraction to it in the wake of the war in Ukraine – the ripple effects of which have been felt far and wide. But my core argument here is that a wider historical perspective – separated from the cycle of 24-seven news and the inevitable dramatization that comes with it – offers a much better grounding for an effective debate on the shortcomings of transnational governance today.

2 Re-evaluating the Role of Trade and Globalization

Extensive studies have been dedicated to the history of globalization which I do not seek to re-write or re-interpret here. Rather, I believe it is vital to restate one simple fact as context to the contemporary debate on transnational governance: specifically, that over the past thirty years two forces have combined to mean that we are more prosperous and more interdependent than ever.

The first is the erosion of physical barriers unleashed by the destruction of the Berlin Wall which has led – in broad terms – to an unprecedented period of political, economic and technological convergence across the world. Flows of finance, goods, services and people across borders have transformed the nature of our societies and economies.

The second, is that this erosion of physical barriers has been coupled with an explosion of virtual connectedness, with the internet providing the platform for what is now often termed hyper-globalization. This is – I would unashamedly suggest – good news. Not least since these inter-connected developments have been associated with the most rapid rise in incomes in history.

Indeed, in a recent article, the International Monetary Fund's Kristalina Georgieva and Gita Gopinath highlighted that these positive forces of integration have "boosted productivity and living standards, tripling the size of the global economy and lifting 1.3bn people out of extreme poverty". By contrast, extreme poverty, more often than not, is because people are disconnected from globalization – leaving them without the infrastructure, education, or access to benefit from the global economy.

I emphasise this remarkable dividend from globalization not to make the case for unfettered markets or neo-liberal policies; rather, to emphasise the true root cause of many – if not all – of the transnational governance challenges that we face today. In short: the past thirty years show us that trade can bring positive change. To suggest otherwise is to disregard recent history and risk a "great retrenchment" that could undermine the great strides made in terms of global prosperity.

Set in this context, the real problem that we must address is the growing disconnect between the problems that bind us as a result of our economic interconnectedness and the ability of governments and institutions to respond in appropriate ways. Unfortunately, while people and systems have become more integrated, governance systems are too often locked into fossilized structures which have failed to keep pace with global developments. The result is that globalization has not been – and is not being – managed correctly.

Financial crises, pandemics, cyber-attacks, climate change, and other global threats are, in many ways, an unfortunate underbelly of globalization. The more connected we are, the more we need to accept that we are exposed to trans-boundary risks; and, by extension, the more we need effective, modern global governance.

3 Analysing the Governance Gap

From a business perspective, four weaknesses stand out in terms of the ability of governments and existing multilateral institutions to adapt to the threats inherent to a hyper-globalized world. The first is that the most significant challenges that arise in today's world are cross-border or global in nature. If the primary purpose of a government is to protect its respective citizens, effective cross-border governance should be a greater focus of their attention.

Second – by extension – none of these threats can be addressed by any one country alone. Even the world's largest countries – such the United States of America or China – do not have the means to fight cross-border risks in isolation. This, of course, does not make for easy domestic politics but the trajectory of the coronavirus pandemic is perhaps the ultimate example of how pursuing disjointed domestic policies is futile in the face of a threat that, by its very nature, knowns no borders. To take just one angle, the long-tail of the pandemic – which has resulted in extensive supply-chain disruptions and associated supply-chain disruptions – is a direct consequence of the general failure of the international community to ensure equitable distribution of COVID-19 vaccines across the world. One, which according to our estimates, has cost the world trillions of dollars in lost output and productivity gains.

The third is that new technologies are evolving at such an unprecedented pace that policymakers and regulators need better ways to map and assess potential threats. And fourth: existing global institutions are unfit for 21st century purpose. To take just one example, international development banks are arguably the best resourced element of today's global institutional system and yet they have proved incapable of moving beyond their original Bretton Woods mandate.

4 A Pathway for Reform

The question is thus what kind of reform do we need to see? Clearly, as a fundamental starting point, a step-change is needed in how governments make the case to voters on the merits of international cooperation. This will not be easy to effect; nor – as we have seen with the now decade-long discussions on reform of the World Trade Organization – is it a straightforward process to reform existing international associations. In short, the risk of statis cannot be understated.

It is in this context that I posit a more pragmatic approach to addressing the yawning global governance gap: new modes and models of cooperations that may have potential to yield immediate dividends in tackling transboundary risks to global peace and prosperity. This, I believe, should start with a new wave of thinking on the role of the private sector in enhancing global governance.

This idea is borne out of my experience over the past five years heading up the world's largest business institution. One of the most striking things I have found in the context of challenges such as climate change, infectious diseases or cybercrime is the difference in the instinctive response within the public and private spheres. In general terms, while the approach of business is to seek cross-border solutions, the reflex of governments tends to be to retreat behind national borders and place short-term domestic interests first.

Given this difference in mindset and approach, I believe it is timely to ask whether some of the deficiencies in transnational cooperation could be addressed by more effective engagement of business. In the academic literature on the evolution of global governance arrangements in different policy areas, six ingredients of successful cooperation are typically identified:

- joint identification of problems;
- shared expertise;
- common action principles;
- an accepted outcome-evaluation process to assess results;
- an ability to adapt instruments; and
- trust in institutions.

What is noticeable, however, is that – aside from a few journal articles on hybrid governance from the 1990s and early 2000s – relatively little attention has been paid to the potential role of business in enhancing these core elements of successful transnational governance. I believe that this is an area that warrants much greater debate. To explain why, let me take three examples in turn.

First, cyber security. While the world's attention is, quite rightly, focused on the real-world conflict in Ukraine, we should not lose sight of the fact that states seeking to intimidate and punish their adversaries are much more likely to use non-military methods – most notably cyber-attacks.

This so-called "grey-zone" aggression, which falls below the threshold of formal conflict, takes place every day – and, increasingly, companies are the primary targets. Indeed, in a survey published at the start of 2022, three-quarters of companies expressed concern about state-sponsored cyber-attacks; while over half were worried about government-led retaliation against business in international diplomatic disputes. It seems reasonable to suggest that these percentages will have increased markedly since the invasion of Ukraine.

This, of course, brings a whole range of dilemmas for business leaders who find themselves exposed to geopolitical risk unlike ever before. But if governments really want to prevent their companies – and, moreover, their critical infrastructure – being crippled by state-sponsored cyber-attacks, they must set up regular consultations about prospective threats.

Establishing such dialogue with executives would enable security officials to alert critical industries to potential threats to which they may be imminently exposed. It would also open a channel for executives to contribute intelligence as regards risks and vulnerabilities to governments. Such links are, moreover, essential preparation for if an attack does occur in enabling businesses, diplomats and security agencies to put up a united front in the face of hostile action.

At the global level, a recent ICC paper has shown clearly that existing institutional arrangements and conventions are often underutilized in defending and in prosecuting malicious actors. Again, the experience and expertise of business – from, if you like, the frontlines of cyberspace – has an important role to play in informing how this existing international architecture can be more effectively deployed and leveraged.

Dialogues between governments and industry won't eliminate grey-zone attacks, but they will remove their sting. In an era in which geopolitics is challenging the very principles of globalisation, that is no mean feat.

The second example I want to cite is the global response to the pandemic. To take the public health response: faced with a rapidly evolving health emergency, the immediate reaction of international agencies and humanitarian organizations was to ask the private sector for charitable donations. That – at one level – is entirely understandable given the lamentable underfunding of the humanitarian sector globally.

Nevertheless, that should not obscure a more fundamental truth: reducing the role of the private sector to that of a piggy bank, is – ultimately – to severely understate the role it can play in assisting the global response to crisis situations. To illustrate, in the context of COVID-19, many promising offers from businesses to put their distribution networks at the service of agencies distributing PPE and, latterly, proven vaccines were frequently declined. While companies who wanted to be able to share best practices around containing the virus – such as workplace reconfigurations or enhanced ventilation systems – unable to find willing interlocutors.

Moreover, we saw institutions such as the IMF and regional development banks calibrating their response to the economic impact of the pandemic based on data with a six-month time lag or theoretical models – while many chambers and local business networks had access to real time information on the actual strains being felt in the real economy.

These examples clearly point to missed opportunities to engage the private sector in response to the various dimensions of the pandemic – and in ways which would, quite clearly, have offered opportunities to improve the necessary global effort to protect lives and livelihoods.

What's more, in a world in which humanitarian crises are increasing in their scale and frequency – and where core government funding for the agencies responsible for responding to them is flat at best – there is a broader question about the role of business in providing in-kind resources as part of a new and durable global humanitarian network. Simply put, this is an idea that deserves much greater thought. Emergency fundraising on an ad-hoc basis is not a sustainable nor, by any means, an optimal response to crisis situations.

The third example I'd like to highlight relates to the food security crisis precipitated by the war in Ukraine. In June 2021, the United Nations successfully brokered the Black Sea Grain Initiative to restore international trade in essential Ukrainian and Russian agricultural products and inputs. This was, without doubt, a tremendous diplomatic achievement: one that was brokered in difficult political circumstances and under great pressure given the growing risk of catastrophic food shortages in the developing world.

But, what perhaps isn't widely known is the role played by the business community – and specifically ICC – in ideating and shaping this landmark diplomatic accord. Lest any readers think that I may be overstating the role business played, let me start by quoting directly from a speech given by the UN Secretary General, Antonio Guterres, to a number of heads of state and foreign ministers during General Assembly week in September 2022:

> On top of this [the climate crisis and impact of the pandemic] we now have the impact of the war in Ukraine. The war has manifested itself in severe challenges for food and for energy – which, of course, further complicates the financial problems faced by developing countries.
>
> I want to thank John Denton who provided me with papers and the ideas that allowed me to negotiate with Putin and Zelenskyy something [the Black Sea Initiative] that was meaningful to address the global food crisis. It was his papers that did that – providing me with the scientific capacity to make proposals that would make sense.

This may seem remarkable when viewed through a classic diplomatic lens but from a logical and pragmatic perspective it makes perfect sense. In short, any diplomatic deal to restore agricultural trade in the context of the war in Ukraine must ultimately work for and with the companies trading in farm products across the value chain – from banks and insurers to shipping lines and commodity traders. The worth of any agreement in this context is ultimately only as good as utility to those businesses operating in the real world.

In this context, rather than guessing what might work and taking a step into the dark in forging a new diplomatic deal, a more effective approach is to work with business to craft arrangements that have the best possible chance of functioning in the real economy. Moreover, this partnership-based approach also has the upside of vesting in the private sector a clear stake in making the implementation of any international outcome work – creating a virtuous cycle from design to implementation.

The UN Secretary General deserves great credit for breaking with "business as usual" diplomacy and engaging the private sector, through ICC, as a genuine partner in the negotiation of the Black Sea deal. Drawing on the insights and expertise of our network, the UN was able to design a diplomatic accord that would get business in the agricultural value chain back into Ukraine and Russia – directly addressing the operational and legal risk resulting from the war.

That's what I'd call modern, multistakeholder multilateralism at its very best.

And precisely the foresight, leadership and, indeed, courage we need to see from the heads of global institutions. In this context, the Black Sea Initiative should not be an outlier in terms of how multilateral institutions and international diplomacy engage with business. It should be seen, rather, as a template for the kind of institutional innovation that we need to see to address the transnational governance failures that so often characterise the response to the interconnected and inherently cross-border challenges we face.

5 Areas for Future Research and Dialogue

None of this, of course, is to suggest that engaging business is a panacea for the deficiencies of multilateral institutions. Rather, my aim is to emphasise the latent potential of business to play a more active role in the response to major global challenges.

In this context, I suggest that there are several areas that warrant further research:

i. What approaches could be used to build the necessary trust within multilateral organizations (and their constituent governments) that business can play a constructive role in global governance and humanitarian efforts?
ii. What systems or modes of engagement could be used to scale and structure the engagement of the private sector in multilateral institutions?

iii. What governance arrangements and checks-and-balances would be needed to properly institutionalise the role of business in multilateral affairs?
iv. What could be the role of business networks, such as ICC, in enabling hybrid systems of governance and decision-making?

As noted previously, these areas have been largely underserved to-date by contemporary research – a result, I believe, of the traditional distinction between public and private spheres when it comes to matters of global governance and international diplomacy.

I hope, in some small way, this article will serve to inspire a new wave of thinking on new modes of multistakeholder or hybrid governance that are far better equipped to tackle the transboundary nature of crises that are a very natural, if unwelcome, biproduct of the world's increasing economic interdependence.

CHAPTER 10

U.S. Trade and Multilateralism

Merit E. Janow[1]

This chapter examines the evolution of U.S. approaches to global economic governance, in particular with respect to international trade policy and multilateralism. We describe herein, an evolution whereby the United States has gone from being a key architect of postwar institutions of international economic policy and the rules-based international trading system to, at this moment, limited executive branch interest in negotiating reciprocal binding trade or economic agreements. Reform of the World Trade Organization (WTO) has been identified as necessary, but after years of failed efforts to advance multilateral trade rounds, dissatisfaction with the functioning of the WTO has grown, and the United States has blocked appointments to the top dispute settlement arm of the WTO, the Appellate Body.

Following the COVID-19 pandemic—which revealed both the importance of international trade and significant vulnerabilities in the supply chain—and an increase in geopolitical tensions, U.S. policy appears to have taken a meaningful pause from pursuing trade agreements.[2] Current U.S. economic priorities center on COVID recovery, competition with China (especially on the technology frontier), support for the clean energy transition, and dealing with a banking crises. In the first two years of the Biden administration, three major pieces of legislation were passed—the CHIPS and Science Act,[3] the Inflation Reduction Act,[4] and the Infrastructure Investment and Jobs Act.[5] Some estimates project over $2 trillion in federal spending over the next ten

1 Merit E. Janow is Dean Emerita and Professor of Practice, International Economic Law & Policy, School of International and Public Affairs, Columbia University.

2 In a recent essay, Alan Wolff argues that trade was essential to addressing COVID. Ventilators, for example, need upward of 1500 parts from some 200 suppliers located around the world. Alan Wolff, 'The Four Horsemen of the Apocalypse at the WTO' [2023].

3 CHIPS and Science Act 2022.

4 Inflation Reduction Act 2022.

5 Infrastructure Investment and Jobs Act 2021.

DOI:10.1163/9789004693722_011

years associated with this legislation in support of R&D, clean energy, health care, competitiveness and innovation.[6]

The president and his cabinet stress the importance of homeshoring, investment nearshoring, and building supply chain resilience with like-minded allies.[7] A number of restrictions have been introduced with respect to trade, investment, and technology exchange with China, with more likely.[8] There is, in effect, a new formulation of what it means to "get the U.S. house in order," and it involves more deeply integrating domestic policy and foreign policy and doing so whilst competing with China. In this landscape, in terms of international economic policy initiatives, the Biden administration has advanced the concept of a new Indo-Pacific Economic Framework for Prosperity (IPEF), with novel areas of focus but no reciprocal market access.

The underlying questions that this essay considers include: Do these developments represent a temporary shift in U.S. domestic and foreign economic priorities away from international trade treaties and strategies, or are they indicative of a fundamental paradigm shift away from economic multilateralism and open markets?

We address:

1. a brief history of U.S. trade policy, focusing on the underlying rationales that motivated those efforts;
2. consideration of factors that have led to the erosion of support away from international trade agreements;
3. evaluation of recent U.S. trade policy;
4. and consideration of areas of potential future action.

At the end of this essay, we propose several policy approaches that arguably offer scope for useful, albeit incremental, steps in support of advancing governance of the international trading system.

6 Justin Badlam, 'The Inflation Reduction Act: Here's What's In It' (*McKinsey*, October 2022) <https://www.mckinsey.com/industries/public-and-social-sector/our-insights/the-inflation-reduction-act-heres-whats-in-it> accessed 30 May 2023.

7 Joseph Biden, 'State of the Union Address' [2023].

8 EU leadership is also calling for a recalibration and de-risking of relations with China. Ursula Von der Leyen, 'Speech by President Von Der Leyen on EU-China Relations to the Mercator Institute for China Studies and the European Policy Centre' (*European Commission*, 20 March 2023) <https://ec.europea.edu/commission/presscorner/detail/en/speech_23_2063>.

1 A (Very) Brief History of U.S. Trade Policy and Underlying Rationales

Under the U.S. constitution, the regulation of international trade is a congressional power that has been, at times, delegated to the executive branch for specific purposes and requires Congressional oversight and approval. As a result, the advancement of international trade agreements between the United States and its trading partners has required both the exercise of presidential leadership and ultimately a necessary degree of congressional support. For most of the postwar period, international trade has been seen as an essential instrument of economic prosperity, a key feature of foreign policy, and an important means of advancing peace and security. Outstanding treatments of U.S. trade policy are found in the work of Douglas Irwin and I.M. Destler.[9] Irwin argues that U.S. trade policy from the establishment of the republic has been aimed at achieving one of three objectives: raising revenues through duties on imports, restricting imports to protect domestic producers, and concluding reciprocity agreements to reduce trade barriers abroad and increase exports. Destler analyzes how trade politics has changed with globalization.

Advancing the economic well-being of the nation has been an important rationale for international trade agreements. As noted above, in the early days of the United States, especially in the absence of national taxing power or a unified nation, international trade (and tariffs) was a major source of revenue. The vision of trade as a driver of growth was advanced by Adam Smith in *The Wealth of Nations*, published in 1776, the same year as the U.S. Declaration of Independence. Smith argued that in markets open to both domestic and foreign competition, when given the freedom to produce and exchange goods as they pleased (free trade), the individual's own self-interest would promote prosperity to a greater degree than would government regulations.[10] In today's parlance, commerce was seen as positive sum, not zero sum.

International trade and market openness have proven to be crucial engines of global economic growth. Mainstream economic thinking has advanced that the countries that have achieved large reductions in poverty are generally those that have experienced rapid economic growth, which in turn has been spurred by openness to international trade. This thinking further holds that outward-looking economies are generally better able to gain from trade

9 *See* Douglas A. Irwin, *Clashing over Commerce* (University of Chicago Press, 2017); I.M. Destler, *American Trade Politics* (University of California Press, 2005).

10 Adam Smith, *The Wealth of Nations* (Penguin, 1986).

as well as weather shocks.[11] The OECD cites evidence that countries that have been open to trade and investment have achieved double the average annual growth of more closed economies.[12] The World Bank holds trade to be the engine of growth that "creates jobs, reduces poverty and increases economic opportunity."[13]

Yet the value of expanding international trade is not just about economic efficiency: it has also been recognized as contributing to liberty, security, and the foreign policy objectives of states. In his magisterial work *America in the World*, Robert Zoellick argues that from the earliest days of independence, Americans have always viewed trade as an expression of liberty. The founders were convinced that new rules of trade could help lead to a changed international system.[14]

In the aftermath of the second world war, the architects of the General Agreement on Tariffs and Trade (GATT) saw an important additional function of trade: advancing international peace. The U.S. government, in outlining the rationale for the draft charter for the International Trade Organization (which ultimately was not accepted by Congress and instead ushered in the GATT), stated:

> The fundamental choice is whether countries will struggle against each other for wealth and power, or work together for security and mutual advantage ... The experience of cooperation in the task of earning a living promotes both the habit and the techniques of common effort and helps make permanent the mutual confidence on which peace depends.[15]

11 Jagdish Bhagwati and Arvind Panagariya, *India's Tryst with Destiny* (Harper Collins, 2012).

12 'Why Open Markets Matter—OECD' (*OECD*) <https://www.oecd.org/trade/understanding-the-global-trading-system/why-open-markets-matter/> accessed April 19, 2023.

13 'Trade has Been a Powerful Driver of Economic Development and Poverty Reduction' (*World Bank*, February 2023) <https://www.worldbank.org/en/topic/trade/brief/trade-has-been-a-powerful-driver-of-economic-development-and-poverty-reduction> accessed 30 May 2023.

14 Robert B. Zoellick, *America in the World* (Hachette UK, 2020). After all, Zoellick observes, the U.S. revolution arose out of protests over British controls and taxes on trade. The founders wanted to change the international economic order—to foster the freedom of American states and private parties to trade as they chose. Robert B. Zoellick, '2019 Gabriel Silver Lecture—American Trade Policy: An Historical Perspective' (*Columbia SIPA*, October 2019) <https://youtu.be/agI58W7ZOMo>.

15 U.S. Department of State, 'Proposals for Consideration by an International Conference on Trade and Employment' (6 December 1945) 1–2.

The authors of an excellent book, *The Genesis of the GATT*, assert that the most important political motivation for the GATT was world peace, especially the idea that flourishing trade between nations would reduce conflict.[16] Cordell Hull, writing in 1934, contended that "the truth is universally recognized that trade between nations is the greatest peace-maker and civilizer in human experience."[17] The GATT treaty framework was built on a recognition of the value of economic interdependence among nations.[18]

To be sure, the United States and the other GATT signatories have always been conscious of the essential character of a sovereign state and its right to consent to any actions that impact domestic policy and the operation of domestic law. From the outset, an important characteristic of the rules of the GATT followed from the premise that the GATT was an instrument of negative rather than positive integration. In other words, countries must agree to tariff reductions or other measures, and only those agreed to (and made effective, in the United States through domestic procedures) would be binding. The GATT and its progeny were not aiming to override domestic law or force convergence of national systems, though in recent agreements, there are some rules that tug in that direction. Instead, the core rules of the GATT require signatories *not* to discriminate, to engage in transparent practices, and to reduce tariffs and specified barriers to trade.

The expansion of international trade and economic interdependence triggered an expansion of multilateral trade agreements. Between 1947 and 1994, there were eight successive multilateral trade rounds that extended the rule coverage from the gradual reduction of tariffs on goods to more ambitious frameworks that also included new rules governing subsidies, services trade, agriculture, intellectual property, investment, technical barriers to trade, sanitary and phytosanitary measures, binding dispute settlement, and much more. As discussed in greater detail herein, the Uruguay Round, completed in 1994, represents a high water mark of trade liberalization and multilateralism. It was also controversial in the United States, and reaching a conclusion took years longer than anticipated. Fundamental to that expansion of multilateralism was the underlying recognition that in an interdependent world, there are issues that simply cannot be addressed by one country acting on its own and therefore require collective action. Moreover, in an interconnected world, policies in one country can have negative and positive externalities across national

16 Douglas A. Irwin, *Genesis of the GATT* (Cambridge University Press, 2009).

17 *Id.*

18 General Agreement on Trade and Tariffs, 'Preamble' <https://www.wto.org/english/res_e/publications_e/ai17_e/gatt1994_preamble_gatt47.pdf>.

borders. Thus, it is necessary for states to come up with frameworks that liberalize trade, clarify rules, limit negative externalities, and create conditions for cooperation and mutual benefit. Such frameworks were undertaken not as an abdication of state sovereignty but rather as a fundamental exercise of it.

In taking the negotiated agreements forward for congressional passage, numerous U.S. presidents have articulated the narrative that domestic prosperity requires an open trading system and engagement with the world. President William J. Clinton, in his remarks on signing the Uruguay Round Agreements, put it this way: "The end of the cold war imposes more than relief. It gives us a responsibility to finally take advantage of the interconnections that exist in the world today. ... We must never run away from the world. We must go into the 21st century convinced that the only way to preserve the American dream is to be involved with the rest of the world."[19]

2 The Erosion of Support for International Trade Negotiations and Treaties

The power and pervasiveness of the ideas outlined above have been fundamental to the exercise of American economic leadership. International trade policy is not just about promoting international trade for its own sake but using trade as an instrument of foreign economic policy, expanding agreements and protocols between the United States and its trading partners as tools of diplomacy. However, binding treaties with domestic effects require congressional approval and public support. Today, that support has eroded, and the debates around globalization, international trade, and a host of related issues are polarized. I would like to point to three broad conditions that have contributed to this current state of affairs: changed domestic economic conditions, the China challenge, and multilateralism in paralysis. We look at these in turn:

2.1 *Changed Domestic Economic Conditions*

The gains from international trade can be enormous, as mainstream economists usually point out, but the effects are diffuse. The pain of dislocations—whether caused by trade or technology—are often localized and enduring. This overall dynamic has occurred in a nation that has seen a steady rise in economic inequality over the past few decades. In the United States, the

19 William J. Clinton, 'Remarks on Signing the Uruguay Round Agreements Act' (8 December 1994) <www.presidency.ucsb.edu>.

rise of inequality since the 1980s is in sharp contrast to the 1950s and 1960s, when every group—most notably those with lower incomes—was advancing in industrialized societies. In 2019, the income of families that ranked in the highest tenth was thirteen times the income of families that ranked the lowest tenth, a ratio that has been rising since around 1980.[20] The picture is similar when looking at wealth inequality—the top 10 percent of Americans in 2021 held nearly 70 percent of U.S. wealth. Income and wealth inequality is higher in the United States than in almost any other developed country.[21]

My colleague Joseph Stiglitz argues that perhaps "the most invidious aspect of America's inequality is that of opportunities: in the U.S. a young person's life prospects depend heavily on the income and education of his parents, even more than in other advanced countries. The American dream is largely a myth."[22] This despair is reflected in surveys of American public attitudes. The majority of U.S. respondents in surveys conducted by the Pew Research Center say that economic conditions are helping people who are wealthy and hurting the poor and middle class. Pew surveys show that seven out of ten Americans also feel that the economic system is unfair and favors the wealthy. However, survey respondents disagree about the sources of these problems and potential solutions.[23]

While the picture may be unclear to most Americans, in an interconnected world, economic globalization, international trade liberalization, technological change, and China have become part of the narrative as to the forces that

---

20 'Income Inequality has been on the Rise since the 1980s, and Continues its Upward Trajectory' (*Peter G. Person Foundation*, December 2022) <http://www.pgpf.org/blog/2022/12/Income-Inequality-Has-Been-on-theRise-since-the1980s-and-Continues-its-Upward-Trajectory>.

21 Anshu Siripurapu, 'The U.S. Inequality Debate' (*Council on Foreign Relations Backgrounder*, 20 April 2022) <http://cfr.org/backgrounder/us-inequality-debate>. Also, 'Trust in America: How do Americans View Economic Inequality?' (*Pew Research Center*, 5 January 2022) <http://Pewresearch.org>. There is also research that suggests that the disparity has stabilized over the past decade, owing to wage growth for the lowest paying jobs rather than median wage workers catching up with those at the top. Researchers from Harvard and MIT looked at data from 1980 to 2020 and found that income inequality peaked in 2012 and then began to stabilize. Ben Steverman, 'America's Inequality Problem Just Improved for the First Time in a Generation' (*Bloomberg*, June 2022) <https://www.bloomberg.com/news/features/2022-06-08/us-income-inequality-fell-during-the-covid-pandemic>.

22 Miles Corak, 'Income Inequality, Equality of Opportunity, and Intergenerational Mobility' (2013) 27(3) *Journal of Economic Perspectives*: 79–102 <https://doi.org/10.2139/ssrn.2314815>.

23 '70% of Americans say U.S. Economic System Unfairly Favors the Powerful' (*Pew Research Center*, 9 January 2020) <http://pewresearch.org>.

have caused dislocation and distress. Various constituencies and individuals have brought these arguments into public discourse with different points of emphasis and some points of overlap and reinforcement. The authors of *Six Faces of Globalization* sketch out six different narratives that point to the strains of globalization, including left-wing and right-wing populist narratives that have found partnership with these themes.[24]

2.2 *The China Challenge*

A second significant factor has been the rise of China and its economic and geopolitical consequences. In an astonishingly short period of time—less than three decades—China came to be a major hub of global manufacturing and exports and the world's second largest economy. In the 1990s, when U.S. manufacturing employment contracted, the role of globalization was heavily debated, but many mainstream economists seemed to coalesce around the view that trade did not have significant negative distributional effects or cause rising wage inequality in developed economies. Instead, the expert literature tended to converge around technological advancement as the more significant factor in labor market changes.[25] The last decade, however, has seen momentum build behind the idea that the surge in goods trade with China was having a bigger impact than technology on American jobs.[26] Several influential studies have revealed that local labor markets exposed to low-income imports from China experienced increased unemployment, especially in manufacturing, and that labor force participation rates remained depressed and unemployment rates "elevated for at least a full decade after the China trade shock commence[d]."[27]

These analyses have generated extensive economic debate as to the extent to which job losses are properly attributed to Chinese (or other) imports and

24 Anthea Roberts and Nicholas Lamp, *Six Faces of Globalization* (Harvard University Press, 2021).

25 *See, e.g.*, Robert C. Feenstra and Gordon H. Hanson, 'Global Production Sharing and Rising Inequality: A Survey of Trade and Wages' (2001) *Handbook of International Trade*, 146–185; Ann Harrison, John McLaren, and Margaret McMillan, 'Recent Perspectives on Trade and Inequality' (2011) (3)(1) *Annu. Rev. Econ.* 261–289.

26 *See* David H. Autor, David Dorn, and Gordon H. Hanson 'The China Shock: Learning from Labor-Market Adjustment to Large Changes in Trade' (2016) 8(1) *Annu. Rev. Econ.* 205–240.

27 David H. Autor, David Dorn, and Gordon H. Hanson, 'The China Syndrome: Local Labor Market Effects of Import Competition in the United States' (2013) 103(6) *American Econ. Rev.* 2121–2168.

the duration and persistence of the imports' effects.[28] Not surprisingly, these questions are far from definitively answered.[29] Much of the current economics literature emphasizes the relative significance of technology.[30] Analyses that take services into account paint a far less bleak picture.

Meanwhile, U.S.-China relations have rapidly deteriorated across a host of policy areas. We should recall that commercial relations between the United States and China were once something of a ballast in the broader relationship between the two countries. China's entry into the WTO in 2001 and the reforms that accompanied it were the result of years of intensive bilateral and multilateral negotiations conducted during the George W. Bush and Clinton administrations. Yet over the past decade, the discourse in Washington has increasingly come to characterize trade with China as heavily disadvantageous for the United States. Official U.S. government documents now characterize China as the most serious strategic competitor faced by the United States.[31]

2.3 *Trade Multilateralism in Paralysis?*

A third factor that has contributed to the erosion of support for expanding international trade rules stems from dissatisfaction by governments with the operation of the WTO and the progress of treaty-based multilateralism. Especially harsh criticism surfaced during the Trump years, when the prevailing attitude towards the WTO might be expressed as: "we tried that, it hasn't worked, time to take back the reins."

---

28 Xavier Jaravel and Erick Sager, 'What Are the Price Effects of Trade? Evidence from the U.S. and Implications for Quantitative Trade Models' (2019) *FEDS* 1–110 (finding that Chinese import competition between 2000–2007 had pro-competitive effects on U.S. firms and generated over $202 billion in consumer benefits through lower prices); Liang Bai and Sebastian Stumpner, 'Estimating U.S. Consumer Gains from Chinese Imports' (2019) 1(2) *American Econ. Rev.* 209–224 (arguing that Chinese imports reduced inflation); Galina Hale, 'How Much Do We Spend On Imports?' (*San Francisco Fed*, January 2019) <https://www.frbsf.org/economic-research/publications/economic-letter/2019/january/how-much-do-we-spend-on-imports/> (estimating that some 56 cents of every dollar spent on Chinese imports in 2018 went to American firms and workers, and finding that about one-third of Chinese imports were intermediate goods used by U.S. firms for global products, thereby helping rather than hurting the American worker).

29 Daron Acemoglu, Gary Anderson, David Beede, Catherine Buffington, Eric Childress, Emin Dinlersoz, Lucia Foster, Nathan Goldschlag, John C. Haltiwanger, and Zachary Kroff, 'Automation and the Workforce: A Firm-Level View from the 2019 Annual Business Survey' (2022). <https://doi.org/10.2139/ssrn.4282509>.

30 *Id.*

31 'National Security Strategy' (*The White House*, October 2022) <https://www.whitehouse.gov/wp-content/uploads/2022/10/Biden-Harris-Administrations-National-Security-Strategy-10.2022.pdf>.

What happened?

The Uruguay Round, the last completed multilateral trade negotiation, however ambitious, did not produce a virtuous cycle of ongoing reforms. With 125 participating countries, the Uruguay Round covered areas that had not previously been subject to multilateral rules and were important for international trade flows—such as agriculture, intellectual property, services, and sanitary and phytosanitary requirements—and it created a two-tiered binding dispute settlement system. It strengthened the framework for trade relations, liberalized markets, buttressed and expanded institutional structures, and covered areas previously exempted from GATT rules. The integration of agriculture, which had been a source of intense conflict between trading partners, as well as textiles and clothing, was thought to initiate a process of ongoing reform. Economic benefits were expected to flow to both developed and developing countries. Predictability of policy and security of market access were supposed to contribute to the dynamic economic gains from the Uruguay Round. The novel inclusion of services and intellectual property under the unified international framework of trade regulation was believed at the time to be a major achievement. In brief, it was envisioned that the implementation of the Uruguay Round agreements would open up new markets, reduce the scope for trade conflict and unilateralism, and create a working organization and an architecture that would be conducive to further liberalization where barriers remained.[32]

The Uruguay Round was also expected to usher in a period when big multilateral negotiating rounds would be less necessary, as it had created a robust "built-in agenda" for further negotiations that would maintain trade liberalization moving forward.[33] By 1996, some countries were calling for further negotiations to commence.[34] Yet it took until November 2001, in the shadow of the tragedy of September 11[t] and following the failed WTO Ministerial in Seattle in 1999, with strong support and advocacy by the United States, for the WTO members to launch the Doha Development Agenda (DDA). As with the Uruguay Round, the negotiations were launched as a "single undertaking,"

32 *See, e.g.*, Arvind Subramanian, *International Trade Policies* (International Monetary Fund, 1994).

33 There were well over 30 items in the original built-in agenda, for example around services and the environment, government procurement, dispute settlement, textiles and clothing, and much more. *See* 'Understanding the WTO—The Uruguay Round' (World Trade Organization, 1994) <https://www.wto.org/english/thewto_e/whatis_e/tif_e/fact5_e.htm> accessed 19 April 2023.

34 *See* https://www.wto.org/english/thewto_e/minist_e/min98_e/slide_e/ur.htm.

meaning that all subjects were to be concluded in a comprehensive package. Once again, the U.S. government played an instrumental role in advancing the DDA, but given the now wide membership of the WTO and the development focus of its agenda, this multilateral round, perhaps more than any other in history, required global buy-in by both developed and developing economies to even get underway.

In the United States, the president then had to press Congress to enact the Trade Act of 2002, which re-established the executive's trade negotiating authority after it had lapsed eight years prior. While seeking congressional support, U.S. officials argued that the administration could be relied upon for pursuing market access and also vigorously enforcing U.S. trade rules. In framing the Doha agenda, U.S. officials stated that "America's trade policies are connected to our broader economic, political and security aims."[35] President Bush was able to secure this authority for an additional five years with a very narrow margin of 215 to 212 in the House of Representatives and a vote of 64 to 34 in the Senate.[36]

The United States was a steadfast supporter of advancing the DDA.[37] Yet, multilateral negotiations proved intractable. Numerous deadlines were missed, and ministerial dialogues faltered repeatedly. By 2015, member countries acknowledged that there was insufficient consensus to keep negotiations going. The failure of the DDA inescapably undermined the credibility of the multilateral system.

There is plenty of blame to ascribe to both developed and developing country members. The *New York Times* summed up the proceedings in an editorial as follows: neither developed economies such as the United States and Europe nor developing countries such as China and India were willing or able to make

35 Robert Zoellick. 'Unleashing the Trade Winds: A Building Block Approach' (2003) 8(1) *Elec. J. of the U.S. Dep't of State.*

36 The Trade Promotion Authority (TPA) expired in July 2007 but remained in effect for agreements that were already under negotiation until their passage in 2011. President Barack Obama was able to secure a third renewal in June 2015.

37 In a joint statement, Ambassador Robert Zoellick and U.S. Agriculture Secretary stated: "The United States believes that this great worldwide venture needs to target grand trade goals: to slash agricultural subsidies and tariffs; to eliminate tariffs on industrial and consumer goods; and to vastly expand opportunities for the fast-emerging services trade. U.S. proposals have backed this vision of global openness, growth and development with bold offers, demonstrating concretely what actions the United States will take to open markets if others join with us." Robert B. Zoellick, 'Statement on the Doha Development Agenda Negotiations' (March 31, 2023) <http://ustr.gov/archive/Document_Library/Press_Releases/2003/March/Zoellick-Veneman_Statement_on_Doha_Negotiations.html>.

the necessary concessions.[38] Several years before the negotiations were officially terminated, a senior U.S. official urged the world to recognize that the Doha Round was doomed and bring it to a close, as negotiators had failed to address the relative roles and responsibilities of advanced and developing countries.[39]

While there were many specific issues that caused the negotiations to ultimately fail, I would also highlight an organizational feature of the WTO: concluding a multilateral round with the then-147 members *by consensus*, as required by the rules of the WTO, proved exceedingly difficult. For Europe and the United States, many of the "easier" issues had been dealt with in previous rounds; average tariff levels were quite low, and the areas under negotiation were among the most intractable. Yet developing countries were unwilling to liberalize without major concessions from developed countries. Securing a consensus of the 147 members of the WTO in order to move ahead required an unattainable combination of diplomacy, coalition building, incentives, and unilateral action.

Powerful constraining undercurrents were at work: the world was still digesting the far-reaching impacts of the Uruguay Round agreements. Put differently, the rule architecture coming out of the Uruguay Round had the positive feature of being more comprehensive than past agreements, but it was tighter and had greater consequences for domestic policy choices than may have generally been understood when it was being negotiated. Moreover, coalition dynamics within the WTO changed with the expansion of its membership. Meanwhile, the only part of the WTO that kept steadily working was dispute settlement. Over time, the dispute settlement system itself became controversial, especially in the United States.

In hindsight, U.S. dissatisfaction with dispute settlement accelerated quickly. For a number of years after the founding of the WTO, the dispute settlement system was characterized as the WTO's "crown jewel."[40] It was actively used by both developed and developing countries. Hundreds of disputes were brought to panels, and still more resolved through consultations in the shadow

38 'Global Trade After the Failure of the Doha Round' (*New York Times*, 1 January 2016) <https://www.nytimes.com/2016/01/01/opinion/global-trade-after-the-failure-of-the-doha-round.html>.

39 Susan Schwab, 'After Doha' (*Foreign Affairs*, April 2011) <https://www.foreignaffairs.com/world/after-doha>.

40 'WTO Disputes Reach 400 Mark' (*World Trade Organization*, 6 November, 2009) <https://www.wto.org/english/news_e/pres09_e/pr578_e.htm>; 'World Trade Review' (World Trade Organization, July 2022).

of dispute settlement. Most of the controversial issues from the GATT period came to be adjudicated under the WTO. But there were always skeptics in the United States who believed that the country had given up too much in agreeing to binding third-party dispute settlement. And there developed a line of cases, especially in trade remedies and safeguards, that generated strong opposition from the U.S. trade bar and dissatisfaction from U.S. trade officials. For a number of years, the United States complained about those rulings in the Dispute Settlement Body (DSB) but complied. It continued to support the system and issue public reports that were on balance more positive than negative about dispute settlement, but also consistently, from the early 2000s, raised a number of serious substantive and procedural criticisms.[41] Of course, governments routinely criticize adverse rulings, so the United States was not alone in that respect.

U.S. frustration with a series of trade remedy, subsidy, and safeguard cases accumulated, and in 2019, the Trump administration took the extreme step of refusing to appoint new members to the Appellate Body, thereby bringing appellate review to a complete halt. It remains halted to this day. Panels continue to operate, but several cases have been appealed into the void, thereby bringing those disputes to a standstill. Since the beginning of 2022, the system has effectively stopped adopting panel reports.

3 U.S. Trade Policy under the Obama, Trump and Biden Administrations

Multilateralism has long coexisted with bilateral and regional initiatives, and the policy dynamic between these different levels of negotiations has been both competitive and reinforcing. The United States first established an FTA with Israel (1985) and then, importantly, with Canada (1988); the latter was utilized to spur interest in the multilateral Uruguay Round. During the Clinton administration, then-Under Secretary of the Treasury Larry Summers characterized U.S. government thinking in a succinct assertion that defined well the attitudes of the day: there should be a strong but rebuttable presumption that

41 'Statements by the United States at the Meeting of the WTO Dispute Settlement Body' (United States Trade Representative) <https://ustr.gov/about-us/policy-offices/press-office/press-releases/2023/january/statements-united-states-meeting-wto-dispute-settlement-body> accessed 19 April 2023.

all forms of liberalization are of value, whether bilateral, regional, or multilateral, as each form drives towards the same end.[42]

This strategic interplay between multilateral, bilateral, and regional predated the Doha Round. The United States started negotiations with a number of countries around FTAs as "building blocks" to multilateralism, and later characterized regional agreements as instruments to deepen ties and seek progress where possible. During the Bush administration, the United States stepped up its bilateral FTA strategy and negotiated thirteen free trade agreements.[43] The Obama administration attempted to advance the Doha agenda, but after narrowly securing trade promotion authority in 2015, it also turned to completing existing FTAs and the Trans-Pacific Partnership (TPP) agreement.

The TPP, negotiated between twelve countries in the Asia-Pacific region (not including China), was the cornerstone of the Obama administration's economic policy in Asia and represented the largest regional trade deal in history.[44] It was aimed at liberalizing trade and binding the United States and like-minded Pacific nations together with sophisticated rules that would help shape trends in the region in the face of growing Chinese influence. Characterized as "open architecture," meaning that other countries could join if they were willing to meet the commitments, the TPP framework broke new ground in its coverage of data and digital economy, services, and state-owned enterprises. Despite having negotiated what many thought to be the "gold standard" of a trade agreement,[45] the Obama administration ultimately did not submit the TPP to Congress before the 2016 election. This decision turned out to be a historic turning point in U.S. trade policy history, the legacy of which still remains very much with us today.

42 *C.f.*, Lawrence Summers. 'Regionalism and the World Trading System' (Federal Reserve Bank of Kansas, 1991); *see also*, James K. Galbraith, 'The 1994 Council of Economic Advisers Report: A Review' (1994) 37(3) *Challenge* 12–16.

43 'The Bush Record—Fact Sheet: President Bush Expanded and Enforced Trade Agreements to Open New Markets for American Products' (*The White House*, December 2008) <https://georgewbush-whitehouse.archives.gov/infocus/bushrecord/factsheets/tradeagreements.html>.

44 Members included Australia, Brunei, Canada, Chile, Mexico, Japan, Malaysia, New Zealand, Peru, Singapore, Vietnam, and the United States. The United States already had bilateral FTAs with a number of these countries.

45 According to Secretary Hilary Clinton, "This TPP sets the gold standard in trade agreements to open free, transparent, fair trade, the kind of environment that has the rule of law and a level playing field." Ian Kullgren, 'Yes Clinton Did Call TPP the 'Gold Standard'' (*Politico*, October 2016) <http://www.politico.com/blogs/2016-presidential-debate-fact-check/2016/10/yes-clinton-did-call-tpp-the-gold-standard-229501>.

During the 2016 presidential campaign, on the Democratic side, TPP was rejected by both leading candidates, Hillary Clinton and Bernie Sanders, and it was also ridiculed and rejected by then-candidate Donald Trump. Trump made plain during the campaign that he thought all trade deals were bad for the United States. He railed against TPP and most particularly NAFTA, which he declared "the worst trade deal maybe ever signed anywhere but certainly ever signed in this country."[46] This seemed to resonate with a significant portion of U.S. public attitudes. As of March 2016, according to Pew surveys, only a bare majority of Americans thought free trade agreements were good for America.[47]

Often when a U.S. president inherits an unpopular trade agreement, there is an effort to make it his own by adding new features thought necessary to correct perceived deficiencies. Instead, the Trump administration quickly pulled out of TPP. However, rather than have the already-concluded TPP die, in a show of exceptional leadership, Japan took the highly unusual step of endorsing the TPP and passing it domestically, which catalyzed its passage among the other ten signatories as the Comprehensive and Progressive Trans-Pacific Partnership (CPTPP).

Interestingly, NAFTA, in contrast, although maligned by candidate Trump, was renegotiated during the Trump administration rather than abandoned. The heart of the revised agreement, called the United States-Canada-Mexico Agreement (USMCA), actually kept the majority of NAFTA provisions in place. It included revised sunset provisions causing the agreement to expire in 2036 and required reauthorization every six years. There were also modifications to several areas, perhaps most dramatically the rules of origin pertaining to the automotive sector and the settlement provisions for investor-state disputes. The new digital provisions were akin to those contained in the TPP.

In general, President Trump, whether on the campaign trail or while in office, opposed most international treaties—he pulled out of TPP, the Paris

46 Emily Stephenson and Amanda Becker, 'Trump Vows to Reopen, or Toss, NAFTA Pact with Canada and Mexico' (*Reuters*, June 2016) <https://www.reuters.com/article/us-usa-election/trump-vows-to-reopen-or-toss-nafta-pact-with-canada-and-mexico-idUSKCN0ZE0Z0>.

47 Bruce Stokes, 'Republicans, Especially Trump Supporters, See Free Trade Deals as Bad for U.S.' (*Pew Research Center*, March 2016) <https://www.pewresearch.org/fact-tank/2016/03/31/republicans-especially-trump-supporters-see-free-trade-deals-as-bad-for-u-s/> While most Democrats supported free trade agreements, most Republicans opposed them, especially among Trump supporters, 67 percent of whom said that free trade was bad for America. The partisan divide paralleled racial, gender, and age divides. White men older than 65 were the staunchest opponents of free trade, while Latinos, African Americans, women, and younger people were the most likely supporters.

Agreement, U.S. participation in the World Health Organization, and the Iran nuclear agreement.

3.1 *Bilateral and Unilateral Measures*

Unsurprisingly, then, trade policy under President Trump moved significantly away from trying to strengthen institutions of global economic governance and became more unilateral. It became more confrontational than in any time since the 1980s. President Trump famously tweeted in 2018, in the context of growing tensions with China, that trade wars were "good and easy to win."[48] In several cases, he employed longstanding tools in new ways, such as using Section 301 of the 1974 Trade Act to attack a variety of intellectual property, investment, and discriminatory trade practices in China or invoking the national security and trade provision of Section 232 of the Trade Expansion Act of 1962 to impose a 25% tariff on steel and a 10% tariff on aluminum imported from Europe.

The actions directed at China launched a more fundamental shift in U.S. policy towards China. The Trump administration appeared to have concluded early in its tenure that the WTO rules were ineffective for dealing with China's alleged unfair trade practices.[49] As a result, bilateral pressure was brought to bear. The U.S. Trade Representative, Robert Lighthizer, inaugurated in August 2017 a domestic 301 action against these perceived unfair Chinese trade practices. A classic trade war followed—the 301 investigation concluded that China was engaging in unfair trade practices; the United States published a list of possible Chinese imports that might be subject to increased tariffs, then imposed tariffs on some portion of those goods and threatened further sanctions; the Chinese government retaliated by imposing tariffs on some U.S. products; further escalation took place on both sides; and eventually they reached a so-called Phase 1 trade agreement. By the end of this period—which ran from 2017 through 2019—Chinese imports amounting to $350 billion were subject to increased tariffs in the United States and approximately $100 billion of U.S. imports into China were covered by increased tariffs. The Phase 1 trade agreement, signed in January 2020, promised $200 billion of additional

48 Donald J. Trump, Twitter. 2 March 2018. "When a country is losing many billions of dollars on trade with virtually every country it does business with, trade wars are good and easy to win." <https://twitter.com/realDonaldTrump/status/969525362580484098>.

49 'Findings of the Investigation into China's Acts, Policies and Practices Related to Technology Transfer, Intellectual Property and Innovation Under Section 301 of the Trade Act of 1974' (Office of the United States Trade Representative, 22 March, 2018) <http://ustr.gov/sites/default/files/Section%20301%20FINAL.PDF>.

purchases of U.S. exports by the end of 2021. In terms of GDP targeted by tariffs, economists have found that the U.S.-China trade war was more substantial than the notorious post-Great Depression Smoot-Hawley tariffs.[50]

What has been the outcome of the U.S.-China trade war? It accelerated a shift in U.S. government policies that has now brought a number of economic policy instruments to bear in a framework that views China as a strategic competitor requiring restrictions on access to U.S. technology and other limitations on investment and commercial activity in the United States and with U.S. allies. Geopolitical developments have caused a further serious deterioration. China's subsequent pledge of friendship with Russia on the eve of Russia's invasion of Ukraine and its ongoing support (although not military, as of this writing) has changed U.S.-China relations profoundly. U.S.-China relations are now in their most strained period since normalization.

The U.S.-China trade war does not yet seem to have had many positive economic outcomes for the United States. First, the starting assumption that trade wars are "good and easy to win" proved quite mistaken. Second, the economic impact of the tariff increases was not, as asserted by the Trump administration, more harmful to China than to the United States.[51] Extensive economic analysis has shown that the impact of the tariffs has been borne by U.S. consumers in the form of higher prices and that the trade war lowered aggregate real income in both the United States and China, although not by a great magnitude.[52] Third, studies suggest that Chinese retaliatory tariffs were particularly targeted to Republican-leaning agricultural counties. The trade war did not pay off well for the Republican party in the 2018 congressional election, "as counties more exposed to the retaliatory tariffs reduced support for Republican candidates."[53] Fourth, studies show that quite apart from the effects of taiffs, policy uncertainty surrounding the trade war spooked the stock market. One study, for example, showed that the market dropped a cumulative 12.9% over a three-day window in the 2018–2019 period.[54] By the end of 2020, the trade war

50 Pablo Fajgelbaum and Amit Khandelwal, 'The Economic Impacts of the U.S.-China Trade War' (2021) 14(1) *Ann. Rev. of Econ.* 205–228.

51 *See* Mary Amiti, Stephen Redding, and David Weinstein, 'Who's Paying for the U.S. Tariffs? A Longer-Term Perspective' (*National Bureau of Economic Research*, January 2020).

52 *See* Pablo Fajgelbaum and Amit Khandelwal, 'The Economic Impacts of the U.S.-China Trade War' (2021) 14(1) *Ann. Rev. of Econ.* 205–228. For a comprehensive analysis of the trade war, *see* Chad P. Bown, 'The U.S.-China Trade War and Phase One Agreement' (2021) <https://doi.org/10.2139/ssrn.3810026>.

53 *Id.* at 208. *See also* Emily Blanchard, Chad Bown, and Davin Chor, 'Did Trump's Trade War Impact the 2018 Election?' (*National Bureau for Economic Research*, March 2019).

54 Mary Amiti, Sang Hoon Kong, and David Weinstein, 'Trade Protection, Stock-Market Returns, and Welfare' (*National Bureau of Economic Research*, March 2021).

was estimated to have lowered the market capitalization of U.S.-listed firms by $1.7 trillion and projected to lower their investment growth by 1.9 percent by the end of 2020.[55] Fifth, at the end of 2021, China still had not purchased the $200 billion of additional exports promised in the Phase 1 deal. The agreement stopped the trade war, but a combination of factors including the global pandemic and the effect of the trade war "battered U.S. manufacturing exports" such that analysts believe that "China was never on pace to meet its purchasing commitments."[56] As of this writing, some five years after the trade war, patterns of trade have shifted to a degree and not in ways that are helpful to core U.S. trade interests. China has reduced its reliance on U.S. suppliers, especially in agriculture, but U.S. farmers still remain highly dependent on the Chinese market.[57]

Trade conflict is not unique to tensions between the United States and China. The United States has a history of contentious trade relations with the countries with which it trades most intensively. Yet the tensions with China have characteristics that are systemic in nature. The underlying logic of U.S. actions seems to have been that the multilateral framework of the WTO was simply unable to take on the crux of the Chinese economic practices of greatest concern to the United States. The affirmative use of unilateral domestic trade tools was the necessary step forward.[58]

---

55 *Id.*

56 Chad P. Bown, 'China Bought None of the Extra $200 Billion of U.S. Exports in Trump's Trade Deal' (*Peterson Institute for International Economics*, July 2022) <https://www.piie.com/sites/default/files/documents/bown-china-us-exports-trade-deal-2022-02.pdf>.

57 In 2022, about 19% of U.S. agriculture exports went to China (up from 14% in 2017), while China's import share from the United States fell from 27 to 18 percent of total agricultural imports. *See* Chad P. Bown and Yilin Wang, 'China is Becoming Less Dependent on American Farmers, but U.S. Export Dependence on China Remains High' (*Peterson Institute for International Economics*, March 2023) <https://www.piie.com/research/piie-charts/china-becoming-less-dependent-american-farmers-us-export-dependence-china>.

58 Moreover, the trade tools were soon coupled with new limitations to foreign investment and technology restrictions aimed at curtailing Chinese access to U.S. technology and forcing selective economic disengagement given China's increasing role as a strategic rival of the United States. See Mark Wu, 'China's Rise and the Growing Doubts Over Multilateralism' *in* Meredith Crowley, *Trade War* (Vox EU, 2019). In the same volume, it is argued in essence that "long-term changes in the relative positions of the U.S. and China in the world economy are the deep drivers behind the eruption of the U.S.-China trade conflict." Crowley summarizes the views in the volume that a global hegemon will underwrite a rules-based system when the benefits of openness vastly exceed the costs but "as the hegemon's power begins to be challenged by the rise of a major competitor, the advantages of a rules-based system wane relative to the gains that can be achieved through power-based bilateral bargaining." *See also*, Aaditya Mattoo and Robert

3.2 *Biden Administration Policies and Priorities*

As described at the outset, the Biden administration did not come into office with an emphasis on global economic governance reform or enhancement. Instead, it has focused primarily on domestic priorities while strengthening relations with U.S. allies and responding to the security crisis faced in Ukraine. The legislative measures passed on semiconductors, climate and energy transition, and infrastructure have been major priorities and achievements. Each of these major bills has significant implications for U.S. competitiveness and foreign economic policy. U.S. trade policy under the Biden administration has stressed standing up for workers' rights, promoting sustainable environmental practices, realigning U.S.-China trade relations, and advancing initiatives and frameworks, notably the geopolitically oriented Indo-Pacific Economic Partnership (IPEF).[59] The administration's tone and approach on trade with allies has been strikingly more diplomatic than that of the Trump administration. While not lifting any of the Trump tariffs on China, it has stepped up engagement with allies and countries viewed as like-minded.

IPEF, negotiated between the United States and thirteen partners, stands as the Biden administration's most significant trade policy initiative.[60] Inaugurated in May 2022, IPEF is organized around four pillars: fair and resilient trade (including labor, digital, and other areas), supply chain resilience, infrastructure decarbonization and clean energy, and advancing a fair economy (with a focus on taxation and anti-corruption). U.S. Trade Representative Katherine Tai has stressed that this is not a traditional trade agreement and will not offer signatories preferential access to the U.S. market. Many analysts see this absence of binding preferential market access features as limiting the likely impact of the agreement and the willingness of negotiating partners to make significant concessions.[61] From a U.S. domestic political perspective, however, the lack of preferential access to the U.S. market improves the prospects that

W. Staiger, 'Trade Wars: What Do They Mean? Why are They Happening Now? What are the Costs?' (2021) 35(103), *Econ. Pol'y* 561–584 (noting why the United States moved away from multilateralism).

59 *See* 'USTR Releases President Biden's 2023 Trade Policy Agenda and 2022 Annual Report' (*United States Trade Representative*, March 2023) <https://ustr.gov/about-us/policy-offices/press-office/press-releases/2023/march/ustr-releases-president-bidens-2023-trade-policy-agenda-and-2022-annual-report>.

60 IPEF partners include Australia, Brunei, Fiji, India, Indonesia, Japan, the Republic of Korea, Malaysia, New Zealand, Philippines, Singapore, Thailand, and Vietnam.

61 Mary Lovely, 'The Trouble with Trans-Pacific Trade' (*Foreign Affairs*, January 2023) <https://www.foreignaffairs.com/united-states/trouble-trans-pacific-trade>.

IPEF can be negotiated and concluded without congressional ratification. This may be an essential feature in the current political environment.

In a speech on the achievements and philosophy of current U.S. trade policy, Ambassador Tai stressed that the Biden administration is ambitious and active. It is developing new mechanisms for building cooperation (such as the U.S.-EU Trade and Technology Council), focusing on practical measures (such as trade facilitation), working on bilateral sectoral issues where possible (such as on critical minerals with Japan and sustainable steel with Europe), and enforcing existing agreements. Drawing once again on the philosophy that has underpinned foreign economic policy since the founding of the United States and that inspired the creation of the Office of the U.S. Trade Representative, Tai concluded that "trade has an undeniable role in promoting freedom and sustaining humanity around the world."[62]

Considering these remarks in the context of U.S. trade policy history, what is notable is the absence of emphasis on further trade liberalization abroad or the negotiation of binding agreements, whether regional or bilateral. American participation at the WTO is not ignored but it is also not emphasized. There is a discernible philosophical throughline, in that U.S. trade policy actions are situated within the traditional themes of liberty and growth and thus suggestive of continuity. Yet at the same time, the instruments and approaches to advance those interests are the ones that can most readily be advanced through executive branch action without congressional approval. The extent to which presidential leadership and political capital is likely to be invoked remains unclear.

Since Joseph Biden came into office, political and security issues have dominated U.S.-China relations, and high-level interaction between trade officials has been very limited. U.S. policies have prioritized strengthening U.S. domestic capacity in key technology areas, limiting Chinese access to U.S. technology, and increasing domestic resilience through enhanced cooperation with like-minded countries. In these and other ways, when it comes to U.S.-China relations, economics and national security have become deeply intertwined. Senior officials have summarized the Biden administration's China policy as "de-risking" rather than decoupling U.S.-China economic relations.[63]

---

62 'Remarks by Ambassador Katherine Tai at American University Washington College of Law' (*United States Trade Representative*, April 2023) <https://ustr.gov/about-us/policy-offices/press-office/speeches-and-remarks/2023/april/remarks-ambassador-katherine-tai-american-university-washington-college-law>.

63 'Remarks by National Security Advisor Jake Sullivan on Renewing American Economic Leadership' (*The White House*, 27 April 2023) <https://www.whitehouse.gov/briefing-room/speeches-remarks/2023/04/27/remarks-by-national-security-advisor-jake-sullivan-on-renewing-american-economic-leadership-at-the-brookings-institution/>.

4 Looking Ahead

This brief review of U.S. multilateralism and trade policy reveals an evolution of approaches that have consistently recognized the importance of trade for economic prosperity but now show limited pursuit of initiatives to expand institutions or rules of global economic governance.

This essay has argued that a combination of factors has contributed to this trend in U.S. policy: public discontent with trade agreements; concerns about job displacement, which is often attributed to imports; the inability of the WTO and its members to advance multilateral trade agreements and address organizational infirmities; dissatisfaction with the dispute settlement system; and profound concerns about China in the global trading system and geopolitically. These all reflect a loss of confidence that the existing system is producing appropriate results in terms of its net impact on the U.S. economy.

Few members of Congress are debating the merits of multilateralism or generating ideas about how best to reform the institutions of the international economic system. Recent U.S. administrations, for their part, have not triggered such congressional debate by seeking new negotiating authority or advocating for expanded international trade frameworks. Other domestic, geopolitical and national security priorities dominate the national legislative and policy agenda.

The focus on domestic economic needs, security, the energy transition and competition on the technology frontier with China is driving the adoption of industrial policies that include, in my view, many admirable priorities including advancing U.S. science and competitiveness and the clean energy transition. Implementation and the disbursement of funds are just underway. Will recent legislation induce significant private sector investment in the United States? Will the tax measures and grants lead to major scientific advancement, accelerate EV use and production, or put a meaningful floor on the contraction of U.S. semiconductor capacity? These are among the intended outcomes. It is important to recognize that, these salutary objectives notwithstanding, recent shifts in U.S. policy might be having worrisome unintended consequences that may intensify with time. The "buy national" and other preferential features are producing friction between the United States and its trading partners. In addition, countries around the world are reacting to U.S. legislation and policy by introducing industrial policies of their own. The U.S. government has traditionally been the enforcer of international rules, challenging foreign practices when deemed discriminatory and unfair for U.S. as well as global competition. Depending on how its industrial policies come to be implemented, the United States now runs of risk of becoming, in the words of one analyst, "just another player in the game, with no justification for its self-dealing" and signaling to developing countries that "their aspirations for development do not matter: only those in the lead now will be allowed to scale the heights of technological production."[64]

The environment in which U.S. foreign economic and trade policy is operating is much altered. If one believes, as I do, that maintaining and enhancing the international trading system remains important, we should ask: are there approaches that offer scope for useful, albeit incremental, steps in support of advancing governance of the international trading system? This essay concludes by identifying four areas for consideration:

First, regional policy frameworks are where further experimentation and competitive dynamics are underway. As noted above, even though the United States did not go forward with the TPP, multiple Asian countries did enter into the CPTPP. The CPTPP has been in effect since 2018 and recently accepted the United Kingdom as a new member.[65] China has applied for membership, raising complicated and provocative issues, given the market access commitments expected of members. In Southeast Asia, some 15 countries have agreed to the Regional Comprehensive Economic Partnership (RCEP). Regional policy frameworks are being established in sectoral areas including around the digital economy. New Zealand, Chile and Singapore have entered into the Digital Economic Partnership (DEPA), an effort to establish building blocks for the governance of digital trade and cross-border payment flows. Members of ASEAN are now considering whether such regional digital partnership frameworks are in their collective interest. These examples of expanding trade policy frameworks suggest ongoing momentum around regionalism—with or without the participation of the United States.

The Biden administration, for its part, is advancing the IPEF. Responses to the concept have been positive. Although only the general contours have been outlined, 13 countries have signed up to be part of the negotiations, which are now vigorously underway. The open question is whether these negotiations will produce meaningful cooperation frameworks that deal with real stresses in the international economic system, such as around supply chains and resiliency, in the absence of market access commitments. Countries also continue

64 *See* Adam Posen, 'Why Current U.S. Industrial Policy is not Just Misguided but Likely to Backfire' (*Foreign Policy*, Spring 2023).

65 'Britain Becomes First European Member of Trans-Pacific Trade Bloc' (*International Institute for Sustainable Development*, April 2023) <https://www.iisd.org/articles/news/britain-becomes-first-european-member-trans-pacific-trade-bloc#:~:text=The%20United%20Kingdom%20became%20the,GDP%20of%20USD%2013.6%20trillion.>.

to reach out to the United States in the hope of triggering binding FTA negotiations.[66] Thus, regional frameworks continue to be a test bed for competitive as well as cooperative experimentation in regionalism.

Second, as others have argued in this volume, I too believe it is necessary to preserve the baseline of openness established by existing institutions and rules, including the WTO, and to continue to seek the advancement of pragmatic approaches at the WTO. There appears to be a growing debate among the WTO membership about the value of so-called "joint statement initiatives," namely methods to allow clusters of countries that agree on a set of priorities to move forward, even in the absence of consensus among all members. Progress of this kind could break a significant impasse that is now facing the WTO. A number of voices are calling for more accommodation of "clubs" of various kinds that can be both inside and outside of the WTO and applied to non-members on a non-discriminatory basis.[67] Plurilateral agreements among coalitions of willing countries represent an avenue for potentially advancing some trade issues.

Third, we should ask ourselves if there are steps possible at the WTO to identify and address sources of systemic friction.[68] Identifying significant sources of friction could be part of a larger conversation around WTO reform. Some of these issues may be addressable case by case; others will likely proceed only if part of a larger overall set of issues. For example, there is growing tension arising from disputes whereby a country invokes the national security exception under article XXI of the GATT. Scholars have put forward ideas around alternative mechanisms that could be created or utilized at the WTO to advance transparency and accountability without invoking dispute settlement.[69] Rules

66 Philippines is reported to have asked the United States to enter into negotiations for an FTA. 'The Philippines calls for FTA' (Inside UStrade.com, 25 April 2023).

67 Bernard M. Hoekman and Petros C Mavroidis, 'Preventing the Bad from Getting Worse: The End of the World (Trade Organization) As We Know It?' (2020) *Eur. Int'l Law Rev.*

68 Unlike the Trump administration, the tone of the Biden administration on the future of the WTO is diplomatic and engaged. This current U.S. posture contributed to a reasonably successful trade ministerial in 2022. Only recently has the US put forward the broad outlines of a proposal on dispute settlement reform. Comprehensive reform of the WTO will surface many intractable issues. It is important to identify areas where reform is needed and those that are creating friction that threatens the very viability or existence of the institution.

69 A creative proposal has been advanced by Bernard Hoekman, Petros Mavroidis and Douglas Nelson that the WTO create a new policy platform for governments to enhance transparency and consider national security-motivated actions with trade impacts. The authors argue that the purpose of such a forum is not to challenge the invocation of national security but to assess such invocations and find an alternative to dispute settlement.

surrounding environmental and R&D subsidies may be ripe for re-engagement, given the new environmental and R&D subsidy regimes being introduced around the world. The reform of the dispute settlement system, both procedurally and substantively, is yet another significant issue area that remains unresolved since the appellate body has stopped operating. These are but a few examples: while there is no agreement among the WTO membership as to what comprises essential areas of WTO reform, it is clear that many countries seek ongoing reforms and the potential agenda is extensive. Consideration of what might comprise WTO-consistent "green" industrial policies is not currently on the agenda but may be worthy of consideration in light of the many actions being introduced around the world to support the energy transition and domestic industry adjustment. Re-engagement around a roadmap of issues and selection of priorities would be a constructive workplan for the future.

Fourth, there is a need to create new forms of regulatory dialogue and consultation in frontier policy areas that currently have no institutional home. In areas including data and the digital economy and emerging technologies such as artificial intelligence, countries are making different domestic policy choices—whether and how to regulate—with significant cross-border consequences. Harmonious governance approaches are needed. Meaningful engagement on these and other policy areas will not only be important but likely require expertise from the private sector and NGOs. As other essays in this volume have argued, more effective collaboration between governments and business executives and NGO participants may offer practical approaches to advance solutions where governments on their own cannot. The future of global economic governance will require experimentation with multi-sector collaboration.

In conclusion, these possibilities for international engagement—be it bilateral, regional, multilateral or new combinations of countries and interests—may differ from and appear more modest than the multilateral trade negotiations of earlier years. Nevertheless, each can contribute to the management of international friction and the ongoing evolution and maintenance of the global trading system. At this moment, that's the name of the game.

See Bernard M. Hoekman, Petros C. Mavroidis, and Douglas R. Nelson. 'Geopolitical Competition, Globalization and WTO Reform' (*World Economy*, February 2023).

Bibliography

'70% of Americans say U.S. Economic System Unfairly Favors the Powerful' (Pew Research Center, 9 January 2020).

'Britain Becomes First European Member of Trans-Pacific Trade Bloc' (International Institute for Sustainable Development, April 2023).

'Findings of the Investigation into China's Acts, Policies and Practices Related to Technology Transfer, Intellectual Property and Innovation Under Section 301 of the Trade Act of 1974' (Office of the United States Trade Representative, 22 March, 2018).

'Global Trade After the Failure of the Doha Round' (New York Times, 1 January 2016) <https://www.nytimes.com/2016/01/01/opinion/global-trade-after-the-failure-of-the-doha-round.html.

'Income Inequality has been on the Rise since the 1980s, and Continues its Upward Trajectory' (Peter G. Person Foundation, December 2022).

'Remarks by Ambassador Katherine Tai at American University Washington College of Law' (United States Trade Representative, April 2023).

'Remarks by National Security Advisor Jake Sullivan on Renewing American Economic Leadership' (The White House, 27 April 2023).

'Statements by the United States at the Meeting of the WTO Dispute Settlement Body' (United States Trade Representative) <https://ustr.gov/about-us/policy-offices/press-office/press-releases/2023/january/statements-united-states-meeting-wto-dispute-settlement-body.

'The Bush Record—Fact Sheet: President Bush Expanded and Enforced Trade Agreements to Open New Markets for American Products' (The White House, December 2008).

'Trade has Been a Powerful Driver of Economic Development and Poverty Reduction' (World Bank, February 2023) <https://www.worldbank.org/en/topic/trade/brief/trade-has-been-a-powerful-driver-of-economic-development-and-poverty-reduction>.

'Trust in America: How do Americans View Economic Inequality?' (Pew Research Center, 5 January 2022).

'Understanding the WTO—The Uruguay Round' (World Trade Organization, 1994).

'USTR Releases President Biden's 2023 Trade Policy Agenda and 2022 Annual Report' (United States Trade Representative, March 2023).

'Why Open Markets Matter—OECD' (OECD) <https://www.oecd.org/trade/understanding-the-global-trading-system/why-open-markets-matter/>.

'World Trade Review' (World Trade Organization, July 2022).

'WTO Disputes Reach 400 Mark' (World Trade Organization, 6 November, 2009).

Amiti, Mary, Sang Hoon Kong, and David Weinstein, 'Trade Protection, Stock-Market Returns, and Welfare' (National Bureau of Economic Research, March 2021).

Amiti, Mary, Stephen Redding, and David Weinstein, 'Who's Paying for the U.S. Tariffs? A Longer-Term Perspective' (National Bureau of Economic Research, January 2020).

Autor, David, David Dorn, and Gordon H. Hanson 'The China Shock: Learning from Labor-Market Adjustment to Large Changes in Trade'-2016 8(1) Annu. Rev. Econ.

Autor, David, David Dorn, and Gordon H. Hanson, 'The China Syndrome: Local Labor Market Effects of Import Competition in the United States'-2013 103(6) American Econ. Rev.

Badlam, Justin 'The Inflation Reduction Act: Here's What's In It' (McKinsey, October 2022) <https://www.mckinsey.com/industries/public-and-social-sector/our-insights/the-inflation-reduction-act-heres-whats-in-it>.

Bai Liang and Sebastian Stumpner, 'Estimating U.S. Consumer Gains from Chinese Imports' (2019) 1(2) American Econ. Rev.

Bhagwati Jagdish and Arvind Panagariya, India's Tryst with Destiny (Harper Collins, 2012).

Biden, Joseph 'State of the Union Address' [2023].

Blanchard, Emily, Chad Bown, and Davin Chor, 'Did Trump's Trade War Impact the 2018 Election?' (National Bureau for Economic Research, March 2019).

Bown, Chad and Yilin Wang, 'China is Becoming Less Dependent on American Farmers, but U.S. Export Dependence on China Remains High' (Peterson Institute for International Economics, March 2023).

Bown, Chad, 'China Bought None of the Extra 200 Billion of U.S. Exports in Trump's Trade Deal' (Peterson Institute for International Economics, July 2022).

Bown, Chad, 'The U.S.-China Trade War and Phase One Agreement'-2021.

Clinton, William, 'Remarks on Signing the Uruguay Round Agreements Act' (8 December 1994).

Corak, Miles 'Income Inequality, Equality of Opportunity, and Intergenerational Mobility' (2013) 27(3) Journal of Economic Perspectives.

Crowley, Meredith Trade War (Vox EU, 2019).

Department U.S. of State, 'Proposals for Consideration by an International Conference on Trade and Employment' (6 December 1945).

Destler, I.M. American Trade Politics (University of California Press, 2005).

Fajgelbaum Pablo and Amit Khandelwal, 'The Economic Impacts of the U.S.-China Trade War'-2021 14(1) Ann. Rev. of Econ.

Feenstra, Robert and Gordon H. Hanson, 'Global Production Sharing and Rising Inequality: A Survey of Trade and Wages'-2001 Handbook of International Trade.

Galbraith, James, 'The 1994 Council of Economic Advisers Report: A Review' (1994) 37(3) Challenge.

General Agreement on Trade and Tariffs, 'Preamble' <https://www.wto.org/english/res_e/publications_e/ai17_e/gatt1994_preamble_gatt47.pdf>.

Harrison, Ann, John McLaren, and Margaret McMillan, 'Recent Perspectives on Trade and Inequality' – 2011 (3)(1) Annu. Rev. Econ.

Hoekman, Bernard and Petros C Mavroidis, 'Preventing the Bad from Getting Worse: The End of the World (Trade Organization) As We Know It?' (2020) Eur. Int'l Law Rev.

Hoekman, Bernard, Petros C. Mavroidis, and Douglas R. Nelson. 'Geopolitical Competition, Globalization and WTO Reform' (World Economy, February 2023).

Inflation Reduction Act 2022.

Infrastructure Investment and Jobs Act 2021.

Irwin, Douglas, Genesis of the GATT (Cambridge University Press, 2009).

Irwin, Douglas, Clashing over Commerce (University of Chicago Press, 2017).

Jaravel Xavier and Erick Sager, 'What Are the Price Effects of Trade? Evidence from the U.S. and Implications for Quantitative Trade Models' (2019) FEDS.

Kullgren, Ian 'Yes Clinton Did Call TPP the 'Gold Standard'' (Politico, October 2016).

Lovely, Mary 'The Trouble with Trans-Pacific Trade' (Foreign Affairs, January 2023).

Mattoo Aaditya and Robert W. Staiger, 'Trade Wars: What Do They Mean? Why are They Happening Now? What are the Costs?'-2021 35(103), Econ. Pol'y.

Posen, Adam 'Why Current U.S. Industrial Policy is not Just Misguided but Likely to Backfire' (Foreign Policy, Spring 2023).

Roberts, Anthea and Nicholas Lamp, Six Faces of Globalization (Harvard University Press, 2021).

Schwab, Susan 'After Doha' (Foreign Affairs, April 2011) <https://www.foreignaffairs.com/world/after-doha.

Siripurapu, Anshu 'The U.S. Inequality Debate' (Council on Foreign Relations Backgrounder, 20 April 2022).

Smith, The Adam Wealth of Nations (Penguin, 1986).

Stephenson, Emily and Amanda Becker, 'Trump Vows to Reopen, or Toss, NAFTA Pact with Canada and Mexico' (Reuters, June 2016).

Steverman, Ben 'America's Inequality Problem Just Improved for the First Time in a Generation' (Bloomberg, June 2022) <https://www.bloomberg.com/news/features/2022-06-08/us-income-inequality-fell-during-the-covid-pandemic.

Stokes, Bruce 'Republicans, Especially Trump Supporters, See Free Trade Deals as Bad for U.S.' (Pew Research Center, March 2016).

Subramanian, Arvind, International Trade Policies (International Monetary Fund, 1994).

Summers, Lawrence 'Regionalism and the World Trading System' (Federal Reserve Bank of Kansas, 1991).

Trump, Donald, Twitter. 2 March 2018.

Von Ursula der Leyen, 'Speech by President Von Der Leyen on EU-China Relations to the Mercator Institute for China Studies and the European Policy Centre' (European Commission, 20 March 2023).

Wolff, Alan, 'The Four Horsemen of the Apocalypse at the WTO' [2023].

Zoellick, Robert, 'Unleashing the Trade Winds: A Building Block Approach'-2003 8(1) Elec. J. of the U.S. Dep't of State.

Zoellick, Robert, America in the World (Hachette UK, 2020).

Zoellick, Robert, '2019 Gabriel Silver Lecture—American Trade Policy: An Historical Perspective' (Columbia SIPA, October 2019).

Zoellick, Robert, 'Statement on the Doha Development Agenda Negotiations' (March 31, 2023).

CHAPTER 11

Democratic Leadership through Transatlantic Cooperation for Trade and Technology Reforms through the EU-US TTC Model?

Elaine Fahey

1 Introduction: the Transatlantic Partnership as the Future of the Constitutionalisation of Global Governance Failures*

The transatlantic partnership is fundamental to the global economy and world security but also to the future of the constitutionalisation (with a small 'c') of global governance. It has long been one of the problem children of global governance – possibly also, as will be outlined here, its great saviours.[1] This is arguably because the EU and US have consistently shaped international approaches to public international law distinctively and differently.[2] While the US has crafted the global order after World War II (WW2) and has consistently promoted EU integration, it is a difficult partnership to credit with much more than this with respect to the global commons and global challenges. For much of the 20th Century, the US was evidently the stronger partner both militarily and economically and arguably dominant in the partnership legally. Even as Europe grew into a larger and more cohesive economic and normative power, the EU has largely relied upon US security might particularly in the 9/11 period and thereafter.[3] This imbalance has arguably been adverse for the development

* The author is grateful to Ivanka Karaivanova for research assistance provided and to the editors for their most helpful and constructive comments.

1 Ernst-Ulrich Petersmann, 'Prevention and Settlement of Transatlantic Economic Disputes: Legal Strategies for EU/US Leadership' in Ernst-Ulrich Petersmann and Mark Pollock (eds), *Transatlantic Economic Disputes: The EU, the US, and the WTO* (Oxford University Press 2003).

2 Jeffrey Dunoff and Mark Pollack, 'International Law and International Relations: Introducing an Interdisciplinary Dialogue' in Jeffrey Dunoff and Mark Pollack (eds), *Interdisciplinary Perspectives on International Law and International Relations: The State of the Art* (Cambridge University Press 2012); Charles Roger, *The Origins of Informality: Why the Legal Foundation of Global Governance are Shifting, and Why It Matters* (Oxford University Press 2020).

3 David O'Sullivan, 'EU-US Relations in a Changing World' in Elaine Fahey (ed), *Routledge Research Handbook on Transatlantic Relations* (1st edn, Routledge 2023).

 | DOI:10.1163/9789004693722_012

of innovation in solving global challenges. Instead, significant human rights challenges have dominated EU reliance upon US legal settlements with respect to civil liberties and security. The EU and US nonetheless constitute two of the leading global figures in trade, economics, agriculture, security. They operate to provide stability as to the liberal global legal order post-WW2, at least until recently when the Trump administration operated a significant deviation from this, particularly as to support for international law and international organisations and they have the capacity in this cooperation to constitutionalise global governance and ameliorate significant previous shortcomings.[4]

The EU actively supported the US pivot to mega-regionals to exclude China and pivot away from the World Trade Organisation (WTO) framework, in particular, the Transatlantic Trade and Investment Partnership (TTIP) during the Trump administration.[5] It spurned a subsequently complex period for EU trade policy, which has framed itself as being based upon 'free and open' trade and competition but has been stymied by a defensive turn to a lexicon of strategic autonomy, digital sovereignty and multiple trade defence instruments. In this new era, the EU has often sought global solutions to global challenges, as part of its constitutional DNA e.g. Article 21 TEU to promote international law, from of the Paris Agreement or the Multilateral Investment Court (MIC) project to reform ISDS globally. Yet these efforts have uniformly not been espoused by the US. In this regard, irrespective of the time period, the EU support for international law and international institutions has remained resolute, but unsupported by the US or US commitment to similar values until recently.

The Ukraine crisis has strengthened relations between the allies. At the same time, however, both structural (the rise of China) and domestic (e.g. 'America first' policy or the strategic autonomy of the EU) factors suggest that the EU-US relationship will weaken over time due to the impact of such factors, in particular on US foreign policy preferences, especially where the EU is strengthening its own foreign policy, including in the area of security and defence.[6] Yet the metrics of the relationship are often shifting across political scientists, political theory and political economy trade and data lawyers and governance scholarship, where the calibration between convergence and divergence has been complex. Within a political cycle, significant variations on the state of transatlantic relations have also followed as well as their

4 Ernst-Ulrich Petersmann in this volume.

5 Gabriel Siles Brugge and Ferdi De Ville, *TTIP: The Truth about the Transatlantic Trade and Investment Partnership* (Polity Press 2015).

6 Marianne Riddervold and Akasemi Newsome, *Transatlantic Relations In Times Of Uncertainty: Crises and EU-US* (1st edn, Routledge 2019).

analysis. Transatlantic Relations as a regional genre have undoubtedly shown themselves to be a vibrant source of dynamic theorisation. The place of actors, powers, competences and institutions form pivotal concepts but also far from objective ideals, imbued often with constructivism.

A Transatlantic Trade and Technology Council (EU-US TTC hereafter), as proposed by the EU in late 2020 to the new Biden administration and already in place by Autumn 2021, could provide an important bedrock from which multilateral ecommerce developments can flourish and evolve global governance significantly.[7] It has express objectives to address complex trade and technology challenges through institutionalisation and explore global policy objectives, outside of a trade negotiation setting. Yet its objectives appear possibly complex where the US refuses to utilise 'binding' trade agreements and increasingly advocates soft law framework solutions. The TTC has notably significant global law-making objectives as will be outlined here-and a significant stakeholder dimension. It constitutes a similar entity or development to that taking place in EU-India relations, where another so-called Trade and Technology Council has also just been established via soft law.[8] Other countries are supposedly following suit on TTCs e.g. India-Singapore and others want to join the TTC as observers.[9] The place of global challenges and global public goods becomes more important to decipher in this era as to its methods, aims and its actors. The European Commission has sought to emphasise the benefits of the TTC as enabling more constructive dialogues on open disputes and cases e.g. steel and aluminium tariffs, thereby widening its strategic operations, benefits and outcomes. The need for multilateral law-making on contemporary critical challenges of data flows and climate change make for uneasy bedfellows but somehow find themselves in this forum. The idea of a new Council with broad-ranging bilateral and multilateral goals is thus difficult to fathom but is also evidence of considerable ambitions to constitutionalise international economic law, explored here.

7 The initial Joint Statement – the so-called Pittsburgh Statement: See European Commission, 'EU-US Trade and Technology Council Inaugural Joint Statement' (Press Release 2021) <https://ec.europa.eu/commission/presscorner/detail/en/STATEMENT_21_4951> accessed 30 June 2023; Chad P Bown, and Cecilia Malmström, 'What is the Transatlantic Trade and Technology Council' (*PIIE*, September 2021) <https://www.piie.com/blogs/trade-and-investment-policy-watch/what-us-eu-trade-and-technology-council-five-things-you-need> accessed 30 June 2023.

8 See European Commission, 'EU-India: Joint press release on launching the Trade and Technology Council' (Press Release 2022) <https://ec.europa.eu/commission/presscorner/detail/en/IP_22_2643> accessed 30 June 2023.

9 Informal discussions with EU Delegation, Washington DC, February 2023.

In terms of trade and economic regulation the EU and US are in many ways moving in different directions. This is the case, in terms of how to regulate big data and big tech in general exposing more fundamental, almost philosophical, divergences in approaches as well as very strong opposing interests, as reflected in disputes over, for example, the EU-US data transfer agreement, the Corporate Sustainability Reporting Directive, and the proposed Directive on corporate sustainability due diligence and many other conflicts. The EU-US Trade and Technology Council might assist but not fundamentally overcome these tensions. Yet regulatory convergence may also be more apparent than real. Five bills (the 'US Antitrust Bills') have been put forward in the US legislature with the aim to regulate digital markets and limit the power of the powerful firms acting on them.[10] As with US antitrust enforcement in digital platform markets, this regulatory sweep might be devised in a way that would limit its effectiveness, not however, diverging significantly from the aims a range of EU legislative measures introduced in recent time such as the Digital Markets Act (DMA) or Digital Services Act (DSA) to address the global challenge of Big Tech power at national level.[11] These developments have been matched by the US Inflation Reduction Act (IRA), with many highly significant subsidies being introduced by the US legal system-and US businesses awash with US subsidies heavily 'courting' EU enterprises increasingly.[12] It is thus a highly complex

10 These bills are: The American Choice and Innovation Online Act (HR 3816, 117th Congress, 11 June 2021), Augmenting Compatibility and Competition by Enabling Service Switching (ACCESS) Act of 2021 (HR 3849, 117th Congress, 11 June 2021), Ending Platform Monopolies Act (HR 3825, 117th Congress, 11 June 2021), Platform Competition and Opportunity Act of 2021(HR 3826, 117th Congress, 11 June 2021), Merger Filing Fee Modernization Act of 2021 (HR 3843, 117th Congress, 11 June 2021).

11 2022 saw two milestones in digital market regulation. On 14 September, the Digital Markets Act (DMA) was adopted. On 19 October, the Digital Services Act (DSA) was adopted. Both regulations are the culmination of the Commission's 2020 Strategy: 'Shaping Europe's Digital Future'. See respectively, Regulation (EU) 2022/2065 of the European Parliament and of the Council of 19 October 2022 on a Single Market For Digital Services and amending Directive 2000/31/EC (Digital Services Act) [2022] OJ L 277/1 and Regulation (EU) 2022/1925 of the European Parliament and of the Council of 14 September 2022 on contestable and fair markets in the digital sector and amending Directives (EU) 2019/1937 and (EU) 2020/1828 (Digital Markets Act) [2022] OJ L 265/1.

12 HR 5376 – Inflation Reduction Act of 2022 Pub. L. 117–169, amounting to $369bn in grants, loans and tax credits for the rollout of renewable energy and clean technologies across the US; See Aime Williams, 'US-Europe trade tensions heat up over green subsidies' *Financial Times* (27 February 2023) <https://www.ft.com/content/0f8bf631-f24c-48da-905f-e37f8dc5d5f8> accessed 23 June 2023; European Commission 'Launch of the US-EU Task Force on the Inflation Reduction Act' (Press Release 2022) <https://ec.europa.eu/commission/presscorner/detail/en/statement_22_6402> accessed 30 June 2023; See David Kleimann and others, 'Europe should answer the US Inflation Reduction Act'

backdrop around which to develop global challenge solutions to shared concerns as to trade and technology, particularly as to supply chains and to unite and evolve global challenges, predominantly unifying against China.

It is also difficult to suggest that the EU and US have in reality engaged substantively on democratic issues as to global challenges through leadership *until* the TTC, which targets a vast range of fairness questions, good practices, higher standards and rule deficit issues on global challenges. This chapter thus makes the case for further evolution of the TTC and for policy goals with the aim of *enhancing* its democratic engagement. It does so principally drawing from EU external relations law developments. It thus addresses the methodology question of 'constitutional failures' of global governance of those addressed in this volume.

Section 2 thus situates the historical failures of transatlantic cooperation, as law-light institution-light 'Business-first' engagement without constitutionalisation ambitions. The chapter then considers the Transatlantic Trade and Technology Partnership negotiations (TTIP) precedent, and its evolution of the treatment of civil society (Section 3). Section 4 assesses the constitutionalisation of EU-US relations in the new EU-US Trade and technology Council (TTC) as a global law-making agenda. The chapter then considers the democratic shortcomings of the TTC and its capacity to evolve stakeholder engagement in the face of significant regulatory divergences e.g. the US Inflation Reduction Act and the EU Digital Markets and Digital Services acts respectively (Section 5), followed by Conclusions.

2 How to Learn from the History of EU-US Cooperation Law-Light Failures?

The role of the United States (US) in crafting the global order after WW2 was decisive and it included the active promotion of EU integration. Over the next 60 or so years, the transatlantic partnership was central to global events through the building of the Western liberal order and all the institutions that went with it. It was an imbalanced and unequal relationship. For much of the period, the US was by far the stronger partner both militarily and economically. In 2004 Jürgen Habermas published the 'Divided West' arguing that the

(2023) Bruegel Policy Contribution 04/2023. EU officials have accused Washington of discriminating against European companies and breaking global trade rules — particularly in the electric vehicle sector, where companies score the full tax credit if they manufacture cars in North America.

'normative authority' of the United States lied in ruins after the Iraq War and called for a European 'counter power'. It was clear in many recent years under the Trump administration that the EU and US alliance had been almost irreparably damaged. A widespread erosion in the place of international organisations was a central touchstone of EU and US tensions on their respective world views, with the EU heavily centering upon institutionalisation.[13] The Eurocentric world of pre-1945 and the resulting shifts of periods of globalisation are of significance.[14] The transatlantic partnership has been far from straightforward legally despite being an obvious basis for global stability of international economic law.

Transatlantic regulatory cooperation has in general been a 'swift' rather than a 'deep' affair, unlike its disputes which often appear to run longer than its agreements.[15] Arising from its last major framework, the New Transatlantic Agenda (NTA) of 1995, by 2003, nine formal binding and non-binding regulatory cooperation agreements had been entered into between the EU and US in areas as diverse as competition, privacy, customs and vetinerary standards.[16] Nonetheless, at whatever stage of its development, transatlantic cooperation has posed major challenges for regulatory independence, transparency and administrative law requirements, confidentiality, multi-level governance and regulatory sovereignty.[17]

Conflict as much as contestation and convergence are easily overplayed or overanalysed. Although a thirst for international cooperation, standards and institutionalisation is seen globally as pivotal to the success of the international economic order, such efforts arguably have often been stymied at transatlantic or domestic level. Ultimately, transatlantic relations are a story of largely cooperative and lively institutional interactions across many individual

13 Elaine Fahey, *Framing convergence with the global order: the EU and the world* (1st edn, Bloomsbury Publishing 2022).

14 Poul Kjaer, 'Does the 'West' still exist? Regulatory Philosophies in a Decentered Global World' in Elaine Fahey (ed), *Imagining the future of good global governance* (2022) City Law School Research Paper 2022/11.

15 See the summary by the Library of the European Parliament, 'Principal EU-US disputes' (Library Briefing, April 2013) <http://www.europarl.europa.eu/RegData/bibliothe que/briefing/2013/130518/LDM_BRI(2013)130518_REV1_EN.pdf> accessed 30 June 2023.

16 On the NTA, see Mark Pollack and others, *The Political Economy of the Transatlantic Partnership* (2003) Working Paper EUI <https://www.eui.eu/Documents/RSCAS/e-texts /200306HMTMvFReport.pdf> accessed 30 June 2023.

17 See Mark Pollack and Gregory Shaffer (eds), *Transatlantic Governance in the Global Economy* (Rowman & Littlefield 2001).

points that perhaps have outgrown traditional typologies of the multi-level nature of EU-US relations.[18]

The sources of bilateral EU-US relations have often been in bilateral regulatory cooperation agreements, as well as Protocols, Exchanges of Letters, thus in both soft and hard law. Law has played a significant role in contemporary transatlantic relations *outside* of the bilateral context which, from the perspective of EU External Relations law, might seem neither conventional nor apparent,[19] e.g. EU *amicus curiae* submissions before the US Supreme Court.[20] Institutions have not been irrelevant. A Transatlantic Legislators Dialogue is on-going since 1972.[21] Transatlantic annual summits have been held since the 1990s, continuing to generate challenges regarding the appropriate EU institutional representation, even after the Treaty of Lisbon and a new European Parliament Liaison Office is situated in Washington DC.[22]

As a result, the bilateral transatlantic relations have been considered to be institutionally modest but also flexible.[23] Views differ substantially on the relative importance of law-light institutional-light framings of the core of the western superpowers alliance, cooperation and engagements-not unimportant to a legal audience-less so other genres of analysis. The EU and US are considered the world's two regulatory great powers and regulatory differences are the most significant impediments to most transatlantic economic activity. In part, as a result, there are common perceptions that the transatlantic regulatory relationship is fraught and that the EU and US are competing to spread their regulations around the world. Non-lawyers claim transatlantic regulatory trade disputes are extremely rare and represent a tiny fraction of transatlantic economic exchange.[24] Many Mutual Recognition Agreements have been

18 Mark Pollack, 'The New Transatlantic Agenda at Ten: Reflections on an Experiment in International Governance' (2005) 43(5) Journal of Common Market Studies 899.

19 Elaine Fahey (ed), *Routledge Research Handbook on Transatlantic Relations* (1st edn, Routledge 2023); Elaine Fahey, 'On The Use of Law in Transatlantic Relations: Legal Dialogues Between the EU and US' (2014) 20 European Law Journal 386.

20 E.g. *Atkins v Virginia* 536 US 304 (2002); *Roper v Simmons* 543 US 551 (2005); *Kiobel v Royal Dutch Petroleum Co* 569 US 108 (2013); *Abitron Austria GmbH et al v Hetronic International Inc.*, Case No 21-1043 (Supr. Ct. Nov. 4, 2022) (*certiorari* granted).

21 I.e. The European Parliament.

22 See Joseph Dunne, 'Connecting the US Congress and the European Parliament: The work and role of the EP Liaison Office in Washington DC' in Fahey, *Routledge Research Handbook on Transatlantic Relations* (n 19).

23 E.g. Pollack (n 18).

24 Alasdair Young, 'The transatlantic regulatory relationship: limited conflict, less competition and a new approach to cooperation' in Fahey, *Routledge Research Handbook on Transatlantic Relations* (n 19); Petersmann, 'Prevention and Settlement of Transatlantic Economic Disputes: Legal Strategies for EU/US Leadership' (n 1); Ernst-Ulrich Petersmann,

alleged to have failed on account of undue power and influence of US federal authorities.[25] As the former EC Trade Commissioner Sir Leon Brittan famously stated, "governments proved to be more eager than their agencies to cooperate."[26] Indeed, many agreements beyond trade have defied characterisation as complex global governance, grounded in soft law and highly complex administrative arrangements. Several post 9/11 bilateral EU-US Agreements in security have been argued to add little to existing Agreements between individual Member States and the US.[27] The Edward Snowdon / NSA surveillance saga caused many to consider the question of the value and merits of transatlantic cooperation through law.[28]

The advent of the Trump administration appeared to give effect to an unprecedented shift in Transatlantic Relations since before World War II – mostly away from institutions-as well as trade wars.[29] This 'unpleasantness' changed swiftly with the Biden administration – at least in tone – e.g. already with the Transatlantic Trade and Technology Council (EUUSTTC) proposed

---

'Transformative Transatlantic Free Trade Agreements without Rights and Remedies of Citizens?' (2015) 18 Journal of International Economic Law 579; Ernst-Ulrich Petersmann, 'CETA, TTIP and TISA: New Trends in International Economic Law' in Stefan Griller, Walter Obwexer and Erich Vranes (eds), *Mega-Regional Trade Agreements: CETA, TTIP, and TISA: New Orientations for EU External Economic Relations* (Oxford University Press 2017); Anthony Gardner, *Stars with Stripes: the essential partnership between the EU and US* (Palgrave Macmillan 2020); Mark Pollack and Gregory Shaffer, *When Cooperation Fails: The International Law and Politics of Genetically Modified Foods* (Oxford University Press 2009).

25 Pollack and others (n 16); See U.S.-EC Mutual Recognition Agreement (MRA) and its six sectoral annexes (of 1997), the U.S.-EC Mutual Recognition Agreement on Marine Safety (of 2001), and the U.S.-EC understanding on Safe Harbour Principles for data privacy protection (of 2000).

26 Schaffer quoting Sir Leon Brittan, 'Transatlantic Economic Partnership: Breaking down the hidden barriers' in George Bermann and others (eds), *Transatlantic Regulatory Cooperation* (Oxford University Press 2000) 13.

27 E.g. Mitsilegas Valsamis, 'The New EU–USA Cooperation on Extradition, Mutual Legal Assistance and the Exchange of Police Data' (2003) 8 European Foreign Affairs Review 515.

28 Gregory Shaffer, 'Globalization and Social Protection: The Impact of EU and International Rules in the Ratcheting Up of U.S. Privacy Standards' (2000) 25 Yale Journal of International Law 1; Anu Bradford, *Brussels Effect: How the European Union rules the World* (Oxford University Press 2020); Joanne Scott, 'From Brussels with Love: the Transatlantic Travels of European Law and the Chemistry of Regulatory Attraction' (2009) 57 The American Journal of Comparative Law 897.

29 Marija Bartl and Elaine Fahey, 'A Postnational Marketplace: Negotiating the Transatlantic Trade and Investment Partnership (TTIP)' in Elaine Fahey and Deirdre Curtin (eds), *A Transatlantic Community of Law: Legal Perspectives on the Relationship between the EU and US legal orders* (Cambridge University Press 2014).

immediately by the European Commission and swiftly implemented and taking effect to be discussed here below – yet still a soft law creation.[30] Transatlantic relations are thus no stranger to evolutions and to a series of innovative hybrid governance or soft law engagement on law-making and soft law outcomes of note and many so-called transatlantic dialogues over the years, even during/ alongside their renowned 'failures'.[31]

3 The TTIP Precedent: Constitutionalising the Place of a Transatlantic Civil Society

In June 2013, the US launched negotiations between the EU and US on a Transatlantic Trade and Investment Partnership (TTIP hereafter) with an ambitious time frame for negotiations to be completed before the end of 2014. With the combined economies of the EU and US accounting for almost 40% of global GDP and approximately a third of global economic trade, the TTIP has thus been touted as a dramatic kick-start to the global political economy. The opening of negotiations on a TTIP was commenced after the Report of the EU-US High Level Working Group on Jobs and Growth (HLWG).[32] There, the suggestion was developed that the negotiations would explore (a) market

---

30 European Commission and High Representative of the Union for Foreign Affairs and Security Policy, 'Joint Communication to the European Parliament, the European Council and the Council: A new EU-US agenda for global change' JOIN (2020) 22 final; European Commission, 'EU-US Trade and Technology Council Inaugural Joint Statement' (Press Release 2021) <https://ec.europa.eu/commission/presscorner/detail/en/statement_21_4951> accessed 30 June 2023; European Commission, 'EU-US launch Trade and Technology Council to lead values-based global digital transformation' (Press Release 2021) <https://ec.europa.eu/commission/presscorner/detail/en/IP_21_2990> accessed 30 June 2023; The White House, 'U.S.-EU Trade and Technology Council Inaugural Joint Statement' (Statement Release 2021) <www.whitehouse.gov/briefing-room/statements-releases/2021/09/29/u-s-eu-trade-and-technology-council-inaugural-joint-statement/> accessed 30 June 2023.

31 Pollack and Shaffer, *Transatlantic Governance in a Global Economy* (n 17) 25–34, 298; Fahey, 'On The Use of Law in Transatlantic Relations: Legal Dialogues Between the EU and US' (n 19); Maria Green Cowles, 'The Transatlantic Business Dialogue: Transforming the New Transatlantic Dialogue' in Pollack and Shaffer, *Transatlantic Governance in a Global Economy* (n 17) 213; Francesca Bignami and Steve Charnovitz, 'Transnational Civil Society Dialogues' in Pollack and Shaffer, *Transatlantic Governance in the Global Economy* (n 17) 275–6.

32 Established after the EU-US Summit in 2011; European Commission, 'Final Report High Level Working Group on Jobs and Growth' (2013) Tradoc 150519 <http://trade.ec.europa.eu/doclib/docs/2013/february/tradoc_150519.pdf> accessed 30 June 2023.

access; (b) regulatory issues and non-tariff barriers, and (c) rules, principles, and new modes of cooperation to address shared global trade challenges and opportunities.

The TTIP purported to develop a multilevel post-national marketplace which would deepen and prospectively *institutionalise* EU-US relations in a range of fields-such as pharmaceuticals, chemicals, public procurement or motor vehicles – also through a Regulatory Cooperation Council with rule-making capacity.[33] The TTIP negotiations expressly involved the discussion of the prospective revision and renegotiations of a broad range of existing EU laws, rules and standards of the *acquis communautaire* to progress far beyond the technical scope of the last EU-US Mutual Recognition Agreement from 1997. This form of institutionalisation and prospective re-negotiation of EU laws, rules and standards was unprecedented in an EU international trade agreement.

Much emphasis has been placed both at the outset and during the TTIP negotiations on the substantive and procedural consent from the European Parliament and US Congress, along with Member State parliaments. From an EU perspective, EU international trade agreements post-Lisbon are *formally* legitimated in a new dynamic of European Parliament scrutiny and enhanced transparency practices of heightened involvement, pursuant to Article 218 TFEU and an Inter-Institutional Framework Agreement. TTIP differed from *historical* EU-US regulatory cooperation and was thus controversial as a mega-regionals project of integration.

The constitutionalisation (with a small 'c') of the role of civil society in EU trade negotiations and also their resulting agreements is an important development in EU law, which began in TTIP, and is important as a moment where the EU ceased to disregard ordinary citizens in high-level trade negotiations.[34] Unlike the European Parliament (EP), civil society actors do not enjoy a formal role under Article 218 TFEU for treaty-making, but have benefitted from the emergence of several venues to provide their input. Whether these entities

33 See Article 43 of the leaked Directives for the negotiation on the Transatlantic Trade and Investment Partnership between the EU and US (Brussels, 17 June, 2013): 'The Agreement will set up an institutional structure to ensure an effective follow up of the commitments under the Agreement, as well as to promote the progressive achievement of compatibility of regulatory regimes'. No. 13/801. See also Elaine Fahey, *The EU as a Global Digital Actor: Institutionalising Data Protection, Digital Trade and Cybersecurity* (Hart Publishing 2022).

34 On constitutionalisation in this fashion, see Jean L Cohen, *Globalization and Sovereignty: Rethinking Legality, Legitimacy, and Constitutionalism* (Cambridge University Press 2012) and Ernst-Ulrich Petersmann in this volume.

actual exert influence or merely constitute a check-box exercise remains to be seen.[35] Civil society actors have indeed challenged the negotiations for the new generation EU FTAs in a number of ways. The lack of information about the negotiations generated civil society organisations on both sides of the Atlantic.[36] The secrecy of the TTIP negotiations gave rise to much concern, even resulting in individual MEPs leaking the negotiation texts 'in the public interest'. Inadequate responses by the Council and Commission to civil society concerns prompted the intervention of the European Ombudsman,[37] resulting in the Commission's decision to publish the EU's textual proposals and position papers, thus making TTIP a unique case of positive shifts towards unprecedented transparency.[38] Significant litigation was also generated by individual parliamentarians working with civil society in the form of a European Citizen Initiative (ECI). During the TTIP negotiations, civil society succeeded in mobilising public opinion and gathering over 3 million signatures for a petition against the conclusion of TTIP and CETA, which resulted in proceedings being taken to the General Court of the EU, seeking annulment of the decision of the Commission to refuse to stop the negotiations.[39] The Court in a broad constitutional reading of the provisions of the Treaty on the democratic life of the Union, held that the Commission's narrow interpretation of law-making that could be stopped so as to preclude negotiations being part of it was incorrect. The Commission thereafter established an Expert Advisory Group specifically for TTIP in order to redress its deficiencies, bringing together business, consumer, labour and health interests,[40] to whom the Commission provided information thereto throughout the negotiations and who were also given

---

35 Isabella Mancini, 'The European Parliament and Civil Society in EU Trade Negotiations: The Untold Story of an Erratic Engagement' (2020) 27 European Foreign Affairs Review 241.

36 See Alasdair Young, 'Not your parents' trade politics: the Transatlantic Trade and Investment Partnership negotiations' (2016) 23 Review of International Political Economy 345.

37 See also Katharina Meissner, 'Democratizing EU External Relations: The European Parliament's Informal Role in SWIFT, ACTA, and TTIP' (2016) 21 European Foreign Affairs Review 269.

38 Mancini, 'The European Parliament and Civil Society in EU Trade Negotiations: The Untold Story of an Erratic Engagement' (n 35); Elaine Fahey, 'On the Benefits of the Transatlantic Trade and Investment Partnership (TTIP) Negotiations for the EU Legal Order: A Legal Perspective' (2016) 43 Legal Issues of Economic Integration 327.

39 Case T-754/14 *Efler and Others v Commission* EU:T:2017:323.

40 European Commission, 'Expert group to advise European Commission on EU-US trade talks' (Press Release 2014) <https://europa.eu/rapid/press-release_IP-14-79_en.htm> accessed 30 June 2023.

the possibility to consult EU negotiating texts, raise questions and provide comments.[41] Despite the progress of TTIP, the latest EU-US trade talks have sparked similar criticism by the civil society actors as to the prevalence of behind-closed-door meetings with big business lobbyists.[42]

The EU-US TTIP negotiations appeared to provide some evidence of responsiveness of EU institutional actors to concerns about shortcomings in the democratic process in EU external relations law and hence about the legitimacy of decision-making in the TTIP negotiations. This responsiveness often goes far beyond what the CJEU appears to demand in its recent case law on international relations and access to documents. Importantly, it also eclipses historical precedents in EU-US relations from the 1990s.[43] It is thus a broadly positive story from a legal and specifically EU law perspective in so far as it contributes positively to our understanding of the place of democratisation of international relations in the supranational EU legal order.

In the era of Big Tech dominance, the place of civil society in theory in solving global challenges in this domain seems highly significant, explored in the next sections, which develop further the plan and actions of the EU-US TTC.

4 The EU-US Trade and Technology Council (TTC): Global Law-Making for Global Challenges (through Soft Law?)

Transatlantic data flows amount to some of the most significant for the global economy.[44] The TTIP, the largest scale form of transatlantic collaboration in recent history, expressly excluded data flows from its negotiations. Its negotiation of e-commerce could have been pivotal given the gap between the Trans-Pacific Partnership (TPP) and EU agreements emerging as to data flows but also the gap emerging as to the regulation of digital trade between the EU and

41 See European Commission, 'Terms of Reference' (July 2015) <https://trade.ec.europa.eu/doclib/docs/2015/july/tradoc_153617.pdf> accessed 30 June 2023.

42 Corporate Europe Observatory, 'TTIP reloaded: big business calls the shots on new EU-US trade talks' (*Corporate Europe Observatory*, February 2019) <https://corporateeurope.org/en/international-trade/2019/02/ttip-reloaded-big-business-calls-shots-new-eu-us-trade-talks> accessed 30 June 2023.

43 E.g. Pollack and Shaffer, Transatlantic Governance in a Global Economy (n 17); Pollack, 'The New Transatlantic Agenda at Ten' (n 18).

44 See US Chamber of Commerce, 'Transatlantic Data Flows: Moving Data with Confidence' (2021) <https://www.uschamber.com/technology/data-privacy/transatlantic-dataflows> accessed 30 June 2023.

US.[45] The US shift towards the need for federal privacy laws has considerably altered this divergence to a degree, noted above. Moreover, after the CJEU struck down the EU-US Privacy Shield in *Schrems* II, the EU and US finally agreed in March 2022 a new Transatlantic Data Privacy Framework principle in March 2022, to include a 'trans-atlantic court' and independent oversight, demonstrating the extraordinary capacity of EU-US relations to lead global challenges debates and evolve transnational views on privacy and courts.[46] The framework even appears to be understood as a pre-condition for the TTC to evolve, prior to meeting 2 in Paris-Saclay in May 2022.[47] It thus provided an extraordinary background from which to begin discussions in the TTC-of a shared commitment to the rule of law through institutions and a clear constitutionalisation of relations between the EU and US on trade and technology.

The EU-US Joint Agenda for Global Change included a TTC, putatively developing a loose institutionalisation of key global challenges. The EU proposed as part of its global change agenda a TTC – centered upon multiple working groups that traverse many fields and multiple competences of EU law, from trade, environment, defence to labour: i.e., Technology Standards Cooperation, Climate and Clean Tech, Secure Supply Chains, ICT Security and Competitiveness, Data Governance and Technology Platforms, Misuse of Technology Threatening Security & Human Rights, Export Controls Cooperation, Investment Screening Cooperation, Promoting SME Access to

---

45 European Commission, 'TTIP: Initial proposal on trade in services, investment and e-commerce' (2015) <http://trade.ec.europa.eu/doclib/docs/2015/july/tradoc_153669.pdf> accessed 30 June 2023; European Commission, 'TTIP: Annexes to the services, investment and e-commerce initial proposal' (2015) <http://trade.ec.europa.eu/doclib/docs/2015/july/tradoc_153670.pdf> accessed 30 June 2023; European Commission, 'A reading guide to the EU proposal on services, investment and e-commerce for the Transatlantic Trade and Investment Partnership' (2015) <http://trade.ec.europa.eu/doclib/docs/2015/july/tradoc_153668.pdf> accessed 30 June 2023; European Parliament, 'TTIP Legislative Train Schedule' (2020) <www.europarl.europa.eu/legislative-train/theme-international-trade-inta/file-ttip-services-investment-and-e-commerce> accessed 30 June 2023; See Mira Burri, 'The Regulation of Data Flows Through Trade Agreements' (2017) 48 Law and Policy in International Business 407.

46 European Commission, 'European Commission and United States Joint Statement on Trans-Atlantic Data Privacy Framework' (Press Release, 2022) <https://ec.europa.eu/commission/presscorner/detail/en/IP_22_2087> accessed 30 June 2023; The White House, 'FACT SHEET: United States and European Commission Announce Trans-Atlantic Data Privacy Framework' (2022) <https://www.whitehouse.gov/briefing-room/statements-releases/2022/03/25/fact-sheet-united-states-and-european-commission-announce-trans-atlantic-data-privacy-framework/> accessed 30 June 2023.

47 Although official evidence of this is difficult to find.

TABLE 11.1 TTC working groups

Working group	Policy topic
1	Technology Standards
2	Climate and Clean Energy
3	Secure Supply Chains
4	Information and Communication Technology and Services (ICTS) Security and Competitiveness
5	Data Governance and Technology Platforms
6	Misuse of Technology Threatening Security and Human Rights
7	Export Controls
8	Investment Screening
9	Promoting Small-and Medium-sized Enterprises (SME) Access to and Use of Digital Tools
10	Global Trade Challenges

SOURCE: EUROPEAN COMMISSION TRADE AND TECHNOLOGY COUNCIL WEBSITE: HTTPS://COMMISSION.EUROPA.EU/STRATEGY-AND-POLICY/PRIORITIES-2019-2024/STRONGER-EUROPE-WORLD/EU-US-TRADE-AND-TECHNOLOGY-COUNCIL_EN

and Use of Digital Technologies and Global Trade Challenges.[48] Notably, seven of the ten working groups address themes that refer to technology either with a security angle or from a competition perspective.[49] What is noticeable is the mission-creep 'evolution' of security between the early meetings, in 2021 into later meetings in 2022 thereafter, as the Ukraine crisis unfolded.

48 See the EU-US Trade and Technology Council Website: <https://futurium.ec.europa.eu/en/EU-US-TTC> accessed 30 June 2023. Elaine Fahey, 'The EU-US Transatlantic Trade and Technology Council: Shifting Multilateralism Through Bilateralism and Institutions?' in Ottavio Quirico and Katarzyna Kwapisz Williams (eds.), *The European Union and the Evolving Architectures of International Economic Agreements* (Springer, forthcoming).

49 Maria Demertzis, 'US-EU relations in the first year of President Biden: a view from Brussels' (*Transatlantic*, December 2021). <https://www.transatlantic.org/wp-content/uploads/2021/12/11-10-2021-Demertzis-US-EU-trade-Challenges-v2.pdf> accessed 30 June 2023.

The TTC is based upon multiple working groups that align with this formula of flexibility for a cross-policy pollination, i.e., Technology Standards Cooperation, Climate and Clean Tech, Secure Supply Chains, ICT Security and Competitiveness, Data Governance and Technology Platforms, Misuse of Technology Threatening Security & Human Rights, Export Controls Cooperation, Investment Screening Cooperation, Promoting SME Access to and Use of Digital Technologies and Global Trade Challenges all grouped to together but also somewhat distinctively apart.[50] The provenance of the groupings and their selection, much like a lot of the TTC, are difficult to fully discern without significant insider insight.

International agreements and standards have heavily informed the work of the TTC which makes for arguably interesting analysis on the depth of their engagement on global challenges.[51] For instance, the instruments referred to span a vast range: the Guidelines for Recipient country Investment Policies Relating to National Security (OECD 2009), the General Agreement on Trade in Services (GATS), the Global Partnership on AI, the First Movers Coalition, Green Digital coalition, OECD AI Recommendation, WTO Government Procurement Agreement (GPA), Declaration on the Future of the Internet (proposed), UN Universal Declaration of Human Rights (UDHR), UN High Commissioner for HR and UN Special Procedures, UN Human Rights Council and WTO Statement on the Trade and Environment Sustainability Structured Discussions are all widely and on multiple occasions referenced.[52] A very

---

50 See the EU-US Trade and Technology Council Website: <https://futurium.ec.europa.eu/en/EU-US-TTC> accessed 30 June 2023.

51 EU-US Inaugural Joint Statement, Brussels. 15 June 2021; EU-US TTC Pittsburgh Statement (First Meeting of TTC). 15 September 2021; EU-US TTC Paris Statement (Second Meeting of TTC). 16 May 2022; EU-US TTC Washington Statement (Third Meeting of TTC). 5 December 2022. See also White House, 'US-EU Joint Statement of the Trade and Technology Council' (Briefing, September 2021) <https://www.whitehouse.gov/briefing-room/statements-releases/2022/12/05/u-s-eu-joint-statement-of-the-trade-and-technology-council/> accessed 30 June 2023.

52 Thanks to Ivanka Karaivanova for assistance on compiling the list that follows: ""Rome Declaration" principles; Outcomes of the World Health Assembly; World Health Organization governance in general; UN 2030 Agenda for Sustainable Development; G20 Common Framework for debt treatment; UNFCCC Paris Agreement; UN Environment Assembly; UN Ocean Conference; UN Intergovernmental Conference on Marine Biodiversity beyond National Jurisdiction; G20/OECD Inclusive Framework on Base erosion and profit shifting (BEPS); World Trade Organization law in general; Galileo – GPS Agreement; Multilateral institutions for democracy, peace, and security in general, including UN Human Rights Council; International humanitarian law; International law, in particular the UN Convention on the Law of the Sea (UNCLOS); UN Security Council Resolution 2254; UN's proposal for an immediate ceasefire in Libya; OHCHR investigations

rough estimate (with counting complicated by multiple divergent references deployed) suggests that over 50 international agreements, instruments or standards are referenced. Whatever about the actual number, it appears a very significant placement of the multilateral at the heart of this bilateral effort to use global instruments as a law-making agenda, albeit couched in soft law and many complex international actors and organizations. It also demonstrated a willingness to look far and wide for solutions to the many cross-cutting themes of the TTC, where the EU had significant legislative infrastructure especially on Tech, the US far less so.

The first post-meeting consensus was that the TTC was off to a 'promising start', but observers also noted that the bar for success in the first meeting was low.[53] The second meeting already appeared ready for significant policy shifts.

---

in Africa; Special Drawing Rights by the IMF for Africa; Joint Comprehensive Plan of Action (JCPOA); 2016 and 2018 Joint Declarations on NATO-EU Cooperation; Coordination in multilateral bodies (in general), including in the WTO; OECD Guidelines with respect to investment screening; General reference to the parties' international obligations and commitments as to trade in dual use goods; promotion of multilateral approach to export controls; OECD Guidelines for Recipient Country Investment Policies Relating to National Security of 2009; Promotion of the respect for human rights and international humanitarian law; Promotion of multilateral approach to export controls and multilateral rules-based trade; Internationally-agreed standards relating to export controls; General Agreement on Tariffs and Trade (GATT); Multilateral export control regimes; Multilateral and international cooperation; OECD Recommendation on Artificial Intelligence; FTAs and unilateral measures that concern fundamental labour rights; Cooperation in the ILO, WTO, and other appropriate multilateral for a; Declaration of the Future of the Internet; International standards activities for critical and emerging technologies; 2021 Ministerial Declaration of the G7 Digital and Technology Ministers' meeting; Internationally-recognized labor rights; International standardisation organisations; International standards regarding AI systems; Facilitation of bilateral and multilateral cooperation; The International Energy Agency ("IEA"); World Trade Organization Agreement on Technical Barriers to Trade (TBT Agreement)/ WTO law/ standardisation; Universal Declaration of Human Rights; Multilateral mechanisms related to data governance and platform governance; G7 Rapid Response Mechanism; Multilateral engagement, including with and within the United Nations, in particular the Office of the United Nations High Commissioner for Human Rights ("OHCHR") and UN Special Procedures; International human rights law; Multilateral engagement, including at the UN; 49th session of the United Nations Human Rights Council; Work in the framework of other international for a; G7 Rapid Response Mechanism ("RRM"); International engagement on investment security issues; Coordinating in the Organisation for Economic Cooperation and Development ("OECD"), International Labour Organization ("ILO"), United Nations, G7, G20, WTO, and other multilateral organizations; ILO's new global forced labour estimate; due diligence guidance & international guidelines; the operation of the network of National Contact Points in the OECD; Cooperate in international fora".

53 Guillaume Van Der Loo, Thijs Vandenbussche, and Andreas Aktoudianakis, 'The EU-US Trade and Technology Council: Mapping the Challenges and Opportunities for

By the third meeting over a year from the first meeting, the Ministerial Joint Statement was already trumpeting the success of the outcomes, centered upon developing economies connectivity and AI, amongst many other, although generally unrelated to legal instruments.[54] In fact, this stems possibly from the fact that the external regulatory landscape was understood to be an advantage for the EU in taking the lead – perhaps so much so as to make the rule-making exercise questionable.[55]

It can be said that the challenges (e.g. digitisation or greening) are all global challenges; they cannot per se be resolved by standards alignment alone by like-minded cooperation however noble minded. Whether the working groups outcomes align well more broadly with the WTO agenda also remains to be seen. The TTC ultimately raises questions as to why reform of WTO should not be key focus. The challenges for civil society engaging with the breadth of the issues proposed and, in this fashion, could be arguably higher than usual.[56]

5 Methods and Means to Improve Democratic and Participatory Aspects of the TTC

5.1 *Deepening and Widening Stakeholder Engagement on Global Challenges*

Whether and what the EU has learned from the TTIP precedents is an important question as to the future of global governance and avoiding policy failures. The initial TTC meeting was plagued by allegations of a lack of transparency for its accordance of excessive influence to the US, allegations that beset many contemporary bilateral and multilateral engagements in the field of trade and technology.[57] Civil society responded adversely to its creation and its initial

Transatlantic Cooperation on Trade, Climate, and Digital' (2021) Egmont Paper 113; Jennifer Hillman and Seara Grundhoefer, 'Can the U.S.-EU Trade and Technology Council Succeed?' (*Council on Foreign Affairs*, 29 October 2021) <www.cfr.org/blog/can-us-eu-trade-and-technology-council-succeed> accessed 30 June 2023; Demertzis, 'US-EU relations in the first year of President Biden: a view from Brussels. Transatlantic' (n 49).

54 White House, 'US-EU Joint Statement of the Trade and Technology Council' (n 51).

55 See Bradford (n 28).

56 Daniel Hamilton, 'Getting to Yes: Making the U.S.-EU Trade and Technology Council Effective (Summary Brief)' (*Transatlantic*, 6 March 2022) <https://www.transatlantic.org/wp-content/uploads/2022/03/TTC-summary-brief-final-March-6-2022.pdf> accessed 30 June 2023.

57 Trans Atlantic Consumer Dialogue (TACD), 'Lack of transparency could thwart the strong consumer safeguards that must be the goal of EU-US cooperation dialogues' (*TACD*, 28

working phases despite its development to avoid the challenges of the EU-US TTIP agreement negotiations, creating upset with civil society as to investment issues, secret courts and a lack of participation.[58] Yet there is much to learn from this era of EU external relations for its deeper engagement and transparency with civil society and stakeholders and its efforts to attempt to bring more into the transatlantic definition of civil society and its unique stakeholders, having prioritised business for so long.[59]

Stakeholder assemblies have been set up to engage with a wide diversity of actors and interest groups in the work of the TTC, moderated by thinktanks. Stakeholders' inputs and suggestions have been included in zoom meetings, supposedly 'creating space for broad exchanges and structured dialogue' and giving stakeholders the opportunity to 'influence the work and priorities of the TTC'. The Stakeholder Assembly in January 2023 aimed to discuss the outcomes of e.g. the third TTC Ministerial Meeting and priorities for 2023 by generating exchanges between a cross-section of stakeholders from government, industry, academia, and civil society on key issues in transatlantic trade and technology policy-making. These assemblies have continued in other specialist areas of TTC work e.g. as to AI policy. The TTC Stakeholder Assembly is part of the stakeholder activities organised by the TTD to increase transparency and stakeholder participation in the TTC workstreams. The purpose of the engagement activities has been in theory to enable an open exchange among stakeholders and to update them on the work progress of the TTC. Stakeholders could ask questions on the TTC to assist them in understanding the current technical work progress, moderated by thinktanks. Stakeholders could also exchange information, concerns, and ideas for future action among each other. Commission officials attended to observe the stakeholder-to-stakeholder exchange and listen to the stakeholders' perspectives in six thematic rooms on zoom. Criticisms can be expressed as to the stakeholder assembly related to its vast array of areas, lack of focus and unduly broad effort to engage with every issue, entailing that any international organisation of engagement however robust nonetheless is doomed to limited effectiveness. Of the 3 TTCs so far at the time of writing, many global challenges policy outcomes were touted by third meeting. Only time will tell as to the effectiveness of its longer term ambitions to formulate solutions to global challenges, not least the sustainability of

---

September 2021) <https://tacd.org/eu-us-organisations-transparency-ttc-pr/> accessed 30 June 2023.

58 Ibid.

59 Bartl and Fahey, 'A Postnational Marketplace: Negotiating the Transatlantic Trade and Investment Partnership (TTIP)' (n 29).

an executive to executive forum twice a year with high-level policy-making as its ambition.

5.2 *Changing the Marginalisation of the EP from EU-US Relations*

One entity not officially to be found within the TTC is the EP. The same can possibly also be said of the US Congress but this argument is not explored here on account of space and also highly variable infrastructures existing in the US as to trade, technology and international relations. The EP is formally not part in any way of the TTC. The TTC has held at the time of writing three 'high-level' political meetings so far, described as executive to executive 'ministerial' meetings steering cooperation within the TTC and guiding its 10 working groups. Yet despites its entirely legal operation outside of the channels of Article 218 TFEU, the question remains why an entity dealing with global challenges and global law-making would be so eager to remain exclusively executive to executive and to continue to exclude parliaments, at least officially? From an EU law perspective, this marginalisation appears complex and indeed easily remedied.

Since 1972 the EP has been regularly participating in a Transatlantic Legislators Dialogue with the US. The EP litigated notoriously the EU-US Passenger Name Records Agreement (PNR) and swiftly rejected the EU-US Transatlantic Terror and Financing Programme (TFTP) giving it much legal prominence in EU-US relations.[60] Yet while individual parliamentarians such as Sophie in 't veld, ex chair of the EP Civil Liberties Committee, have been litigating civil liberties issues in transatlantic security agreements, they were notably not supported by the EP as a whole. The EP did not issue recommendations on the opening of EU-US trade negotiations in 2019 and the EP notably even rejected a draft resolution recommending the opening of Trump-era EU-US trade talks (on both industrial goods and conformity assessment relating to concerns as to the Trump administration, Eastern European country visas for the US). In 2020, the Parliament's INTA Committee eventually approved the mini-tariff agreement (lobsters) with the US with no amendments but it stood out as a peculiar and hostile engagement in a complex era of EU-US relations.[61]

60 Elaine Fahey, 'Of "One Shotters" and "Repeat Hitters": A Retrospective on the Role of the European Parliament in the EU-US PNR Litigation' in Fernanda Nicola and Bill Davies (eds), *EU Law Stories: Contextual and Critical Histories of European Jurisprudence, Law in Context* (Cambridge University Press 2017).

61 In 2019, the Parliament adopted a resolution on the allocation of a share of the EU quota for hormone-free beef to the US. In 2021, INTA adopted an opinion on EU-US trade relations, as part of a resolution on the future of EU-US relations adopted by Parliament on 6 October 2021; See European Parliament Legislative Observatory, 'Motion for a resolution on the future of EU-US relations' 2021/2038(INI); European Parliament Legislative

The place of the Washington DC Liaison Office as a conduit for law-makers and Big Tech alike appears increasingly salient as it seeks to raise its profile, its 'go-between' activities and technical functions. Again, the EP is still not part of this TTC forum as an executive to executive forum-first, which appears unaligned with the institutional evolution of the EP. This would mark a highly significant shift towards the form of 'citizen sovereignty' outlined by Steinbach in this volume in particular, as a shift in how global challenges are formulated and engaged with.[62]

5.3 *Reframing Participation of Civil Society, Industry* and *the EP*

The TTC has a range of engagement strategies for stakeholders. The 'mission creep' of the TTC appears to generate ever more problematic stakeholder engagement as a result. A TTC Stakeholder Assembly was organised by the Trade and Technology Dialogue (TTD) which adopts the EU international relations lexicon of dialogues with stakeholders, increasingly found in EU trade negotiations and resulting agreements as it leads important innovations through its deeper trade agenda. Vast stakeholder series of events are part of the TTC. One may say that it is a confusing series of alphabetised meetings called the TTD, meant to support the TTC. The sheer range of issues and topics considered by the TTD by zoom-using breakout rooms-is particularly remarkable and easily accused of being ill focused given the massive number of topics covered by the TTC.[63] The lack of formal accountability here appears striking so far with stakeholder sessions run by thinktanks for the EU. High level US

Observatory, 'Opening of negotiations of an agreement with the USA on conformity assessment' COM(2019)0015; European Parliament Legislative Observatory, 'Opening of negotiations of an agreement with the USA on the elimination of tariffs for industrial goods' COM(2019)0016; European Parliament, 'Resolution on the EU/USA Agreement on the allocation of a share in the tariff rate quota for imports of high-quality beef' (2019) 10681/2019 – C9-0107/2019 – 2019/0142M(NLE).

62 See further Armin Steinbach in this volume.

63 TTD outlined in writing its Stakeholder Participation Policy for 31 January 2023: 'The purpose of the engagement activities is to enable an open exchange among stakeholders and to update them on the work progress of the TTC. During the first part of this event, stakeholders will be able to ask questions on the TTC to assist them in understanding the current technical work progress. During the second part of the event, stakeholders will be able to exchange information, concerns, and ideas for future action among each other in dialogue. Please note European Commission officials will be present to observe the stakeholder-to-stakeholder exchange and listen to the stakeholders' perspectives in the six thematic rooms. This Stakeholder Assembly is part of the stakeholder activities organised by the TTD to increase transparency and stakeholder participation in the TTC workstreams.'

administration, professional lobbyists and/or thinktanks and EU institutions – but not the EP – entail a clear dominance of non-EU-institutional 'thinking' and limited concern for fundamental rights or the EU public interest-and a very particular view of the development of policy on global challenges.[64] The EP has received briefings on the TTC from the Commission, although this information is very difficult to discern publicly. The EP INTA Trade committee has received outsized prominence in EU-US relations matters on account of the significance of digital trade. However, democratic scrutiny has been repeatedly mentioned by the EP as to the TTC-albeit via EPRS briefings rather than via a resolution; members of the EP have described the work of the TTC as being 'modest' to date-which could readily change.[65] Future TTC meetings on global challenges could make these models for engagement worthy of more reflection, analysis and development.

5.4 *The EU 'in' the US: Institutions and Diplomacy Ratcheting Upwards*

The exclusion of the EP formally is very notable given the EU's ratcheting up of institutions and diplomacy in the US post-DSA and DMA. An array of factors are all combining to change traditional attitudes in the Congress on the need to deepen EU-US cooperation. It was only in 2010 that one side established a dedicated structure with the explicit task of channeling and deepening ties between the EU and US legislatures-a European Parliament Liaison Office (EPLO) – still with no US equivalent.[66] The EPLO sits alongside physically the European External Action Service (EEAS) in Washington DC in the same building but notably on the floor below it. EPLO Washington DC has added an important 'hard' dimension to institutionalising the EU-US inter-parliamentary relationship.[67] Aside from the EEAS office in Washington DC and the EPLO in Washington DC alongside it, the EU recently opened its new EEAS office in San Francisco, California, as a self-professed global centre for digital technology and innovation.[68] Its mission was said

64 European Parliament, 'European Parliament resolution of 24 November 2010 on the Anti-Counterfeiting Trade Agreement (ACTA)' (P7_TA(2010)0432). First Reading, (EP-PE_TC1-COD(2005)0127).

65 'EU-US Trade and Technology Council: Modest progress in a challenging context' (*European Parliament*, 10 February 2023). <https://epthinktank.eu/2023/02/10/eu-us-trade-and-technology-council-modest-progress-in-a-challenging-context/> accessed 30 June 2023.

66 Dunne, 'Connecting the US Congress and the European Parliament: The work and role of the EP Liaison Office in Washington DC' (n 22).

67 Ibid.

68 The opening of the office was said to be as a result of the 2021 EU-US Summit shared commitment to strengthen transatlantic technological cooperation and is a core part

to be to promote EU standards and technologies, digital policies and regulations and governance models, and to strengthen cooperation with US stakeholders, including by advancing the work of the EU-US Trade and Technology Council.[69] The office was said to work under the authority of the EU Delegation in Washington, DC, in close coordination with Headquarters in Brussels and in partnership with EU Member States consulates in the San Francisco Bay Area-but again without any mention of or reference to the EP.[70] This model of developing further diplomacy 'islands' appears to contradict many of the tenets of the direction of EU-US engagement to widen and deepen its subjects, objects and actors.

6 Conclusions

Transatlantic relations is a seemingly endless tale of decades of complex bilateralism and multilateralism failures. It has been marked by a dominance of soft law and hybrid governance, not necessarily always a clear or positive impact upon multilateralism per se. What is global law-making policy in a mired multilateral world may constitute for many blue-sky reflection-but in reality the TTC marks the most significant shift in global governance thinking on trade and technology in the 21st century to date, even where the definition of public goods is under strain and where increasingly data flows defy characterisation. A transatlantic alignment of lexicon, policy and ambitions through bilateral cooperation should mark the future of global governance shifts. On

of the Conclusions on Digital Diplomacy. See Council of the European Union, 'EU digital diplomacy: Council agrees a more concerted European approach to the challenges posed by new digital technologies' (18 July 2022) <https://www.consilium.europa.eu/en/press/press-releases/2022/07/18/eu-digital-diplomacy-council-agrees-a-more-concerted-european-approach-to-the-challenges-posed-by-new-digital-technologies/#:~:text=The%20Council%20today%20approved%20conclusions,the%20geopolitical%20balance%20of%20power> accessed 30 June 2023.

69 European External Action Service, 'US/Digital: EU opens new Office in San Francisco to reinforce its Digital Diplomacy' (September 2022) <https://www.eeas.europa.eu/eeas/usdigital-eu-opens-new-office-san-francisco-reinforce-its-digital-diplomacy_en> accessed 30 June 2023.

70 It was to be headed by Gerard de Graaf, a senior Commission official who has worked extensively on digital policies, most recently on the EU's landmark new platform laws, the Digital Services Act and Digital Markets Act. See European Commission, 'Digital Services Package: Commission welcomes the adoption by the European Parliament of the EU's new rulebook for digital services' (Press Release, 2022) <https://ec.europa.eu/commission/presscorner/detail/en/IP_22_4313> accessed 30 June 2023.

one level, the TTC represents an important and positive institutionalisation of the outcomes of the failed TTIP negotiations and many lessons learned from many transatlantic experiments in global governance. Yet it is only a step in the right direction and considerably more can be done to evolve the precedent of the TTIP era. Developing global challenges through institutions and deeper and wider engagement marks an important step in constitutionalisation – but with much that can be done to enhance it. The capacity for this convergence to evolve further and to align bilaterally, particularly through institutions, could become pivotal going forward as to global law-making. This chapter has outlined a range of policy formulations and evolutions that can readily be implemented.

The TTC it is notably not the only recent Council proposed by the EU – as noted, there is the new EU-India Trade Council. These new Councils represent a new modus operandi for the EU to engage with complex large third country partners through executive to executive engagement, meeting agency counterparts regularly in close groups in an era of EU trade policy deepening its stakeholder and civil society ambit overall. The TTC has a vast range of policy-making activities, traversing many areas of EU law. Their selection and future is difficult to understand in EU trade and data policy seemingly pivoting to executive-led soft law in some arenas and then towards more robust global courts such as a Transatlantic Data Review Court in others. Still, however, there is an effort to learn from the TTIP precedent-which must and can be taken further. Above all, they are characterised by more outreach and a deeper understanding of the need for multilevel engagement-and to think 'bigger' about the nature of democratic engagement in global challenge policy development. Yet, such intergovernmental and non-transparent collaboration of executives and businesses risks also being 'captured' by rent-seeking interest groups influencing negotiations on new product and production standards and subsidies in their favour to the detriment of general consumer welfare and total citizen welfare. There is clearly some constitutional danger or risk of regulatory capture of the TTC.[71] So far, the TTC may reflect more the business-driven, neo-liberal US tradition of economic regulation than Europe's multilevel economic constitutional approaches to regulating 'market failures' (like information asymmetries and abuses in the Internet and ecommerce) and related 'governance failures' (like insufficient protection of fundamental rights in data regulations).[72] However, European first-mover advantage in the field

71 See Ernst-Ulrich Petersmann in this volume.

72 Ibid.

of tech and data privacy and its important constitutional evolutions in stakeholder engagement may indicate that the outcomes of the TTC are complex to evaluate at this juncture.

Bibliography

Bartl, M and Fahey, E, 'A Postnational Marketplace: Negotiating the Transatlantic Trade and Investment Partnership (TTIP)' in Fahey, E and Curtin, D (eds), *A Transatlantic Community of Law: Legal Perspectives on the Relationship between the EU and US legal orders* (Cambridge University Press 2014).

Bignami, F and Charnovitz, S, 'Transnational Civil Society Dialogues' Pollack, M and Shaffer, G (eds), *Transatlantic Governance in the Global Economy* (Rowman & Littlefield 2001).

Bown, C P and Malmström, C, 'What is the Transatlantic Trade and Technology Council' (*PIIE*, September 2021) <https://www.piie.com/blogs/trade-and-investment-policy-watch/what-us-eu-trade-and-technology-council-five-things-you-need> accessed 30 June 2023.

Bradford, A, *Brussels Effect: How the European Union rules the World* (Oxford University Press 2020).

Brugge, G S and De Ville, F, *TTIP: The Truth about the Transatlantic Trade and Investment Partnership* (Polity Press 2015).

Burri, M, 'The Regulation of Data Flows Through Trade Agreements' (2017) 48 Law and Policy in International Business 407.

Cohen, J L, *Globalization and Sovereignty: Rethinking Legality, Legitimacy, and Constitutionalism* (Cambridge University Press 2012).

Corporate Europe Observatory, 'TTIP reloaded: big business calls the shots on new EU-US trade talks' (*Corporate Europe Observatory*, February 2019) <https://corporateeurope.org/en/international-trade/2019/02/ttip-reloaded-big-business-calls-shots-new-eu-us-trade-talks> accessed 30 June 2023.

Council of the European Union, 'EU digital diplomacy: Council agrees a more concerted European approach to the challenges posed by new digital technologies' (18 July 2022) <https://www.consilium.europa.eu/en/press/press-releases/2022/07/18/eu-digital-diplomacy-council-agrees-a-more-concerted-european-approach-to-the-challenges-posed-by-new-digital-technologies/#:~:text=The%20Council%20today%20approved%20conclusions,the%20geopolitical%20balance%20of%20power> accessed 30 June 2023.

Cowles, M G, 'The Transatlantic Business Dialogue: Transforming the New Transatlantic Dialogue' in Pollack, M and Shaffer, G (eds), *Transatlantic Governance in the Global Economy* (Rowman & Littlefield 2001).

Demertzis, M, 'US-EU relations in the first year of President Biden: a view from Brussels' (*Transatlantic*, December 2021). <https://www.transatlantic.org/wp-content/uploads/2021/12/11-10-2021-Demertzis-US-EU-trade-Challenges-v2.pdf> accessed 30 June 2023.

Dunne, J and Pollack, M, 'International Law and International Relations: Introducing an Interdisciplinary Dialogue' in Dunoff, J and Pollack, M (eds), *Interdisciplinary Perspectives on International Law and International Relations: The State of the Art* (Cambridge University Press 2012).

Dunne, J, 'Connecting the US Congress and the European Parliament: The work and role of the EP Liaison Office in Washington DC' in Fahey, E (ed), *Routledge Research Handbook on Transatlantic Relations* (1st edn, Routledge 2023).

European Commission and High Representative of the Union for Foreign Affairs and Security Policy, 'Joint Communication to the European Parliament, the European Council and the Council: A new EU-US agenda for global change' JOIN (2020) 22 final.

European Commission, 'A reading guide to the EU proposal on services, investment and e-commerce for the Transatlantic Trade and Investment Partnership' (2015) <http://trade.ec.europa.eu/doclib/docs/2015/july/tradoc_153668.pdf> accessed 30 June 2023.

European Commission, 'Digital Services Package: Commission welcomes the adoption by the European Parliament of the EU's new rulebook for digital services' (Press Release, 2022) <https://ec.europa.eu/commission/presscorner/detail/en/IP_22_4313> accessed 30 June 2023.

European Commission, 'EU-India: Joint press release on launching the Trade and Technology Council' (Press Release 2022) <https://ec.europa.eu/commission/presscorner/detail/en/IP_22_2643> accessed 30 June 2023.

European Commission, 'European Commission and United States Joint Statement on Trans-Atlantic Data Privacy Framework' (Press Release, 2022) <https://ec.europa.eu/commission/presscorner/detail/en/IP_22_2087> accessed 30 June 2023.

European Commission, 'EU-US launch Trade and Technology Council to lead values-based global digital transformation' (Press Release 2021) <https://ec.europa.eu/commission/presscorner/detail/en/IP_21_2990> accessed 30 June 2023.

European Commission, 'EU-US Trade and Technology Council Inaugural Joint Statement' (Press Release 2021) <https://ec.europa.eu/commission/presscorner/detail/en/STATEMENT_21_4951> accessed 30 June 2023.

European Commission, 'Expert group to advise European Commission on EU-US trade talks' (Press Release 2014) <https://europa.eu/rapid/press-release_IP-14-79_en.htm> accessed 30 June 2023.

European Commission, 'Final Report High Level Working Group on Jobs and Growth' (2013) Tradoc 150519 <http://trade.ec.europa.eu/doclib/docs/2013/february/tradoc_150519.pdf> accessed 30 June 2023.

European Commission, 'Launch of the US-EU Task Force on the Inflation Reduction Act' (Press Release 2022) <https://ec.europa.eu/commission/presscorner/detail/en/statement_22_6402> accessed 30 June 2023.

European Commission, 'Terms of Reference' (July 2015) <https://trade.ec.europa.eu/doclib/docs/2015/july/tradoc_153617.pdf> accessed 30 June 2023.

European Commission, 'TTIP: Annexes to the services, investment and e-commerce initial proposal' (2015) <http://trade.ec.europa.eu/doclib/docs/2015/july/tradoc_153670.pdf> accessed 30 June 2023.

European Commission, 'TTIP: Initial proposal on trade in services, investment and e-commerce' (2015) <http://trade.ec.europa.eu/doclib/docs/2015/july/tradoc_153669.pdf> accessed 30 June 2023.

European External Action Service, 'US/Digital: EU opens new Office in San Francisco to reinforce its Digital Diplomacy' (September 2022) <https://www.eeas.europa.eu/eeas/usdigital-eu-opens-new-office-san-francisco-reinforce-its-digital-diplomacy_en> accessed 30 June 2023.

European Parliament Legislative Observatory, 'Motion for a resolution on the future of EU-US relations' 2021/2038(INI).

European Parliament Legislative Observatory, 'Opening of negotiations of an agreement with the USA on conformity assessment' COM (2019) 0015.

European Parliament Legislative Observatory, 'Opening of negotiations of an agreement with the USA on the elimination of tariffs for industrial goods' COM (2019) 0016.

European Parliament, 'European Parliament resolution of 24 November 2010 on the Anti-Counterfeiting Trade Agreement (ACTA)' (P7_TA(2010)0432). First Reading, (EP-PE_TC1-COD(2005)0127).

European Parliament, 'EU-US Trade and Technology Council: Modest progress in a challenging context' (*European Parliament*, 10 February 2023). <https://epthinktank.eu/2023/02/10/eu-us-trade-and-technology-council-modest-progress-in-a-challenging-context/> accessed 30 June 2023.

European Parliament, 'Resolution on the EU/USA Agreement on the allocation of a share in the tariff rate quota for imports of high-quality beef' (2019) 10681/2019 – C9-0107/2019 – 2019/0142M(NLE).

European Parliament, 'TTIP Legislative Train Schedule' (2020) <www.europarl.europa.eu/legislative-train/theme-international-trade-inta/file-ttip-services-investment-and-e-commerce> accessed 30 June 2023.

EU-US Trade and Technology Council Website: <https://futurium.ec.europa.eu/en/EU-US-TTC> accessed 30 June 2023.

Fahey, E, (ed), *Routledge Research Handbook on Transatlantic Relations* (1st edn, Routledge 2023).

Fahey, E, 'Of "One Shotters" and "Repeat Hitters": A Retrospective on the Role of the European Parliament in the EU-US PNR Litigation' in Nicola, F and Davies, B (eds), *EU Law Stories: Contextual and Critical Histories of European Jurisprudence, Law in Context* (Cambridge University Press 2017).

Fahey, E, 'On the Benefits of the Transatlantic Trade and Investment Partnership (TTIP) Negotiations for the EU Legal Order: A Legal Perspective' (2016) 43 Legal Issues of Economic Integration 327.

Fahey, E, 'On The Use of Law in Transatlantic Relations: Legal Dialogues Between the EU and US' (2014) 20 European Law Journal 386.

Fahey, E, *Framing convergence with the global order: the EU and the world* (1st edn, Bloomsbury Publishing 2022).

Fahey, E, *The EU as a Global Digital Actor: Institutionalising Data Protection, Digital Trade and Cybersecurity* (Hart Publishing 2022).

Gardner, A, *Stars with Stripes: the essential partnership between the EU and US* (Palgrave Macmillan 2020).

Hamilton, D, 'Getting to Yes: Making the U.S.-EU Trade and Technology Council Effective (Summary Brief)' (*Transatlantic*, 6 March 2022) <https://www.transatlantic.org/wp-content/uploads/2022/03/TTC-summary-brief-final-March-6-2022.pdf> accessed 30 June 2023.

Hillman, J and Grundhoefer, S, 'Can the U.S.-EU Trade and Technology Council Succeed?' (*Council on Foreign Affairs*, 29 October 2021) <www.cfr.org/blog/can-us-eu-trade-and-technology-council-succeed> accessed 30 June 2023.

Kjaer, P, 'Does the 'West' still exist? Regulatory Philosophies in a Decentered Global World' in Fahey, E (ed), *Imagining the future of good global governance* (2022) City Law School Research Paper 2022/11.

Kleimann, D and others, 'Europe should answer the US Inflation Reduction Act' (2023) Bruegel Policy Contribution 04/2023.

Library of the European Parliament, 'Principal EU-US disputes' (Library Briefing, April 2013) <http://www.europarl.europa.eu/RegData/bibliotheque/briefing/2013/130518/LDM_BRI(2013)130518_REV1_EN.pdf> accessed 30 June 2023.

Mancini, I, 'The European Parliament and Civil Society in EU Trade Negotiations: The Untold Story of an Erratic Engagement' (2020) 27 European Foreign Affairs Review 241.

Meissner, K, 'Democratizing EU External Relations: The European Parliament's Informal Role in SWIFT, ACTA, and TTIP' (2016) 21 European Foreign Affairs Review 269.

O'Sullivan, D, 'EU-US Relations in a Changing World' in Fahey, E (ed), *Routledge Research Handbook on Transatlantic Relations* (1st edn, Routledge 2023).

Petersmann, E-U, 'CETA, TTIP and TISA: New Trends in International Economic Law' in Griller, S, Obwexer, W, and Vranes, E (eds), *Mega-Regional Trade Agreements: CETA, TTIP, and TISA: New Orientations for EU External Economic Relations* (Oxford University Press 2017).

Petersmann, E-U, 'Prevention and Settlement of Transatlantic Economic Disputes: Legal Strategies for EU/US Leadership' in Petersmann, E-U and Pollock, M (eds), *Transatlantic Economic Disputes: The EU, the US, and the WTO* (Oxford University Press 2003).

Petersmann, E-U, 'Transformative Transatlantic Free Trade Agreements without Rights and Remedies of Citizens?' (2015) 18 Journal of International Economic Law 579.

Pollack, M and Shaffer, G (eds), *Transatlantic Governance in the Global Economy* (Rowman & Littlefield 2001).

Pollack, M and Shaffer, G, *When Cooperation Fails: The International Law and Politics of Genetically Modified Foods* (Oxford University Press 2009).

Pollack, M, 'The New Transatlantic Agenda at Ten: Reflections on an Experiment in International Governance' (2005) 43(5) Journal of Common Market Studies 899.

Pollack, M, Shaffer, G and others, *The Political Economy of the Transatlantic Partnership* (2003) Working Paper EUI <https://www.eui.eu/Documents/RSCAS/e-texts/200306HMTMvFReport.pdf> accessed 30 June 2023.

Riddervold, M and Newsome, A, *Transatlantic Relations In Times Of Uncertainty: Crises and EU-US* (1st edn, Routledge 2019).

Roger, C, *The Origins of Informality: Why the Legal Foundation of Global Governance are Shifting, and Why It Matters* (Oxford University Press 2020).

Scott, J, 'From Brussels with Love: the Transatlantic Travels of European Law and the Chemistry of Regulatory Attraction' (2009) 57 The American Journal of Comparative Law 897.

Shaffer, G, 'Globalization and Social Protection: The Impact of EU and International Rules in the Ratcheting Up of U.S. Privacy Standards' (2000) 25 Yale Journal of International Law 1.

Sir Leon Brittan, 'Transatlantic Economic Partnership: Breaking down the hidden barriers' in Bermann, G and others (eds), *Transatlantic Regulatory Cooperation* (Oxford University Press 2000).

The White House, 'FACT SHEET: United States and European Commission Announce Trans-Atlantic Data Privacy Framework' (2022) <https://www.whitehouse.gov/briefing-room/statements-releases/2022/03/25/fact-sheet-united-states-and-european-commission-announce-trans-atlantic-data-privacy-framework/> accessed 30 June 2023.

The White House, 'U.S.-EU Trade and Technology Council Inaugural Joint Statement' (Statement Release 2021) <www.whitehouse.gov/briefing-room/statements-releases/2021/09/29/u-s-eu-trade-and-technology-council-inaugural-joint-statement/> accessed 30 June 2023.

The White House, 'US-EU Joint Statement of the Trade and Technology Council' (Briefing, September 2021) <https://www.whitehouse.gov/briefing-room/statements-releases/2022/12/05/u-s-eu-joint-statement-of-the-trade-and-technology-council/> accessed 30 June 2023.

Trans Atlantic Consumer Dialogue (TACD), 'Lack of transparency could thwart the strong consumer safeguards that must be the goal of EU-US cooperation dialogues' (*TACD*, 28 September 2021) <https://tacd.org/eu-us-organisations-transparency-ttc-pr/> accessed 30 June 2023.

US Chamber of Commerce, 'Transatlantic Data Flows: Moving Data with Confidence' (2021) <https://www.uschamber.com/technology/data-privacy/transatlantic-dataflows> accessed 30 June 2023.

Valsamis, M, 'The New EU–USA Cooperation on Extradition, Mutual Legal Assistance and the Exchange of Police Data' (2003) 8 European Foreign Affairs Review 515.

Van Der Loo, G, Vandenbussche, T, and Aktoudianakis, A, 'The EU-US Trade and Technology Council: Mapping the Challenges and Opportunities for Transatlantic Cooperation on Trade, Climate, and Digital' (2021) Egmont Paper 11.

Williams, A, 'US-Europe trade tensions heat up over green subsidies' *Financial Times* (27 February 2023) <https://www.ft.com/content/0f8bf631-f24c-48da-905f-e37f8dc5d5f8> accessed 23 June 2023.

Young, A, 'Not your parents' trade politics: the Transatlantic Trade and Investment Partnership negotiations' (2016) 23 Review of International Political Economy 345.

Young, A, 'The transatlantic regulatory relationship: limited conflict, less competition and a new approach to cooperation' in Fahey, E (ed), *Routledge Research Handbook on Transatlantic Relations* (1st edn, Routledge 2023).

CHAPTER 12

Can the WTO Dispute Settlement System Be Revived?

Options for Addressing a Major Governance Failure of the World Trade Organization

Peter Van den Bossche

1 Introduction[1]

The dispute settlement system of the World Trade Organization ('WTO'), which for many years was lauded as the jewel in the crown of this organization, is a mere shadow of its former self in 2023. The current crisis of the WTO dispute settlement system – a bold, but now aborted, experiment with the rule of law in international trade relations – is a major governance failure of the WTO. Recognizing the importance and urgency of addressing this failure, WTO Members agreed at the Ministerial Conference in June 2022 to conduct discussions 'with the view to having a fully and well-functioning dispute settlement system accessible to all Members by 2024'.[2] To this end, Members have been engaged since February 2023 in an intensive process of informal, small and larger-group meetings referred to as the Molina Process. In this chapter, I will first briefly recall the past successful functioning of the WTO dispute settlement system and its recent demise because of the paralysis of the Appellate Body ('AB'). I will subsequently discuss the unsuccessful attempt in 2019 to avoid the current crisis ('the Walker Process') and the establishment and operation of an alternative system for appellate review ('the MPIA'), before assessing – based on the information available – the chances of success of the ongoing Molina Process. In conclusion, I will review the options available to overcome the current crisis of WTO dispute settlement and address this major governance failure of the WTO.

1 I wish to acknowledge the able research assistance of Manuj Gupta, West Bengal National University of Juridical Sciences, Kolkata, India.

2 WTO Ministerial Conference, MC12 Outcome Document, adopted on 17 June 2022, WT/MIN(22)/24, dated 22 June 2022, para. 4.

2 The Road from Success to Failure

2.1 *The Success of WTO Dispute Settlement*

One of the most notable features of the WTO is its dispute settlement system. Its establishment in 1995 was one of the main achievements of the Uruguay Round of Multilateral Trade Negotiations (1986–1994).[3] With its compulsory jurisdiction, mandatory pre-litigation consultations, appellate review, strict time frames for proceedings, and surveillance and enforcement of compliance, the WTO dispute settlement system is in many respects unique among international dispute resolution systems.

Since its initiation in 1995, the WTO dispute settlement system has been the most frequently used system for the resolution of State-to-State disputes. To date, WTO Members have brought 618 disputes to the WTO for resolution.[4] To date, the WTO dispute settlement system has been used, as a party or third party, by 111 of the 164 WTO Members, and it has been used by developed and developing countries alike.[5] While the United States ('US') and the European Union ('EU') have been the most frequent complainants (as well as the most frequent respondents), the system has often been used by other WTO Members to see legal rights prevail over economic and other might.[6] On 1 September 2023, a total of 290 panel reports and 148 AB reports had been issued and circulated.[7] When compared with other state-to-state dispute resolution systems, such as the International Court of Justice ('ICJ') or the International Tribunal for the Law of the Sea ('ITLOS'), this reveals a very high level of activity. In the period from 1 January 1995 to 1 September 2023, the ICJ rendered 90 judgments and 7 advisory opinions.[8] The ITLOS, an international tribunal with

3 Understanding on Rules and Procedures Governing the Settlement of Disputes ('Dispute Settlement Understanding' or 'DSU'), Annex 2 of the Marrakesh Agreement Establishing the World Trade Organization, https://www.wto.org/english/tratop_e/dispu_e/dsu_e.htm.

4 See https://www.worldtradelaw.net/databases/searchcomplaints.php.

5 See 'Dispute settlement activity – some figures' (World Trade Organization). <https://www.wto.org/english/tratop_e/dispu_e/dispustats_e.htm> accessed 20 September 2023; https://www.worldtradelaw.net/databases/complaintscomplainant.php.

6 J. Lacarte and P. Gappah, 'Developing Countries and the WTO Legal and Dispute Settlement System', (2000) 3(3) Journal of International Economic Law 395, 400.

7 'WTO Panel Reports' (WorldTradeLaw.net). <https://www.worldtradelaw.net/databases/wtopanels.php> accessed 20 September 2023; 'WTO Appellate Body Reports and other appellate decisions' (WorldTradeLaw.net). <https://www.worldtradelaw.net/databases/abreports.php> accessed 20 September 2023.

8 'Judgments, Advisory Opinions and Orders' (International Court of Justice). <https://www.icj-cij.org/decisions?type=2&from=1995&to=2023&sort_bef_combine=order_DESC> accessed 20 September 2023; Judgments, Advisory Opinions and Orders' (International

jurisdiction limited to a specific field of international law like the WTO dispute settlement system, has rendered in total 30 judgments, advisory opinions and orders of removal since its establishment in 1996.[9] While the law applied by WTO panels and the AB is highly technical, the issues raised in many WTO disputes are often politically sensitive, as they concern the legality under WTO law of domestic legislation and policies for the protection of core societal values and interests, such as public health, public morals, environmental protection, employment, economic development and national security. The rulings in many WTO disputes have attracted much interest, receiving high praise as well as sharp criticism from WTO Member governments, economic operators, and civil society. Finally, but most importantly, it should be noted that the WTO dispute settlement system has not only been used frequently and has 'produced' many rulings on politically sensitive issues, but it also has an excellent record of compliance with its rulings.[10]

2.2 *A Crisis Looming since Long*

While in the early years of the WTO dispute settlement system, WTO Members often expressed their satisfaction with its functioning, there were, nevertheless, a number of crisis moments (e.g., the *Helms-Burton Act* national security crisis in 1997, the Articles 21.5/22.6 DSU sequencing crisis in 1999, and the *amicus curiae* brief crisis in 2000).[11] Also, while expressing satisfaction with the operation of the dispute settlement system, WTO Members tabled many proposals for its reform, both before and during the early stages of Doha Round negotiations in the first half of the 2000s.[12] Some of these proposals were aimed at a further judicialization of the system, while others reflected a desire to introduce greater Member (i.e., political) control over WTO dispute settlement. Note that Claude Barfield of the American Enterprise Institute, wrote in 2001 that the WTO dispute settlement system is 'substantively and politically unsustainable' and that its powers would have to be curbed. Further, Claus-Dieter Ehlermann, the first European AB member, stated in 2002 that the WTO dispute settlement system is threatened by a dangerous institutional

---

Court of Justice). <https://www.icj-cij.org/decisions?type=4&from=1995&to=2023&sort_bef_combine=order_DESC> accessed 20 September 2023.

9 'Contentious Cases' (International Tribunal for the Law of the Sea). <https://www.itlos.org/en/main/cases/contentious-cases/ and https://www.itlos.org/en/main/cases/advisory-proceedings/> accessed 20 September 2023.

10 See https://www.worldtradelaw.net/databases/summary.php.

11 Peter Van den Bossche and Werner Zdouc, *The Law and Policy of the World Trade Organization*, (5th edn, CUP 2022) 1015, 416 and 423.

12 Ibid, p. 194–95.

imbalance between the weak legislative and the successful judicial branch of the WTO.[13]

From the beginning of the 2010s, the WTO dispute settlement came under an ever-increasing pressure. A major crisis was looming for several, related reasons.[14] *First*, the workload of panels and the AB significantly augmented due to the increased size and the complexity of the disputes brought to the WTO for resolution, while the financial and other resources made available for dispute settlement fell short. *Second*, the paralysis of the 'legislative' branch of the WTO made Members seek change to WTO law through adjudication, rather than negotiations. This paralysis also made it impossible for Members to 'correct' alleged errors by the AB in the interpretation of WTO law. *Third*, some Members, and in particular the US, increasingly made antagonistic allegations of judicial overreach by the AB and accused it of unacceptable disregard of procedural rules, in particular the 90-day time frame for appellate review. *Fourth* and finally, the US took overt as well as covert action affecting the independence and impartiality of AB members, primarily in the context of the process of reappointment of AB members. While its gravity was unexpected, the current crisis had been looming for years.

2.3 *The Existential Crisis*

The current crisis was triggered by the blockage of the Trump administration of the process of appointment (or reappointment) of AB members. Due to this blockage, the AB, ordinarily seven strong, had only one member left on 11 December 2019 and was thus rendered unable to hear and decide any new appeals filed from then onwards.[15] Subsequently, the term of the one remaining member expired on 30 November 2020. Since then, the AB has been a court without judges.

The US has blocked the appointment process because it has fundamental concerns regarding the AB and its functioning.[16] The most significant of these

13 Claude E. Barfield, 'Free Trade, Sovereignty, Democracy: The Future of the World Trade Organization' (2001) 2(2) Chicago Journal of International Law, Article 13, 403, 410; Claus-Dieter Ehlermann, *Some Personal Experiences as Member of the Appellate Body of the WTO*, Policy Papers, RSC No. 02/9 (European University Institute, 2002), para 124.

14 See Van den Bosscche and Zdouc (n 11), 424.

15 Of the 13 appeals pending before the Appellate Body on 11 December 2019, only three were still decided. The other ten appeals remained pending.

16 The United States set out its concerns in detail in February 2020 in United States Trade Representative, *Report on the Appellate Body of the World Trade Organization* <https://ustr.gov/sites/default/files/Report_on_the_Appellate_Body_of_the_World_Trade_Organization.pdf> accessed 20 September 2023.

concerns is that the AB added to or diminished the rights and obligations of WTO Members under the WTO agreements. It accuses the AB of 'judicial activism' on matters relating to anti-dumping measures, subsidies, countervailing measures, safeguard measures and technical barriers to trade. The US argues, in particular, that the AB case law limits its ability to counteract the importation of goods, which harms its domestic industry, and contends that other Members use litigation to obtain what they have not achieved through negotiation. In addition, according to the US, the AB disregarded the rules of WTO dispute settlement by:

(1) exceeding the mandatory 90-day time limit for appellate review (without the consent of the parties);
(2) allowing outgoing AB members to complete work on appeals to which they had been assigned before the end of their term;
(3) issuing 'advisory opinions' on issues not necessary to resolve the dispute;
(4) reviewing factual findings of panels and, in particular, panel findings on the meaning of the respondent's domestic law; and
(5) treating its rulings as binding precedent.

It should be noted that most of these concerns regarding the functioning of the AB had already been raised by the US under the Obama and the George W. Bush administrations respectively. However, only the Trump administration saw fit to paralyse the AB and deprive WTO Members of appellate review of panel reports.

The US blockage of the appointment process of AB members, however, did not only paralyze the AB but also plunged the entire WTO dispute settlement system into an existential crisis. Pursuant to Article 16.4 of the DSU, when a panel report is appealed, it can only be adopted by the WTO Dispute Settlement Body ('DSB'), and become legally binding, once the AB has completed its appellate review. To prevent adverse rulings in panel reports from becoming legally binding, the losing parties in WTO disputes have since December 2019 systematically appealed panel reports to the dysfunctional AB. This has been most appropriately referred to as 'appealing into the void' and, as a result, most disputes brought to the WTO in recent years have remained in a legal limbo, i.e., unresolved. Only five of the 29 panel reports circulated since 11 December 2019 have been adopted by the DSB.[17] Twenty of the panel reports were appealed

17 See Panel Report, *China – AD on Stainless Steel Products (Japan)*, WT/DS601/R, adopted 28 July 2023; Panel Report, *US – Safeguards on Washers*, WT/DS546, adopted 28 April 2023; Panel Report, *EU – Steel Safeguard Measures (Turkey)*, WT/595/R, adopted 31 May 2022; Panel Report, *Costa Rica – Avocados*, WT/DS524/R, adopted 31 May 2022; Panel Report, *United States – Anti-dumping and countervailing duties on ripe olives from Spain*, WT/DS577/R, adopted 20 December 2021. Note that the panel reports in *Colombia – Frozen*

into the void.[18] With regard to the remaining four panel reports, parties are still to decide whether to appeal.[19] It is obvious that in view of the significant risk of disputes remaining unresolved, there are few incentives for WTO Members to have recourse to the WTO dispute settlement system. Not surprisingly, the number of new disputes brought to the WTO for resolution in 2020, 2021, 2022 and 2023 (as of 1 September) fell to 5, 9, 7 and 4 respectively, while in 2018, it was 39.[20] The end of appellate review by the AB has severely undermined the effectiveness and credibility of the entire WTO dispute settlement system.

3 The 2019 Attempt to Address the US Concerns by Reforming the AB

3.1 *The Walker Process*

Faced with a possible collapse of the WTO dispute settlement system, no less than 22 WTO Members and the African Group tabled, in the period from November 2018 to June 2019, either individually or jointly, position papers with proposals for the reform of the AB to address the concerns raised by the US. On 26 November 2018, the EU, China, Canada, India, Norway, New Zealand, Switzerland, Australia, the Republic of Korea, Iceland, Singapore and Mexico submitted a communication to the WTO General Council (WT/GC/W/752/Rev. 2) setting out proposals for amendments to WTO appellate review. On the same day, the European Union, China, and India submitted a second communication to the General Council (WT/GC/W/753) setting out proposals for additional amendments, particularly with regard to institutional issues concerning the AB. However, at the General Council meeting of 12 December 2018, the US

Fries, WT/DS591/R and *Turkey – Pharmaceutical Products*, WT/DS583/R were the subject appeal arbitration under Article 25 of the DSU, and the underlying disputes were thus brought to a legally binding resolution. See below, Section 4. Note that in four disputes in which a panel had been established, the parties reached a mutually agreed solution in these disputes. This was the case in 2023 in *China – AD/CVD on Barley* (DS598) (complaint by Australia); in *India – Additional Duties* (DS585) (complaint by the United States); and in *US – Steel and Aluminium* (DS547) (complaint by India); and in 2021 in *Canada – Wine (Australia)* (DS537) (complaint by Australia).

18 See 'WTO Panel Reports' (WorldTradeLaw.net). <https://www.worldtradelaw.net/databases/wtopanels.php> accessed on 20 September 2023. There are currently appeals of 22 panel reports pending before the paralyzed Appellate Body. See https://www.worldtradelaw.net/static.php?type=dsc&page=currentcases.

19 Ibid.

20 See https://www.worldtradelaw.net/databases/searchcomplaints.php.

curtly rejected these proposals as not addressing the concerns it had raised.[21] Subsequently, Honduras (in January and February 2019, WT/GC/W/758, /759, /760 and /761), Chinese Taipei (in February 2019, WT/GC/W/763 and /763/Rev.), Brazil, Paraguay and Uruguay (in March and April 2019, WT/GC/W/767 and /767/Rev.), Japan, Australia and Chile (in April 2019, WT/GC/W/768 and /768/Rev), Thailand (in April 2019, WT/GC/W/769) and the African Group (in June 2019, WT/GC/W/776) submitted position papers to the General Council setting out further proposals, varying in detail and approach, for amending WTO appellate review. Some of these position papers, such as the first position paper referred to above, i.e., the paper by the European Union, China, Canada, India, and others, were rather 'sceptical' about the legitimacy of the concerns raised by the US and made proposals which firmly safeguarded the key features of WTO appellate review. Other position papers, such as the paper by Japan, Australia and Chile, or the paper by Brazil, Paraguay and Uruguay were more sympathetic to the US concerns and proposed to alter some key features of WTO appellate review. Finally, the position paper of Thailand, or the position papers of Honduras tried to strike a middle ground. In parallel with formal discussions on these proposals in the General Council, Members engaged in frequent and informal discussions under the leadership of Ambassador David Walker of New Zealand, the Chair of the WTO Dispute Settlement Body (the 'Walker Process') in 2019. However, the US did not actively participate in these discussions and did not put forward any specific proposals for changes to address the concerns regarding the functioning of the AB it had raised.

3.2 *The Draft General Council Decision on the Functioning of the Appellate Body of October 2019*

In October 2019, two months before the AB was expected to become dysfunctional, the discussions among WTO Members on amending WTO appellate review, i.e., the Walker Process, resulted in a draft General Council Decision on the Functioning of the Appellate Body.[22] As stated by Ambassador Walker, the draft Decision was aimed at 'seeking workable and agreeable solutions to

21 On the US reaction to the Communication from the EU, China, Canada, India and others, see Statements by the United States at the Meeting of the WTO General Council on 12 December 2018 (agenda items 7 and 8). https://geneva.usmission.gov/2018/12/12/statements-items-7-and-8-by-the-united-states-at-the-meeting-of-the-wto-general-council/.

22 General Council, Informal Process on Matters related to the Functioning of the Appellate Body – Report by the Facilitator, H.E. Dr. David Walker (New Zealand), Agenda Item 4, Annex, JOB/GC/222, dated 15 October 2019.

improve the functioning of the Appellate Body', in the hope of avoiding the paralysis of the AB as from December 2019.[23]

The draft Decision *inter alia*, addressed: (1) the US concern regarding judicial activism by stating that, pursuant to Articles 3.2 and 19.2 of the DSU, AB rulings 'cannot add to or diminish the rights and obligations provided in the covered agreements'; (2) the US concern regarding binding precedent by stating that precedent is 'not created through WTO dispute settlement proceedings', but that consistency and predictability in the interpretation of WTO law is 'of significant value to Members'; (3) the US concern regarding advisory opinions rendered by the AB by stating that the latter may only address issues raised by the parties to the extent necessary to resolve the dispute; (4) the US concern regarding appellate review of panel findings on the meaning of municipal law by stating that the meaning of municipal law is to be treated as a matter of fact and, therefore, pursuant to Article 17.6 of the DSU, not subject to appellate review; (5) the US concern regarding the 90-day time frame for appellate review by stating that, pursuant to Article 17.5 of the DSU, the AB is obligated to issue its report within ninety days of the notice of appeal and that this time frame can only be extended with the agreement of the parties; and (6) the US concern regarding Rule 15 of the Working Procedures by providing that only the DSB can authorise outgoing AB Members to complete the disposition of an appeal after the expiry of their term in office, provided that the hearing in the appeal took place prior to the expiry of the term.[24]

The draft Decision was a carefully constructed compromise, which preserved the core features of the WTO appellate review while addressing US concerns. It was a good-faith effort of the WTO membership (minus one) to avert the crisis. However, any hope that it would be successful in doing so was short-lived. At the General Council meeting of 15 October 2019, the US rejected offhand the draft Decision as insufficient in addressing its concerns. According to the US, WTO Members failed to discuss what it considered to be the most important question, namely, why did the AB come to feel it could operate outside of its mandate?[25]

At the General Council meeting of 9 December 2019, two days before the AB became paralysed, the EU ambassador to the WTO, Amb. João Aguiar Machado, stated that:

23 Ibid., Agenda Item 4, para. 1.9.

24 Van den Bossche and Zdouc (n 11), 428.

25 See Statement by Ambassador Dennis Shea (US) at the WTO General Council meeting of 15 October 2019, Item 4, https://geneva.usmission.gov/2019/10/15/statements-by-the-united-states-at-the-wto-general-council-meeting/.

> [T]he European Union wishes to emphasise that [the Appellate Body] has served well all Members in an independent, highly professional and, given the circumstances, very efficient manner. The European Union, therefore, would like to commend all the present and past members of the Appellate Body on their work, as well as the staff working on the Appellate Body's secretariat.[26]

The US position on the functioning of the Appellate Body arguably reflects: (1) its strong disagreement with especially those parts of the AB case law which, in its view, restricts its ability to protect the domestic industry from import competition by using trade remedy measures; and (2) its desire to return to a pre-WTO kind of dispute settlement that would not restrain the use economic power to 'resolve' disputes with other countries, and especially China.

With the rejection of the draft General Council Decision, the impasse was complete and the paralysis of the AB on 11 December 2019, unavoidable. From 2020 to 2022, WTO Members made no new concerted efforts to reform WTO appellate review.[27] Many Members, including the European Union, China, and India, disagree with the US that the AB systematically engaged in judicial activism or demonstrated consistent and malicious disregard for procedural and institutional rules.[28] Almost all WTO Members were, and still are, of the view

26 See Statement by Ambassador João Aguiar Machado (EU) at the WTO General Council meeting on 9 December 2019, Item 5, WT/GC/W/791, dated 9 December 2019.

27 Note, however, that on 27 March 2020, 16 WTO Members, including Australia Brazil, Canada, China, the European Union and Mexico announced that they had reached an agreement on the *Multi-Party Interim Appeal Arbitration Arrangement under Article 25 of the DSU*, commonly referred to as the 'MPIA', which became effective on 30 April 2020, when it was notified to the DSB. See Statement on a Mechanism for Developing, Documenting and Sharing Practices and Procedures in the Conduct of WTO Disputes, Addendum, JOB/DSB/1/Add. 12, dated 30 April 2020, at https://trade.ec.europa.eu/doclib/docs/2020/april/tradoc_158731.pdf. At the DSB meeting of 28 June 2020, the European Union delivered a statement explaining that the MPIA is an interim arrangement intended: 'to preserve, in disputes among Members participating in the MPIA, a functioning and two-step dispute settlement process, as envisaged by the DSU'. According to the United States, the MPIA 'incorporates and exacerbates some of the worst aspects of the Appellate Body's practices'. The MPIA has currently has 25 parties, representing WTO Members, but to date no appeal of a panel report has been heard and decided under the MPIA.

28 See e.g. Amb. Joao Aguiar Machado (European Union), 'Statement at the WTO General Council meeting on 15 and 16 October 2019 on Informal Process on Matters Related to the Functioning of the Appellate Body – Report by the Facilitator'(Permanent Mission of the European Union to the World Trade Organization, 16 October 2019) <https://eeas.europa.eu/delegations/world-trade-organization-wto/68955/eu-statement-ambassador-joão-aguiar-machado-general-council-meeting-15-and-16-october-2019_en>

that whatever legitimate concerns the US might have regarding the functioning of the AB, these concerns did not justify the obstruction of the appointment process, which resulted in the paralysis of the AB and plunged the entire WTO dispute settlement system into crisis. This is clearly demonstrated by the fact that WTO Members, at every regular DSB meeting of the past years, have requested the DSB to launch the appointment process of AB members without delay. At the DSB meeting of 19 September 2023, 130 WTO Members supported such a request.[29] In response to this request, the US stated, as it had done in response to all similar requests in the past, that its longstanding concerns with WTO dispute settlement 'remain unaddressed' and that it therefore does not support the proposed decision.[30] However, it should be noted that the Biden administration, unlike the Trump administration, has shown readiness to discuss the reform of the WTO dispute settlement. At the DSB meeting of 27 April 2022, the US ambassador to the WTO, Amb. Maria Pagán stated:

> The United States supports WTO dispute settlement reform. ... I can appreciate the benefits of a system that effectively meets the needs of Members. WTO dispute settlement currently fails in this regard ... My delegation has been, and will continue to be, hard at work, meeting with Members to better understand the interests of all Members.[31]

In the months that followed this statement, the United States did indeed engage in multiple bilateral meetings with other WTO Members to ensure, as

accessed 20 September 2023; Amb. ZHANG Xiangchen (China), 'Statement at the WTO General Council meeting on 15 & 16 October 2019 on Informal Process on Matters Related to the Functioning of the Appellate Body – Report by the Facilitator' <http://wto.mofcom.gov.cn/article/meetingsandstatements/201807/20180702770676.shtml.> accessed 20 September 2023.

29 See DSB Meeting of 19 September 2023, at <https://www.wto.org/english/news_e/news23_e/dsb_19sep23_e.htm> accessed 24 September 2023. This was the 68th time that such request was tabled.

30 See U.S. Statements at the July 28, 2023, DSB Meeting, at US Mission Geneva, 'Statements by the United States at the Meeting of the WTO Dispute Settlement Body' (US Mission to International Organizations in Geneva, 28 July 2023) <https://uploads.mwp.mprod.getusinfo.com/uploads/sites/25/2023/07/Jul28.DSB_.Stmt_.as_.deliv_.fin_-1.pdf> accessed 20 September 2023.

31 See US Mission Geneva, 'U.S. Statement by Ambassador Maria Pagán at the WTO Dispute Settlement Body Meeting, Geneva' (US Mission to International Organizations in Geneva, 27 April 2022) <https://geneva.usmission.gov/2022/04/27/us-statement-by-ambassador-maria-pagan-at-the-wto-dsb-meeting/> accessed 20 September 2023.

Amb. Pagán explained, 'a true reform discussion' on WTO dispute settlement that 'reflects the real interests of Members'.[32]

4 The Establishment and Operation of an Alternative System for Appellate Review

4.1 *The Multi-party Interim Appeal Arbitration Arrangement*

While committed to finding a solution to the AB crisis, but, having abandoned any hope of doing so any time soon, a group of Members, at the initiative of the European Union, reached in March 2020, an agreement on the Multi-Party Interim Appeal Arbitration Arrangement, commonly referred to as the 'MPIA'.[33] The MPIA, which came into effect on 30 April 2020 among 19 Members, provides for a temporary alternative procedure for appellate review under Article 25 of the DSU and is intended 'to preserve, in disputes among Members participating in the MPIA, a functioning and two-step dispute settlement process, as envisaged by the DSU'.[34] On 1 September 2023, twenty-six WTO Members were a party to the MPIA, including Brazil, Canada, China, the EU, Japan and Mexico, i.e. six of the ten most frequent users of the WTO dispute settlement system.[35]

Under the MPIA, which is a political rather than a legally binding arrangement, Members commit not to appeal panel reports to the paralysed AB (i.e., agree not to appeal panel reports into the void), but instead to resort to appellate arbitration under Article 25 of the DSU.[36] As stated in the MPIA, appeal

32 Ibid.

33 See Statement on a Mechanism for Developing, Documenting and Sharing Practices and Procedures in the Conduct of WTO Disputes, Addendum, JOB/DSB/1/Add.12, dated 30 April 2020.

34 See European Union, 'Statement at the Regular DSB meeting' (Permanent Mission of the European Union to the World Trade Organization, Agenda point 13, 29 June 2020) <https://www.eeas.europa.eu/delegations/world-trade-organization-wto/eu-statement-regular-dispute-settlement-body-meeting-29_en> accessed 20 September 2023.

35 When comparing the number of MPIA parties (26) with the number of WTO Members (164), one should consider that also the 27 Member States of the European Union are WTO Members, and that it could therefore be argued that 53 Members, or almost 1/3 of WTO Members, are a 'party' to the MPIA.

36 See Statement on a Mechanism for Developing, Documenting and Sharing Practices and Procedures in the Conduct of WTO Disputes, Addendum, Multiparty Appeal Interim Arbitration Arrangement Pursuant to Article 25 of the DSU, paras. 1–2 and Annex 1, para. 15, JOB/DSB/1/Add.12, dated 30 April 2020. Since the MPIA is a political, rather than legally binding, arrangement, MPIA parties will adopt in every single dispute between them a legally binding appeal arbitration agreement, referred to as 'Agreed Procedures for

arbitrations under the MPIA are to a large extent governed, with any necessary adjustments, by the provisions of the DSU and other rules and procedures applicable to appellate review under the DSU, such as the Working Procedures for Appellate Review.[37] At the same time, the MPIA contains some procedural innovations to enhance procedural efficiency and streamline the proceedings, such as page limits, time limits, deadlines and the length and number of hearings as well as regarding claims under Article 11 of the DSU (i.e., claims regarding a panel's failure to make an objective assessment of the facts).[38]

Under the MPIA, appeals are dealt with by three arbitrators selected randomly from a pool of ten. This pool of ten arbitrators is made up of persons of recognised authority and demonstrated expertise.[39] The appeal arbitrators are to review only issues of law, may only address the issues necessary to resolve the dispute, and cannot add to or diminish the rights and obligations provided in the covered agreements.[40] Pursuant to Article 25.3, second sentence, of the DSU, the appeal arbitration awards are final and binding on the parties.[41] Article 21 of the DSU, regarding the surveillance of implementation, including compliance proceedings, as well as Article 22 thereof, regarding compensation and arbitration on the suspension of concessions, apply to arbitration awards emanating from Article 25 procedures, and therefore also to MPIA procedures.

In its statement on the MPIA at the DSB meeting of 29 June 2020, the US objected to any arrangement that would 'perpetuate the failings' of the AB.[42] According to the US, the MPIA 'incorporates and exacerbates some of the worst aspects of the Appellate Body's practices', and it does so by:

Arbitration under Article 25 of the DSU', and they will do so within 60 days of the establishment of the panel. See, e.g., Agreed Procedures for Arbitration under Article 25 of the DSU, *Colombia – Frozen Fries*, WT/DS591/3, dated 15 July 2020.

37 See Statement on a Mechanism for Developing, Documenting and Sharing Practices and Procedures in the Conduct of WTO Disputes, Addendum, Multiparty Appeal Interim Arbitration Arrangement Pursuant to Article 25 of the DSU, Annex 1, para.11, JOB/DSB/1/Add.12, dated 30 April 2020.

38 See ibid., para. 12.

39 See ibid., para. 7, and Annex 2. The list of MPIA arbitrators was communicated to WTO Members in JOB/DSB/1/Add.12/Suppl.5, dated 3 August 2020. See also Geneva Trade Platform, 'Multi-Party Interim Appeal Arbitration Arrangement (MPIA)' <https://wtoplurilaterals.info/plural_initiative/the-mpia/> accessed 20 September 2023.

40 See ibid., Preamble and Annex 1, paras. 8–10.

41 Note that the panel report appealed will be attached to the appeal arbitration award and that the non-appealed findings of the panel report will, as a result, also become binding.

42 See US Mission Geneva, 'Statements by the United States at the Meeting of the WTO Dispute Settlement Body' (US Mission to International Organizations in Geneva, Agenda item 13, 29 June 2020) <https://geneva.usmission.gov/2020/06/29/statements-by-the-united-states-at-the-june-29-2020-dsb-meeting/> accessed 20 September 2023.

(1) weakening the mandatory deadline for completing AB reports;
(2) contemplating appellate review of panel findings of fact;
(3) failing to reflect the limitation on appellate review to those findings necessary to resolve the dispute;
(4) promoting the use of precedent by identifying 'consistency' (regardless of correctness) as a guiding principle for decisions; and
(5) encouraging arbitrators to create a body of law through litigation.[43]

The US considered that 'the numerous departures from the DSU highlight that at least some Members prefer an appellate 'court' with expansive powers, instead of the more narrow appellate review envisioned by Members in the DSU'.[44]

4.2 *Appeal Arbitration under the MPIA and Otherwise to Date*

The MPIA entered into force in May 2020. The first recourse to appeal arbitration under the MPIA was, however, only in October 2022, when Colombia appealed the panel report in *Colombia – Frozen Fries* (DS591) (complaint by the EU).[45] In earlier disputes between MPIA parties, such as *Canada – Wine* (DS537) (complaint by Australia) or *Costa Rica – Avocados* (DS524), the parties either reached a mutually agreed solution or the panel report was not appealed. The appeal arbitrators in *Colombia – Frozen Fries* circulated their award on 21 December 2022.[46]

As noted above, appeal arbitration under the MPIA 'will be based on the substantive and procedural aspects of Appellate Review pursuant to Article 17 of the DSU', but also provides for some novelties to enhance the procedural efficiency of appeal proceedings. The question thus arises of how much of the appeal arbitration procedure, as it was applied in *Colombia – Frozen Fries*, differed from the appellate review procedure under Article 17 of the DSU.[47] One must note that the appeal arbitrators issued their award within 74 days of the filing of the notice of appeal, i.e., well within the mandatory 90-day timeframe, and that the report was only 39 pages long. During the last ten years of

43 See ibid.

44 See ibid.

45 Notification of an Appeal by Colombia under Article 25 DSU, *Colombia –Frozen Fries*, WT/DS591/7, dated 10 October 2022.

46 Award of the Arbitrators, Arbitration under Article 25 of the DSU, *Colombia – Frozen Fries*, WT/DS591/ARB25, dated 21 December 2022.

47 See on this, the reflections of Joost Pauwelyn, one of the appeal arbitrators in *Colombia – Frozen Fries*, at Joost Pauwelyn, 'The MPIA: What's New (Part III)' (International Economic Law and Policy, 21 February 2023)<https://ielp.worldtradelaw.net/2023/03/the-mpia-whats-new-part-iii.html> accessed 20 September 2023.

its operation, the AB seldom managed to respect the 90-day timeframe and its reports were always much longer. Pursuant to paragraph 12 of the Agreed Procedures in *Colombia – Frozen Fries*, the arbitrators set a word limit on the appellant and appellee submissions of 27,000 words or 40 per cent of the word count of the appealed panel report, and on third participant submissions of 9000 words.[48] Such word limit on submissions may be helpful as it obliges parties to focus on the essence of their arguments on appeal. However, it may also necessitate the later filing of additional memoranda to clarify and elaborate arguments which were underdeveloped in the submissions.[49] The arbitrators in *Colombia – Frozen Fries* also set time limits of 30 to 35 minutes and 7 minutes on oral statements of the participants and third participants respectively.[50] This is, however, merely the continuation of a long-established AB practice.

Pursuant to paragraph 13 of the Agreed Procedures in *Colombia – Frozen Fries*, the appeal arbitrators also invited Colombia and the EU 'to consider refraining from making [Article 11] claims'.[51] The consideration of such claims that the panel failed to make an objective assessment of the facts, was notoriously time-consuming for the AB. In the event that a party would nevertheless decide to bring Article 11 claims, that party was requested to 'set forth succinctly' in its appeal: (1) whether and how the alleged panel error was raised before the Panel, in particular during the interim review stage; (2) in what way the Article 11 claim is an issue necessary for the resolution of the dispute; and (3) in what way the alleged panel error is not simply an appreciation of a

48 See Agreed Procedures for Arbitration under Article 25 of the DSU, Revision, *Colombia – Frozen Fries* (DS591), WT/DS591/3/Rev.1, dated 22 April 2022; and Pre-Arbitration Letter, dated 19 September 2022, Section 1, attached as Annex 2 to the Additional Procedures for Arbitration under Article 25 of the DSU, Adopted by the Arbitrators on 19 October 2022, which itself is Annex A-2 to the Award of the Arbitrators, Arbitration under Article 25 of the DSU, *Colombia – Frozen Fries*, WT/DS591/ARB25/Add.1, dated 21 December 2022.

49 In 2015, the Chair of the AB had discussed with WTO Members the possibility of introducing limits on the length of submissions, but at that time this idea was, after initial support, eventually not favourably received by Members and subsequently dropped.

50 Additional Procedures for Arbitration under Article 25 of the DSU, Adopted by the Arbitrators on 19 October 2022, para. 23, which is attached as Annex A-2 to the Award of the Arbitrators, Arbitration under Article 25 of the DSU, *Colombia – Frozen Fries*, Annex A-2, WT/DS591/ARB25/Add.1, dated 21 December 2022.

51 See Agreed Procedures for Arbitration under Article 25 of the DSU, Revision, *Colombia – Frozen Fries* (DS591), WT/DS591/3/Rev.1, dated 22 April 2022, para. 13; and Pre-Arbitration Letter, dated 19 September 2022, Section 3, attached as Annex 2 to the Additional Procedures for Arbitration under Article 25 of the DSU, Adopted by the Arbitrators on 19 October 2022, which itself is Annex A-2 to the Award of the Arbitrators, Arbitration under Article 25 of the DSU, *Colombia – Frozen Fries*, WT/DS591/ARB25/Add.1, dated 21 December 2022.

factual issue (within the exclusive domain of panels).[52] Colombia refrained in its appeal from making any Article 11 claims of error. However, whether this is because it was discouraged to do so by the arbitrators is an open question. Under paragraph 13, appeal arbitrators cannot prevent or prohibit parties from making Article 11 claims, but paragraph 13 may nevertheless be useful in limiting such claims by rendering it more onerous to make them.

Another noteworthy procedural novelty in the appeal arbitration procedure in *Colombia – Frozen Fries* is the pre-hearing conference. This pre-hearing conference was convened by the arbitrators six days before the actual hearing. The purpose of this pre-hearing conference was to assist the arbitrators in identifying the issues to be addressed at the hearing, and to avoid issues that are not within their mandate, were not necessary for the resolution of this dispute, or where not contested between the parties.[53] Also, the pre-hearing conference gave the arbitrators an opportunity to signal to the parties what they would like the parties to focus on at the hearing. Time will tell how useful such pre-hearing conferences are in narrowing down the issues that need to be discussed at the hearing.

The word limits on submissions, discouraging of Article 11 claims and the pre-hearing conference may all have contributed to the fact that the appeal arbitrators in *Colombia – Frozen Fries* were able to issue a short award in record time.[54] However, it should be noted that the appeal in *Colombia – Frozen Fries* was a small appeal in a dispute on one single measure raising only a few issues of limited complexity. It remains to be seen whether these procedural innovations will work as well in much larger appeals raising more complex and politically more sensitive issues. Also, small is not always beautiful and fast is often dangerous, certainly in the convoluted world of international trade disputes.

52 Ibid. The arbitrators noted that these requirements are "without prejudice to the question of whether (and, if so, under what conditions) such claims fall within the appeal mandate set out in Article 17.6 of the DSU and/or paragraph 9 of the Agreed Procedures".

53 Award of the Arbitrators, Arbitration under Article 25 of the DSU, *Colombia – Frozen Fries*, WT/DS591/ARB25/Add.1, dated 21 December 2022, [1.11 – 1.12].

54 A procedural innovation on *Colombia – Frozen Fries*, which will not have contributed to the shortness of the report or the appellate process, but is a welcome, albeit modest, step in ensuring more transparency in appellate proceedings, is the online recording of the opening statements at the oral hearing of the parties and some of the third parties. See Additional Procedures for BCI Protection and Partial Public Viewing of the Hearing, Adopted by the Arbitrators on 1 November 2022, Annex A-3 to the Award, para. 2. For the recording, see https://www.wto.org/english/tratop_e/dispu_e/material_e/ds591_arb25.mp4.

At present, there are eight disputes between MPIA parties in which Agreed Procedures for Arbitration under Article 25 of the DSU have been adopted, and in which, if the panel report is appealed, appeal arbitration under the MPIA will allow a dispute to be brought to a legally binding conclusion.[55] Whether the procedural innovations in the *Colombia – Frozen Fries* will also lead to shorter and faster reports in these cases, some of which are much more complex and politically sensitive, remains to be seen, but it is certainly worthwhile to try it out and, where necessary, further develop these and other procedural innovations.

Finally, it should be noted that apart from appeal arbitration under the MPIA, appeal arbitration can also be made available on an *ad hoc* basis under Article 25 of the DSU in disputes involving one or more WTO Members, which are not MPIA parties. In *EU – Steel Safeguard Measures* (*Turkey*) (DS595) and *Turkey – Pharmaceutical Products* (*EU*) (DS583), the EU and Turkey (which is not an MPIA party) agreed, in the course of the panel proceedings, that they would not appeal the panel reports to the paralyzed AB, but would instead, in case of an appeal, have recourse to *ad hoc* appeal arbitration under Article 25 of the DSU. The procedural rules for *ad hoc* appeal arbitration agreed to by the EU and Turkey in these disputes were almost identical to the rules under the MPIA. However, there was one exception which related to the appeal arbitrators. In *EU – Steel Safeguard Measures* (*Turkey*) the arbitrators would be two former AB members and in *Turkey – Pharmaceutical Products* (*EU*) the reverse. Only the panel report in the latter case was appealed. The arbitrators in this appeal circulated their Award on 25 July 2022.[56] At the DSB meeting of 29 August 2022, the US, while observing that the Agreed Procedures for Appeal Arbitration between the EU and Turkey 'provided for an arbitration that incorporated many of the most troubling practices of appellate review under the Appellate Body', it nevertheless welcomed 'the agreement of the parties on a way forward in this dispute'.[57]

---

55 See Geneva Trade Platform, 'Multi-Party Interim Appeal Arbitration Arrangement (MPIA)' <https://wtoplurilaterals.info/plural_initiative/the-mpia/> accessed 20 September 2023.

56 Award of the Arbitrators, Arbitration under Article 25 of the DSU, *Turkey – Pharmaceutical Products* (*EU*), WT/DS583/ARB25, dated 25 July 2022.

57 US Mission Geneva, 'Statements by the United States at the August 29, 2022, DSB Meeting' (US Mission to International Organizations in Geneva, 30 August 2023) <https://geneva.usmission.gov/2022/08/30/statements-by-the-united-states-at-the-august-29-2022-dsb-meeting/> accessed 20 September 2023.

5 Ongoing Efforts to Restore the Dispute Settlement System (the Molina Process)

5.1 *Main Features of the Molina Process*

As mentioned above, the WTO Members committed themselves, at the Twelfth Ministerial Conference in Geneva in June 2022, to conduct discussions 'with the view to having a fully and well-functioning dispute settlement system accessible to all Members by 2024'.[58] While not much happened during the first six months after the Ministerial Conference, since February 2023, there have been frequent small-group and larger-group meetings of Members to discuss how to revive the WTO dispute settlement system, and thus fulfil the June 2022 ministerial mandate. These informal meetings have been convened – at the request of a group of WTO Members – by Marco Tulio Molina, the Deputy Permanent Representative of Guatemala to the WTO, and are therefore commonly referred to as the 'Molina Process'. As an indication of the intensity of this Process, in April and May 2023, Molina held no less that 57 meetings.[59] The ambition of Molina is to find 'practical solutions' to the WTO dispute settlement crisis by the Ministerial Conference to be held in Abu Dabi in February 2024.[60]

The Molina Process is different in several respects from the Walker Process, the informal negotiations conducted in 2019 to avert the paralysis of the AB. First, the Molina Process addresses the functioning of the entire WTO dispute settlement system, and not only the functioning of the AB, as was the case for the Walker Process. This is a positive development, as many of the (real or perceived) problems with appellate review have their origin in, or are related to, problems with other elements of the WTO dispute settlement. Second, unlike the Walker Process, the US is an active participant in the Molina Process. It is obviously only with the active participation of the US, that there can be any hope to overcome a crisis triggered by the US. Third, while in the context of the Walker Process, many Members, either individually or collectively, tabled position papers, which were publicly available, the 70-plus proposals made by Members in the context of the Molina Process are kept confidential. At the DSB meetings in March, May, and July 2023, Molina briefed, in general terms, WTO

58 WTO Ministerial Conference, MC12 Outcome Document, adopted on 17 June 2022, WT/MIN(22)/24, dated 22 June 2022, para. 4.

59 See DSB Meeting of 30 May 2023, at <https://www.wto.org/english/news_e/news23_e/dsb_30may23_e.htm> accessed 24 September 2023.

60 Ibid.

Members on the informal meetings convened by him, but did not give any specific information on the reform proposals tabled by the Members.[61]

At the DSB meeting of 28 July 2023, Molina reported that Members had continued to 'actively participate in the intense programme of meetings' on dispute settlement reform, and had reached 'an understanding on 80% of the issues under consideration'.[62] According to Molina, these issues were ripe to move to the drafting process, which was to start over the summer break.[63] Another 10% of the issues under consideration were 'close to reaching the level of maturity needed for the drafting process'.[64] However, on the remaining 10%, Molina reported that Members 'still hold different conceptual views about how to tackle them'. He did not indicate which these highly controversial issues were but announced that he would continue his consultation efforts after the summer break with the aim of reaching a common understanding on these issues.[65] Molina reported to the WTO Members that he was 'convinced that despite the conceptual differences, members can find a solution at the technical level that can reconcile their interests and concerns'.[66] One would, of course, expect Molina to strike an optimistic tone, but wonders whether his optimism is justified.

5.2 *Will the Molina Process Be Successful?*

On a number of issues on the reform agenda, such as the use of alternative dispute resolution (ADR) methods and the streamlining of the panel process, there may indeed be a growing consensus.[67] However, if the reporting from

---

61 See for the DSB meeting of 31 March 2023, at <https://www.wto.org/english/news_e/news23_e/dsb_31mar23_e.htm> accessed on 24 September 2023; the DSB meeting of 30 May 2023, at <https://www.wto.org/english/news_e/news23_e/dsb_30may23_e.htm> accessed on 24 September 2023; the DSB meeting of 28 July 2023, at <https://www.wto.org/english/news_e/news23_e/dsb_28jul23_e.htm.> accessed on 24 September 2023. Note that at the DSB meeting of 19 September 2023, the Molina Process was not on the agenda. See <https://www.wto.org/english/news_e/news23_e/dsb_19sep23_e.htm.> accessed on 24 September 2023.

62 See DSB Meeting of 28 July 2023, at <https://www.wto.org/english/news_e/news23_e/dsb_28jul23_e.htm.> accessed on 24 September 2023.

63 Ibid.

64 Ibid.

65 Ibid.

66 Ibid.

67 Regarding the streamlining of the panel process, it may well possible to reach agreement on: (1) panel establishment at the first DSB meeting; (2) one rather than two meetings of the parties with the panel; (2) word limits for written submissions and time limits for meeting of the parties with the panel; (4) sharing with the parties the questions of the panel in advance of the meeting of the parties with the panel; (5) adherence to

Ravi Kanth of The Third World Network, in April and June 2023,[68] on some of the core reform proposals of the US and the reactions of other Members to these proposals is accurate, the resolution of the WTO dispute settlement crisis is still a long way off. Not surprisingly, the most controversial US proposal relates to the appellate review in WTO dispute settlement.

First, the US would want to make appellate review optional. While it reportedly does not provide any details on how exactly this would be achieved, the general idea would be that a panel report could only be appealed when both parties would agree on this. Also, appellate review would no longer be done by a standing body, as the AB, but by an *ad hoc* review adjudicator or adjudicators selected via a mechanism agreed by the parties. It is unlikely that there will be many cases in which both parties will agree to allow for appellate review. In all but a few cases, one of the parties considers itself to be the 'winner' at the panel stage and will not initiate appeal proceedings which may endanger this 'win'. It is a fact that in many AB proceedings, the 'winning' party cross-appealed some panel findings it did not agree with, but this party would not have cross-appealed in the absence of an appeal initiated by the 'losing' party. Moreover, in the (very) few disputes in which both parties would agree on appellate review, the parties would subsequently have to agree on whom to appoint as review adjudicator(s). It is unclear whether in case of disagreement between parties on the review adjudicator(s), it would be for the WTO Director General to appoint her/him(them). More importantly, appellate review by an *ad hoc* adjudicator or adjudicators would not ensure the consistency of the case law, which is one of the main functions of appellate review. The EU and other major players in the WTO, including China, Brazil, and India, have stressed that the WTO dispute settlement system must be a system providing for effective appellate review of panel reports. A WTO dispute settlement system providing for voluntary appeal review by an *ad hoc* adjudicator or adjudicators is therefore unlikely to be acceptable to them.

---

timeframes; and (6) allowing the panel to invite parties to focus on certain claims or exclude certain claims.

68 See Ravi Kanth, 'WTO: In a radical overhaul, US proposes single-tier dispute settlement system' (Third World Network (TWN) Info Service on WTO and Trade Issues, 26 April 2023)<https://twn.my/title2/wto.info/2023/ti230414.htm> accessed on 24 September 2023; Ravi Kanth, 'WTO: US proposals on dispute settlement reform could hurt smaller countries' (Third World Network (TWN) Info Service on WTO and Trade Issues, 27 April 2023) <https://twn.my/title2/wto.info/2023/ti230415.htm> accessed on 24 September 2023; and Ravi Kanth, 'WTO: UK, US raise controversial proposals on DS reform' (Third World Network (TWN) Info Service on WTO and Trade Issues, 2 June 2023) <https://twn.my/title2/wto.info/2023/ti230602.htm.> accessed on 24 September 2023.

Second, adding insult to injury, the US reportedly proposes to reduce drastically the scope of appellate review. Pursuant to Article 17.6 of the DSU, the scope of appellate review by the AB comprises all 'issues of law covered in the panel report and legal interpretations developed by the panel.' The US proposes to limit appellate review to instances in which the appellant contends that the panel: (a) was guilty of gross misconduct, bias, or serious conflict of interest, or otherwise materially violated the rules of conduct; (b) seriously departed from a fundamental rule of procedure; or (c) manifestly exceeded its powers, authority or jurisdiction, and any of these acts by the panel materially affected the decision and threatens the integrity of the process. This is not truly an appellate review as it will not allow parties to challenge a panel's interpretation and application of WTO law but is much more in the nature of an annulment procedure, as it exists in ICSID arbitration. Note, however, that under ICSID rules, there are more and broader grounds for annulment than the US proposes. As this would only be an appellate review in name, this proposal on the scope of appellate review is, as the proposal on voluntary appellate review, unacceptable for the EU and many other WTO Members.

Among the other reported proposals of the US, there are some that may receive a more positive reception from other Members. This is the case, for example, for the proposal to improve, and give more importance to, the interim review of panel reports, in the hope that this would allow for, and encourage, parties to settle disputes before a panel adopts and makes its final report public. Such an improved interim review would also empower panels to make better decisions as parties would point out mistakes and shortcomings in the interim report, which the panel could then subsequently address. While giving more importance to interim review would be useful, many Members may mistrust the US' undeclared goal when making this proposal. Is it the US' aim to reduce the instances in which panels clearly and publicly pronounce on what is and what is not WTO-consistent, and increase the instances in which disputes do not get resolved on the basis of the law but through negotiations in which the US can fully exploit its economic and other powers?

Truly puzzling is the US proposal to give Members more power to correct what it considers erroneous interpretations of WTO law, i.e., interpretations that add to or diminish the rights and obligations of Members. Already now, Members have the authority, pursuant to Article IX:2 of the WTO Agreement, to adopt 'authoritative interpretations'; pursuant to Article XII to amend existing provisions; or, finally, pursuant to Article IX:1, to adopt new rules. To date, Members have made no use of this authority to correct erroneous interpretations by the dispute settlement bodies, because the consensus among Members to correct the interpretations was always lacking. While the losing party in a dispute may consider certain interpretations of WTO law to be erroneous, it is unlikely that the winning party in that dispute shares that opinion and joins the consensus to overturn an interpretation favorable to it. It is unclear how US wants to give more power to Members to correct what it considers wrong interpretations of WTO law. But it is safe to assume that it would not advocate abandoning the firmly established WTO practice of taking decisions by consensus.

The US has reportedly also advocated changes in the rules on panel composition and the Rules of Conduct so that only panelists with the appropriate level of expertise and integrity would serve on panels. No Member would disagree that panelists must have these qualifications, but many would argue that the integrity of panelists has certainly not been a problem in the past and that there is, therefore, no need for any rule change. With regard to the role of the WTO Secretariat in supporting WTO adjudicators, it has been reported that US wishes to limit that role to the administration of the proceedings and legal support that is responsive to the submissions of the parties (i.e., no 'creative' thinking on what the correct interpretation of the legal provision at issue is). Most surprisingly here is, however, that US calls for more legal expertise at the Secretariat. The WTO Secretariat lawyers arguably constitute the most experienced group of international trade lawyers anywhere. Many WTO Members are likely to consider this US proposal as a call for more lawyers who share the US government's position on the interpretation and application of WTO law.

Finally, the US has reportedly proposed to exclude, from the jurisdiction of the WTO dispute settlement system, disputes relating to measures adopted for the protection of national security. The mere invocation of the national security exception would then place a challenged measure outside the reach of rules-based adjudication. While such limitation of jurisdiction may be appealing to some WTO Members, other Members may be expected to object strongly to such limitation as it would give Members a blank cheque to adopt any trade restrictive measure they wish.

6 Options Available to Overcome the WTO Dispute Settlement Crisis

In considering the future of WTO dispute settlement and, more generally, the future of international trade dispute resolution, several options are, at least in theory, available to WTO Members. One option is to abandon WTO dispute settlement in favor of dispute resolution under bilateral or regional trade agreements. Many of these agreements provide for a dispute resolution procedure.

With some exceptions,[69] there has, however, been very limited use made of the dispute resolution mechanisms under bilateral and regional trade agreements. This is arguably because these mechanisms are untested, usually less elaborate, and lack the institutional support that the WTO provides for dispute resolution. Also, there is, unlike in the context of the WTO, only limited, if any, peer pressure to comply with adverse rulings. If disputes arise between parties of bilateral or regional trade agreements, these parties usually prefer to resolve them through diplomatic means, or, where possible, to bring these disputes to the WTO for resolution.[70]

Faced with the crisis of the WTO dispute settlement system, countries may reconsider their position on the use of dispute resolution mechanisms under bilateral and regional trade agreements, and have more frequent recourse to it. However, to date, there has been no notable increase in the number of disputes brought to bilateral or regional dispute resolution mechanisms.[71] Also, some trade relations that give rise to frequent disputes, such as, for example, the trade relations between the US and the EU on the one hand and China on the other hand, are not subject to any bilateral or regional trade agreement, and dispute resolution under such agreement is therefore not an option.

Another option available to WTO Members for resolving trade disputes is to employ diplomatic methods of dispute resolution, such as mediation and conciliation, rather than legal methods, i.e., judicial settlement and arbitration. As mentioned above, such alternative dispute resolution ('ADR') is currently being discussed in the context of the Molina Process. While there are, undoubtedly, disputes in which ADR is appropriate, many WTO Members, and, in particular, the economically or otherwise less powerful Members, would not consider such voluntary, non-binding, and ultimately power-based (rather than rules-based) methods of dispute resolution, as a desirable alternative to WTO

69 A notable exception is dispute resolution in the context of the United States-Mexico-Canada Agreement (USMCA) (formerly NAFTA). See 'CUSMA Dispute' (The Secretatiat Canada-Mexico-United States, 22 September 2023) <https://can-mex-usa-sec.org/secretariat/disputes-litges-controversias.aspx?lang=eng.> accessed on 24 September 2023.

70 E.g., *Thailand – Customs and Fiscal Measures on Cigarettes from the Philippines* (DS371). This dispute could have been dealt with under the ASEAN Enhanced Dispute Resolution Mechanism, but instead was brought to the WTO.

71 For an overview of complaints under bilateral and regional trade agreements, see https://www.worldtradelaw.net/databases/ftacomplaints.php. Note that in September 2023, a dispute between New Zealand and Canada was, for the first time, resolved under the dispute resolution mechanism of the Comprehensive and Progressive Agreement for Trans-Pacific Partnership (CPTPP), See CPTPP Panel Report, *Canada – Dairy Tariff Rate Quota Allocation Measures*, 5 September 2023, https://www.worldtradelaw.net/document.php?id=dsc/fta/canada-dairytrq(dsc)(cptpp)(panel).pdf.

adjudication. It should be noted that Article 5 of the DSU already provides, since 1995, for the possibility of Members to have recourse to mediation and conciliation, and that very little use has been made of this possibility.[72] Against the background of the current crisis of WTO dispute settlement, recourse to mediation or conciliation may, however, be more appealing in some disputes between some Members.

An oft-discussed option for overcoming the current WTO dispute settlement crisis is to abandon appellate review under Article 17 of the DSU and limit WTO dispute settlement to a single-stage adjudication by panels. This option was most prominently advocated by Bernard Hoekman and Petros Mavroidis, who propose a single-stage dispute settlement by a standing panel body of 15 members, which decides specific cases in panels of three, randomly selected panel body members.[73] The idea of having a standing panel body, rather than *ad hoc* panels, to adjudicate WTO disputes was already advanced by the EU as early as 1998.[74] The establishment of a standing panel body would be a very welcome improvement to the WTO dispute settlement system, as it will make the system more judicial in nature. It would, however, not make appellate review redundant. Even with a standing panel body, appellate review would still be needed. WTO dispute settlement concerns State-to-State disputes, often on matters of high political sensitivity and/or great legal complexity. In such disputes, a second bite of the apple, i.e., appellate review, is very useful in ensuring that a well-considered decision is made and that the losing party is (more) willing to accept this decision. Also, there is no reason to assume that an adverse panel finding would be more 'acceptable' to Members, and especially the US, than an adverse AB finding. Moreover, as mentioned above, for many WTO Members, and in particular the EU, appellate review is an essential, indispensable feature of WTO dispute settlement, and any proposal to dispose of appellate review is therefore unlikely to be accepted.

The obvious option for overcoming the current crisis of WTO dispute settlement is to reform the AB and WTO appellate review with the aim of addressing the concerns of US, which triggered the crisis. As mentioned above, this is what WTO Members attempted to do in 2019 in the context of the Walker Process, which led to the draft General Council Decision on the Functioning

72 Van den Bossche and Zdouc (n 11), 436.

73 Bernard M. Hoekman and Petros C. Mavroidis, 'To AB or not the AB? Dispute Settlement in WTO Reform' [2020] 23 JIEL 1, 12.

74 See, e.g., *Contribution of the European Communities and its Member States to the Improvement of the WTO Dispute Settlement Understanding*, Communication of the European Communities, NT/DS/W/1, dated 13 March 2002.

of the Appellate Body. This good faith effort to address the concerns of the US was, however, summarily rejected by the latter. Nevertheless, the 2019 draft General Council Decision should be the starting point of any negotiations on the reform of the AB and WTO appellate review. A number of the changes set out in the draft Decision were subsequently taken up in the MPIA, and some of them have already been put into practice by the arbitral tribunal in *Colombia – Frozen Fries,* the first MPIA case. However, it is unlikely that those changes will suffice to address the US concerns and resolve the crisis. While the proposals that the US reportedly tabled in the context of the Molina process regarding voluntary appellate review and its very limited scope gives little hope that an agreement on reform can be reached currently. Among the changes, in addition to those already reflected in the draft General Council Decision and the MPIA, is the adoption by a resurrected AB of a more deferential standard of appellate review. In the past, the AB always conducted a full and *de novo* review of the legal issues on appeal. This is how it, correctly, understood its mandate under the DSU. Thomas Cottier, one of the current MPIA arbitrators, has proposed that the AB should rather adopt a standard of reasonableness when reviewing panel findings on legal issues.[75] This means that the AB would uphold an appealed panel finding when it considered that finding to be 'reasonable', and would, in that case, restrain from developing its own reasoning on the legal issue concerned. The AB would thus show much more deference to a panel's reasoning and findings. However, for appeals of panel findings on legal issues of a constitutional nature, such a deferential standard of appellate review would, according to Cottier, not be appropriate. For appeals of such findings, he proposes to maintain full and *de novo* review by the AB. As Cottier concedes, it may not be easy to distinguish panel findings on constitutional issues, which would be subject to full and *de novo* appellate review, from other panel findings, which would be subject to the much more deferential standard of reasonableness.

Among the other possible changes to appellate review, which are not already reflected in the Draft General Council Decision or the MPIA, are: (1) a more reasonable and flexible time frame for appellate review (because, while swift dispute resolution is important, time pressure should not prevent careful consideration of all issues on appeal); (2) an increase in the number of AB members (to allow for more appeals to be heard simultaneously and for the AB membership to be more 'representative' of membership in the WTO); (3) fixed

75 Thomas Cottier, 'Recalibrating the WTO Dispute Settlement System: Towards New Standards of Appellate Review' [2021] 24 JIEL 515, 524.

6 to 8 year non-renewable terms in office for AB members (to better ensure the independence and impartiality of AB Members); (4) 'law clerks' assigned to, and supporting, individual AB members rather than having lawyers from an AB Secretariat providing support to a division hearing an appeal (as proposed by the US to limit undue influence of the Secretariat over the decisions by the AB); (5) guidelines for the AB on treaty interpretation, for going beyond and/or deviating from the rules on treaty interpretation of the Vienna Convention of the Law of Treaties (such as, for example, giving more importance to the negotiating history of the WTO agreements and not having recourse to other international law in giving meaning to WTO provisions); and (6) providing for oversight over the AB and its decisions (either by a dispute settlement review committee composed of delegates of WTO Members or by a special a-political legal expert group). None of the above-mentioned possible changes is likely to gather enthusiastic support from all Members.

Finally, the last option to be mentioned for overcoming the current crisis of WTO dispute settlement is the option Members have now chosen, namely to reform the whole dispute settlement system. As discussed above, the ongoing Molina Process, unlike the 2019 Walker Process, deals with the reform of WTO dispute settlement as a whole, rather than focusing on appellate review only. As mentioned, this is a welcome development as many of the concerns raised regarding the AB are related to what happens (or does not happen) in the earlier and later stages of the WTO dispute settlement process. WTO Members have already been discussing how to improve the consultation stage, the panel stage, and the implementation and enforcement stages of the dispute settlement process since 1997 in the context of the DSU review negotiations and subsequently, since 2002, in the context of the Doha Development Round negotiations on DSU reform. Members can now build on these negotiations, and the progress in the ongoing discussions, which Marco Molina referred, at the DSB meeting of July 2023, is undoubtedly related – primarily, if not exclusively – to changes to the panel stage of the dispute settlement process. An agreement on useful improvements to the panel stage is certainly within reach. However, without an agreement on how to reform appellate review, the current crisis of WTO dispute settlement will not be overcome.

7 Conclusion

The WTO dispute settlement system, imperfect as it was, worked remarkedly well until it no longer did because of the refusal of the US to allow for the appointment of new AB members. This refusal led. in December 2019, to the paralysis of the Appellate Body and resulted in an existential crisis of the WTO dispute settlement system. This crisis is a major governance failure of the WTO. In these times of polycrisis (the climate crisis; the geopolitical confrontation between the US and China; the war in Ukraine; the social and economic impact of digitalization on the production of goods and services; the rise of populist anti-globalism and economic nationalism; and the weaponization of trade) a multilateral system for the rules-based resolution of trade disputes is more needed than ever.

The options available to Members to address this failure are diverse and include disposing of appellate review, reforming appellate review, and reforming the entire WTO dispute settlement system. WTO Members committed themselves at the WTO Ministerial Conference in June 2022 to conduct discussions with the view to having 'a fully and well-functioning dispute settlement system accessible to all Members by 2024'. Since February 2023, serious efforts to this end have been undertaken in the context of the Molina Process. The proposals tabled by Members in this context are confidential, but from what is known of them, there seems little hope that Members will be able to come to an agreement, in particular, on appellate review. The AB of yesteryear is unlikely to make a comeback, but for many WTO Members, a reformed WTO dispute settlement system must provide for genuine and effective appellate review. From what it is known of the proposals it tabled, this is not something the US is ready to agree to. Also, it is unlikely that the US will allow the dispute settlement crisis to be resolved without a 'correction' of the alleged errors of interpretation by the AB of provisions of, in particular, the Anti-Dumping Agreement, the SCM Agreement, and the Agreement on Safeguards. Such correction requires, however, consensus among WTO Members, which is unlike to be attained. At the core of the problem of the WTO dispute settlement is the institutional imbalance between the adjudicative function of the WTO, which used to work well, and the rule-making function, which underperformed due to the practice of consensus decision-making in the WTO. Addressing this imbalance is essential if one wants to overcome the dispute settlement crisis in the long term.

WTO Members have occasionally surprised the world by finding some middle ground on divisive issues allowing for a pragmatic solution to a challenging problem. While I hope to be proven wrong, it is unlikely that Members will be able to come to an agreement on 'a fully and well-functioning dispute settlement system accessible to all Members' any time soon. For the foreseeable future, the best option for WTO Members for remedy, at least partially and among the willing, is to have recourse to appeal arbitration under the MPIA.

The latter can, and should, be used as a testing ground for how appellate review could be done differently, and possibly better, than the AB did.

Bibliography

Barfield, C. *Free Trade, Sovereignty, Democracy: The Future of the World Trade Organization* (American Enterprise Institute Press, 2001), 1–68.

Barfield, Claude E. 'Free Trade, Sovereignty, Democracy: The Future of the World Trade Organization' (2001) 2(2) Chicago Journal of International Law 403.

Claus-Dieter Ehlermann, *Some Personal Experiences as Member of the Appellate Body of the WTO*, Policy Papers, RSC No. 02/9 (European University Institute, 2002). 14.

Cottier, Thomas 'Recalibrating the WTO Dispute Settlement System: Towards New Standards of Appellate Review' [2021] 24 JIEL 515.

Hoekman Bernard M. and Petros C. Mavroidis, 'To AB or not the AB? Dispute Settlement in WTO Reform' [2020] 23 JIEL 1.

Joost Pauwelyn, 'The MPIA: What's New (Part III)' (International Economic Law and Policy, 21 February 2023) <https://ielp.worldtradelaw.net/2023/03/the-mpia-whats-new-part-iii.html> accessed 20 September 2023.

Julio Lacarte and Petina Gappah, 'Developing Countries and the WTO Legal and Dispute Settlement System', (2000) 3(3) JIEL 395.

Ravi Kanth, 'WTO: In a radical overhaul, US proposes single-tier dispute settlement system' (Third World Network (TWN) Info Service on WTO and Trade Issues, 26 April 2023)<https://twn.my/title2/wto.info/2023/ti230414.htm> accessed on 24 September 2023.

Ravi Kanth, 'WTO: UK, US raise controversial proposals on DS reform' (Third World Network (TWN) Info Service on WTO and Trade Issues, 2 June 2023) <https://twn.my/title2/wto.info/2023/ti230602.htm.> accessed on 24 September 2023.

Ravi Kanth, 'WTO: US proposals on dispute settlement reform could hurt smaller countries' (Third World Network (TWN) Info Service on WTO and Trade Issues, 27 April 2023) <https://twn.my/title2/wto.info/2023/ti230415.htm> accessed on 24 September 2023.

Van den Bossche Peter and Werner Zdouc, *The Law and Policy of the World Trade Organization*, (5th edn, CUP 2022), 173–336.

Van den Bossche, Peter 'Appellate Body: Dispute Settlement of the World Trade Organization (WTO)', in *Max Planck Encyclopedia of Public International Law* (*MPEPIL*) (OUP, 2020) <https://brill.com/display/book/edcoll/9789047418184/Bej.9789004145634.1-704_001.xml.> accessed 20 September 2023.

Van den Bossche, Peter 'Is there a Future for the WTO Appellate Body and WTO Dispute Settlement?', in Freya Baetens and Stefaan Van den Bogaert (eds), *The EU and the WTO: Ever the Twain Shall Meet, Liber Amicorum Marco Bronkers*, (Kluwer, 2023), 193–208.

Van den Bossche, Peter *The Demise of the WTO Appellate Body: Lessons for Governance of International Adjudication?*, WTI Working Paper No. 02/2021

CHAPTER 13

EU and UN Proposals for Reforming Investor-State Arbitration

*Maria Laura Marceddu**

What are international investment agreements (IIAs) for? Although clearly interlinked, the functions and provisions of IIAs do not always match. Arguably, the drafting of investment rules depends on the function(s) attributed to and expected to be performed by investment treaties. The problem, however, is that the main function of investment treaties remains a moving target: is it to attract and protect investment? Is it to subject host countries to certain principles of conduct? Or is it to pursue economic development? While one does not necessarily have to exclude the other, without a clear purpose the interpretative activity of arbitral tribunals has often impinged, perhaps unintentionally, on a wide range of domestic policy sensitivities. Indeed, arbitral tribunals have found themselves in the position of assessing what constitutes a *normal* exercise of host states' regulatory powers according to what investment protection obligations prescribe, often without factoring other interests and needs in the process.

This lack of purpose and its resulting foreign interference from arbitral tribunals in domestic sensitivities have become increasingly noticeable. The dissatisfaction with investment arbitration has grown considerably both in academia and the generable political debate. While it may be difficult to identify a precise time when the malaise first arose, states' dissatisfaction with the investment adjudication system has become increasingly hard to hide. The crisis reached its peak during the 2010s when some states withdrew from the ICSID Convention, and others decided to terminate their BITs. A widespread dissatisfaction that emerged at many levels and from multiple fronts put so much pressure on the investment system that the economic neoliberal tenet according to which foreign capitals deliver prosperity in the forms of more growth and jobs began to tremble. Albeit neoliberalism remains resilient, its narrative is no longer sufficient to accept unreservedly that foreign

* Visiting Max Weber Fellow at the European University Institute. Maria.marceddu@kcl.ac.uk.

interferences at the domestic level risk jeopardizing the accommodation of economic prosperity with non-economic needs.

The re-orientation processes that have been instated in the last decade within the investment system have attempted to respond to this pressure, although the processes are quite broad in scope and offer many angles of analysis. Looking at these processes of reform retrospectively, one particularly convincing and somewhat original perspective of analysis is to understand whether, and if so the extent to which, non-economic concerns had been factored into the reform process. To this end, a constitutionally-oriented reform appears the most apt to address the issue. This chapter thus developed accordingly around the concept of justice and articulates in the following three stages. The analysis begins by outlining the emergence of a growing sense of dissatisfaction within the investment system and the directions of reform taken so far (Section 1). It then moves to elaborate on the concept of justice as a premise for ensuring the pursuit of more satisfactory reform processes. In so doing, it assesses the progresses of three key players, the European Union (EU) and the United Nations (UN) – both United Nation Commission on International Trade Law (UNCITRAL) and United Nation Commission on Trade and Development (UNCTAD) – in pursuing a constitutionally-oriented reform (Section 2). In light of the analysis provided, the third and last section critically discusses the limits of these approaches and the questions that remain unanswered (Section 3).

1 From Dissatisfaction towards Reform

Over the last twenty years (2000–2020), a growing dissatisfaction has acutely emerged against one of the less palatable features of the investment system: the mechanism for resolving investment disputes, i.e. investment arbitration or investor-state arbitration.[1] Investment arbitration consists of a small group of arbitrators sitting impermanent tribunals chosen to decide disputes between foreign investors and governments. These tribunals deliver decision that are often inconsistent, costly, lengthy, opaque and present very narrow grounds to be challenged. As Sornarajah warns, it is hard to pinpoint a precise time when the malaise against investor-state arbitration first arose, but states' dissatisfaction with the investment adjudication system became increasingly

1 The terms 'investment arbitration' or 'investor-state arbitration' will be used interchangeably in this contribution.

hard to ignore.[2] It is around the 2000s, when the number of claims reached the four-digit stratosphere, that the effect of IIAs became more noticeable, especially in light of the wave of lawsuits that arose in the context of the NAFTA. The crisis reached its peak during the 2010s when some states withdrew from the ICSID Convention, and others decided to terminate their BITs.[3] UNCTAD studies have set 2008 as the moment where the IIA regime evolved from an era of proliferation to an era of reorientation, as a consequence of three key lessons learned by the countries during the years. Firstly, it became manifest that IIAs 'bite' because of their far-reaching implications at domestic level. Secondly, even when attaining at their main purpose – i.e. attract foreign capitals – they display evident limitations as far as their underused potential as investment promotion and facilitation tools is concerned, perhaps overshadowed by their main focus currently on investment protection and litigation. Lastly, IIAs pose a range of challenges for capacity building, but even more prominently for policy and systemic coherence.[4]

The problems of policy coherence are intrinsically related to one of the most controversial points of the arbitral tribunal's interpretative activity: the assessment of whether the host state's conduct in question might (or not) constitute a normal exercise of its regulatory powers according to what is prescribed by the investment agreement in question. Such a broader interpretative power has generated the potential effect of deterring host states from changing their domestic regulatory framework to escape even the prospect itself of being hit with (costly) investment claims. This phenomenon is known as 'regulatory chill' and is one of the manifestations that most vividly have revealed the far-reaching implications of investment arbitration.

The problems with investment arbitration, however, go beyond the problem of regulatory chill and encompass issues such as the lack of transparency, of

---

2 Muthucumaraswamy Sornarajah, *Resistance and Change in the International Law on Foreign Investment* (CUP 2015).

3 Bolivia, Ecuador, and Venezuela withdrew from the ICSID convention in 2007, 2009, and 2012 respectively. In 2014, Indonesia announced its intention to terminate its BITs. South Africa has begun a similar programme of termination: it terminated its BIT with Belgium-Luxembourg in 2012 and issued cancellation notices for its BITs with Germany and Switzerland.

4 UNCTAD, *World Investment Report 2015 – Reforming the International Investment Regime: An Action Menu* (2015), 125 available at https://unctad.org/system/files/official-document/wir2015ch4_en.pdf (WiR 2015); see also Meeting Report, Investment Treaties in a State of Flux: Strategies and opportunities for developing countries, available at https://www.iisd.org/system/files/meterial/IISD%209th%20Annual%20Forum%20Meeting%20Report%20English.pdf.

balance between the interests of investors and host states, and of predictability and consistency – just to name a few. Some processes of reforms have aimed to address these issues like the UNCITRAL process to increase transparency in treaty-based investor-State arbitrations under the UNCITRAL Rules, culminating in the transparency rules of 2014;[5] and the 2012 UNCTAD investment policy framework for sustainable development that flagged options for reform of investor–State arbitration.[6]

Several attempts of reform in investment arbitration have tried to achieve greater protection for a state that finds itself caught between a potential financial obligation towards investors and a public policy obligation to its citizens. The public policy obligation is particularly revealing of a persistent dissatisfaction vis-à-vis investment arbitration that is inextricably linked to a global tendency of disillusionment towards free markets. This disillusionment is the result of neo-liberalizing policies instated in the first decade of the 2000s, which, in principle, aimed to normalize legally binding constraints by drawing on the normative ideas of comparative advantage (enhanced social well-being), consumer freedom (opportunity to consume goods and services from any place), and rule of law (as a mean to cabin the tendency of governments to stray from the range of acceptable responses).[7] Economically, this was associated with a strong normative preference for 'free market' and 'free trade' and tended to valorise material prosperity as a central human good.[8] In practice, however, ideas such as the ability of the market to correct itself, the advantages of economic liberalisation, and the emphasis on the right to property became hard to justify in light of market failures, especially when the costs of these failures have to be borne by societies. This appears even more cumbersome within the investment system and the limits placed on states' capacity to solve redistributive problems in case of failed economic investments.[9]

5 United Nations Commission on International Trade Law Rules on Transparency in Treaty-based Investor-State Arbitration and Arbitration Rules (as revised in 2010, with new article 1, paragraph 4, as adopted 16 December 2013), UN GAOR Sixty-Eighth Session Agenda item 79, UN Doc. A/68/462 (2013) art. 1(2).

6 UNCTAD, *Investment Policy Framework for Sustainable Development* (IPFSD) (2012) available at https://unctad.org/system/files/official-document/diaepcb2012d5_en.pdf. (IPFSD 2012).

7 David Schneiderman, *Resisting Economic Globalization* (Palgrave 2013) 36–39.

8 Andrew Lang, *World Trade Law After Neoliberalism* (OUP 2011).

9 See Schneiderman (n 7) at 50 commenting on the Argentinian cases CMS, L&G, Enron, Suez: 'equal treatment with citizens is tolerated only so long as treatment does not fall below certain minimum level, at which point investors are to be granted priority in the wake of financial collapse of the state'.

The effects of this neoliberal wave of globalisation in the investment regime are quite specific. In the regime of international investment, the constraint of sovereignty brought about by globalisation is characterised by two main characteristics. First, the inherent nature of investment agreements that impose standards of governance on states, but no obligations on investors. This could be seen as a consequence of the impact that the deregulatory instincts of neoliberalism have had on strengthening peculiar forms of state intervention in the enforcement of contracts and property rights.[10] And second, the Investor-State mechanism, a *sui generis* mechanism of dispute resolution with adjudicators (arbitrators) selected and appointed by the disputing parties. These two characteristics are often described by the advocates of the system as the historically necessary conditions for the establishment of substantive guarantees and a neutral forum, in contrast to the prejudiced domestic courts of host states. In fact, in these investment tribunals investors are given the possibility to seek direct enforcement of the international substantive rights granted in the underpinning agreement – that is, the right to be treated in a fair and just manner by public authorities of host states, and not to be subject to illegal expropriations or to measures having equivalent effect – and eventually obtain monetary damages. This responds to the neoliberalism prioritization of wealth creation, preservation, and economic efficiency as primary goals of policy and is furthermore corroborated by the fact that the main purpose of investment agreements is (and has been since their very beginning) the protection and promotion of investment, as clearly stated in their title, which generally reads as 'agreement between the Government of the state X and the Government of the state Y on the reciprocal *promotion* and *protection* of investments'.

These characteristics are problematic for many reasons. To begin with, the lack of obligations on investors does not sanction for or offer remedies in case of investments that failed to perform efficiently. As things stand, even in the presence of failed investments, the regime operates as a meaningful constraint on politics with tribunals called to assess whether states' behaviours conform to what is prescribed by the investment treaty in question and whether such behaviours is ultimately the cause for the investment's failure.[11] The systemic inability to hold investors liable does not provide for non-market based solutions and is unavoidably exposed to the criticism that it creates imbalances and is inattentive to alternative social values, thus questioning the effectiveness in

10 Lang (n 8).

11 A case in point is *Biwater Gauff (Tanzania) v Tanzania* (Award, 24 July 2008) ARB/05/22. See also the disputes emerged against Spain (but also Czech Republic, Italy) in the renewable energy context.

delivering the promised material prosperity.[12] This appears to be even more problematic if one considers that the negative economic consequences are borne by societies (i.e. citizens and consumers) potentially twice. Firstly, because of the negative impact a failed investment may have locally; secondly, investment claims argued upon failed economic operations risk penalising states that act in ways deviating from the standard rational model prescribed by investment agreements. Indeed, failed investments, or negative effects on the delivery of the investments, remain somehow seen as a consequence of the alterations introduced in the investment environment by states changes.

Although economic globalization is hard to resist, the unaccountability for market failures revealed a chronic weakness of the economic neoliberalism tenet. As Schneiderman argues, the investment rules regime aims to establish thresholds of tolerable behaviours promoting a culture of marketing seemingly freed from the control of politics.[13] This logic finds confirmation in the fact that the system's approach is to punish deviant governments with large damage awards in case of unusual commercial behaviours that negatively impact the investment – political choices nuisances included. Investment treaty norms and procedures thus become a matter of concern because they leave scarce, if any, room, for accommodating foreign investments with needs that go beyond the purely economic sphere – for example, health, environmental, social and labour issues. The consequences of this logic are increasingly hard to hide. Even the general public has come to grasp how investments norms impinge on a wide range of domestic policies and on sovereignty sensitivities in unprecedented ways. A few countries remained supportive of classic liberalism as its central body of doctrine,[14] and an increasing number of states have recently initiated a process of reform of their investment agreements to strengthen the defensive character of their treaties. By reasserting their control over the interpretation and application of investment treaties,[15] states have attempted to place their treaties more in line with other policy objectives.

Here lies the problem with many processes of reform. Largely ignoring the substantive injustices that the systemic asymmetries have generated, the gist of the problem has predominantly been framed in procedural terms. From this perspective, it is the margin of judicial discretion voluntarily bestowed

12 Lang (n 8) 1–7.

13 Schneiderman (n 7) 51.

14 Jurgën Kurtz, 'NGOs, the Internet and International Economic Policy Making: The Failure of the OECD Multilateral Agreement on Investment' (2002) 3 Melbourne Journal of International Law 213, 223.

15 Andreas Kulick (ed), *Reassertion of Control over the Investment Treaty Regime* (CUP 2016).

by states to adjudicating bodies that has frequently required arbitral tribunals to engage in some type of minimal law-making.[16] This, in turn, has resulted in interpretations far beyond parties' predictions over the possible implications their treaty may have, and which is perceived as the point where intervention is most acutely needed. The wave of initiatives and proposals for reform, either institutionally mandated (e.g., the work of the UNCITRAL Working Group III) or commenced by scholars and civil society organizations concur to reform investment arbitration procedurally. These attempts of reform remain praiseworthy and are likely to mitigate some of the problems affecting investment arbitration. However, a more interesting and often neglected angle would be to look at the reform processes of the past fifteen years to ascertain whether, and the extent to which, non-economic concerns have been factored in the process. I would argue that time is ripe for a justice-oriented reform to address the investment system issues, but it seems the current processes of reform only partially hit this mark, as I will discuss in the following section.

2 From Reform towards Justice

Following on a growing sense of dissatisfaction, the official reform initiatives have sought to intervene on those points of friction (whether real or perceived) that trigger public criticism against the legitimacy of investment arbitration. They introduced textual clarifications, focused on increasing transparency and public participation with a view to enhancing coherence and consistency in arbitrator decision-making. While these are important concerns, the current reform initiatives overlook the central issues with the process and structure of the investment arbitration system.[17] The special status accorded to foreign investors remains unaltered, as does the power of arbitrators to decide arbitration claims on the basis of adherence to investment agreements' norms, and allocate public funds accordingly, albeit the reform processes made it more disciplined. The proposed reforms lack a vision of justice that would review and discipline IIAs as instrument to foster development without questioning

16 Laurence Helfer and Anne-Marie Slaughter, 'Why States Create International Tribunals: A Response to Professors Posner and Yoo' (2005) 93 California Law Review 899.

17 Gus van Harten, 'The European Commission and UNCTAD Reform Agendas: Do They Ensure Independence, Openness, and Fairness in Investor–State Arbitration?', in Steffen Hindelang, and Markus Krajewski (eds), *Shifting Paradigms in International Investment Law: More Balanced, Less Isolated, Increasingly Diversified* (OUP 2016) 129.

sovereign sensitivities and, therefore, seeking compensation from public budgets.

In this section, I will review the approaches of the EU, UNCITRAL and UNCTAD towards reforming investment arbitration from the perspective of justice, intended as a constitutionally-anchored principle. For present purposes, justice is intended as justification as proposed by Forst. From this standpoint, justice is the premise from where the input is derived to ensure legitimacy (output), instead of a utilitarian source that could deliver legitimacy anyway. The logical starting point of the analysis is the same as that of legal and economic constitutionalism. Rules and 'welfare' must be justified by a vision of justice where (potential) voluntary, informed consent is given by reasonable individuals. The input legitimacy is based on methodological individualism rather than by utilitarian output-legitimacy only. Simply put, the assumption is that that IIAs are instruments to foster development. They certainly seek to attract and protect FDIs but cannot be constrained exclusively by an utilitarian output-legitimacy that would focus one-sidedly on investor interests and neglect the non-economic interests. While legitimacy remains the common aim, the framing is different. Legitimacy can be achieved through a vision based on justice or utility. If the former, justification for action (the investment) is derived from an ideal (justice) to be realized through an economic program (investment) effected through and by the rule of law (development and inclusion of non-economic factors). If the latter, justification for action (the investment) is derived from the merely pursuit of a utility (economic profit) effected through and by economic rules (protection of investments and investors).

When using the expression 'justification for action' in the context of investments, I rely on Forst's conception of the 'right to justification'.[18] According to his theory, members of societies plagued by multiple types of domination have a legitimate claim on the various dominators for 'the resources necessary to establish a minimally justified democratic order'.[19] Beyond that, at the maximal level he defends a dialogic analogue of Rawls's Difference Principle: the transnational basic structure must be such that it survives 'the (qualified) veto right of the worst off'.[20] The basis of this qualified veto right is the same as the basis for domestic and international justice, and corresponds to the foundation of morality as such – namely, the right to justification. According to this right to justification, all actions affecting others in morally relevant ways, all claims of justice against others, and all laws and norms need to be justifiable

18 Rainer Forst, *The Right to Justification* (Columbia University Press 2011).

19 ibid, 263.

20 ibid, 265.

in reciprocal and general ways. The ideal of reciprocity at work here is particularly congruent in investment law, where there is a risk that one (foreign investors) arrogates to oneself a specific status one denies to others (domestic investors). Moreover, reciprocity serves also as the foundation to justify the attainment of investment (and investors) protection as well as the pursuit of host state's development. If the development dimension is missing, however, FDIs would pursue an utilitarian output-legitimacy that leaves no space for non-economic factors.[21]

A plausible explanation of investment arbitration resistance to a justice justification finds indirect confirmation also in the work of St John concerning the rise of investment arbitration. According to her findings, investment arbitration was a 'strange idea on the [World] Bank's part', and the insertion of ISDS clauses was not deliberately sought or imposed from investors.[22] Specifically, investment arbitration was a framework created by international officers to kick off a gradual institutional development that eventually culminated in investment arbitration and established a pro-ISDS constituency along the way.[23] The success of investment arbitration can be explained by the fact that institutions persist. Even when they generate consequences that are unintended or unreasonable (from a justice perspective) as it happened with investment arbitration, actors will pursue transformative institutional changes rather than abandoning it. The current efforts to reform investor-state dispute settlement undertaken by the European Union, UNCITRAL and UNCTAD constitute to a large extent a confirmation of this persistence. All official reform processes aim to correct some systemic disfunctions without dismantling investment arbitration or radically altering its inner fibre, or at least this appears not to be the direction these reform processes are taking anytime soon.

Despite these limitations, it is possible to investigate whether traces of justice as the right to justification are detectable in the current efforts of reform. By investigating the extent to which these efforts are addressing the call to factor non-economic needs in the process, it would be possible to understand whether the investment system persists orbiting around non-economic needs or whether it is moving closer, albeit slowly, to more reasonable 'justice choices' to address the central problems with the process and institutional

21 On the point see also Chapter 3, where Armin Steinbach argues with reference to constitutional economics that mutual agreeability of constitutional arrangements for all members of society implies positing 'consumer sovereignty' and 'citizen sovereignty'.

22 'There was almost no demand from investors for this type of arbitration'. Taylor St John, *The Rise of Investor-State Arbitration* (OUP 2018) 3.

23 ibid, 13.

structure of investment arbitration. In the spirit of the questions raised by this book, I will proceed reviewing the recent approaches taken by the European Commission, UNCTAD and UNCITRAL from the perspective of justice-oriented choices. To this end, for the EU, I will concentrate on the Commission Concept Paper released in September 2015 – *Investment in TTIP and beyond – The path for reform* – and on the investment protection agreements (IPAs) negotiated by the Commission. As regards the UNCITRAL reform approach, I will investigate the work carried out by Working Group (WG) II to increase transparency (2009–2014), and by WG III (2017-ongoing) to (i) identify concerns regarding ISDS; (ii) consider whether reform is desirable; and, if so, (iii) develop recommendations. As regards UNCTAD, my focus will be on the 2012 investment policy framework for sustainable development that flagged options for reform of investor–State arbitration, on the 2015 Action Menu for Reforming the International Investment Regime, and on the 2018 UNCTAD's Reform Package.

The remaining of this section will thus develop in the following three stages. First, it investigates justice as openness. In democratic adjudicative processes, powers like those of arbitrators reviewing matters of public interest and issuing compensation from public funds need to be exercised publicly to ensure accountability and fairness. Second, it considers justice as a procedure. Unlike other adjudicative systems, investment arbitration lacks institutional safeguards of judicial independence and procedural fairness. To this end, institutionalization and judicialization are advanced, especially by the European Commission, as remedies to enduring systemic malaise. Third, justice is conceived as a remedy to failures and social injustice. The investment arbitration system is rather asymmetric given that access is permitted to the claimant investor and the respondent government, but other parties, whose rights or interests may be affected by the decision-making, have no standing in the process.

2.1 *Justice as Openness*

In democratic adjudicative processes, powers like those of arbitrators reviewing matters of public interest and issuing compensation from public funds need to be exercised publicly to ensure accountability and fairness. With great powers come great responsibilities; secrecy is fundamentally misplaced in investment treaty arbitration where arbitrators regularly review decisions of legislatures, governments, and courts on matters of public interest and where they award compensation from public funds.[24] Investment arbitration allows

24 Gus Van Harten, 'Investment Treaty Arbitration, Procedural Fairness, and the Rule of Law' in Stephan Schill (ed), *International Investment Law and Comparative Public Law* (OUP 2010); Gus Van Harten, *Investment Treaty Arbitration and Public Law* (OUP 2007) 159–75.

for information to be kept confidential, up to a point where confidentiality can extend to all documents produced throughout the proceedings and even to mere existence of the arbitration. Shielding information from the public unavoidably generates an increasing sense of suspicion towards the ways arbitral tribunals operate and their lack of openness. This poses particular problems in terms of their accountability, risks jeopardizing the legality, and undermines the development of systemic consistency and predictability.

The lack of openness is a long-standing concern, and transparency has often been depicted as its appropriate remedy. Albeit a general principle of transparency does not exist in international law, domestic systems do recognize its legal value. Transparency operates as a vehicle through which tribunals could inform the public about both how arbitrations are decided, and enable government to elucidate their impacts on domestic level. The release of documents to the public domain provides for a channel through which government and the public might interact, and potentially intervene – e.g. through amicus curiae submission.

In this context, it is reasonable to expect commitment towards transparency and openness from both the UN and the EU. In principle, all three systems here considered advocate for access to documents, public hearings, and for granting forms of participation to third parties. The Commission's approach is the most assertive in this regard. The EU IPAs introduced full, mandatory transparency of the arbitration process. This is the default option, to be attained either via the UNCITRAL Rules on Transparency or through supplementary provisions. This means that all documents (submissions by the disputing parties, decisions of the tribunal) will be made publicly available, all hearings will be open to the public, and interested parties (NGOs, trade unions) will be able to make submissions.[25]

UNCITRAL's approach is remarkable on many fronts, although there exist some limitations, mostly of practical nature. Starting in 2009, the UNCITRAL WG II worked for more than four years on the elaboration of new standards favouring greater transparency in investment arbitration. Eventually, the process culminated in July 2013 with the adoption of the Rules on transparency in treaty-based investor-State arbitration.[26] The 2013 Rules consist of a

25 European Commission, Concept Paper *Investment in TTIP and beyond – the path for reform, Enhancing the right to regulate and moving from current ad hoc arbitration towards an Investment Court* (2015) 2.

26 UNCITRAL, 'Report of the United Nations Commission on International Trade Law Forty-sixth session (8–26 July 2013)' UN GAOR Sixty-Eighth Session Supplement No. 17, UN Doc. A/68/17 (UNCITRAL Rules on Transparency), para III.A.

formulation of transparency standards that states are encouraged to use.[27] They comprise eight articles that reverse the presumption of confidentiality in investment treaty arbitration in favour of a presumption of openness[28] and can operate autonomously or as an integral component of the UNCITRAL Arbitration Rules.[29] As per Article 1, the Rules can be applied to any arbitration initiated under the UNCITRAL Arbitration Rules and based on investment treaties 'concluded on or after 1 April 2014'.[30] The Rules do not apply retroactively to those agreements signed off before the cut-off date, for which the contracting parties are expressly required to 'opt-in' to their application'.[31] This constitutes the most critical aspect of the Rules: they only apply to those arbitrations conducted under the UNCITRAL Arbitration Rules and which are based on an investment treaty concluded on or after 1 April 2014, unless the parties have opted out of the Rules. Simply put, this means that for the thousands of treaties concluded before April 2014, the Rules will not apply, unless the parties have expressly agreed to do so. To remedy this shortcoming in scope, the WG II considered different options to ensure the wider applicability of the Rules and eventually came up with the United Nations Convention on Transparency in Treaty-based Investor-State Arbitration, also known as the Mauritius Convention.[32] The Convention offers a means for states to consent to the application of the Rules to treaties pre-dating April 2014. Article 2 of the Convention applies the Rules on transparency, regardless of whether conducted under UNCITRAL arbitration rules, on the condition that the respondent and home state are party to the Convention or the respondent is party and the claimant agrees to apply the Rules on transparency. The Convention was adopted by the UN General Assembly on 10 December 2014[33] and entered into force on 18 October 2017, having three instruments of ratification, acceptance, approval or accession – coming respectively from Canada, Mauritius and

27 UNCITRAL, 'Report of Working Group II (Arbitration and Conciliation) on the work of its fifty-third session (Vienna, 4–8 October 2010)' UN Doc. A/CN.9/712.

28 Stephan Schill, 'Editorial: Five Times Transparency in International Investment Law' (2014) 15 The Journal of World Investment & Trade, 363.

29 Claudia Reith, 'The New UNCITRAL Rules on Transparency 2014: Significant Breakthrough or a Regime Full of Empty Formula?' (2015) 4 Yearbook on International Arbitration, 127.

30 UNCITRAL Rules on Transparency (n 26).

31 ibid art. 1(2)(a) and (b). See also UNCITRAL, 'Report of Working Group II (Arbitration and Conciliation) on the work of its fifty-eighth session (New York, 4–8 February 2013)' UN Doc. A/CN.9/765, para 17.

32 UNCITRAL, 'Report of the United Nations Commission on International Trade Law Forty-seventh session (7–18 July 2014)' UN GAOR Sixty-Ninth Session Supplement No. 17 UN Doc. A/69/17, para 106.

33 UNGA Res 69/116 (18 December 2014) UN Doc. A/RES/69/116.

Switzerland. As of June 2023, the Mauritius Convention counts nine parties and a higher number of signatories states (23), while the UNCITRAL Rules on transparency feature more than a hundred IIAs. Ultimately, the very question as to their effectiveness depends on their general acceptance.

Perhaps surprising to many, UNCTAD took a soft stance towards the improvement of transparency in investment arbitration, delivering at times some helpful statements but, on the whole, falling short of commitments. Transparency is firstly advocated for investors (in both 2012 and 2015 reform plans): 'investment policies should be [...] embedded in an institutional framework based on the rule of law that adheres to high standards of public governance and ensures predictable, efficient and transparent procedures for investors'.[34] It is conceded, however, that 'transparency of ISDS claims could enable broader and informed public debate as well as a more adequate representation of stakeholder interests, prevent non-transparent deals and stimulate balanced and well-reasoned arbitral decisions.' Greater transparency can be attained by, for example, granting public access to arbitration documents (including settlement agreements) and arbitral hearings and allowing the participation of interested non-disputing parties such as civil society organizations.[35] As Van Harten argued, these were helpful statements by UNCTAD but they fell short of a clear commitment to openness in investment treaty arbitration.[36] Transparency remains a precondition for attracting investments, even though UNCTAD recognizes its potential contribution 'to facilitate dialogue between public and private sector stakeholders, including companies, organized labour and non-governmental organizations (NGOs).'[37] On this point, it is interesting to note that UNCTAD insists (in 2012, 2015 and then again in 2018) on the fact that the reform process itself 'should be a transparent multistakeholder engagement, allowing all stakeholders to voice their opinion and to propose contributions'.[38] On the whole UNCTAD's engagement tends to remain at a superficial level, albeit it recognised the potential of transparency at treaty-making level. It attempts to take some steps to address the lack of openness, in a manner that delivers more positive results at policymaking level – i.e. renders the reform process more transparent and open to inputs from all involved stakeholders – than at investment arbitration level.

34 WiR 2015 (n 4) 129.

35 IPFSD 2012 (n 6), UNCTAD's Reform Package fort he International Investment Regime 2018 (Reform Package 2018).

36 Van Harten (n 17) 137–8.

37 IPFSD 2012 (n 6) 12.

38 WiR 2015 (n 4) 165–168.

2.2 *Justice as Procedure*

Unlike other adjudicative systems, investment arbitration provides for a peculiar form of adjudication that lacks the institutional safeguards of judicial independence and procedural fairness. As such, it 'holds little additional value in the presence of well-established and well-functioning domestic legal systems'.[39] This type of critique is frequently derived from one of the historically distinctive features of arbitration: the disputants' power to select their own adjudicators. Claimants and respondents, in fact, have the power to constitute arbitral tribunals by appointing one member of the tribunal each in case of a three-adjudicator tribunal, or to jointly appoint one sole arbitrator. As it has often been argued, the problem with party's right to appoint arbitration is that it leans close to an ad hoc 'private' dispute resolution system and does not offer the same guarantees of independence and impartiality as a state court. The lack (whether real or perceived) of the institutional safeguards of independence and impartiality, which are otherwise present in the adjudicative functions, renders investment arbitration an anomaly and unavoidably instil the suspect of inappropriate bias in the system.

The problem with impartiality and independence is compound in nature. Beyond the powers arbitrators use during the dispute settlement procedures, and the perplexity over the arbitrators' appointment process,[40] a crucial concern resides in the fact that the same individuals are not precluded from acting as counsel in different cases (the so-called 'double-hat' phenomenon). As Crawford has put it, the problem is that there exist:

> Situation[s] in which one day you are presenting an expert opinion on a particular point, the next day you are acting as counsel on the same point of investment law, and the day after you are sitting as an arbitrator in a case which raises that very point, [and this] undoubtedly give[s] rise to difficulties, however much personal integrity the individuals display.[41]

---

39 ibid.

40 Some scholars have even called for a 'moral hazard' associated with party-appointed arbitrators. See in this sense: Charles N Brower and Charles B Rosenberg, 'The Death of the Two-Headed Nightingale: Why the Paulsson–van Den Berg Presumption that Party-Appointed Arbitrators are Untrustworthy is Wrongheaded' (2013) 29 Arbitration International 7.

41 James Crawford, 'Keynote Address: International Protection of Foreign Direct Investments: Between Clinical Isolation and Systematic Integration' in Rainer Hofmann and Christian J Tams (eds), International Investment Law and General International Law: From Clinical Isolation to Systemic Integration? (1st edn, Nomos Verlagsgesellschaft 2011) 21.

One rather obvious explanation for lack of independence and impartiality in investment arbitration is that characteristics like tenure, fixed remuneration, prohibition of concurrent work, etc do not feature in the arbitrator's profile. Unsurprisingly, the reform proposals, especially the most recent ones, are particularly vocal in addressing the shortcomings of the lack of independence and impartiality. A point where the three reform proponents concentrate, albeit with different nuances, is the strengthening of independence and impartiality of adjudicators through institutional design. Specifically, they converge on the need to narrow and discipline arbitrator conducts, along with the establishment of a more institutionalized and judicialized system, especially as far as the European Commission and UNCITRAL are concerned.

Among the points of convergence between the work carried out by the Commission and UNCITRAL there are a code of conduct for arbitrators, the establishment of a structured and permanent judicial process with tenured adjudicators, and a new system of appointment. The Commission's short-to-medium term proposal to move from arbitration is the investment court system (ICS), which now features in a number of international investment agreements – notably, in the Comprehensive Economic and Trade Agreement (CETA) with Canada (2017), the EU-Singapore Investment Protection Agreement (2018) and the EU-Vietnam Investment Protection Agreement (2018) and, in principle, in the agreement with Mexico.[42] The ICS is a two-tier system that comprises a first instance tribunal and an appellate tribunal, both of which are composed of permanent adjudicators appointed by a Joint Committee of representatives from the EU and its treaty partners. The ICS still combines elements typical of investment arbitration as we have known it so far, especially as far as enforcement is concerned, with some significant adjustments such as (but not limited to) the standing status of the tribunal, the imposition of a code of conduct on its members, the members' tenured position, their fixed remuneration and their appointment, which is no longer at the discretion of the litigating parties (i.e. the investor and the host state).

42 European Union–Canada Comprehensive Economic and Trade Agreement (CETA) (signed 30 October 2016, entered into force 21 September 2017 provisionally); Free Trade Agreement between the European Union and the Republic of Singapore (entered into force 21 November 2019), Investment Protection Agreement, Framework Agreement on Partnership and Cooperation between the European Union and the Republic of Singapore (signed 19 October 2018, not yet entered into force); Free Trade Agreement between the European Union and the Republic of Vietnam (entered into force 1 August 2020), Investment Protection Agreement between the European Union and the Republic of Vietnam (signed 30 June 2019, not yet entered into force); New EU-Mexico Agreement in principle (as of 21 April 2018).

This approach is further refined in the long-term solution advanced by the EU, predominantly in the context of the UNCITRAL negotiations, in the form of a multilateral investment court (MIC) clearly modelled upon the WTO dispute settlement system. The multilateral court is composed of permanent adjudicators and aims to provide a judicial procedural framework for investor-state dispute settlements but will not intervene in the underlying substantive laws (e.g. bilateral investment agreements), which remain part of the investment agreements the court is called to interpret and apply.[43]

The proposals advanced by the UNCITRAL WG III in the context of the ISDS reform process are complementary to the ICS, especially as far as the permanent character of the adjudication system and selection process of adjudicators are concerned. There is agreement around the idea of electing tribunal members through an intergovernmental body voting from a list of nominated candidates and to ensure diversity of legal expertise, gender, regional representation, and language. There is flexibility in the establishment of the tribunal depending on geographical representation, following any variation in the number of participating States, as well as in caseload.[44] There is room for accommodating part-time employments, although WG III is firm on the need to adopt a rule 'regarding parallel activities that would be prohibited'.[45]

On this last point and still within the UNCITRAL process of reform, a development worth mentioning is the drafting of a code of conduct in ISDS, an idea that was explored by UNCITRAL WG III following on Algeria's input.[46] After preparing some background work and collecting Member States' comments, delegates at WGIII's 38th session (October 2019) suggested that the Secretariats ICSID and UNCITRAL cooperate in preparing model provisions for a code of conduct for adjudicators.[47] This joint effort led to the release of a first version

43 UNCITRAL Working Group III, 'Possible reform of investor State dispute settlement (ISDS): Submission from the European Union Union and its Member States' (24 January 2019) UN Doc A/CN.9/WG.III/WP.15.

44 UNCITRAL Working Group III, 'Possible reform of investor-State dispute settlement (ISDS) Standing multilateral mechanism: Selection and appointment of ISDS tribunal members and related matters', Note by the Secretariat (8 December 2021) UN Doc A/CN.9/WG.III/WP.213, para 18.

45 ibid, para 21.

46 UNCITRAL Working Group III, 'Settlement of Commercial Disputes: Possible Future Work on Ethics in International Arbitration', Note by the Secretariat' (29 April 2016), UN Doc A/CN.9/808; UNCITRAL Working Group III, 'Possible Future Work in the Field of Dispute Settlement: Ethics in International Arbitration' *Note by the Secretariat* (13 April 2017),UN Doc A/CN.9/916.

47 UNCITRAL, Report of Working Group III (Investor-State Dispute Settlement Reform) on the work of its 38th session (Vienna, 14–18 October 2019) UN Doc A/CN.9/1004.

of the Code in May 2020. Based on the feedback received from interested stakeholders, a second version of the Code was published in April 2021, a third version was published in September 2021, followed by a fourth version in July 2022, and a fifth version in November 2022. In May 2023, ICSID and UNCITRAL published advanced drafts of the texts to be presented to UNCITRAL at its 56th annual session, in the course of which the Code has formally been adopted.

The Code consists of 12 articles, which provide definitions (art.1), explain the applicability of the Code (art.2) along with more substantive obligations for adjudicators (art. 4–9), pre-appointment interviews and fees (art.10 and art. 11). The Code is concluded with a provision addressing the fundamental issue of its enforcement (art. 12). The Code constitutes a remarkable attempt to enhance confidence in the independence and impartiality of ISDS adjudicators. As stressed in Art.3, the Code attempt to enhance even the appearance itself of confidence: 'the obligation not to: [...t]ake any action that creates the *appearance* of a lack of independence or impartiality'.[48] As the commentary explains, an arbitrator must remain vigilant and be proactive in ensuring that he or she does not instil an impression of bias and should make continued efforts to not create a perception of bias. The Code marks an interesting turning point in tackling the concern of double hatting of arbitrators and the risk it poses to their independence and impartiality. Despite the positive impact this type of reform might generate on perceptions, it is an exercise in discipline that remains focused on an individual level, hence the importance of appearances, and largely continue to ignore 'the foundational role of safeguards of adjudicative independence in domestic courts, international courts, and some other systems of arbitration'.[49]

UNCTAD epitomises this aspect of individuality of the reform processes even more vividly. It does not appear particularly concerned about the conflict of interests (WiR 2015), although it does embrace the creation of a roster from which to appoint adjudicators. UNCTAD acknowledges that the institutional set-up of the investment arbitration system generates a more perceivable sense of illegitimacy, albeit impartiality and independence are not mentioned in this context. Its reform-action menus refer to the need of selecting independent arbitrators,[50] and ensuring that adjudicators are fully independent, impartial, free from conflicts of interest and 'affordable' to the parties. This need could be

48 UNCITRAL Working Group III, 'Draft code of conduct for arbitrators in international investment dispute resolution and commentary', Note by the Secretariat (April 2023), UN Doc A/CN.9/1148 (for discussion purposes only).

49 Gus Van Harten (n 17) 131–132.

50 WiR 2015 (n 4) 128.

met, for example, by creating rules on qualifications, conduct and/or remuneration of arbitrators (e.g. through a code of conduct).[51] Yet UNCTAD expresses no concern about the systemic structure underpinning arbitrators' appointments and falls short of discussing the need of independence and impartiality as systemic safeguards.

If compared to the other two players, UNCTAD's approach remains cautious and lays out a more limited option for a system with permanent / quasi permanent arbitrators or an appellate system:

> An appellate body with permanent judges, appointed by States from a pool of eminent jurists, would allow the appeals facility to become an authority capable of delivering consistent – and balanced – opinions, which would rectify some of the legitimacy concerns about the current ISDS regime.[52]

The attempt is probably to engage in a critical analysis of the existing reform proposals; UNCTAD appears somehow persuaded that the tenured character of adjudicators would be congenial to mitigate some concerns levelled against investment arbitration. The element of addressing the lack of independence and impartiality as institutional safeguards, however, is almost entirely dismissed. What seems to transpire from UNCTAD is that 'ad hoc mechanisms would be easier to realize and involve lower costs',[53] whereas 'an appellate body with the authority to issue rulings with the force of precedents [and therefore a MIC or potentially any permanent tribunals] could place new limitations on the sovereignty of contracting parties through the establishment of an independent body of jurisprudence'.[54] It is interesting that the establishment of an independent body of jurisprudence is perceived as a threat (*limitations*) to the sovereign powers of the contracting parties. UNCTAD sees little value of systemic coherence and predictability that an appeal facility might bring. Rather, it assumes that the inherent power of precedent possessed by an appellate tribunal would amount to more constraints on litigants than those deriving from ad hoc decision issued by arbitral tribunals.

51 ibid, 148; Reform Package 2018 (n 35) 50.

52 Reform Package 2018 (n 35), 53.

53 ibid.

54 WiR 2015 (n 4) 148.

2.3 *Justice as a Remedy to Market Failures and Social Injustices*

One of the main problems with investment arbitration is the imbalanced allocation of rights and responsibilities not only between investors and states, but also among investors, states, and other affected third parties. As things stand, investment agreements give full rights for standing to foreign investors (claimants) and governments (respondents) but leave out third parties, despite the effects an investment may have on them. Examples of 'third parties' could be Indigenous communities in whose land arrives 'a corporation from a faraway place to pursue an investment';[55] or domestic investors in competition with foreign competitors. None of those who fall under the 'third party' category is entitled to full standing in the investment adjudication even though their rights or interests could be affected by the investment and are likely to be even more affected by a decision of an arbitral tribunal.

Regardless of the extent to which three (or one) selected individuals, 'drawn from lists of academics and international lawyers almost unknown outside their highly specialized field',[56] undertake the assessment of domestic policy choices, the expansion of the rights of private persons vis-à-vis the regulatory capacity of governments remains undeniable. Albeit it is not accurate to describe investment arbitration as the forum where 'investors always win',[57] it is surely true that there are certain features, peculiar to the investment arbitration system only, that aggravate the imbalance between public and private sensitivities.[58] What states have found particularly disturbing, especially when they are due to comply with awards that placed enormous strain on public finances, is the need to provide justifications to their citizens. Governments found themselves in the uncomfortable position of justifying to their citizens not only that arbitrators were considered more suitable than the domestic legal system to solve investment disputes[59] but also, and perhaps more challengingly, that the decisions they deliver were fair.

---

55 *Bear Creek v Peru*, ARB/14/21 (Dissenting opinion of Prof. P. Sands, 30 November 2017) para 7.

56 Anthony Depalma, 'Nafta's Powerful Little Secret; Obscure Tribunals Settle Disputes, but Go Too Far, Critics Say' *The New York Times* (11 March 2001).

57 'Developments and Reform of Investor-state Dispute Settlement – Q&A with Meg Kinnear', available at: http://bit.ly/2hQDKYf.

58 Specifically, as Wells has argued, the problem has been in the lack of symmetry in ISDS, 'with protection for investors but not for host governments': Louis Wells, 'Backlash to Investment Arbitration: Three Causes' in Michael Waibel, Asha Kaushal, Kyo-Hwa Liz Chung and Claire Balchin (eds), *The Backlash Against Investment Arbitration: Perceptions and Reality* (Kluwer Law International 2010).

59 Protests against ISDS have been organised in Canada, France, Germany, United Kingdom, as well as in the United States and Canada.

This part concentrates on justice as a remedy to market failures and social injustice and attempts to assess how the reform processes are responding to market failures, especially when the costs of these failures have to be borne by societies. From this standpoint, market failures refer to investments that failed to attain and deliver the economic prosperity expected. Social injustices, instead, refer to those situations where a market failure– i.e. an investment failure – produced harmful effects on third parties, like societies and consumers, with no standing rights. Arbitral proceedings tend to acknowledge, and rightly so, that market failure might occur. The same cannot be argued as far as social injustices are concerned. The assessment of an investment failure is based on what the underpinning investment agreement prescribed, albeit it does contain obligations for investors but might raise questions as to whether the investment's failure is a consequence of states' behaviours that deviate from their obligations vis-à-vis the foreign investor in question. By way of oversimplification, if the host state has breached what is prescribed by the investment agreement, the investor is entitled to compensation. However, in case of investments that failed to perform efficiently, the investor may incur in contractual liability, but no remedies for consumers or citizens are envisioned. In the presence of failed investments non-market-based solutions are still marginal, if not entirely absent, and leave third parties to bear the negative consequences twice. Firstly, because of the negative impact a failed investment may have locally; secondly, because of their marginalization during the proceedings. In this sense, the injustice derives from the fact that those whose rights or interests have been affected have no standing in the process.

As things stand, market failures and social injustices have been treated separately, with the former being taken into account and the latter being largely overlooked. The point I would like to investigate in the remainder of this section is whether the reform processes have attempted to address the problem as a compound one, so accounting for both market failure and social injustices.

One proposal around which all the three players converge is the possibility for third parties to submit amicus curiae briefs, which have the potential to raise public interests that go beyond the host state, and which can include the perspective of other stakeholders. Their contribution, however, remain somewhat limited in addressing the problem of injustice. As the Latin words indicate, amicus curiae is a 'friend of the court,' and is not a party to the proceeding. Arbitral tribunals have often allowed amici participation only on the conditions of a manifest interest within the scope of the dispute and on the safeguard of the integrity of the process.[60] Moreover, it remains unclear the extent to which these briefs are ultimately taken into account in the final award.

An area where the EU and UNCITRAL approaches diverge is the possibility of having counterclaims (against investors), which remains a grey area to say the least. The UNCITRAL WG III investigated the issue of counterclaims among possible reform solutions only once in its 39th Session (2020). On that occasion, the WG III noted that there have been a few ISDS cases in which respondent States had filed counterclaims, some of which were accepted by arbitral tribunals and some of which were dismissed on grounds of lack of jurisdiction or merits.[61] The WG remained fairly open to explore the possibility that claims might be brought against an investor, as long as there exists a legal basis for doing so.[62] The governments of Morocco and South Africa were particularly vocal in insisting on the possibility to enable the host State to submit a counterclaim if an investor failed to comply with one or more of its obligations under the treaty to address the imbalance in the existing ISDS mechanisms.[63] In that context, the WG III had considered formulating 'clauses for use by States in their offer to arbitrate in investment treaties', which could reduce, if not eliminate, uncertainty about the consent of the parties as well as any connection requirement, whether factual or legal.[64] The EU appears rather close to the possibility of counterclaims, especially considering that CETA expressly precludes issues of domestic laws (including EU law) from the jurisdiction of arbitral tribunals and requires tribunals to accept the interpretation of domestic laws by courts or other authorities of treaty parties as a matter of fact (Art.8.31). The EU choice to safeguard the exclusive authority of its internal judicial system over issues of domestic laws would preclude investment arbitral tribunals from entertaining counterclaims based on domestic law – as could well be the case, for example, for environmental counterclaims in the investment context. Due to its devotion to the sanctity of the Court of Justice of the European Union, this may sound like an EU peculiarity, but it is rather common among states. For example, the India's 2015 Draft Model BIT included language that would have provided for counterclaims:

60 *Encavis and Others v Italy*, ARB/20/39 (Procedural Order N.2, 21 May 2022) para 41.

61 UNCITRAL Working Group III, 'Possible reform of investor-State dispute settlement (ISDS) Multiple proceedings and counterclaims', Note by the Secretariat (22 January 2020) UN Doc. A/CN.9/WG.III/WP.193, para 37.

62 ibid, para 32.

63 ibid, para 34.

64 ibid, para 44.

> A party may initiate a counterclaim against the Investor or Investment for a breach of the obligations [corruption, disclosure, taxation, compliance with host state law] before a tribunal established under this Article and seek as a remedy suitable declaratory relief, enforcement action or monetary compensation.

This language, however, was later dropped in India's new 2016 Draft Model BIT. These ambiguities notwithstanding, there is at least one interesting novelty put forward by the EU in CETA that deals with market failures, as enshrined in paragraph 4 of CETA Article 8.10, which reads:

> When applying the above fair and equitable treatment obligation, a Tribunal *may* take into account whether a Party made a specific representation to an investor to induce a covered investment, that created a legitimate expectation, and upon which the investor relied in deciding to make or maintain the covered investment, but that the Party subsequently frustrated.

This provision signals a radical shift from the traditional drafting of FET. The change from the usual perspective is enshrined in the term 'may'. Even in the case of the frustration of legitimate expectations (by the host state to the detriment of the investor), the tribunal is not necessarily bound to consider this as a violation of the treatment of investors' provisions. Differently put, even in the presence of a market failure, the tribunal can take the negative impact on the investment into consideration, but this 'giving thought to' is not binding. What seems important to retain for present purposes is that the breadth of a tribunal's discretion is considerably limited. The change of perspective lies in the fact that the tribunal is no longer bound to take the legitimate expectations' component into consideration, or at least not exclusively, nor should investors expect the tribunal to do so. The agreement provides for a right to regulate provision to safeguard state's regulatory autonomy, but no reference is found in case of potentially negative consequences on third parties.[65]

Another proposal worth mentioning is the creation of an advisory centre for the prevention, avoidance, and management of investment disputes, as well as for the collection and promotion of best practices. As articulated in its 43rd session, the WG III identified a list of possible services that an advisory centre

65 In CETA, third parties are mentioned in the context of intellectual property regulation (art. 20.32) and in the chapter on Trade and Labour as part of collaborative activities (art. 23.7).

could render. This list is built around two main pillars. First, the centre should provide assistance in mediation and other alternative dispute resolution methods (ADR); and support during dispute settlement proceedings. Second, the centre should function as a forum for sharing of best practices, including on pre-dispute and dispute avoidance services, mediation and other forms of ADR, as well as legal and policy advisory services.[66] The interesting part is that, beyond respondent states – with precedence given to LDCs, developing countries and more broadly states with limited financial capacities or in situation of political turmoil – the list of possible beneficiaries may be extended to small-medium enterprises and, depending on the scope of services, to amici curiae and/or other potential intervenors. While there is no express reference to those affected by an investment that have no standing in a dispute, the inclusion of 'potential intervenors' leaves hope for a centre where affected parties are allowed to raise their instances. This by no means implies a systemic reconfiguration, but at least might provide a venue to be heard, albeit with clear limitations.

UNCTAD's line of action remains somehow less consistent if compared to UNCITRAL and the European Commission approaches. UNCTAD does recognize that most IIAs are asymmetrical in that they set out obligations only for States and not for investors. Among possible reform options, it insists on the need to strengthen ADR as a dispute prevention mechanism, for example by making it a compulsory step before the commencement of investment arbitration.

Taking stock of a global trend advocating for rebalancing, UNCTAD identifies two broad sets of options: raising the obligations to comply with domestic laws to the international level and designing corporate social responsibility (CSR) clauses.[67] For example, it reports that some recent IIAs contain provisions to foster responsible investment by requiring investors to comply with environmental assessment screening procedures prior to establishment of the investment and to conduct social impact assessments of potential investments and to maintain an environmental management system and meet international certification standards.[68] In a similar vein, there are some IIAs which set

66 UNCITRAL Working Group, 'Possible reform of investor-State dispute settlement (ISDS) – Advisory Centre', Note by the Secretariat (3 December 2021) UN Doc. A/CN.9/WG.III/WP.212, para 19.

67 Reform Package 2018 (n 35) 65–8.

68 Reciprocal Investment Promotion and Protection Agreement Between the Government of the Kingdom of Morocco and the Government of the Federal Republic of Nigeria (signed on 3 December 2016), art. 8.

out consequences for investors' failure to comply with investor obligations – e.g. subjecting them to civil actions before the courts of their home State in case of acts leading to significant damage, personal injuries or loss of life in the host State.[69] While the overview provided is accurate, the report simply surveys some states' measures introduced to correct the systemic imbalances without entering in the merit of their impact.

All reform processes recognize that the investment arbitration is characterized by problems of symmetry, or rather of lack of, but none of them has framed the narrative in terms of market failures and social injustices as two sides of the same coin. Some reforms seem to point towards more rebalancing but, as they stand, none of them intends to engage into a systemic restructuring.

3 From Justice towards Remaining the Same

In this chapter I discussed whether appropriate steps have been taken to reform the system in a more justice-oriented fashion. Although the future does not have to be bleak, the path is fraught with uncertainties. Much of what the reforms in international investment agreements since 2004 have tried to achieve is greater protection for a state that finds itself caught between a potential financial obligation to an investor and a public policy obligation to its citizens. While the path towards the expansion of state's regulatory autonomy has potential, it is insufficient to address problems like social injustices.

In some instances, the reform processes took stock of the developments occurred in the last twenty years and remain limited merely to codifying the existing practice of arbitral tribunals rather than truly call for radical reforms. The changes introduced by global reform processes are laudable, especially when they have rendered investment arbitration more open and impartial; but they are inadequate when it comes to addressing the structural problems long affecting the investment regime. The elephant in the room is, in fact, the asymmetry of the investment system, which assigns only rights to investors and only obligations to states and that, as a consequence, generates social injustices.

Interesting novelties are sometimes advances by single states, albeit not unreservedly. The reform proposals are attempting, quite successfully, to limit investors' rights and accord greater protection to states in international investment disputes; but they only do so by shifting the interpretative power of arbitrators from one flexible wording to another within a given BIT, thus

69 ibid, art 20.

reducing the positive impact a permanent adjudication body might exercise in the long term, as 'feared' by UNCTAD. Attempts to protect the right of states to regulate, albeit celebrated as radical changes, only apparently tackle the imbalances, and actually leave the systemic structure intact. It almost looks like that according to these attempts of reform 'everything must change so that everything can stay the same'.[70] In the absence of radical systemic interventions, these reforms are likely to crystalize the systemic asymmetry which, by design, assigns only rights to investors and only obligations to states.

Acknowledgements

I am most grateful to Ernst Ulrich Petersmann and Armin Steinbach for their very helpful comments and exchanges. All opinions and errors remain mine.

Bibliography

Brower CN and Rosenberg CB, 'The Death of the Two-Headed Nightingale: Why the Paulsson–van Den Berg Presumption that Party-Appointed Arbitrators are Untrustworthy is Wrongheaded' (2013) 29 Arbitration International 7.

Crawford J, 'Keynote Address: International Protection of Foreign Direct Investments: Between Clinical Isolation and Systematic Integration' in R Hofmann and CJ Tams (eds), *International Investment Law and General International Law: From Clinical Isolation to Systemic Integration?* (1st edn, Nomos Verlagsgesellschaft 2011).

Depalma A, 'Nafta's Powerful Little Secret; Obscure Tribunals Settle Disputes, but Go Too Far, Critics Say' *The New York Times* (11 March 2001).

Developments 'Developments and Reform of Investor-state Dispute Settlement – Q&A with Meg Kinnear', available at: http://bit.ly/2hQDKYf.

Di Lampedusa T, *The Leopard* (1958).

European Commission, Concept Paper – Investment in TTIP and beyond – the path for reform, Enhancing the right to regulate and moving from current ad hoc arbitration towards an Investment Court (2015).

Forst R., *The Right to Justification* (Columbia University Press 2011).

Giorgetti C, 'The Draft Code of Conduct for Adjudicators in Investor–State Dispute Settlement: A Low-hanging Fruit in the ISDS Reform Process' (2023) 14 Journal of International Dispute Settlement, 176.

70 Tomasi di Lampedusa, *The Leopard* (1958).

Helfer L. and Slaughter AM, 'Why States Create International Tribunals: A Response to Professors Posner and Yoo' (2005) 93 California Law Review 899.

Kulick A. (ed), *Reassertion of Control over the Investment Treaty Regime* (CUP 2016).

Kurtz J, 'NGOs, the Internet and International Economic Policy Making: The Failure of the OECD Multilateral Agreement on Investment' (2002) 3 Melbourne Journal of International Law 213, 223.

Lang A, *World Trade Law After Neoliberalism* (OUP 2011).

Muthucumaraswamy, Sornarajah M. *Resistance and Change in the International Law on Foreign Investment* (CUP 2015).

Reith C, 'The New UNCITRAL Rules on Transparency 2014: Significant Breakthrough or a Regime Full of Empty Formula?' (2015) 4 Yearbook on International Arbitration, 127.

Schill S, 'Editorial: Five Times Transparency in International Investment Law' (2014) 15 The Journal of World Investment & Trade, 363.

Schneiderman D., *Resisting Economic Globalization* (Palgrave 2013).

St John T., *The Rise of Investor-State Arbitration* (OUP 2018).

UNCTAD, *Investment Policy Framework for Sustainable Development* (*IPFSD*) (2012) available at https://unctad.org/system/files/official-document/diaepcb2012d5_en.pdf.

UNCTAD, *World Investment Report 2015 – Reforming the International Investment Regime: An Action Menu* (2015), 125 available at https://unctad.org/system/files/official-document/wir2015ch4_en.pdf.

Van Harten G, 'Investment Treaty Arbitration, Procedural Fairness, and the Rule of Law' in S Schill (ed), *International Investment Law and Comparative Public Law* (OUP 2010).

Van Harten G, 'The European Commission and UNCTAD Reform Agendas: Do They Ensure Independence, Openness, and Fairness in Investor–State Arbitration?', in S Hindelang, and M Krajewski (eds), *Shifting Paradigms in International Investment Law: More Balanced, Less Isolated, Increasingly Diversified* (OUP 2016).

Van Harten G., *Investment Treaty Arbitration and Public Law* (OUP 2007) 159.

Wells L, 'Backlash to Investment Arbitration: Three Causes' in M Waibel, A Kaushal, K-H Liz Chung and C Balchin (eds), *The Backlash Against Investment Arbitration: Perceptions and Reality* (Kluwer Law International 2010).

CHAPTER 14

Systematic Rivalries and Multilevel Governance in Asia: a Constitutional Perspective

Julien Chaisse

1 Introduction

This chapter examines the limits and possibilities for multilateral and regional cooperation within Asian regulatory competition, 'constitutional failures' to protect human rights and cross-border aggregate public goods, and domination of legal frameworks for transnational governance by systemic rivalries and hegemonic power politics. In identifying and analysing the approach of Asian regulators among the three competing models driving global governance trends, this chapter investigates the persistence of existing value differences between North American, European, and Asian policy regimes. The key lines of inquiry include whether diverse regional approaches represent an adequate substitute for the multilevel governance of public goods;[1] the optimal design of multilateral constitutional rules to manage systemic divergence (e.g. formation of plurilateral agreements within the World Trade Organization (WTO); and potential paths to strengthening United Nations (UN) and European security systems via clarification of customary legal rules regarding collective countermeasures by democratic alliances against UN Security Council (UNSC) veto abuse and military aggression.[2]

1 Ernst-Ulrich Petersmann, 'Constitutional Pluralism, Regulatory Competition and Transnational Governance Failures' in A. Steinbach and E.U. Petersmann (eds), *Constitutionalism, Transnational Governance Failures and Policy Responses* (This book).

2 Collective countermeasures are adopted by third countries on serious breaches of international law. Despite growing use, the permissibility of countermeasures remains unresolved under customary international law. Art. 54 of the Responsibility of States for Internationally Wrongful Acts does not prejudice third countries' rights from implementing countermeasures at the behest of an injured country. However, the International Law Commission's commentary on the act noted that insufficient state practice on collective countermeasures existed with no well-established right under Art. 48 for states to undertake collective countermeasures; inserting a provision to permit countermeasures by non-injured countries would be inappropriate. See Michael N Schmitt and Sean Watts, 'Collective Cyber Countermeasures?' (2021) 12 Harvard National Security Journal 373, 385–397.

This chapter employs the methodologies of constitutionalism and constitutional economics to examine multidimensional failures in the provision of transnational public goods. By incorporating constitutional economics, a broader and more corrective lens is employed, moving beyond the narrow considerations of localised cost-benefit analyses towards advocating for legislative, administrative, and independent judicial protections of the rule of law and equal rights at the transnational level. Constitutional designs emphasise optimal rules of higher rank that are founded on consensus, free political will, and inclusive democratic institutions. Additionally, the insights of constitutional economics fill the gaps left by public choice scholars, who advocate for salutary forms of regulatory competition but fail to account for power biases that facilitate the abuse of jurisdictional competition and transnational governance failures. In light of policy failures increasingly shifting from the domestic government to transnational governance levels, incorporating insights from constitutional economics emphasises the importance of implementing legislative, administrative, and adjudicative protection of the rule of law and equal rights at the transnational level.

The rationale for this chapter's focus on the Asian perspective flows from a few essential facts. Along with Europe and the United States (US), Asia accounts for the lion's share of global carbon emissions.[3] Global cooperation must transcend geopolitical rivalries to prevent more than 140 million climate refugees by 2050.[4] Despite a relatively delayed arrival to regional economic formation globally, the Asia-Pacific region has been the most active region during the last decade. This region not only boasts of having the world's highest number of free trade agreements (FTAs) but is also home to two of the world's largest FTAs: the Comprehensive and Progressive Agreement for Trans-Pacific Partnership (CPTPP) and Regional Comprehensive Economic Partnership (RCEP).[5] Additionally, the Indo-Pacific Economic Framework (IPEF) was

3 EPA, 'Global Greenhouse Gas Emissions Data', (*US Environmental Protection Agency*, 15 February 2023) <https://www.epa.gov/ghgemissions/global-greenhouse-gas-emissions-data> accessed 26 June 2023.

4 World Bank, 'Climate Change could Force over 140 Million to Migrate Within Countries by 2050: World Bank Report' (*World Bank*, 19 March 2018) <https://www.worldbank.org/en/news/press-release/2018/03/19/climate-change-could-force-over-140-million-to-migrate-within-countries-by-2050-world-bank-report> accessed 26 June 2023.

5 See, for example, Julien Chaisse, 'The Regional Comprehensive Economic Partnership's Investment Chapter: One Step Forward, Two Steps Back?' (2020) 271 Columbia FDI Perspectives 1; Julien Chaisse and others, 'Drafting Investment Law: Patterns of Influence in the Regional Comprehensive Economic Partnership (RCEP)' (2022) 25 Journal of International Economic Law 110.

launched in 2022, creating the potential for further regional economic and regulatory integration. In addition to examining the origins of trade pact proliferation in the Asia-Pacific region, this chapter traces future trajectories of regional economic cooperation by highlighting several major trends: the US pivot to Asia, China-US rivalry, competition and convergence across regional blocs, non-traditional agreements, such as the Digital Economy Partnership Agreement (DEPA) and IPEF, and the role of small open economies.

The chapter begins by elucidating the systemic rivalries and multilevel governance of public goods, followed by an exposition of the Asian approach to safeguard the benefits of a rule-based and liberal trading system. This involves an analysis of the challenges faced by Asia in the context of a multilevel governance system and its confrontation with systemic rivalries. Additionally, the chapter addresses how the RCEP and CPTPP protect the advantages of a rule-based and liberal trading system, while also considering the potential impact of the IPEF as a game changer.

2 Navigating Complexities: the Interplay of Systemic Rivalries and Multilevel Governance in the Provision of Public Goods

This section emphasises the importance of multilevel governance, as it includes both local and international authorities working together to effectively tackle the complex challenges arising from globalisation and competition. Fostering cooperation and coordination across different governance levels ensures that public goods with varying externalities are appropriately managed, leading to efficient and equitable resource allocation and policy implementation. Effective provisions of public goods depend on the governance level, which then relies on the extent of externalities of a particular public good. Thus, the local council will govern the provision of public goods with externalities limited to a locality, such as lighthouses. In contrast, public goods with cross-border externalities, such as biodiversity, will require international governance.[6] Globalisation has engendered competition among public actors and political economies of varying hierarchies, impacting the provision of public goods. A potential remedy to this issue is multilevel governance of public goods, wherein power is allocated to authorities within and beyond national borders through established norms. By contrast, systemic rivalries address these challenges by focusing on market

6 See Liesbet Hooghe, Gary Marks and Arjan Schakel, 'Multilevel Governance' in Daniele Caramani (ed), *Comparative Politics* (OUP 2020) 194.

participants' roles rather than adhering to a formal institutionalism approach. For instance, the European Commission has labelled China as "a systemic rival promoting alternative models of governance", even though the existing global governance structure also presents difficulties.[7]

Systemic rivalry and multilevel governance of public goods are susceptible to convergence and divergence. In terms of convergence, both systemic rivalries and multilevel governance of public goods involve multiple actors. For systemic rivalries, these actors take the form of states, whereas, for multilevel governance, these actors take the form of multiple levels of government as well as non-governmental actors. Additionally, rivalry for resources or other strategic objectives might motivate one another. Both may also include cooperation and collaboration among the parties involved. Governments may need to collaborate to manage existing disputes and avoid further escalation when structural rivals exist. In a system with several levels of governance, diverse players may have to collaborate to successfully offer public goods. As for the differences, the primary objective of systemic rivalry is to further one's interests, while multilevel governance aims to produce public goods for the benefit of all concerned parties. In contrast to systemic rivalries, which often result in one side prevailing at the cost of the other, it frequently entails striking a balance between opposing interests and finding areas of agreement. Systemic rivalries include the use or threat of force, while multilevel governance generally depends on negotiation and collaboration.

Multilevel governance of public goods and systemic rivalry have certain points in common but are also diverse regarding their features and objectives. Multilevel governance emphasises collaboration and the provision of public goods, in contrast to the systemic rivalries driven by rivalry and self-interest. This part attempts to showcase *first* the Asian challenges to multilevel governance of public goods and *second*, explain the systemic rivalries.

2.1 *Public Goods in Asia: Balancing National and Regional Interests*

The Asian challenges of multilevel governance of public goods include explaining how the current multilevel governance system in Asia faces contemporary challenges in the region. This part showcases *first*, the meaning of multilevel governance of public good; *second*, the reason for the erosion of this concept; *third*, the Asian approach to transnational aggregate public goods; *fourth*, the

7 European Commission, 'Joint Communication to the European Parliament, the European Council and the Council: EU-China – A Strategic Outlook' JOIN (2019) 5 final, 1.

comparison of European constitutionalism and Asian countries; and *last*, the need for global cooperation due to Asian actions.

2.1.1 Multilevel Governance of Public Goods

The multilevel governance of public goods may be characterised as a type of transnational constitutionalism. This constitutionalism establishes institutional and normative frameworks that aim to reconcile various political economies for administrating localised public goods with the requirement for synchronised and structured preservation of collective public goods, like public health, human rights, and climate change mitigation.[8] It establishes and regulates governing institutions and rules of a legal hierarchy for the collective provision of public goods. It also does not pertain to a solitary form of multilevel relationship between national and transnational entities; rather, it encompasses a spectrum of legal pluralism that contemplates the subordination of domestic to transnational rules (and vice versa).

A key aspect of multilevel governance of public goods is the integration of national legislatures, executives, judiciaries, and independent regulatory bodies within a broader constitutional framework, which legally restricts their collective governance. This is achieved through multilevel regulatory institutions, which incorporate judicial remedies to safeguard transnational public goods. The European Union (EU) exemplifies such a dynamic, with member States' national constitutions functioning within a more extensive set of constitutional law obligations for public goods, jointly overseen by the European Court of Human Rights (ECHR) and the EU Court of Justice. Furthermore, this constitutionalism demands innovations in transnational legitimacy formation and democratic accountability mechanisms to surmount governance, market, and constitutional failures that have arisen in recent years.

The undersupply of public goods is directly connected to numerous humanitarian crises in contemporary history. Despite the need for transnational collaboration in increasing access to essential goods, the current institutional and normative frameworks have led to failures that challenge the legitimacy

8 See Petersmann, 'Constitutional Pluralism, Regulatory Competition and Transnational Governance Failures' (n 1) ('Globalization requires complementary, multilevel constitutionalism constituting, limiting and justifying multilevel governance of transnational PGs. European law illustrates how path-dependent 'constitutionalism 1.0' is based on (1) national constitutional contracts (like the 1789 French Declaration of the Rights of Man and the Citizen), (2) national Constitutions, (3) democratic legislation and (4) administrative and judicial protection of rule-of-law for the benefit of citizens; it can be extended to international law and institutions for legally constituting *transnational PGs*, which no single state can protect without rules-based international cooperation.').

of the global rules-based system. Without enhanced accountability mechanisms, their provision will be susceptible to narrow interest groups, hegemonic power politics, and mercantilist protectionism. These factors risk undermining human and democratic rights while exacerbating environmental and public health crises.

2.1.2 Erosion of Multilevel Governance of Public Goods

Numerous forces have led to the erosion of the multilevel governance of public goods, including heterogeneous national preferences and geopolitical tensions. Institutions of authority and their problem-solving capacities have struggled to keep pace with fundamental knowledge and technological transformations, creating a gap between deterritorialised networks and territorially-bound regulatory and governance systems. Within this gap have arisen failures from markets, governments and constitutional frameworks designed to place checks and balances on power politics and human nature. Governance failures occur nationally and transnationally, and influence each other. The US withdrawal from the 2015 Paris Agreement and its trade war with China exemplify actions that have undermined international cooperation. On the other end of the spectrum, international organisations, like the EU, have previously failed to vigorously uphold their legal obligations to address rule-of-law violations.[9]

The absence of effective legal safeguards against global collective action problems and competing preferences for managing transnational public goods can partly be explained by the inadequate implementation of the rule of law, human rights and climate change mitigation into the national legal architectures of States. The 2022 US Inflation Reduction Act demonstrates protectionist policies and trade discrimination in the service of environmental goals. Such trends are also evident in the BRICS countries, like China's and India's refusal to phase out coal-generated electricity by 2050. Despite the existence of 'global commons' to promote universal access, ineffective transnational judicial remedies and accountability mechanisms will continue to undermine public goods' effective governance. Attempts to reduce government and market failures through competition have also been undermined. Instead of a level-playing field where jurisdictional competition leads to the most effective

9 Lili Bayer, 'Brussels Drags out Poland and Hungary Rule-of-Law Probes' (*Politico*, 16 October 2018) <https://www.politico.eu/article/brussels-drags-out-poland-and-hungary-rule-of-law-probes/> accessed 21 October 2022.

solution, the law is circumvented through power imbalances that aggravate unequal distributions of resources and erode public trust in institutions.[10]

2.1.3 Governing Transnational 'Aggregate Public Goods': an Asian Perspective

Contrasting to the European constitutionalism approach, China approaches aggregate public goods with its feet in two boats. Nationally, China's single-party government's political structure insulates the country's political elites and military from legal constitutionalism restraints. China's political economy also influences its approach to governing transnational public goods. Ineffective national constitutional and judicial remedies for citizens to challenge human and political rights suppression create localised conditions that obstruct the provision of aggregate public goods, like political opposition. Nevertheless, China has successfully participated in international governance bodies with constitutional features, like the UNSC and WTO dispute settlement system. This is partly because these bodies lack adequate, independent judicial remedies and multilateral rules to protect non-discriminatory conditions of competition, guarantee citizens' human and democratic rights, and ensure the provision of aggregate public goods necessary to maintain stable environmental conditions.

China's governance of market public goods is filtered through a state-capitalist system that has selectively adopted UN human rights treaties to protect the Chinese Communist Party's political monopoly. Its constitution does not effectively constrain this monopoly, which aggravates government-induced market failures, fuelled by opaque corruption and asymmetrical rights structures within oligarchic governance systems. Despite subsidy schemes distorting global competition and a lack of independent judicial protections, China, as a totalitarian state-capitalist country, is not outright abandoning rules-based systems' advantages. Rather, value conflicts and geopolitical rivalries have precipitated a shifting landscape in trade and foreign policy programs with significant implications for adequate provisions of these aggregate public goods. For example, the RCEP, which entered into force in China and 14 Asia-Pacific countries on 1 January 2022, and China's political dominance of bilateral infrastructure and financing deals regarding its 'Belt and Road' (BRI) development strategy,[11] reflect regulatory competition to other regional

10 Anne Case and Angus Deaton, *Deaths of Despair and the Future of Capitalism* (Princeton University Press 2020).

11 The BRI is a development plan, primarily aiming to promote economic cooperation and connectivity between Asia, Europe, and Africa. The effort includes building infrastructure projects, and is anticipated to result in a rise in trade and investment among participating

economic partnerships, like the CPTPP. This disregard for global rules that limit the market, governance and constitutional failures coincides with a rise of 'authoritarian alliances' across Eurasia juxtaposed by regional trade partnerships between Western democracies and global south nations with varying national development priorities.[12]

2.1.4 Multilevel Constitutionalism in Asia and Europe: Uncovering the Divergences

European multilevel constitutionalism, applies transnationally by extending domestic constitutional principles to EU foreign policy and security matters. Increased transparency and predictability of EU foreign policies are achieved by embedding human rights, democracy, the rule of law and compliance with international sustainable development goals (SDGs) into policy-making via Arts. 3 and 21 of the Treaty on European Union.

National and EU powers are limited through the institutionalisation of multilevel regulatory agencies of a higher legal rank and democratic and judicial remedies for governance failures related to competition, environmental stewardship and monetary policy. To the extent that 'regulatory competition' exists among EU and European Free Trade Area member states, governance failures from diverging regulatory systems are constrained by constitutional law principles enshrined in the cooperation among European courts, national courts, and transnational institutions. Despite a trajectory of evolving constitutionalism that started over a half-century ago, similar efforts to progressively limit transnational governance failures through aligning national constitutions with new global realities have not been followed outside of Europe. Asia's national constitutions also often fail to check abuses of power and collective action problems that have been addressed in Europe via constitutional reforms. There are several reasons why the multilevel judicial protection of rights via regional agreements does not exist in Asia. Post-feudal and colonial regimes

---

nations, and the creation of new economic prospects for them. Additionally, by linking nations and areas that are historically physically divided from one another, the BRI might assist to increase economic development and eliminate poverty in participating countries. Furthermore, the initiative is considered a means through which China can demonstrate its leadership internationally, while also expanding its influence in the area and beyond, promoting its internal overcapacity, and boosting its access to resources, markets and key positions. See, for example, Julien Chaisse and Jamieson Kirkwood, 'Chinese Puzzle: Anatomy of the (Invisible) Belt and Road Investment Treaty' (2020) 23 Journal of International Economic Law 245.

12 Petersmann, 'Constitutional Pluralism, Regulatory Competition and Transnational Governance Failures' (n 1).

in Asia represent relatively new constitutional approaches that differ from their European counterparts. While European and North American democracies emphasise individualist foundations based on equal freedoms and rights, Asian legal traditions embrace communitarianism within hierarchies and public good protections through 'duties' attributed to the state.[13]

In addition to general issues of power politics and procedural difficulties of amending constitutions, there are systematic differences between market economies and state-capitalist countries, which lack independent judicial protections and constitutional restraints on totalitarian regimes' the anti-competitive conduct and human rights abuses. China's 'non-democratic constitutionalism' model creates conflicts resulting in a fragmented framework for legal accountability. This is reflected by China's adoption of the International Covenant on Economic, Social and Cultural Rights but not the International Covenant on Civil and Political Rights. This constitutionalism, deriving legitimacy primarily through state consent, diverges from EU multilevel constitutionalism and the UN's 'constitutional governance model', whose foundations of legitimacy rest on human and democratic rights. The management approach to economic and environmental regulation common to state-capitalist countries also tends to be less restrained by multilevel constitutionalism.

Without the constitutional constraints of common market freedoms, customs union rules and judicial remedies applicable to executive decision-making, authorities in Asia and elsewhere can justify violations of ratified international treaties by invoking so-called sovereignty powers. Constitutional nationalism elsewhere, along with a broader trend of the power-oriented, intergovernmental pursuit of national self-interests, also creates an environment undermining the potential ability of UN and WTO law to impose constitutional constraints on abuses of public power among states acting as trading partners with Asia. The inadequacy of the UN and WTO's constitutional framework for legislative procedures and judicial remedies to address competition, environment and social concerns also represents a constitutional failure on the transnational level due to the absence of legal principles capable of protecting aggregate public goods. While European law has responded to the emergence of transnational public goods wrought by globalisation with multilevel constitutionalism supporting rule-based cooperation, Asia's limited number of constitutional democracies undermines the formation of multilevel judicial

13 Ernst-Ulrich Petersmann, 'Lessons from European Constitutionalism for Reforming Multilevel Governance of Transnational Public Goods in Asia?' in Julien Chaisse (ed) *Sixty Years of European Integration and Global Power Shifts: Perceptions, Interactions and Lessons* (Hart Publishing 2020) 217.

protections of the rule of law due to the absence of citizen-driven enforcement mechanisms of constitutional guarantees of market freedoms alongside civil, political, economic and social rights.

2.1.5 Global Cooperation under Pressure: the Impact of Asia

While China has embraced domestic legal reforms and complies with the majority of WTO rules and dispute settlement rulings, several recent actions have eroded global cooperation. These developments are part of a broader trend signalling the return of hegemonic, mercantilist, and neoliberal interest group power politics, undermining international cooperation frameworks. Because national constitutional and governance failures increasingly translate into parallel failures on a transnational level, China's rejection of legal constitutionalism undermines global cooperation and the effective governance of transnational public goods. In addition, totalitarian policy-making facilitates a wide array of anti-competitive practices, including disguised subsidies and trade sanctions. These, directly and indirectly, discriminatory policies receive the state's blessing, despite conflicting with WTO subsidy rules and the rules-based international system's foundational principles. Ineffective constitutional and judicial remedies in authoritarian states also fail to preserve non-discriminatory conditions of competition. Simultaneously, inadequate multilevel governance remedies to address market distortions have led market economies to increasingly resort to countermeasures, resulting in a bifurcated global trade system that undermines global cooperation and rights protections. The political domination of bilateral deals among BRI development partners and authoritarian regimes also represents direct competition with existing, rules-based global trading and investment regimes.

Clear examples of power politics and national interest influencing decisions to explicitly disregard the embedded liberalism within WTO law exist. Furthermore, China's limited cooperation with the World Health Organization's attempts at ascertaining the COVID-19 pandemic's origins highlights how power politics can dominate UN institutions at the expense of global public goods. China has also disregarded UN and WTO sustainable development obligations through illegal extensions of sovereign rights in the South China Sea and disregarded a 2016 arbitral award under the Law of the Sea Convention (UNCLOS).

While China is not the only actor undermining UN and WTO systems and multilevel governance, geopolitical rivalries and constitutional nationalism between authoritarian and democratic countries are substantial catalysts of eroding global cooperation, particularly on SDGs and public goods. As a response to totalitarian Chinese state capitalism, democratic states are forming alliances to reaffirm and defend the liberal, rules-based international system from military threats and disregard for invading and enforcing human and constitutional rights by independent judicial bodies.

2.2 *Asia's Power Struggle: Examining Superpower Rivalries*

Systemic rivalries are an analytical framework enabling the attribution of responsibility for market, governance, and constitutional failures across complex multilevel governance systems with rules-based, state-controlled and business-determined dimensions. Rather than merely following formal institutional distributions of authority, actor-based and rules-oriented perspectives situate the conduct of diverse public and private entities within existing institutions and normative regimes. The actors include governments, public and private authorities, and intergovernmental and supranational entities. Systemic rivalries manifest through business-driven economic regulation, constitutionally unbound state capitalism and rules-based governance systems promoting non-discriminatory trade and democratic and human rights guarantees. They exist within a globalised, interdependent world where provisions of transnational public goods are prone to broadly defined governance failures that incorporate the relationships between market actors, governments, international organisations and supranational entities across various political, economic, social, environmental and technological dimensions.

2.2.1 Systemic Rivalry and Its Implications for Multilevel Governance of Public Goods

Failures to preserve public goods are common in both democratic and non-democratic regimes. Mismatches between the domestic policy-making process and the multilevel governance of public goods cause these failures. Further, corrupted elites and undemocratic institutions, nations with internal democratic legitimacy may also harm transnational public goods. One example of the latter is the US Supreme Court restricting the administrative discretion of national environmental regulators to address climate change. International organisations may also act in a manner that undermines their democratic legitimacy while domestic policy arenas traditionally within national governance regimes become more deterritorialised. While all UN member states utilise constitutionalism to protect national public goods, globalisation has produced transnational public goods requiring a multilevel constitutional governance system that is still a work in progress. EU treaty constitutionalism complements the national constitutions of EU member states through a series of multilevel governance rights, rules and institutions. However, Europe's multilevel constitutionalism is the exception. Power politics endemic to systemic rivalries also permeate international agreements, leading to deficiencies in fairness and efficiency. Despite formal recognitions of the multilevel framework response to collective action problems, practical shortcomings allow such problems to persist, particularly in the context of the rule of law, security and climate policy.[14]

2.2.2 Rivalries and Resonance in Asia?

Opting for economic collaboration among authoritarian governments rooted in power politics, rather than participating in global cooperation through multilateral institutions, exemplifies how Asian nations aim to capitalise on the benefits of rules-based, liberal trading systems amid the decline of multilevel trade governance. A case in point is the BRI, a significant instrument of Chinese economic statecraft, which encompasses approximately 64% of the global population and 30% of the world's GDP.[15] In addition to serving as a stimulus for China's domestic economy and labour force and an avenue to increase international use of China's currency, the BRI also represents a channel for laying the foundations of an alternative trade regime based on bilateral power-politics that excludes multilateral rules, independent judicial remedies and guarantees of citizens' rights[16] – this aligns with the path pursued by increased Sino-Russian and pan-Eurasian cooperations.[17] The BRI has also been framed as a source of 'new ideas and plans for reform of the global governance system'.[18] Regulations establishing international commercial courts and dispute resolution services for BRI-related projects raise open questions about the degree of divergence or coherence with established international legal and institutional practices. Coupled with Russia's dominant influence in Eurasia, China's political dominance of bilateral BRI infrastructure projects, financial networks, and their linkages to regional Asian institutions create a Sino-Russia bloc based on power politics, economic cooperation and selective adherence to multilateral rules and human rights obligations. Concurrently, China has framed the BRI as an effort toward providing global and regional public goods, including

---

14 Inge Kaul, *Providing Global Public Goods: Managing Globalization* (OUP 2003).

15 Office of the Leading Group for Promoting the Belt and Road Initiative, *The Belt and Road Initiative Progress, Contributions and Prospects* (1st edn, Foreign Languages Press Co Ltd 2019) 88.

16 Petersmann, 'Constitutional Pluralism, Regulatory Competition and Transnational Governance Failures' (n 1).

17 ibid.

18 Carla P Freeman and Mie Ōba 'Bridging the Belt and Road Divide' (*Carnegie Endowment for International Peace*, 10 October 2019) <https://carnegieendowment.org/2019/10/10/bridging-belt-and-road-divide-pub-80019> accessed 24 January 2023.

free trade, and governance sensitive to the contributions of developing countries.[19] Central and Southeast Asia are two areas where the BRI prompts the emergence of Asia-based systemic rivalries. For instance, China is currently a major force shaping Southeast Asia's future.[20] Yet, through the Association of Southeast Asian Nations (ASEAN), Southeast Asian nations are seeking to offset China's overwhelming influence by diversifying investment and trade sources while pursuing partnerships and security impacts with international partners.[21] China is currently ASEAN's closest partner; linked institutions, such as the Asian Infrastructure Investment Bank, provide platforms and channels for assistance with technical and financial matters and fora for discussions and meetings between parties.

China's economic statecraft, through BRI projects, represents a revival of political and economic forces originally meant to be restrained by rules-based market competition and independent dispute resolution. Limited competition and non-transparent subsidy practices allow China to export competition distortions on world markets while deploying trade sanctions or restrictions for political reasons. These developments mirror the rising influence of authoritarian state capitalism and anti-competitive practices that create government-induced market failures and conflict with multilateral obligations to adhere to a rules-based trading system built on non-discrimination and fairness. While the BRI deals' terms often lack transparency,[22] this mode of development and its associated rules of the game begs questions about whether new norms, regulations and practices will be compatible with previous standards or capable of transforming national markets into transnational ones. To the extent China attempts to attach strings to the BRI for geopolitical purposes, dynamic shifts could emerge in democratic and authoritarian alliances vying over political power and control of multilevel governance regimes.

---

19 ibid.

20 Sophie Boisseau du Rocher, *The Belt and Road: China's "Community of Destiny" for Southeast Asia?* (Ifri 2020) 14.

21 Freeman and Ōba (n 19).

22 Some of the projects included in the BRI have been called opaque, which has led to criticism towards the BRI. This is often due to concerns over the projects' funding and administration, as well as worries regarding the viability of the debt and the possible repercussions on the people in the area. In general, the criticisms levelled against the BRI projects for their lack of transparency underscore the need for more open and participatory decision-making procedures, as well as more specific information on the funding and administration of these projects.

2.2.3 Connecting Asia to the World: Systemic Rivalry between Europe, the US, and China

In reaction to totalitarian power politics and the disdain for global laws supporting non-discriminatory commerce and human and democratic rights, the EU and the US have undertaken programmes that promote coordinated and cooperative policy-making and alignment on issues like trade and climate remediation, which has become more institutionalised and comprehensive following the implementation of formal mechanisms, like the EU-US Dialogue on China.[23] In 2019, the EU classified China as a 'systemic rival', requiring 'a flexible and pragmatic whole-of-EU approach enabling a principled defence of interests and values'.[24] This strategy was informed by three main challenges: local infringement of freedoms, rights, and market opportunities by the Chinese leadership; coercive tactics within the region; and growing assertiveness by extending BRI strategies into Europe.[25] Global interdependencies and tensions in the EU-China systemic rivalry are evidenced in the currently stalled Comprehensive Agreement on Investment (CAI). Despite the potential of significant concessions on discriminatory investment policies, sanctions and counter-sanctions reflecting ongoing concern over human rights violations underline the ongoing constitutional and governance failures as a result of systemic rivalries unchecked by adequate multilevel constitutional safeguards.[26] The CAI also highlights that rivalries and geopolitical power politics not only exist between opposing authoritarian and democratic alliances but also among them. These tensions have persisted following the US Inflation Reduction Act's adoption, which pursues the decarbonisation of the US economy through discriminatory tax credits, domestic content requirements and trade discrimination.

In addition to more recent pledges of support for Russia in February 2022, China and Russia have strengthened their strategic partnerships through bilateral economic relations and improved cooperation in international

23 Shaohua Yan, 'Transatlantic Policy Coordination on China and Its Limitations' (2022) 92 China International Studies 65.

24 Commission (n 8).

25 Steven Blockmans and Weinian Hu, 'Systemic Rivalry and Balancing Interests' (*CEPS*, 21 March 2019) <https://www.ceps.eu/ceps-publications/systemic-rivalry-and-balancing-interests-chinese-investment-meets-eu-law-belt-and-road/> accessed 24 January 2023.

26 Frederick Kliem, 'Finding the Middle Ground: EU-China Relations' (*Hinrich Foundation*, 6 December 2022) <https://www.hinrichfoundation.com/research/article/sustainable/eu-china-relations/> accessed 24 January 2023.

organisations.[27] Meanwhile, close trade relationships between China and democratic states have been weaponised for political gain and to the detriment of treaty obligations and the integrity of the multilevel governance of public goods. Thus, following the US' illegal trade war against China, both have since entered into a 'bilateral opt-out' of WTO legal and dispute settlement obligations via discriminatory reciprocity negotiations that excluded third-party adjudication.[28]

2.2.4 Geopolitical Rivalries Impact on UN and WTO Law and the SDGs

Systemic rivalries accelerate hegemonic power politics, undermining global rules seeking to preserve SDGs and aggregate public goods through limitations on the market, governance, and constitutional failures. Unilateral and coordinated responses to 'authoritarian alliances' among China, Russia, and other Eurasian countries risk accelerating economic fragmentation, which entrenches obstacles to multilevel governance and magnifies tensions between diverse national development priorities. Because localised and regional actions increasingly result in extraterritorial effects, domestic and national solutions are inadequate to address transnational problems and the side effects emerging from complex and interdependent systems of exchange of goods, services, and financial capital.[29] Transnational governance failures perpetuate and are undermined by national constitutionalism, which attempts to retain its grip on rule setting and manage the disruptive processes of globalisation, technological intermediation, and legal and economic interconnectedness. Parties enmeshed in geopolitical rivalries resist the constitutionalisation of foreign policy powers for many reasons. For totalitarian, state-capitalist nations seeking to preserve political monopolies, constitutionalisation risks imposing constraints on abuses of powers that could lead to the promotion of citizen-driven solutions that undermine the legitimacy of previously unaccountable leaders. Democratic nations can be plagued by welfare nationalism; regulatory capture by business interests and neo-liberal interest group politics disrupt the rules-based world trading system and are incentivised to continue perpetuating the *status quo* despite short-term, narrow interests being put before the common

---

27 Liliana Popescu and Razvan Tudose, 'The Dragonbear and the Grey Rhinos – The European Union Faced with the Rise of the China-Russia Partnership' (2021) 21 Romanian Journal of European Affairs 130, 135.

28 Petersmanfn, 'Constitutional Pluralism, Regulatory Competition and Transnational Governance Failures' (n 1).

29 Inger-Johanne Sand, 'Polycontextuality as an Alternative to Constitutionalism' in Christian Joerges, Inger-Johanne Sand and Gunther Teubner (eds), *Transnational Governance and Constitutionalism* (Hart Publishing 2004) 48.

interests of an international polity. Geopolitical rivalries also risk fomenting populist power politics that undermine the effectiveness of multilevel governance of public goods through failures to hold governments democratically and legally accountable for violations of treaties, upholding the transnational rule of law and compulsory third-party dispute settlements.[30]

2.2.5 Geopolitical Rivalries: Uncovering the Path-Dependent Value Conflicts

The persistence of path-dependent geopolitical rivalries creates obstacles for global cooperation in achieving SDGs. Intergovernmental power politics and prioritisation of national interests exploit inadequacies of UN and WTO law to legally constrain market distortions and human rights abuses while resisting efforts to reform multilevel constitutional frameworks to address hegemonic mercantilism and climate change. Factors such as Russian aggression, politically-motivated interruptions in Sino-US environmental dialogue, and rejection of regional human rights regimes disrupt the multilevel governance of public goods and challenge democratic constitutionalism to respond within international law constraints.

Historical and political path dependencies underlie geopolitical rivalries that hinder global cooperation. Therefore, it is improbable that managerial, mission-oriented approaches can effectively address the interconnected governance, market, and constitutional failures at the heart of these conflicts.[31] Such governance is ill-suited to address the collective action problems obstructing necessary transnational cooperation on the provision of globalised, aggregate public goods and the facilitation of digital markets. It also lacks the legitimacy and strength of bottom-up, democratic social regulations required to overcome top-down failures to regulate state-owned enterprises (SOEs). As totalitarian power politics reject rules-based legal restraints on non-discriminatory competitive actions and abuses of political and social human rights, democratic states increasingly respond via coordinated countermeasures and collective defence alliances within UN and WTO law.

Simultaneously, certain elements of WTO law, which perpetuate power imbalances between rent-seeking business entities and political party monopolies, hinder the effective restraint of welfare nationalism and other discriminatory, state-controlled governance systems. Although healthy regulatory

30 Ernst-Ulrich Petersmann, 'The 2018 Trade Wars as a Threat to the World Trading System and to Constitutional Democracies' (2018) 10 Trade, Law and Development 179.

31 Petersmann, 'Constitutional Pluralism, Regulatory Competition and Transnational Governance Failures' (n 1).

competition can potentially stimulate the adoption of socially advantageous and economically efficient structures, insufficient transnational governance leads to the exploitation of dominant positions, compromising equitable jurisdictional competition. Power politics and unregulated unilateral transgressions of WTO trade remedy regulations persistently contribute to the fragmentation of the multilateral, rules-based trading system into regionally-based political alliances. As transnational governance failures exacerbate the unequal distribution of economic resources and public goods, the diminishing trust and perceived legitimacy of political elites and institutions will further erode the rule of law and democratic, citizen-centric accountability mechanisms essential for advancing social welfare and public goods.

The various stages of institutional, political, and economic failures that have given rise to the EU's current system of rights and obligations provide lessons for Asian countries, which are increasingly adopting legislation and international agreements protecting a wide range of rights and obligations related to the governance of public goods.[32] First, limitations on economic and political 'markets' arise from the fact that they are socially and legally constructed. Historically and empirically, human rights, the rule of law, democracy, and republicanism are the constitutional core principles that are most effective in limiting failures to protect public goods and general consumer and citizen welfare.[33] Empirically speaking, constitutional rights that facilitate localised and decentralised civil society support for transnational public goods are more effective governance tools for addressing globalisation than state-centred and power-oriented models disconnected from legal, democratic, and judicial accountability.[34] For legal instruments to perform their social regulation and construction functions properly in a multilevel context, strong constitutional protections for citizens and non-governmental actors are required to overcome ineffective transnational democratic institutions and a singular polity. Multilevel constitutionalism must enable legal and policy priorities that reflect democratic, localised preferences of people. Such citizen-driven, 'bottom-up network governance' provides a more robust framework for limiting abuses and failures of 'top-down chessboard governance' through increased democratic pressure for solutions to common public goods crises

32 Petersmann, 'Lessons from European Constitutionalism for Reforming Multilevel Governance of Transnational Public Goods in Asia?' (n 14) 226.

33 Roland Pierik and Wouter Werner (eds), *Cosmopolitanism in Context. Perspectives from International Law and Political Theory* (CUP 2010).

34 Anne-Marie Slaughter, *The Chessboard and the Web: Strategies of Connection in a Networked World* (Yale University Press 2017).

that transcend political and economic interest groups. Stronger rights, citizens' participation and remedies within multilevel governance systems are also necessary to ensure a transnational legal order that provides adequate incentives for public goods protection and imposes limitations on collective action problems and abuses of public and private power. These goals are achievable through measures, including joint administration of public pool resources, 'republican countervailing rights' and judicial remedies of citizens, and the transformation of 'pure public goods' into 'club goods' that reduce free-riding through reciprocity requirements.[35]

3 Asia's Response to the Challenges of Rules-Based and Liberal Trading Systems: an Examination of Regional Approaches

Regional cooperation in Asia has emerged rapidly in the last decade. RCEP, CPTPP and IPEF are the current cooperative arrangements actively managing free trade in the region. This part analyses *first* how RCEP and CPTPP can help in protecting the rules-based and liberal system and *second* how IPEF can emerge as a potential game-changer in transforming the approach.

3.1 *Asia's Mega Regionals and the Rules-Based and Liberal Systems*

In examining how the CPTPP and the RCEP arrangements can aid the protection of the rules-based and liberal system, this section shall briefly discuss two recent plurilateral initiatives. Thereafter, it shall explore and outline the pros of having a rules-based and liberal system. Recognising that such advantages bring unique challenges, the next part of this chapter shall briefly delve into the challenges posed by a system of this kind. Lastly, the author shall discuss how the RCEP and CPTPP help maximise and strengthen a liberal rules-based system's advantages.

3.1.1 Innovative Plurilateral Initiatives: Asia's Response to Evolving Trade Challenges

In addition to conventional regional accords, Asia has established non-traditional agreements in response to the rise in protectionist measures. Countries in the Asia-Pacific region are increasingly adopting club-membership agreements, which involve a limited number of participating nations. One

---

35 Elinor Ostrom, *Governing the Commons: The Evolution of Institutions for Collective Action* (1st edn, CUP 1990); Elinor Ostrom, *Understanding Institutional Diversity* (Princeton University Press 2005).

such example is the Digital Economy Partnership Agreement (DEPA), signed by Singapore, Chile, and New Zealand on 12 June, 2020.[36] Notably, Canada, South Korea, and China have also expressed interest in joining this agreement. The agreement, whose provisions mirror that of the CPTPP,[37] represents an attempt to create best practices and regulations on digital trade and facilitation,[38] and addresses existing and upcoming technologies. Crucially, the chapter on emerging trends and technologies is a crux of the DEPA,[39] because digital trade, as one of the most dynamic sectors in the world, will play a significant role in trade and investment, whilst driving the growth of e-commerce and cross-border payments by utilising technologies, including blockchain technology.[40] It should be noted that although accession is open on terms that all parties have agreed upon, in reality, only WTO members can accede to the agreement.[41]

Another example is the Declaration on Trade in Essential Goods for Combating the COVID-19 Pandemic (the Declaration). Launched on 15 April 2021, it is based on the Joint Ministerial Statement affirming commitment to ensuring supply chain connectivity, initially signed in March 2020 between Singapore and New Zealand. It further develops the statement's pledges. Among other obligations, participating countries must facilitate the movement of essential goods, including sanitary products, by removing tariffs and disallowing export restrictions.[42] Similar to the DEPA, the Declaration is open to accession by WTO members, which have also submitted their acceptance of the document.

---

36 New Zealand Foreign Affairs & Trade, 'Overview' (*New Zealand Foreign Affairs & Trade*) <https://www.mfat.govt.nz/en/trade/free-trade-agreements/free-trade-agreements-in-force/digital-economy-partnership-agreement-depa/overview/> accessed 26 June 2023.

37 Dan Ciuriak and Robert Fay, 'The Digital Economic Partnership: Should Canada Join?' (2022) Centre for International Governance Innovation Policy Brief No 171, 1, 7 <https://www.cigionline.org/static/documents/PB_no.171.pdf> accessed 26 June 2023.

38 Michael A Peters, 'Digital Trade, Digital Economy and the Digital Economy Partnership Agreement (DEPA)' (2022) 55 Educational Philosophy and Theory 1, 6 <https://www.tandfonline.com/doi/epdf/10.1080/00131857.2022.2041413?needAccess=true&role=button> accessed 26 June 2023.

39 Ciuriak and Fay (n 38) 5.

40 Peters (n 39) 7.

41 New Zealand Foreign Affairs & Trade (n 37).

42 Library of Congress, 'New Zealand; Singapore: New Declaration on Trade in Essential Goods for Combating the COVID-19 Pandemic' (*Library of Congress*, 17 April 2020) <https://www.loc.gov/item/global-legal-monitor/2020-04-17/new-zealand-singapore-new-declaration-on-trade-in-essential-goods-for-combating-the-covid-19-pandemic/> accessed 26 June 2023.

Asia's response to the challenges of rules-based and liberal trading systems has been multifaceted, involving both traditional and non-traditional agreements. The emergence of plurilateral initiatives, such as the DEPA and the COVID-19 Declaration, demonstrates the region's adaptability and commitment to addressing contemporary global challenges. By embracing innovative approaches and fostering cooperation among participating countries, these regional agreements exemplify Asia's dedication to sustaining a rules-based and liberal trading system.

3.1.2 Obstacles to Multilateralism: Power Politics and Constitutional Nationalism

The liberal rules-based system constitutes a series of multilateral rules, judicial remedies and human and democratic rights guarantees, that are created and enforced by relevant public and private stakeholders. This brings many advantages. The system is key in most SDGs' materialisation, including global poverty reduction and sustainable development. It also devises the required international cooperation to deal with the deterritorialisation of public goods and the subsequent failures to protect them, which are progressively out of the reach of national governing structures and constitutions. Within the WTO, the monitoring of domestic policies with the Trade Policy Review mechanism encourages domestic and multilateral transparency.[43] Further, compliance with its compulsory legal dispute settlement mechanism limits protectionism and potential escalations of trade conflicts, whilst preserving the international system's security and predictability.

However, the system is facing numerous challenges globally. Constitutional nationalism and hegemonic power politics have exacerbated weaknesses in global governance systems struggling to address abusive regulatory competition, national security restrictions on international treaty obligations, and shifting global realities. Constitutional reform efforts targeting UN and WTO governance and global climate remediation have been resisted, due to geopolitical power politics and constitutional nationalism. Additionally, these proposed reforms' limited scope and structural limitations of existing multilevel governance systems fail to implement constitutional governance models that adequately protect human rights, the rule of law and democratic accountability mechanisms, thus exacerbating the above-mentioned challenges in delaying and obstructing efforts to maintain and expand rules-based,

43 World Trade Organization, 'Principles of the Trading System' (*World Trade Organization*) <https://www.wto.org/english/thewto_e/whatis_e/tif_e/fact2_e.htm> accessed 24 January 2023.

multilevel governance systems necessary to address transnational public goods challenges across various dimensions. Compulsory judicial remedies have also not been pursued to address international human rights law enforcement and other protections of democratic rights and rule of law.[44]

Government accountability and effective judicial remedies covering transnational relations remain elusive despite compulsory adjudication mechanisms. Examples include the ongoing US obstruction of the WTO Appellate Body and Russia's disregard of 2022 judicial orders.[45] Proposals to enhance the rules-based, liberal system have also been prevented by UNSC veto powers abuse and disruption of WTO dispute settlement mechanisms via illegal veto practices.[46] These reflect that power politics remains the primary impediment to UN and WTO law's ability to limit collective action problems, protect human rights and provide and protect public goods by implementing effective multilevel constitutionalism.

Real and perceived national security risks have also challenged the rules-based system. International health pandemics have prompted the rare exercise of UNSC action to call for extended suspensions of armed conflicts globally and the extension of humanitarian assistance to conflict zones.[47] However, globalisation has also created the potential for the weaponisation of interdependence by dominant political actors,[48] prompting the invocation of national security exemptions to treaty obligations. Such disguised protectionisms result from geopolitical 'chessboard governance' that has fostered abusive regulatory competition and effective obstruction of multilevel constitutional restraints on governance, market and constitutional failures.[49]

3.1.3 Safeguarding the Benefits of Rules-Based and Liberal Systems through RCEP and CPTPP

Despite diverse, unilateral state actions undermining UN and WTO law and explicit disregard for treaty obligations to protect public goods, states and

44 Ernst-Ulrich Petersmann, 'China and the Future of International Economic Law: European Perspectives on the Way Forward' (2022) EUI LAW Working Paper 2022/13, 1, 8 <https://cadmus.eui.eu/bitstream/handle/1814/75146/LAW_WP_2022_13.pdf?sequence=1> accessed 26 June 2023.

45 ibid.

46 Petersmann, 'Constitutional Pluralism, Regulatory Competition and Transnational Governance Failures' (n 1).

47 UNSC Res 2565 (26 February 2021) UN Doc S/RES/ 2565.

48 Henry Farrell and Abraham L Newman, 'Weaponized Interdependence: How Global Economic Networks Shape State Coercion' (2019) 44 International Security 42, 47–58.

49 Slaughter (n 35).

actors globally persist in pursuing the rules-based, liberal trading system. It is estimated that the RCEP, which represents the biggest trade bloc in history and accounts for approximately 30% of the world's population and global GDP at the time of signing,[50] and the CPTPP together will offset global losses from the US-China trade war, excluding China and the US. In addition to improved economic efficiencies, these new agreements create linkages across North and Southeast Asia, covering technology, manufacturing, agriculture, and natural resources.[51]

The RCEP is potentially central to regional integration by standard-setting for all ASEAN economies. Instead of the successful economic integration of geopolitical rivals, regional cooperation among affinity partners through the RCEP and the CPTPP represents a 'second-best' building block approach, inviting wider participation from countries seeking to reinvigorate their economies post-pandemic. The CPTPP's openness has created opportunities and challenges. Achieving SDGs and spurring many nations' economic growth will require liberalised international markets, which provide stability and predictability.

The RCEP's flexible structure reflects that micro, small and medium enterprises (SMEs) constitute more than 90% of business organisations. It provides measures to reduce bureaucracy, addressing globalisation-related issues facing businesses and facilitating access to funds from the BRI. Unlike the CPTPP, the RCEP includes no guidance on SOEs or state subsidies. Labour provisions and environmental protections are also absent or inadequate to align with all parties' Paris Agreement commitments and pledges under the 2030 SDG Agenda.

The two agreements will optimise the North and Southeast Asian economies, linking their technological, manufacturing, agriculture, and natural resources strengths.[52] Absent a delayed US entry into the RCEP or TPP, US involvement in future growth across the Pacific will largely hinge on the IPEF's scope and success.

---

50 Zeeshan Khan and others, 'The Roles of Export Diversification and Composite Country Risks in Carbon Emissions Abatement: Evidence from the Signatories of the Regional Comprehensive Partnership Agreement' (2021) 53 Applied Economics 4769.

51 Peter A Petri and Michael Plummer, 'RCEP: A New Trade Agreement that will Shape Global Economics and Politics' (*Brookings*, 16 November 2020) <https://www.brookings.edu/blog/order-from-chaos/2020/11/16/rcep-a-new-trade-agreement-that-will-shape-global-economics-and-politics/> accessed 24 January 2023.

52 ibid.

3.2 *Indo-Pacific Economic Framework (IPEF): a Game Changer?*

In 2022, US President Joe Biden officially launched the IPEF, a US-led region-wide economic development negotiation platform. With the Indo-Pacific forecasted to account for the most significant share of global growth over the next three decades, the IPEF seeks to establish novel regulations pertaining to trade, digital markets, supply chains, and infrastructure initiatives. This platform involves 14 Indo-Pacific partners, collectively representing an estimated 40% of the global GDP.[53] Depending on its execution, the IPEF's framework offers a potential platform for the plurilateral promotion of SDGs and public goods governance. Potentially, it is a solution to the insufficient constitutional frameworks regarding transnational public goods, and also an alliance mechanism of democratic countries to defend the liberal, rules-based international system. Cooperations from countries with diverse backgrounds could also alleviate adverse effects such as hegemony, mercantilism, and neoliberalism. Nevertheless, the framework has several characteristics that create possibilities and challenges for transforming multilevel governance of public goods.

3.2.1 Indo-Pacific Economic Framework in Context: Asia's Noodle Bowl of Trade Agreements

During times of crises, trade and foreign direct investment flow, thanks to well-designed FTAs. However, the abundance of overlapping and complicated FTAs in East Asia risks becoming cumbersome and hindering trade.[54] This is the spaghetti bowl phenomenon of economic agreements, or the 'noodle bowl' effect, as referred to in Asia (Figure 14.1).[55]

Notably, the proliferation of transactions has raised transaction costs, especially for SMEs, which can afford them the least because of the FTAs' complicated rules and variable tariffs.[56] The proliferation of bilateral and multilateral agreements also undermines efforts to reach a more comprehensive agreement on world trade.

---

53 Department of Commerce, 'Indo-Pacific Economic Framework' (*US Department of Commerce*) <https://www.commerce.gov/ipef/indo-pacific-economic-framework/> accessed 26 June 2023.

54 Ganesh Wignaraja and Masahiro Kawai, 'Tangled up in Trade? The "Noodle Bowl" of Free Trade Agreements in East Asia' (*CEPR*, 15 September 2009) <https://cepr.org/voxeu/columns/tangled-trade-noodle-bowl-free-trade-agreements-east-asia> accessed 26 June 2023.

55 See, for example, Julien Chaisse and Shintaro Hamanaka, 'The 'Noodle Bowl Effect' of Investment Treaties in Asia: The Phenomenon, the Problems, the Practical Solutions' (2018) 33 ICSID Review – Foreign Investment Law Journal 501.

56 Wignaraja and Kawai (n 55).

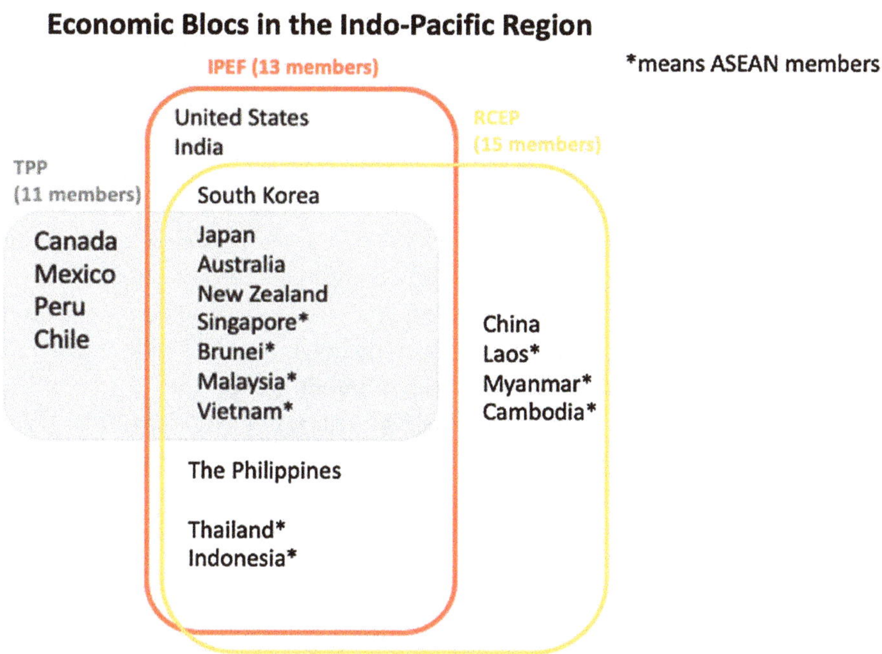

FIGURE 14.1 IPEF and the noodle bowl of agreements
SOURCE: ELABORATED BY THE AUTHOR FROM VARIOUS PUBLIC SOURCES

The 'noodle bowl' effect is *per se* bad as it skews markets and threatens trade regulations' coherency. Companies must comply with many intricate international treaties, which adds to their transaction costs. If strong states can demand better terms from partners, they also introduce asymmetries.[57]

This effect is a villain to regional agreements as Asia is currently crisscrossed by dozens of frequently wildly inconsistent bilateral agreements, as opposed to having a single, integrated set of trade rules that apply equally to all governments.[58] Each has its standards for administrative procedures, non-tariff trade policy reforms, and rules for tariff reduction.[59] Therefore, it complicates trade negotiations, especially the IPEF.

---

57 Jong Woo Kang, 'The Noodle Bowl Effect: Stumbling or Building Block' (2015) ADB Economic Paper Working Series No 446, 1 <https://www.adb.org/sites/default/files/publication/172902/ewp-446.pdf> accessed 24 January 2023.

58 Jeffrey Wilson, 'Can the TPP Fix the "Noodle Bowl" of Asian Free Trade Agreements?' (*Australian Institute of International Affairs*, 25 February 2016) <https://www.internationalaffairs.org.au/australianoutlook/can-the-tpp-fix-the-noodle-bowl-of-asian-free-trade-agreements/> accessed 24 March 2023.

59 ibid.

3.2.2 The Genesis of the Indo-Pacific Economic Framework and Its Purpose

First, by treating the IPEF as an executive agreement, the Biden administration seeks to bypass congressional approval that has stymied similar deals in the US and abroad.[60] Parties to the negotiation can select among the pillars for negotiation while being bound to the agreement on all 'modules' within each pillar. The US is currently considering applying 'early harvest' to the IPEF, which allows narrow agreements on individual pillars to take effect immediately upon agreement instead of entering into force following comprehensive agreements on all IPEF pillars.[61] This flexibility heightens the likelihood of successful plurilateral progress on transnational public goods.

Contrasting to China's inroads across Asia and into Europe via its BRI, the IPEF seeks to 'build bridges between the Indo-Pacific and the Euro-Atlantic'.[62] Concurrently, broader acknowledgements of transnational public goods are reflected in commitments to seek cooperation with China in areas, like climate change.[63] Consequently, although the Sino-American relationship has been plagued by antagonism and mistrust,[64] the IPEF potentially showcases multilevel governance on public goods, where both countries' opposing interests are put aside, and a consensus is reached. Similarly, the collaboration between Indo-Pacific countries demonstrates Asian countries' acknowledgement of the rules-based, liberal trading systems' benefits, despite the challenges multilevel governance faces in the region. A focus on the promotion of sustainable and durable infrastructure also reflects a rhetorical commitment to a path more reminiscent of the Paris Agreement than 'America First' (the Inflation Reduction Act notwithstanding).

---

60 Aridan Arasasingham and others, 'Unpacking the Indo-Pacific Economic Framework Launch' (*CSIS*, 23 May 2022) <https://www.csis.org/analysis/unpacking-indo-pacific-economic-framework-launch> accessed 26 June 2023.

61 Seonjou Kang, 'Indo-Pacific Economic Framework for Prosperity: Assessing Its Economic and Strategic Prospects' (*Institute of Foreign Affairs and National Security*, 17 October 2022). <https://www.ifans.go.kr/knda/com/fileupload/FileDownloadView.do?storgeId=c61b04e5-0182-4c75-ad21-828ecacfb855&uploadId=171808451876783456&fileSn=1> accessed 24 January 2023.

62 National Security Council, Executive Office of the President, 'Indo-Pacific Strategy of the United States' (*White House*, February 2022) 1, 10 <https://www.whitehouse.gov/wp-content/uploads/2022/02/U.S.-Indo-Pacific-Strategy.pdf> accessed 24 January 2023.

63 ibid 5.

64 Shin-wha Lee, 'Middle Power Conundrum amid US-China Rivalry' (*East Asia Forum*, 1 January 2022) <https://www.eastasiaforum.org/2022/01/01/middle-power-conundrum-amid-us-china-rivalry/> accessed 26 June 2023.

While continuing with a more competitive posture toward China established under the Trump administration, the IPEF rhetorically shifts from a more confrontational approach toward closer engagement with allies and capacity-building. India's inclusion within the IPEF also creates opportunities and obstacles for implementing a rules-based, liberal economic framework within the Indo-Pacific region. The strategy document specifically cites 'India's continued rise and regional leadership' as critical elements of success for the framework. Structural deficits in multilevel governance institutions, pre-existing geopolitical and systemic rivalries, and ongoing military conflict in Ukraine represent key obstacles to the successful implementation of the IPEF's vision of an open, interconnected, and sustainable Indo-Pacific economic bloc. One major limitation of the negotiations of IPEF is the exclusion of potential tariff reductions,[65] a primary tool for facilitating market access in international trade agreements. This creates challenges for participating countries in identifying the precise economic gains associated with IPEF and incorporating clear costs and/or benefits into their analysis.

Critics of the IPEF have suggested it is primarily intended to reduce the regional influence of China, given the ongoing Sino-US rivalry, with numerous member states indicating that the framework should surpass geopolitical rivalries and seek an effective and mutually beneficial economic bloc for all participant economies.[66] Protectionist populists, labour groups and environmental advocates, which have previously lobbied against the TPP, have raised similar concerns regarding the prospect of outsourcing highly-skilled trades and the rigour of multilateral labour and environmental standards.[67]

While the IPEF aligns with India's Indo-Pacific orientation and 'Act East' policy focus, welfare nationalism and cronyism in key Indian economic sectors undermine the free and open regime outlined in the IPEF strategy document.[68] The Ukrainian war has also placed India in a difficult position due to its reliance on Russian weaponry and military equipment.[69] Despite moves to implement the IPEF as an executive agreement, congressional resistance

65 Su-Lin Tan, 'The Indo-Pacific Economic Framework: What It is – and Why It Matters' (*CNBC*, 25 Mary 2022) <https://www.cnbc.com/2022/05/26/ipef-what-is-the-indo-pacific-framework-whos-in-it-why-it-matters.html> accessed 26 June 2023.

66 Riad A Ajami, 'Strategic Trade and Investments Framework and Geopolitical Linkages across Asia-Pacific Economies' (2022) 23 Journal of Asia-Pacific Business 183.

67 ibid.

68 Ritesh Kumar Singh, 'Adani Affair is a Warning to New Delhi to Clean up its Act too' (*Nikkei Asia*, 13 February 2023) <https://asia.nikkei.com/Opinion/Adani-affair-is-a-warning-to-New-Delhi-to-clean-up-its-act-too> accessed 26 June 2023.

69 Ajami (n 67).

to the Biden administration's Build Back Better infrastructure program may create obstacles in deploying political and financial support for foreign infrastructure development.[70] It also risks being overturned by subsequent administrations with minimal legal obstacles.[71] In the absence of available resources for States to meet their infrastructure demands, BRI may be the most practical alternative.

4 Conclusion

The Eurasian political power dynamics and insufficient collective security standards within the UN and WTO hinder international collaboration and coordination in addressing transnational challenges, such as anti-competitive behaviour, human rights violations, and inadequate protection of public goods. The liberal, rules-based international economic system is undermined by national rivalry, as evidenced by the US-China trade war, military assertiveness, tensions among WTO members, and collective economic sanctions imposed on Russia. Moreover, the UN and WTO's flawed legal safeguards, failing to curb market, governance, and constitutional failures, intensify regulatory competition among neoliberal, state-capitalist, and ordo-liberal governance frameworks.

The US and EU's unilateral actions against Russia in its invasion of Ukraine and response to perceived governance inadequacies represent a rational reaction to insufficient multilevel governance mechanisms and the opportunistic exploitation of these weaknesses for protectionist or geopolitical power play purposes. On the one hand, Europe's multilevel constitutionalism provides valuable insights into reforming the governance of global public goods and achieving SDGs more effectively. For instance, the adoption of "treaty constitutions" by all EU member states, which supplements national constitutions by offering multilevel guarantees of human and democratic rights and judicial remedies, serves as one such lesson. These institutional checks and balances,

70 Jacob Pramuk and Christina Wilkie, 'House Democrats Scramble Late into the Night to Win Support for Biden's Economic Plans' (*CNBC*, 5 November 2021) <https://www.cnbc.com/2021/11/05/house-aims-to-vote-on-build-back-better-infrastructure-bills.html> accessed 26 June 2023.

71 David Uren, 'Is the US really Committed to Its New Indo-Pacific Economic Initiative?' (*ASPI*, 31 May 2022) <https://www.aspistrategist.org.au/is-the-us-really-committed-to-its-new-indo-pacific-economic-initiative/> accessed 26 June 2023.

market rules, rule-of-law requirements, and constitutionally protected rights limit failures across market, governance, and constitutional dimensions.

Concurrently, Asia's constitutional reform endeavours, influenced by diverse cultural histories, democratic preferences, and legal traditions, continue to evolve. Simultaneously, the constitutional failures of Europe's experiments in constitutionalising multilevel governance of public goods highlight the rationale for Asian countries to acknowledge their self-interest in constitutional obligations to restrict hegemonic power politics from undermining international law and multilateral treaty protections of global public goods.

To successfully extend constitutionalism to the multilevel governance of transnational public goods, it is essential to ensure input and output legitimacy through mechanisms for democratic and legal accountability to citizens and representative institutions. The 2009 Treaty of Lisbon, which outlines complementary principles that recognise the underlying functional, legal, and democratic sources of accountability and legitimacy, is regarded as the gold standard.

The multilevel governance of public goods faces significant challenges, including systemic rivalries and the emergence of collective actions, which negatively impact global cooperation, an essential element for providing public goods. Furthermore, the governance structure has inherent shortcomings. The crucial question is whether plurilateralism or European-style multilevel constitutionalism will emerge as a superior or second-best alternative for governing public goods, acknowledging that both approaches can positively contribute to public goods provision.

It is vital to recognise that Europe and Asia each have their unique versions of multilevel constitutionalism, with neither being perfect. Instead of asserting one as superior to the other, it is more prudent to view both plurilateralism and multilevel constitutionalism as complementary alternatives, working together to address the complex challenges facing the multilevel governance of public goods. In instances where plurilateral reform strategies emerge as the most effective alternative for achieving multilevel governance of public goods, mechanisms of "SDG conditionality" and greenhouse gas reduction commitments must be incorporated as the price of entry for future market access to preserve the benefits of rules-based, liberal trading systems.

Bibliography

Books

Boisseau du Rocher S, *The Belt and Road: China's "Community of Destiny" for Southeast Asia?* (Ifri 2020) 14.

Kaul I, *Providing Global Public Goods: Managing Globalization* (OUP 2003).

Ostrom E, *Governing the Commons: The Evolution of Institutions for Collective Action* (1st edn, CUP 1990).

Ostrom E, *Understanding Institutional Diversity* (Princeton University Press 2005).

Pierik R and Werner W (eds), *Cosmopolitanism in Context. Perspectives from International Law and Political Theory* (CUP 2010).

Slaughterhouse AM, *The Chessboard and the Web: Strategies of Connection in a Networked World* (Yale University Press 2017).

Book Chapters

Petersmann EU, 'Constitutional Pluralism, Regulatory Competition and Transnational Governance Failures' in A. Steinbach and E.U. Petersmann (eds), *Constitutionalism, Transnational Governance Failures and Policy Responses* (This book).

Petersmann EU, 'Lessons from European Constitutionalism for Reforming Multilevel Governance of Transnational Public Goods in Asia?' in Chaisse J (ed) *Sixty Years of European Integration and Global Power Shifts: Perceptions, Interactions and Lessons* (Hart Publishing 2020) 217.

Sand IJ, 'Polycontextuality as an Alternative to Constitutionalism' in Joerges C, Sand IJ and Teubner G (eds), *Transnational Governance and Constitutionalism* (Hart Publishing 2004) 48.

Journal Articles

Ajami RA, 'Strategic Trade and Investments Framework and Geopolitical Linkages across Asia-Pacific Economies' (2022) 23 Journal of Asia-Pacific Business 183.

Case A and Deaton A, *Deaths of Despair and the Future of Capitalism* (Princeton University Press 2020).

Chaisse J and Hamanaka S, 'The 'Noodle Bowl Effect' of Investment Treaties in Asia: The Phenomenon, the Problems, the Practical Solutions' (2018) 33 ICSID Review – Foreign Investment Law Journal 501.

Chaisse J and Kirkwood J, 'Chinese Puzzle: Anatomy of the (Invisible) Belt and Road Investment Treaty' (2020) 23 Journal of International Economic Law 245.

Chaisse J and others, 'Drafting Investment Law: Patterns of Influence in the Regional Comprehensive Economic Partnership (RCEP)' (2022) 25 Journal of International Economic Law 110.

Chaisse J, 'The Regional Comprehensive Economic Partnership's Investment Chapter: One Step Forward, Two Steps Back?' (2020) 271 Columbia FDI Perspectives 1.

Farrell H and Newman AL, 'Weaponized Interdependence: How Global Economic Networks Shape State Coercion' (2019) 44 International Security 42, 47–58.

Petersmann EU, 'The 2018 Trade Wars as a Threat to the World Trading System and to Constitutional Democracies' (2018) 10 Trade, Law and Development 179.

Popescu L and Tudose R, 'The Dragonbear and the Grey Rhinos – The European Union Faced with the Rise of the China-Russia Partnership' (2021) 21 Romanian Journal of European Affairs 130, 135.

Schmitt MN and Watts S, 'Collective Cyber Countermeasures?' (2021) 12 Harvard National Security Journal 373, 385–397.

Yan S, 'Transatlantic Policy Coordination on China and Its Limitations' (2022) 92 China International Studies 65.

Others

Arasasingham A and others, 'Unpacking the Indo-Pacific Economic Framework Launch' (*CSIS*, 23 May 2022) <https://www.csis.org/analysis/unpacking-indo-pacific-economic-framework-launch> accessed 27 March 2023.

Bayer L, 'Brussels Drags out Poland and Hungary Rule-of-Law Probes' (*Politico*, 16 October 2018) <https://www.politico.eu/article/brussels-drags-out-poland-and-hungary-rule-of-law-probes/> accessed 21 October 2022.

Blockmans S and Hu W, 'Systemic Rivalry and Balancing Interests' (*CEPS*, 21 March 2019) <https://www.ceps.eu/ceps-publications/systemic-rivalry-and-balancing-interests-chinese-investment-meets-eu-law-belt-and-road/> accessed 24 January 2023.

Ciuriak D and Fay R, 'The Digital Economic Partnership: Should Canada Join?' (2022) Centre for International Governance Innovation Policy Brief No 171, 1, 7 <https://www.cigionline.org/static/documents/PB_no.171.pdf> accessed 27 March 2023.

Department of Commerce, 'Indo-Pacific Economic Framework' (*US Department of Commerce*) <https://www.commerce.gov/ipef/indo-pacific-economic-framework/> accessed 27 March 2023.

EPA, 'Global Greenhouse Gas Emissions Data', (*US Environmental Protection Agency*, 15 February 2023) <https://www.epa.gov/ghgemissions/global-greenhouse-gas-emissions-data> accessed 27 March 2023.

European Commission, 'Joint Communication to the European Parliament, the European Council and the Council: EU-China – A Strategic Outlook' JOIN (2019) 5 final, 1.

Freeman CP and Mie Ōba 'Bridging the Belt and Road Divide' (*Carnegie Endowment for International Peace*, 10 October 2019) <https://carnegieendowment.org/2019/10/10/bridging-belt-and-road-divide-pub-80019> accessed 24 January 2023.

Hooghe L, Marks G and Schakel A, 'Multilevel Governance' in Daniele Caramani (ed), *Comparative Politics* (OUP 2020) 194.

Kang JW, 'The Noodle Bowl Effect: Stumbling or Building Block' (2015) ADB Economic Paper Working Series No 446, 1 <https://www.adb.org/sites/default/files/publication/172902/ewp-446.pdf> accessed 24 January 2023.

Kang S, 'Indo-Pacific Economic Framework for Prosperity: Assessing Its Economic and Strategic Prospects' (*Institute of Foreign Affairs and National Security*, 17 October 2022). <https://www.ifans.go.kr/knda/com/fileupload/FileDownloadView.do?storgeId=c61b04e5-0182-4c75-ad21-828ecacfb855&uploadId=171808451876783 45&filеSn=1> accessed 24 January 2023.

Khan Z and others, 'The Roles of Export Diversification and Composite Country Risks in Carbon Emissions Abatement: Evidence from the Signatories of the Regional Comprehensive Partnership Agreement' (2021) 53 Applied Economics 4769.

Kliem F, 'Finding the Middle Ground: EU-China Relations' (*Hinrich Foundation*, 6 December 2022) <https://www.hinrichfoundation.com/research/article/sustainable/eu-china-relations/> accessed 24 January 2023.

Lee S, 'Middle Power Conundrum amid US-China Rivalry' (*East Asia Forum*, 1 January 2022) <https://www.eastasiaforum.org/2022/01/01/middle-power-conundrum-amid-us-china-rivalry/> accessed 27 March 2023.

Library of Congress, 'New Zealand; Singapore: New Declaration on Trade in Essential Goods for Combating the COVID-19 Pandemic' (*Library of Congress*, 17 April 2020) <https://www.loc.gov/item/global-legal-monitor/2020-04-17/new-zealand-singapore-new-declaration-on-trade-in-essential-goods-for-combating-the-covid-19-pandemic/> accessed 27 March 2023.

National Security Council, Executive Office of the President, 'Indo-Pacific Strategy of the United States' (*White House*, February 2022) 1, 10 <https://www.whitehouse.gov/wp-content/uploads/2022/02/U.S.-Indo-Pacific-Strategy.pdf> accessed 24 January 2023.

New Zealand Foreign Affairs & Trade, 'Overview' (*New Zealand Foreign Affairs & Trade*) <https://www.mfat.govt.nz/en/trade/free-trade-agreements/free-trade-agreements-in-force/digital-economy-partnership-agreement-depa/overview/> accessed 27 March 2023.

Office of the Leading Group for Promoting the Belt and Road Initiative, *The Belt and Road Initiative Progress, Contributions and Prospects* (1st edn, Foreign Languages Press Co Ltd 2019) 88.

Peters MA, 'Digital Trade, Digital Economy and the Digital Economy Partnership Agreement (DEPA)' (2022) 55 Educational Philosophy and Theory 1, 6 <https://www.tandfonline.com/doi/epdf/10.1080/00131857.2022.2041413?needAccess=true&role=button> accessed 27 March 2023.

Petersmann EU, 'China and the Future of International Economic Law: European Perspectives on the Way Forward' (2022) EUI LAW Working Paper 2022/13, 1, 8 <https://cadmus.eui.eu/bitstream/handle/1814/75146/LAW_WP_2022_13.pdf?sequence=1> accessed 27 March 2023.

Petri PA and Plummer M, 'RCEP: A New Trade Agreement that will Shape Global Economics and Politics' (*Brookings*, 16 November 2020) <https://www.brookings.edu/blog/order-from-chaos/2020/11/16/rcep-a-new-trade-agreement-that-will-shape-global-economics-and-politics/> accessed 24 January 2023.

Pramuk J and Wilkie C, 'House Democrats Scramble Late into the Night to Win Support for Biden's Economic Plans' (*CNBC*, 5 November 2021) <https://www.cnbc.com/2021/11/05/house-aims-to-vote-on-build-back-better-infrastructure-bills.html> accessed 27 March 2023.

Singh RK, 'Adani Affair is a Warning to New Delhi to Clean up its Act too' (*Nikkei Asia*, 13 February 2023) <https://asia.nikkei.com/Opinion/Adani-affair-is-a-warning-to-New-Delhi-to-clean-up-its-act-too> accessed 27 March 2023.

Tan SL, 'The Indo-Pacific Economic Framework: What It is – and Why It Matters' (*CNBC*, 25 Mary 2022) <https://www.cnbc.com/2022/05/26/ipef-what-is-the-indo-pacific-framework-whos-in-it-why-it-matters.html> accessed 27 March 2023.

UNSC Res 2565 (26 February 2021) UN Doc S/RES/ 2565.

Uren D, 'Is the US really Committed to Its New Indo-Pacific Economic Initiative?' (*ASPI*, 31 May 2022) <https://www.aspistrategist.org.au/is-the-us-really-committed-to-its-new-indo-pacific-economic-initiative/> accessed 27 March 2023.

Wignaraja G and Kawai M, 'Tangled up in Trade? The "Noodle Bowl" of Free Trade Agreements in East Asia' (*CEPR*, 15 September 2009) <https://cepr.org/voxeu/columns/tangled-trade-noodle-bowl-free-trade-agreements-east-asia> accessed 27 March 2023.

Wilson J, 'Can the TPP Fix the "Noodle Bowl" of Asian Free Trade Agreements?' (*Australian Institute of International Affairs*, 25 February 2016) <https://www.internationalaffairs.org.au/australianoutlook/can-the-tpp-fix-the-noodle-bowl-of-asian-free-trade-agreements/> accessed 24 March 2023.

World Bank, 'Climate Change could Force over 140 Million to Migrate Within Countries by 2050: World Bank Report' (*World Bank*, 19 March 2018) <https://www.worldbank.org/en/news/press-release/2018/03/19/climate-change-could-force-over-140-million-to-migrate-within-countries-by-2050-world-bank-report> accessed 27 March 2023.

World Trade Organization, 'Principles of the Trading System' (*World Trade Organization*) <https://www.wto.org/english/thewto_e/whatis_e/tif_e/fact2_e.htm> accessed 24 January 2023.

Index

www.ingramcontent.com/pod-product-compliance
Lightning Source LLC
Chambersburg PA
CBHW071327230926
51849CB00002B/333